THE NEW YORK RANGERS

Broadway's Longest-Running Hit

By

John Kreiser and Lou Friedman

Consulting Editor: John Halligan

Foreword By Neil Smith

SAGAMORE PUBLISHING

Champaign, IL

Interior Design: Michelle Summers
Editor: Susan McKinney
Jacket and Cover Design: Deborah Bellaire
Proofreader: Phyllis L. Bannon

ISBN: 1-57167-041-6
Library of Congress catalog card number: 96-71293

We have made every effort to trace the ownership of copyrighted photos. If we have failed to give adequate credit, we will be pleased to make changes in future printings.

Printed in the United States.

This book is dedicated to everyone who has been a part of the Rangers over the first 70 years, and to the millions for whom the Rangers have been an integral part of life.

———————————————

THANK YOU

CONTENTS

ACKNOWLEDGMENTS

JOHN & LOU WOULD LIKE TO THANK THE FOLLOWING:

A book of this size and type cannot come about without the efforts of a large number of people who want it to succeed.

We have to start with John Halligan, the Rangers' long-time director of public relations, whose love of the Rangers is exceeded only by his class and dignity. John was the "godfather" of this project, pointing out interesting corners of Rangers history that might otherwise have gone unexplored and constantly working with us to make this a better book. We are more indebted to him than we can express.

A huge tip of the cap to all of the folks at Sagamore Publishing. Mike Pearson got an education in New York Rangers hockey; we got one in dealing with a top-class editor. Thanks also to Peter Bannon, who did much of the initial legwork with the Rangers, as well as Michelle Summers and Susan McKinney of the production department, Monica Cundiff in marketing and Jim Sheppard of the sales staff. Also thanks to Mr. Public Relations, Dave Kasel, whose hard work resulted in making this book available.

We're also indebted to Neil Smith and his staff with the Rangers. We've had the good fortune to deal with Neil since his arrival in New York in 1989, and it's safe to say that few people have more respect for Rangers history than he has. Thanks also to Kevin Kennedy for making this project work from the Rangers' end, as well as to Kevin's assistant, Jim Pfeifer. Rob Koch, our point man, was every bit as good at handling our requests as Brian Leetch is at manning the point on the Rangers' power play. Thanks also to John Rosasco, Frank Buonamo and the rest of the PR staff, who went out of their way to help.

We would also like to thank Phil Pritchard, Jeff Davis, and especially Craig Campbell at the Hockey Hall of Fame in Toronto for allowing us access to their vast resource materials, as well as to Andy McGowan of the NHL office in New York. Thanks also to Barry Watkins at MSG Network and Bill Shannon of the New York Sports Museum & Hall of Fame for their valuable help. We'd also be remiss not to acknowledge the dozens of men and women who have covered the Rangers during their 70 seasons, ranging from people like Jim Burchard, Al Laney and Joe Nichols, who chronicled the Rangers when they were young, to today's writers, reporters and broadcasters—many of whom we are pleased to call our friends and who were kind enough to take part in our survey to determine the Rangers' most magical moments and biggest deals.

JOHN WOULD ALSO LIKE TO THANK THE FOLLOWING:

Thanks to the staff at the Floral Park and Elmont Public Libraries, who provided invaluable assistance in researching this book; to friends like Scott Carey, Bill Kamski, Bob Kopp and John Marchese, with whom I lived and died with the Rangers more years ago than I'd like to remember, to former colleagues (and long-time friends) Ken Rappoport and Barry Wilner for their encouragement and suggestions and to my writing partner for making this work a joy. I am also indebted to my parents, Joe and Dawn Kreiser, who used to put me to sleep to the sound of Bert Lee's Ranger broadcasts; to my children, Kathy, Kevin, Patty, Theresa and Matthew, for not complaining when Daddy wasn't around for much of the spring and summer, and especially to my wonderful wife, Helen, who gave me inspiration when I needed it most.

LOU WOULD ALSO LIKE TO THANK THE FOLLOWING:

The Connetquot (Oakdale/Bohemia) Public Library for their various resource materials; my friends and various in-laws (who know I didn't fall off the face of the planet) for their patience while I masqueraded as an author (especially Weeb); Nancy Brommer for excellent travel arrangements on short notice; Fred Christensen, computer guru of the highest order; Ken Rappoport of The Associated Press for giving me the chance to see the sport of hockey from a whole new perspective; those players, media folks, and staff involved in hockey who have enriched my life; my writing partner, who survived a cranky intestine and several other distractions while planning and working on this tome; my late parents, Bertram & Jacqueline Friedman, for putting me on this planet; and finally, my lovely wife Denise, whose love and support during the course of putting this book together were both needed and greatly appreciated.

FOREWORD

By Neil Smith

Few things during my seven years of running the New York Rangers have pleased me as much as the chance to delve into the history of the franchise. From the era of Lester Patrick, the Cooks and Frank Boucher, to the revitalization of the team under Emile Francis and stars like Rod Gilbert and Ed Giacomin in the late 1960s, to the current era, being a Ranger has always been something special. Given the realities of hockey in the 1990s, it's sometimes easy to overlook that fact.

What John Kreiser and Lou Friedman have done in this book is give Ranger fans a way of remembering just how special the Rangers always have been, in a format that offers something unique for every generation. Some will enjoy taking a stroll down memory lane with yearly snapshots of the early seasons, when the Rangers first earned their distinction as "The Classiest Team In Hockey" and a game at the Garden was as much a social occasion as a sporting event. Those of us who learned about hockey in the 1960s and 1970s will savor remembrances of the heroes of our youth, reliving events that still stand out in our memories. Younger fans can learn about the history behind the Rangers and the people and events that have shaped them into the team you know today.

Neil Smith

But this book is not just a recitation of numbers and dates, goals and assists (though they're all here, too). It's also a look at the people and events that have helped make the Rangers so special. You'll find the names you know—portraits of everyone from Bill Cook to Bryan Hextall to Brad Park to Mark Messier—and highlights of the biggest events in the Rangers' 70 seasons. But there's also a look at a lot of the people and happenings you might not have known about: Goalie Davey Kerr making the cover of *Time* Magazine in the late 1930s and Monty Hall (of "Let's Make A Deal" fame) serving as a Ranger broadcaster in the late 1950s, are just two examples.

This book is more than just a history of a hockey team. It's a portrait of a franchise that has been an integral part of the world's premier city for seven decades, and a tribute to the people who have helped make it what it is today.

"TEX'S RANGERS"
The Birth of a Franchise

It may not sound romantic, but if you're a Rangers fan (and if you're reading this, there's a good chance you are), you have a bootlegger and a Texas boxing promoter to thank for the birth of your team.

William B. "Big Bill" Dwyer, who made lots of money selling moonshine, was sold on the idea of buying an NHL team for New York. The seller was Thomas J. Duggan, who had rights to sell two Canadian-based franchises to the United States. Dwyer struck a deal to buy the Hamilton Tigers and move them into the brand new Madison Square Garden, which was run by Tex Rickard. They were named the New York Americans, and started play in 1925.

Rickard, a boxing promoter, liked what he saw of the fast-paced sport, and with the encouragement of Garden president Col. John S. Hammond, decided to purchase an expansion team for the following season, much to the chagrin of the Americans, who had forged a verbal agreement that they would be the Garden's only hockey tenant.

The $50,000 investment was christened "Tex's Rangers," and the moniker stuck with the team. Rickard used boxing publicist Johnny Bruno to promote the Rangers, and it led to some near-disastrous ideas. Bruno changed the names of Lorne Chabot and Oliver Reinikka to "Chabotsky" and "Ollie Rocco," respectively, to appeal to the city's varied ethnicity. That was

Tex Rickard brought the Rangers to the Garden.
Photo courtesy of the Hockey Hall of Fame.

Tex Rickard was so impressed with the way the Americans drew at the Garden that he got his own NHL team. Photo courtesy of the Hockey Hall of Fame.

shelved quickly. Bruno's next big idea got him fired. It never happened, but Bruno thought a staged kidnapping of Rangers right wing Bill Cook should take place three days before opening night, and of course, Cook would be "found" in time to take the opening faceoff.

It was Rickard who brought in Conn Smythe to assemble the team, fired him before their first training camp, and settled on Lester Patrick.

And the rest—70 years and counting—is history.

1926 1927

New York Rangers

TIME CAPSULE

- **September 23, 1926:**
  Heavyweight challenger Gene Tunney wrested the title away from Jack Dempsey in Philadelphia.

- **April 7, 1927:**
  Secretary of Commerce Herbert Hoover broadcast from Washington, the first time television was demonstrated. The demonstration took place in New York.

- **May 20, 1927:**
  Aviator Charles Lindbergh took off from Mitchel Field (Long Island), New York for Paris, France, and arrived 33 hours later.

1926-1927

FINAL STANDINGS

American Division	W	L	T	PTS	GF	GA
RANGERS	25	13	6	56	95	72
Boston	21	20	3	45	97	89
Chicago	19	22	3	41	115	116
Pittsburgh	15	26	3	33	79	108
Detroit	12	28	4	28	76	105

Canadian Division Winner—Ottawa Senators

PLAYOFF RESULTS
Semifinals: Boston defeated Rangers (most goals) 3-1
LEADING PLAYOFF SCORERS
Bill Cook (1-0-1)

Taffy Abel (0-1-1)

STANLEY CUP CHAMPION
Ottawa Senators

SEASON SNAPSHOT

Most Goals:
Bill Cook (33)

Most Assists:
Frank Boucher (15)

Most Points:
Bill Cook (37)

Most Penalty Minutes:
Ching Johnson (66)

Most Wins, Goaltender:
Lorne Chabot (22)

Lowest Goals-Against Average:
Lorne Chabot (1.56)

Most Shutouts:
Lorne Chabot (10)

NHL Award Winners:
Bill Cook (Art Ross Trophy)

2

The 1926-27 Season in Review

Tex's Rangers began here, and 70 years and four Stanley Cups later, they're still as popular as they were on opening night. Of course, there weren't as many broken hearts in this era. Opening night at Madison Square Garden was as glitzy a production as anything at one of the nearby theaters, and the Rangers helped make the night memorable by pitching a 1-0 shutout at the Montreal Maroons. It was just the beginning. This brand new team wound up winning the American Division by a hearty 11 points over second-place Boston. Hal Winkler tended goal in the opener, but it was Lorne Chabot who saw the bulk of netminding duties, finishing with a 1.56 goals-against average and 10 shutouts. Bill Cook scored 33 goals, added four assists, and won the Art Ross Trophy as the NHL's top scorer by one point over Chicago center Dick Irvin. How good was this team? In 44 games, it had just one three-game losing streak and a single two-game losing streak. Conversely, it had a pair of four-game and three-game winning streaks. In the playoffs, the Rangers advanced to the semifinals by virtue of fin-

The 1926-27 Ranger team. Photo courtesy of the Hockey Hall of Fame.

ishing first, where they faced the Bruins in a two-game, total-goals series for a berth in the championship round. The two teams played a scoreless tie in Boston, but the Bruins defeated the Rangers 3-1 before a packed house at the Garden, spoiling the perfect storybook season. But not for long.

MAGIC MOMENT *Opening Night*

There was electricity in the air at the one-year-old Madison Square Garden on November 16, 1926, as New York's second hockey team made its way onto the ice for its NHL debut. Tex Rickard's newly-named Rangers were ready to start, and were looking to take the Cup in their first season. That didn't happen. But what did happen was an exciting, entertaining brand of sport that would keep loyal followers coming back. On opening night, a crowd of more than 13,000 witnessed a 1-0 victory over the Montreal Maroons, a game that saw Bill Cook score the first of his 33 goals. Frank Boucher, who won the Lady Byng Trophy seven times, got into the only fight of his NHL career when he duked it out with "Bad Bill" Phillips. Though Lorne Chabot carried the bulk of the workload in goal during the season, it was Hal Winkler who won this game by shutting out the Maroons. Between-periods entertainment was provided by actress Lois Moran, who also dropped the first puck, and figure skating star Katy Schmidt. Referee Lou Marsh used a dinner bell (a short-lived experiment by the league) to stop play for penalties. The games back then started at 8:45 p.m., to coincide with curtain time at the various Broadway theaters nearby.

Hal Winkler shut out the Montreal Maroons 1-0 in the Rangers' first game. Photo courtesy of the Bill Galloway Collection/Hockey Hall of Fame.

3

RANGER LEGEND
Bill Cook

Right wing Bill Cook was the key to several Rangers "firsts." He scored the first goal in franchise history, the only goal of the team's first game. It came at 18:37 of the second period and gave the Blueshirts a 1-0 home victory against the Montreal Maroons. He was the first captain in Rangers history, and wore the "C" from opening night until he retired in 1937. Cook led the team in scoring the first season and three more after that. He was the first player from the Rangers to make the NHL's first All-Star team, as chosen by the writers. He was so honored for three seasons (1930-31, 1931-32, and 1932-33, the first three seasons

Bill Cook was the Rangers' first captain. Photo courtesy of Imperial Oil-Turofsky/Hockey Hall of Fame.

that All-Star teams were voted), and was on the second All-Star team in 1933-34. Cook was the first of only two Rangers to win the Art Ross Trophy for leading the league in scoring, and did so twice, in the first two Stanley Cup seasons (Bryan Hextall was the other, in 1942). Though he didn't score the first Stanley Cup-clinching goal; that honor went to his center, Frank Boucher. But Cook did score a dramatic overtime goal—and the only goal of the game—to give the Rangers their second Cup in 1933. His 33 goals in the first season and again in 1931-32 stood as a team record until Andy Bathgate got 40

in 1958-59. Cook spent most of his career on a line with Boucher in the middle, and brother Fred (better known as Bun) on the left, making him part of the team's first brother combination as well. It was the same threesome who played in the old WCHL; the Cook brothers played in Saskatoon and Boucher in Vancouver. When the league folded, Conn Smythe brought them all to New York. Cook retired after the 1936-37 season with a tidy 228 goals and 366 points, and two engravings on Lord Stanley's Cup. One more first: Cook was the first career Ranger to be elected into the Hockey Hall Of Fame (1952).

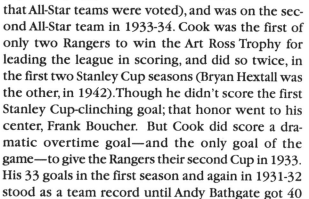

Bill Cook File

- **BORN:**
  October 9, 1896; Brantford, Ontario
- **ACQUIRED:**
  Signed as an original Ranger
- **FIRST SEASON WITH RANGERS:**
  1926-27
- **BEST SEASON WITH RANGERS:**
  1929-30, 44 GP, 29-30-59, 56 PIM

- **TOTALS WITH RANGERS:**
  Regular season: 475 GP, 228-138-366, 386 PIM
  Playoffs: 46 GP, 13-13-26, 76 PIM
- **HONORS:**
  Art Ross Trophy 1926-27, 1932-33;
  First-team All-Star, 1930-31, 1931-32, 1932-33;
  Second-team All-Star, 1933-34

CURTAIN CALL

Conn Smythe

Many people forget that Conn Smythe was the architect who put together this original batch of Rangers. Smythe was hired by Tex Rickard and Col. John Hammond to help develop the franchise and serve as the team's first general manager. Smythe raided the folding WCHL to pick up several players who would be key to the Rangers' early success. But Smythe didn't get along with Rickard, and especially Hammond, and was let go before training camp even opened. Hammond thought Smythe was not experienced enough to run the team, and the breaking point came when Smythe thought Babe Dye, who wound up scoring 202 goals

Conn Smythe was the first man hired to build the Rangers but was replaced by Lester Patrick before the first puck dropped. Photo courtesy of the Imperial Oil-Turofsky/Hockey Hall of Fame.

in his 269-game NHL career, "was not the type of player we needed." After Smythe's ouster from the Rangers, he headed north to Toronto and built the Maple Leafs into a powerhouse. Smythe had an eye for young talent, as demonstrated by Toronto's "Kid Line" of Charlie Conacher, Joe Primeau, and Busher Jackson, but the Maple Leafs won only one Stanley Cup (1932) during the time the Rangers won three.

NEW YORK Ice Exchange

The first season in franchise history was built with several WCHL players after that league folded. Included in this group were Murray Murdoch, Ching Johnson, and Taffy Abel. The Cook brothers, Frank Boucher, Lorne Chabot, and others were all looking for places to play and landed on Broadway. Those who were only around for the first season: Stan Brown, Ollie Reinikka, and Reg Mackey. After things didn't work out with initial boss Conn Smythe, another Western League recruit was brought in to replace him. Tex Rickard and Col. John Hammond took Chicago Blackhawks coach Barney Stanley's suggestion and signed Lester Patrick to be the team's first coach and general manager—and the rest is history. Patrick also played one game during the season (not in goal, as he would do in the 1928 playoffs), and was scoreless, although he did get on the scoresheet with two penalty minutes.

Lester Patrick had to suit up for a game on defense in 1926-27.

—1927  1928—

TIME CAPSULE

- **September 30, 1927:**
  Babe Ruth slugged his record-setting 60th home run for the New York Yankees.

- **November 13, 1927:**
  The Holland Tunnel, America's first underwater tunnel, was opened to traffic, linking New Jersey with Manhattan.

- **May 5, 1928:**
  Amelia Earhart became the first woman to fly an airplane across the Atlantic Ocean.

1927-1928

FINAL STANDINGS

American Division	W	L	T	PTS	GF	GA
Boston	20	13	11	51	77	70
RANGERS	19	16	9	47	97	79
Pittsburgh	19	17	8	46	67	76
Detroit	19	19	6	44	88	79
Chicago	7	34	3	17	68	134

Canadian Division Winner—Montreal Canadiens

PLAYOFF RESULTS

Quarterfinals: Rangers defeated Pittsburgh (most goals) 6-4

Semifinals: Rangers defeated Boston (most goals) 5-2

Finals: Rangers defeated Montreal Maroons 3-2

LEADING PLAYOFF SCORER

Frank Boucher (7-1-8)

STANLEY CUP CHAMPION

NEW YORK RANGERS

SEASON SNAPSHOT

Most Goals:
Frank Boucher (23)

Most Assists:
Bun Cook (14)

Most Points:
Frank Boucher (35)

Most Penalty Minutes:
Ching Johnson (146)

Most Wins, Goaltender:
Lorne Chabot (19)

Lowest Goals-Against Average:
Lorne Chabot (1.80)

Most Shutouts:
Lorne Chabot (11)

NHL Award Winners:
Frank Boucher (Lady Byng Trophy)

The 1927-28 Season in Review

The Rangers picked up where they left off after winning the American Division in their first season by winning their first three games in the 1927-28 season. But aside from a four-game winning run at the end of January, they couldn't piece together more than two wins in a row during any other part of the season. There was a run of eight straight games between February 7-28 where a shutout was involved: Lorne Chabot won three of those games, lost two, and the other three ended up scoreless ties. Chabot had 11 shutouts on the season, winning eight. Frank Boucher led the team with 35 points, while defenseman Ching Johnson had a team-high 146 penalty minutes. In the playoffs, the Rangers beat the Pittsburgh Pirates in the quarterfinals in a two-game, total-goals series 6-4. In the semifinals, they outscored Boston 5-2 in the same format. Then, in just their second season of existence, the Rangers were competing for the Stanley Cup against the Montreal Maroons. The Blueshirts had to play every game of the best-of-five finals at the Montreal Forum, while the circus took

Lorne Chabot had 11 shutouts, but was injured in the playoffs. Photo courtesy of the Hockey Hall of Fame.

over the Garden. The Rangers lost the first game 2-0, won the second 2-1 in overtime as coach Lester Patrick saved the day by serving as an emergency goaltender, and lost Game 3 by a 2-0 score. Twice facing elimination, the Rangers rallied for a 1-0 victory in Game 4 before Boucher scored the Cup-winner in Game 5 as they beat the Maroons 2-1 to capture the Stanley Cup in only their second year of existence.

MAGIC MOMENT *April 7, 1928*

Lester Patrick's heroics helped the Rangers win their first Stanley Cup.

The Rangers came into Game 2 of the finals against the Montreal Maroons at the Forum still looking for their first goal of the series when disaster struck. After making 15 saves in a scoreless first period, goalie Lorne Chabot was hit in the left eye by Nels Stewart's shot early in the middle period. Chabot was taken to Royal Victoria Hospital for treatment, leaving the Rangers without a goalie. Patrick asked Montreal counterpart Eddie Gerard for permission to use one of two goalies sitting in the stands (Ottawa's Alex Connell, one of the NHL's leading netminders, or minor-leaguer Hughie McCormick) as a substitute. Gerard refused the Rangers both times. When Frank Boucher—half jokingly—said to Patrick that he should suit up, the 43-year-old Silver Fox took off his suit and donned the pads. Patrick stopped five shots during the rest of the period to keep the game scoreless after 40 minutes. Bill Cook scored 30 seconds into the third period, only to be answered by Stewart at 12:40. The teams headed into overtime, where Patrick and Maroons counterpart Clint Benedict each stopped three shots. But Frank Boucher fired the fourth Ranger shot and beat Benedict. The victory tied the series and that gutty performance by Patrick spurred the Rangers to their first championship.

RANGER LEGEND
Frank Boucher

As the center for the Cook brothers on the Rangers' famous "A-Line" (named after the subway that ran under the old Garden), and later as coach and general manager, Frank Boucher was a guiding force for the Rangers for more than a quarter-century. Boucher led the Rangers in goals (23) and points (35) during their first championship season, and would lead the team in scoring for the next two seasons as well. It was he who suggested that Lester Patrick suit up as goalie in Game 2 of the finals when Lorne Chabot was injured, a move that helped the Rangers win their first Stanley Cup. One of four brothers to play in the NHL, Boucher was a star in the Western Canada Hockey League and was part of the exodus to the NHL that marked the demise of the league after the 1925-26 season. Boucher stands 13th on the team's all-time scoring list, but only led the team once —in 1927-28—in goals scored. Boucher ended his playing career after 14 seasons, and the highlight was scoring the Cup-clinching goal against the Montreal Maroons in the fifth and final game of the 1928 finals, giving the Broadway Blueshirts an NHL championship in only their second year of existence. Starting in 1928, Boucher won the Lady Byng Trophy for four consecutive seasons for skillful and gentlemanly play; in all, he won the hardware in seven out of eight seasons. Because he won so often, the NHL finally gave him the trophy outright, and created a new one for subsequent honorees. Boucher had only one fight in his NHL career—in the very first game at Madison

Square Garden, when he took on Montreal Maroons forward Merlyn "Bad Bill" Phillips. After retiring as a player, Boucher went on to coach the Rangers for more than nine seasons, succeeding Lester Patrick, and was the man in charge when they won the Cup in 1940. He also succeeded Patrick as general manager, and wound up spending more than 25 years working for the Rangers in some capacity. Boucher was elected to the Hockey Hall Of Fame in 1958.

Frank Boucher File

BORN:
October 7, 1901; Ottawa, Ontario
ACQUIRED:
Purchased from Boston, which had acquired him after the breakup of the WHL, May 1926.
FIRST SEASON WITH RANGERS:
1926-27
BEST SEASON WITH RANGERS:
1929-30, 42 GP, 26-36-62, 16 PIM

TOTALS WITH RANGERS:
Regular season: 533 GP, 152-261-413, 114 PIM
Playoffs: 53 GP, 16-18-34, 12 PIM
HONORS:
Lady Byng Trophy, 1927-28, 1928-29, 1929-30, 1930-31, 1932-33, 1933-34, 1934-35;
First-team All-Star, 1932-33, 1933-34, 1934-35, 1941-42 (as coach);
Second-team All-Star, 1930-31

CURTAIN CALL

Early Presidents

John S. Hammond was the first president of the Rangers, and some would argue that it was he, and not Tex Rickard, with whom original GM Conn Smythe disagreed, leading to Smythe's departure from the Rangers before their first training camp. Hammond was the driving force in convincing Rickard to put ice-making equipment into the Garden, and then in persuading him to land the Rangers. He also lured Lester Patrick to take the reins of the team. Hammond stayed as president of the Rangers until the end of the 1931-32 season. After a two-year absence in that position (filled by William F. Carey and John Reed Kilpatrick), Hammond returned for a one-season stint before leaving Broadway for good. Kilpatrick was the only other team president to serve more than one interrupted term; he took over after Hammond left in 1935, and stayed in charge until the end of the 1959-60 season, a span of 25 years, the longest tenure for a president in team history.

John Reed Kilpatrick had the longest tenure of any team president in Rangers' history.

NEW YORK Ice Exchange

Alex Gray was among the few newcomers in 1927-28. Photo courtesy of Hockey Hall of Fame.

The new faces on the roster were Alex Gray, who had seven regular-season goals and one playoff tally, Patsy Callighen, who was pointless in 36 regular-season games and nine playoff games, and Laurie Scott, who had one assist in 23 games and saw no playoff action. Gray left after the season for Toronto, and was out of the NHL after one more year. Three players who wore Ranger Blue in the inaugural season were gone from the roster for the Stanley Cup year: Stan Brown, Ollie Reinikka and Reg Mackey. With the franchise only two years old, there wasn't a lot of player movement—not in an era when teams were only allowed to carry 12 players (not counting goaltenders) on their rosters. Taffy Abel played the fewest amount of regular-season games (23).

The Patricks:
New York Hockey's Royal Family

The Rangers have always prided themselves on being a family—and no family has meant more to them than the Patricks. Maybe there would be a National Hockey League if the Patricks hadn't come along, but there would certainly be no New York Rangers as we know them without Lester Patrick and his descendants.

Amazingly, though, the Patricks almost weren't involved with the Rangers. When Col. John S. Hammond obtained a franchise to compete with the Americans in Madison Square Garden beginning in 1926-27, he signed Conn Smythe to manage the team. Lester Patrick, already a hockey legend, was busy overseeing the breakup of the Western Canada Hockey League, which had fallen on hard financial times. But Tex Rickard, who ran the Garden, had met with Lester in the spring of 1926 and was impressed; when Smythe and Hammond had a falling out, Patrick got a telegram from Hammond inviting him to come to New York and discuss an offer to coach the team—an offer that was likely triggered by Rickard, who wanted his new Garden to be the "in" place on the New York sporting scene and felt Patrick was the man to make the Rangers a high-class team. He was right.

Lester inherited a good nucleus from Smythe, including the Cook brothers, Bill and Bun, Frank Boucher, and goaltender Lorne Chabot. He added to that nucleus and then showed he knew what to do with talent by coaching the Rangers to a first-place finish in the American Division in their debut season. Even though the Bruins upset them in the playoffs, the Rangers and their fans had started

Lester Patrick is the only man to have his name on the Stanley Cup with two of his sons in the same year.

a long and beautiful friendship.

At least as important as Lester's ability as a coach and general manager was his ability to sell the game to the local writers, most of whom knew little about hockey. His efforts to court sportswriters earned him the sobriquet "The Silver Fox," though it's hard to say whether the name had more to do with his gray hair or his hockey wisdom.

Lester did more than coach the Rangers to the 1928 Stanley Cup. When goalie Lorne Chabot was hurt in Game 2 of the finals against the Montreal Maroons, and Patrick's request to use Ottawa's Alex Connell was denied, Lester put on the pads himself and backstopped the Rangers to a 2-1 overtime victory that sparked them to their first championship.

The Rangers stayed in contention and won their second Cup in 1933, as Patrick kept the nucleus of his original team together while building a farm system to provide the

next wave of talent. As players like the Cook brothers, Frank Boucher and Ching Johnson departed in the mid- and late 1930s, they were replaced by a new crop, including two of Lester's sons.

Lynn Patrick, who went on to play on a high-scoring line with Phil Watson and Bryan Hextall, joined the Rangers in 1934—though as he admitted in Eric Whitehead's book *The Patricks: Hockey's Royal Family:* "One man I did not impress [in training camp] was Lester. However, Bill and Bun Cook apparently saw something Lester didn't and told him he'd be crazy not to sign me." It took him a few games to show he was more than the boss's son, but Lynn eventually became an All-Star.

Muzz Patrick was better known as a boxer, winning the Canadian Amateur heavyweight title and appearing as a boxer at the Garden before he ever donned a Ranger jersey. He joined his brother with the Blueshirts in 1937 as a defenseman and both were part of the 1940 championship team.

That team was coached by Boucher, because the elder Patrick had decided the previous spring to step down as coach. He remained as general manager, though, and with a young, talented team backed by a well-stocked farm system, the Rangers appeared set to dominate for years.

Then came World War II. Muzz and Lynn Patrick enlisted in the U.S. Army, while Lester tried to operate a team that had lost its best talent. By 1943, most of his veterans were off to the war and his farm system was decimated. He sought permission to suspend operations, but was convinced by the other owners to continue icing a team. He did, but the Rangers floundered— and even the return of his former stars after the war didn't help.

On February 22, 1946, Lester Patrick walked into the office of Gen. John Reed Kilpatrick, the president of Madison Square Garden, and tendered his resignation, saying, "It's time I stepped down." On December 3, 1947, he was honored at Lester Patrick Night, celebrating his years of service to the Rangers and his election to the Hockey Hall of Fame.

Neither Lynn nor Muzz had gotten their legs back after the war, and both went into coaching. Lynn Patrick succeeded Boucher as coach in December 1948 and led the Rangers to the finals in 1950. But the Game 7 loss to Detroit in double overtime turned out to be Lynn's last game with the Rangers. He went back to western Canada to coach Lester's minor-league team—but no sooner had he moved than Boston boss Art Ross called and asked him to coach the Bruins. He eventually became their general manager.

Muzz Patrick also succeeded Boucher behind the bench. It came in 1954, after Boucher had returned to coaching when Bill Cook stepped down. Muzz coached for 1 1/2 seasons, then succeeded Boucher as GM in the summer of 1955. The Rangers made the playoffs for three straight years in the late 1950s, but couldn't hold a big lead in 1958-59 and finished fifth behind Toronto. During the early 1960s, the two Patricks' teams were doomed to fight for the scraps left by the NHL's other four clubs.

Muzz was gone in 1964, moved upstairs to help oversee the transition to the new Madison Square Garden. Lynn left the Bruins in 1966 and went on to help build the St. Louis Blues.

Muzz Patrick was an amateur boxing champion before joining the Rangers' defense.

Just as Lynn Patrick followed in Lester's skate tracks, so did Lynn's son, Craig. A fairly successful checking forward as a player, Craig left his real mark off the ice, first as an assistant coach with the 1980 U.S. Olympic team and then with the Rangers. He joined the team as director of operations shortly after the stunning U.S. gold medal victory, coached the team into the 1981 semifinals and was named general manager that summer—hiring his former Olympic boss, Herb Brooks, as coach.

Patrick built some excellent teams, but they were unable to get past the Islanders in the playoffs. He went behind the bench again after relieving Brooks in 1985, but the team struggled and he was succeeded by Phil Esposito in the summer of 1986. He joined Pittsburgh as general manager in 1989 and assembled the team that won back-to-back Stanley Cups in 1991 and 1992.

Craig Patrick became the third generation of Patricks to coach the Rangers before becoming general manager.

—1928 1929—

IME CAPSULE

- **October 9, 1928:**
  The New York Yankees completed a sweep of the St. Louis Cardinals with a 7-3 victory to win their second straight World Series.

- **May 16, 1929:**
  The first Academy Awards ceremony took place, with *Wings* winning the award for best picture.

- **June 30, 1929:**
  Golfer Bobby Jones won the U.S. Open.

1928-1929

FINAL STANDINGS

American Division	W	L	T	PTS	GF	GA
Boston	26	13	5	57	89	52
RANGERS	21	13	10	52	72	65
Detroit	19	16	9	47	72	63
Pittsburgh	9	27	8	26	46	80
Chicago	7	29	8	22	33	85

Canadian Division Winner—Montreal Canadiens

PLAYOFF RESULTS

Quarterfinals: Rangers defeated Americans (most goals) 1-0

Semifinals: Rangers defeated Toronto 2-0

Finals: Boston defeated Rangers 2-0

LEADING PLAYOFF SCORER

Butch Keeling (3-0-3)

STANLEY CUP CHAMPION

Boston Bruins

SEASON SNAPSHOT

Most Goals:
Bill Cook (15)

Most Assists:
Frank Boucher (16)

Most Points:
Frank Boucher (26)

Most Penalty Minutes:
Bun Cook (70)

Most Wins, Goaltender:
John Ross Roach (21)

Lowest Goals-Against Average:
John Ross Roach (1.48)

Most Shutouts:
John Ross Roach (13)

NHL Award Winners:
Frank Boucher (Lady Byng Trophy)

The 1928-29 Season in Review

As they did the previous season, the Rangers finished second in the American Division to the Boston Bruins, but they improved from 47 points to 52, mostly thanks to the stingiest defense in team history. The Rangers set franchise records both for fewest goals scored in a season (72) and fewest allowed (65)—and that includes a nine-goal game for and a nine-goal game against. New netminder John Ross Roach had a lot to do with the low goals-against total. Roach stepped in for Lorne Chabot, who went to the Toronto Maple Leafs, played every game, and accrued a team-record 13 regular-season shutouts. Roach's 21 wins represented just over 25% of his Ranger NHL victory total. This was the only season of the first five for the Rangers that they gained at least one regular-season victory over every opponent. The team was streaky during the season, enjoying feast (an 8-1-2 stretch mid-December to mid-January) and enduring famine (4-7-4 in their last 15 games). Bill Cook led goal scorers with 15, while Frank Boucher led the team with 16 assists and 26 points. Trying to defend the Cup, the Rangers faced the rival Americans in the quarterfinals

Frank Boucher (#7), facing off with Detroit's Stan McCabe, led the Rangers with 26 points.

in a total-goals series, and after a scoreless tie in the opener, the Blueshirts ousted their co-tenants by winning the second game 1-0 in double overtime. The semifinals, now a best-of-three series, saw the Rangers sweep Toronto. They lost to the Bruins in the finals in two straight games. It was the first Stanley Cup final that featured two U.S.-based teams.

MAGIC MOMENT *March 21, 1929*

The Rangers beat Roy Worters and the Americans in 1928-29.

Long before the Islanders came into being, the Rangers had a fierce rivalry with the New York Americans. Both teams called Madison Square Garden home, and fought for the attention of the fans and newspapers. That's why the players couldn't wait to start their quarterfinal series against the Americans (a scenario that draws parallels to the 1975 preliminary series against the Islanders: first-time playoff meeting, natural rivals, short series). The expected goaltending duel between the Rangers' John Ross Roach and the Americans' Roy Worters was the focal point of the series. Roach had 13 shutouts during the season, while Worters' brilliance earned him the Hart Trophy as the regular-season MVP. Both goalies were unbeatable in the opener of the total-goals series, which ended in a scoreless tie, and put up goose eggs again through regulation time in Game 2. The first overtime was scoreless, and as the second extra session dragged on, it looked as if no one might ever score. Finally at 9:50 of the second overtime, Butch Keeling beat Worters for the only goal of the game and series—and a most satisfying Ranger victory was complete.

RANGER LEGEND
John Ross Roach

What do you do when you win the Stanley Cup with a goalie who won 19 games, had a goals-against average of 1.80 and posted 11 shutouts? If you're coach/GM Lester Patrick, you replace him with a goalie who would wind up with 21 wins, a 1.48 goals-against average and 13 shutouts. Patrick made a tough decision to let Lorne Chabot go after he was injured in the finals against the Maroons following a superb season, but Chabot's replacement, John Ross Roach, made Patrick look like a genius. Roach, a pickup from Toronto, played four seasons for the Blueshirts, won 80 games, posted a 2.26 goals-against average and recorded 30 shutouts. His best season was his first, and his worst was the following year, when he finished at .500 with a 3.25 goals-against average and just one shutout. He kept the team near the top of the NHL mountain, as they made the finals and semifinals twice each during his four-year tenure. But Roach, who won a Stanley Cup as a member of the 1922 Toronto St. Patricks as a rookie, never got that second chance to drink from the Cup. His shining moment came in the 1929 playoffs, when he blanked the Americans twice and allowed the Maple Leafs only one goal as the Rangers advanced to the finals. Roach lost both games to the Bruins, though he gave up just two goals in each. Roach was the fourth goalie to play for the Blueshirts, after Hal Winkler, Chabot and Patrick, but in Patrick's time as GM, there would be 16 different netminders on Broadway. Roach wound up his 14-year career in Detroit—sold there by Patrick for $11,000—and re-

John Ross Roach set a team record with 13 shutouts in 1928-29. Photo courtesy of the Hockey Hall of Fame.

tired after the 1934-35 season with 491 games played, 218 wins, 204 losses and 69 ties, a 2.46 goals-against average, and 58 shutouts. When the Rangers beat the Red Wings in the 1933 semifinals on the way to their second Stanley Cup, the opposing netminder was—yes—Roach.

John Ross Roach File

- **BORN:**
  June 23, 1900; Fort Perry, Ontario
- **ACQUIRED:**
  From Toronto for Lorne Chabot prior to the 1928-29 season.
- **FIRST SEASON WITH RANGERS:**
  1928-29

- **BEST SEASON WITH RANGERS:**
  1928-29, 44 GP, 21-13-10, 1.48 goals-against average, 13 shutouts
- **TOTALS WITH RANGERS:**
  Regular season: 180 GP, 80-63-37, 2.26 goals-against average, 30 shutouts
  Playoffs: 21 GP, 5 series won, 4 series lost, 2.10 goals-against average, 4 shutouts

CURTAIN CALL

Frank Calder

NHL President Frank Calder presided over numerous rules changes.

Frank Calder, the first president of the NHL, instituted several rules changes that helped shape the league in its formative years, including lifting a previous salary cap, establishing uniform game starting times and enacting the loaning of spare goaltenders for backup purposes. He even helped the media by making it mandatory for all teams to have proper facilities for the press available at every game: "at least 10 centrally located seats from which all parts of the rink are plainly visible, adjacent to telegraph wires and telephone communication with minor officials." Other rules which helped shape the NHL: Jersey numbers on the players' backs became mandatory in 1930; the official scorer was introduced as a permanent fixture in 1926 (prior to that, the League relied on independent reports to compile statistical information). The four-sided scoreboard clock was introduced in 1931, while five years later, the green light was put into use; it automatically locked out the opportunity to illuminate the red goal light at the end of each period, thus minimizing arguments about goals scored at the buzzer.

NEW YORK Ice Exchange

Of the four Rangers who joined the team the previous season, only Billy Boyd was still with the team at the start of 1928-29, but he didn't last long, as he was traded to the Americans during the season. Also dispatched were Patsy Callighen, Alex Gray and Laurie Scott. More importantly, Lorne Chabot, the goalie whose acrobatics helped the Blueshirts win the Stanley Cup the previous year, was also gone, landing in Toronto (he wound up playing for six different teams). John Ross Roach took over between the pipes, and the Rangers never skipped a beat, getting at least as far as the semifinals in the four seasons with Roach in goal. Other new bodies included Butch Keeling (from Toronto), who led the team with three playoff goals. Also with the team were Sparky Vail, Myles Lane, Russ Oatman (from the Maroons) and Jerry Carson (from the Canadiens), who cumulatively totaled six goals to the cause.

Butch Keeling proved to be a valuable addition up front.

Ranger Lists

Single-Season Shutout Leaders

Name	No.	Season
John Ross Roach	13	1928-29
Lorne Chabot	11	1927-28
Lorne Chabot	10	1926-27
Ed Giacomin	9	1966-67
John Ross Roach	9	1931-32
Dave Kerr	8	1935-36
Dave Kerr	8	1937-38
Dave Kerr	8	1939-40
Ed Giacomin	8	1967-68
Ed Giacomin	8	1970-71

—1929 1930—

TIME CAPSULE

- **November 29, 1929:**
  The first ever successful flight over the South Pole was completed by Lt. Commander Richard E. Byrd.

- **March 13, 1930:**
  From an observatory in Flagstaff, Arizona, the ninth planet of our solar system, Pluto, was discovered.

- **June 7, 1930:**
  Gallant Fox captured the Triple Crown by winning the Belmont Stakes.

1929-1930

FINAL STANDINGS

American Division	W	L	T	PTS	GF	GA
Boston	38	5	1	77	179	98
Chicago	21	18	5	47	117	111
RANGERS	17	17	10	44	136	143
Detroit	14	24	6	34	117	133
Pittsburgh	5	36	3	13	102	185

Canadian Division Winner—Montreal Maroons

PLAYOFF RESULTS

Quarterfinals:Rangers defeated Ottawa (most goals) 6-3

Semifinals: Montreal Canadiens defeated Rangers 2-0

LEADING PLAYOFF SCORERS

Murray Murdoch (3-0-3) Butch Keeling (0-3-3)

STANLEY CUP CHAMPION

Montreal Canadiens

SEASON SNAPSHOT

Most Goals:
Bill Cook (29)

Most Assists:
Frank Boucher (36)

Most Points:
Frank Boucher (62)

Most Penalty Minutes:
Ching Johnson (82)

Most Wins, Goaltender:
John Ross Roach (17)

Lowest Goals-Against Average:
John Ross Roach (3.25)

Most Shutouts:
John Ross Roach (1)

NHL Award Winners:
Frank Boucher (Lady Byng Trophy)

The 1929-30 Season in Review

There was no ebb or flow to the season for the Rangers, rather, a frustrating group of fits and starts. They managed a four-game winning streak in mid-January, which came on the heels of a three-game losing streak. Otherwise, it was win a couple here, lose two there, throw in a few ties—you get the picture. The only consistency came when the Blueshirts faced Boston and Toronto. They managed one tie against each, losing the other five games to the Bruins and three to the Maple Leafs. The Rangers ended their season by tying five of their last eight games, including four in a row. Half a loaf is better than none, hockey people will say, but it's either the whole loaf or no bread when the playoffs roll around. The Rangers broke bread with Ottawa in the quarterfinals, and doubled them 6-3 in the two-game, total-goals series. That put them into the semifinals against the Canadiens, but New York couldn't get its offense untracked, losing to Montreal 2-1 in overtime in the Forum and 2-0 at the Garden. Frank Boucher was tops in regular-season scoring

The Rangers' "A-line" with Frank Boucher and the Cook brothers, combined for 79 goals in 1929-30.

with 62 points (26 goals, 36 assists), a total no Ranger player matched or surpassed until Andy Bathgate picked up 66 points in 1955-56, a span of 26 years. John Ross Roach's numbers weren't good compared to the previous season: 17 wins (vs. 21), a 3.25 goals-against average, up from 1.48, and just one shutout, 12 less than the previous season.

MAGIC MOMENT *A String Of Ties*

John Ross Roach was in goal when the Rangers played four straight ties. Photo courtesy of the Hockey Hall of Fame.

The Rangers accomplished something in 1929-30 that they had never done before and haven't repeated since: They played four consecutive tie games. The Blueshirts have had seasons where they had 21 ties (1950-51), 18 ties (1954-55) and two seasons with 16 (1952-53 and 1969-70). But in a season where they played to just 10 deadlocks, four of them came consecutively. The streak started at Madison Square Garden on February 27, when they played to a 1-1 draw against the Blackhawks. They then went on the road for a four-game trip, of which the first three games ended up deadlocked. They gained a point in Toronto on March 1 with a 3-3 tie. The next night in Detroit, they drew 2-2 with the Red Wings. Finally, two nights later in the Windy City, they tied Chicago, also 2-2. The string was snapped four nights later in Montreal, where the Blueshirts absorbed a 6-0 pounding by the Canadiens. In all, eight of their 10 ties came during a season-ending 2-6-8 stretch and enabled the Rangers to make the playoffs almost literally a point at a time.

RANGER LEGEND
Murray Murdoch

Murray Murdoch was a fixture in Lester Patrick's line up for his entire NHL career, spanning 11 seasons and 508 games. The left wing wasn't a prolific scorer (only 84 goals worth), but his longevity was the mark that latter-day players compared themselves to. Murdoch never missed a game in his Blueshirts career, and only two other original Rangers lasted as long as Murdoch: Bill Cook retired along with Murdoch after the 1936-37 season (though missing 33 games along the way), and Frank Boucher played 12 consecutive seasons and 518 total games (not counting the short comeback in 1943-44). Murdoch was used primarily as a checking wing, allowing the Cook brothers and Frank Boucher to work their magic with the puck. His biggest scoring output came in the 1933-34 season, when he tallied 17 goals and 27 points. There were only two other seasons when Murdoch's goal total reached double figures (13 in 1929-30, 14 in 1934-35), and in his final season, he had 14 assists but no goals. In seven seasons, Murdoch finished either fifth or sixth in team scoring. He finished fourth during his 17-goal season, and finished eighth twice. In a bit of irony, he wound up 11th in scoring in his 11th and final season; two slots below Murdoch sat Bill Cook,

Murray Murdoch never missed a game during his NHL career.

who managed only one goal and five points in 21 games. Murdoch was there from the very beginning of the franchise, and headed for retirement with a pair of Stanley Cup championship rings. Murdoch's playing career ended on Broadway, but he took his act north to New Haven, where he went on to a long and successful coaching career at Yale University.

Murray Murdoch File

BORN:
May 19, 1904; Lucknow, Ontario
ACQUIRED:
Signed as original Ranger
FIRST SEASON WITH RANGERS:
1926-27

BEST SEASON WITH RANGERS:
1933-34, 48 GP, 17-10-27, 29 PIM
TOTALS WITH RANGERS:
Regular season: 508 GP, 84-108-192, 197 PIM
Playoffs: 55 GP, 9-12-21, 28 PIM

CURTAIN CALL
Alphabet Soup

Leo Quenneville, a forward whose NHL career lasted all of 25 games, isn't noted for what he did for the Rangers (three assists), but for his name. Quenneville is the only player in Rangers history whose last name starts with the letter Q. There are five other NHL retired players whose surname starts with the 17th letter of the alphabet: Bill and Max Quackenbush, Joel Quenneville, John Quilty and Pat Quinn. There were five players in the 1995-96 *NHL Media Guide & Record Book* currently active who are filed under Q: Dan Quinn, Ken Quinney, Deron Quint, Stephane Quintal and Jean-Francois Quintin. But Q isn't the only rarity, letter-wise, in Ranger history. There has only been one player on the roster in the 70 years of New York hockey whose last name started with Y—Tom Younghans, who skated for the Blueshirts in the 1981-82 season. Younghans is one of 16 NHL "Y" players, including seven whose last name is Young; 12 of the 16 are retired.

Tom Younghans is the only Ranger whose name started with a "Y." Leo Quenneville is the only name to start with a "Q."

NEW YORK Ice Exchange

Taffy Abel was the first regular skater to be dealt away. Photo courtesy of the Hockey Hall of Fame.

The first trade of GM Lester Patrick's regime involving a regular position player took place, as Taffy Abel was sent to the Chicago Blackhawks for Ralph Taylor, who played only 24 games for the Rangers and scored two of his four career goals before exiting the NHL. Patrick was reluctant to trade his top stars, showing loyalty to those who served the team well. That would be a pattern that would continue throughout Rangers history. Several newcomers made the squad, including Roy (Leroy) Goldsworthy, Leo Quenneville, Orville Heximer, Leo Reise Sr., Bill Regan and Harry Foster. Of the bunch, only Regan played another season on Broadway. Goldsworthy, Heximer and Foster used the Rangers as their NHL launching point. Aside from Abel, missing from the previous year's team were Billy Boyd, Jerry Carson, Myles Lane and Russ Oatman.

Ranger Lists

Rangers undefeated and winless seasons against other Original Six teams

Team, Undefeated seasons **(us)**, Winless seasons **(ws)**

Boston Bruins, (us) 1989-90 **(ws)** 1929-30, 1930-31, 1976-77, 1982-83, 1983-84, 1984-85, 1988-89

Chicago Blackhawks, (us) 1928-29, 1975-76, 1978-79, 1981-82, **(ws)** 1982-83, 1984-85, 1985-86, 1990-91, 1995-96

Detroit Red Wings, (us) 1982-83, 1983-84, 1985 86, 1989-90, 1992-93, **(ws)** 1988-89, 1990-91, 1993-94,

Montreal Canadiens, (us) 1985-86, **(ws)** 1927-28, 1943-44, 1972-73, 1974-75, 1975-76, 1979-80, 1984-85, 1986-87, 1988-89, 1989-90

Toronto Maple Leafs, (us) 1982-83, 1984-85, 1993-94, 1995-96, **(ws)** 1929-30, 1933-34, 1975-76, 1991-92

—1930  1931—

TIME CAPSULE

- **September 27, 1930:**
  By winning the U.S. Amateur tournament, Bobby Jones became the first player to win golf's Grand Slam.

- **March 3, 1931:**
  President Herbert Hoover signed a congressional act making "The Star-Spangled Banner" the national anthem.

- **May 1, 1931:**
  The world's tallest building, the Empire State Building, officially opened in New York City.

1930-1931
FINAL STANDINGS

American Division	W	L	T	PTS	GF	GA
Boston	28	10	6	62	143	90
Chicago	24	17	3	51	108	78
RANGERS	19	16	9	47	106	87
Detroit	16	21	7	39	102	105
Philadelphia	4	36	4	12	76	184

Canadian Division Winner—Montreal Canadiens

PLAYOFF RESULTS

Quarterfinals: Rangers defeated Montreal Maroons (most goals) 8-1

Semifinals: Chicago defeated Rangers (most goals) 3-0

LEADING PLAYOFF SCORERS
Paul Thompson (3-0-3)

Bill Cook (3-0-3)

STANLEY CUP CHAMPION
Montreal Canadiens

SEASON SNAPSHOT

Most Goals:
Bill Cook (30)

Most Assists:
Frank Boucher (27)

Most Points:
Bill Cook (42)

Most Penalty Minutes:
Ching Johnson (77)

Most Wins, Goaltender:
John Ross Roach (19)

Lowest Goals-Against Average:
John Ross Roach (1.98)

Most Shutouts:
John Ross Roach (7)

NHL Award Winners:
Frank Boucher (Lady Byng Trophy)

NHL All-Stars:
Bill Cook, RW (First Team);
Lester Patrick, Coach (First Team);
Ching Johnson, D (Second Team);
Frank Boucher, C (Second Team);
Bun Cook, LW (Second Team)

There was never any tide turning for the Rangers during the season. With two exceptions, they were never more than two games above .500 or two games below .500, the two exceptions being January 8 and the final day of the season (March 17), the only times they got as far as three games above the break-even mark. A 7-2-2 run was followed by an 0-5-3 slide, including four losses in a row—all by one goal. Goaltender John Ross Roach did what he could to help stem the tide. Of the 16 losses he absorbed, nine were by a single goal. He wound up with a 1.98 goals-against average and seven shutouts. But that didn't stop the Rangers from losing nine games at Madison Square Garden, the most in any season until the war ravaged the team in 1942. Bill Cook led the goal-scoring parade with 30. The Rangers had three players who tallied plenty of penalty minutes: Ching Johnson led the way with 78 minutes, and Bun Cook and Joe Jerwa each had 72. The playoffs started well for the Blueshirts, as the Montreal Maroons turned out to be quarterfinals patsies. The Rangers, with Bill Cook and Paul Thompson scoring three goals each, socked the Maroons in a two-game, most-goals series 8-1. But they should have saved some of those goals for the semifinals, as the Chicago Blackhawks ended the Rangers' season by outscoring them 3-0 in their two-game series.

Bill Cook was a first-team All-Star with 30 goals in 1930-31.

Magic Moment

100 Wins

It took almost five full seasons and exactly 218 games to accomplish, but on March 10, 1931, the New York Rangers recorded the 100th victory in franchise history. Their 3-1 win over the Detroit Falcons at Madison Square Garden gave them a century's worth of victories, to go along with 75 losses and 43 ties. Those first five seasons represent about 5% of the overall franchise wins. After 70 seasons of hockey, the Rangers are 22 wins away from the 2,000th victory in team history, a number surpassed only by Boston, Montreal and Toronto. After 70 years, Broadway's longest-running hit has a lifetime regular-season record of 1,978 wins, 1,955 losses and 731 ties in 4,664 games played. The Blueshirts have more wins against Chicago (228) than anybody else. They also have more than 200 victories against Boston (215) and Detroit (207). The team the Rangers have the fewest wins against is Anaheim (one win in four tries). The Rangers have lost the most games to Montreal (293), and have lost to the other "Original Six" teams at least 200 times each.

RANGER LEGEND
Bun Cook

Left wing Fred "Bun" Cook was usually overshadowed by big brother Bill, but he was an integral part of the Rangers' most explosive line, which featured his brother on the right side and Frank Boucher in the middle. The younger Cook had his offensive moments in the sun, and was quite consistent. In 1926-27, the Rangers' first season, Bun wound up third in team scoring to his two linemates. The next four seasons found him fourth, second, third and fourth again in the points column. His career-high goal mark was 24 during the 1929-30 season, and during the 1931-32 playoffs, he tore it up with six goals and two assists in seven games. Cook was also aggressive, and though he didn't match teammate Ching Johnson's penalty-minute numbers, he made it quite clear that he would not let anybody take any liberties with either himself or his teammates. His Blueshirt career regular-season numbers didn't compare badly to those of his older brother. Bill scored only 73 more points with the Rangers than Bun, who played 45 fewer games. Bun's 293 career points on Broadway put him 37th on the Rangers all-time scoring list. Both brothers played in 46 playoff games, and the goal totals were close (Bill had 13, Bun notched 12), but Bill had 13 assists, while his sibling had but four. Bill also was more aggressive in postseason play, with 76 penalty minutes compared to Bun's 56. Cook left the Rangers after 10 seasons, played one more year in Boston, then retired at the end of the 1936-37 sea-

Like his brother, Bun Cook was an original Ranger and made the Hall of Fame.

son. It took 43 years to achieve the same honor as his brother, but finally in 1995, Bun joined Bill in the Hockey Hall Of Fame.

Bun Cook File

- **BORN:**
  September 18, 1903; Kingston, Ontario
- **ACQUIRED:**
  Signed as original Ranger
- **FIRST SEASON WITH RANGERS:**
  1926-27
- **BEST SEASON WITH RANGERS:**
  1929-30, 43 GP, 24-18-42, 55 PIM

- **TOTALS WITH RANGERS:**
  Regular season: 433 GP, 154-139-293, 436 PIM
  Playoffs: 46 GP, 12-4-16, 56 PIM
- **HONORS:**
  Second-team All-Star, 1930-31

CURTAIN CALL

Philadelphia Quakers

Talk about a bad franchise. The Pittsburgh Pirates, after four seasons, left western Pennsylvania and headed East to Philadelphia, where they became the Quakers. A more apt moniker was not to be found. The Pirates left Pittsburgh after a season that featured five wins, three ties and 36 losses. Their only season in Philadelphia produced the worst 44-plus game season in NHL history. The Quakers, whose loss total included the Rangers' six-game sweep, won only four games all season. They again lost 36, showing everyone they did have some consistency, and tied four times for a meager 12 points. It's no wonder that the team folded after the 1930-31 season. But believe it or not, there were worse teams in the early years of the NHL, most notably the 1917 Montreal Wanderers, who lost five of their first six games before they had to disband because their home rink, the Montreal Arena, burned to the ground. At least they had an excuse.

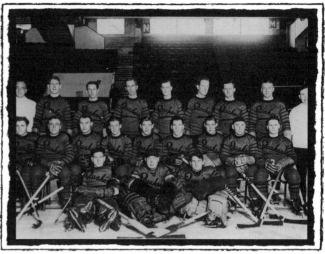

The Rangers swept the Quakers in their lone NHL season. Photo courtesy of the Hockey Hall of Fame.

NEW YORK
Ice Exchange

The core of the previous season's squad remained intact, as nine players were back for another campaign. The changes that GM Lester Patrick made were numerous, but mainly peripheral ones. Bodies out: Sparky Vail, Frank Waite, Ralph Taylor, Leo Reise Sr., Orville Heximer and Harry Foster. The last two went to Boston, the others ended their NHL careers. Bodies in: Frank Peters, Bill Kenny, Gene Carrigan, Sam McAdam (for four games), Joe Jerwa, Henry Maracle and Eddie Rodden, who came from the Bruins. Of those newcomers, only Jerwa (who went to Boston after the season) and Carrigan (St. Louis bound) played in the NHL for a stretch after the season. Jerwa, who lasted nine years in the league, wound up sixth in team scoring with four goals and seven assists, and had 72 of his 338 penalty minutes with the Blueshirts. Also, Paul Thompson, who had been with the team since its inception, was traded to Chicago after the season. He is the brother of long-time Boston Bruins goaltender Cecil "Tiny" Thompson.

Paul Thompson was dealt after a seven-goal seven-assist season.

—1931 1932—

⌛ TIME CAPSULE

- **October 25, 1931:**
  The George Washington Bridge opened to traffic, giving New Yorkers and New Jerseyites a commuter path across the Hudson River.

- **March 1, 1932:**
  Aviator Charles Lindbergh's son, Charles Jr., was kidnapped from his home in Hopewell, N.J.

- **August 14, 1932:**
  The U.S. picked up its 16th and final gold medal at the Summer Olympics in Los Angeles, the most gold medals of any competing country.

1931-1932
FINAL STANDINGS

American Division	W	L	T	PTS	GF	GA
RANGERS	23	17	8	54	134	112
Chicago	18	19	11	47	86	101
Detroit	18	20	10	46	95	108
Boston	15	21	12	42	122	117

Canadian Division Winner—Montreal Canadiens

PLAYOFF RESULTS

Semifinals: Rangers defeated Montreal Canadiens 3-1

Finals: Toronto defeated Rangers 3-0

LEADING PLAYOFF SCORER

Frank Boucher (3-6-9)

STANLEY CUP CHAMPION

Toronto Maple Leafs

SEASON SNAPSHOT

Most Goals:
Bill Cook (33)

Most Assists:
Frank Boucher (23)

Most Points:
Bill Cook (47)

Most Penalty Minutes:
Ching Johnson (106)

Most Wins, Goaltender:
John Ross Roach (23)

Lowest Goals-Against Average:
John Ross Roach (2.33)

Most Shutouts:
John Ross Roach (9)

NHL All-Stars:
Bill Cook, RW (First Team);
Ching Johnson, D (First Team);
Lester Patrick, Coach (First Team)

The 1931-32 Season in Review

Rookie defenseman Ott Heller helped the Rangers make the finals in 1931-32.

This season was perfectly divided in half: For the first 24 games, the Rangers looked like a Stanley Cup champion, while in the second half, they had the makings of a last-place team. Fortunately for the Rangers, their strong first half was enough to carry them to the American Division title, seven points ahead of second-place Chicago. The Rangers were the only team in the division to finish over .500, and scored 22 more goals than they allowed (incredibly, Boston, in last place with 42 points, scored five more goals than it gave up). The Blueshirts had only three losses and four ties to go with their 17 wins in the first half, but stumbled home in the second half, going just 7-14-3. Bill Cook matched his career-high of 33 goals and led the team with 47 points. John Ross Roach posted a 2.33 goals-against average and recorded nine shutouts during the regular season. The Rangers started the playoffs in the semifinals against the Montreal Canadiens, and won the best-of-five series 3-1 after dropping the opening game. That moved them into the finals against the Toronto Maple Leafs and former teammate Lorne Chabot, their starting goaltender in the 1928 championship season. If Chabot was looking for revenge, he got it, as the Maple Leafs swept the Rangers in three straight games, scoring six goals in each. The sweep sealed the fate of Roach, who was peddled to Detroit during the off-season and replaced by Andy Aitkenhead.

MAGIC MOMENT

April 9, 1932

The Rangers put themselves in the NHL record book once again, this time with some help from the Toronto Maple Leafs. When these two teams met for the Cup, they accomplished a league first when two players registered hat tricks in the same finals game. The Leafs took a commanding 2-0 lead in the best-of-five series by winning the first two games, 6-4 at Madison Square Garden and 6-2 in Boston, the Rangers' home for Game 2 when they had to vacate the Garden after the circus came to town. Game 3 in Toronto was another high-scoring affair, with the Maple Leafs clinching the Cup with a 6-4 victory. Toronto's Busher Jackson, part of the Leafs' "Kid Line" with Charlie Conacher and Joe Primeau, pumped three goals past John Ross Roach. Not to be outdone, the Rangers' big line of the Cook Brothers and Frank Boucher was also going strong, and it was Boucher who lit the red light scoring the Rangers' first playoff hat trick, by beating ex-teammate Lorne Chabot three times. Unfortunately for Ranger fans, Boucher's outburst wasn't enough, as the Rangers became the first team to be swept in a best-of-five series. The Leafs fulfilled a vow by

Frank Boucher had the first playoff hat trick in Rangers history, but it couldn't prevent a sweep.

Conn Smythe, who had been let go by the Rangers in favor of Lester Patrick, that he would someday build a better team than the one he left.

From the beginnings of hockey, there's always been a role for the tough defenseman—one who would get himself involved in the front of the net and in the corners. The Rangers had such a stalwart in Ivan "Ching" Johnson, a 28-year-old who came on board at the start of the franchise. Johnson was not counted on to be an offensive threat, though he did add the odd goal. The number that tells the most about his style of play is the penalty-minutes count: 798 in 403 games. Johnson led the team in penalty minutes in eight of his 11 seasons with the Blueshirts, including seven of the first eight—in 1934-35, he had only had 34 penalty minutes, but they came in just 26 games, as he missed most of the season with injuries. Johnson was let go by the Rangers after the 1936-37 season, but walked across the hall at the Garden and earned another shot with the Americans, playing a final season before retiring and adding 10 penalty minutes for the Blueshirts' archrivals, for a career total of 808. Johnson also had 159 minutes in 54 career playoff games for the Rangers, along with seven points. But by today's standards, those numbers would hardly raise an eyebrow. Only three pre-1960 players are listed in the all-time penalty minutes leaders (1,500 minutes minimum): Ted Lindsay, Gordie Howe and Bill Gadsby. Johnson wound up seventh on the Rangers' all-time penalty minutes list, though. Johnson did make an occasional contribution at the other end of the ice, scoring 38 goals and 86 points during his time in Broadway Blue. Four times an NHL All-Star, Johnson was enshrined into the Hockey Hall Of Fame along with teammate Frank Boucher in 1958.

Johnson also took up officiating after his retirement, serving as a linesman in the old Eastern Hockey League. During one game, he forgot he was wearing a striped shirt and nailed an onrushing forward with a stiff bodycheck. Asked what caused him to do it, he replied, "Instinct, I guess."

Ching Johnson File

- **BORN:**
  December 7, 1897; Winnipeg, Manitoba
- **ACQUIRED:**
  Signed as original Ranger
- **FIRST SEASON WITH RANGERS:**
  1926-27
- **BEST SEASON WITH RANGERS:**
  1932-33, 48 GP, 8-9-17, 127 PIM

- **TOTALS WITH RANGERS:**
  Regular season: 403 GP, 38-48-86, 798 PIM
  Playoffs: 54 GP, 5-2-7, 159 PIM
- **HONORS:**
  First-team All-Star (1931-32, 1932-33)
  Second-team All-Star (1930-31, 1933-34).

CURTAIN CALL

The Tennis Series

The Toronto sweep in the finals was dubbed "The Tennis Series" by local scribes. There was a solid reason, aside from the 6-4, 6-2 and 6-4 tennis lookalike scores. France won tennis' Davis Cup in 1932, and the decisive match was between Jean Borotra and Ellsworth Vines. Borotra won the match by the identical 6-4, 6-2 and 6-4 scores, giving France its fifth straight Davis Cup title. It was the first championship for the Maple Leafs, but according to NHL records, it was the fourth title to be captured by a team representing the Ontario city. In 1914, the Toronto Blueshirts beat the Montreal Canadiens. Four years later, the Toronto Arenas beat the Vancouver Millionaires of the old National Hockey Association. And four years after that, the Toronto St. Patricks beat the Millionaires again, but had to rally from two one-game deficits in the best-of-five series, despite having all five games at home.

Ex-Ranger Lorne Chabot beat his former team in the 1932 Finals, known as the "Tennis Series". Photo courtesy of the Imperial Oil-Turofsky/Hockey Hall of Fame.

NEW YORK Ice Exchange

Art Somers had 11 goals in his first season with the Rangers.

GM/coach Lester Patrick did some wheeling and dealing to better his team. He traded Paul Thompson and Bill Kenny to Chicago for Art Somers and Vic Desjardins, and also sent Joe Jerwa to Boston for Norman "Dutch" Gainor. Two future stars on defense were brought up to help: Earl Seibert and Ott Heller. Doug Brennan and Hib Milks were also first-year Blueshirts along for the ride. Four players played their last NHL games this season: Henry Maracle, Frank Waite, Sam McAdam and Frank Peters. Also, for the first time in franchise history, everyone on the roster participated in both regular-season and playoff action, unlike the past where players filled in during the season, only to be left out when the Stanley Cup run began. Desjardins and Milks missed one playoff game each, while everyone else played all seven games.

Ranger Lists
All-Star Defensemen

Ching Johnson
First team: 1931-32, 32-33
Second team: 1930-31, 33- 34

Earl Seibert
First team: 1934-35

Art Coulter
Second team: 1937-38, 38-39, 39-40

Ott Heller
Second team: 1940-41

Hy Buller
Second team: 1951-52

Bill Gadsby
First team: 1955-56, 57-58, 58-59
Second team: 1956-57

Doug Harvey
First team: 1961-62

Harry Howell
First team: 1966-67

Jim Neilson
Second team: 1967-68

Brad Park
First team: 1969-70, 71-72, 73-74
Second team: 1970-71, 72-73

Brian Leetch
First team: 1991-92
Second team: 1990-91, 93-94, 95-96

—1932  1933—

TIME CAPSULE

- **November 8, 1932:**
  Franklin D. Roosevelt defeated incumbent Herbert Hoover to win election as the 32nd president of the United States.

- **March 13, 1933:**
  Banks across the country reopened after a bank holiday declared by President Roosevelt.

- **July 6, 1933:**
  Baseball's first All-Star Game was held at Comiskey Park in Chicago. The highlight of the American League's 4-2 victory was Babe Ruth's home run.

1932-1933

FINAL STANDINGS

American Division	W	L	T	PTS	GF	GA
Boston	25	15	8	58	124	88
Detroit	25	15	8	58	111	93
RANGERS	23	17	8	54	135	107
Chicago	16	20	12	44	88	101

Canadian Division Winner—Toronto

PLAYOFF RESULTS

Quarterfinals: Rangers defeated Montreal Canadiens (most goals) 8-5

Semifinals: Rangers defeated Detroit (most goals) 6-3

Finals: Rangers defeated Toronto 3-1

LEADING PLAYOFF SCORER

Cecil Dillon (8-2-10)

STANLEY CUP CHAMPION

NEW YORK RANGERS

SEASON SNAPSHOT

Most Goals:
Bill Cook (28)

Most Assists:
Frank Boucher (28)

Most Points:
Bill Cook (50)

Most Penalty Minutes:
Ching Johnson (127)

Most Wins, Goaltender:
Andy Aitkenhead (23)

Lowest Goals-Against Average:
Andy Aitkenhead (2.33)

Most Shutouts:
Andy Aitkenhead (3)

NHL Award Winners:
Bill Cook (Art Ross Trophy)
Frank Boucher (Lady Byng Trophy)

NHL All-Stars:
Frank Boucher, C (First Team);
Bill Cook, RW (First Team);
Ching Johnson, D (First Team);
Lester Patrick, Coach (First Team)

The 1932-33 Season in Review

The question for the season was whether the Rangers would bounce back after the disappointing sweep in the previous spring's finals by Toronto. They did. The Blueshirts were 14-6-4 at the halfway point, with new goalie Andy Aitkenhead posting three shutouts. Those would be his only blankings, as the team played sub-.500 hockey in the second half (9-11-4), and three of those nine victories were against the rival Americans, who were winless against the Rangers (0-5-1). Aitkenhead still posted a respectable 2.33 goals-against average while Bill Cook picked up his second Art Ross Trophy with 28 goals and 50 points. Brother Bun was second in goal-scoring with 22, and the only other goal-scorer to hit double figures was Cecil Dillon, who bagged 21. Frank Boucher won his fifth Lady Byng Trophy in six seasons with 35 points and only four minutes in the penalty box. The Rangers then faced the Canadiens in a two-game, most-goals quarterfinal playoff series, and advanced by outscoring the Habs 8-5. In the semifinals, the Rangers faced the renamed Detroit Red

Cecil Dillon had 21 regular-season goals and eight in the playoffs.

Wings (formerly the Falcons), and in a similar series, the Rangers doubled the goal output of Detroit, advancing to the finals by a 6-3 total score. Playwrights couldn't have put together a better script for the finals, because the Rangers were playing the Maple Leafs again. This time, though, the outcome was different: With the Maple Leafs coming off a grueling semifinal series against Boston and beginning the finals with no rest, the Rangers rolled to their second Stanley Cup by beating the weary Leafs in four games.

MAGIC MOMENT   *April 13, 1933*

The Rangers were happy to see Toronto as their opponent in the Stanley Cup finals—what better way to exact revenge for the Maple Leafs' sweep of the previous spring? They would also face the goalie who helped win them their first Cup five years earlier—Lorne Chabot. The Blueshirts had only one home game for the finals before the circus took over the Garden, but they did have a huge advantage. Toronto played a six-overtime game 18 hours prior to facing off with the Rangers. It was the second-longest overtime game in NHL history (Ken Doraty beat Boston's Tiny Thompson at 4:46 of the sixth overtime for the only goal of the game). Toronto's sluggishness was evident in the opening game at the Garden, a 5-1 Ranger victory. Back in Toronto, the Rangers shrugged off Doraty's early goal in Game 2 and tallies by Ott Heller, Bill Cook and Babe Siebert were enough for a 3-1 win. After losing the third game 3-2, Andy Aitkenhead and Chabot matched zeroes in Game 4 through the regulation 60 minutes. The game stayed scoreless until Cook took a pass from Butch Keeling during a power play and stuffed the puck past Chabot at 7:33 of overtime, giving the Rangers their second championship.

L. To R. Earl Seibert, Andy Aitkenhead, Ching Johnson, Frank Boucher, Bun Cook, and Bill Cook at the Cup presentation.

29

RANGER LEGEND
Andy Aitkenhead

General manager Lester Patrick had a knack for introducing a new goalie to his team, and having that goalie perform well. A prime example of this talent was Andy Aitkenhead. One of a scant few NHL players born in Scotland, Aitkenhead, nicknamed "The Glasgow Gobbler," spent all three years of his NHL career on Broadway with the Blueshirts. Patrick had so much faith in Aitkenhead's ability—and so little in John Ross Roach after being swept in the 1932 finals—that he peddled Roach to the Detroit Falcons (later the Red Wings) and gave Aitkenhead the No. 1 job. Aitkenhead had a first season that was right out of a dream, posting solid totals (23 wins, a 2.33 goals-against average and three shutouts), and backstopping the team to a Stanley Cup championship. Though Aitkenhead would never duplicate those numbers again, he posted a respectable three-year won-lost total of 47-43-16, with a 2.42 goals-against average and 11 shutouts in the regular season. He played every game in his first two seasons on Broadway, both in the regular season and in the playoffs. His postseason mark was 6-3-1, with a 1.48 goals-against average (only 15 goals allowed in 10 games) and three shutouts, including a 1-0 overtime victory in the 1933 Cup clincher. After helping the Rangers win it all in his first season, Aitkenhead and his teammates lost to the Montreal Maroons the following season in the quarterfinals in a two-game, total goals series. The two teams played to a scoreless tie at the Montreal Forum, and the Blueshirts lost by a 2-1 score at the Garden. After the first 10 games of the 1934-35 season, Aitkenhead was 3-7-0 with a 3.70 goals-against average. No one could figure out why he had slipped so badly, but it prompted Patrick to make a deal for Dave Kerr (another solid goaltending pick up) and release Aitkenhead from further duties with the Blueshirts. He never played in the NHL again.

Andy Aitkenhead File

- **BORN:**
  March 6, 1904; Glasgow, Scotland
- **ACQUIRED:**
  Product of Rangers organization.
- **FIRST SEASON WITH RANGERS:**
  1932-33

- **BEST SEASON WITH RANGERS:**
  1932-33, 48 GP, 23-17-8, 2.33 goals-against average, 3 shutouts
- **TOTALS WITH RANGERS:**
  Regular season: 106 GP, 47-43-16, 2.42 goals-against average, 11 shutouts
  Playoffs: 10 GP, 6-2-2, 1.48 goals-against average, 3 shutouts

CURTAIN CALL

Harry Westerby

Harry Westerby was the Rangers' trainer for their first three Stanley Cup teams. Photo courtesy of the Hockey Hall of Fame.

Only three faces appear in the team pictures of each of the Rangers' first three Stanley Cup champions: Lester Patrick (as player/coach and general manager), Frank Boucher (player and coach) and Harry Westerby. Who's Harry Westerby? Even then, every team needed a trainer; someone who could stitch cuts quickly, repair skates and jerseys, and tend to the players' medical needs. For the Rangers, that someone was Westerby. He also handled the job of traveling secretary—booking train and hotel reservations, which all trainers were responsible for in that particular era. Westerby worked for the team until 1946, when Tom McKenna took over. McKenna stayed for two years, and then Frank Paice began nearly three decades as trainer when he stepped in at the start of the 1948-49 season. If McKenna's name looks familiar to baseball fans, that's because he was also a trainer for the New York Mets in their early years.

NEW YORK Ice Exchange

Gord Pettinger won four Stanley Cups, including one in his only season with the Rangers.

Only five original Rangers were on the team when Bill Cook scored the overtime goal to give them their second Cup: Cook, his brother Bun, Frank Boucher, Ching Johnson and Murray Murdoch, who would spend 11 seasons with the team. After being swept by the Maple Leafs in the '32 finals, GM Lester Patrick rid himself of goalie John Ross Roach (to Detroit) and promoted Andy Aitkenhead. Left wing Alex "Babe" Siebert (no relation to Earl Seibert) was brought over from the Montreal Maroons. Center Gord Pettinger came from Detroit in the Roach trade, stayed for one season, won a Cup, and then went back to Detroit. Pettinger had a charmed career: In eight NHL seasons, he was on four Cup-winning teams. Also new to the roster were Ozzie Asmundson, and bit player Carl Voss. Out of the mix were Norman "Dutch" Gainor, Vic Desjardins and Hib Milks.

Ranger Lists

Stanley Cup-Winning Goals

1927-28
Frank Boucher
Montreal Forum
vs. Montreal Maroons

1932-33
Bill Cook
Maple Leaf Gardens
vs. Toronto

1939-40
Bryan Hextall
Maple Leaf Gardens
vs. Toronto

1993-94
Mark Messier
Madison Square Garden
vs. Vancouver

—1933 1934—

TIME CAPSULE

- **December 5, 1933:**
  Congress passed the 21st Amendment, repealing Prohibition.

- **May 23, 1934:**
  Dr. Wallace Carothers of DuPont Laboratories developed a synthetic fiber known as nylon.

- **June 14, 1934:**
  Max Baer won the world heavyweight boxing championship with a TKO over Primo Carnera.

1933-1934
FINAL STANDINGS

American Division	W	L	T	PTS	GF	GA
Detroit	24	14	10	58	113	98
Chicago	20	17	11	51	88	83
RANGERS	22	20	6	50	120	113
Boston	18	25	5	41	111	130

Canadian Division Winner—Toronto Maple Leafs

PLAYOFF RESULTS

Quarterfinals: Montreal Maroons defeated Rangers

(most goals) 2-1

LEADING PLAYOFF SCORERS

Vic Ripley (1-0-1)

Cecil Dillon (0-1-1)

STANLEY CUP CHAMPION

Chicago Blackhawks

SEASON SNAPSHOT

Most Goals:
Bun Cook (18)

Most Assists:
Frank Boucher (30)

Most Points:
Frank Boucher (44)

Most Penalty Minutes:
Ching Johnson (86)

Most Wins, Goaltender:
Andy Aitkenhead (21)

Lowest Goals-Against Average:
Andy Aitkenhead (2.35)

Most Shutouts:
Andy Aitkenhead (7)

NHL Award Winners:
Frank Boucher (Lady Byng Trophy)

NHL All-Stars:
Frank Boucher, C (First Team);
Lester Patrick, Coach (First Team);
Bill Cook, RW (Second Team);
Ching Johnson, D (Second Team)

The 1933-34 Season in Review

Earl Seibert had 13 goals in 1933-34, then a team record for defensemen.

If they hadn't been coming off a Stanley Cup championship, the Rangers' regular-season would have been a good one. They never lost more than two games in a row, and had a pair of three-game winning streaks, but there were difficulties. The Rangers lost their opening game for the first time in franchise history (4-3 at Toronto), and dropped four of their next five games. But then things clicked, and they lost only three of their next 18 games, including a six-day span in early December in which Andy Aitkenhead pitched three consecutive shutouts, winning two and tying one. They scored 75 goals in their 21 wins, only 46 in their 19 losses and eight draws. One of those ties matched the team record for the highest scoring tie game, a 5-5 deadlock at the Garden against Toronto on Feb. 1 (the other 5-5 draw was on the opening night of the 1929-30 season at Detroit). Bun Cook led the team in scoring with 18 goals. The Rangers headed into the playoffs with only one win in their last six games, and their bad fortune carried over into their two-game, total-goals series with the Montreal Maroons. The Rangers and Maroons were scoreless in the first game at the Forum, but the Maroons got the better of the second game at the Garden, beating the Rangers 2-1 to end their season.

MAGIC MOMENT

Milestones

"Moments" is more like it, because even though the season was not a success for the Rangers on a team level, it turned out to be memorable for several players who hit personal milestones. Bill Cook and Frank Boucher both notched their 300th NHL points during the season—with every point for both coming in a Rangers sweater.

Bill Cook (above) and Frank Boucher notched their 300th NHL points in 1933-34.

Boucher would go on to score another 113 points while on Broadway, and Cook would pick up another 66. Other notable numbers include Butch Keeling's 150th point, and Ching Johnson setting the stage for his latter-day predecessors by hitting penalty minute No. 700. Keeling didn't join the Rangers until the 1928-29 season; he averaged 25 points a season in his first six years. Johnson played no favorites in the playoffs, as he topped the 150-minute post-season penalty minute mark during the series with the Maroons. The next player who would hit the 300-point mark for the Blueshirts was Lynn Patrick, who turned the trick during the 1941-42 season. Phil Watson and Bryan Hextall were the only other pre-1950 players who managed 300 Ranger points.

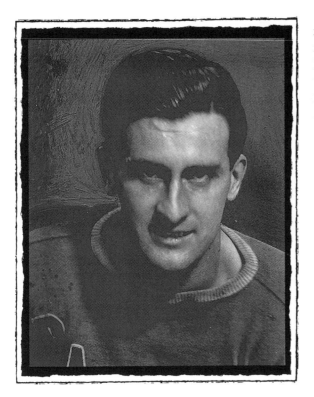

Lester Patrick was one of the first people in hockey to realize the talent pool for adding young players to a winning organization stretched past the Canadian junior leagues. Toledo, Ohio-born and bred Cecil Dillon came to the Rangers in 1931 when Patrick obtained him from the Montreal Maroons system along with Babe Siebert and Art Somers. Dillon made a strong first impression when he finished second in team scoring that season with 23 goals and 48 points. He became the first player other than Bill Cook or Frank Boucher to finish in the top two in scoring for the Blueshirts. More impressive was the following season, when Dillon was one of three 20-goal scorers, along with the Cook brothers. He led the team during the Stanley Cup playoffs with eight goals and two assists (the team-record eight playoff goals wasn't equaled until 1971 and wasn't topped until 1994). During his first three seasons, Dillon had 14 postseason points in 17 games. He played eight full seasons for the Rangers, led the team in scoring for three straight years (1936, 1937, 1938), and finished second in two other years. Dillon averaged 20 goals per season during his time on Broadway, joining Bill Cook as the only other Ranger who could make that claim during the early years. His durability was never a problem. Dillon never missed a regular-season game on Broadway (384 games), and only missed the last six playoff games in his last season (34 of 40). Dillon wound up in Detroit after the 1938-39 season. And when the Rangers won the Stanley Cup the next season, Dillon called it quits. His career numbers averaged out to one goal for every 3.7 games he played—impressive numbers in a low-scoring era. He wound up two points shy of 300 for his NHL career, but that was more than compensated for by having his name on Lord Stanley's trophy.

Cecil Dillon File

BORN:
April 26, 1908; Toledo, Ohio

ACQUIRED:
Obtained from the Montreal Maroons with Babe Siebert and Art Somers prior to the 1931-32 season.

FIRST SEASON WITH RANGERS:
1931-32

BEST SEASON WITH RANGERS:
1938-39, 48 GP, 21-18-39, 6 PIM

TOTALS WITH RANGERS:
Regular season: 409 GP, 160-121-281, 93 PIM
Playoffs: 34 GP, 13-8-21, 12 PIM

HONORS:
First-team All-Star, 1937-38

CURTAIN CALL

Ottawa Senators

This was the last NHL season for the Senators until they rejoined the league as part of the 1992 NHL expansion. The original Senators, an NHL powerhouse before the Rangers joined the league, were very gracious to the Rangers while the two were in the league. The Rangers, with the notable exception of their inaugural 1926-27 season (where they were 0-3-1), dominated the Senators each year. After the first season, the Rangers compiled a 17-3-8 record against the boys from Canada's capital–and they picked up right where they left off in 1992. In the 14 meetings between the two teams from 1992-96, the Rangers have won all but one game (the loss was on October 22, 1995—the last loss at the Garden before they embarked on their record-tying 24-game home unbeaten streak). The Rangers did very well against the defunct teams of their time (the New York/Brooklyn Americans, St. Louis Eagles, Philadelphia Quakers, Pittsburgh Pirates, Montreal Maroons, and, more recently, the California Golden Seals and Cleveland Barons). Their combined record against all these now non-existent teams is 152-58-36.

The Ottawa Senators faded from powerhouse to cellar-dwellars before dropping out of the NHL. Photo courtesy of Bill Galloway Collection/Hockey Hall of Fame.

NEW YORK Ice Exchange

Only two players who were on the 1933 Stanley Cup regular-season roster did not stay around to defend their title: bit player Carl Voss (who didn't suit up for the playoffs) and Gord Pettinger, who went on to win two championships with Detroit and one with Boston. Babe Siebert played only 13 games before he was sent to Boston. Several new faces dotted the roster for the season, but only two stuck around for the playoff ouster by the Maroons: Vic Ripley, who had five goals in 35 games, and Duke Dutkowski, who made the last stop of his 10-year career after stints in Chicago and with the Americans. Bit players who didn't see next season on Broadway included Dan Cox, Jean Pusie, Albert Leduc and Lorne Carr—the same Lorne Carr who would send the Rangers home from the playoffs in 1938 with a famous overtime goal as a member of the rival Americans.

Lorne Carr didn't do much as a Ranger in 1933-34, but came back to haunt them four years later. Photo courtesy of the Hockey Hall of Fame.

Ranger Lists

Rangers Who Were a Part of Two or More Stanley Cup Teams

Lester Patrick
Spare goalie, coach, GM
1928, 1933, 1940
Frank Boucher
Center, coach
1928, 1933, 1940
Harry Westerby
Trainer
1928, 1933, 1940
Ching Johnson
Defense
1928, 1933
Bill Cook
Right Wing
1928, 1933
Bun Cook
Left Wing
1928, 1933
Murray Murdoch
Left Wing
1928, 1933
Ott Heller
Defense
1933, 1940

—1934 1935—

TIME CAPSULE

- **December 9, 1934:**
  The New York Giants beat the Chicago Bears 30-13 in the famous "Sneaker Game" at the Polo Grounds to win their first NFL championship.

- **May 24, 1935:**
  Baseball's first night game was played at Crosley Field as the host Cincinnati Reds beat the Philadelphia Phillies.

- **August 14, 1935:**
  Senior citizens were first able to receive benefit payments thanks to President Roosevelt's signing of the Social Security Act.

1934-1935
FINAL STANDINGS

American Division	W	L	T	PTS	GF	GA
Boston	26	16	6	58	129	112
Chicago	26	17	5	57	118	88
RANGERS	22	20	6	50	137	139
Detroit	19	22	7	45	127	114

Canadian Division Winner—Toronto

PLAYOFF RESULTS
Quarterfinals: Rangers defeated Canadiens (most goals) 6-5
Semifinals: Maroons defeated Rangers (most goals) 5-4
LEADING PLAYOFF SCORER
Lynn Patrick (2-2-4)
STANLEY CUP CHAMPION
Montreal Maroons

SEASON SNAPSHOT

Most Goals:
Cecil Dillon (25)

Most Assists:
Frank Boucher (32)

Most Points:
Frank Boucher (45)

Most Penalty Minutes:
Earl Seibert (86)

Most Wins, Goaltender:
Dave Kerr (19)

Lowest Goals-Against Average:
Dave Kerr (2.54)

Most Shutouts:
Dave Kerr (4)

NHL Award Winners:
Frank Boucher (Lady Byng Trophy)

NHL All-Stars:
Frank Boucher, C (First Team);
Earl Seibert, D (First Team);
Lester Patrick, Coach (First Team)

The 1934-35 Season in Review

This season was a three-act play: bad start, great middle, terrible finish. The Rangers' story started with 10 losses in their first 14 games. It got better when they went on a 17-3-5 tear, including a franchise-record seven-game road winning streak. Unfortunately, the season ended on a 1-7-1 downer before the playoffs started. For the second time in franchise history, the Blueshirts allowed more goals than they scored (137-139), which caused GM Lester Patrick to make yet another goaltending change. After going 3-7-0 to start the season, Andy Aitkenhead was given the boot. Percy Jackson stood in for one game, and then Dave Kerr was imported from the Americans. Except for one game the following year, Kerr played every game for the next six-plus seasons. Patrick brought his oldest son, Lynn, aboard, and he finished seventh on the team in scoring in his rookie season (9-13-22), but led the team in the playoffs with two goals and two assists. Frank Boucher led the team in scoring for the fifth time and won the Lady Byng Trophy for the seventh time. Teammate Cecil Dillon could have been a candidate for Boucher's trophy. He led the team

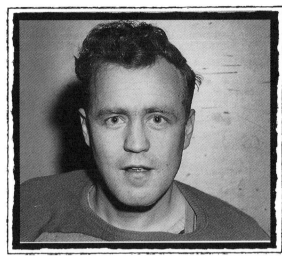

Frank Boucher led the Rangers in scoring for the last time in 1934-35.

with 25 goals and had only four penalty minutes (Boucher had just two). In the playoffs, the Rangers eked out a 6-5 total-goals series with the Montreal Canadiens, and then barely lost to the Montreal Maroons 5-4 (total goals) in the semifinals, with the Maroons going on to win the Stanley Cup.

MAGIC MOMENT   *First Penalty Shots*

Bun Cook missed on the first penalty shot in Ranger history.

The NHL instituted a penalty shot for the first time in 1934-35, giving a freebie to anyone fouled during a breakaway. The Rangers were involved in seven penalty shots during the season. They were 0-4 as shooters, while their goaltenders stopped two of the three attempts they faced. The first penalty shot in Rangers history came on November 15, 1934, when Detroit's Ebbie Goodfellow missed against Percy Jackson, who was playing his only game while filling the gap between Andy Aitkenhead and Dave Kerr. Goodfellow's was one of the rare misses in Detroit's 8-2 thrashing of New York at the Olympia. Three nights later, Bun Cook became the first Ranger to attempt a penalty shot. He missed against St. Louis Eagles netminder Bill Beveridge, but the Rangers still won the game 5-0 at Madison Square Garden. Cook was stopped again on December 8, and Bert Connolly was halted twice in an eight-day span in January. The only successful shooter against the Blueshirts was Canadiens forward Armand Mondou, who beat Aitkenhead in a 5-3 Ranger loss at the Forum on December 4. It wasn't until January, 1936, that Connolly became the first Ranger to connect on a penalty shot.

RANGER LEGEND
Earl Seibert

Defenseman Earl Seibert (no relation to Babe Siebert) launched his 15-year NHL career with the Rangers in 1931, spending his first four-plus seasons on Broadway. He was not afraid to shoot the puck, collecting 27 goals in 202 games, good offensive numbers in an era where defensemen weren't expected to score much. Seibert wasn't afraid to get his nose dirty either, racking up 338 penalty minutes. Seibert missed seven games in his first two full seasons on Broadway, and none in his last two. His best offensive season for the Blueshirts was in 1933-34, when he scored 13 goals and added 10 assists to finish sixth in team scoring. Yet, it was a year later that Seibert was voted to the first team of NHL All-Stars. He was the fourth defenseman in Rangers history to score a playoff goal, after Ching Johnson, Taffy Abel and Leo Bourgault. He took home two championship rings in his long career: one with the Rangers in 1933 and the other with the Chicago Blackhawks in 1938 after being dealt for Art Coulter. While in the Windy City, he was reunited with another former Ranger, Paul Thompson, though they never teamed up on Broadway (Thompson was traded just prior to Seibert joining the Blueshirts). Seibert ended his career with Detroit, and retired at the end of the 1945-46 season. The final numbers: 652 regular-season games played, 89 goals, 187 assists, 276 points, 768 penalty minutes. In 66 playoff games, he had eight goals, nine assists and 66 penalty minutes. Seibert became a member of the Hockey Hall of Fame in 1963, becoming the seventh inductee to have worn a Ranger uniform.

Earl Seibert File

- **BORN:**
  December 7, 1911; Kitchener, Ontario
- **ACQUIRED:**
  Product of Rangers organization.
- **FIRST SEASON WITH RANGERS:**
  1931-32
- **BEST SEASON WITH RANGERS:**
  1933-34, 48 GP, 13-10-23, 21 PIM

- **TOTALS WITH RANGERS:**
  Regular season: 202 GP, 27-41-68, 338 PIM
  Playoffs: 21 GP, 2-2-4, 38 PIM
- **HONORS:**
  First-team All-Star, 1934-35

CURTAIN CALL
The "Four-R" Chain

Lester Patrick developed what he coined the "Four-R" chain in the early 1930s as a feeder system for developing young talent. The four R's refer to: 1. The New York RANGERS (National Hockey League). 2. The Philadelphia RAMBLERS (International-American League). 3. The New York ROVERS (Eastern Amateur League). 4. The Alberta ROAMERS (Canadian juniors). Players who came up through the "4-R" system included Bryan Hextall, Alex Shibicky, Phil Watson, Neil and Mac Colville and Lynn and Muzz Patrick. Starting with the "Four-R's", and continuing through the Guelph Biltmores, the Providence Reds, Buffalo Bisons, Omaha Knights, the Denver Rangers and today's Binghamton Rangers, the Broadway Blueshirts have had a solid farm system through most of their history. With the exception of the mid-90s, when free agency has flourished, a majority of the major talent that has donned Rangers' blue has been homegrown.

The New Haven Ramblers were part of the "4-R" system.

NEW YORK
Ice Exchange

Family ties played no part in GM/coach Lester Patrick's decision to bring his son, Lynn, up to play in the big leagues. It was strictly a need for some offense, and Lynn fared quite well in his rookie season after a slow start, ending any feelings of nepotism. The Rangers also found their goaltender for the next several seasons when they fleeced the Americans of Dave Kerr, who went on to star for the 1940 Stanley Cup team. Otherwise, the core personnel remained the same from the previous season, and aside from Patrick and rookie forward Bert Connolly, most of the changes involved the third-line forwards and fifth and sixth defensemen. Gone from last season were Ozzie Asmundson, Dan Cox, Duke Dutkowski, Jean Pusie, Albert Leduc, Lorne Carr and Doug Brennan. Vic Ripley was traded to St. Louis. Also on board were Charlie Mason, Alex Levinsky, Bill MacKenzie and Harold Starr. Levinsky and the traded Ripley were the only two Rangers who suited up in the regular season but missed out on postseason action.

Lynn Patrick quickly proved that nepotism had nothing to do with his being in the NHL.

39

—1935  1936—

⧗ TIME CAPSULE

- **November 9, 1935:**
  John L. Lewis established the Congress of Industrial Organizations, better known as the C.I.O.

- **June 12, 1936:**
  The Republican party nominated Alf Landon and Col. Frank Knox as its presidential ticket.

- **August 16, 1936:**
  Closing ceremonies took place at the Summer Olympics in Berlin, where American Jesse Owens starred.

1935-1936
FINAL STANDINGS

American Division	W	L	T	PTS	GF	GA
Detroit	24	16	8	56	124	103
Boston	22	20	6	50	92	83
Chicago	21	19	8	50	93	92
RANGERS	19	17	12	50	91	96

Canadian Division Winner—Montreal Maroons

PLAYOFF RESULTS
Rangers did not qualify

STANLEY CUP CHAMPION
Detroit Red Wings

SEASON SNAPSHOT

Most Goals:
Cecil Dillon (18)

Most Assists:
Frank Boucher (18)

Most Points:
Cecil Dillon (32)

Most Penalty Minutes:
Ching Johnson (58)

Most Wins, Goaltender:
Dave Kerr (18)

Lowest Goals-Against Average:
Dave Kerr (2.02)

Most Shutouts:
Dave Kerr (8)

NHL All-Stars:
Lester Patrick, Coach (First Team);
Cecil Dillon, RW (Second Team)

The 1935-36 Season in Review

The addition of Art Coulter boosted the Rangers' defense, but not enough to make the playoffs.

The Rangers wound up as the odd team out in a three-way scramble for two playoff berths, missing out on postseason play for the first time in the franchise's history (and the only time until the team was ravaged by World War II). By the numbers, it wasn't a bad season: They finished over .500 (19-17-12), ended up in a tie with Boston and Chicago at 50 points, and trailed American Division champions Detroit by only six points. Unfortunately for the Rangers, they had fewer wins than the Bruins and Blackhawks, and fourth-place teams, even ones who were two games over .500, didn't make the playoffs at that time. On the plus side, the Blueshirts dominated Boston like they never had before, winning six of eight matchups. It was the third time they beat the Bruins in a season series, but the first by more than one game. Cecil Dillon led the team in scoring for the first of three consecutive seasons, notching 18 goals and 32 points. Except for one game played (and won) by Bert Gardiner, Dave Kerr spent the whole season between the pipes. Kerr posted eight shutouts and a 2.02 goals-against average. The playoff miss proved to be a pit stop for the Rangers; they went on to six straight playoff appearances starting next season, appearing in two Stanley Cup finals and winning one championship.

MAGIC MOMENT   *January 16, 1936*

A Ranger first took place on January 16, 1936 in a game at Madison Square Garden against the Toronto Maple Leafs. Bert Connolly was awarded a penalty shot, and he would face off one-on-one against Toronto netminder George Hainsworth. It was Connolly's third attempted penalty shot with the Rangers; he had missed the previous two (including one the previous season against Hainsworth at Toronto). This time, Connolly made it count, and it stood as the only goal of the game as the Rangers beat the Maple Leafs 1-0 on the first successful penalty shot in Blueshirts history. The Blueshirts have had 17 successful regular-season penalty shots in their history in 39 attempts. They're one for two in postseason attempts, with Alex Shibicky missing in 1937 and Anders Hedberg connecting in 1981. Three Rangers have attempted three penalty shots: Connolly, Shibicky (two for three) and Don Murdoch (one for three). Mike Richter is pretty unflappable when he faces penalty shots. He hasn't allowed one in four regular-season attempts, but the stop most fans remember was in Game 3 of the 1994 finals

Bert Connolly was the first Ranger to score on a penalty shot. Photo courtesy of the Hockey Hall of Fame.

in Vancouver, when his split save on Pavel Bure's attempt propelled the Blueshirts to a huge road win, and eventually, the Stanley Cup.

The Rangers echoed today's newer teams: Start with experience from other clubs, and then build with youth developed from within. Alex Shibicky is a case in point. He stepped right in and played 18 games in 1935-36, his rookie season, then kept going until the war temporarily halted his career in 1942. Shibicky was teamed with the Colville brothers, Neil and Mac to form the "Bread Line," and his goal production steadily increased, from four to 11 to 17 to a career-high 24 in 1938-39. In four of his six full pre-war seasons, he had at least 30 points by season's end. Shibicky earned the distinction of being the second player in NHL history to attempt a penalty shot in a Stanley Cup playoff game. It took place on April 13, 1937 at the Olympia against Detroit's Earl Robertson in the fourth game of the finals, with Robertson making the save. The first shot was two weeks earlier, when Lionel Conacher of the Maroons also missed, going against Boston's Tiny Thompson. Shibicky's playoff goal total also progressed to a career-high three in 1939, but he only had two assists in 10 career Stanley Cup final-round games. He slumped (by his previous numbers) the next two seasons, then rebounded for 20 goals (and three playoff goals) in 1941-42. He got his career-high point total in 1937-38, when he combined for 17 goals and 18 assists for 35 points.

After fulfilling his military duty, Shibicky returned for one more season (1945-46), had 10 goals and five assists in 33 games, and retired afterwards. He was one of the few Rangers to end his career with more goals than assists, but as the old axiom goes, goal scorers are supposed to score goals.

Alex Shibicky File

- **BORN:**
  May 19, 1914; Winnipeg, Manitoba
- **ACQUIRED:**
  Product of Rangers organization
- **FIRST SEASON WITH RANGERS:**
  1935-36

- **BEST SEASON WITH RANGERS:**
  1937-38, 48 GP, 17-18-35, 26 PIM
- **TOTALS WITH RANGERS:**
  Regular season: 322 GP, 110-91-201, 161 PIM
  Playoffs: 40 GP, 12-12-24, 12 PIM

CURTAIN CALL
Celebrity Row

With the likes of Spike Lee and Woody Allen at courtside, it sometimes looks like the Knicks have the monopoly on celebrities in the stands these days. Of course, the Rangers have their share of celebrity fans, including Tim Robbins and Susan Sarandon. But in the pre-World War II era, the "Classiest Team in Hockey" was the toast of the celebrity capital of the world. Regulars at the Garden included the likes of Lucille Ball and Desi Arnaz, Humphrey Bogart, Cab Calloway (he used to duck in for a period or two between appearances and would introduce players to the audience when he performed), the Duke and Duchess of Windsor, Jack LaRue and George Raft. Many Canadian-born celebrities, such as Michael J. Fox and Alan Thicke, have grown up following hockey, and their presence in Hollywood—along with Wayne Gretzky's trade to the Los Angeles Kings in 1988—brought other celebrities out to enjoy the game. Rocker Neil Young's father Scott is a famed hockey writer and winner of the Lester Patrick Trophy. "Peanuts" creator Charles M. Schulz plays in a senior league, and often features hockey cartoons in his daily strips. Most involve Snoopy and Woodstock playing on Woodstock's frozen birdbath. Schulz is a member of the U.S. Hockey Hall of Fame.

Cab Calloway was among the celebrities who frequented the Garden in the early years of the Rangers.

NEW YORK
Ice Exchange

One reason for the absence from postseason play was a major turnover in personnel. An even 10 new faces showed themselves during part or all of the season: Butch Keeling, Glenn Brydson, Howie Morenz, Alex Shibicky, Art Coulter, Neil & Mac Colville, Thomas "Vern" Ayres, Babe Pratt & Phil Watson. Shibicky, Watson, Coulter (from Chicago), Pratt and the Colville brothers would be the base of the next generation of Ranger champions. Among those who departed were Art Somers, Alex Levinsky, Vic Ripley and Bill MacKenzie. Morenz, a future Hall of Famer who spent a season in Chicago before coming to the Rangers, was returned to the Montreal Canadiens, for whom he had starred for many years. The following season, Morenz broke his leg, went into the hospital for surgery, and died five weeks later of a heart attack.

The Colville brothers and Alex Shibicky all joined the Rangers in 1935-36.

Ranger Lists
Players Who Played For Both the Rangers & the Americans

Lorne Chabot	G
Dave Kerr	G
Joe Miller	G
Chuck Rayner	G
Oscar Asmundson	C
Thomas "Vern" Ayres	D
Bill Boyd	RW
Lorne Carr	RW
Duke Dutkowski	D
Pat Egan	D
Orville Heximer	LW
Fred Hunt	RW
Ching Johnson	D
Norm Larson	RW
Charley Mason	RW
Bill Regan	D
Leo Reise Sr.	D
Laurie Scott	F
Fred Thurier	C

1936 1937

TIME CAPSULE

- **October 6, 1936:**
  The New York Yankees routed the New York Giants 13-5 to capture the World Series in six games.

- **November 3, 1936:**
  Franklin D. Roosevelt was reelected as president of the United States, beating Alf Landon.

- **May 6, 1937:**
  The Hindenburg disaster took place, as the German dirigible exploded into flames over Lakehurst, N.J., while much of a horrified nation listened on radio.

1936-37

FINAL STANDINGS

American Division	W	L	T	PTS	GF	GA
Detroit	25	14	9	59	128	102
Boston	23	18	7	53	120	110
RANGERS	19	20	9	47	117	106
Chicago	14	27	7	35	99	131

Canadian Division Winner—Montreal Canadiens

PLAYOFF RESULTS

Quarterfinals: Rangers beat Toronto 2-0

Semifinals: Rangers beat Montreal Maroons 2-0

Finals: Detroit beat Rangers 3-2

LEADING PLAYOFF SCORER

Neil Colville (3-3-6)

STANLEY CUP CHAMPION

Detroit Red Wings

SEASON SNAPSHOT

Most Goals:
Cecil Dillon (20)

Most Assists:
Neil Colville (18)

Most Points:
Cecil Dillon (31)

Most Penalty Minutes:
Ott Heller/Joe Cooper (42)

Most Wins, Goaltender:
Dave Kerr (19)

Lowest Goals-Against Average:
Dave Kerr (2.21)

Most Shutouts:
Dave Kerr (4)

NHL All-Stars:
Cecil Dillon, RW (Second Team)

The 1936-37 Season in Review

After missing the postseason for the first time in franchise history, the Rangers wound up in the Stanley Cup finals. You wouldn't believe it though, based on their regular-season play, which saw them finish under .500 for the first time in franchise history (19-20-9). They actually started out well, going 12-9-3 in the first half of the season. But they faltered in the second half, stumbling home with a 7-11-6 mark. The team had tremendous success against Toronto, winning five of six. But they were just 1-5-2 against Detroit, the eventual Cup champions. Cecil Dillon led the team in scoring for the second straight season with 31 points, and Dave Kerr played every minute of every game and

Lester Patrick coached the Rangers to the finals in 1936-37.

posted four shutouts and a fine 2.21 goals-against average. Nobody expected the Blueshirts to go far in postseason play, but they made short work of the Maple Leafs and the Maroons, sweeping both in the best-of-three series. The Cup finals against Detroit went the full five games, with the last four played in the Olympia due to the circus. The Rangers won their only game at the Garden by a whopping 5-1 score, lost the second game 4-2, won a 1-0 duel in Game 3, and then were shut out in the final two games by Earl Robertson, who never played a regular-season game for the Red Wings during his career. The Red Wings became the first U.S.-based team to defend a Stanley Cup championship successfully.

MAGIC MOMENT December 16, 1936

Alex Shibicky beat Mike Karakas on a penalty shot, one of two in the same game.

While making the Stanley Cup finals after missing the play-offs is an accomplishment unto itself, the Rangers had another memorable moment during a 2-0 victory over the Americans at the Garden on December 16, 1936. For the first time in franchise history, there were two penalty shots awarded in the same game, one for each team. Both shooters missed, as Dave Kerr stopped the Americans' Hap Emms, and Neil Colville was stopped by Earl Robertson. The only other Ranger game with two penalty shots, one by each side, took place on February 1, 1937, less than two months later. During a 6-1 rout of Chicago at the Garden, Alex Shibicky beat Blackhawks goalie Mike Karakas, while Dave Kerr stopped Paul Thompson. The double penalty-shot trick also happened on February 16, 1986, but this time, both chances went to the Rangers. Pierre Larouche and Mike Ridley both failed to convert against Detroit netminder Corrado Micalef. The Rangers still beat the Red Wings 3-1 at the Garden.

RANGER LEGEND
Neil Colville

Neil Colville spent his entire NHL career, all 12 years of it, wearing Broadway Blue. He was there for the good times (a Stanley Cup championship in 1940), and the not-so-good times (five straight post-season misses in the late '40s). The Edmonton native made a one-game debut in 1935-36, then became a full-time player the following season. He never hit the top of the team scoring list, but in his first five full seasons, you would find him either second or third when the final scoring totals came out, and he improved point-wise every season of those five (from 28 points to 36, 37, 38, and a career-high 42 in 1940-41). Most of the time, he played on a line with brother Mac on his right side and Alex Shibicky on his left. Coach/GM Lester Patrick compared the speed that Colville's line had to that of the team's famous "A-Line," featuring the Cook brothers and Frank Boucher. Colville just missed hitting the 100-goal plateau, ending his Ranger career with 99 regular-season tallies. He also never managed to score 20 goals in any one season, though he came close in 1939-40 when he tallied 19. Colville was better suited for the playoffs. His best postseason year was the 1939-40 championship season, in which he had two goals and seven assists, which tied him with Phil Watson as the team's postseason points leader. In Stanley Cup finals career play, Colville had three goals and four assists in 11 games. After a "forced" retirement following the

1941-42 season to join the Armed Forces, Colville came back to the Blueshirts at the end of the 1944-45 season, and played another four full seasons before quitting for good in 1949. Colville was honored in 1967 when he was voted into the Hockey Hall of Fame.

Neil Colville File

- **BORN:**
  August 4, 1914; Edmonton, Alberta
- **ACQUIRED:**
  Product of Rangers organization
- **FIRST SEASON WITH THE RANGERS:**
  1935-36
- **BEST SEASON WITH RANGERS:**
  1940-41, 48 GP, 14-28-42, 28 PIM

- **TOTALS WITH RANGERS:**
  Regular season: 464 GP, 99-166-265, 213 PIM
  Playoffs: 46 GP, 7-19-26, 33 PIM
- **HONORS:**
  Second-team All-Star, 1938-39, 1939-40; All-Star Game, 1948-49

CURTAIN CALL

Joe Nichols

It wasn't true that Joe Nichols was part of the furniture at the old Garden. But it must have seemed that way to the Ranger faithful of the 1930s, '40s and '50s. From 1931 to 1958, Nichols was at the Garden for every home game but one (a draft board physical exam broke the streak), covering the highs and lows of the Rangers for *The New York Times,* the paper for which he wrote for more than four decades. In a recollection published in the program of the final contest at the old Garden in February 1968, Nichols remembered the artistry of the Cook brothers and Frank Boucher, the exploits of defensemen like Ching Johnson and the skills of visiting players like Eddie Shore and Maurice Richard. As for a game that stood out, Nichols cited the 1938 playoff contest in which the Americans beat the Rangers 3-2 in four overtimes to win their last playoff series. Lorne Carr's goal at 1:30 in the morning was the game-winner, and as Nichols noted, "The game was the first hockey story to make page one of *The New York Times.*"

NEW YORK Ice Exchange

Howie Morenz's stay in the Big Apple didn't last long. The long-time Montreal Canadiens star, who came to the Rangers midway through 1935-36 was dealt back to his long-time team by Lester Patrick. Tragically, Morenz broke his leg during a regular-season game and died five weeks later from a heart attack. Time continued to run down on several of the Rangers' original stars. Bun Cook was dealt to Boston, where he played a final season before retiring. It was also the last season for two other original Rangers: Bun's brother, Bill, who played only 21 games, and Murray Murdoch. In

The Rangers released Ching Johnson after the 1936-37 season, only to see him join the Americans.

their stead, youngsters like Mac and Neil Colville, Phil Watson and Babe Pratt, all of whom got their introduction to the NHL the previous season won full-time jobs. Four other newcomers played sparingly: Joe Krol, Eddie Wares, Clint Smith and Bryan Hextall. Krol and Wares didn't even make the team the following season, but Smith and Hextall went on to productive careers with the Rangers and were part of the 1940 championship team.

Ranger Lists

Rangers Who Wore Three Different Jersey Numbers

Name	Jersey Numbers
John Davidson	00, 30, 35
Phil Esposito	5, 12, 77
Jack "Tex" Evans	3, 30, 5
Mark Janssens	27, 47, 15
Kilby MacDonald	14, 8, 2
Larry Mickey	9, 12, 18
Clint Smith	10, 20, 14
Doug Soetaert	1, 31, 33
Irv Spencer	21, 16, 15

—1937 1938—

TIME CAPSULE

- **October 10, 1937:**
  The New York Yankees beat the New York Giants 4-2 to win the World Series in five games.

- **April 10, 1938:**
  The German army occupied and annexed Austria.

- **May 2, 1938:**
  Our Town, Thornton Wilder's novel, won a Pulitzer Prize for drama.

1937-1938

FINAL STANDINGS

American Division	W	L	T	PTS	GF	GA
Boston	30	11	7	67	142	89
RANGERS	27	15	6	60	149	96
Chicago	14	25	9	37	97	139
Detroit	12	25	11	32	99	133

Canadian Division Winner—Toronto

PLAYOFF RESULTS
Quarterfinals: Americans defeated Rangers 2-1
LEADING PLAYOFF SCORERS
Clint Smith (2-0-2),

Neil Colville (2-0-2)

Bryan Hextall (2-0-2)
STANLEY CUP CHAMPION
Chicago Blackhawks

SEASON SNAPSHOT

Most Goals:
Cecil Dillon (21)

Most Assists:
Phil Watson (25)

Most Points:
Cecil Dillon (39)

Most Penalty Minutes:
Art Coulter (80)

Most Wins, Goaltender:
Dave Kerr (27)

Lowest Goals-Against Average:
Dave Kerr (2.00)

Most Shutouts:
Dave Kerr (8)

NHL All-Stars:
Cecil Dillon, RW (First Team);
Lester Patrick, Coach (First Team);
Dave Kerr, G (Second Team);
Art Coulter, D (Second Team)

The 1937-38 Season in Review

The Rangers changed their tendencies in 1937-38; this time, they got off to a slow start, then finished strong. After opening the season 3-5-1, the Blueshirts reeled off five straight wins, tied the Canadiens, then beat the Maroons. They lost only seven of their last 26 games (16-7-3), and in that stretch, ripped off a pair of five-game winning streaks and a four-game winning streak. They did all this without Bill Cook, who retired prior to the season, but several players chipped in offensively to help register the most wins in franchise history (27) by setting a team scoring record with 149 goals. Cecil Dillon led a balanced scoring attack with 21 goals, and Phil Watson was tops with 25 assists. Neil Colville, Alex Shibicky and Bryan Hextall each had 17 goals, and Lynn Patrick (15), Clint Smith (14) and Mac Colville (14) also hit double figures. Dave Kerr, in his fourth season with the team, again played every minute of every game, finishing with a 2.00 goals-against average and eight shutouts. Art Coulter, the team's second captain, spent the most time in the penalty box—80 minutes worth. The Rangers finished second to Boston and met the Americans (who were in the Canadian Division) in the playoffs. The teams split the first two games and the rubber match

Neil Colville (left) had 17 goals as part of a balanced attack.

went into four overtimes before the Amerks' Lorne Carr—an ex-Ranger—beat Kerr to send his former team home for the summer.

Magic Moment *March 27, 1938*

By 1938, it was obvious which hockey team was New York's favorite. The Rangers had dominated the Americans both on the ice and at the box office, so there was much anticipation when the two teams squared off in the playoffs for the second and final time. The Americans, who had finished second in the Canadian Division, were the road team in the opener of the best-of-three series, but stunned the sellout crown by winning 2-1 on Johnny Sorrell's goal at 1:25 of the second overtime. The Rangers evened the series with a 4-3 "road" win and appeared headed for victory in the third game when goals by Alex Shibicky and Bryan Hextall put them ahead 2-0. But the Americans got third-period goals from Lorne Carr and Nels Stewart to send the game into overtime. Lots of overtime. The game, which began at 8:45 p.m., was scoreless through the first three overtimes, then ended abruptly when Carr scored the most famous goal in Americans history, beating Davey Kerr 40 seconds into the fourth overtime

Lorne Carr's goal won the longest game ever at the Garden.

for a 3-2 victory. Lester Patrick's reaction after losing the longest game in Garden history: He crossed the ice, greeted long-time Ranger Ching Johnson, who had gone over to the Amerks after being cut the previous spring, and shook his hand. It was Johnson's last hurrah—and the last big moment for the Americans, who folded four years later.

RANGER LEGEND
Clint Smith

Though not as well known to many Ranger fans such as Bill Cook or Frank Boucher, Clint Smith was still nearly as valuable to the Rangers. Smith was a Ranger for 281 games, and made his NHL debut in the 1936-37 season, when he played two games and scored a goal. His second full season in 1938-39 was his career year, when he led the team in scoring with 41 points (21 goals, 20 assists), and captured the Lady Byng Trophy with just two penalty minutes. A Blueshirt for the first seven years of his 11-year career, Smith racked up 80 goals and 195 points. Amazingly, he only had 12 penalty minutes during his tenure with the team and just 24 for his regular-season career; incredibly, he took just two penalty minutes in 44 career playoff games, with 30 of those contests in a Rangers sweater. Only Buddy O'Connor had as few Ranger penalty minutes in a like number of games played (238). In Smith's first full season, he finished second to Cecil Dillon in team scoring with 14 goals and 37 points. Smith was only the sixth player in team history to finish either first or second in scoring—the first five were Bill Cook, Frank Boucher, Bun Cook, Phil Watson and Cecil Dillon. He was a part of the 1940 Cup team (and picked up his two playoff penalty minutes in the finals), and spent his last four seasons in Chicago, where he retired after the 1946-47 season. Smith posted better playoff numbers with the Blackhawks. In

14 games, he had six goals and nine assists. One of nine Rangers to wear three different jersey numbers during his tenure (10, 20, 14), Smith was elected to the Hockey Hall of Fame in 1991, the 29th player who entered with the Rangers included on his playing résumé.

Clint Smith File

- **BORN:**
  December 12, 1913; Assiniboia, Saskatchewan
- **ACQUIRED:**
  Product of Rangers organization
- **FIRST SEASON WITH RANGERS:**
  1936-37
- **BEST SEASON WITH RANGERS:**
  1938-39, 48 GP, 21-20-41, 2 PIM

- **TOTALS WITH RANGERS:**
  Regular season: 281 GP, 80-115-195, 12 PIM
  Playoffs: 30 GP, 4-5-9, 2 PIM
- **HONORS:**
  Lady Byng Trophy, 1938-39

CURTAIN CALL

Time Magazine

Goaltender Dave Kerr became the first hockey player to be featured on the cover of *Time* when he appeared on the March 14, 1938 issue. It would be more than 20 years later before a second hockey player (Maurice Richard) would be featured on the front page of the national newsweekly. Hockey was a new, non-American sport—something that magazines would rarely bother with, but that didn't stop the local media from covering the Rangers. There were at one time 11 daily tabloids in New York City, so the press coverage was one to rival Montreal or Toronto. But magazine coverage of the sport was still minimal, even with *Sports Illustrated*, who preferred baseball and football. What changed everything was the arrival of Wayne Gretzky. The kid with the memorable last name provided more talent for the league to promote and celebrate since Bobby Orr. Gretzky, who signed with the Rangers in July 1996, also was media-friendly, and knew the impact he would have on the sport by his willingness to promote the game. Gretzky started appearing on magazine covers, which helped propel hockey's budding popularity.

Dave Kerr was the first NHL player to make the cover of Time *Magazine.*

NEW YORK Ice Exchange

Muzz Patrick joined brother Lynn as a Ranger in 1937-38.

Four roster spots changed hands: lesser lights Joe Krol and Eddie Wares were out, Johnny Sherf (one playoff game only), Larry Molyneaux and Bobby Kirk were in. More prominently, Bill Cook, the best right wing the Rangers had up until this point, had retired after playing only 21 games the year before. Also gone was Ching Johnson, who was let go by GM Lester Patrick after the 1936-37 season. He walked across the hall and found a job with the Americans for one season before calling it quits. Finally, Frank Boucher hung up his skates after 18 games, though he wound up making a short comeback in the 1943-44 season. The most prominent addition to the roster was Lester's son Murray (better known as Muzz), a rugged defenseman who had been an amateur boxing champion. He joined his brother Lynn and wound up spending five seasons as a player with the Rangers—plus many more as a coach and general manager.

Ranger Lists

Most Victories, Pre 70-Game Season

29 - 1941-42 (48 games)

27 - 1937-38 (48 games)

27 - 1939-40 (48 games)

26 - 1938-39 (48 games)

25 - 1926-27 (44 games)

23 - 1931-32 (48 games)

23 - 1932-33 (48 games)

WINNING TRADITIONS . . .

New York Rangers and the United States Postal Service

UNITED STATES POSTAL SERVICE™

Continue the winning tradition with United States Postal Service's Priority Mail

The Rangers and the Americans

The New York Americans are little more than an historical footnote now, another of the NHL franchises that exists only in the memory of the fans who watched them and the history books that chronicled them. But for 15 years, they fought the Rangers both on the ice and off, and though they ultimately lost both battles, they hold a unique place in New York hockey history.

The Americans were the Garden's first hockey team. They joined the NHL in 1925-26, a team imported from Hamilton, Ontario by "Big Bill" Dwyer and managed by Tommy Gorman. Their opening night on December 15, 1925—the first hockey game ever played in the brand-new Madison Square Garden, was an international event, featuring a Canadian band, a host of foreign dignitaries and players in star-spangled uniforms. They lost to the powerful Montreal Canadiens and wound up fifth, despite 22 goals from Billy Burch. But the Americans' success at the box office convinced Garden management to get its own team.

Thus, beginning in the winter of 1926, New York had two hockey clubs playing in the same building. With the NHL going from seven teams to 10, the New York squads were split up, with the Rangers in the American Division and the Americans (for purposes of balance) wound up in the Canadian Division. The two teams couldn't have been more dissimilar. The Rangers were the Yankees of the NHL—a team identified with winning and class. The Rangers always made the playoffs, while postseason play for the

The Americans called it quits after the 1941-42 season.

Americans was a sometime thing. The Americans, despite having the capable Gorman (and later Red Dutton) running the team, became the NHL's version of the Brooklyn Dodgers of that era—lovable losers.

The two teams met in the opening round of the 1929 playoffs, where little Roy Worters almost ended the Rangers' reign as Stanley Cup champs by himself. The teams played to a scoreless tie in the first game and the Blueshirts needed Butch Keeling's goal in double overtime—the only tally of the series—to win Game 2 and the series. But as the 1930s went on, the Americans faded.

They had an excellent first line at one time, with Art Chapman centering for Lorne Carr and Dave "Sweeney" Schriner (who won back-to-back scoring titles in 1935-36 and 1936-37 for sub-.500 teams), but were also the home for the NHL's unwanted—guys who got old before their time. One of the unwanted was Ching Johnson,

who went from the Rangers to the Americans after the 1936-37 season when Lester Patrick released him.

Johnson got the last laugh when the two clubs met in the opening round of the playoffs in 1938 and Carr's goal in the fourth overtime gave the Americans the game and the series.

That game was a sellout, but big crowds were something the Americans only drew when they played the Rangers. With the team not winning and not drawing, Dutton announced that for the 1941-42 season, the team would be known as the Brooklyn Americans, practicing at the Brooklyn Ice Palace but playing at the Garden. But if the move was designed to spark some civic pride in the borough's hockey fans, it flopped.

With World War II raging, the Americans finally went under before the 1942-43 season; Dutton, in an ironic twist of fate, wound up presiding over their demise as the second president of the NHL.

1938 1939

NEW YORK RANGERS

TIME CAPSULE

- **October 9, 1938**
  The New York Yankees beat the Chicago Cubs 8-3 to complete a four-game sweep for their third straight World Series championship.

- **October 30, 1938:**
  War of the Worlds made its broadcast debut; Orson Welles' radio play wreaked havoc, as many thought the broadcast was real.

- **December 11, 1938:**
  The New York Giants won their second NFL championship, beating the Green Bay Packers 23-17 at the Polo Grounds on Hank Soar's third-quarter touchdown.

1938-1939

FINAL STANDINGS

	W	L	T	PTS	GF	GA
Boston	36	10	2	74	156	76
RANGERS	26	16	6	58	149	105
Toronto	19	20	9	47	114	107
NY Americans	17	21	10	44	119	157
Detroit	18	24	6	42	107	128
Montreal	15	24	9	39	115	146
Chicago	12	28	8	32	91	132

PLAYOFF RESULTS
Semifinals: Boston defeated Rangers 4-3

LEADING PLAYOFF SCORER
Alex Shibicky (3-1-4)

STANLEY CUP CHAMPION
Boston Bruins

SEASON SNAPSHOT

Most Goals:
Alex Shibicky (24)

Most Assists:
Ott Heller (23)

Most Points:
Clint Smith (41)

Most Penalty Minutes:
Art Coulter (58)

Most Wins, Goaltender:
Dave Kerr (26)

Lowest Goals-Against Average:
Dave Kerr (2.19)

Most Shutouts:
Dave Kerr (6)

NHL Award Winners:
Clint Smith (Lady Byng Trophy)

NHL All-Stars:
Art Coulter, D (Second Team)
Neil Colville, C (Second Team)

The 1938-39 Season in Review

With the NHL now down to seven teams, the Rangers returned to their usual form, getting off to a fast start by winning their first four games and 13 of their first 19. But in what had become typical fashion, they slumped toward the end of the season, winning just three of their final 13 games. Still, they wound up second to Boston and were the only team besides the Bruins to finish over .500. Lady Byng Trophy winner Clint Smith led the team with 41 points while spending only two minutes in the penalty box. For the fourth straight season, Dave Kerr tended goal in every game; he wound up with a 2.19 goals-against average and six shutouts. The offense opened up, finishing second in the league in scoring and enabling the Rangers to win nine games by four or more goals. They matched the previous franchise-high with 149 goals scored. Seven players hit double figures in goals scored, with Alex Shibicky topping all scorers with 24. The only team they couldn't handle was Boston, losing five of eight games. The Blueshirts wound up 16 points behind the Bruins when the regular season closed, and sat 11 points ahead of third-place Toronto. The Rangers met Boston in the semifinals in the first-ever

Clint Smith won the Lady Byng Trophy and led the Rangers in scoring.

best-of-seven playoff series in NHL history, and the Bruins won Game 7 on Mel "Sudden Death" Hill's third overtime goal of the series. The season marked the end of Lester Patrick's coaching regime. He turned over the reins to Frank Boucher for the 1939-40 season, but remained in the general manager's role until stepping down in 1946—again in favor of Boucher.

MAGIC MOMENT   April 2, 1939

Mel Hill's three overtime goals sank the Rangers.

Mel Hill was a rookie forward on a Boston powerhouse that featured players like Milt Schmidt, Woody Dumart and Bill Cowley. But for one spring, he was the most timely scorer in hockey history. Because the Bruins and Rangers had finished 1-2 in the standings, their "reward" was a best-of-seven series for a trip to the Cup finals. Hill almost single-handedly put the Bruins into the title round, scoring overtime goals for a 2-1 win in the opener and a 3-2 triumph in Game 2. After the Rangers rallied from a three-game deficit to force a seventh game in Boston, Hill did it again. Eight minutes into the third extra period, he took a pass from Bill Cowley and beat Dave Kerr to send the Bruins to the finals on their way to the Stanley Cup. "I just happened to get super-hot in that series with New York," said Hill, who earned the sobriquet "Sudden Death" for his efforts. Describing the game-winner, he said, "I got the puck from Cowley and held it for a second, then I flipped the puck up on the short side." The Rangers who came one goal short of becoming the first team ever to win a series after losing the first three games, exacted revenge the following spring, beating Boston in six games on their way to the championship.

RANGER LEGEND
Art Coulter

After spending his first four-plus NHL seasons in Chicago, Art Coulter was traded to the Rangers, and stayed on for more than six seasons. While he was on the roster for a full season, the Rangers never missed postseason play. It was more than a coincidence, because Coulter was regarded as a solid, stay-at-home, hard-hitting type of defenseman who could score the odd goal or two. When Bill Cook, the only captain the Rangers had ever had, decided to retire after the 1936-37 season, coach/GM Lester Patrick bestowed the captain's "C" upon Coulter, who wore it until his retirement. Coulter, Bill Cook and Mark Messier are the only Rangers to captain Stanley Cup teams on Broadway. Dave Kerr and Coulter were the only players on the 1940 Stanley Cup championship team who were imported from outside the Rangers organization (Kerr came from the Americans). Coulter contributed 85 regular-season points and seven playoff points to the Rangers' cause. He never failed to score at least one goal in any season on Broadway, and his biggest numbers came in the 1940-41 season, when he scored five goals and added 14 assists for 19 points. Coulter also spent some time in the penalty box while with the Blueshirts, 332 minutes' worth. Three times a second-team All-Star selection, Coulter finished his 11-year career with 30 goals, 82 assists, 112 points and 543 penalty minutes, as well as a pair of Stanley Cup rings (he also was a member of the 1934 champion Blackhawks). He retired after the 1941-42 season, and was elected to the Hockey Hall of Fame in 1974, the 17th member of the Rangers to be so honored.

Art Coulter File

- **BORN:**
  May 31, 1909; Winnipeg, Manitoba
- **ACQUIRED:**
  From Chicago for Earl Seibert, January 1936
- **FIRST SEASON WITH RANGERS:**
  1935-36
- **BEST SEASON WITH RANGERS:**
  1940-41, 35 GP, 5-14-19, 42 PIM

- **TOTALS WITH RANGERS:**
  Regular season: 287 GP, 18-67-85, 332 PIM
  Playoffs: 37 GP, 2-5-7, 60 PIM
- **HONORS:**
  Second-team All-Star, 1937-38, 1938-39, 1939-40

CURTAIN CALL

Hollywood on Ice

Before he made Gone With the Wind, Clark Gable had been tapped to play a hockey star.

But for a studio's decision, Phil Watson and Babe Pratt might have become movie stars. Metro-Goldwyn-Mayer had planned a movie called *The Great Canadian*, starring Clark Gable as a hockey hero. The studio got Lester Patrick to allow the use of the Garden for location shots, and obtained permission to use Watson and Pratt as doubles in the hockey scenes. Watson was to double for Gable (he even grew a pencil-thin mustache like the star), and Pratt for the villain, whose role had not been filled. Pratt, convinced he was handsomer than Watson, reportedly told Patrick he should have been Gable's double. Patrick is said to have replied that Gable wouldn't risk having someone as handsome as Pratt acting as his double. Unfortunately, neither player got his 15 minutes of fame, as the movie was eventually canceled. Gable did bounce back from that loss to star in a flick of some note: *Gone With the Wind*. Among hockey movies that have been made over the years, perhaps the best known is *Slapshot*, starring Paul Newman. It was the film that also introduced the cartoonish Hanson Brothers to film and hockey fans.

NEW YORK Ice Exchange

Larry Molyneaux earned a regular spot in 1938-39.

GM/Coach Lester Patrick had no trouble keeping track of two of his sons, now that Muzz was playing full-time on the Rangers' blue line. The youngest Patrick earned a full-time job after playing one regular-season game in 1937-38. Larry Molyneaux, who had a two-game tryout with the Rangers a season earlier, also earned a regular spot in the lineup. The biggest loss was forward Butch Keeling, who quietly put up 136 goals in 455 games over 10 seasons for the Rangers. New York was now devoid of any members of the original Rangers, but Lester Patrick had put together the core of a team that would eventually win the Stanley Cup a year later. Besides Muzz Patrick, the only newcomer to see significant playing time was George Allen, who had six goals and 12 points in 19 games, getting some ice because Lynn Patrick missed 13 games. Joe Krol and Billy Carse also had one-game cameos. In league terms, the biggest move was the decision by the Montreal Maroons to fold, leaving the NHL as a one-division, seven-team league with two franchises in New York.

Ranger Lists

Most Goals in a Road Game

March 16, 1939 N.Y. Americans	11-5
December 4, 1976 Minnesota	11-4
March 24, 1978 Washington	11-4
October 25, 1984 New Jersey	11-2
November 25, 1992 Pittsburgh	11-3
October 12, 1976 Minnesota	10-4

—1939 1940—

TIME CAPSULE

- **September 3, 1939:**
  France and Great Britain declared war on Germany, while the United States remained neutral.

- **December 10, 1939:**
  The Green Bay Packers won the NFL championship with a 27-0 pasting of the New York Giants.

- **May 6, 1940:**
  John Steinbeck won the Pulitzer Prize for his book *The Grapes of Wrath*.

1939-1940

FINAL STANDINGS

	W	L	T	PTS	GF	GA
Boston	31	12	5	67	170	98
RANGERS	27	11	10	64	136	77
Toronto	25	17	6	56	134	110
Chicago	23	19	6	52	112	120
Detroit	16	26	6	38	90	126
NY Americans	15	29	4	34	106	140
Montreal	10	33	5	25	90	167

PLAYOFF RESULTS

Semifinals: Rangers beat Boston 4-2

Finals: Rangers beat Toronto 4-2

LEADING PLAYOFF SCORERS

Phil Watson (3-6-9)

Neil Colville (2-7-9)

STANLEY CUP CHAMPION

NEW YORK RANGERS

SEASON SNAPSHOT

Most Goals:
Bryan Hextall (24)

Most Assists:
Phil Watson (28)

Most Points:
Bryan Hextall (39)

Most Penalty Minutes:
Art Coulter (68)

Most Wins, Goaltender:
Dave Kerr (27)

Lowest Goals-Against Average:
Dave Kerr (1.60)

Most Shutouts:
Dave Kerr (8)

NHL Award Winners:
Dave Kerr (Vezina Trophy);
Kilby MacDonald (Calder Trophy)

NHL All-Stars:
Dave Kerr, G (First Team);
Bryan Hextall, RW (First Team);
Frank Boucher, Coach (Second Team);
Art Coulter, D (Second Team);
Neil Colville, C (Second Team)

The 1939-40 Season in Review

This Ranger group was a dynamite team, one of the best teams ever to skate on Broadway. They started off 1-4-3, but after that, everything clicked. From November 28 until January 14, the Blueshirts went undefeated, winning 14 games (10 of them in a row) and tying three. After the streak was snapped with a 2-1 loss in Chicago, the Rangers won their next five for a 19-1-3 string. Under rookie coach Frank Boucher, the team also became innovative. They pulled Kerr in the last minute of the Chicago loss, but GM Lester Patrick didn't know about it beforehand, and his yells alerted both the Blackhawks and the referee, who blew the play dead. Boucher was also the creator of the "box defense" while the team was shorthanded. There were 13 players who appeared in at least 43 games and hit double figures in points. Facing the Bruins in the playoff semifinals, Vezina Trophy winner Dave Kerr allowed one goal in the Rangers' four victories. In the finals for the sixth time in franchise history, they faced the Toronto Maple Leafs. The Rangers managed to get in two home games before the circus took over, and won both. Toronto won the next two games at Maple Leaf Gardens to tie the series. The pivotal fifth game went to

The Colville Brothers, Mac (left) and Neil (center) and Alex Shibicky gave the Rangers a solid line behind the Watson-Lynn Patrick-Hextall unit.

double overtime tied at 1-1 before Muzz Patrick scored at 11:43, giving the Rangers the series lead. They trailed 2-0 in Game 6, but rallied to force overtime; Bryan Hextall's goal at 2:07 gave the Rangers the third Stanley Cup in their 14-year history.

MAGIC MOMENT *April 13, 1940*

It was later sung derisively for so long, but "Nineteen-Forty" still converted into a championship for the Blueshirts. On April 13, the Rangers, again tossed out of their home for the circus, were ahead of the Toronto Maple Leafs in the Stanley Cup finals three games to two. The Rangers came into the game relaxed—maybe too relaxed, as Syl Apps and Nick Metz staked Toronto to a 2-0 lead. GM Lester Patrick came into the dressing room after the first period, sat down quietly and is said to have told his team, "Let's get down to business. I've made arrangements for a victory party. Don't let me down." They didn't. In the third period, Neil Colville and Alf Pike scored in a two-minute span to draw New York even. Naturally, 60 minutes couldn't produce a winner, so into overtime they went. And unlike Game 5, when Muzz Patrick put a stake in Toronto's heart at 11:43 of double overtime, the demise of the Maple Leafs in Game 6 was quick. Bryan Hextall clinched the Rangers' third Stanley Cup in 14 years by beating Broda just 2:07 into the extra session on assists from

Bryan Hextall's overtime goal gave the Rangers their third Stanley Cup.

Phil Watson and Dutch Hiller, making Boucher a champion in his first year behind the bench. Little did Ranger fans know that it would be 54 years before the Cup would return to Broadway.

RANGER LEGEND
Dave Kerr

The rival New York Americans decided that they could do better than to have Dave Kerr in net, so the Rangers brought him on board in 1934 with GM Lester Patrick's intent that the revolving door policy of goalies would cease. Kerr did his job, as he tended net for seven seasons on Broadway, posting 40 regular-season shutouts and winning the Vezina Trophy in 1939-40 as the Blueshirts won it all. Kerr played the last 37 games of the 1934-35 season, his first wearing Ranger blue. The next season, he played all but one game, with Bert Gardiner getting the nod (and the win) in the other. He then started every game for his last five seasons on Broadway. Kerr, who was the first hockey player ever to be featured on the cover of *Time* Magazine, would have his finest hour in the 1940 playoffs—and it wasn't even the final round against Toronto in which he stood out, it was the semifinals against the Bruins in which he shone brightest. After shutting out the B's 4-0 in the opener at home, Kerr and the Rangers lost the next two games in Boston. After that, Kerr took charge. He posted back-to-back shutouts, both by 1-0 scores with one in each city, and is one of only two goalies in Rangers history to post consecutive playoff shutouts (Mike Richter did it in 1994). Lifetime, Kerr played 11 seasons for the Maroons, Americans and Rangers, posting regular-season totals of 203 wins, 51 shutouts and a 2.17 goals-against average. Surprisingly, his playoff record was under .500 (18-19-3), but he still had a sparkling 1.74 goals-against average with eight shutouts (seven as a Ranger) and a Stanley Cup championship to his credit. Kerr played only one more season after the 1940 championship, stunning the Rangers by announcing his retirement following the 1940-41 campaign.

Dave Kerr File

- **BORN:**
  January 11, 1910, Toronto, Ontario
- **ACQUIRED:**
  From the New York Americans, December 1934
- **FIRST SEASON WITH RANGERS:**
  1934-35
- **BEST SEASON WITH RANGERS:**
  1939-40, 48 GP, 27-11-10, 1.60 goals-against average, 8 shutouts

- **TOTALS WITH RANGERS:**
  Regular season: 324 GP, 157-110-57, 2.07 goals-against average, 40 shutouts
  Playoffs: 32 GP, 18-19-3, 1.99 goals-against average, 7 shutouts
- **HONORS:**
  Vezina Trophy, 1939-40
  First-team All-Star, 1939-40
- **NHL MILESTONES:**
  51 shutouts

CURTAIN CALL

The NHL On NBC

NBC included the Rangers in the first-ever hockey telecast in the United States. On February 25, the future peacock network presented the Rangers-Canadiens game from Madison Square Garden. The game was televised using only one camera in a fixed position. Only a couple of hundred people were able to watch—because there were only approximately 300 television sets in the city. The game was the second indoor sporting event broadcast on the tube; the first was a track meet at the Garden that was broadcast the night before. The event went across W2XBS, the experimental TV station of NBC, then the dominant radio network. Skip Walz was calling the action, but he went by his stage name of "Bill Allen." As a reference point: At the time, there were 11 newspapers in New York fighting for readership. The first cablecasts of Rangers hockey took place in the early 70s, when Viacom Cablevision in Islip (Long Island) picked up home broadcasts of both the Rangers and the Knicks—commercial free (those were the days).

NEW YORK Ice Exchange

For the first time in their history, the Rangers started the season without Lester Patrick behind the bench. Patrick had stepped down as coach, naming former star center Frank Boucher to replace him. Boucher inherited a largely set lineup, largely due to the "4-R" talent system that Patrick put together early in the '30s. Only two Rangers on this Cup-winning team came from other clubs: goalie Dave Kerr (from the rival Americans) and defenseman Art Coulter (from Chicago). Everybody else came up through the Roamers, Rovers and/or Ramblers to get to the big club. The best addition was Kilby MacDonald, who won the Calder Trophy as the NHL's top rookie. Defenseman Larry Molyneaux, who played in 43 games the prior season, was gone from the Stanley Cup roster, as were Joe Krol and Bill Carse. In their stead came Johnny Polich and Stan Smith (one game each), and Cliff Barton (three games). Smith made one playoff appearance, while the others never saw postseason ice. Cecil Dillon went to Detroit before the season, and George Allen was Chicago-bound. Six Rangers played all 48 games, and Smith came in for a playoff game that Alex Shibicky missed. Otherwise, every regular played in all 12 postseason games.

Kilby MacDonald won the Calder Trophy in 1939-40.

Ranger Lists

Career Playoff Shutout leaders

Name	# of shutouts
Dave Kerr	7
Mike Richter	6
John Ross Roach	5
Andy Aitkenhead	3
Lorne Chabot	2
John Vanbiesbrouck	2
Joe Miller	1
Jim Henry	1
Chuck Rayner	1
Ed Giacomin	1
John Davidson	1
Glen Hanlon	1

—1940 1941—

TIME CAPSULE

- **November 5, 1940:**
  Franklin D. Roosevelt won an unprecedented third term as president, demolishing Wendell Willkie in one of the most lopsided elections ever.

- **December 8, 1940:**
  The Chicago Bears smashed the Washington Redskins, 73-0, in the NFL championship game, the biggest rout in pro football history.

- **June 22, 1941:**
  Germany invaded the Soviet Union, with whom it had previously made a non-aggression pact.

1940-1941
FINAL STANDINGS

	W	L	T	PTS	GF	GA
Boston	27	8	13	67	168	102
Toronto	28	14	6	62	145	99
Detroit	21	16	11	53	112	102
RANGERS	21	19	8	50	143	125
Chicago	16	25	7	39	112	139
Montreal	16	26	6	38	121	147
NY Americans	8	29	11	27	99	186

PLAYOFF RESULTS
Toronto defeated Rangers 2-1
LEADING PLAYOFF SCORERS
Neil Colville (1-1-2)

Mac Colville (1-1-2)

Babe Pratt (1-1-2)
STANLEY CUP CHAMPION
Boston Bruins

SEASON SNAPSHOT

Most Goals:
Bryan Hextall (26)

Most Assists:
Neil Colville (28)

Most Points:
Bryan Hextall (44)

Most Penalty Minutes:
Babe Pratt (52)

Most Wins, Goaltender:
Dave Kerr (21)

Lowest Goals-Against Average:
Dave Kerr (2.60)

Most Shutouts:
Dave Kerr (2)

NHL All-Stars:
Bryan Hextall, RW (First Team)
Ott Heller, D (Second Team)

The 1940-41 Season in Review

T he Rangers played most of the 1940-41 season as if they were living off the previous spring's Stanley Cup triumph. After starting off 2-0-2, including a 3-2 victory over the Americans, the Rangers were a model of inconsistency, playing well in fits and starts while going 8-12-5 over the first 25 games. A pair of four-game unbeaten streaks sandwiched around a pair of road losses was an indication that the Rangers were coming around, but a four-game losing streak began to make Garden fans nervous about even reaching the playoffs. But with nine games to go in the season, New York finally caught fire. A five-game winning streak eased the Garden faithful's fears about the playoffs, and after a loss in Detroit, the Rangers finally climbed above .500 by closing with three more victories, all at home. The line of Bryan Hextall, Lynn Patrick, and Phil Watson powered the offense, with Hextall scoring 26 times to lead a parade of seven players in double digits; while Dave Kerr, though not quite up to his Vezina Trophy-winning form of 1939-40, got tougher as the season went on. Their playoff opponents were the Red Wings, and the best-of-three series went to the limit.

Neil Colville led the Rangers with 28 assists in 1940-41.

Detroit won the opener 2-1 in overtime on a goal by Gus Giesebrecht. The Rangers stayed alive with a 3-1 win at the Garden, but the Wings advanced with a 3-2 victory in the third and deciding game at the Olympia.

Magic Moment
November 2, 1940

Phil Watson's goal capped a late Ranger outburst that won the season opener in Toronto.

Talk about returning to the scene of your greatest triumph. The NHL schedule-maker sent the Rangers to Maple Leafs' Gardens for their 1940-41 season opener—less than seven months after the Blueshirts had left Toronto as Stanley Cup champions following an overtime triumph in Game 6 of the finals. The season-opener also appeared headed for overtime; the teams were tied 1-1 with less than 90 seconds left on goals by Alex Shibicky and the Leafs' Gordie Drillon. But just as they had done in the spring, the Rangers came through when it counted. Defenseman Babe Pratt scored with 1:26 left to break the tie. With the Leafs now desperate, Bryan Hextall, who scored the overtime goal against Turk Broda to win the Cup, beat him again with 1:05 left for a 3-1 lead. Phil Watson added some window-dressing by scoring with one second left as the Rangers went home with a 4-1 victory—a lovely way to start the defense of their championship. They were probably just as happy the game didn't go into overtime: Of the 13 games that went into extra time that season, the Rangers lost five and tied eight.

RANGER LEGEND
Bryan Hextall

Like the New York Yankees of the 1940s, the Rangers had their own version of "Old Reliable." Tommy Henrich's equivalent on ice was Bryan Hextall, who showed up for work every night and gave everything he had. Hextall played every game for seven straight seasons, a streak interrupted only by World War II. The war also ended his streak of scoring 20 or more goals at six seasons—matching an NHL record at the time. Hextall had a cup of coffee with the Rangers in 1936-37 before hooking on for good the next season and scoring 17 goals. He connected 20 times in 1938-39 and had at least 21 in each of the next five seasons. But none of those goals will ever compare to the one he scored on April 13, 1940 at Maple Leaf Gardens. Hextall's backhander beat Turk Broda at 2:07 into overtime, giving the Rangers their third Stanley Cup—their last championship until 1994. Two seasons later, Hextall had another "last" when he became the last Ranger to win the Art Ross Trophy as the NHL's leading scorer while leading the Rangers to first place, the last time they finished on top of the overall standings until 1991-92. Hextall was a durable, consistent scorer who also loved to hit; in 1942-43, writer James Hendy called Hextall "the greatest right wing in hockey today" and termed him "a fire-eater on the ice who hands out more body checks than 99 percent of the defensemen." Hextall stayed home in Saskatchewan in 1944-45 for war defense work, and was hampered in 1945-46 by an illness that threatened his career. But he came back in 1946-47 to score 20 goals while again playing every

game, then called it quits after a 1947-48 campaign in which a knee injury helped limit him to 8 goals. Hextall was inducted into the Hall of Fame in 1969. Two of his sons, Bryan and Dennis, played for the Rangers in the late 1960s and early 1970s, while grandson Ron is one of the NHL's top goaltenders.

Bryan Hextall File

- **BORN:**
  July 31, 1915; Grenfell, Saskatchewan
- **ACQUIRED:**
  Product of Rangers organization
- **FIRST SEASON WITH RANGERS:**
  1936-37
- **BEST SEASON WITH RANGERS:**
  1942-43, 50 GP, 27-32-59, 28 PIM

- **TOTALS WITH RANGERS:**
  Regular season: 449 GP, 187-175-362, 227 PIM
  Playoffs: 37 GP, 8-9-17, 19 PIM
- **HONORS:**
  Art Ross Trophy, 1941-42
  First-team All-Star, 1939-40, 1940-41, 1941-42
  Second-team All-Star, 1942-43
  West Side Assn. Rangers MVP, 1943-44

CURTAIN CALL
The Rangers Victory Song

Photo courtesy of the Hockey Hall of Fame.

Hockey fans weren't the only ones inspired by the Rangers' march to the 1940 Stanley Cup. J. Fred Coots, the popular composer of *Love Letters In The Sand*, watched the Rangers beat Toronto in the finals and was so taken by their four overtime victories that he felt moved to write a special song for his new heroes. Thus was born the *Rangers Victory Song*. "Just keep your stick on the puck, and don't lay down with your luck, that's the *Rangers Victory Song,*" he wrote. Team officials liked the song so much that they had it played every time the Rangers took the ice at the old Garden. The song lasted longer than most of Coots' other ditties, even making the move to the new Garden in 1968 and outlasting everything from team ownership changes to The Beatles and the Disco Age. A galaxy of Ranger stars skated out onto Garden ice to the strains of the Victory Song during the 40+ years it was used—but ironically, the one thing they never were able to do was record the ultimate victory, another Stanley Cup triumph, until 1994.

NEW YORK Ice Exchange

Talk about staying with the players who've succeeded for you: GM Lester Patrick stuck with the same 15 regulars (14 skaters and one goaltender) who won the Stanley Cup in 1940. Only defenseman Art Coulter (35) played less than 40 games, while six Rangers played all 48 games and four others missed just one contest each. Stan Smith played eight games in his second and last cup of coffee with the team, while Bill Juzda, who returned to the team after the war, had a five-game trial. Herb Foster (4), Johnny Polich (2) and Bill Allum (1) were the only other players to see any action. Goaltender Dave Kerr played in every game for the fifth straight season, then stunned the Rangers after the playoffs by announcing his retirement. Kerr, who finished his Ranger career with 40 regular-season shutouts and seven in the playoffs, played every regular-season game except one (in 1935-36) from his arrival in 1934-35 until he called it quits—a team durability standard that's not likely to be broken.

1940-41 was Dave Kerr's last season in the NHL.

Ranger Lists
Playoff Records vs. Original Six Teams

Montreal
No. Series: 14
Record: 7-7
Last meeting: 1996-W

Boston
No. Series: 9
Record: 3-6
Last meeting: 1973-W

Toronto
No. Series: 8
Record: 5-3
Last meeting: 1971-W

Chicago
No. Series: 5
Record: 1-4
Last meeting: 1973-L

Detroit
No. Series: 5
Record: 1-4
Last meeting: 1950-L

—1941— 1942—

TIME CAPSULE

- **October 5, 1941:**
  Brooklyn catcher Mickey Owen was unable to handle what would have been a game-ending third strike to Tommy Henrich in Game 4 of the World Series; the Yankees rallied for four runs, turning a 4-3 loss into a 7-4 victory.

- **December 7, 1941:**
  The Japanese attacked Pearl Harbor in Hawaii, killing about 3,000 Americans and triggering the United States' entry into World War II.

- **December 21, 1941:**
  The Chicago Bears downed the New York Giants 37-9 to win the NFL championship.

1941-1942
FINAL STANDINGS

	W	L	T	PTS	GF	GA
RANGERS	29	17	2	60	177	143
Toronto	27	18	3	57	156	138
Boston	25	17	6	56	160	118
Chicago	22	23	3	47	145	155
Detroit	19	25	4	42	140	147
Montreal	18	27	3	39	134	173
Brooklyn	16	29	3	35	133	175

PLAYOFF RESULTS
Semifinals: Boston defeated Rangers 4-2
LEADING PLAYOFF SCORERS
Alex Shibicky (3-2-5)

Phil Watson (1-4-5)

Neil Colville (0-5-5)
STANLEY CUP CHAMPION
Toronto Maple Leafs

SEASON SNAPSHOT

Most Goals:
Lynn Patrick (32)

Most Assists:
Phil Watson (37)

Most Points:
Bryan Hextall (56)

Most Penalty Minutes:
Babe Pratt (65)

Most Wins, Goaltender:
Jim Henry (29)

Lowest Goals-Against Average:
Jim Henry (2.98)

Most Shutouts:
Jim Henry (1)

NHL Award Winners:
Bryan Hextall (Art Ross Trophy)

NHL All-Stars:
Bryan Hextall, RW (First Team);
Lynn Patrick, LW (First Team);
Frank Boucher, Coach (First Team);
Phil Watson, C (Second Team)

The 1941-42 Season in Review

(L. to R.) Bryan Hextall, Phil Watson, Lynn Patrick. Hextall led the NHL in scoring with Patrick finishing second and Watson coming in fourth.

The Rangers' 16th NHL season turned out to be one to remember, as the Blueshirts rallied from a slow start to finish first for the third time in their history. The Rangers lost their first four home games on the way to a 3-5-0 start, but got hot around Thanksgiving and stayed that way for the next 10 weeks. The line of Phil Watson centering for Lynn Patrick on the left and Bryan Hextall on the right turned into the NHL's top offensive unit, with Hextall (56 points) edging Patrick (55 points, including a league-high 32 goals) for the scoring title and Watson (52 points) finishing fourth. A 20-4-1 streak put the Rangers into first place and they managed to stay on top despite a late 4-7-1 slide that made a final-night victory in Chicago a necessity. The 5-1 win at Chicago Stadium enabled the Rangers to finish three points ahead of Toronto. Unfortunately for the Rangers, the playoff system of that era had the first- and second-place teams meeting in a best-of-seven series for an automatic berth in the finals. Lester Patrick predicted a six-game Ranger triumph; he had the right series length but the wrong winner. The Leafs opened the series with a win at home, won Game 2 at the Garden, and the Rangers never caught up. They got within 3-2 by winning Game 5 to send the series back

to Toronto. Third-period goals by Alf Pike and Watson tied Game 6 at 2-2 and overtime appeared imminent, but Nick Metz beat rookie goalie Jim Henry with six seconds left in regulation to win the series. By the next autumn, World War II had decimated the Rangers, leaving just the shadow of a first-place team.

MAGIC MOMENT | *March 15, 1942*

Alex Shibicky scored his 100th career goal as the Rangers wrapped up first place.

The Rangers appeared to have a lock on first place for most of the season, but a final-month slump combined with a surge by Toronto left them needing a victory on the final night of the season to assure themselves of the regular-season championship. The Rangers' task appeared tougher: They had to play the fourth-place Blackhawks in Chicago, while Toronto, which trailed the Blueshirts by one point, visited the Garden to take on the last-place Americans. But the Rangers wound up having little trouble with the Hawks. Lynn Patrick scored his league-leading 31st and 32nd goals, Bryan Hextall had a goal and an assist to wrap up the scoring title and Alex Shibicky tallied his 100th NHL goal as the Rangers coasted to a 5-1 victory. It marked the second straight season in which the Rangers had avoided being shut out, and their total of 177 goals was just two short of the post-1926 record of 179 set by Boston in 1929-30. Just in case their fellow New Yorkers needed some help, the Americans, playing what turned out to be the final game in franchise history, shredded the Leafs 6-3.

Perhaps more than any other defenseman of his era, Babe Pratt believed that the best defense was a good offense; by the standards of his time, Pratt may have been the game's premier offensive defenseman. One of his offensive marks (most assists) stood for 21 years and wasn't broken until well after the schedule had expanded from 50 games to 70. There was little doubt even when he was young that Pratt was going to be a star: At age 17, he played for teams in five different leagues and helped all of them win championships. Ranger scout Al Ritchie called Pratt "the finest prospect I have ever seen" and Ritchie knew what he was talking about—the young defenseman turned pro with the Philadelphia Ramblers (a Ranger farm team) in 1935, and by January 1936, he was a Ranger. Pratt, who at 6-foot-3 and 195 pounds was one of the biggest players of his era, learned alongside Blueshirt stalwarts Ching Johnson, Art Coulter and Ott Heller and became one of the keys to the 1940 championship squad. Pratt was paired with Heller during the 1939-40 season and the two were on ice for only 17 goals against during the 48-goal schedule. Pratt, who loved the New York social scene as much as its hockey environment, nearly became a movie star, too—he was tapped to double for the villain of a movie in which Clark Gable was to play a hockey hero, but MGM wound up scrapping the movie. Prior to the 1942-43 season, Pratt was dealt to Toronto, where he continued to star. He won the Hart Trophy as the league's MVP in 1943-44 while setting a scoring mark for defensemen with 57 points in 50 games, and scored the Cup-winning goal in Game 7 of the 1945 finals against Detroit. Pratt was suspended 16 games for gambling during the 1945-46 season, and after 31 games with Boston the next season, he was gone from the NHL for good. Not that he stopped playing: He was named MVP in the Pacific Coast League from 1947-48 through 1950-51 before finally retiring in 1953. He was voted into the Hockey Hall of Fame in 1966.

Babe Pratt File

BORN:
January 7, 1916; Stoney Mountain, Manitoba

ACQUIRED:
Product of Rangers organization

FIRST SEASON WITH RANGERS:
1935-36

BEST SEASON WITH RANGERS:
1941-42, 47 GP, 4-24-28, 65 PIM

TOTALS WITH RANGERS:
Regular season: 307 GP, 27-97-124, 299 PIM
Playoffs: 39 GP, 7-10-17, 70 PIM

CURTAIN CALL

Goodbye Americans

Right from the moment the Rangers arrived in New York, the Big Apple's first team, the Americans, became second-class citizens. With Madison Square Garden owning the Rangers, the Americans were the tenants—and as any New Yorker will tell you, it's better to own than rent. While the Rangers were living up to their nickname, "The Classiest Team In Hockey," the Americans became the poor relatives, a team largely made up of hand-me-downs from other teams. Not that there weren't some big moments for the folks in the star-spangled uniforms. Probably the biggest came in 1938, when they ousted the Rangers in the playoffs on Lorne Carr's goal in the fourth overtime. The attendance was announced as 16,340—about 400 more than the Garden's capacity. But by the early 1940s, the Americans were the sad sacks of the NHL, and even Red Dutton's move to rechristen the team as the Brooklyn Americans (practicing in Brooklyn but playing at the Garden) in 1941 didn't spark any interest. World War II hastened their demise, and in an ironic twist of fate, Dutton presided over their dismemberment as president of the NHL.

Red Dutton (L.) tried his best as a player and executive, but the Americans went out of business after the 1941-42 season.

NEW YORK Ice Exchange

World War II was under way, but the fighting had little immediate effect on the NHL. The first Ranger to leave was Muzz Patrick, who joined the U.S. Army after Pearl Harbor. One move that did have an effect on the Rangers was Dave Kerr's

Grant Warwick won the Calder Trophy in 1941-42.

surprising decision to retire just one year after backstopping the Rangers to the Stanley Cup. But rookie "Sugar" Jim Henry stepped in and won 29 games with a 2.98 goals-against average, enabling the Rangers to finish first. Another newcomer who played a key role was Grant Warwick, who had 16 goals and 33 points in 44 games to win the Calder Trophy as the NHL's top rookie. Bill Juzda took Patrick's place on the back line, while Alan Kuntz added 10 goals in 31 games up front. Two players who didn't return from the disappointing 1940-41 squad were Dutch Hiller and 1940 Calder winner Kilby MacDonald, both of whom were sold.

The War Years

Through their first 16 seasons in the National Hockey League, the Rangers more than lived up to the sobriquet of "The Classiest Team In Hockey." They won three Stanley Cups, finished first three times and missed the playoffs only once. Their farm system had enabled Lester Patrick to fill in the gaps as his original stars got older, and the first-place finish in 1941-42 portended more success for years to come.

World War II put an end to all that. The war is a defining moment in Rangers history. More so than any other NHL team, the Rangers were devastated by the conflict.

After the 1941-42 season, goalie Jim Henry went into the Canadian Navy, while other stars like the Colvilles and Alex Shibicky entered the Canadian Army; Lynn Patrick had entered the U.S. Army. Lester Patrick, thinking that the NHL might cease opera-

The Colville brothers and Alex Shibicky played with the Ottawa Army Commandos during the war.
Photo courtesy of Bill Galloway Photo Collection.

tion during the war or that his players would all be drafted, discontinued one of his top farm teams, the Philadelphia Ramblers, selling off the players to other organizations. These players helped other teams keep their farm systems going while leaving the Rangers without a reserve of talent.

The Rangers collapsed so badly in 1942-43 that Patrick wanted to suspend operations before the 1943-44 season. But with the Americans now gone (after the 1941-42 season), the other five teams didn't want to lose another club and talked Lester into icing a team.

Patrick probably wished he hadn't; with almost all their regulars gone to the war effort, the 1943-44 Rangers won just six times in 50 games, the worst showing in team history. They won only 11 times in 1944-45 and just 13 in 1945-46—finally leading to Patrick's departure. Frank Boucher rebuilt the farm system in the late '40s and early '50s, but the Rangers were never the same again.

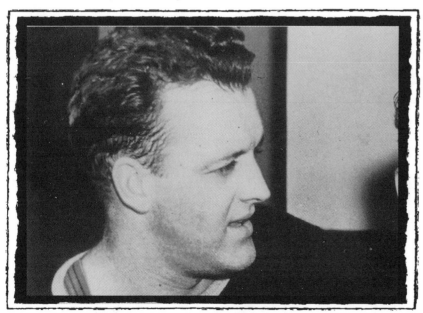

Lynn Patrick enlisted in the U.S. Army after the 1941-42 season.

—1942 NEW YORK RANGERS 1943—

TIME CAPSULE

- **October 5, 1942:**
  The St. Louis Cardinals beat the New York Yankees 4-2 to win the World Series in five games.

- **May 5, 1943:**
  Postmaster Frank Walker inaugurated a postal-zone numbering system to speed up mail delivery.

- **July 19, 1943:**
  Rome was bombed by more than 500 Allied planes.

1942-1943
FINAL STANDINGS

	W	L	T	PTS	GF	GA
Detroit	25	14	11	61	169	124
Boston	24	17	9	57	195	176
Toronto	22	19	9	53	198	159
Montreal	19	19	12	50	181	191
Chicago	17	18	15	49	179	180
RANGERS	11	31	8	30	161	253

PLAYOFF RESULTS
Rangers did not qualify

STANLEY CUP CHAMPION
Detroit Red Wings

SEASON SNAPSHOT

Most Goals
Bryan Hextall (27)

Most Assists
Lynn Patrick (39)

Most Points
Lynn Patrick (61)

Most Penalty Minutes
Vic Myles (57)

Most Wins, Goaltender:
Jimmy Franks (5)

Lowest Goals-Against Average:
Jimmy Franks (4.48)

Most Shutouts:
Bill Beveridge (1)

NHL All-Stars:
Bryan Hextall, RW (Second Team);
Lynn Patrick, LW (Second Team)

The 1942-43 Season in Review

World War II did what their NHL opponents never could: make the Rangers look like a bad team. They tried to get by on offense, but paid the defensive consequences, especially following the trade of defenseman Babe Pratt just before the start of the season. With Jim Henry in the Canadian Navy, the Rangers tried five goalies—none of them very effective. Jimmy Franks, who was previously with Detroit, led the team with five victories. The Rangers gave up double figures in goals twice in the first four games of the season, the first times that had happened in team history, and saw it happen twice more before the end of the season. They did not win a game from New Year's Eve until February 21, a span of 19 games in which they went 0-14-5 before beating Montreal 6-1. They managed to win at least twice against everybody except Detroit, against whom the Rangers posted a 1-7-2 mark. The Blueshirts never lost more than five in a row, and had a three-game winning streak at Christmas time. Seven players hit double figures in goal scoring, but only Bryan Hextall (27) and team-leading scorer Lynn Patrick (22) topped the 20-goal mark. The Rangers didn't spend much time in the penalty box. Vic Myles led the team with 57 penalty minutes, the only player to go over the 50-minute level. This marked only the second time in franchise history that the Rangers missed the postseason, and things were only going to get worse; the war-ravaged Blueshirts missed the playoffs for five straight seasons.

World War II began to take its toll on the Rangers in 1942-43. Photo courtesy of the Hockey Hall of Fame.

MAGIC MOMENT

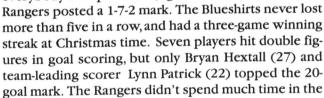

Goal No. 2,000

Bryan Hextall scored the 2,000th goal in Ranger history in the 1942-43 home opener.

It took three games for the Rangers to pick up their first of 11 wins for the season, but the Blueshirts hit another milestone on November 7, 1942 when they faced Montreal in their home opener. The second of their four goals in a 4-3 victory over the Canadiens marked the Rangers' 2,000th tally in regular-season play. The goal scorer was Bryan Hextall. It was his second goal of the game, and came at 18:28 of the first period on assists from Phil Watson and Lynn Patrick. It took the Blueshirts 751 games over the span of 16-plus seasons to hit the mark. Owing to the steadily lengthening schedule, the Rangers needed only a little more than 11 seasons to double that feat, as they picked up their 4,000th goal on December 19, 1955 during a 3-3 tie at the Garden vs. Toronto, a span of 760 games. Toronto was also the victim of the 10,000th goal in Rangers history. On March 15, 1980, the Rangers hit the mark during an 8-4 triumph at Maple Leaf Gardens. After 70 full seasons, the Rangers have 14,694 goals. If they get on an offensive roll, they may hit the 15,000-goal mark toward the end of the 1996-97 season.

RANGER LEGEND
Ott Heller

Erhardt Henry (Ott) Heller lasted 15 years with the Rangers, a number surpassed only by Rod Gilbert (18 years) and Harry Howell (17). Heller came up in 1931, and was the only player in history to be a part of the second and third Ranger Stanley Cup teams. He also lasted through the early stages of World War II, so Heller saw both ends of the spectrum with the early Rangers. But Heller's 15 seasons in the NHL represent only about half of his professional hockey career. He started in 1928 with the Kitchener Green Shirts, and then moved to the Springfield (Mass.) Indians the following season before coming to New York. After the Rangers, there were stops in Indianapolis and Cleveland. He finally quit hockey after playing for the Barons at the end of the 1954-55 season. That meant Heller played professional hockey for an incredible 27 straight seasons. While in Indianapolis, he took on the role of player-coach. Some of his proteges who hit the big time include Terry Sawchuk, Fred Glover and brothers John and Larry Wilson. Heller started his career as a right wing before switching to the blue line before the call up to the Blueshirts. When he first arrived, he was paired with Ching Johnson, allowing the veteran Johnson to rush the puck a little more, then teamed with Babe Pratt to form an almost impregnable duo during the 1939-40 championship season. He played solid defense, and still managed to score 55 goals during his tenure. Heller's best season offensively was in one of the Rangers worst seasons — 1943-44. when he

scored eight goals and added 27 assists for 35 points (all career highs). He was captain of the team for three seasons (1942-45), the third player in team history to wear the "C" after Bill Cook and Art Coulter. Heller retired to his farm in Kitchener, and passed away in 1980 at the age of 70.

Ott Heller File

- **BORN:**
  October 11, 1921; Kitchener, Ontario
- **ACQUIRED:**
  Product of Rangers organization.
- **FIRST SEASON WITH THE RANGERS:**
  1931-32
- **BEST SEASON WITH RANGERS:**
  1943-44, 50 GP, 8-27-35, 29 PIM

- **TOTALS WITH RANGERS:**
  Regular season: 647 GP, 55-176-231, 465 PIM
  Playoffs: 61 GP, 6-8-14, 61 PIM
- **HONORS:**
  Second-team All-Star, 1940-41
  West Side Assn. Rangers MVP, 1942-43

CURTAIN CALL

Dudley "Red" Garrett

Red Garrett became the first NHL player to die in World War II. Photo courtesy of the Hockey Hall of Fame.

Red Garrett, who came to the Rangers from Toronto in the Babe Pratt trade, was recognized as the first NHL player to be killed in World War II. Garrett, a Toronto native born on July 24, 1924, played in 23 games for the Rangers in the 1942-43 season, and had one goal, one assist and 18 penalty minutes—not bad totals for a promising 19-year-old. He was honored by hockey for his service by having the American Hockey League's rookie award named after him. Of course, he was not the only Ranger to have an award named after him. The Lester Patrick Award, given to those who demonstrate outstanding service to hockey in the United States, was named after the first leader of the Blueshirts. Garrett just happened to be the first Ranger with an award in his honor. The Rangers started giving out their own awards to their players, and the first such award started the previous season, with the founding of the West Side Association Rangers' MVP Trophy. The first winner was Lynn Patrick, who won for a second straight time this season. It is the oldest active local award for the team.

NEW YORK Ice Exchange

World War II took its toll on the Rangers. Key players found themselves lacing up combat boots instead of hockey skates, as Alex Shibicky, Art Coulter, Jim Henry and the Colville brothers all left for the war. Four goalies tried, but couldn't replace Henry: Jimmy Franks (who led the team with five wins and the lowest goals-against average: 4.48), Bill Beveridge (four wins and the only shutout for the Blueshirts in the last of his nine seasons with five teams), Steve Buzinski (a 2-6-1 record in his only NHL season) and Lionel Bouvrette (six goals allowed in his only game in the NHL). Also gone was star defenseman Babe Pratt, who was dealt to Toronto for Hank Goldup and Red Garrett just before the start of the season. Unfortunately for the Rangers, there was one deal that never came off: In the late 1960s, Frank Selke Jr. reportedly said his father, Montreal GM Frank Selke, had tried to trade rookie Maurice Richard to the Rangers for Phil Watson—but the deal fell through.

Steve Buzinski tried to fill the hole in goal.

—1943  1944—

TIME CAPSULE

- **December 24, 1943:**
  General Dwight D. Eisenhower was appointed Supreme Commander of Allied Forces for the European invasion.

- **March 6, 1944:**
  Berlin was ambushed by U.S. pilots, who dropped 2,000 tons of bombs on the city.

- **June 6, 1944:**
  The beginning of the Normandy invasion took place as over four million Allied troops, 4,000 ships and 3,000 planes stormed in.

1943-1944
FINAL STANDINGS

	W	L	T	PTS	GF	GA
Montreal	38	5	7	83	234	109
Detroit	26	18	6	58	214	177
Toronto	23	23	4	50	214	174
Chicago	22	23	5	49	178	187
Boston	19	26	5	43	223	268
RANGERS	6	39	5	17	162	310

PLAYOFF RESULTS
Rangers did not qualify

STANLEY CUP CHAMPION
Montreal Canadiens

SEASON SNAPSHOT

Most Goals:

Bryan Hextall (21)

Most Assists:

Bryan Hextall (33)

Most Points:

Bryan Hextall (54)

Most Penalty Minutes:

Bob Dill (66)

Most Wins, Goaltender:

Ken McAuley (6)

Lowest Goals-Against Average:

Ken McAuley (6.20)

The 1943-44 Season in Review

The six victories the Rangers managed to garner stands as the lowest seasonal win total of a still-existing franchise in NHL history since the Blueshirts joined in 1926. Only the defunct Philadelphia Quakers (4) and Pittsburgh Pirates (5) were worse, and they played only 44 games. Of course, the biggest reason for the poor season was World War II. No Neil Colville, no Alex Shibicky, no Jim Henry ... oh well, you get the idea. Poor Ken McAuley. He played every minute of every game in net and wound up with a 6.20 goals-against average. After setting a franchise record with 11 losses to open the season, they managed a tie before losing three more games. Finally, in their 16th game, the Rangers beat Boston 6-4. That started a burst of four wins in five games. Then after losing seven more in a row, the Rangers won two straight. They then managed four more ties in their final 21 games, but no more wins. Combine that season-ending slide with four losses to start the 1944-45 season, and the Rangers set a team futility mark of 25 games without a win (over two seasons). The Blueshirts also allowed the opposition to hit double figures in goals seven times. Two of their six wins were in Toronto, the other four at home to Boston (twice), Detroit and Chicago. As

Bryan Hextall led the Rangers with 21 goals in 1943-44.

for Montreal, the Rangers managed just one tie in their 10 contests with the Habs. This season marked the lowest point total (17) in the 70-year history of the franchise.

MAGIC MOMENT — January 23, 1944

Ken McAuley was the victim of Detroit's 15-0 rout.

The present Rangers hope they never have to go through a night like the 1943-44 squad went through on January 23 in Detroit. It was at the old Olympia that Detroit put the worst hurting on the New York franchise in its 70 seasons, to the tune of 15-0. Before a crowd of 12,293, the Red Wings scored two goals in the first period and five more in the second for a 7-0 lead. Then the dam really burst: Ken McAuley, who finished with 43 saves, was beaten eight times in the third period. Every Red Wing player who dressed, except for goalie Connie Dion and defenseman Cully Simon, had at least one point. Dion, who was only five games back from his stint in the Canadian Army, had to make just nine saves. Gordie Howe had a hat trick, and Murray Armstrong, Carl Liscombe and Don Grosso each scored twice. It could have been worse. The Red Wings beat McAuley a 16th time, but the goal was disallowed because the final horn had sounded just before the puck went into the net. In a season where the Rangers allowed at least 10 goals in seven games, this was the worst of them all. One oddity was that the loss technically didn't go on Frank Boucher's ledger. He was attending his brother's funeral, so Lester Patrick went back behind the bench for one night.

RANGER LEGEND
Ab DeMarco

Albert George (Ab) DeMarco was one of the Rangers' slickest centermen. Though his career was short-lived and devoid of any playoff action, he still managed almost a point-a-game average. DeMarco joined the Rangers in 1943 after three years with Chicago, Toronto and Boston. He finished fourth, on the team in scoring that season despite only playing 36 of 50 games. It led to his leading the team in scoring the following two seasons, while the Blueshirts were going through the lean years when the war stripped the team of a big part of its major talent base. Scoring was at a premium then, and only two other players aside from DeMarco scored at least 20 goals in two of the four seasons he played: Bryan Hextall (21 goals in 1943-44, 20 goals in 1946-47) and Grant Warwick (20 goals in 1944-45, 20 goals in 1946-47). DeMarco averaged a shade under 17 goals a season for his time on Broadway. His best effort was in the 1944-45 season, when he notched career highs in goals (24), assists, (30) and points (54), which earned him the fourth West Side Association Most Valuable Player award. DeMarco's fourth and final Ranger season saw him with only nine goals and 19 points while missing 16 games. He is one of a handful of Rangers who have played in 150 regular-season games without seeing playoff action. His seven-year career ended with 72 goals and 93 assists. He retired after the 1947 season, but his son and namesake carried on Ranger tradition. Albert Thomas DeMarco carved out a niche as an offensive-minded defenseman. He joined the Rangers in 1969, played on Broadway for four seasons, and stuck around in the NHL for another five seasons with five other teams. So as one Ab wound up his NHL career on Broadway, another Ab launched his there.

Ab DeMarco File

- **BORN:**
  May 10, 1916; South Bay, Ontario
- **ACQUIRED:**
  Trade from Boston prior to 1943-44 season
- **FIRST SEASON WITH RANGERS:**
  1943-44

- **BEST SEASON WITH RANGERS:**
  1944-45, 50 GP, 24-30-54, 10 PIM
- **TOTALS WITH RANGERS:**
  Regular season: 182 GP, 67-86-153, 36 PIM
  Playoffs: Did not participate
- **HONORS:**
  West Side Assn. Rangers MVP, 1944-45

CURTAIN CALL
Versatile Boucher

Frank Boucher made a brief comeback in 1943-44, getting to play with the red line he helped institute.

General manager Frank Boucher was one of hockey's most versatile thinkers, and one of his ideas shaped hockey as we know it today. Boucher was the driving force behind the implementation of the center-ice red line, which was put in place for the start of the 1943-44 season. Previously, the rule was that the puck couldn't be passed from inside the defensive zone; it had to be carried out. But Boucher convinced the Board of Governors that the red line would speed up the game, so the league had the six arenas put a red stripe at center ice. Defensemen were now able to pass the puck out of their zone to center ice, bringing more flow and speed to a game that had become choppy. Little did Boucher know that he would soon be testing his creation. Since the war had taken most of the Rangers' young, promising talent, Boucher decided that he would help the team by coming out of retirement and playing. With the Rangers desperate for players, Boucher shook off five years of inactivity and surprised everyone with how spry he looked and played. Boucher played in 15 games, and wound up with four goals and 10 assists for 14 points. Not bad for a coach.

NEW YORK Ice Exchange

Every team suffered through losses of personnel to World War II, but it seemed no one was hit harder than the Rangers, who used players too young or too old to be drafted. Don Raleigh, a talented 17-year-old, managed 15 games before he broke his jaw and missed the rest of the season. With most of their stars tied up with the war effort, the season wore on with Bryan Hextall, Dutch Hiller, Ott Heller and Ab DeMarco holding the fort. This season, as well as the other war years, found players who normally would not be on an NHL roster. Some of those who were a part of the 1943-44 roster who got (as the late Andy Warhol put it) their "15 minutes of fame:" Art Strobel, Max Labovitch, Jack Mann, Lloyd Mohns, Bob McDonald, Hank Dyck, Tony Demers, Archie Fraser, Jimmy Jamieson, Hank D'Amore, Chuck Sands, Tommy Dewar, Aldo Palazzari, Roger Leger and Bob Dill. Only Mann and Dill returned for appearances during the 1944-45 season.

Don Raleigh made his Ranger debut in 1943-44 as a 17-year-old.

Ranger Lists

Father/Seasons
Lester Patrick: 1927-28
Son/Seasons
Lynn: 1934-43, 1945-46
Muzz: 1937-41, 1945-46

Father
Lynn Patrick
Son/Seasons
Craig: Coach 1980-81; 1985
GM 11/80 to 7/86

Father/Seasons
Ab DeMarco: 1943-47
Son/Seasons
Ab: 1969-73

Father/Seasons
Bryan Hextall:
1936-44, 1945-48
Son/Seasons
Bryan: 1962-63
Dennis: 1967-69

Father/Seasons
Leo Reise: 1929-30
Son/Seasons
Leo: 1952-54

—1944 1945—

TIME CAPSULE

- **November 7, 1944:**
  Franklin D. Roosevelt was re-elected president for a record fourth term.

- **May 8, 1945:**
  The Germans unconditionally surrendered, ending the European phase of World War II.

- **August 6, 1945:**
  The first atomic bomb used in war was dropped on Hiroshima, Japan. The Japanese surrendered to the Allies nine days later.

1944-1945
FINAL STANDINGS

	W	L	T	PTS	GF	GA
Montreal	38	8	4	80	228	121
Detroit	31	14	5	67	218	161
Toronto	24	22	4	52	183	161
Boston	16	30	4	36	179	219
Chicago	13	30	7	33	141	194
RANGERS	11	29	10	32	154	247

PLAYOFF RESULTS
Rangers did not qualify

STANLEY CUP CHAMPION
Toronto Maple Leafs

SEASON SNAPSHOT

Most Goals:
Ab DeMarco (24)

Most Assists:
Ab DeMarco (30)

Most Points:
Ab DeMarco (54)

Most Penalty Minutes:
Bob Dill (69)

Most Wins, Goaltender:
Ken McAuley (11)

Lowest Goals-Against Average:
Ken McAuley (4.94)

Most Shutouts:
Ken McAuley (1)

The 1944-45 Season in Review

As the war continued, so did the Rangers' problems. Scoring goals? That was a problem. They tallied only 154 times, second-fewest (to Chicago) in the league. Ab DeMarco led the team with 24 goals and 54 points. Grant Warwick was the only other Blueshirt to hit the 20-goal mark. Preventing goals? Problem. Ken McAuley, who qualified for combat pay based on the volume of pucks that he faced, was better than the previous season, raising his victory total from 6 to 11 and dropping his goals-against average from 6.20 to 4.94, but still seeing far too many shots playing behind a badly depleted lineup. McAuley played in 46 games, with Doug Stevenson going winless in the other four contests. The only problem the Rangers didn't have was losing. Though the Blueshirts cut their losses from 39 to 29 and showed considerable improvement from the previous season, they still finished last, one point behind Chicago. The losing tested the resolve of GM Lester Patrick and coach Frank Boucher. Both men realized that most of their talent was off defending their respective countries, so they forged on and waited for the veteran players to return and the new talent to establish themselves. Warwick finished second in scoring for the first of three straight years, and Phil Watson came back from a year away and scored 11 goals.

Ott Heller was one of the few Ranger veterans left by 1944-45.

MAGIC MOMENT January 18-19, 1945

When you mix train travel with winter weather, you can get some long delays (as any rider of the Long Island Railroad or Metro North can vouch for). Since the Rangers traveled by train in the 1940s, it's not surprising that problems sometimes arose. One such weather-related difficulty for the Rangers took place on January 18, 1945, when they were supposed to play the Red Wings in Detroit. Weather-related problems caused the Rangers' train to be delayed. And while 7,687 brave souls sat in the Olympia waiting for either a game to begin or a cancellation to be announced, time passed. The Blueshirts finally arrived, and it was decided to play the game, one which the Red Wings won handily, coasting to a 7-3 triumph. The game started at 11:13 p.m., but the Rangers showed no effects of their long trek in the first period, skating off with a 2-2 tie after 20 minutes, with one of their goals coming on a penalty shot by Fred Thurier against Harry Lumley. But they ran out of gas after the first intermission, surrendering three goals in the second period and two more in the third before Phil Watson's consolation marker at the end. The buzzer

Fred Thurier scored on a penalty shot in a 7-3 loss at Detroit that started well after 11 p.m. when the Rangers' train was delayed.

ending the game finally went off at 12:56 a.m. on January 19, making it the only regular-season game in team history that took more than one day to complete (though ironically, in terms of playing time, it was one of the fastest they've ever been involved in).

RANGER LEGEND
Phil Watson

Phil Watson was not a redhead, but he earned his nickname of "Fiery" for continuously seeing red. He possessed what others would kindly call an unpredictable temper. Born in Montreal, Watson's playing rights belonged to the Canadiens; the rules in pre-expansion days allowed Montreal to have the rights to French-Canadian youngsters who were born or playing in the province of Quebec. But GM Lester Patrick put in a claim for him, saying that Watson's Scottish father altered his ancestry for the purposes of the rule. The NHL ruled in Patrick's favor, and Watson was Ranger property. He joined the Blueshirts during the 1935-36 season, and spent his entire career on Broadway, except the 1943-44 season, when he played for the hometown Canadiens due to wartime restrictions in Canada that forced him to stay north of the border. He spent most of his years centering Lynn Patrick and Bryan Hextall. The best of his 12 seasons was in 1941-42, where he had 15 goals and 52 points, finishing fourth in the scoring race. But his biggest goal total came in his final season, 1947-48, when he agreed to coach Frank Boucher's request to switch from center to left wing and responded with 18 goals. After he retired, Watson bided his time, and when Muzz Patrick took over as GM from Boucher in 1955, his first act was to call his old road roommate and offer him the job as coach. During his four-plus years, the hot seat got pretty warm for Watson, who had a long-running public feud with his goalie, Gump Worsley, and didn't hesitate to criticize his players in the newspapers. Though the

Phil Watson was one of the most fiery Rangers ever, as both a player and coach.

Rangers made the playoffs for three straight years under Watson, they couldn't hang on to a big lead in 1958-59 and wound up missing postseason play—with Watson ripping his players in the press down the stretch, hoping the tactic would light a fire under them. It didn't. After irking players and management once too often, Watson was let go in November 1959. He coached Boston in 1961 for 1 1/2 seasons, before his act wore thin there, too.

Phil Watson File

- **BORN:**
  April 24, 1914; Montreal, Quebec
- **ACQUIRED:**
  Product of Rangers organization.
- **FIRST SEASON WITH RANGERS:**
  1935-36
- **BEST SEASON WITH RANGERS:**
  1941-42, 48 GP, 15-37-52, 58 PIM

- **TOTALS WITH RANGERS:**
  Regular season: 546 GP, 127-233-360, 471 PIM
  Playoffs: 45 GP, 7-20-27, 49 PIM
- **HONORS:**
  Second-team All-Star, 1941-42

CURTAIN CALL

Name Dropping

Odd names have always been a staple in sports, especially hockey. For every Doug Wilson or Larry Robinson who played in the league, there was an Ari Haanpaa or Yip Radley to match. The following people actually have played for the Rangers at one point or another in the team's 70-year history, and the names (or nicknames) certainly weren't changed to protect the innocent: Hib Milks, Bing Juckes, Odie Lowe, Hy Buller, Sparky Vail, Taffy Abel, Orville Heximer, Duke Dutkowski, Church Russell, Mel Read, Jean Paul Denis (is there a last name?), Bucko McDonald, Bronco Horvath, Steve Kraftcheck, Zellio Toppazzini, Dolph Kukulowicz, Ants Atanas, Ulf Sterner, Wally Hergesheimer, Orland Kurtenbach, Sheldon Kannegeisser, Randy Legge, Hartland Monahan, John Bednarski, Reijo Ruotsalainen, Mikko Leinonen, and of course, the infamous Per Djoos. OK, stop snickering.

Unusual names like Hib Milks are a staple of sports, and the Rangers are no exception.

NEW YORK Ice Exchange

Bodies flew left and right as the Rangers tried to cope with the lack of talent brought on by the war. GM Lester Patrick cleaned house after the 1943-44 collapse, ushering out Art Strobel, Max Labovitch, Lloyd Mohns, Bob McDonald, Hank Dyck, Tony Demers, Archie Fraser, Jimmy Jamieson, Hank D'Amore, Chuck Sands, Tommy Dewar, Aldo Palazzari and Roger Leger. The most prominent returnees were Jack Mann (6 games) and Bob Dill (48 games: 9-5-14). Patrick fired a lot of blanks with all the bodies he imported to keep the franchise afloat. The newest wartime heroes included Hal Cooper (for eight unproductive games), Jim Drummond (two games), and Len Wharton and Alex Ritson (one game each). However, one legitimate star came back from the war, ready to resume his career: Neil Colville, managed to play four games and secure one assist and one minor penalty.

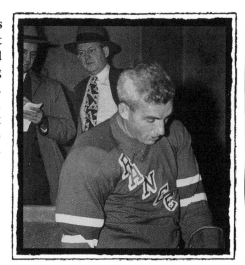

Neil Colville was the first of the Rangers to return after World War II.

—1945 1946—

TIME CAPSULE

- **September 2, 1945**
  Japan signed the formal document of surrender aboard the U.S.S. Missouri in Tokyo Bay.

- **February 15, 1946**
  The world's first electronic digital computer was developed by scientists in Philadelphia.

- **July 2, 1946:**
  African-Americans voted for the first time in Mississippi primaries.

1945-1946
FINAL STANDINGS

	W	L	T	PTS	GF	GA
Montreal	28	17	5	61	172	134
Boston	24	18	8	56	167	156
Chicago	23	20	7	53	200	178
Detroit	20	20	10	50	146	159
Toronto	19	24	7	43	174	185
RANGERS	13	28	9	35	144	191

PLAYOFF RESULTS

Rangers did not qualify

STANLEY CUP CHAMPION

Montreal Canadiens

SEASON SNAPSHOT

Most Goals:
Ab DeMarco (20)

Most Assists:
Ab DeMarco (27)

Most Points:
Ab DeMarco (47)

Most Penalty Minutes:
Phil Watson (43)

Most Wins, Goaltender:
Chuck Rayner (12)

Lowest Goals-Against Average:
Chuck Rayner (3.75)

Most Shutouts:
Chuck Rayner/Jim Henry (1)

NHL Award Winners:
Edgar Laprade (Calder Trophy)

The 1945-46 Season in Review

It was another season of recovery from the war for the Rangers, who could only manage to improve from 11 to 13 victories. Positives were few and far between: They had a 2-0-2 streak just after Christmas, and won their final two games. The not-so-positives: Those final two wins marked their only multiple-game winning streak for the season. They had a pair of six-game winless streaks (going 0-5-1 in both), a five-game winless streak, and a five-game losing streak. They provided good competition to four of the other five teams; going 4-4-2 against Detroit; the exception was a 1-8-1 showing against Montreal. Chuck Rayner carried the load in goal, posting a 3.75 goals-against average. Jim Henry did appear in 11 games to give Rayner a break, but only won once and tied twice while losing seven. Edgar Laprade posted 15 goals and 19 assists in his first season, enough to win the Calder Trophy, while center Ab DeMarco led the team in scoring with 20 goals and 47 points. This smallish bunch of players wasn't quite physical enough, since the highest penalty-minute total belonged to Phil Watson with 43 minutes. Nobody else had 30 minutes in the box. It was the third straight season that the Rangers finished last in every statistical category. Not a great way for general manager Lester Patrick to end his tenure; he announced his resignation on February 21, but stayed on as a vice president of Madison Square Garden.

Ab DeMarco led the Rangers in goals in 1945-46.

MAGIC MOMENT *March 17, 1946*

The Rangers' definition of torture in 1945-46 was having to play Montreal. The Canadiens went 8-0-1 in their first nine meetings with the Blueshirts, and the only non-victory for the Habs was a scoreless tie on New Year's Eve at the Garden. But with nothing to lose, since their season was ending, the Rangers delighted another big crowd at the Garden by finally ending the Canadiens' hex with an 8-5 triumph. The eight goals represented a season-high for the Rangers and was the most allowed all season by Vezina Trophy winner Bill Durnan. Rookie Cal Gardner had two goals, giving him six in the season's final four games. Phil Watson and Tony Leswick also had a pair for the Rangers, while Bill Moe and Rene Trudell had one apiece. Gardner scored twice and Moe once in the first period to give the Rangers an early lead, and goals by Trudell and Watson in the second period made it 5-0 before Toe Blake finally beat Chuck Rayner. Despite the fact that the Rangers had been out of the playoff race for weeks, a near-capacity crowd of 15,115 turned out to say so long to another season, giving the Rangers a record season attendance of 359,920, an average of 14,397 fans per game.

Cal Gardner had two goals as the Rangers closed their season on a high note.

RANGER LEGEND
Edgar Laprade

Edgar Laprade was one of those rare athletes with a plan. He knew at an early age just how he wanted his hockey career to go, and he set out to achieve his goals. Playing junior hockey for the Port Arthur (Ontario) Bear Cats, Laprade won an Allan Cup (Canadian seniors) championship in his first season with the club in 1938. The Rangers tried to persuade him to turn professional, but Laprade refused, sticking with the Bear Cats until he had to serve a two-year stint in the Canadian Army, where he played on the hockey team. When Laprade was discharged in 1945, he finally signed a contract with the Blueshirts. Three weeks after his 26th birthday, Laprade made his NHL debut. At the end of his first season, he had 15 goals, 34 points and the Calder Trophy as rookie of the year. Laprade finished third in team scoring that season, and would finish in the top three in each of the next four years. His most memorable season came in 1949-50, when he scored 22 goals and added 22 assists to lead the team in scoring while winning the Lady Byng Trophy. He also had three goals and eight points in the Rangers' near-championship playoff run. But Laprade decided to retire after the 1951-52 season; even though he was just 32 years old. He compared his decision to boxer Joe Louis in the respect that Louis left the game while he was on top. Laprade, whose family owned a sporting goods business in Port Arthur, also wanted to go out on his own terms. His motives were strictly to spend more time with his business and family. But when the Rangers started off with a lot of injuries and slumps in 1952-53,

GM Frank Boucher went up to Port Arthur and—though it took over two months of cajoling—got Laprade to come back to Broadway. He stayed another three seasons before retiring for good at the end of the 1954-55 season—after playing his 500th game, a milestone that only four previous Rangers had reached. Laprade was inducted into the Hockey Hall of Fame in 1993.

Edgar Laprade File

- **BORN:**
  October 10, 1919; Mine Center, Ontario
- **ACQUIRED:**
  Product of Rangers organization
- **FIRST SEASON WITH RANGERS:**
  1945-46
- **BEST SEASON WITH RANGERS:**
  1947-48, 59 GP, 13-34-47, 7 PIM

- **TOTALS WITH RANGERS:**
  Regular season: 500 GP, 108-172-280, 42 PIM
  Playoffs: 18 GP, 4-9-13, 4 PIM
- **HONORS:**
  Calder Trophy, 1945-46
  Lady Byng Trophy, 1949-50
  West Side Assn. Rangers MVP, 1948-49, 1949-50
  All-Star Game, 1947-48, 1948-49, 1949-50, 1950-51

CURTAIN CALL
The War Heroes Come Home

When World War II took its toll on the Rangers' roster in 1942, GM Lester Patrick asked the NHL if the team could suspend operations until the war ended. The other five teams persuaded Patrick and the Rangers to keep operating. After the war finally ended, 49 players returned to their respective NHL teams, including six key members of the Rangers. It was good for the Rangers to see both Jim Henry and Chuck Rayner back between the pipes after a succession of wartime netminders failed to stem the tide. Neil Colville, who managed to get into four games in the previous season, played in all but one in 1945-46. Brother Mac also returned from duty, as did Alex Shibicky and Muzz Patrick. The problem was that these heroes had aged a few years and weren't the same players they had been before the war. Neil Colville managed only five goals and four assists, while brother Mac had seven goals and 13 points. Shibicky had 10 goals and 15 points in only 33 games, while Patrick managed two assists in 24 games. The

Mac Colville rejoined his brother on the Rangers after the war.

goaltending duo also showed some postwar rust: Rayner had 12 wins and a 3.75 goals-against average while Henry went 1-7-2 with a 4.10 goals-against average. Each goalie registered one shutout.

NEW YORK
Ice Exchange

Most of the newer players on the team were the old players. Six World War II veterans returned to wear the Blueshirt: Neil and Mac Colville, Alex Shibicky, Muzz Patrick, Chuck Rayner and Jim Henry. Netminder Ken McAuley retired after two seasons in which he saw a career's worth of rubber. This season marked the debut of rookie Edgar Laprade, and the brief return (three games worth) of Bryan Hextall, who missed the entire 1944-45 season due to the war, then was idled by a liver ailment that threatened to end his career. Other brief appearances were made by Alan Kuntz (who played 45 games for the Rangers spread out over two war-displaced seasons), Hal Brown (13 career games) and Bill Juzda (another war veteran). A pair of Freds never got a shot (to continue) from last season: Fred Thurier, fourth highest point-getter in 1944-45, wasn't given a chance to repeat his efforts, and fifth-leading point scorer Fred Hunt also didn't return.

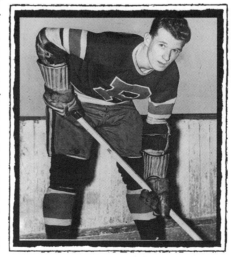

Alan Kuntz played 45 games in two seasons with the Rangers.

—1946 1947—

TIME CAPSULE

- **December 15, 1946**
  The Chicago Bears defeated the New York Giants 24-14 to win the NFL Championship.

- **April 11, 1947:**
  Jackie Robinson of the Brooklyn Dodgers became the first black player to play major-league baseball.

- **June 23, 1947:**
  The Taft-Hartley Labor Act was passed by Congress despite the veto of the controversial bill by President Harry S. Truman.

1946-1947
FINAL STANDINGS

	W	L	T	PTS	GF	GA
Montreal	34	16	10	78	189	138
Toronto	31	19	10	72	209	172
Boston	26	23	11	63	190	175
Detroit	22	27	11	55	190	193
RANGERS	22	32	6	50	167	186
Chicago	19	37	4	42	193	274

PLAYOFF RESULTS
Rangers did not qualify

STANLEY CUP CHAMPION
Toronto Maple Leafs

SEASON SNAPSHOT

Most Goals:
Tony Leswick (27)

Most Assists:
Edgar Laprade (25)

Most Points:
Tony Leswick (41)

Most Penalty Minutes:
Bill Juzda (60)

Most Wins, Goaltender:
Chuck Rayner (22)

Lowest Goals-Against Average:
Chuck Rayner (3.05)

Most Shutouts:
Chuck Rayner (5)

The 1946-47 Season in Review

New blood took the Rangers into the 1946-47 season, as Lester Patrick, the team's general manager since its inception in 1926, stepped down. In his stead came Frank Boucher, who was already installed as coach. Also new was an increase in the schedule, from 50 to 60 games. The Rangers started off 3-2-1 before the roof caved in—in the form of an eight-game winless streak (0-7-1). They then won five of six, but fell apart again by winning just one of their following 11 games. Their best stretch came between January 4 and February 19, when they posted a 11-5-0 record. But from that point on, they won just one game prior to the season finale—a 1-10-1 stretch that cost them any shot at a playoff berth. Offensively, four players hit the 20-goal mark, including leading scorer Tony Leswick, who had a team-high 27 goals. Other 20-goal scorers were Grant Warwick, Bryan Hextall, and Church Russell. Chuck Rayner played all but two games in goal and posted five shutouts and a 3.05 goals-against average. There were only two players (Leswick and Bill Juzda) who surpassed 50 penalty minutes, a sign that Boucher's club would have to get stronger the next season if the team was going to go anywhere. They did, and in the process, doubled the amount of players who had at least 50 penalty minutes.

Bryan Hextall bounced back from illness with 21 goals in 1946-47.

MAGIC MOMENT
February 1, 1947

As a rule, goaltenders are supposed to stay put. Their main job is to block shots and clear away rebounds. Oh, occasionally they play the puck, but only in order to get it to a defenseman. They were never supposed to move the puck up for offensive purposes. Well, somebody forgot to tell Chuck Rayner this creed of early netminding. On February 1, 1947, Rayner abandoned his cage with the puck in his possession during a 2-1 loss at Montreal. Not only did he leave the crease to play the puck, he rushed into the Montreal zone just like a forward, and attempted to score the tying goal while his net remained open for any Montreal player to attempt an empty-net tally. Rayner didn't just try this trick once, he did it THREE times. Unfortunately for Rayner and the Rangers, all the strategy yielded was some oohs and aahs from the Forum crowd. Rayner wasn't the last Ranger goalie to try to put the puck in the other net. In the late 1960s and early 1970s, Ed Giacomin, one of the first of the modern goaltenders who consistently left his crease to play the puck, often tried to shoot the disc into a vacated net, once hitting the post. Rayner actually did score several goals during his career as a goaltender, but never accomplished the feat in the NHL.

Chuck Rayner tried leading rushes in addition to his goaltending chores.

RANGER LEGEND
Tony Leswick

His nickname was "Tough Tony," and his 420 minutes in the sin bin during six seasons with the Rangers are testimonial enough to the way Tony Leswick earned that tag. Leswick could be compared to Vic Hadfield, who played tough when he had to, but had enough offensive capabilities to be plenty useful at the offensive end of the ice. Leswick averaged more than 18 goals per season, along with 84 penalty minutes. Like most of his teammates at the time, Leswick wasn't a big guy, standing only 5-foot-6 1/2 and weighing just 160 pounds. But his dogged determination kept him in the NHL for 12 years—though his training as an amateur boxer didn't hurt, either. An unnamed Toronto Maple Leaf once described Leswick as someone "who gets under your arms, between your legs and annoys the life out of you in general"—a perfect description of a penalty killer, and Leswick teamed up with Edgar Laprade to form one of the best defensive duos in the league. He joined the Rangers at the start of the 1945-46 season after a two-year hitch in the Canadian Navy, and learned his hockey in Cleveland of the AHL under former Ranger legend Bill Cook. Leswick led the Rangers in scoring in his second season, and was no worse than fourth in scoring every year he was there except his final season (1950-51). He was traded after that season by GM Frank Boucher to Detroit for minor-league prospect Gaye Stewart, and it was with the Red Wings that Leswick accomplished his career highlight, scoring only the second overtime goal in the seventh game of a Stanley Cup final series to give Detroit the championship in 1954. He finished his career in Chi-

cago, and retired in 1958. Leswick averaged more than a penalty minute a game during his Rangers tenure, and wound up with 900 for his career, in addition to three Stanley Cup rings.

Tony Leswick File

- **BORN:**
  May 17, 1923; Humboldt, Saskatchewan
- **ACQUIRED:**
  Product of Rangers organization
- **FIRST SEASON WITH RANGERS:**
  1945-46
- **BEST SEASON WITH RANGERS:**
  1946-47, 59 GP, 27-14-41, 41 PIM

- **TOTALS WITH RANGERS:**
  Regular season: 368 GP, 113-89-202, 420 PIM
  Playoffs: 18 GP, 5-6-11, 20 PIM
- **HONORS:**
  Second-team All-Star, 1949-50
  All-Star Game, 1947-48, 1948-49, 1949-50, 1950-51

CURTAIN CALL
Uniform Change

For the first 20 years of their existence, the Rangers stayed with the same basic uniform design—featuring the familiar diagonal R-A-N-G-E-R-S and blue, red and white color scheme. There had been some occasional tinkering with the style of the letters and the players' numbers, but the design remained the same. All that changed in 1946-47, when the Rangers made the first major uniform change in their history. Instead of spelling out R-A-N-G-E-R-S in large letters, the uniform front was dominated by large numerals, with the team name spelled out in a half-moon in smaller letters over the numerals. The pants, stockings and colors all remained the same. The club reverted back to the regular design the following season and kept the traditional look until 1976-77, when new GM John Ferguson totally overhauled the uniform, putting the team's crest on the front of the jersey. That design lasted just two seasons until the team returned to its traditional design, which is still in use today.

(L. to R.) Eddie Kullman, Edgar Laprade, Tony Leswick. The Rangers altered their uniforms for the 1946-47 season.

NEW YORK
Ice Exchange

Frank Boucher was the second man to hold the post of Rangers coach, and at the start of the season, he could say the same thing about being the general manager, too. Boucher was named by outgoing coach/GM Lester Patrick to take over his slot behind the bench in 1939, and was given the second job after the only GM the Rangers ever had (not counting Conn Smythe) decided to step down. The Rangers also started the season without long-time defenseman Ott Heller, who had ended his NHL career after 15 seasons. Also, after four teams and seven seasons, Ab DeMarco said that 1946-47 would be his last season. They ended the season with another of the glory boys calling it quits, as Mac Colville came back from the war in 1945, and played two more years before calling it a career.

Frank Boucher took over as GM in 1946.

Ranger Lists

Rangers who played at least 150 regular games & no playoff games

Paul Ronty, C
260 games

Ab DeMarco, C
182 games

Aldo Guidolin, D
182 games

Hy Buller, D
179 games

John Hanna, D
177 games

—1947 1948—

TIME CAPSULE

- **October 14, 1947:**
  Captain Chuck Yeager piloted the world's first supersonic aircraft.

- **December 7, 1947:**
  Joe Louis earned a split decision over "Jersey Joe" Walcott for the heavyweight championship.

- **August 16, 1948:**
  Babe Ruth, arguably the greatest player in baseball history, died of throat cancer.

1947-1948 FINAL STANDINGS

	W	L	T	PTS	GF	GA
Toronto	32	15	13	77	182	143
Detroit	30	18	12	72	187	148
Boston	23	24	13	59	167	168
RANGERS	21	26	13	55	176	201
Montreal	20	29	11	51	147	169
Chicago	20	34	6	46	195	225

PLAYOFF RESULTS
Semifinals: Detroit defeated Rangers 4-2
LEADING PLAYOFF SCORERS
Tony Leswick (3-2-5)   Phil Watson (2-3-5)

Buddy O'Connor (1-4-5)   Edgar Laprade (1-4-5)
STANLEY CUP CHAMPION
Toronto Maple Leafs

SEASON SNAPSHOT

Most Goals:
Buddy O'Connor/Tony Leswick (24)
Most Assists:
Buddy O'Connor (36)
Most Points:
Buddy O'Connor (60)
Most Penalty Minutes:
Tony Leswick (76)
Most Wins, Goaltender:
Jim Henry (17)
Lowest Goals-Against Average:
Jim Henry (3.19)
Most Shutouts:
Jim Henry (2)
NHL Award Winners:
Buddy O'Connor
(Hart Trophy, Lady Byng Trophy)
NHL All-Stars:
Chuck Rayner, G (Second Team);
Tony Leswick, LW (Second Team)
Rangers In All-Star Game:
Pat Egan, D; Edgar Laprade, C;
Tony Leswick, LW; Buddy O'Connor, C;
Chuck Rayner, G.

The 1947-48 Season in Review

After five years without getting a sniff of postseason play, the Rangers finally put it together and managed to see the playoffs from the inside. Oh, they still did their fair share of losing, especially late in the season. After winning their opener, the Blueshirts lost three straight, won the next two, and then lost four in a row. They then went on the tear that earned them a playoff berth, going 8-1-3 in their next dozen games, including a 5-0-1 run on the road. There was a stretch at the start of February in which they tied five of six games (and lost the other). What could have killed them was a season-ending stretch in which they won once in their last nine games (1-7-1). But the Montreal Canadiens were having a worse season, and the Rangers edged the Habs by four points for the final playoff berth. Buddy O'Connor, heisted by Frank Boucher from Montreal, led the team in assists (36) and points (60), and tied Tony Leswick with 24 goals. He just missed winning the Art Ross Trophy as the NHL's top scorer, finishing one point behind Montreal's Elmer Lach. In a reversal of the previous season, Jim Henry got the bulk of the work in net, while partner Chuck Rayner spent most

Jim Henry carried the bulk of the goaltending chores in 1947-48.

of the season trying to stay ready. Rayner's readiness paid off: He was the chosen one when the Rangers met the Detroit Red Wings in the semifinals. But they didn't last long, as the Wings disposed of the Rangers in six games.

MAGIC MOMENT
March 17, 1948

St. Patrick's Day 1948 turned out to be a lucky one for the Rangers: It was the night they clinched their first playoff appearance in six years. It's not like the Rangers came in on a roll; they were 0-6-1 in their previous seven games and were trying to fend off the Montreal Canadiens, who had missed the playoffs just twice since the Rangers entered the NHL in 1926. But the Canadiens struggled for most of the season, relying solely on the famed "Punch Line" of Maurice Richard, Toe Blake and Elmer Lach. Despite the crowd of 16,431 at Chicago Stadium rooting against them, the Rangers glided into the playoffs by polishing off the last-place Blackhawks 5-2. Eddie Kullman gave the Rangers an early lead and Buddy O'Connor scored one goal and set up another as the Rangers went ahead 3-0. Pete Conacher scored for the Blackhawks late in the second period, but goals by Edgar Laprade and Tony Leswick in the final period put the game away. Conacher beat Chuck Rayner in the final minute, but it didn't matter. It was only the fourth victory of the season for Rayner, who spent most of the year backing up his friend, Jim Henry.

Eddie Kullman's goal started the Rangers on their way to a playoff-clinching win in Chicago.

RANGER LEGEND
Buddy O'Connor

Herbert William "Buddy" O'Connor's first season with the Rangers was more than a little bit fruitful. All he did was lead the team in scoring in the regular season, tie for the playoff lead in scoring, and capture both the Hart Trophy as the league's most valuable player and the Lady Byng Trophy as the league's most gentlemanly player. It was the first of only two times that anyone in league history has captured those two trophies in the same season (Wayne Gretzky did it in 1980). O'Connor barely missed an awards hat trick, finishing one point behind Montreal's Elmer Lach in the race for the Art Ross Trophy (1948 was the first year an actual trophy was awarded for winning the scoring title). The Rangers were so impressed with O'Connor's play that they gave him a $500 bonus—matching the money he would have received if he had beaten Lach for the scoring title. O'Connor was only the second player in NHL history to win two awards in the same season; in 1938-39, Boston netminder Frank Brimsek snagged both the Vezina Trophy (best goaltender) and the Calder Trophy (rookie of the year)—both of which are easier to win because the Vezina is limited to goalies and the Calder is limited to rookies. O'Connor, who was another smallish member of the Blueshirts (5'7", 145 lbs.), came from Montreal with Frank Eddolls for Hal Laycoe, Joe Bell and George Robertson in the summer of 1947. While with Montreal, O'Connor picked up 78 goals in 276 games, but Canadiens GM Frank Selke still traded

him, and admitted that the Rangers probably got the better of the deal. O'Connor had only 30 penalty minutes in his first seven seasons in the league and finished with just 40—including playoffs—in his 10-year career.

Buddy O'Connor File

- **BORN:**
  June 21, 1916; Montreal, Quebec
- **ACQUIRED:**
  Traded by Montreal with Frank Eddolls for Hal Laycoe, Joe Bell and George Robertson, Aug. 11, 1947.
- **FIRST SEASON WITH RANGERS:**
  1947-48
- **BEST SEASON WITH RANGERS:**
  1947-48, 60 GP, 24-36-60, 8 PIM

- **TOTALS WITH RANGERS:**
  Regular season: 238 GP, 62-102-164, 12 PIM
  Playoffs: 6 GP, 1-4-5, 0 PIM
- **HONORS:**
  Hart Trophy, 1947-48
  Lady Byng Trophy, 1947-48
  West Side Assn. Rangers MVP, 1947-48

CURTAIN CALL
Lester Patrick Night

In the first of many nights honoring those who served the Rangers well throughout their careers, Lester Patrick was feted on December 3, 1947 at Madison Square Garden prior to the game against Toronto. Patrick served as coach for the first seven years of the Rangers, and was the general manager for their first 20 years. Patrick was toasted prior to the game at a midtown restaurant, where he received several gifts—including a check for $1,500 from the other five teams that was given to him under the condition that only his wife could spend the money. Patrick, who was choked up by the accolades afforded him, said that it "was the most wonderful moment of my life." *The New York Times* put it best about the always chatty Patrick: "It finally happened–Lester Patrick was at a loss for words." The only damper on the night came after the festivities: The Toronto Maple Leafs spoiled the party with a 4-1 victory, the Rangers' only loss in a 12-game span.

Lester Patrick was honored with his own night on December 3, 1947.

NEW YORK
Ice Exchange

August 11, 1947 marked one of GM Frank Boucher's finest hours, as he swiped Buddy O'Connor and Frank Eddolls from Montreal for Hal Laycoe, Joe Bell and rookie George Robertson. The trade nearly didn't happen: Lester Patrick opposed it and tried to get team president John Reed Kilpatrick to veto it. The deal was approved only when Boucher put his job on the line. O'Connor gave the Rangers their best play at center since their prewar powerhouse days, while Eddolls, a future captain, fortified the blue line with his playmaking skills and leadership. Eddie Kullman made his debut, finishing fifth in scoring with 15 goals and 32 points. It was to be Grant Warwick's last season in New York (he went to Boston), and the first of three seasons for another rookie callup, a defenseman by the name of Fred Shero. Interestingly, four players did not appear in a regular-season game, but made at least one appearance in the playoffs—Ken Davies, Duncan Fisher, Jack Lancien and Nick Mickoski. Fisher and Mickoski each had an assist in the six-game loss to Detroit.

Nick Mickoski saw full-time action in the 1948 playoffs.

Ranger Lists

First-Round Playoff Exits

1926-27	Boston	Most goals 1-3
1933-34	Maroons	Most goals 1-2
1937-38	Americans	3 games
1938-39	Boston	7 games
1940-41	Detroit	3 games
1941-42	Toronto	6 games
1947-48	Detroit	6 games
1955-56	Montreal	5 games
1956-57	Montreal	5 games
1957-58	Boston	6 games
1961-62	Toronto	6 games
1966-67	Montreal	4 games
1967-68	Chicago	6 games
1968-69	Montreal	4 games
1969-70	Boston	6 games
1974-75	Islanders	3 games
1977-78	Buffalo	3 games
1983-84	Islanders	5 games
1984-85	Philadelphia	3 games
1986-87	Philadelphia	6 games
1988-89	Pittsburgh	4 games
1990-91	Washington	6 games

—1948 1949—

IME CAPSULE

- **November 2, 1948:**
  President Harry Truman pulled off one of the greatest upsets in American political history by winning re-election over New York Gov. Thomas Dewey.

- **December 15, 1948:**
  Former State Department official Alger Hiss was indicted by a federal grand jury on two counts of perjury.

- **June 22, 1949:**
  Ezzard Charles defeated Jersey Joe Wolcott to become the heavyweight champion of the world.

1948-1949

FINAL STANDINGS

	W	L	T	PTS	GF	GA
Detroit	34	19	7	75	195	145
Boston	29	23	8	66	178	163
Montreal	28	23	9	65	152	126
Toronto	22	25	13	57	147	161
Chicago	21	31	8	50	173	211
RANGERS	18	31	11	47	133	172

PLAYOFF RESULTS
Rangers did not qualify

STANLEY CUP CHAMPION
Toronto Maple Leafs

SEASON SNAPSHOT

Most Goals:
Edgar Laprade (18)

Most Assists:
Buddy O'Connor (24)

Most Points:
Buddy O'Connor (35)

Most Penalty Minutes:
Tony Leswick (70)

Most Wins, Goaltender:
Chuck Rayner (16)

Lowest Goals-Against Average:
Chuck Rayner (2.70)

Most Shutouts:
Chuck Rayner (7)

NHL Award Winners:
Pentti Lund (Calder Trophy)

NHL All-Stars:
Chuck Rayner, G (Second Team)

Rangers In All-Star Game:
Neil Colville, C; Edgar Laprade, C;
Tony Leswick, LW

The 1948-49 Season in Review

Coming off their first playoff appearance in six years, the Rangers had reason for optimism as they entered the season. But their season suffered a severe jolt on October 8, 1948, when four players, Buddy O'Connor, Edgar Laprade, Frank Eddolls and Bill Moe, were injured when a truck hit their car. All four were unconscious when they reached the hospital; O'Connor's broken ribs and Eddolls' severed knee tendon proved to be the most serious injuries. O'Connor, coming off an MVP season, was gone for 14 games, while Eddolls, one of their top defensemen, was out for 34 contests and Laprade missed four. The injuries triggered a 3-11-5 start that left the Rangers reeling and they never recovered; an injury to their top scorer, Don Raleigh, assured New York of another non-playoff season. The problems came up front: New York had a league-low 133 goals and thanks to the injuries, had no 20-goal scorer—the only time that happened between 1935-36 and the lockout season of 1994-95. The Rangers' only spurt was a 4-0-1 run that was capped by Chuck Rayner's 2-0 shutout victory in Montreal on Christmas night. That game came four nights after GM/coach Frank

An auto accident that injured Buddy O'Connor and three other regulars ruined the 1948-49 season.

Boucher installed Lynn Patrick behind the bench to enable himself to concentrate on finding talent. The 36-year-old Patrick became the NHL's youngest coach, but it was Rayner who kept the Rangers from total collapse: He posted all 18 of the Rangers' victories, seven by shutout, had a 2.70 goals-against average and was named a second-team All-Star.

MAGIC MOMENT *December 25, 1948*

From 1930 to 1948, the only one more reliable at Christmastime than the Rangers was Santa Claus. Winning on Christmas Night was a Ranger tradition, and despite the plague of injuries that had virtually ruined their season before it started, 1948 was no exception. The Rangers came into the Montreal Forum on their biggest roll of the season, a 4-0-1 streak, and extended the unbeaten run to six games with a 2-0 victory. Chuck Rayner, who had started the hot streak by blanking Detroit 13 days earlier, got the shutout as the Rangers continued their Christmas celebration. The victory extended their holiday streak to 14-0-1 and marked the third straight season that the Rangers celebrated Christmas with a 2-0 shutout. Ironically, Rayner was even better the next year at the Forum, but had to settle for a scoreless tie despite what *The Hockey News* praised as "The best goaltending performance of the season." The win over Montreal marked the end of the Rangers' holiday hex over the NHL; they went 9-9-3 in their last 21 games on Christmas until the league stopped playing on the holiday in the early 1970s.

Chuck Rayner's 2-0 shutout at Montreal continued the Rangers' Christmas streak.

He lasted but three seasons on Broadway, but Pentti Lund was the first Finnish-born player to have a major impact on the Rangers. Lund came to Canada as a six-year-old and got his hockey training in North America. Lund won the Eastern Amateur League scoring title with the Boston Olympics in 1946-47 and starred at Hershey of the AHL the next season. He joined the Rangers in the summer of 1948, and after a slow start, Lund began to score. Frank Boucher put him with Edgar Laprade and Tony Leswick on what was quickly dubbed "The Three-L Line," and the hard-shooting wing wound up with 14 goals and 16 assists—paltry totals by today's standards perhaps, but enough to earn Lund the Calder Trophy as the NHL's top rookie. The highlight of his career came in 1949-50, when his 18 goals helped the Rangers make the playoffs—and his all-around play brought the

Rangers within a goal of the Stanley Cup. Lund outplayed Maurice "The Rocket" Richard in the semifinals against Montreal, shutting him out in four of the five games and recording a hat trick in New York's 4-1 victory in Game 3. Lund continued to produce in the finals against Detroit and wound up as the leading scorer in the playoffs, a feat not accomplished again by a Ranger until Brian Leetch did it in 1994. Unfortunately for both Lund and the Rangers, that was his last big moment in the Big Apple. He slumped to just four goals and 16 assists for 20 points in 1950-51 and was dealt back to Boston after the season at the behest of his former coach, Lynn Patrick, who had moved from the Big Apple to the Hub. An eye injury early in the 1951-52 season forced Lund to retire prematurely; he went on to become the long-time sports editor of the *Thunder Bay* (Ontario) *Times-News*.

Pentti Lund File

- **BORN:**
  December 6, 1925, Karijoki, Finland
- **ACQUIRED:**
  Trade from Boston with Billy Taylor for Grant Warwick, Summer 1948
- **FIRST SEASON WITH RANGERS:**
  1948-49

- **BEST SEASON WITH RANGERS:**
  1948-49, 14-16-30, 16 PIM
- **TOTALS WITH RANGERS:**
  Regular season: 182 GP, 36-41-77, 38 PIM
  Playoffs: 12 GP, 6-5-11, 0 PIM
- **HONORS:**
  Calder Trophy, 1948-49

CURTAIN CALL

Gladys Goodding

For generations, she was the answer to the trivia question, "Who played for the Rangers, the Knicks and the Dodgers?" The answer was Gladys Goodding, the organist for two generations of Madison Square Garden fans from the early 1940s to the late 1950s, as well as at Ebbets Field during the Dodgers' heyday in Brooklyn. Gladys would welcome fans, players and even the newspapermen who covered the Rangers with their favorite songs as they entered the building. It was a ritual that the general public at the Garden didn't realize, but it went on night after night. Her favorite tune? Without a doubt it was *The Rangers Victory Song*, which premiered after the 1939-40 championship season and was played for the Blueshirts as they took the ice at the start of every period. Asked once if she knew how many times she had played *The Rangers Victory Song*, she replied: "I can't count that high."

NEW YORK
Ice Exchange

The Rangers' slow start helped convince GM/coach Frank Boucher that he was wearing one too many hats. That's why, although his team was riding its best streak of the season, Boucher stepped down on December 21 in favor of Lynn Patrick, Lester's son and a former teammate. But the same offensive troubles that made Boucher's life miserable as coach plagued the Rangers under Patrick as well, despite the emergence of rookie Pentti Lund as the NHL's top rookie. Boucher opened up the Garden's checkbook to land another top acquisition, shelling out $70,000 and two players (Ed Kullman and Elwyn Morris) to Providence of the AHL to acquire defenseman Allan Stanley. He was joined on the back line by another newcomer, Dunc Fisher, who had played in one playoff game the previous spring. Chuck Rayner finally had the goaltending job to himself when Boucher dealt Jim Henry to Chicago. Among the players coming from Chicago: a diminutive goaltender named Emile Francis whose impact on the Rangers proved to be immense.

Pentti Lund and Allan Stanley finished 1-2 in the Calder Trophy voting.

—1949 1950—

TIME CAPSULE

- **October 9, 1949:**
  The New York Yankees captured the World Series by beating the rival Brooklyn Dodgers.

- **October 24, 1949:**
  The United Nations headquarters was dedicated in Manhattan.

- **April 23, 1950**
  The first NBA championship was won by the Minneapolis Lakers, as they defeated the Syracuse Nationals. George Mikan starred for the Lakers.

1949-1950
FINAL STANDINGS

	W	L	T	PTS	GF	GA
Detroit	37	19	14	88	229	164
Montreal	29	22	19	77	172	150
Toronto	31	27	12	74	176	173
RANGERS	28	31	11	67	170	189
Boston	22	32	16	60	198	228
Chicago	22	38	10	45	203	244

PLAYOFF RESULTS
Semifinals: Rangers defeated Canadiens 4-1

Finals: Red Wings defeated Rangers 4-3

LEADING PLAYOFF SCORER
Pentti Lund (6-5-11)

STANLEY CUP CHAMPION
Detroit Red Wings

SEASON SNAPSHOT

Most Goals:
Edgar Laprade (22)

Most Assists:
Tony Leswick/Don Raleigh (25)

Most Points:
Edgar Laprade/Tony Leswick (44)

Most Penalty Minutes:
Gus Kyle (143)

Most Wins, Goaltender:
Chuck Rayner (28)

Lowest Goals-Against Average:
Chuck Rayner (2.62)

Most Shutouts:
Chuck Rayner (6)

NHL Award Winners:
Chuck Rayner (Hart Trophy)
Edgar Laprade (Lady Byng Trophy)

NHL All-Stars:
Chuck Rayner, G (Second Team)
Tony Leswick, LW (Second Team)

Rangers In All-Star Game:
Pat Egan, D; Edgar Laprade, C;
Tony Leswick, LW; Buddy O'Connor, C;
Chuck Rayner, G.

The Rangers entered the 1949-50 season with only one play-off appearance under their belts since 1942, and wound up having their best season since winning the Cup 10 years earlier. The biggest difference may have been an attitude adjustment: The smallish Rangers weren't backing off from anybody, and Gus Kyle saw to that with a team-leading 143 penalty minutes. Kyle's muscle enabled Tony Leswick to concentrate on offense, and he responded by increasing his goal total from 13 to 19. Edgar Laprade was the only Ranger to crack the 20-goal mark (22), and wound up tied with Leswick as high scorer. But goalie Chuck Rayner was the team's true hero. On a club that finished three games under .500, Rayner finished with a 2.62 goals-against average and six shutouts, earning the Hart Trophy as the league's most valuable player (though ironically, he was only a Second-team All-Star). Despite two seven-game losing streaks, the Rangers managed to make the playoffs, where they were expected to be little more than a pit stop for the second-place Montreal Canadiens. But in a major upset, the Rangers knocked out the Canadiens in five games. They almost wound up doing the same to the Detroit Red Wings in the finals. Despite having to play their two "home" games in Toronto due to the circus, the Rangers led the series 3-2, and

Edgar Laprade led the Rangers with 22 goals in 1949-50.

had leads in Games 6 and 7. But the Red Wings, the regular-season champions, rebounded each time and took the Cup on Pete Babando's double-overtime goal in the deciding game at the Olympia. Little did Ranger fans know that the upset win over the Canadiens would be the team's last in a playoff series until 1971.

MAGIC MOMENT
April 23, 1950

Even Don Raleigh's two overtime goals in the finals weren't enough to beat Detroit.

When the Rangers met the Detroit Red Wings in the finals, they wouldn't face either Gordie Howe (facial injuries) or the Garden (circus time). They lost Game 1 in Detroit, then split their two "home" games in Toronto. Back in Detroit, they fought off a 3-1 third-period deficit to win Game 4 in overtime on a goal by Don Raleigh. The Blueshirts led 1-0 in Game 5 until Ted Lindsay tied the game with two minutes left in regulation. Again, it was Raleigh to the rescue in overtime, and the Rangers were one win away from their first title in a decade. The Rangers led 4-3 in the third period of Game 6, but Lindsay and Sid Abel scored, and the series was tied. The Rangers took an early 2-0 lead in Game 7, only to see the Red Wings pull even with a pair of power-play goals. New York went ahead 3-2 on a goal by Buddy O'Connor, but the Wings tied it again late in the second period and a scoreless third period sent the game into overtime. New York's Nick Mickoski hit the post in the first extra period. In the second overtime, Detroit's Pete Babando fired a backhander after George Gee won a draw. Rayner never saw the puck until it was past him. And at 8:31 of double overtime in Game 7 of the finals, the Rangers' season finally ended. A final irony: Three years later, Babando became a member of the Rangers.

RANGER LEGEND
Chuck Rayner

There were times where Chuck Rayner must have felt he was wearing a bullseye on his sweater instead of the diagonal "Rangers" his teammates wore. Rayner joined the Rangers at the start of the 1945-46 season, and was only fortunate enough to see postseason play twice while on Broadway (1948 and 1950). But Rayner made his mark as one of the best Ranger netminders ever. His five shutouts in 1946-47 led the league in that category. He never played in front of a big, rugged group of defensemen, but his goals-against average slowly dropped. His best season was in 1949-50, when he posted a 2.62 average and six shutouts, which helped the Rangers make the playoffs and almost netted them the Stanley Cup. For that performance, he was awarded the Hart Trophy as the MVP of the league, only the second goalie to receive the honor (Roy Worters of the Americans was the first). He shared netminding chores with Jim Henry in his first three seasons, an oddity for two reasons: It was still too early in league history for teams to be able to afford carrying two goalies on the major-league roster, and Henry and Rayner were friends and business partners. Both were involved in a resort hotel in Ontario, and their wives were tight friends, too. But GM Frank Boucher felt he could only keep one of the two, and Henry was the one sent away—to Chicago for another netminder who was sent right down to New Haven: Emile Francis. Rayner was never the same after a knee injury sustained

in the 1951-52 season and was gone after only 20 games in 1952-53; his replacement, Gump Worsley, won the Calder Trophy. Twenty years after his retirement, he became the 13th goalie to enter the Hockey Hall of Fame in 1973.

Chuck Rayner File

- **BORN:**
  August 11, 1920; Sutherland, Saskatchewan
- **ACQUIRED:**
  Awarded to Rangers after breakup of the Brooklyn Americans
- **FIRST SEASON WITH RANGERS:**
  1945-46
- **BEST SEASON WITH RANGERS:**
  1949-50, 69 GP, 28-30-11, 2.62 goals-against average, 6 shutouts

- **TOTALS WITH RANGERS:**
  Regular season: 377 GP, 123-181-73, 2.99 goals-against average, 24 shutouts
  Playoffs: 18 GP, 9-9-0, 2.63 goals-against average, 1 shutout
- **HONORS:**
  Hart Trophy, 1949-50
  All-Star Game, 1949-50, 1950-51, 1951-52
  West Side Assn. Rangers MVP, 1945-46, 1946-47, 1948-49
- **NHL MILESTONES:**
  25 Shutouts

CURTAIN CALL

William J. Macbeth Trophy

The William J. Macbeth Trophy honored one of the first known hockey writers in New York. "Bunk" Macbeth was also instrumental in convincing "Big Bill" Dwyer to buy the Americans. Macbeth passed away in 1937, and a piece of hardware was made in his honor to salute the winner of the season series between the Rangers and Americans, or intra-city champions, as they were referred to in those times. It may as well have been called the Rangers Trophy, since they won it every season until the Americans disbanded in 1942. Even had there been a trophy for season-series winners following the Rangers' inception in 1926, the Americans would have been clear-cut winners only in 1933-34, when they took four of six games from their Garden rivals. After the Americans folded, the Rangers presented the trophy to their most valuable player in the playoffs. When the Rangers missed postseason play, the hardware remained idle. The first playoff MVP to be awarded the trophy was Phil Watson for his efforts in the 1948 playoffs.

The Macbeth Trophy was originally given to the winner of the Rangers-Americans series.

NEW YORK Ice Exchange

Long-time trainer Frank Paice joined the Rangers in 1949. Photo by Paul Bereswill.

Most of the changes in the Rangers roster from the previous season were on the periphery. Only one of the top 10 scorers of 1948-49, Clint Albright, did not return. Gus Kyle made his rookie debut and led the team with 143 penalty minutes. Jean Paul Lamirande, and Jack Lancien, both of whom missed the previous season, made it back to see regular-season and playoff action. Jack Gordon only played one regular-season game, but appeared in nine of the 12 postseason contests. This also marked the final NHL season of Fred Shero's three-year career, all of them with the Blueshirts. This season also marked the debut of a new Ranger not on the active roster: Frank Paice, who had served as trainer for the minor-league Rovers, moved up to the big club—where he stayed for more than 25 years. Paice replaced Tom McKenna, who later wound up on the New York Mets.

Ranger Lists
Stanley Cup– Winning Goals Against the Rangers

1929 @ MSG

by Bill Carson/Boston

1932 @ Toronto

by Ace Bailey/Toronto

1937 @ Detroit

by Marty Barry/Detroit

1950 @ Detroit

by Pete Babando/Detroit

1972 @ MSG

by Bobby Orr/Boston

1979 @ Montreal

by Jacques Lemaire/Montreal

The All-Ranger Team
First Era (1926-50)

Center
Frank Boucher
(1926-44)

The best playmaker of his era and the only Ranger to have played for or coached each of the first three Cup winners, centering the No. 1 line on the 1928 and 1933 championship teams and coaching the 1940 squad. He won the Lady Byng Trophy so often (seven times in eight years) that the NHL finally gave it to him and had a new trophy struck.

Goaltender
Dave Kerr
(1934-41)

As the first Ranger goaltender to win the Vezina Trophy (and for 54 years, the last to backstop a Stanley Cup winner), Kerr ranks as the best netminder of the Rangers' early days. He still holds the Rangers' playoff record with seven shutouts. He allowed just over two goals per game in seven full seasons on Broadway while recording 40 shutouts in 324 games played.

Defense
Ching Johnson
(1926-37)

As the Rangers' first tough guy, he was an early fan favorite. Johnson, whose real first name was Ivan, was among the premier bodycheckers in an era where the style of play was vastly different than it is today. No Ranger may have loved to hit more; few have done it as well. Johnson was a two-time First-team All-Star and a key member of two Cup winners.

Defense
Art Coulter
(1935-42)

Coulter wrote the book on playing stay-at-home defense: He rarely ventured into the offensive zone and scored only 18 goals in 287 games as a Ranger. But the strong, silent rearguard was a three-time second-team All-Star, an anchor of the 1940 Cup-winning squad and the man chosen to succeed Bill Cook as team captain in 1937.

Art Coulter

Wing
Bill Cook
(1926-37)

It was appropriate that Cook scored the first goal in franchise history. He's still the only Ranger to lead the NHL in scoring twice (1926-27 and 1932-33) and was one of the most feared snipers of his day. He teamed with brother Bun and Boucher to form the "A Line" (named for the subway under the old Garden), the first great scoring unit in Rangers history.

Wing
Bryan Hextall
(1936-48)

Hextall holds two distinctions: He's the last Ranger to win the scoring title, edging teammate Lynn Patrick with 56 points in 1941-42, and had the last Cup-winning goal in team history (1940) until the 1993-94 squad ended the drought. Hextall had 187 goals for the Rangers and would have scored far more had the war not intervened.

Coach
Lester Patrick
(1926-39)

"The Silver Fox" is more responsible than anyone else for the building of the Rangers. He coached two Cup winners and built the team that won a third title. He sold the game to New Yorkers and the local media, turning Madison Square Garden into THE place to see and be seen while constructing and leading "The Classiest Team In Hockey."

Lester Patrick

1950 NEW YORK RANGERS 1951

TIME CAPSULE

■ **October 7, 1950:**
The New York Yankees completed a sweep of the Philadelphia Phillies for their second of five straight World Series titles.

■ **February 26, 1951:**
Congress adopted the 22nd Amendment to the Constitution, stipulating that no one may be elected to more than two terms as President.

■ **April 11, 1951:**
President Harry S. Truman relieved Gen. Douglas MacArthur of his post as supreme commander of forces in Korea, replacing him with Gen. Matthew Ridgeway.

1950-1951
FINAL STANDINGS

	W	L	T	PTS	GF	GA
Detroit	44	13	13	101	236	139
Toronto	41	16	13	95	212	138
Montreal	25	30	15	65	173	184
Boston	22	30	18	62	178	197
RANGERS	20	29	21	61	169	201
Chicago	13	47	10	36	171	280

PLAYOFF RESULTS
Rangers did not qualify

STANLEY CUP CHAMPIONS
Toronto Maple Leafs

SEASON SNAPSHOT

Most Goals:
Nick Mickoski (20)

Most Assists:
Don Raleigh (24)

Most Points:
Nick Mickoski/Don Raleigh (39)

Most Penalty Minutes:
Tony Leswick (112)

Most Wins, Goaltender:
Chuck Rayner (19)

Lowest Goals-Against Average:
Chuck Rayner (2.83)

Most Shutouts:
Chuck Rayner (2)

NHL All-Stars:
Chuck Rayner, G (Second Team)

Rangers In All-Star Game:
Chuck Rayner, G;
Tony Leswick, LW;
Edgar Laprade, C

The 1950-51 Season in Review

After nearly winning the Stanley Cup the previous spring, the Rangers entered 1950-51 with lots of optimism under new coach Neil Colville—and fell flat right out of the gate. They split their first two games, then went 0-8-7 (including three straight shutouts in one stretch) in their next 15 before beating Montreal on November 22, making the rest of the season an uphill climb. Most of the blame for the club's struggles fell on the offense. New York had only one 20-goal scorer (Nick Mickoski) and no one managed as many as 40 points as the team finished last in scoring. Injuries hurt, too: Center Don Raleigh went down with a knee injury before the stretch drive. Still, thanks to the goaltending of Chuck Rayner, a second-team All-Star, and their domination of last-place Chicago, the Rangers bounced back into contention for the final playoff berth. They were in good shape after beating Chicago 3-1 at the Garden on March 7, but the offense then gave out again as the Rangers went 0-6-1 in their next seven games, including five straight losses, before whipping the lowly Blackhawks 5-2 in the season finale. That wasn't enough; the Rangers wound up one point behind Boston, beginning a streak of disappointments that was to last for five years.

The line of Ed Slowinski, Don Raleigh and Nick Mickoski was the Rangers' best in 1950-51.

MAGIC MOMENT *Frank Boucher Night*

Perhaps it was appropriate that the Rangers picked Valentine's Day to show Frank Boucher just how much he meant to the franchise. Boucher had played for two Stanley Cup winners, coached another, and was trying to build a fourth as general manager when he was honored for 25 years of service as the quintessential Ranger. He was showered with gifts (including a car and a television set) and tributes from the likes of Mayor Vincent Impellittieri, NHL president Clarence Campbell and his old linemates, Bill and Bun Cook. After listening to the tributes, Boucher told the crowd that he and his wife "would cherish this for the rest of our lives." Putting on his general manager's hat, Boucher also cherished the easy 5-1 victory over lowly Chicago that followed the ceremonies; unlike Lester Patrick Night four years earlier, when the Rangers were whipped by Toronto, they remembered to win the game as well. Boucher stayed on as general manager

Frank Boucher was honored for 25 years as a Ranger.

through 1954-55, but was unable to get the team back to the playoffs, though the talent he left behind was the nucleus of the Rangers' rise in the late 1950s.

RANGER LEGEND
Frank Eddolls

Frank Eddolls refused to allow a lack of size to keep him from becoming a solid NHL defenseman. He wound up in New York partly due to Montreal boss Frank Selke's sense of fairness. Selke felt it wasn't right to keep Eddolls and Buddy O'Connor in the minors just because the Canadiens were overstocked, and in what more than one pre-expansion writer called "the best trade ever made by the Rangers," they came to Broadway in the summer of 1947 for Hal Laycoe, Joe Bell, and George Robertson. Whatever Eddolls lacked in size (at 5-8 and 175, he was the Reijo Ruotsalainen of his day, size-wise), he more than made up for with skills, smarts, and leadership. Eddolls was regarded as one of the smartest (and best-dressed) players of his day during his five seasons in New York. He spent his last full season as captain of the Rangers, stepping down when he took over briefly as coach of Saskatoon of the old Pacific Coast League after Bill Cook moved behind the Rangers' bench. Just before the 1952-53 season, the Rangers sold Eddolls back to Montreal to enable him to coach Buffalo of the AHL. Eddolls built the Bisons into a first-place team and was named AHL Coach of the Year, a performance that earned him a chance to coach the moribund Blackhawks—at age 33. The Blackhawks let him go after repeating their last-place finish of the previous season, so Eddolls returned to Buffalo and served terms as coach and GM, helping build the Bisons into an AHL powerhouse. He appeared to be in line for a long career as a successful hockey executive, but fate had other ideas: Eddolls, then 40, collapsed and died of a heart attack while playing golf in August 1961.

Frank Eddolls File

- **BORN:**
  July 5, 1921, Lachine, Quebec
- **ACQUIRED:**
  Traded from Montreal with Buddy O'Connor for Hal Laycoe, Joe Bell, and George Robertson, August 11, 1947
- **FIRST SEASON WITH RANGERS:**
  1947-48

- **BEST SEASON WITH RANGERS:**
  1947-48, 58 GP, 6-13-19, 16 PIM
- **TOTALS WITH RANGERS:**
  Regular season: 260 GP, 18-34-52, 88 PIM
  Playoffs: 13 GP, 0-1-1, 4 PIM
- **HONORS:**
  All-Star Game, 1951-52

CURTAIN CALL

Trying Everything

Teams will do anything to end a losing streak. In the case of the Rangers, "anything" included a hypnotist. With the team mired in a winless streak that would reach 15 games, someone (Stan Saplin, the team's publicist, was the chief suspect) mentioned that a Dr. David Tracy had successfully implanted athletes with a positive psyche via hypnosis. The hypnotist accepted an invitation to try out his specialty on the players, and came into the locker room prior to the November 15 game with Boston at the Garden. He appeared to have Tony Leswick mesmerized as teammates looked on with a mixture of amusement and amazement. Garden fans were amazed as the Rangers looked sharp, staying even with Boston until Bill Quackenbush broke the spell when he bounced a puck past Chuck Rayner in the final minute and gave the Bruins a 4-3 win. That was all for Dr. Tracy, though he kept trying to convince the Rangers that he realized his mistake. "You've got to let me at the 'goolie,'" he insisted. "He's not relaxed."

Tony Leswick was a receptive subject for hypnotist David Tracy.

NEW YORK Ice Exchange

Coming off a near-miss in the Stanley Cup finals, the Rangers were stunned when coach Lynn Patrick resigned not long after the season ended. Patrick had worked out a deal with his father, Lester, to go back and coach in Victoria, British Columbia—but he was no sooner settled in a new house when he accepted an offer from

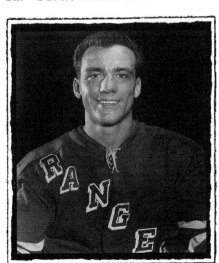

Zellio Toppazzini had 14 goals in his first season as a Ranger.

Art Ross to coach the Bruins. GM Frank Boucher turned to another former Ranger star, Neil Colville, to replace him. On the ice, the search was on for offense, and the Rangers tried to find some both from within the organization and via trades. The best newcomer was rookie Reg Sinclair, who popped in 18 goals, second on the team, and tied with Don Raleigh for tops on the club with 39 points. His 70 penalty minutes also put him among the team leaders, and he was one of only five Rangers to play in all 70 games under the new expanded schedule. The best acquisition was Zellio Toppazzini, who contributed 14 goals and 13 assists in 55 games after being acquired from Boston.

Ranger Lists

Rangers captains who have coached the team

Bill Cook
Captain 1926-37
Coach 1951-53

Neil Colville
Captain 1945-48
Coach 1950-51

Red Sullivan
Captain 1957-61
Coach 1962-65

Phil Esposito
Captain 1975-78
Coach 1986-87 and 1989

—1951  1952—

TIME CAPSULE

- **October 3, 1951:**
  Bobby Thomson of the New York Giants hit "The Shot Heard Around The World," a three-run homer in the bottom of the ninth that gave the Giants a 5-4 victory over the Brooklyn Dodgers for the National League pennant.

- **November 10, 1951:**
  The first transcontinental direct-dial telephone service began when a call was placed from New Jersey to California.

- **April 8, 1952:**
  President Harry S. Truman issued an order preventing the shutdown of the nation's steel mills.

1951-1952
FINAL STANDINGS

	W	L	T	PTS	GF	GA
Detroit	44	14	12	100	215	133
Montreal	34	26	10	78	195	164
Toronto	29	25	16	74	168	157
Boston	25	29	16	66	162	176
RANGERS	23	34	13	59	192	219
Chicago	17	44	9	43	158	241

PLAYOFF RESULTS
Rangers did not qualify

STANLEY CUP CHAMPION
Detroit Red Wings

SEASON SNAPSHOT

Most Goals:
Wally Hergesheimer (26)

Most Assists:
Don Raleigh (42)

Most Points:
Don Raleigh (61)

Most Penalty Minutes:
Hy Buller (96)

Most Wins, Goaltender:
Chuck Rayner (18)

Lowest Goals-Against Average:
Chuck Rayner (3.00)

Most Shutouts:
Chuck Rayner (2)

NHL All-Stars:
Hy Buller, D (Second Team)

Rangers In All-Star Game:
Chuck Rayner, G
Frank Eddolls, D;
Don Raleigh, C;
Reg Sinclair, LW;
Gaye Stewart, LW

For the second year in a row, the Rangers had their quest for a playoff berth spoiled by the Boston Bruins, who used a late 4-1-1 surge (the one loss was to the Rangers) to move past the Blueshirts into fourth place in the final 10 days of the season. A 6-12-5 start, along with poor health, was enough to convince Neil Colville to hand over the coaching reins to the man he succeeded as captain, Bill Cook. The Rangers perked up by Christmas and battled the Bruins for the final playoff berth the rest of the way, despite a knee injury that sidelined starting goaltender Chuck Rayner for the final five weeks of the season (Rayner was first injured in mid-December, but hid the injury for nearly two months until surgery was needed) and a shoulder injury that KO'd defenseman Allan Stanley for seven weeks. They pulled even with the Bruins on March 12, when they set a slew of team offensive records in routing Chicago 10-2 at the Garden. But a pair of losses to Toronto, combined with the Bruins' late hot streak, was enough to send the Rangers home early. The individual highlight belonged to Don Raleigh, who finished second in the NHL in assists with

Reg Sinclair was a 20-goal scorer for the Rangers in 1951-52.

42 and fourth in scoring with 61 points, tying Lynn Patrick's team record. Wally Hergesheimer led the Rangers with 26 goals, but Ed Slowinski (21) and Reg Sinclair (20) were the only others to hit the 20-goal mark.

Magic Moment   March 12, 1952

Every game counted as the Rangers battled for a play-off berth down the stretch in 1952, so having the last-place Blackhawks come to town was an opportunity not to be missed. The Rangers appeared to have the game in hand with a 3-0 lead late in the second period before Chicago's Bill Mosienko and Jimmy Peters scored to cut the margin to one goal with plenty of time left. With the crowd fearing a collapse, the Rangers did the opposite, putting the game away with an offensive burst that shattered a host of team marks. The Rangers scored seven times in the final 13:10 for a 10-2 victory, their first double-digit output in a decade. Four of the goals came in a 2-minute, 10-second span, breaking another team mark set in 1942. Rookie Wally Hergesheimer had three of the seven goals, all in a 7:30 span, against a defenseless goalie Harry Lumley, who wound up facing 51 shots. The last two tallies capped off the four-goal explosion that had been started by Don Raleigh at 12:10. The winning goalie was Emile Francis, who later went on to play a much bigger role in Ranger history.

Wally Hergesheimer scored three times in the Rangers' seven-goal burst.

RANGER LEGEND
Don Raleigh

At just under 6 feet tall and barely 150 pounds, Don Raleigh's nickname just had to be "Bones." But whatever Raleigh lacked in heft, he more than made up for in skill and heart. Raleigh became the youngest player ever to skate for the Rangers when he took part in 15 games as a 17-year-old in 1943-44. He made a good impression before a broken jaw ended his season, then went back to school—and it took some fancy talking by Frank Boucher to lure him back to the NHL. Boucher's trip proved to be well worth the effort: Raleigh became only the third Ranger to be given No. 7 after Phil Watson retired and did nothing but add to the luster of the most famous number in team history. "There is something special about No. 7 on the Rangers" Watson said of the decision. "We had to pick a class guy to wear it." They did. In only his fourth game, Raleigh set a league record by assisting on three goals in an 81-second span, and later in the same season, he scored four times in a game. Raleigh also became the first player ever to score back-to-back overtime goals in the same final-round series when he connected twice against Detroit in 1950; he nearly had a third overtime winner, but his shot in the second extra period of Game 7 hit the post just before Pete Babando's game-winner. Unfortunately for the Rangers, Raleigh's career was slowed by injury: He was leading the team in scoring in 1948-49 before a knee injury ended his

Don Raleigh had his best season with 61 points in 1951-52.

season, and a broken wrist ruined his 1952-53 season. A Civil War devotee and poetry buff, he was one of the most popular Rangers ever and was named captain in November 1953, serving for two seasons until stepping down prior to his final NHL campaign.

Don Raleigh File

- **BORN:**
  June 27, 1926, Kenora, Ontario
- **ACQUIRED:**
  Signed from University of Manitoba, 1947
- **FIRST SEASON WITH RANGERS:**
  1943-44
- **BEST SEASON WITH RANGERS:**
  1951-52, 70 GP, 19-42-61, 14 PIM

- **TOTALS WITH RANGERS:**
  Regular season: 535 GP, 101-219-320, 96 PIM
  Playoffs: 18 GP, 6-5-11, 6 PIM
- **HONORS:**
  West Side Assn. Rangers MVP, 1950-51
  All-Star Game, 1954-55

CURTAIN CALL
March 23, 1952

The 3,254 fans who showed up for the 1952 season finale against Chicago didn't get the Ranger victory they expected. Instead, they got to see history being made. With Ed Slowinski scoring three times, the Rangers led 6-2 with less than 14 minutes left when Bill Mosienko took a pass from Gus Bodnar and snapped a shot past rookie goalie Lorne Anderson at 6:09. It didn't look like much—until Bodnar fed Mosienko for another goal just 11 seconds later. It took just 10 seconds for Mosienko to beat Anderson again, this time converting feeds from Bodnar and George Gee for his third goal in 21 seconds. Not only did Mosienko eclipse the individual mark for fastest three goals of 1:04 set by Detroit's Carl Liscombe in 1938, he broke the *team* mark of three goals in 24 seconds set by the Montreal Maroons in 1932. The

Bill Mosienko's three goals in 21 seconds is still an NHL record.

Garden crowd loudly cheered Mosienko's feat, but the fans were less happy when Sid Finney tied the game with 6:10 to play and scored in the final minute to give Chicago a 7-6 victory. Mosienko's mark has stood unchallenged for more than 40 years. The biggest loser was Anderson, a youngster up from the Rovers whose third NHL game turned out to be his last.

NEW YORK
Ice Exchange

The biggest change in 1951-52 came on December 6, when Neil Colville turned over the coaching reins to his former teammate, Bill Cook. Colville was taking the Rangers' continuing struggles hard: He had been reduced to a milk diet because his stomach was bothering him so badly. On the ice, the Rangers brought up two rookies who made an immediate impression: Wally Hergesheimer set a team mark for goals by a first-year player with 26, while Hy Buller tied a team mark for points

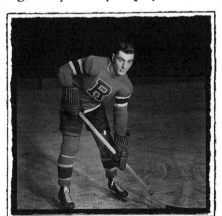

Hy Buller tied a team record for points by a defenseman as a rookie in 1951-52.

by a defenseman with 35. The Rangers also added scoring up front from Paul Ronty and Gaye Stewart, while two heroes of the run to the Stanley Cup finals in 1950, Buddy O'Connor (Montreal) and Tony Leswick (Detroit) were dealt away. It was also the last full season for two other 1950 heroes: goalie Chuck Rayner, who was never the same after undergoing knee surgery in February, virtually taking the Rangers' playoff chances with him, and defenseman Frank Eddolls, who resigned his captaincy early in the season and played only 42 games before beginning his coaching career by stepping in for Cook in Saskatoon.

Ranger Lists

Rangers who have worn No. 7

Frank Boucher
1926-38

Phil Watson
1938-43; 1944-48

Don Raleigh
1948-56

Red Sullivan
1956-61

Guy Gendron
1961-62

Rod Gilbert
1962-77
(Number retired)

—1952 1953—

TIME CAPSULE

- **September 23, 1952:**
  Rocky Marciano won his 43rd consecutive bout without a loss, defeating Jersey Joe Walcott to win the heavyweight championship.

- **November 4, 1952:**
  Republican Dwight Eisenhower defeated Democrat Adlai Stevenson and was elected as the 34th President of the United States.

- **March 18, 1953:**
  Baseball's Boston Braves moved to Milwaukee, setting in motion a wave of franchise shifts that saw the Dodgers and Giants leave New York five years later.

1952-1953
FINAL STANDINGS

	W	L	T	PTS	GF	GA
Detroit	36	16	18	90	222	133
Montreal	28	23	19	75	155	148
Boston	28	29	13	69	152	172
Chicago	27	28	15	69	169	175
Toronto	27	30	13	67	156	167
RANGERS	17	37	16	50	152	211

PLAYOFF RESULTS
Rangers did not qualify

STANLEY CUP CHAMPIONS
Montreal Canadiens

SEASON SNAPSHOT

Most Goals:
Wally Hergesheimer (30)

Most Assists:
Paul Ronty (38)

Most Points:
Wally Hergesheimer (59)

Most Penalty Minutes:
Hy Buller (73)

Most Wins, Goaltender:
Gump Worsley (13)

Lowest Goals-Against Average:
Gump Worsley (3.06)

Most Shutouts:
Gump Worsley (2)

NHL Award Winners:
Gump Worsley (Calder Trophy)

Rangers In All-Star Game:
Hy Buller, D;
Leo Reise Jr., D

The 1952-53 Season in Review

It was just one of those years. The Rangers started the season on the road, as usual, this time hitting all five opposition cities before their Garden opener, and went 0-4-1. The bad start was a harbinger of things to come. Featuring a lineup that was studded with newcomers, most of them untried youngsters from their growing farm system, the Rangers won just six times in their first 38 games and finished 17 points behind fifth-place Chicago. Things would have been even worse if the Rangers hadn't done well against the Boston Bruins—they went 7-5-2 against their New England rivals and 10-32-14 against the other four teams. The Rangers never won more than twice in a row and their longest unbeaten streak was only four games—a win and three ties. Wally Hergesheimer led the team with 30 goals and 59 points, but no other Ranger was able to hit the 20-goal mark and only center Paul Ronty (54) had more than 40 points. The good news for Garden fans was that help was on the way. GM Frank Boucher's efforts to build up the farm system began to pay off, as Gump Worsley stepped in for long-time netminder Chuck Rayner and played well enough to

Wally Hergesheimer led the Rangers with 30 goals and 59 points.

earn the Calder Trophy. Two other future Hall of Famers, Harry Howell and Andy Bathgate, also made their NHL debuts, with Howell stepping out of juniors and right into a regular berth on the blue line, where he stayed for 17 seasons. The future was looking brighter—but that wasn't much consolation for Garden fans, who saw the team again miss the playoffs.

Magic Moment   *January 11, 1953*

The Montreal Canadiens were on their way to another Stanley Cup, while the Rangers again were headed toward an early summer. For one night, though, the two sides switched roles. Before an enthused (and doubtless amazed) gathering at the Garden, the Rangers embarrassed their long-time tormentors, routing the Canadiens 7-0. It was a night of firsts: the first victory for the Rangers over the Canadiens in 1952-53, and the first shutout in the career of rookie goaltender Gump Worsley, who was still regarded as a fill-in for injured started Chuck Rayner at the time but went on to win the Calder Trophy as the NHL's top rookie. It was also the worst defeat suffered by the Habs since the Rangers had beaten them 9-0 at the Garden nearly four years earlier. Jack Stoddard had two goals for New York as the Rangers scored more than five goals for the first time in 1952-53; 11 days later, they got eight in a rout of Detroit (a game in which Wings fans mocked their team by chanting for more Ranger goals), then needed five games to score their next seven goals.

Jack Stoddard scored twice in the Rangers' biggest win of the season.

115

RANGER LEGEND
Allan Stanley

In an era where players routinely make a million dollars or more, $70,000 might seem like peanuts. But there were gasps around the NHL when Rangers GM Frank Boucher paid that amount (plus two players) to Providence of the AHL for Allan Stanley, a 22-year-old defenseman who was counted on to fortify the Blueshirts' blue line. Stanley more than lived up to his buildup, playing with poise and confidence rarely seen in rookies. Despite the late start and an injury that hampered him later in the season, Stanley was the runner-up to teammate Pentti Lund for the Calder Trophy as the league's top rookie. One of Stanley's biggest attributes was also his biggest liability with Ranger fans: He wasn't flashy, and as a result, his skating, passing, and shooting skills were sometimes lost on the gatherings at the Garden. Perhaps his finest moments as a Ranger came in the 1950 playoffs, when he had seven points in 12 games and was regarded by coach Lynn Patrick as the best player on the ice in the final-round loss to Detroit. He was even chosen as captain in December 1951 when Frank Eddolls stepped down. But the Rangers' continued struggles and Stanley's lack of flash began to grate on the Garden faithful. They hooted him so unmercifully that GM Frank Boucher at one point even announced that Stanley would play only road games, then decided to send him to the Rangers' farm team in Vancouver in 1953-54. "Boucher made it clear to me it wasn't because of my play," Stanley remembered years later. "I was hurt and relieved at the same time, but I knew I'd get another chance." Stanley rejoined the Rangers the next season, but was soon dealt to Boston, where Patrick was now in charge. He later played for Chicago but his best days came in Toronto, where he was a key member of the Leafs' Cup-winners in the early 1960s. Stanley wound up with exactly 100 career goals, four Stanley Cup rings, and a berth in the Hall of Fame.

Allan Stanley File

- **BORN:**
  March 1, 1926, Timmins, Ontario
- **FIRST NHL SEASON:**
  1948-49
- **ACQUIRED:**
  Trade from Providence (AHL) for Ed Kullman, Elwyn Morris and cash, December 1948
- **FIRST SEASON WITH RANGERS:**
  1948-49

- **BEST SEASON WITH RANGERS:**
  1950-51, 70 GP, 7-14-21, 75 PIM
- **TOTALS WITH RANGERS:**
  Regular season: 307 GP, 23-56-79, 272 PIM
  Playoffs: 12 GP, 2-5-7, 10 PIM
- **NHL MILESTONES:**
  1,244 Games Played

CURTAIN CALL

The Quebec Rangers?

GM Frank Boucher admitted the Rangers talked about playing some games in Quebec.

Had the Rangers made the playoffs in 1953, they might have wound up playing their home games in Quebec—along with a handful the following season. GM Frank Boucher admitted in mid-January that while no one from Quebec had directly approached the club, "it's not such a fantastic idea, and it might be one way to find out whether Quebec City could support big-time hockey." The memory of not having a home game in the 1950 finals due to the circus was fresh in Boucher's mind, though he admitted that he was "thinking out loud as a hockey man" and not speaking on behalf of anyone connected with Madison Square Garden or the Rangers. The *Quebec Chronicle-Telegraph* wrote that "a reliable Montreal informant" told him the Rangers would use the new Coliseé for any playoff games in 1953 and as many as 15 home games in 1953-54—and that Jean Beliveau, then a star with the Quebec Aces, might become a Ranger as part of the deal. Unfortunately, that part of the story never came true.

NEW YORK Ice Exchange

Ranger fans definitely needed programs in 1952-53. GM Frank Boucher's hunt for young talent began to pay off, as no fewer than 14 newcomers made their Ranger debuts. Three of them—goalie Gump Worsley, defenseman Harry Howell, and forward Andy Bathgate—went on to become members of the Hockey Hall of Fame, while forwards Dean Prentice and Ron Murphy turned

Harry Howell began his Ranger career in 1952-53. He played more games as a Ranger than anyone else.

into solid NHL forwards. Worsley's emergence and continuing injury problems spelled the end for popular goaltender Chuck Rayner, who played only 20 games, going 4-9-7 with one shutout and a 2.90 goals-against average. Perhaps the most ironic addition was the midseason purchase of forward Pete Babando from Chicago—less than three years after Babando's goal in double overtime beat the Rangers in Game 7 of the Stanley Cup finals for Detroit. The most famous departure was Bill Cook; the Ranger legend, now their coach, called it quits after the season.

1953 1954

TIME CAPSULE

- **October 5, 1953:**
  The New York Yankees won their fifth straight World Series, beating the Brooklyn Dodgers 4-3 to wrap up a six-game victory over their local rivals.

- **February 23, 1954:**
  Polio vaccinations in schools took place for the first time.

- **March 20, 1954:**
  LaSalle, led by Tom Gola, beat Bradley to win the NCAA basketball championship.

1953-1954
FINAL STANDINGS

	W	L	T	PTS	GF	GA
Detroit	37	19	14	88	191	132
Montreal	35	24	11	81	195	141
Toronto	32	24	14	78	152	131
Boston	32	28	10	74	177	181
RANGERS	29	31	10	68	161	182
Chicago	12	51	7	31	133	242

PLAYOFF RESULTS
Rangers did not qualify

STANLEY CUP CHAMPION
Detroit Red Wings

SEASON SNAPSHOT

Most Goals:
Wally Hergesheimer (27)

Most Assists:
Paul Ronty (33)

Most Points:
Paul Ronty (46)

Most Penalty Minutes:
Ivan Irwin (109)

Most Wins, Goaltender:
Johnny Bower (29)

Lowest Goals-Against Average:
Johnny Bower (2.60)

Most Shutouts:
Johnny Bower (5)

NHL Award Winners:
Camille Henry (Calder Trophy)

Rangers In All-Star Game:
Leo Reise Jr., D;
Paul Ronty, C;
Wally Hergesheimer C

The 1953-54 Season in Review

The Broadway Boys came up with their best season since 1941-42. They didn't finish above .500, but they were only two games off the mark (they were three below in 1949-50, when they went to the seventh game of the finals). Unfortunately, this still meant no playoffs for the 10th time in 12 years—but there were several positive signs indicating that the Rangers were about to shake the malaise that had dogged them since wartime. For instance, they started the season with a five-game road trip—one game in each city— and gained a win and a tie, a better showing than in many past seasons. The first half of the season had 10 wins and six ties in 35 games, but in the second half, the Rangers got on their best sustained roll in years, going 19-12-4, the first time they finished a half-season over .500 since the first half of the 1947-48 season (13-

Muzz Patrick took over as coach midway through 1953-54.

12-5). Wally Hergesheimer led the team with 27 goals, and Paul Ronty was tops in assists (33) and points (46). Johnny Bower tended goal the entire season, and with offense on the increase, posted a very respectable 2.60 goals against and five shutouts. He allowed more than four goals in only seven games. The Blueshirts would suffer a setback the following season, but then rebound to make the playoffs for three straight years. Even so, GM/coach Frank Boucher removed himself from the bench after 39 games, and handed the reins to Muzz Patrick.

MAGIC MOMENT January 20, 1954

There were few true moments of magic involving the Rangers between 1942 and 1956, but one took place on January 20, 1954, when Doug Bentley came out of retirement to join his brother Max as Ranger teammates—and what a show Doug put on. It was the only home game in the usual hell of mid-January, and the Rangers hosted the Bruins. The fact that they beat Boston by an 8-3 count was secondary to what Doug Bentley did in his first game on Broadway as a Ranger. Bentley had a goal and three assists, one of which came on a goal by his brother. It was the only season for the tandem on the Rangers, and despite his spectacular debut, Doug wound up scoring just one more goal and assisting on seven others in 20 games before calling it quits for good. Max played in 57 games and had 14 goals and 18 assists. Ironically, there was another brother combo behind the bench that night, as Muzz Patrick was coaching the Rangers, and brother Lynn was running the Bruins. It was the fourth and final season of Lynn's coaching tenure in Boston before he went on to serve as GM.

Max (L.) and Doug (R.) Bentley. Doug Bentley produced four points in his NHL comeback, one on an assist to brother Max. Photo courtesy of the Hockey Hall of Fame.

RANGER LEGEND
Camille Henry

He stood about 5-foot-6 and weighed less than 150 pounds, but Camille Henry actually used his size to his advantage. He was so shifty that bigger players often couldn't draw a bead on him to inflict punishment. Henry put up such impressive goal totals in juniors and the minors that GM Frank Boucher gave him a shot with the Blueshirts in 1953 as a power-play specialist. This meant that Henry logged very little ice time, and had to make the most of it. He did, scoring 24 goals—20 of them on the power play—and added 15 assists to give him 39 points and the Calder Trophy as rookie of the year. Henry scored four of those goals on March 13 in Detroit's Olympia, the first and only Ranger to do so. His prowess also cost Terry Sawchuk his third straight Vezina Trophy, as the Rangers won the game 5-2. However, Henry's world was rocked when Boucher sent him down to the minors the next season because he simply wasn't producing. Henry was even put on waivers, but no one would pay the $15,000 price tag. He caught two breaks: Muzz Patrick took over for Boucher, and Parker MacDonald got hurt. In 1956, Patrick gave Henry a second chance, but Henry went right back to Providence. But when January rolled around, Henry was back in the NHL to stay. "Camille The Eel" was one of the game's greatest tip-

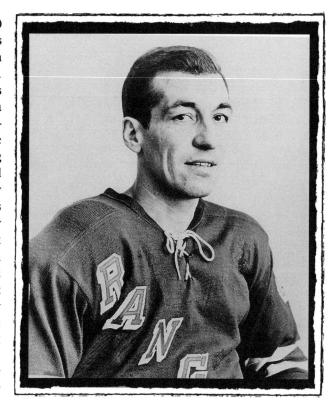

in artists and scored as many as 37 goals in a season for the Rangers before being dealt to Chicago in 1964-65. He retired after the 1969-70 season, finishing his career with 279 goals and 249 assists for 528 points while toiling for the Rangers, Chicago and St. Louis. Henry wanted to coach in the Rangers' organization, but when that opportunity wasn't available, he took a job as the first coach of the New York Raiders of the newly formed WHA. That only lasted one season (as did the Raiders, who moved to Cherry Hill, N.J.), and Henry left the sport, except to fill in as a color commentator on Canadian hockey broadcasts.

Camille Henry File

- **BORN:**
  January 31, 1933; Quebec City, Quebec
- **ACQUIRED:**
  Product of Rangers organization
- **FIRST SEASON WITH RANGERS:**
  1953-54
- **BEST SEASON WITH RANGERS:**
  1962-63, 66 GP, 37-23-60, 8 PIM

- **TOTALS WITH RANGERS:**
  Regular season: 637 GP, 256-222-478, 78 PIM
  Playoffs: 16 GP, 3-7-10, 5 PIM
- **HONORS:**
  Calder Trophy, 1953-54
  Lady Byng Trophy 1957-58

CURTAIN CALL
December 20, 1953

One of the nastiest incidents in Garden history took place on December 20, 1953 during the Rangers' 3-1 victory over Montreal. New York's Ron Murphy slashed Montreal star Bernie "Boom-Boom" Geoffrion, who took exception and swung his stick like a baseball bat. The Boomer connected with Murphy's head, giving him a concussion and a broken jaw. After commissioner Clarence Campbell passed sentence (Geoffrion was suspended for the next seven Rangers-Canadiens meetings, Murphy for the next four), Montreal forward Maurice "Rocket" Richard spoke out in a column he wrote for *Samedi Dimanche*, a French-language newspaper in Montreal. He ripped Campbell, saying the penalty to his teammate was too harsh. Campbell immediately took action, forcing Richard to forsake his journalistic musings and apologize publicly for his outburst. Campbell also took $1,000 from him as a bond to dissuade further outbursts, with the promise to return the money if Richard behaved.

Ron Murphy and Boom-Boom Geoffrion were suspended after a stick-swinging incident.

NEW YORK
Ice Exchange

Johnny Bower had a spectacular NHL debut in 1953-54.

Frank Boucher came back for his second go-around behind the bench. He replaced Bill Cook after the 1952-53 season, but lasted only until January, when he vacated the bench after 39 games (and a 13-20-6 record) to concentrate solely on his GM's desk. He handed off the coaching responsibilities to Muzz Patrick, who would last through the rest of the season and all of the following one. The captaincy also changed hands, as Allan Stanley relinquished the "C" to Don Raleigh on November 4. Johnny Bower took over the goaltending chores and posted a 2.60 goals-against average and five shutouts. The biggest offensive buzz was from Camille Henry's callup (and 24 goals—enough to win the Calder Trophy), while defenseman Jack "Tex" Evans returned after a one-year absence. It was also to be the second and final season in the career of defenseman Leo Reise Jr., who wound up 3-5-8 with 71 penalty minutes during the season, and 7-20-27 with 124 minutes of penalty time for his career.

Ranger Lists

Calder Trophy Winners

Kilby MacDonald
1939-40

Grant Warwick
1941-42

Edgar Laprade
1945-46

Pentti Lund
1948-49

Gump Worsley
1952-53

Camille Henry
1953-54

Steve Vickers
1972-73

Brian Leetch
1988-89

— 1954 1955 —

TIME CAPSULE

- **September 29, 1954:**
  Willie Mays made one of the most famous catches in World Series history, running down a 460-foot drive by Vic Wertz in the opening game at the Polo Grounds. The Giants went on to win the game and sweep the series.

- **December 2, 1954:**
  Sen. Joseph McCarthy was condemned in a vote by fellow U.S. senators for his actions in his anticommunist witch hunt.

- **May 2, 1955:**
  Tennessee Williams was awarded the Pulitzer Prize for his drama, *Cat On A Hot Tin Roof.*

1954-1955

FINAL STANDINGS

	W	L	T	PTS	GF	GA
Detroit	42	17	11	95	204	134
Montreal	41	18	11	93	228	157
Toronto	24	24	22	70	147	135
Boston	23	26	21	67	169	188
RANGERS	17	35	18	52	150	210
Chicago	13	40	17	43	161	235

PLAYOFF RESULTS
Rangers did not qualify

STANLEY CUP CHAMPION
Detroit Red Wings

SEASON SNAPSHOT

Most Goals:
Danny Lewicki (29)

Most Assists:
Danny Lewicki (24)

Most Points:
Danny Lewicki (53)

Most Penalty Minutes:
Jack Evans (91)

Most Wins, Goaltender:
Gump Worsley (15)

Lowest Goals-Against Average:
Gump Worsley (3.03)

Most Shutouts:
Gump Worsley (4)

NHL All-Stars:
Danny Lewicki, LW (Second Team)

Rangers In All-Star Game:
Harry Howell, D;
Paul Ronty, C;
Don Raleigh, C.

The 1954-55 Season in Review

No one knew that the misery and suffering would end after this season, and the Rangers' play showed no indication of a potential turnaround. They jumped out of the gate with wins in five of their first eight games, then hit the wall with a six-game winless streak. After rebounding with a 3-2-3 run, they slid out of the playoff chase by going winless in the next 14 games (eight losses, six ties). And after snapping that streak with a win, they went 0-4-2 in the following six games. To put a cap on their misery, their record between January 30 and March 6 was 1-10-4. The poor showing triggered a postseason shakeup, as GM Frank Boucher was ousted, coach Muzz Patrick took Boucher's spot, and Phil Watson was chosen by Patrick to coach the following season. The brightest spot on the team was Danny Lewicki, who managed to lead the Blueshirts in scoring in his first season with the team with 29 goals and 53 points. Andy Bathgate's first full season netted him 20 goals and 20 assists. Only four other Rangers managed at least 10 goals, and one was newly acquired Pete Conacher. After a year in the minors, Gump Worsley came back up and took his job back from Johnny Bower. In 65 games, Worsley posted a respectable 3.03 goals-against average and four shutouts.

Paul Ronty was one of three Rangers in the All-Star Game. Photo by Bill Jacobellis.

MAGIC MOMENT   January 19, 1955

Gump Worsley's 2-0 shutout of the Detroit Red Wings on January 19, 1955 was one of the greatest goaltending efforts ever seen at the Garden. The powerful Red Wings, on their way to another Stanley Cup, pelted Worsley with 51 shots. The little goalie stopped every one of them. It's believed to be the most shots ever turned aside by a Ranger goalie in a shutout. Andy Bathgate took care of the offense, beating Terry Sawchuk at 1:17 of the second period to give the Rangers the lead, then adding an insurance tally with 2:50 remaining in the game. The shutout came during one of the best stretches of Worsley's Hall of Fame career, a six-game span in which he allowed only eight goals. It started on January 12, when the Rangers and Maple Leafs played a scoreless tie at the Garden. Worsley then allowed just two goals in a 6-2 win over Chicago and was beaten three times in a 3-0 loss at Detroit on January 16. After his 51-save effort gave the Rangers a split of the home-and-home series with the Wings, Worsley was a 3-1 loser in Boston on January 22, but silenced the Hub fans the next night by recording his third shutout in 12 days, blanking the Bruins 2-0.

Gump Worsley stopped 51 shots to blank Detroit, one of three shutouts in a 12-day stretch.

RANGER LEGEND
Danny Lewicki

Danny Lewicki became a member of the Rangers because his previous team thought he was a case of a square peg not fitting into a round hole. He was signed by Toronto in time to start the 1950-51 season with the club and had an excellent rookie season with the Maple Leafs, scoring 16 goals. The problem for Lewicki was that both Leafs owner Conn Smythe and coach Joe Primeau thought he wasn't the right kind of player for their team. Lewicki wasn't a physical player, and though he was willing to take a hit in traffic to make a play, he wasn't the kind of player who would run somebody or get them involved in a fight. Frustrated because of Lewicki's lack of physical play, Smythe sold Lewicki to the Rangers for $15,000. The Maple Leafs knew that Lewicki was quite capable of scoring, as the Blueshirts would soon find out. He joined the Rangers for the 1954-55 season, and was hot from the start, scoring 11 goals in his first 15 games and 18 goals in his first 33 games. He wound up with 29 tallies for the season, just four short of Bill Cook's team mark, a total that included five game-winners and a pair of game-tying tallies. Unfortunately for Lewicki and the Rangers, he never scored like that again. Lewicki had 18 goals in each of the next two seasons, then managed just 11 in 1957-58. Those numbers added up to the end of Lewicki on Broadway. He finished out his playing career with one season with the Blackhawks, and retired in 1959. He was one of the only players in the NHL who had come to the Rangers with three different championships under his belt. He was on the 1948

Memorial Cup champion Port Arthur Bruins. In 1950, he was a part of the Toronto Marlboros, who captured the Allan Cup, and then one year later, he was a member of the 1951 Stanley Cup champion Toronto Maple Leafs.

Danny Lewicki File

- **BORN:**
  March 12, 1931; Fort William, Ontario
- **ACQUIRED:**
  From the Toronto Maple Leafs for $15,000 prior to the 1954-55 season.
- **FIRST SEASON WITH RANGERS:**
  1954-55

- **BEST SEASON WITH RANGERS:**
  1954-55, 70 GP, 29-24-53, 8 PIM
- **TOTALS WITH RANGERS:**
  Regular season: 280 GP, 76-90-166, 107 PIM
  Playoffs: 16 GP, 0-4-4, 8 PIM
- **HONORS:**
  West Side Assn. Rangers MVP, 1954-55;
  All-Star Game, 1955-56

CURTAIN CALL
Time Change

When the Rangers first came into the NHL, they set the starting time for their home games at Madison Square Garden for 8:45 p.m. to coincide with the Broadway shows going on around them. After a short time, they moved the starting time up 15 minutes, to 8:30. But with attendance sliding, management tried something new on January 9, 1955, changing the starting time of a Sunday night game against the Canadiens to 7 p.m. The result was the largest crowd of the season, as 13,607 turned out to watch their heroes absorb a 7-1 thrashing. Management took a cue from the large crowd and changed six consecutive Sunday home games to 7 p.m. starts. Those changes began on February 13, when they again hosted Montreal. The only difference was the result, a 4-1 Ranger win. The crowd that night numbered 11,859, and the Rangers realized that starting earlier was better for their fans. The Sunday night game time stayed at 7 p.m. well into the 1970s before inching up to 7:35, matching what had become their regular weeknight faceoff time. That lasted until 1996-97, when the starting time was moved back to 7:05.

The Rangers had success moving the starting time of Sunday games at the Garden to 7p.m.

NEW YORK
Ice Exchange

GM Frank Boucher started the season as the last link to the original Rangers; he ended it out of work. Another non-playoff season cost Boucher his job, ending a tenure with the team that dated to 1926. On the ice, Danny Lewicki made his Rangers debut, and wound up leading the team in goals and points. The roster was large; 29 players saw action in a Ranger sweater. One was Glen Sonmor, later the coach of the Minnesota North Stars, who ended his two-season, 28-game NHL career with the Rangers. Gump Worsley and Johnny Bower traded places in goal, with Worsley getting back to the NHL for keeps, while defenseman Allan Stanley and forward Nick Mickoski were traded to Chicago during the season for Bill Gadsby and Pete Conacher. Those who didn't return to Broadway after the season included Dick Bouchard, Bill McCreary, Jackie McLeod, "Wild" Bill Ezinicki, Vic Howe, Paul Ronty (traded to Montreal) and Bob Chrystal. Finally, Edgar Laprade retired after having scored 108 goals during his 500 games in 10 years with the Rangers.

Pete Conacher came to the Rangers from Chicago with Bill Gadsby.

Ranger Lists

Ranger coaches who never played for the team

John Ferguson
1976-77
Jean-Guy Talbot
1977-78
Craig Patrick
1980-81, 1984-85
Herb Brooks
1981-82 — 1984-85
Ted Sator
1985-86
Tom Webster
1986-87
Wayne Cashman
1986-87
Michel Bergeron
1987-88 — 1988-89
Roger Neilson
1989-90 — 1992-93
Ron Smith
1992-93
Mike Keenan
1993-94
Colin Campbell
1994-95 — Present

—1955  1956—

TIME CAPSULE

- **September 21, 1955:**
  Rocky Marciano retained his heavyweight boxing crown by defeating Archie Moore.

- **October 4, 1955:**
  The Brooklyn Dodgers won their only World Series by beating the New York Yankees 2-0 in Game 7 behind the pitching of Johnny Podres.

- **April 19, 1956:**
  Actress Grace Kelly married Prince Rainier of Monaco.

1955-1956

FINAL STANDINGS

	W	L	T	PTS	GF	GA
Montreal	45	15	10	100	222	131
Detroit	30	24	16	76	183	148
RANGERS	32	28	10	74	204	203
Toronto	24	33	13	61	153	181
Boston	23	34	13	59	147	185
Chicago	19	39	12	50	155	216

PLAYOFF RESULTS

Semifinals: Montreal beat Rangers 4-1.

LEADING PLAYOFF SCORER

Bill Gadsby (1-3-4)

STANLEY CUP CHAMPION

Montreal Canadiens

SEASON SNAPSHOT

Most Goals:
Dean Prentice/Andy Hebenton (24)

Most Assists:
Andy Bathgate (47)

Most Points:
Andy Bathgate (66)

Most Penalty Minutes:
Lou Fontinato (202)

Most Wins, Goaltender:
Gump Worsley (32)

Lowest Goals-Against Average:
Gump Worsley (2.90)

Most Shutouts:
Gump Worsley (4)

NHL All-Stars:
Bill Gadsby, D (First Team)

Rangers In All-Star Game:
Danny Lewicki, LW

The 1955-56 Season in Review

The Rangers pulled a total turnaround from the previous season's disaster by finishing the 1955-56 season over .500 for the first time since 1941-42. Streaks of 6-0-1 and 8-3-1 made it obvious well before the end of the season that the Rangers were on their way to the playoffs for the first time since 1950. What caused the turnaround? Some fresh blood in the front office and behind the bench didn't hurt, as Phil Watson became coach when his former teammate, Muzz Patrick was kicked upstairs to the general manager's office, replacing Frank Boucher. The Rangers also profited from a balanced attack, led by Andy Bathgate's team-record 66 points. With four players hitting the 20-goal mark, 10 in double-figures and defenseman Bill Gadsby setting a team mark with 51 points on the blue line, Gump Worsley enjoyed some offensive support for the first time in his career. He responded with a stellar 2.90 goals-against average and four shutouts. Whatever the cause, the 17-victory increase set a team record that's been surpassed only twice—a 19-win jump from 1994-95 to 1995-96 (22 wins to 41), and an 18-game leap from 1992-93 to Stanley Cup No. 4 in 1993-94 (34 to 52). But in what

Larry Popein(L) and Dean Prentice were two of 10 Rangers in double figures in goals in 1955-56.

may have been a bad omen, the Rangers finished their season with back-to-back losses to Montreal, their first-round opponents. The Rangers stunned the Canadiens by winning Game 2 in Montreal to even the series, but dropped the next three contests against the eventual Cup champions.

MAGIC MOMENT
March 22, 1956

Gordie Bell backstopped the only Ranger victory in the 1956 playoffs. Photo courtesy of Hockey Hall of Fame.

Gump Worsley played every minute of every game in 1955-56, the last Ranger netminder to do so, and set a team record by earning 32 victories, a mark that lasted until Ed Giacomin came along in the late 1960s. Thus, when Worsley's sore knee hampered him during the playoffs, the Rangers had no reliable backup. Enter 31-year-old Gordie Bell, who had played eight games for the Toronto Maple Leafs 10 years earlier before returning to the minors. Bell was recalled from Trois Rivieres and struggled during a 7-1 series-opening loss in which he and Worsley both saw action. Coach Phil Watson opted to go with Bell for Game 2, and the result was a stunning 4-2 series-tying victory, the Rangers' first triumph at the Forum since January 30, 1954. With the series heading back to New York, the surprising victory had the Rangers dreaming of an upset. Unfortunately, Bell's magic didn't make the trip: The Canadiens posted 3-1 and 5-3 victories at the Garden before wrapping up the series with a 7-0 rout at home. The victory was Bell's last moment of glory—he never played in the NHL again.

"Leapin' Louie" Fontinato made his NHL debut with the Rangers in February 1955, and immediately became a crowd favorite for his toughness and willingness to protect smaller teammates—something that hadn't been seen at the Garden in years. He earned the "Leapin" tag because he would leap in amazement when a penalty was called on him. Though he toned down the leaping after the misconduct penalties began to pile up, it didn't completely stop him if the time was right. For instance, in a game against Montreal in 1957, teammate Andy Hebenton was in a tussle with Montreal's Jean-Guy Talbot, and Hebenton managed to pull Talbot's sweater off. Noticing the jersey laying on the ice, Fontinato leaped and landed blades-first on the sweater. After a few more jumps, the sweater was sliced to ribbons. For that transgression, he was given a misconduct, fined $25 by the league, and billed $25 by the Canadiens to replace the shredded jersey. He antagonized and fought anyone, be it superstars like Gordie Howe and Maurice Richard, or a "busher" (his term). He didn't limit his fisticuffs to opponents, though. He once targeted the Boston Garden crowd in one of the wildest scenes ever during a game. On March 15, 1958, Fontinato got into a fight in the penalty box with Boston's Vic Stasiuk (both teams sat in the same box back then). Some fans came down and got involved with Fontinato, who then—with teammates and Bruins in tow—jumped into the stands. After seven seasons, Fontinato was sent to Montreal in the deal that brought Doug Harvey to New York as a player-coach. His career ended on St. Patrick's Day in 1962, when in a game against his former teammates, he missed connections while trying to check Vic Hadfield and crashed head-first into the boards. He suffered a broken neck and temporary paralysis, but eventually recovered.

Lou Fontinato File

- **BORN:**
  January 20, 1932; Guelph, Ontario
- **ACQUIRED:**
  Product of Rangers organization
- **FIRST SEASON WITH RANGERS:**
  1954-55

- **BEST SEASON WITH RANGERS:**
  1955-56, 70 GP, 3-15-18, 202 PIM
- **TOTALS WITH RANGERS:**
  Regular season: 418 GP, 22-57-79, 939 PIM
  Playoffs: 15 GP, 0-1-1, 19 PIM

CURTAIN CALL
The Longest Trip

The Rangers made two trips to the Olympia during their marathon road trip. Photo courtesy of the Hockey Hall of Fame.

The arrival of the ice show in January traditionally meant it was time for the Rangers to hit the road for a week or two. After expansion, this was usually the time to head for the West Coast, but in the pre-expansion era, it wasn't unusual for the Rangers to tour the entire league, hitting some cities more than once. However, no trip in team history was longer than the marathon tour they endured in January 1956. After stomping the Canadiens 6-1 at home on January 11, the Rangers began the longest trip in team history the next night in Detroit, where they were demolished 6-0 by the Red Wings. They stayed on the road until their visit to Chicago on January 29, then came home to host Toronto on February 1. The nine-game tour of the NHL included three visits to Chicago, two each to Toronto and Detroit, and single stops in Boston and Montreal. Thanks to wins in the last two games (at Toronto and Chicago), the Rangers wound up their trip with a 4-4-1 mark. Ironically, their trip wasn't even the longest in the league that season—Chicago had a 10-game swing that ended just before the Rangers' trip began.

NEW YORK Ice Exchange

Once again, a Patrick was in charge of the Rangers' fortunes. This time, though, the man on the hot seat was Muzz Patrick, son of the Rangers' patriarch, who moved from coach to general manager when Frank Boucher (who succeeded Lester Patrick as coach and later as GM) was let go. The younger Patrick wasted no time bringing in former teammate Phil Watson as coach. The volatile Watson had to do without high-scoring wing Camille Henry, who missed the season with an injury, but got a boost from three newcomers as the farm system continued to produce. Andy Hebenton connected for 24 goals in his first NHL season while playing every game—beginning a streak of 630 straight regular-season appearances. Guy Gendron and Bronco Horvath also turned in productive seasons. The Rangers' best outside acquisition was Dave Creighton, who had 21 goals and 51 points after coming over from Toronto.

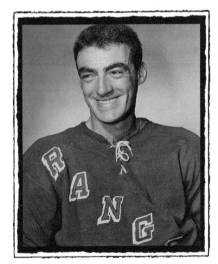

Guy Gendron was a productive newcomer in 1955-56.

— 1956  1957 —

TIME CAPSULE

- **October 8, 1956:**
  Don Larsen of the New York Yankees pitched the first perfect game in World Series history, beating the Brooklyn Dodgers 2-0.

- **November 6, 1956:**
  Dwight Eisenhower beat Adlai Stevenson for the second straight time to win reelection as president.

- **January 21, 1957:**
  NBC carried the first nationally televised videotaped broadcast, a recording of President Dwight Eisenhower's inauguration ceremonies.

1956-1957

FINAL STANDINGS

	W	L	T	PTS	GF	GA
Detroit	38	20	12	88	198	157
Montreal	35	23	12	82	210	155
Boston	34	24	12	80	195	174
RANGERS	26	30	14	66	184	227
Toronto	21	34	15	57	174	192
Chicago	16	39	15	47	169	225

PLAYOFF RESULTS
Semifinals: Canadiens beat Rangers 4-1

LEADING PLAYOFF SCORER
Camille Henry (2-3-5)

STANLEY CUP CHAMPION
Montreal Canadiens

SEASON SNAPSHOT

Most Goals:
Andy Bathgate (27)

Most Assists:
Andy Bathgate (50)

Most Points:
Andy Bathgate (77)

Most Penalty Minutes:
Lou Fontinato (139)

Most Wins, Goaltender:
Gump Worsley (26)

Lowest Goals-Against Average:
Gump Worsley (3.24)

Most Shutouts:
Gump Worsley (3)

NHL All-Stars:
Bill Gadsby, D (Second Team)

Rangers In All-Star Game:
Bill Gadsby, D;
Dave Creighton, C;
Red Sullivan, C

The 1956-57 Season in Review

Gump Worsley posted all 26 of the Rangers' victories in 1956-57.

Coming off their first playoff appearance in six seasons (and their first over-.500 season since 1941-42), the Rangers slipped back down below .500 at 26-32-12. Fortunately for them, it didn't matter. They finished comfortably in fourth place, so postseason play beckoned for consecutive years for the first time since 1940-41 and 1941-42. After opening the season by winning four of six, the Rangers hit a 10-game tailspin that included a tie, six straight losses, and three more ties before a win at Boston. After that streak ended, they played .500 hockey for the rest of the season, despite four separate three-game losing streaks. Half of their 12 ties came against the lowly Blackhawks, against whom the Rangers compiled a 7-1-6 mark. Conversely, they lost 10 of 14 games to regular-season champion Detroit. For the second straight season, Andy Bathgate led the team in scoring, garnering 77 points and a team-high 27 goals. Andy Hebenton, with 21, was the only other Blueshirt to break the 20-goal mark. Gump Worsley played in all but two games, posting all 26 of the team's victories, compiling a 3.24 goals-against average and three shutouts and giving the Rangers solid goaltending despite the fact that they allowed more goals than any other team in the NHL. As they had the year before, the Rangers had the misfortune to play the Montreal Canadiens in the semifinals. The result was a repeat of the previous season, with the Canadiens winning five games on their way to the Stanley Cup.

MAGIC MOMENT — March 28, 1957

Andy Hebenton's overtime goal gave the Rangers their only playoff win.

Though the Rangers lost in the playoff semifinals to Montreal, their lone victory in the five-game series was a moment to remember. The Canadiens won the opener, and Game 2 at the Garden was tied 2-2 after 60 minutes. Jacques Plante stood tall for the Habs, while Gump Worsley kept the Rangers in the game. And then, it happened. Red Sullivan led the Blueshirts on a rush down center ice and sent a pass to Andy Hebenton on right wing. Montreal defenseman Bob Turner seemingly had Hebenton out of the play, but Hebenton kept right on going, squeezing through Turner's check. He came in on Plante, and let go a backhander from about 15 feet out. Plante had the net covered, except for about four square inches above his left shoulder on the short side. The puck must have had eyes, for it found those four inches (with an inch to spare) and sent 15,925 Rangers fans home happy and voiceless. It was the Rangers' first overtime win at the Garden since Alf Pike's goal won the opener of the 1940 finals against Toronto; unfortunately for the Rangers, this time, they were unable to capitalize on the momentum from Hebenton's goal and dropped the next three games.

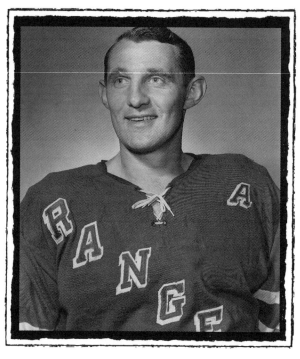

In an era where defensemen were supposed to stay at home, Bill Gadsby's penchant for playmaking made him an NHL standout. Gadsby broke into the NHL in 1946 as a member of the Blackhawks with a reputation of thinking offense first (a no-no at the time), and collected 45 goals and 180 points in eight seasons in Chicago, then among the NHL's weakest teams. He also collected coaches before coming to Broadway; Gadsby played for five different men in the Windy City: Johnny Gottselig, Charlie Conacher, Ebbie Goodfellow, Sid Abel and ex-Ranger Frank Eddolls. Gadsby was traded to the Rangers in November 1954 along with Pete Conacher for Allan Stanley, Nick Mickoski and minor-leaguer Dick Lamoureux. The move to the Big Apple was just what Gadsby needed: Coach Phil Watson instilled the confidence that Gadsby often lacked in Chicago. Watson and GM Muzz Patrick wanted Gadsby as a steadying influence on the growing number of youngsters on the Blueshirts' roster. Watson encouraged Gadsby to play offensively, and paired him (most of the time) with Tex Evans, a defensive-minded defenseman. It was a superb move, as Gadsby turned into one of the NHL's highest-scoring defensemen, mostly due to his passing abilities: He had 51 points in 1955-56 (9 goals, 42 assists) and again in 1958-59 (5 goals, 46 assists), while earning first-team All-Star honors three times in four seasons. But when Watson was let go as coach early in the 1959-60 season, Alf Pike, his replacement, wasn't as thrilled with Gadsby. Patrick had a deal worked out with Detroit to send Gadsby and Eddie Shack to the Red Wings for Red Kelly and Billy McNeil. But the two Detroit players, particularly Kelly, balked at the idea of playing in New York and threatened to retire, so the deal was killed. The arrival of Doug Harvey in the summer of 1961 finally spelled the end of Gadsby's stay in New York: he was sent to Detroit for Les Hunt (who never played an NHL game) and cash. Gadsby played five more seasons in the Motor City, ultimately finishing his 21-year career in 1966 having played in 1,248 games without winning a Stanley Cup. He was inducted into the Hall of Fame in 1970.

Bill Gadsby File

- **BORN:**
  August 8, 1927; Calgary, Alberta
- **ACQUIRED:**
  Acquired with Pete Conacher from the Chicago Blackhawks for Allan Stanley, Nick Mickoski and Dick Lamoureux, November, 1954.
- **FIRST SEASON WITH RANGERS:**
  1954-55
- **BEST SEASON WITH RANGERS:**
  1955-56, 70 GP, 9-42-51, 84 PIM

- **TOTALS WITH RANGERS:**
  Regular season: 457 GP, 58-212-270, 411 PIM
  Playoffs: 16 GP, 2-8-10, 10 PIM
- **HONORS:**
  First-team All-Star, 1955-56, 1957-58, 1958-59
  Second-team All-Star, 1956-57
  All-Star Game, 1956-57, 1957-58, 1958-59, 1959-60, 1960-61
  West Side Assn. Rangers MVP, 1955-56
- **NHL MILESTONES:**
  1,248 Games Played

CURTAIN CALL
The NHL on CBS

Even though NBC carried the first hockey telecast in 1940 when the Rangers hosted Montreal, the telecast was limited to the New York area—and to those few who were able to afford a television set. But in the 1950s, more people owned televisions, and CBS decided to fill Saturday afternoon programming during the winter by broadcasting NHL games from coast to coast. The Rangers hosted the first telecast on January 5, 1957, beating the Chicago Blackhawks 4-1. CBS

The Rangers were part of the NHL's debut on CBS.

broadcast nine more weeks of nationwide hockey coverage, and the Rangers were involved in four of those games, including three of the first four. They won in 5-4 in Detroit on January 12, won 5-3 in Boston on January 26, and lost 5-4 to the Red Wings at the Garden on February 2. CBS expanded the package the next season, becoming the first U.S. network to air an NHL Game of the Week and giving the Rangers 10 exposures. CBS picked up the package again in the late 1960s, going as far as to air final-round games in prime time. NBC picked up hockey in the 1970s after CBS dropped the package, but interest waned and hockey disappeared from network television in the late 1970s until ABC and then Fox revived the concept in the early 1990s.

NEW YORK Ice Exchange

Roster changes were minimal, as they should have been. GM Muzz Patrick was smart enough to know that you don't rip apart a team that landed in postseason play for the first time in six years. That didn't mean that this season's roster was a carbon copy of last season's. Eight of the nine top scorers from last season were back for another year—only Wally Hergesheimer wasn't around; he went to Chicago. New faces to the roster included Red Sullivan (from the Blackhawks), Parker MacDonald, Larry Cahan and Gerry Foley. Foley and MacDonald each wound up with seven goals in their rookie seasons. Bronco Horvath lasted only seven games into the season before he wound up in Montreal. Bruce Cline's 30-game season was his only NHL career action. The remaining 17 roster players all played in the playoffs, although MacDonald only played in one game. Everyone else, except defenseman Cahan (three games) played all five playoff games.

Red Sullivan joined the Rangers as a player in 1956-57 and later served as their coach.

—1957 1958—

TIME CAPSULE

■ **September 25, 1957:**
10,000 Army paratroopers were dispatched to Central High School in Little Rock, Arkansas to enforce desegregation, as ordered by President Eisenhower.

■ **October 10, 1957:**
The Braves won their first World Series since moving to Milwaukee in 1953, blanking the New York Yankees 5-0 in Game 7.

■ **March 25, 1958:**
Sugar Ray Robinson regained the middleweight boxing title for an unprecedented fifth time, defeating Carmen Basilio.

1957-1958
FINAL STANDINGS

	W	L	T	PTS	GF	GA
Montreal	43	17	10	96	250	158
RANGERS	32	25	13	77	195	188
Detroit	29	29	12	70	176	207
Boston	27	28	15	69	199	194
Chicago	24	39	7	55	163	202
Toronto	21	38	11	53	192	226

PLAYOFF RESULTS
Semifinals: Boston defeated Rangers 4-2

LEADING PLAYOFF SCORER
Andy Bathgate (5-3-8)

STANLEY CUP CHAMPION
Montreal Canadiens

SEASON SNAPSHOT

Most Goals:
Camille Henry (32)

Most Assists:
Andy Bathgate (48)

Most Points:
Andy Bathgate (78)

Most Penalty Minutes:
Lou Fontinato (152)

Most Wins, Goaltender:
Gump Worsley (21)

Lowest Goals-Against Average:
Gump Worsley (2.32)

Most Shutouts:
Gump Worsley (4)

NHL Award Winners:
Camille Henry (Lady Byng Trophy)

NHL All-Stars:
Bill Gadsby, D (First Team);
Andy Bathgate, RW (Second Team);
Camille Henry, LW (Second Team)

Rangers In All-Star Game:
Andy Bathgate, RW; Bill Gadsby, D;
Dean Prentice, LW

The 1957-58 Season in Review

Maybe it was the gloves: The 1957-58 Rangers were the first team to paint their gloves to match their uniforms. (every team but Detroit quickly followed suit). Whatever the reason, coach Phil Watson drove the Rangers to their best finish since the 1941-42 team came in first overall, as the team finished second while making the playoffs for the third straight year. The Rangers matched the franchise record set two seasons earlier by winning 32 games. The wins and losses came in bunches: a streak of one win in 10 games was followed by an unbeaten streak of five games. That was followed by an eight-game winless run, but the Rangers turned their season around by losing only four of their final 21 games (13-4-4). They even split the season series with Montreal, the first time in a decade that the Canadiens had not dominated the Rangers. Andy Bathgate led the offense with 78 points, and Camille Henry's 32 goals were a team high. Andy Hebenton added 21 as the Rangers' top nine scorers all hit double figures in goals. Gump Worsley and Marcel Paille split the goaltending chores almost equally, but Worsley had the better goals-against average (2.32), and recorded the only four shutouts.

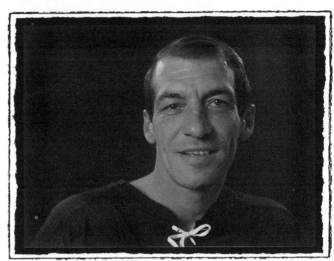

Camille Henry led the Rangers with 32 goals.

When the playoffs came, the Rangers were paired against the Boston Bruins, the only team to beat them in the season series. The teams split the first four games before the Bruins rolled to 6-1 and 6-2 victories, ending the Rangers' best season since World War II much too early.

MAGIC MOMENT   *March 8, 1958*

Though the Rangers had improved through the 1950s and now ranked among the NHL's better teams, one thing they still had trouble doing was beating Montreal at the Forum. A rare Forum win was a treat to be savored, and the Rangers came to Montreal for the final time in 1957-58 trying to win the season series in their least-favorite building—a feat they hadn't accomplished in a decade. Things looked bleak when the Rangers entered the third period trailing 2-1. But the littlest Ranger, Camille Henry, gave them a big spark early in the third period when he broke in alone on Jacques Plante, was hauled down from behind by Tom Johnson and awarded a penalty shot by referee Red Storey. Henry deked left, drew Jacques Plante out of his net and tucked the puck into the bottom left-hand corner before crashing into the boards. It was his 30th goal of the season and his first ever on a penalty shot. The goal sparked the Rangers and Guy Gendron beat Plante again midway through the final period to give the Rangers a 3-2 victory. They finished 3-2-2 at the Forum that season, their last winning mark at hockey's most famous building until they went 1-0-2 in 1971-72.

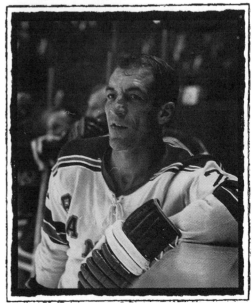

Camille Henry's penalty-shot goal sparked the Rangers to a memorable win at the Forum. Photo by Barton Silverman.

RANGER LEGEND
Red Sullivan

George "Red" Sullivan was a natural leader, and a verbal exchange between Sullivan (then with the Blackhawks) and Rangers coach Phil Watson convinced both Watson and GM Muzz Patrick to get Sullivan; he came to the Rangers for Ron Murphy and Wally Hergesheimer during the summer of 1956. Sullivan spent the final five seasons of his 11-year career with the Rangers. He wasn't a prolific scorer (only 59 goals on Broadway and 107 for his career), but what made him so useful to the Rangers were his heart and determination. Sullivan was used quite effectively as a penalty-killer, and he performed the task well by confounding the opposing power-play unit. His best season on Broadway came in 1958-59, when he netted 21 goals and added 42 assists for 63 points, which put him second in team scoring to Andy Bathgate. But Sullivan was a leader, so much so that he was named team captain in his second season and wore the "C" until his retirement. And after his retirement, he wound up staying involved with the Rangers (and hockey, in general) in a big way. After a little more than one season as coach of the Kitchener farm team of the Eastern Professional Hockey

Photo by Barton Silverman.

League. Sullivan was named Rangers coach on December 28, 1962. Muzz Patrick, who was doing both jobs, decided to concentrate solely on his GM duties, which gave the (then) 33-year-old rookie coach little time to get adjusted. Sullivan stayed behind the bench until mid-December 1965. Unfortunately for Sullivan, his desire to be the best wasn't reflected in his record as coach. He compiled a record of 58-103-35 at the helm of the Rangers, a .385 winning percentage. He was replaced on December 5, 1965 by Emile Francis, who decided to add the coaching responsibilities to his job as general manager.

Red Sullivan File

- **BORN:**
  December 24, 1929; Peterborough, Ontario
- **ACQUIRED:**
  From the Chicago Blackhawks for Ron Murphy and Wally Hergesheimer prior to the 1956-57 season.
- **FIRST SEASON WITH RANGERS:**
  1956-57

- **BEST SEASON WITH RANGERS:**
  1958-59, 70 GP, 21-42-63, 56 PIM
- **TOTALS WITH RANGERS:**
  Regular season: 322 GP, 59-150-209, 300 PIM
  Playoffs: 6 GP, 1-2-3, 4 PIM
- **HONORS:**
  All-Star Game, 1956-57, 1958-59, 1959-60, 1960-61;
  Players' Player Award, 1959-60

CURTAIN CALL
Reichert/Maslow

Arthur Reichert and Saul Maslow are as much a part of Madison Square Garden history as any of the teams that have played there. Reichert, a CPA by profession, spent more than 60 years as a Garden goal judge, beginning with the semipro New York Rovers in the early 1930s. He moved up to the Rangers in 1945 and spent the next 46 years watching the Rangers from a small stool behind the net. His partner for many of those years was Saul Maslow, who became involved with hockey in 1932 as the assistant trainer of an amateur team while still in school. He was on hand for the Rangers' triumph in 1940. "I made 25 cents an hour scraping the ice," said Maslow, who became an off-ice official after that season. Reichert once said he remembered being overruled just three times in his 60 seasons—though he and the Rangers didn't always see eye-to-eye. On January 31, 1965, Reichert ruled that a Detroit shot went into the net. Rangers coach Emile Francis came down from the bench to argue and a rhu-

Arthur Reichert was a fixture at Ranger games for more than 40 years. Photo courtesy of NHL Images.

barb broke out, with Ranger players eventually climbing into the stands to protect their coach. Though team president Bill Jennings wanted Reichert removed, replays of the shot showed the call was correct—as usual.

NEW YORK Ice Exchange

Muzz Patrick's biggest move of the season was to bring up a backup for netminder Gump Worsley. It was partially designed to give Worsley some much needed rest—and also partially due to coach Phil Watson's constant prodding of Worsley; he felt having another goalie around would serve to remind the Gumper who was boss. Enter Marcel Paille, who split the goaltending chores almost evenly with Worsley—Gump played in 37 games, Paille in 33. Paille's presence appeared to have the desired effect on Worsley, who had the best statistical season of his Ranger career. Except for the 1942-43 season (the first

Danny Lewicki had 11 goals in his final season with the Rangers.

with World War II in full swing), the Rangers had never distributed their goaltending duties so evenly. It was the last season in the Big Apple for forward Danny Lewicki, whose goal production fell to 11, and for defenseman Jack "Tex" Evans. Guy Gendron was traded to Montreal after the season, and Gerry Foley, a regular for two seasons, was returned to the minors; he didn't surface in the NHL again until 1968-69, when he played briefly for Los Angeles.

Ranger Lists

Best Record vs. Opponent, One Season (Minimum 6 Games)

6-0-0 - vs. New Jersey
1993-94
6-0-0 - vs. Philadelphia
1971-72
6-0-0 - vs. Los Angeles
1971-72
6-0-0 - vs. Buffalo
1971-72
6-0-0 - vs. Minnesota
1970-71
5-0-1 - vs. Pittsburgh
1970-71
7-1-0 - vs. Detroit
1941-42
10-2-2 - vs. Boston
1959-60
10-3-1 - vs. Chicago
1955-56
9-3-1 - vs. Boston
1960-61

—1958 1959—

TIME CAPSULE

- **October 9, 1958:**
  The New York Yankees scored four runs in the eighth inning and beat the Milwaukee Braves 6-2 to win the World Series in seven games.

- **December 28, 1958:**
  The Baltimore Colts beat the New York Giants 23-17 at Yankee Stadium for the NFL championship in the first overtime game in league history.

- **February 3, 1959:**
  Rock-and-roll stars Buddy Holly, Richie Valens and "The Big Bopper" died in an airplane crash.

1958-1959

FINAL STANDINGS

	W	L	T	PTS	GF	GA
Montreal	39	18	13	91	258	158
Boston	32	29	9	73	205	215
Chicago	28	29	13	69	197	208
Toronto	27	32	11	65	189	201
RANGERS	26	32	12	64	201	217
Detroit	25	37	8	58	167	218

PLAYOFF RESULTS

Rangers did not qualify

STANLEY CUP CHAMPION

Montreal Canadiens

SEASON SNAPSHOT

Most Goals:
Andy Bathgate (40)

Most Assists:
Andy Bathgate (48)

Most Points:
Andy Bathgate (88)

Most Penalty Minutes:
Lou Fontinato (149)

Most Wins, Goaltender:
Gump Worsley (26)

Lowest Goals-Against Average:
Gump Worsley (3.07)

Most Shutouts:
Gump Worsley (2)

NHL Award Winners:
Andy Bathgate (Hart Trophy)

NHL All-Stars:
Bill Gadsby, D (First Team)
Andy Bathgate, RW (First Team)

Rangers In All-Star Game:
Bill Gadsby, D; Red Sullivan, C;
Camille Henry, LW; Andy Bathgate, RW

The 1958-59 Season in Review

The 1958-59 season was one of the cruelest campaigns ever for Ranger fans. The Garden crowd had become accustomed to making the playoffs, and for the first four months of the season, it looked like the Rangers would have a chance (perhaps even the best chance) to end the Montreal Canadiens' run of three straight Stanley Cups. With Andy Bathgate shattering all of the team's offensive records on the way to a 40-goal, 88-point season that earned him the Hart Trophy as the NHL's Most Valuable Player, the Rangers entered the final 20 games of the season more concerned about finishing second than making the playoffs. But a 5-0 victory at Detroit proved to be the high-water mark of the season. A 6-3 defeat at Chicago on February 7 triggered a six-game losing streak as Toronto began climbing in the standings. Still, the Rangers' playoff berth seemed secure (tickets were already being sold) after wins over Chicago and Detroit left them just a game under .500. But with coach Phil Watson wearing down his regulars and battling goaltender Gump Worsley in the papers, the Rangers forgot how to win. They dropped five straight games, including a damaging weekend sweep by the Leafs. A 5-2 victory at Detroit on the final Saturday of the season gave them some hope entering the season finale against Montreal, but a 4-2 loss to the Canadiens at the Garden capped a season that started with promise and ended in disaster.

Bill Gadsby was a first-team All-Star for the third time as a Ranger in 1958-59.

MAGIC MOMENT   *Bobby Hull in Ranger Blue*

A young Bobby Hull scored 14 goals as a Ranger on a tour of Europe. Photo courtesy of NHL Images.

When Bobby Hull came to the Rangers' camp well into the twilight of his career, New Yorkers had to wonder: What would it have been like to have "The Golden Jet" in his prime? The Rangers actually *did* have him for a few brief weeks in the spring of 1959—the only problem was that the games didn't count. Hull was among a handful of players added to the Rangers for an exhibition tour of Europe following the 1959 Stanley Cup playoffs. The Rangers and Boston Bruins played 23 games in a variety of European locales, including London, Geneva and Paris, with the Rangers winning 11, losing nine and tying three. Hull and another add-on, former Ranger Eddie Shack, shared the team lead with 14 goals apiece. Hull's biggest game came midway through the tour in Zurich, Switzerland, when he scored four times in a 7-6 victory. The players each got $1,000 for the tour—a stipend that, in the Rangers' case, helped make up for the money they didn't get by missing the playoffs. The only bad part for the Rangers came after they got home: They didn't get to keep Hull, then one of the NHL's up-and-coming superstars.

139

RANGER LEGEND
Andy Bathgate

In 1982, John Halligan, the Rangers' long-time public relations director, produced the most accurate appraisal of Andy Bathgate. "Quite simply," he wrote, "Andy Bathgate *was* the New York Rangers during his heyday, from the mid-1950s to the early 1960s. He was the Rangers' first superstar since before World War II, a hero to Ranger fans in an era that produced some highs, some lows, but no overwhelming successes." Bathgate led the Rangers in scoring for eight straight seasons, a team mark that may never be eclipsed. Goalies feared his slap shot, but he was an excellent passer who piled up far more assists than goals and had an excellent wrist shot and a fine backhander. Bathgate needed three cracks to make the NHL for good, but became a 20-goal scorer in 1954-55, a 30-goal man in 1957-58, and the Rangers' first 40-goal scorer in 1958-59, when he won the Hart Trophy as league MVP with 40 goals and 88 points on a team that missed the playoffs. Three years later, Bathgate became the first Ranger in two decades to lead the league in scoring, finishing in a tie with Bobby Hull (who got the Art Ross Trophy because he scored more goals) and

leading the Rangers to a surprising playoff berth; his penalty-shot goal against Detroit on March 14 still ranks as one of the most memorable moments in Rangers history. Bathgate had 35 goals (11 during a 10-game goal-scoring streak) and 81 points in 1962-63, but the Rangers finished far out of the playoffs and rumors began to fly that Bathgate could be had for the right offer. Bathgate continued to average more than a point a game in 1963-64, but with the Rangers still floundering, GM Muzz Patrick decided it was time to rebuild. Patrick risked the fans' ire by sending Bathgate and Don McKenney to Toronto for Dick Duff, Bob Nevin and three prospects. Ironically, the trade worked out for both sides: Bathgate wound up on a Cup-winner, while Nevin and defensemen Rod Seiling and Arnie Brown were keys to the rise of the Rangers in the late 1960s. Bathgate played his last NHL game in 1971 and was inducted into the Hockey Hall of Fame in 1978.

Andy Bathgate File

- **BORN:**
  August 28, 1932, Winnipeg, Manitoba
- **ACQUIRED:**
  Product of Rangers organization
- **FIRST SEASON WITH RANGERS:**
  1952-53
- **BEST SEASON WITH RANGERS:**
  1958-59, 70 GP, 40-48-88, 48 PIM
- **TOTALS WITH RANGERS:**
  Regular season: 719 GP, 272-457-729, 444 PIM
  Playoffs: 22 GP, 9-7-16, 39 PIM

- **HONORS:**
  Hart Trophy, 1958-59
  First-team All-Star, 1958-59, 1961-62
  Second-team All-Star, 1957-58, 1962-63
  All-Star Game, 1957-58, 1958-59, 1959-60, 1960-61, 1961-62, 1962-63, 1963-64
  West Side Assn. Rangers MVP, 1956-57, 1957-58, 1958-59, 1962-63
  Players' Player Award, 1962-63
- **NHL MILESTONES:**
  1,069 Games Played

CURTAIN CALL
Monty Hall

Before he was making deals, Monty Hall was part of the Rangers' broadcast team.

Long before the rest of America knew him as the genial host of "Let's Make A Deal," New Yorkers knew Monty Hall as a member of the Rangers' broadcast team. Hall, an excellent athlete in high school and at the University of Manitoba, was a young TV host of NBC shows such as "Byline: Monty Hall" and "Bingo," but he also spent a couple of seasons handling the between-periods duties on Rangers broadcasts. Hall grew up in Winnipeg and his NBC bio at the time says he remembers "those little Bathgate kids" as having a lot of promise. His first hockey idol was Hall of Fame defenseman Babe Pratt, who married the girl next door to him, and schoolmate Wally Stanowski, who played three seasons for the Rangers in the early 1950s, was his all-time favorite player.

Hall started his broadcasting career in Winnipeg, moved to Toronto and reached New York in 1956. His background in the sport—and his connections to Rangers past and present— brought an interesting perspective to Ranger broadcasts.

NEW YORK
Ice Exchange

Clear the track! Here comes Shack! Eddie Shack, one of hockey's most colorful personalities, made his NHL debut with the Rangers in 1958-59. Coach Phil Watson expected big things from Shack, who was brought to New York to add muscle to a lightweight team. Shack piled up 109 penalty minutes, but managed only 7 goals and 14 assists, far below expectations, and played only one more full season in the Big Apple. Another rookie, defenseman John Hanna, played all 70 games, as did forward Jim Bartlett, who joined the team from Montreal. Earl Ingarfield, a center who was among the most popular Rangers of the 1960s, also made his NHL debut, though he scored only once in 35 games. Wally Hergesheimer, who had been dealt away a couple of years earlier, came back and played 22 games, but had only three goals and called it quits.

Eddie Shack began his long NHL career as a Ranger in 1958-59.

Ranger Lists
Brothers who have played for the Rangers:

Andy and Frank Bathgate

Gordie and Joe Bell

Doug and Max Bentley

Mac and Neil Colville

Bill and Bun Cook

Brian and Ray Cullen

Peter and Chris Ferraro

Gilles and Norm Gratton

Bryan and Dennis Hextall

Harry and Ron Howell

Gus and Bill Kyle

Dave and Don Maloney

Kelly and Kevin Miller

James and Stephen Patrick

Lynn and Muzz Patrick

Grant and Billy Warwick

—1959 1960—

TIME CAPSULE

- **September 15, 1959:**
  President Dwight D. Eisenhower welcomed Soviet Premier Nikita Krushchev to the United States for a round of meetings.

- **January 4, 1960:**
  A six-month strike ended when the United Steel Workers and the nation's steel companies agreed to a wage increase.

- **June 20, 1960:**
  Floyd Patterson became the first boxer in history to regain the world heavyweight championship when he knocked out Ingemar Johansson.

1959-1960
FINAL STANDINGS

	W	L	T	PTS	GF	GA
Montreal	40	18	12	92	255	178
Toronto	35	26	9	79	199	195
Chicago	28	29	13	69	191	180
Detroit	26	29	15	67	186	197
Boston	28	34	8	64	220	241
RANGERS	17	38	15	49	187	247

PLAYOFF RESULTS
Rangers did not qualify

STANLEY CUP CHAMPION
Montreal Canadiens

SEASON SNAPSHOT

Most Goals:
Dean Prentice (32)

Most Assists:
Andy Bathgate (48)

Most Points:
Andy Bathgate (74)

Most Penalty Minutes:
Lou Fontinato (137)

Most Wins, Goaltender:
Gump Worsley (8)

Lowest Goals-Against Average:
Gump Worsley (3.57)

Most Shutouts:
Marcel Paille (1)

NHL All-Stars:
Dean Prentice, LW (Second Team)

Rangers In All-Star Game:
Andy Bathgate, RW;
Bill Gadsby, D;
Red Sullivan, C.

The 1959-60 Season in Review

Maybe it was the trip to Europe the previous spring, or maybe the late-season collapse that preceded it, but the Rangers never got untracked in 1959-60. The Blueshirts lost their first four games, won only twice in the first 13 contests and just three times in the opening 23. Then, they played their most successful hockey, winning the next four of five and capturing six of nine outings. But except for a three-game winning streak in that group, this team couldn't even manage back-to-back victories the entire season. Surprisingly, they played .500 hockey against the eventual Stanley Cup champion Canadiens (6-6-2), but were dismal against the other four teams, including a 1-11-2 record against Chicago. The slow start prompted GM Muzz Patrick to change coaches, a move which came (ironically) the day after their third win. On November 12, fiery Phil Watson was out, and Alf Pike was in. This season marked the first time the Rangers used five goalies during the regular season (Gump Worsley, Marcel Paille, Al Rollins, Jack McCartan and Joe Schaefer). As usual, Andy Bathgate led the team in scoring, but the only other bright spot for the season was the play of left

Andy Bathgate (L.) led the Rangers with 74 points in 1959-60.

wing Dean Prentice, who picked up 32 goals and a second-team All-Star berth. This also marked the final season of the reign of team president John Reed Kilpatrick, who had been in charge since 1935.

MAGIC MOMENT   *November 1, 1959*

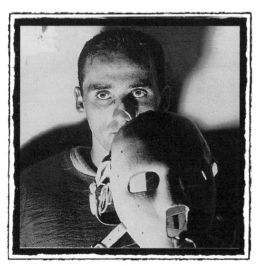

Jacques Plante was the first goaltender to wear a mask.

Who was that masked man who tended goal for the Montreal Canadiens on the night of November 1, 1959? Why, none other than Jacques Plante. Though Montreal Maroons goalie Clint Benedict first wore a leather mask to protect a broken nose in the 1930s, it was Plante who made the mask a standard part of his equipment. With the Rangers facing the Canadiens at the Garden, Andy Bathgate let go with a backhander that caught Plante under his right eye, opening up a seven-stitch cut. When Plante returned to the ice, he was carrying a plastic mask he sometimes used in practice. Coach Toe Blake had refused to allow Plante to wear the facegear during the game, but relented when Plante said he wouldn't go back into the net without it. Plante stopped 26 shots the rest of the way, and the Canadiens won the game 3-1. Plante wore the mask from that night on, and others were soon to follow. Among the early converts were the Rangers; one month later, GM Muzz Patrick mandated that all Ranger goaltenders on the farm or in junior hockey must wear a Plante-type mask. Patrick felt that goalies would be more confident if their faces were protected, and also felt that the mask would serve as a deflector of shots.

143

Dean Prentice spent off-seasons early in his career working in the Canadian gold mines as a dynamite carrier. It was harder to determine which packed the bigger wallop: the dynamite, or opponents such as Ted Lindsay. Prentice was a smart hockey player who knew what it took to stay in the NHL—he did so for 22 seasons. The first 11 of those were spent on Broadway. He came up as a rookie in 1952 (along with Andy Bathgate), and became a reliable checking forward and penalty killer. Prentice did learn how to score along the way, though he skipped a level of training. He came right out of junior hockey (Guelph Biltmores), and straight to Broadway, but thanks to his coach at Guelph, ex-Ranger Alf Pike, he was able to make the transition to the big leagues faster and smoother than others in his position. Prentice picked up a career-high 32 goals in the 1959-60 season, and earned a second-team All-Star berth. Prentice averaged almost 18 goals a season for the Rangers, and hit the 20-goal mark four times. But he was most noted for his defensive play, and that, along with his excellent penalty-killing capabilities, is what kept him employed in the NHL for such a long period of time. He was traded after 11 seasons with the Rangers, and spent the rest of his career bouncing from team to team, playing in Boston, Detroit, Pittsburgh and Minnesota, where he retired at the end of the 1973-74 season. His career numbers: 1,378 games played, 391 goals, 469 assists, 860 points. In 54 career playoff

games, he added 13 goals and 17 assists. The only thing Prentice didn't accomplish during his long career was getting his name on Lord Stanley's Cup.

Dean Prentice File

- **BORN:**
  October 5, 1932; Schumacher, Ontario
- **ACQUIRED:**
  Product of Rangers organization
- **FIRST SEASON WITH RANGERS:**
  1952-53
- **BEST SEASON WITH RANGERS:**
  1959-60, 70 GP, 32-34-66, 43 PIM

- **TOTALS WITH RANGERS:**
  Regular season: 666 GP, 186-236-422, 263 PIM
  Playoffs: 19 GP, 2-7-9, 10 PIM
- **HONORS:**
  Second-team All-Star, 1959-60
  All-Star Game, 1957-58, 1962-63
  West Side Assn. Rangers MVP, 1959-60
- **NHL MILESTONES:**
  1,378 Games Played

CURTAIN CALL

Jack McCartan

Twenty years before the 1980 "Miracle On Ice" at Lake Placid, there was the miracle of 1960 at the Winter Olympics in Squaw Valley, Calif. Like their counterparts two decades later, the U.S. team also stunned the world by winning a gold medal. The 1960 team may have had an even tougher road, since the earlier team had to beat Canada in addition to the usual powerhouses such as the Soviet Union and Czechoslovakia. The goalie of that team was Jack McCartan, on leave from a stint in the Army. McCartan then was given permission to go to the Rangers, who held his NHL rights, for a five-game tryout. His NHL debut on March 6, 1960 at the Garden was more than just a sporting event; even *Life* magazine was there to photograph McCartan, who penned a first-person review of his NHL debut. The Olympic hero gave the crowd what it wanted, stoning the Red Wings and Gordie Howe 3-1. McCartan played three more games, finishing his tryout with a 2-1-1 record and a 1.75 goals-against average. He shut out Chicago in his 1960-61 debut, but wound up with a 4.91 goals-against average in seven games that season. He never played in the NHL again.

Olympic hero Jack McCartan was superb in his NHL debut.

NEW YORK Ice Exchange

GM Muzz Patrick didn't do much tinkering with his top players of the previous season, so most of the roster moves came from the lesser lights getting a chance to shine or be dimmed. Patrick did have a lot of players get on the ice for the Rangers during the season: 25, as opposed to 18 the previous season. Players who made their Ranger debuts and played in subsequent season(s) for the Blueshirts included Brian Cullen and Noel Price (from Toronto), Irv Spencer, Mel Pearson, Bob Kabel and Dave Balon. Parker MacDonald was sent to Detroit during the season, as was Art Stratton. In fact, the only two players on the roster who didn't play any other seasons on Broadway were Ian Cushenan (17 games) and Bill Sweeney (4 games). Patrick also gave Olympic hero goalie Jack McCartan a five-game tryout in March.

Dave Balon got his first taste of the NHL with the Rangers in 1959-60.

—1960 1961—

TIME CAPSULE

- **October 13, 1960:**
  Bill Mazeroski's home run in the bottom of the ninth inning gave the Pittsburgh Pirates a 10-9 victory over the New York Yankees in Game 7 of the World Series.

- **November 8, 1960:**
  John Kennedy narrowly defeated Richard Nixon and was elected the 35th president of the United States.

- **May 5, 1961:**
  Alan Shepard became the first American in space when he made a successful flight aboard the Project Mercury capsule Freedom VII.

1960-1961
FINAL STANDINGS

	W	L	T	PTS	GF	GA
Montreal	41	19	10	92	254	188
Toronto	39	19	12	90	234	176
Chicago	29	24	17	75	198	180
Detroit	25	29	16	66	195	215
RANGERS	22	38	10	54	204	248
Boston	15	42	13	43	176	254

PLAYOFF RESULTS
Rangers did not qualify

STANLEY CUP CHAMPION
Chicago Blackhawks

SEASON SNAPSHOT

Most Goals:
Andy Bathgate (29)

Most Assists:
Andy Bathgate (48)

Most Points:
Andy Bathgate (77)

Most Penalty Minutes:
Lou Fontinato (100)

Most Wins, Goaltender:
Gump Worsley (20)

Lowest Goals-Against Average:
Gump Worsley (3.29)

Most Shutouts:
Gump Worsley (1)

Rangers In All-Star Game:
Andy Bathgate, RW;
Bill Gadsby, D;
Andy Hebenton, RW;
Red Sullivan, C

The 1960-61 Season in Review

For the third straight season, the Rangers sat and watched four other teams take part in the quest for the Stanley Cup—part of a stretch in which they missed postseason play seven times in eight years. However, they did post some decent numbers in certain categories. For instance, the Blueshirts wound up playing .500 hockey at home (15-15-5). They matched a team record by scoring 204 goals for the season, equaling their franchise high of 1955-56. When the Rangers didn't have to deal with the teams north of the border, they were fine. Against the three other U.S.-based teams (Boston, Chicago, Detroit), they had a record of 18-17-7. But it was No, Canada when they played Montreal or Toronto. Their combined record against the twosome was a woeful 4-21-3. After winning their first two games, and carrying a 4-5-0 mark after nine contests, the Rangers hit the skids with an 0-7-1 slump. That was followed later in the season by a 1-7-1 skid and an 0-5-1 run. Andy Bathgate shone again, leading the Rangers in scoring for the sixth straight season with 29 goals and 48 assists for 77 points, putting him fourth in the NHL scoring race. Gump Worsley was 20-28-8

Lou Fontinato spent 100 minutes in the penalty box in 1960-61.

for the season, with a 3.29 goals-against average and one shutout. Before the season, John Bergen was appointed team president, replacing Gen. John Reed Kilpatrick. The third straight non-playoff finish ended Alf Pike's tenure behind the bench; he resigned with a .378 winning percentage.

MAGIC MOMENT *November 27, 1960*

Rod Gilbert made his NHL debut in 1960-61.

A lot of kids get called up from their junior teams (or minor-league teams) for a look-see. Some impress right off the bat and are labeled as prospects, others are just up for the proverbial cup of coffee. Anyone who attended the game at the Garden on November 27, 1960, got to see one of those prospects. It was just for one game, due to an injury to Earl Ingarfield. The Rangers were hosting the Chicago Blackhawks, and wound up playing to a 3-3 tie. What made the game special was that it was the night that Rod Gilbert made his NHL debut. Head coach Alf Pike juggled his lines due to Ingarfield's injury, and Gilbert played with Dean Prentice and Andy Bathgate, who was switched from right wing to the middle. Gilbert wound up with an assist, the first of his franchise-record total of 615. Gilbert came back up for the playoffs the next season, getting the call when Ken Schinkel was hurt, scored two goals in his second playoff game, and the rest is history. He went on to become the Rangers' all-time leading scorer—the only player in team history to record more than 400 goals and 1,000 points.

If Andy Hebenton could have bottled whatever it was that kept him going on and on, he would have become an instant millionaire. Hebenton, who joined the Rangers at the start of the 1955-56 season, held a record of some consequence during his playing career. He bested Johnny Wilson's mark of 580 consecutive games played by getting into 630 straight games over eight seasons with the Rangers and one with Boston. He also never missed a playoff game during his NHL time (22 games). Murray Murdoch held the previous record for the Blueshirts with 508 games in a row—11 straight seasons, all in a Ranger uniform. Hebenton had always dreamed of scoring 200 NHL goals, but fell 11 shy of the mark. He hit his career-high of 33 goals in 1958-59, and surpassed the 20-goal mark in five of his eight seasons

on Broadway. But after slumping to 15 goals in 1962-63, GM Muzz Patrick didn't protect Hebenton in the waiver draft before the following season. Boston picked him and he played the next season for the Bruins, notching 12 goals and setting the NHL mark for endurance by playing all 70 games for the ninth straight season. But it was his last season in the NHL. The Bruins sent him to the minors in 1964-65, then traded him the following season to Toronto's minor-league club in Victoria. Hebenton went on to play several more seasons in the minors before finally retiring. Incredibly, from March 10, 1952 (in juniors), through Dec. 29, 1965 (in Victoria), Hebenton never missed a game, 1,000 in all, spanning the Pacific Coast Hockey League, the Western Hockey League, and the NHL. Hebenton collected only 75 penalty minutes in his eight seasons in New York, and eight more minutes in Boston, earning the Lady Byng Trophy in 1957. Not bad for a former box lacrosse player. Hebenton also was the first recipient of the West Side Association's Players' Player Award, an honor he won for three straight seasons.

Andy Hebenton File

- **BORN:**
  October 3, 1929; Winnipeg, Manitoba
- **ACQUIRED:**
  Product of Rangers organization
- **FIRST SEASON WITH RANGERS:**
  1955-56
- **BEST SEASON WITH RANGERS:**
  1958-59, 70 GP, 33-29-62, 8 PIM

- **TOTALS WITH RANGERS:**
  Regular season: 560 GP, 172-225-397, 75 PIM
  Playoffs: 22 GP, 6-5-11, 8 PIM
- **HONORS:**
  Lady Byng Trophy 1956-57
  Players' Player Award, 1958-59, 1959-60, 1960-61

CURTAIN CALL
Home Sweet Home

GM Muzz Patrick had a smile on his face when the 1960-61 NHL schedule landed on his desk. There was good reason: For the first time since the team's opening game in November 1926, the Rangers got to start the season at the Garden. "It's a good break," Patrick beamed after finding out the Rangers would open at home against Boston on October 5. They made the most of the opportunity, nipping the Bruins 2-1. In all, the Rangers opened on the road for 33 straight seasons, going 14-15-4 while starting in Detroit 11 times, in Toronto seven times, in Montreal seven (five against the Canadiens, two against the Maroons), in Chicago six times, and once each in Philadelphia and St. Louis (against the defunct Quakers and Eagles, respectively). Amazingly, the opening-night win over Boston marked the first time the Rangers had ever played the Bruins in a season-

GM Muzz Patrick was elated when the Rangers finally got to open at home in 1960-61.

opener; they did not open a season at Boston until 1964-65. In all, the Rangers opened at home just 20 times in their first 70 seasons, often falling into a hole that they were unable to dig out of. And why did the Rangers finally get to start the season at home in 1960? Because (happily for them) the rodeo moved out.

NEW YORK
Ice Exchange

If Muzz Patrick wanted a unique idea, he could have installed a revolving door into the Rangers' locker room at the Garden. Ten bodies exited from the previous season, and 12 new ones were eager to take their places. The most notable retiree was Red Sullivan, who quit after 11 years with Boston, Chicago and the Rangers. Two of the other nine departees eventually wound up with expansion teams after spending time in the minors: Larry Popein, part of a successful line with Andy Bathgate

Jean Ratelle scored his first two Ranger goals in a three-game tryout in 1960-61. Photo by Barton Silverman.

for several years, eventually played for Oakland in the Seals' inaugural season (1967-68), while left wing Mel Pearson became a Penguin in their first year in Pittsburgh. Other bye-byes included the names of Price, Cushenan, Bownass and MacDonald. The newcomers included Jean Ratelle (who played three games in his first NHL action). Johnny Wilson, whose consecutive-game mark was later broken by teammate Andy Hebenton, came from Toronto, while Floyd Smith headed south from Boston to Broadway.

Ranger Lists

Ranger Goalies on the NHL's All-Time Shutout List:

Terry Sawchuk
103 career/1 with Rangers
All-Time Ranking: 1

Jacques Plante
82 career/5 with Rangers
All-Time Ranking: 4

Lorne Chabot
73 career/21 with Rangers
All-Time Ranking: 8

Harry Lumley
71 career/0 with Rangers
All-Time Ranking: 9

John Ross Roach
58 career/30 with Rangers
All-Time Ranking: 12

Ed Giacomin
54 career/49 with Rangers
All-Time Ranking: 15

Dave Kerr
51 career/40 with Rangers
All-Time Ranking: 16

Gump Worsley
43 career/24 with Rangers
All-Time Ranking: 19

—1961 1962—

IME CAPSULE

- **October 1, 1961:**
  Roger Maris of the New York Yankees hit his 61st home run, a solo shot off Boston's Tracy Stallard at Yankee Stadium, to break Babe Ruth's single-season record.

- **February 20, 1962:**
  John Glenn became the first American to orbit the earth, circling the globe three times aboard Friendship 7.

- **March 2, 1962:**
  Wilt Chamberlain of the Philadelphia Warriors set an NBA record by scoring 100 points in a game against the New York Knicks at Hershey, Pennsylvania.

1961-1962

FINAL STANDINGS

	W	L	T	PTS	GF	GA
Montreal	42	14	14	98	259	166
Toronto	37	22	11	85	232	180
Chicago	31	26	13	77	217	186
RANGERS	26	32	12	64	195	207
Detroit	23	33	14	60	184	219
Boston	15	47	8	38	177	306

PLAYOFF RESULTS
Semifinals: Toronto defeated Rangers 4-2
LEADING PLAYOFF SCORER
Earl Ingarfield (3-2-5)

Rod Gilbert (2-3-5)

Dave Balon (2-3-5)
STANLEY CUP CHAMPION
Toronto Maple Leafs

SEASON SNAPSHOT

Most Goals:
Andy Bathgate (28)

Most Assists:
Andy Bathgate (56)

Most Points:
Andy Bathgate (84)

Most Penalty Minutes:
Al Langlois (90)

Most Wins, Goaltender:
Gump Worsley (22)

Lowest Goals-Against Average:
Gump Worsley (2.97)

Most Shutouts:
Gump Worsley (2)

NHL Award Winners:
Doug Harvey (Norris Trophy)

NHL All-Stars:
Doug Harvey, D (First Team),
Andy Bathgate, RW (First Team)

Rangers In All-Star Game:
Gump Worsley, G, Doug Harvey, D,
Andy Bathgate, RW

The 1961-62 Season in Review

After missing the playoffs for four straight seasons, GM Muzz Patrick knew his team needed a major shakeup. He started right at the top, getting a coach and a star defenseman in one package by acquiring 36-year-old Doug Harvey from Montreal. With Harvey showing that age had not diminished his skills, the Rangers overcame a 10-game losing streak at midseason to battle Detroit for the final playoff spot. The teams were tied when the Wings came to the Garden on March 14; the Rangers took command in the race with a 3-2 victory when Andy Bathgate beat Hank Bassen on a third-period penalty shot, and wound up four points ahead of Detroit, earning their first playoff berth since 1958 as they met Toronto. The Leafs won the first two games at home, but the Rangers, sparked by 20-year-old Rod Gilbert, won the next two games at Madison Square Garden to pull even. Gump Worsley did everything he could in Game 5, making 55 saves before Red Kelly's goal 4:23 into the second overtime won the game for Toronto. The Leafs closed out the Rangers in Game 6. The Rangers wound up with two first-team All-Stars in Harvey, who also won the Norris Trophy as the NHL's top defenseman, and Bathgate, the league's top right wing and co-winner (with Bobby Hull) of the scoring title.

Andy Bathgate celebrates his 200th goal with Red Sullivan (L).

MAGIC MOMENT
March 14, 1962

Andy Bathgate's penalty shot vs. Detroit is one of the most famous goals in Ranger history.

The Detroit Red Wings came to the Garden on March 14 with a chance to make history—and to break a tie with the Rangers for the final playoff berth. The Wings' Gordie Howe did make history, scoring a spectacular shorthanded goal at 17:10 of the second period for his 500th career tally (and earning a standing ovation from the Garden faithful). But it was the Rangers who went home with two points and fourth place, thanks to one of the most memorable plays in Garden history. With the score tied 2-2 late in the third period, Dean Prentice was going in on a breakaway when goalie Hank Bassen slid his stick across the ice to break up the play. The Rangers were awarded a penalty shot—the first seen at the Garden since 1956. Though Prentice should have taken the shot, referee Eddie Powers mistakenly allowed Andy Bathgate to take it. Unlike Powers, Bathgate made no mistakes, deking Bassen and flicking a backhand into the net for the winning margin. The ovation literally rocked the Garden—while the victory started a 3-1-1 season-ending streak that put the Rangers into the playoffs.

RANGER LEGEND
Doug Harvey

The Montreal Canadiens thought 14 seasons in the NHL were enough for Doug Harvey. Luckily for the Rangers, the 36-year-old Harvey had other ideas. In an unprecedented deal, the Rangers got a coach and a future Hall of Fame defenseman in one package when they worked out a swap that sent fan favorite Lou Fontinato to Montreal for Harvey, who inked a three-year contract as player-coach for a then-enormous $75,000. Harvey had won nine Norris Trophys as the NHL's top defenseman primarily for his skill at controlling the tempo of the game. He quickly showed he had lost little on the blue line, becoming the first Ranger ever to win the Norris Trophy. With Harvey running the attack, Andy Bathgate tied for the NHL scoring lead and three other Rangers broke the 20-goal barrier. As coach, Harvey said he

Doug Harvey (#2) was the first Ranger to win the Norris Trophy.

intended to make the Rangers' style of play more like the Canadiens'—and while New York certainly didn't have Montreal's talent, Harvey did pilot them to their first playoff berth since 1957-58. Harvey gave up the coaching reins prior to his second season, but though his offensive numbers improved—he led all NHL defensemen with 39 points—Garden critics began to blame him for the team's struggles. Those struggles continued in the third season: Harvey had only two assists in 14 games when he opted to be released by the Rangers, rather than retire or go to the minors. Though it looked like his career was over, Harvey returned to the ice, went to the minors and eventually made it back to the NHL, playing a limited but effective role for St. Louis well after turning 40.

Doug Harvey File

- **BORN:**
  December 19, 1924, Montreal, Quebec
- **ACQUIRED:**
  Traded from Montreal for Lou Fontinato, June 1961
- **FIRST SEASON WITH RANGERS:**
  1961-62
- **BEST SEASON WITH RANGERS:**
  1962-63, 68 GP, 4-35-39 92 PIM

- **TOTALS WITH RANGERS:**
  Regular season: 151 GP, 10-61-71, 144 PIM
  Playoffs: 6 GP, 0-1-1, 2 PIM
- **HONORS:**
  Norris Trophy, 1961-62
  First-team All-Star, 1961-62
  All-Star Game, 1961-62, 1962-63
- **NHL MILESTONES:**
  1,113 Games Played

CURTAIN CALL
Rod Gilbert's Magic Night

Few Broadway stars have ever broken in with the kind of splash that Rod Gilbert made. Gilbert was a 20-year-old injury callup who had played in just one NHL game when he joined the Rangers for Game 3 of their playoff series against Toronto, getting a chance when Ken Schinkel broke his toe. Gilbert had an assist in the Rangers' 5-4 victory in Game 3, but Game 4 was all his—a sign that a new era was at hand. Gilbert set off an explosion in the old Garden just 41 seconds into the game when he picked off Allan Stanley's pass and beat Johnny Bower with a 20-foot slap shot. Later in the period, he got his second goal on a backhander, triggering a 4-2 victory that evened the series at 2-2. "It was like a dream," Gilbert remembered years later. "After the period was over, I went over to (Rangers GM) Muzz Patrick, who was handling the line shifts because Doug Harvey was player-coach, and I said, 'Pinch me. I want to make sure I'm not dreaming.'" The Rangers lost the series in six games, but Gilbert finished with five points in four games—convincing the Rangers that he was ready for the NHL.

Rod Gilbert starred against Toronto in his first playoff series.

NEW YORK
Ice Exchange

When GM Muzz Patrick signed Doug Harvey as player-coach, he promised that Harvey would be given a free hand in reshaping the team, which had missed the playoffs for three straight seasons. Harvey wasted little time in doing just that. The first player he brought to the Big Apple was his Montreal defense partner, Al Langlois, who came in a deal that sent John Hanna to the Canadiens. "Leapin' Lou" Fontinato also went to the Canadiens as payment for Harvey. With a logjam on the blue line, former All-Star Bill Gadsby wound up as the odd man out, going to Detroit in a deal for Les Hunt and cash. At Harvey's insistence, the Rangers plucked former Blueshirt Guy Gendron, who chipped in with 14 goals. Rangers fans also got a look at better days to come with glimpses of three newcomers: Vic Hadfield, Jean Ratelle and Rod Gilbert. Hadfield, drafted from Chicago, provided toughness while Ratelle and Gilbert, boyhood friends from the Montreal area who had had brief trials the previous season, contributed speed and skating ability.

Vic Hadfield joined the Rangers from Chicago in 1961-62.

—1962 1963—

TIME CAPSULE

- **October 1, 1962:**
  Two men were killed as violence broke out after James Meredith became the first black to attend classes at the University of Mississippi. Federal marshals escorted Meredith to his classes.

- **October 16, 1962:**
  The New York Yankees edged the San Francisco Giants 1-0 in Game 7 to win their second straight World Series.

- **May 7, 1963:**
  Telstar II was launched from Cape Canaveral, Florida. The satellite relayed television signals between the United States and Europe.

1962-1963

FINAL STANDINGS

	W	L	T	PTS	GF	GA
Toronto	35	23	12	82	221	180
Chicago	32	21	17	81	194	178
Montreal	28	19	23	79	225	183
Detroit	32	25	13	77	200	194
RANGERS	22	36	12	56	211	233
Boston	14	39	17	45	198	281

PLAYOFF RESULTS

Rangers did not qualify

STANLEY CUP CHAMPION

Toronto Maple Leafs

SEASON SNAPSHOT

Most Goals:
Andy Bathgate (28)

Most Assists:
Andy Bathgate (56)

Most Points:
Andy Bathgate (84)

Most Penalty Minutes:
Doug Harvey (92)

Most Wins, Goaltender:
Gump Worsley (22)

Lowest Goals-Against Average:
Gump Worsley (3.30)

Most Shutouts:
Gump Worsley (2)

NHL All-Stars:
Andy Bathgate, RW (Second Team)

Rangers In All-Star Game:
Andy Bathgate, RW;
Doug Harvey, D;
Dean Prentice, LW;
Gump Worsley, G

The 1962-63 Season in Review

Red Sullivan took over for Muzz Patrick as coach on December 28, 1962.

Coming off their first trip to the playoffs since 1958, the Rangers went backward instead of forward. They never suffered a long losing streak, like the previous season's 10-game disaster. Instead, they put themselves and their fans through a different kind of torture. The Blueshirts never lost more than three games in a row during the season, but did so seven times. They had only one winning streak as long as three games and won back-to-back games only three other times. Some of this took place under new coach Muzz Patrick, as player-coach Doug Harvey decided to give up one of his jobs. But on December 28, 1962 Muzz left the bench duties in the hands of Red Sullivan, a fan favorite who had retired a couple of years earlier. It was feast or famine for the Rangers at the Garden. They wound up five games under .500 at home (12-17-6) at home, but only gave up three more goals than they scored (110-107). Only six of those home games were one-goal affairs (the home team lost five of them), which meant a lot of blowouts. New York had 13 home games decided by three or more goals, winning eight of them. Andy Bathgate led the way in scoring for the eighth straight (and final) time with 81 points, but it was Camille Henry who topped the goal-scoring list with 37. Bathgate did set a team (and modern-day NHL) record by scoring goals in 10 straight games. Gump Worsley appeared in all but three games, and in his final season on Broadway, posted a 3.30 goals-against average and two shutouts despite little defensive support.

MAGIC MOMENT *January 5, 1963*

There was some question at the time as to whether Andy Bathgate's 10-game goal scoring streak set an NHL record, but there was no question about the shot that gave Bathgate the longest goal-scoring streak in Rangers' history. As Bathgate's streak approached double figures in December 1962, the NHL went to the trouble of putting out a press release documenting that Harry "Punch" Broadbent had set the league mark with a 16-game streak in 1921-22 during which he scored 25 goals. Montreal's Joe Malone had a 14-gamer in 1917-18, while teammate Newsy Lalonde scored in 13 straight games in the 1920-21 season and Ottawa's Cy Denneny had goals in a dozen consecutive games in the 1917-18 season. The league did allow that a 10-game streak would be a "modern-day record" covering the time since the NHL took possession of the Stanley Cup in 1926. Bathgate had scored one goal in each of nine straight games when the Rangers arrived in Montreal on January 5, 1963, equaling a mark set by Maurice Richard, Bernie Geoffrion and Bobby Hull.

Andy Bathgate set a team record in 1962-63 by scoring in 10 straight games.

Bathgate made it 10 straight games with a blast from the right wing that "had some pepper on it" said Canadiens goalie Jacques Plante. For good measure, Bathgate scored again in the third period to give the Rangers a 2-2 tie.

One of the most colorful characters to ever lace up the skates, Gump Worsley was also among the last of a dying breed: the maskless goalie. He was among the last goaltenders to opt for a face mask making the move not long before he retired in 1974 after spending most of his 21 seasons in the NHL looking shooters straight in the eye—sort of the Craig MacTavish of his time. Worsley started his career with the Rangers in 1952-53 and played well enough to earn the Calder Trophy as rookie of the year while amassing 13 wins, a 3.06 goals-against average and two shutouts. Johnny Bower displaced him the next season, but Worsley won his job back in 1954-55 and kept it for nine seasons before being traded to the Montreal Canadiens. It was there that Worsley was

a part of four Stanley Cup teams. He later finished his career in Minnesota, splitting time with another former Ranger netminder, Cesare Maniago. His career numbers spanning 21 seasons: 335-353-151 and a 2.90 goals-against average. Worsley had two seasons in New York in which his goals against average was below 3.00, and in both (1957-58 and 1961-62), the Rangers made the playoffs. He won the Vezina Trophy twice, both times with Montreal, in 1966 and again in 1968, and not so coincidentally, the Canadiens won the Cup in both seasons. He finished his Ranger career with 24 shutouts, and his NHL career with 43, putting him 19th on the all-time shutout list. Arguably, Worsley's best season with the Blueshirts was in 1961-62. He played in 60 of the 70 games, and though his record was only 22-27-9, his goals against average was 2.97 and the team surprised almost everyone by making the playoffs. Worsley's best game as a Ranger may have been in Game 5 of the 1962 semifinals, where he made 55 saves at Maple Leaf Gardens before losing 4-3 to Toronto in double overtime. Wearing a mask (as he did very late in his career) didn't dull Worsley's senses. He was always quick with a quip, but he had one war that took more out of him than his goaltending duties: his weight. Worsley was constantly fighting the battle of the bulge. It was the only battle he didn't mind losing once in a while.

Gump Worsley File:

- **BORN:**
  May 14, 1929; Montreal, Quebec
- **ACQUIRED:**
  Product of Rangers organization
- **FIRST SEASON WITH RANGERS:**
  1952-53
- **BEST SEASON WITH RANGERS:**
  1957-58, 37 GP, 21-10-4,
  2.32 goals-against average, 4 shutouts

- **TOTALS WITH RANGERS:**
  Regular season: 583 GP, 204-271-101,
  3.10 goals-against average, 24 shutouts
  Playoffs: 22 GP, 6-16, 4.16 goals-against
  average, 0 shutouts
- **HONORS:**
  Calder Trophy, 1952-53
  West Side Assn. Rangers MVP, 1962-63
- **NHL MILESTONES:**
  862 Games Played, 335 Victories, 43 Shutouts

CURTAIN CALL

Bill Jennings

William Jennings launched a new era both for the Rangers and the NHL in 1962 when he became the fifth president in the club's history. Jennings, a lawyer by trade, was a go-getter who pushed hard for the expansion that has turned the NHL into more than just a regional league. He chaired two NHL committees (finance and expansion) and headed the Board of Governors from 1968-70. Jennings persuaded the NHL to put an office in New York and was instrumental in establishing the Lester Patrick Award for "Outstanding Service to Hockey in the United States." He won the award in 1971, five years after its inception. He was also instrumental in paving the way for the arrival of the New York Islanders, lowering the territorial indemnification fee in order to keep the upstart World Hockey Association from putting a team into the Nassau Coliseum. Jennings is one of nine administrators elected to both the Canadian and U.S. Hockey Halls of Fame. He retired after 19 seasons with the Rangers and died on August 17, 1981 at the age of 60.

William Jennings was the prime architect of the NHL expansion.

NEW YORK Ice Exchange

After two straight seasons of appearing in one regular-season game (plus four playoff games the previous spring), Rod Gilbert made the full-time leap to Manhattan, scoring 11 goals and 31 points in his first full season with the Rangers. Another soon-to-be long-time Ranger also made his rookie debut: defenseman Jim Neilson, who only missed one game, and scored 16 points (five goals). Leon Rochefort started his 15-year NHL career with the 1962-63 Blueshirts, while Don McKenney came from Boston in a trade for Irv Spencer. And in one of several father-son combinations on the Blueshirts, rookie Bryan Hextall, son of the former Ranger star, spent 21 games on his first NHL team, and collected two assists. Off the ice, Doug Harvey decided that one job was enough, opting to let Muzz Patrick take over the coaching duties while he concentrated on playing.

Jim Neilson made a successful NHL debut in '62-63. Photo by Paul Bereswill.

Patrick ran the team until December 28, when Red Sullivan stepped behind the bench. Also, John J. Bergen left the presidency of the team, and was replaced by William M. Jennings, who would reside in the top spot for the next 19 seasons.

—1963 [NEW YORK RANGERS] 1964—

TIME CAPSULE

- **October 2, 1963:**
  Sandy Koufax of the Los Angeles Dodgers set a World Series record by striking out 15 batters in the opening game against the New York Yankees. The Dodgers went on to sweep the series in four games.

- **November 22, 1963:**
  President John F. Kennedy was assassinated in Dallas. Vice President Lyndon Johnson was sworn in as president.

- **February 25, 1964:**
  Challenger Cassius Clay (later Muhammad Ali) stopped Sonny Liston in Miami Beach to take the world heavyweight title.

1963-1964

FINAL STANDINGS

	W	L	T	PTS	GF	GA
Montreal	36	21	13	85	209	167
Chicago	36	22	12	84	218	169
Toronto	33	25	12	78	192	172
Detroit	30	29	11	71	191	204
RANGERS	22	38	10	54	186	242
Boston	28	40	12	48	170	212

PLAYOFF RESULTS

Rangers did not qualify

STANLEY CUP CHAMPION

Toronto Maple Leafs

SEASON SNAPSHOT

Most Goals:
Camille Henry (29)
Most Assists:
Andy Bathgate (43)
Most Points:
Phil Goyette (65)
Most Power-Play Goals:
Camille Henry (9)
Most Shorthanded Goals:
Val Fonteyne (2)
Most Penalty Minutes:
Vic Hadfield (151)
Power Play:
40/253, 15.8%, 6 SHGA
Penalty-Killing:
162/206, 78.6%, 3 SHG
Most Wins, Goaltender:
Jacques Plante (22)
Lowest Goals-Against Average:
Jacques Plante (3.38)
Most Shutouts:
Jacques Plante (3)
Rangers In All-Star Game:
Harry Howell, D;
Camille Henry, LW;
Andy Bathgate, RW

The 1963-64 Season in Review

After missing the playoffs in 1962-63, GM Muzz Patrick rolled the dice in a big off-season trade with Montreal, dealing away fan favorite Gump Worsley in a huge swap that brought All-Star goaltender Jacques Plante and forwards Phil Goyette and Don Marshall to New York to join their former Canadien teammate, Doug Harvey. The deal looked good early on: Plante and the Rangers shut out Detroit in the home opener on October 16 and blanked the Bruins in Boston eight days later for their third straight victory. But after splitting their first eight games, the Rangers lost seven straight, were undefeated in four games and then went winless in nine to fall out of the playoff race. Not even a 10-3-2 run in January made much of a difference, so in February, Patrick

Despite acquiring Jacques Plante, the Rangers missed the playoffs.

gambled again, sending the Rangers' top gun, Andy Bathgate, along with forward Don McKenney to Toronto for a five-player package that included veterans Bob Nevin and Dick Duff, plus rookie defensemen Arnie Brown and Rod Seiling. Plante had the satisfaction of beating his old team in Montreal on March 7 and shutting them out (a 0-0 tie) in New York the next night, but those were the last points the Rangers earned; they lost their last six games and managed only to finish ahead of Boston to avoid the cellar.

MAGIC MOMENT   October 16, 1963

Jacques Plante celebrates shutout in home opener.

Ranger fans were curious to see if the big trade with Montreal would make a difference; a crowd of 15,240 for the home opener against Detroit was their largest for a Garden debut in 16 years. For one night, at least, the trade was everything the Rangers and their fans had hoped it would be. Led by goaltender Jacques Plante, the key to the trade, the Rangers wound up with a satisfying 3-0 victory over the Red Wings. Phil Goyette, who had come to the Rangers with Plante, got the first goal just 55 seconds into the game, while Rod Gilbert and ex-Red Wing Val Fonteyne connected about five minutes apart in the second. But the night really belonged to Plante, who had been under siege while making 102 saves in road losses at Chicago and Montreal. "Jake The Snake" kept the crowd roaring with a 34-save performance that earned him a standing ovation from the big crowd as the clock counted down. The flamboyant Plante, termed by coach Red Sullivan as "the best goalie in the league" the day before, jumped for joy at the final buzzer as his new teammates congratulated him on his 59th career shutout and first victory as a Ranger.

Jacques Plante was the biggest name to come to New York in the Rangers' big deal with Montreal, but Phil Goyette proved to be the most effective player by far over the long term. Goyette played for four Cup-winning teams in Montreal, but generally was confined to the checking line and eventually fell victim of the Canadiens' surplus of talent in the middle—there wasn't much ice time left on a team whose first two centers were Jean Beliveau and Henri Richard. No such problem existed with the Rangers, where "The Professor" (his nickname in Montreal) wasted little time moving in as the first-line center. Goyette tied an NHL record on October 21, 1963, with four first-period assists against Boston and finished in the top 10 in scoring with 65 points. The quick development of another French-Canadian, Jean Ratelle, bumped Goyette back to the second line, but the slick center teamed with fellow ex-Canadien Donnie Marshall and ex-Maple Leaf Bob Nevin to form "The Smoothies," one of the best-skating two-way lines Garden fans have ever seen. Goyette's offensive production dropped off in 1964-65 and 1965-66, but he rebounded with a team high 61 points in 1966-67, helping the Rangers end their playoff drought, and posted 25 goals and 65 points the next season as the Rangers soared to second place. Goyette lasted one more season before being sent to St. Louis in 1969. But after being dealt by the Blues to Buffalo, he wound up finishing his career back in New York, when the Rangers dealt for him again in 1972 after Ratelle broke his ankle in March. He played in 13 playoff games, and the Rangers made the finals for the first time in 23 years.

Phil Goyette File

- **BORN:**
  October 31, 1933; Lachine, Quebec
- **ACQUIRED:**
  From Montreal with Jacques Plante and Don Marshall for Gump Worsley, Leon Rochefort, Len Ronson and Dave Balon, June 1963
- **FIRST SEASON WITH RANGERS:**
  1963-64

- **BEST SEASON WITH RANGERS:**
  1976-68; 73 GP, 25-40-65, 10 PIM
- **TOTALS WITH RANGERS:**
  Regular Season: 397 GP, 98-231-329, 51 PIM
  Playoffs: 26 GP, 2-4-6, 10 PIM
- **HONORS:**
  Players' Player Award, 1963-64

CURTAIN CALL

Sal Messina

His name isn't listed on the team's all-time roster, but Sal Messina was a Ranger long before he became one of the NHL's longest-lasting radio analysts. Like the Mullen brothers, two other New Yorkers who made it big in the NHL, Messina started his hockey career on roller skates, playing goal on the sidewalks of Astoria. He switched to ice hockey as a teen and was good enough that his team, West New York (N.J.), pressured GM Muzz Patrick into giving him a tryout at the Garden. The Rangers ultimately put Messina on their negotiating list after he turned pro with the Long Island Ducks of the old Eastern League. Messina got an invitation to training camp in 1963 and wound up being signed as a practice goalie. He traveled with the team, but never got into a game; his closest call came in Montreal when Plante, a former Canadien, got sick on the morning before facing his old team.

"Red Light" (as he was playfully dubbed by long-time broadcast partner Marv Albert) never did get into an NHL game as a goaltender, but has spent more than two decades analyzing the Rangers' wins and losses as a broadcaster—a career he never dreamed about.

NEW YORK
Ice Exchange

Gump Worsley was tired of facing a fusillade of shots every night in New York, while Montreal had grown tired of Jacques Plante's idiosyncrasies, so the two clubs exchanged goalies in the summer of 1963. The Rangers also traded Leon Rochefort and Dave Balon, while receiving a pair of slick-skating veterans, Phil Goyette and Don Marshall. But perhaps the biggest trade in team history to that point took place in February, when the Rangers dealt star right wing Andy Bathgate, their top scorer in each of the previous eight seasons, along with Don McKenney, to Toronto.

Rod Seiling was part of the five-player package the Rangers received in the Andy Bathgate deal.

Of the five players they got back, three—forward Bob Nevin and defensemen Arnie Brown and Rod Seiling—went on to have productive careers with the Rangers. Bathgate got a reward, too—the Leafs won the Stanley Cup. Two other key Rangers also departed. Andy Hebenton, who had played in every game during the past eight seasons, was exposed in the waiver draft and claimed by Boston, where he broke the NHL's consecutive games-played record 21 games into the season. The Rangers also released defenseman Doug Harvey after just 14 games; their former coach and star, now 38, had just two assists before being let go.

Ranger Lists
Most Road Losses, One Season
26
1975-76
26
1984-85
25
1963-64
25
1965-66
23
1952-53
23
1954-55
23
1959-60
23
1960-61
23
1980-81

Emile Francis

Emile Francis started his hockey career at age 11 by trading a bicycle for a pair of hockey gloves. That early deal was a sign of what lay ahead.

Francis spent 18 seasons as a professional goaltender, beginning in 1942 and ending in 1960. He spent some time with the Rangers and Blackhawks, but for most of his career, he was a successful minor-leaguer. His ports of call ranged from east (Washington) to west (Seattle) and a variety of cities in between. He also served in the Canadian army, and played and managed semipro baseball teams in Saskatchewan.

Francis' baseball stint also included handling day-to-day operations and scouting duties, which enabled him to get a taste of what it took to run a team. When he finally hung up his pads, Rangers GM Muzz Patrick wasted little time getting him into the organization. At that time, NHL teams owned junior clubs; the Rangers' team was Guelph in the Ontario Hockey Association, and that's where Francis got his start as both coach and manager. He later joined the Rangers as Patrick's assistant, and on October 30, 1964, became general manager.

Francis had helped develop players like Rod Gilbert and Jean Ratelle during his days at Guelph; he also nurtured Vic Hadfield, Jim Neilson and Rod Seiling and drafted players like Brad Park, Walt Tkaczuk, Bill Fairbairn and Ron Greschner. His biggest move came in the summer of 1965, when he traded four players to Providence of the American Hockey League for minor-league goaltender Ed Giacomin.

As the rebuilt Rangers began to rise in the standings, Francis used the fruits of his farm system to acquire complementary veterans such as Pete Stemkowski, Bruce MacGregor, Dale Rolfe and Bobby Rousseau. From 1967-75, the Francis-built (and usually Francis-coached) Rangers made the playoffs every season. They got to the finals in 1972, but with Ratelle hobbled by a broken ankle, they fell to Boston in six games.

Emile Francis coached more games than anyone in Rangers history.

A proud man who once battled his own fans while disputing a call by goal judge Arthur Reichert, Francis continued to try to find the combination that would win the Stanley Cup. He began a major shakeup in 1975 by letting Giacomin go to Detroit on waivers, then dealing Park and Ratelle to Boston for Phil Esposito and Carol Vadnais. Injuries, always a Ranger trademark, combined with the fallout from the roster moves, helped cost Francis his job on January 6, 1976.

Francis had three coaching stints with the Rangers, and still holds the club records for games coached and victories. He finished 1975-76 as a vice president with the Rangers, then went to St. Louis as coach and general manager. After seven seasons with the Blues, he moved to Hartford, where he was GM for six seasons before retiring in 1989.

Francis helped develop players like Walt Tkaczuk (18) and dealt for others like Pete Stemkowski (21). Photo by Paul Bereswill.

—1964 1965—

TIME CAPSULE

October 15, 1964:
The St. Louis Cardinals beat the New York Yankees 7-5 in Game 7 to win their first World Series championship since 1946.

November 3, 1964:
Lyndon Johnson routed Barry Goldwater to win a full term as president after succeeding John F. Kennedy a year earlier following Kennedy's assassination.

March 8, 1965:
The first American combat forces landed in South Vietnam to guard the U.S. Air Force base at Da Nang.

1964-1965

FINAL STANDINGS

	W	L	T	PTS	GF	GA
Detroit	40	23	7	87	224	175
Montreal	36	23	11	83	211	185
Chicago	34	28	8	76	224	176
Toronto	30	26	14	74	204	173
RANGERS	20	38	12	52	179	246
Boston	21	43	6	48	166	253

PLAYOFF RESULTS

Rangers did not qualify.

STANLEY CUP CHAMPION

Montreal Canadiens

SEASON SNAPSHOT

Most Goals:
Rod Gilbert (25)
Most Assists:
Rod Gilbert (36)
Most Points:
Rod Gilbert (61)
Most Power-Play Goals:
Camille Henry (13)
Most Shorthanded Goals:
Don Marshall (3)
Most Penalty Minutes:
Arnie Brown (145)
Power Play:
55/321, 17.1%, 9 SHGA
Penalty-Killing:
224/267, 83.9%, 7 SHG
Most Wins, Goaltender:
Jacques Plante/Marcel Paille (10)
Lowest Goals-Against Average:
Jacques Plante (3.37)
Most Shutouts:
Jacques Plante (2)
Rangers In All-Star Game:
Harry Howell, D;
Camille Henry, LW;
Rod Gilbert, RW

After four coaching changes in the past three seasons, upper management decided to make a different kind of move, opting to reassign GM Muzz Patrick to help with the upcoming move to the new Madison Square Garden. Assistant GM Emile Francis moved into the top job, with Red Sullivan still behind the bench. The club seemed to respond early, and was one game over .500 after a 4-1 victory at Chicago on December 6. But a 1-10-2 slide over the next month evaporated any playoff hopes, and a 1-9-1 slump in late January and early February forced Francis to start planning for the future. Jacques Plante, whose acquisition in the summer of 1963 had led to great expectations, started well enough, but wound up being assigned to the Rangers' minor-league team in Baltimore in favor of journeyman Marcel Paille. The season's best news

Don Marshall had 20 goals in 1964-65, his second season with the Rangers.

was the continuing development of Rod Gilbert, who led the team with 25 goals and 61 points, good for seventh in the league in scoring. But only two other players (Camille Henry and Don Marshall) were able to score as many as 20 goals, making things tough on whoever was in the nets. Only an 8-5-1 mark against the lowly Bruins kept the Rangers out of the cellar, and Francis knew he had a lot of work ahead.

MAGIC MOMENT   *January 27, 1965*

From its inception, the NHL could have stood for "North Americans-only Hockey League." Though an occasional European-born skater such as Finnish-born former Ranger Pentti Lund, made it to the NHL, these players had moved across the Atlantic at an early age and received their hockey training in Canada. All that changed in January 1965, when the Rangers called up forward Ulf Sterner from their farm team in Baltimore. Sterner, the first European-bred player to sign an NHL contract, was Sweden's top player and earned his promotion after excelling in the Central League and the AHL. His debut was a success: The Rangers beat Boston 5-2 and Sterner played adequately, though he had an apparent goal disallowed by an offside call. But the 6-2, 185-pounder was targeted for abuse by opposing teams, who felt they would be able to intimidate Sterner because he was unaccustomed to the physical style of NHL play. He lasted just four games before returning

Ulf Sterner was the NHL's first Swedish born-and-bred player.

to the minors, and eventually went back to Sweden—but every European to make the NHL since then owes him a debt of gratitude as a trailblazer.

Photo by Barton Silverman.

"The Chief" played in the first NHL game he ever attended when he made the Rangers as a not-quite-21-year-old in October 1962. His partner and tutor was Hall of Famer Doug Harvey, who had won the Norris Trophy the previous season. Harvey did his work well, because Neilson went on to spend more than a decade on the Rangers' blue line, repaying the instruction he got from Harvey by serving as one of the tutors for Brad Park when he joined the team in 1968 ("Jimmy seemed like Father Time when I got here," Park remembered later, even though Neilson was all of 28 at the time). Neilson was speedy enough to play forward as a youngster (he was on left wing for his first NHL goal against Boston's Ed Johnston in 1962), and though he was never the major offensive force that Park became, Neilson was an adept puck-carrier who was also plenty effective in his own zone. At 6-foot-2 and 200 pounds, Neilson was big enough to move opposing forwards out of the slot, yet quick enough to join the rush when need be. He hit double figures in goals only once, getting 10 in 1968-69 (when he was named a second-team All-Star), but in typical Neilson style, was quietly effective offensively. His best years came when he was paired with Rod Seiling, another quiet-but-effective player, in a unit that would have been the prime pairing on a lot of clubs but was a superlative No. 2 duo for the Rangers behind Park and Dale Rolfe. Neilson scored 60 goals and added 238 assists in his 12 seasons in the Big Apple before finishing up his career by spending four more years with California and Cleveland, reaching an NHL milestone by playing more than 1,000 games.

Jim Neilson File

- **BORN:**
  November 28, 1941; Big River, Saskatchewan
- **ACQUIRED:**
  Product of Rangers organization
- **FIRST SEASON WITH RANGERS:**
  1962-63
- **BEST SEASON WITH RANGERS:**
  1968-69, 76 GP, 10-34-44, 95 PIM

- **TOTALS WITH RANGERS:**
  Regular season: 810 GP, 60-238-298, 786 PIM
  Playoffs: 65 GP, 1-17-18, 61 PIM
- **HONORS:**
  Second-team All-Star, 1967-68
  All-Star game, 1966-67, 1969-70, 1970-71
- **NHL MILESTONES:**
  1,023 Games Played

CURTAIN CALL

Marcel Paille

As a backup goaltender in the one-goalie era, Marcel Paille was usually like the Maytag repairman: He had a lot of time on his hands. Paille spent most of his NHL career watching someone else play goal for the Rangers until 1964-65, when the Rangers' displeasure with Jacques Plante gave him a shot at the top job. Wearing No. 23 (the only Ranger goalie ever to do so), Paille struggled along with his team, finishing with a 10-21-7 record and a 3.58 goals-against average in 39 games (six more than Plante played). Though Paille didn't get a shot at the starting job the next season, he played a key role in filling it: He was one of four players whom GM Emile Francis peddled to Providence of the AHL in exchange for a minor-league goaltender named Ed Giacomin. Paille spent several more seasons in the minors, and even got a chance to play in the Garden again as a visitor with the Philadelphia Blazers of the fledgling World Hockey Association before finally calling it quits in 1973.

Marcel Paille bridged the gap between Jacques Plante and Ed Giacomin.

NEW YORK Ice Exchange

New GM Emile Francis knew that he faced a major reconstruction project in order to turn the Rangers into a contender; that meant giving playing time to some younger players and finding more youthful talent. Arnie Brown and Rod Seiling, two young defensemen acquired from Toronto in the Andy Bathgate deal the previous February, both took regular turns throughout the season and showed the skills that eventually made them NHL regulars. Another player obtained in that deal, Dick Duff, was sent to Montreal for speedy forward Billy Hicke. With an eye toward putting together a club capable of playing a more physical style, Francis dealt team captain Camille Henry, the NHL's smallest player, to Chicago in February for Doug

Doug Robinson came from Chicago for Camille Henry.

Robinson, a big left wing who averaged a point a game for the rest of the season after coming to New York, plus left wing John Brenneman and defenseman Wayne Hillman. Francis and coach Red Sullivan gave numerous other youngsters a chance to play; perhaps the most popular was center Lou Angotti, who became a crowd favorite with his hustle.

Ranger Lists

Longest Home Winless Streaks

10
1/30/44 - 3/19/44

9
12/31/42 - 2/18/43

9
11/29/64 - 1/3/65

9
2/15/96 - 3/24/96

8
11/12/44 - 12/27/44

8
12/1/54 - 12/26/54

—1965 NEW YORK RANGERS 1966—

TIME CAPSULE ———————————————————

- **November 9, 1965:**
  The lights went out for millions of people in the Northeast, as a 13-hour blackout brought the region to a standstill.

- **January 31, 1966:**
  President Lyndon Johnson announced that American pilots had resumed their bombing raids on North Vietnam after a 38-day hiatus in hopes of furthering peace talks.

- **April 28, 1966:**
  The Boston Celtics beat the Los Angeles Lakers in Game 7 of the NBA Finals, enabling coach Red Auerbach to retire with his eighth straight championship.

1965-1966 FINAL STANDINGS

	W	L	T	PTS	GF	GA
Montreal	41	21	8	90	239	173
Chicago	37	25	8	82	240	187
Toronto	34	25	11	79	208	187
Detroit	31	27	12	74	221	194
Boston	21	43	6	48	174	275
RANGERS	18	41	11	47	195	261

PLAYOFF RESULTS
Rangers did not qualify

STANLEY CUP CHAMPION
Montreal Canadiens

SEASON SNAPSHOT

Most Goals:
Bob Nevin (29)

Most Assists:
Bob Nevin (33)

Most Points:
Bob Nevin (62)

Most Power-Play Goals:
Don Marshall (10)

Most Shorthanded Goals:
Bob Nevin/Don Marshall (1)

Most Penalty Minutes:
Reg Fleming (122)

Power Play:
44/282, 15.6%, 2 SHGA

Penalty-Killing:
219/282, 77.7%, 2 SHG

Most Wins, Goaltender:
Cesare Maniago (9)

Lowest Goals-Against Average:
Cesare Maniago (3.50)

Most Shutouts:
Cesare Maniago (2)

Rangers In All-Star Game:
Harry Howell, D;
Vic Hadfield, LW;
Rod Gilbert, RW

The 1965-66 Season in Review

Reggie Fleming added much-needed muscle up front. Photo by Barton Silverman.

For the first half of the 1960s, the Rangers had the Boston Bruins to keep them out of the NHL cellar. In 1965-66, even that didn't work. After going 5-5-4 in their first 14 games, the Rangers fell apart, winning only once between Thanksgiving and Christmas and costing coach Red Sullivan his job. GM Emile Francis went behind the bench, but it didn't help as the losses kept coming. Captain Bob Nevin had an excellent season with 29 goals and 33 assists for 62 points, good for eighth in the NHL scoring race, and Don Marshall added 26 goals, but the Rangers were undone by their defense and penalty-killing. Neither Ed Giacomin nor Cesare Maniago was able to take command in the nets and the penalty-killers coughed up 62 goals. The Rangers were also hurt by a back injury that side-lined Rod Gilbert for the second half of the season, forcing him to undergo surgery. Among the few positive notes were the blossoming of center Jean Ratelle into a 20-goal scorer and the continued development of young defensemen Jim Neilson, Arnie Brown and Rod Seiling. But the Rangers were able to win as many as two games in a row only twice all season, and an 0-6-1 streak before a closing-night victory over Montreal dropped them into last place for the first time since 1959-60.

MAGIC MOMENT — *March 12, 1966*

Unfortunately for the Rangers, they found themselves in the path of Bobby Hull's quest for immortality once too often. Hull hit the 50-goal mark, then the NHL record, with 13 games still remaining in 1965-66 and the pressure on him to break it was immense. Too immense, actually; the Blackhawks were shut out by Toronto, Montreal and, finally, the Rangers, who blanked Hull and the Hawks 1-0 at the Garden on March 9 behind Cesare Maniago. The Rangers started well in the return match at Chicago Stadium three nights later, taking a 2-0 lead after two periods as Maniago and the Rangers kept the lid on the sellout crowd at Chicago Stadium. But early in the third, Hull set up Chico Maki for the Hawks' first goal, and now the crowd was alive. With Harry Howell in the penalty box, Hull fired a low 30-foot wrist shot just as Eric Nesterenko charged the net. Maniago did the split as Nesterenko flashed by, tipping the goaltenders' stick—and the puck flew into the back of the net for No. 51, setting off one of the great eruptions in the old building's history and making Hull the first to break the 50-goal mark. To add insult to injury for the Rangers, the Hawks scored twice more to win the game, 4-2.

Bobby Hull got his record-setting 51st goal against the Rangers.

Shock was a kind term for the feeling Bob Nevin had when he was dealt from the Toronto Maple Leafs to the Rangers in February 1964. "In those days, going from the Leafs to the Rangers was like being shipped to Siberia. I almost quit hockey," Nevin said years later. Luckily for the Rangers, he didn't. Not only did Nevin help New York fans forget Andy Bathgate, he went on to become one of the key elements in Emile Francis' rebuilding of the team. "Nevin was the guy we had to get in the Bathgate deal," said Francis, the Rangers' assistant GM when the deal was made. Nevin became team captain within a year of arriving on Broadway, and was lauded by then-coach Red Sullivan as "the best captain I've ever played with or coached." Nevin's offensive skills had taken a back seat in Toronto, where he spent much of his time as the defensive forward on a unit that included Frank Mahovlich and Red Kelly, but they came to the forefront in New York, where he posted five 20-goal seasons, including a 31-goal campaign in 1968-69. His best offensive seasons came when he was paired with center Phil Goyette and left wing Don Marshall, a trio known as "The Smoothies." Nevin's last goal for the Rangers was his most memorable: He scored 9:07 into overtime to beat Toronto in Game 6 of the 1971 quarterfinals, giving the Rangers their first playoff series win in 21 years. He was dealt to Minnesota that summer for Bobby Rousseau and went on to play five more seasons in the NHL with the North Stars and Los Angeles Kings, finishing his career with more than 300 goals and 700 points while playing in 1,128 games before retiring in 1976.

Bob Nevin File

- **BORN:**
  March 18, 1938; South Porcupine, Ontario
- **ACQUIRED:**
  From Toronto with Dick Duff, Rod Seiling, Arnie Brown, and Bill Collins for Andy Bathgate and Don McKenney, Feb. 22, 1964.
- **FIRST SEASON WITH RANGERS:**
  1963-64

- **BEST SEASON WITH RANGERS:**
  1965-66, 69 GP, 29-33-62, 10 PIM
- **TOTALS WITH RANGERS:**
  Regular Season: 505 GP, 168-174-342, 107 PIM
  Playoffs: 33 GP, 6-12-18, 8 PIM
- **HONORS:**
  All-Star Game, 1966-67, 1968-69
  West Side Assn. Rangers MVP, 1965-66
- **NHL MILESTONES:**
  1,128 Games Played

CURTAIN CALL

The Lester Patrick Trophy

More than any other sport, hockey has a long and formidable list of trophies. The Rangers added to that collection in 1966 when they donated the Lester Patrick Trophy, named for the patriarch of the franchise, to honor "Outstanding Service To Hockey In The United States." The Patrick Trophy was conceived and developed by Bill Jennings, the long-time governor of the Rangers (and a 1971 recipient) and resides at Madison Square Garden. Jack Adams, who coached the Red Wings during their heyday in the 1950s, was the initial recipient. The list of winners over the years includes hockey immortals like Bobby Hull, Bobby Orr, Wayne Gretzky and Gordie Howe, Ranger greats such as Frank Boucher, Murray Murdoch and Rod Gilbert, builders like Emile Francis and Gen. John Kirkpatrick, as well as New Yorkers who have made a name in hockey like the Mullen brothers, Brian and Joe, and Bill Chadwick, a local product who went on to a Hall of Fame career as a referee.

Three Lester Patrick Award winners; (L. to R.) Bill Chadwick, Donald Clark and Tommy Ivan.

NEW YORK
Ice Exchange

Emile Francis knew that any contending team needed a star goaltender, something he knew the Rangers didn't have. With nothing to lose, he rolled the dice and shipped four players to Providence of the AHL in exchange for Ed Giacomin, a solid minor-leaguer who had never been given a shot in the NHL. But Francis didn't put all his eggs in Giacomin's basket; he also reeled in lanky Cesare Maniago and veteran Don Simmons, hoping that one or the other could help plug the hole in net. None of the three could win the job in 1965-66, a prime reason why coach Red Sullivan was sacked in December. With his team going nowhere fast, Francis relieved Sullivan and put himself behind the bench.

Cesare Maniago had 2 shutouts in 1965-66.

Francis, always seeking more size, added one of the NHL's toughest players at midseason when he sent Johnny McKenzie to Boston for Reggie Fleming. Forward Garry Peters came over from Montreal and got a full-season shot, but produced only seven goals; numerous other youngsters also got chances as Francis continued his talent search.

—1966  1967—

TIME CAPSULE

- **November 11, 1966:**
  The last mission of the Gemini space series was launched, with astronauts Jim Lovell and Edwin "Buzz" Aldrin making a successful rendezvous with a target vehicle.

- **January 15, 1967:**
  The Green Bay Packers won the first Super Bowl, defeating the Kansas City Chiefs 35-10 at the Los Angeles Memorial Coliseum.

- **March 25, 1967:**
  Sophomore center Lew Alcindor, later known as Kareem Abdul-Jabbar, led UCLA to the NCAA basketball title, capping an unbeaten season by beating Dayton 79-64 in the title game.

1966-1967
FINAL STANDINGS

	W	L	T	PTS	GF	GA
Chicago	41	17	12	94	264	170
Montreal	32	25	13	77	252	188
Toronto	32	27	11	75	204	211
RANGERS	30	28	12	72	188	189
Detroit	27	39	4	58	212	241
Boston	17	43	10	44	182	253

PLAYOFF RESULTS
Montreal defeated Rangers 4-0
LEADING PLAYOFF SCORER
Rod Gilbert (2-2-4)
STANLEY CUP CHAMPION
Toronto Maple Leafs

SEASON SNAPSHOT

Most Goals:
Rod Gilbert (28)
Most Assists:
Phil Goyette (49)
Most Points:
Phil Goyette (61)
Most Power-Play Goals:
Don Marshall (8)
Most Shorthanded Goals:
Ken Schinkel (2)
Most Penalty Minutes:
Reg Fleming (146)
Power Play:
35/199, 17.6%, 4 SHGA
Penalty-Killing:
169/199, 85.1%, 4 SHG
Most Wins, Goaltender:
Ed Giacomin (30)
Lowest Goals-Against Average:
Ed Giacomin (2.61)
Most Shutouts:
Ed Giacomin (9)
NHL Award Winners:
Harry Howell (Norris Trophy)
NHL All-Stars:
Ed Giacomin, G (First Team);
Harry Howell, D (First Team);
Don Marshall, LW (Second Team)
Rangers In All-Star Game:
Ed Giacomin, G; Harry Howell, D;
Jim Neilson, D; Rod Gilbert, RW;
Bob Nevin, RW

The 1966-67 Season in Review

The rebuilding job by coach/GM Emile Francis paid off in a playoff berth. After a slow start, the Rangers got a spark from a rare win at Montreal in mid-November and went on their biggest hot streak in years, grabbing a share of first place on Christmas Night with a 1-0 victory at Chicago as Ed Giacomin won a goaltending duel with Denis DeJordy. Giacomin, booed lustily by Garden fans during his rookie season, became a big crowd favorite by recording nine shutouts and winning an All-Star berth. He got plenty of help from Harry Howell, who at 34 enjoyed the best season of his career, winning the Norris Trophy as the NHL's top defenseman. The offense got a boost when Francis coaxed Bernie "Boom Boom" Geoffrion out of retirement; the Boomer added some of-

Harry Howell won the Norris Trophy in 1966-67. Photo by Barton Silverman.

fense (17 goals in 58 games) and a large dose of leadership in the locker room. The Rangers ran out of gas down the stretch and wound up fourth, earning a first-round meeting with Montreal. They stunned the Canadiens by jumping to a 4-1 lead in the opener behind two goals by Geoffrion, but the Canadiens recovered for a 6-4 win and went on to sweep the series, winning the last game on John Ferguson's overtime goal after Red Berenson's shot had hit the post. Still, for the first time in years, Rangers fans knew their team finally was on the road to respectability.

MAGIC MOMENT November 12, 1966

When Emile Francis convinced Bernie "Boom-Boom" Geoffrion to make a comeback after two seasons in retirement, the Boomer's long-time coach, Montreal's Toe Blake, didn't think his former star could do it. That was more than enough incentive for Geoffrion, who wanted to show his old coach, his old team and his old fans that he could still play. He got his chance in the Rangers' 11th game of the season—and made the most of it. Though Montreal native Rod Gilbert had two goals, Geoffrion was the true star on this night at the Forum. He scored on a third-period breakaway to break the game open, set up Harry Howell for the clincher late in the third period—and then led cheers in the dressing room after his goal and three assists led New York to a 6-3 victory—just their third triumph of the season. "We can beat them if we just believe," he boomed after the game. "We're as good as any club in the league." The Rangers believed, and with Geoffrion providing both offense and

A Geoffrion-led victory in Montreal sparked the Rangers' season.

leadership, the Rangers went on a 15-4-3 surge, their best spurt in years, that helped put them into the playoffs for the first time since 1962.

RANGER LEGEND
Harry Howell

No player has worn a Ranger jersey for as many games as Harry Howell. Few have worn it as well. Howell wasn't flamboyant, wasn't an attacker who happened to be wearing a defenseman's jersey. He came to the Rangers right out of junior hockey in 1952 (something rarely done at the time) and didn't leave until 1969. Garden fans booed him at first, feeling he wasn't rough enough, then grew to appreciate him as an honest hockey player who gave his best every night. Typical Howell: In 1955, he became the youngest captain in team history at age 22; he asked to be relieved two years later because he felt he wasn't playing well enough. The Rangers' struggles and Howell's quiet effectiveness kept him from getting much recognition until 1966-67, when at the age of 34 he enjoyed the best offensive season of his career and won the Norris Trophy as the NHL's top defenseman while leading the Rangers back into the playoffs. He was the most respected of Rangers by his teammates, management, and opponents. "Harry was a fine player when he first came up and he's been outstanding for at least a dozen years," remembered former coach and GM Muzz Patrick. "He's not doing anything different now. He's just being noticed because the team is winning." Howell played with the Rangers for 17 seasons through 1968-69, but with a bad back limiting his effectiveness, he knew his days were numbered. Rather than retire, as GM Emile Francis suggested, Howell asked to be traded. Francis complied, and Howell played with California and Los

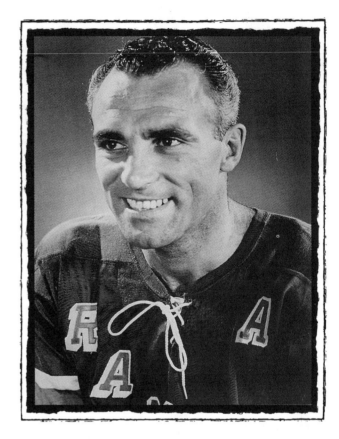

Angeles, finishing with the Kings in 1972-73 after 1,411 games—the most ever by a player without winning a Stanley Cup. He was inducted into the Hockey Hall of Fame in 1979.

Harry Howell File

- **BORN:**
  December 28, 1932; Hamilton Ontario
- **ACQUIRED:**
  Product of Rangers organization
- **FIRST SEASON WITH RANGERS:**
  1952-53
- **BEST SEASON WITH RANGERS:**
  1966-67, 70 GP, 12-28-40, 54 PIM
- **TOTALS WITH RANGERS:**
  Regular Season: 1,160 GP, 82-263-345, 1,147 PIM
  Playoffs: 34 GP, 2-3-5, 30 PIM

- **HONORS:**
  Norris Trophy, 1966-67
  First-team All-Star, 1966-67
  All-Star Game, 1954-55, 1963-64, 1964-65, 1965-66, 1966-67, 1967-68
  West Side Assn. Rangers MVP, 1963-64
  Players' Player Award, 1964-65, 1966-67
- **NHL MILESTONES:**
  1,411 Games Played

CURTAIN CALL

January 25, 1967

Local writers called it "A Night To Howell." More precisely, it was the first night ever given by the Rangers to an active player—and it came in the middle of Harry Howell's finest season in New York. Howell's family flew in from Hamilton, Ontario (another 50-person delegation from his home town missed the ceremony because Kennedy Airport was fogged in). Former teammates Lou Fontinato and Red Sullivan stepped out of a new car given to Howell, who received a myriad of other gifts, including three vacations and a special medal from New York City Mayor John Lindsay. The celebration came two games after Howell became the first Ranger ever to play 1,000 games with the team—and was held on the same night that he was voted onto the first-half All-Star team. In all, it took Howell six trips in a station wagon to take home all the gifts (not counting the car). To put the icing on the cake, the Rangers beat Boston 2-1.

Harry Howell was the first active Ranger honored with a special night. Photo by Barton Silverman.

NEW YORK Ice Exchange

When Emile Francis first joined the Rangers, he realized that one of their major failings was a lack of size. That's why he wasted little time grabbing center Orland Kurtenbach in the preseason waiver draft. Kurtenbach provided the kind of size up the middle that the Rangers hadn't had in years, serving as a top-flight enforcer for a lineup that was still relatively small up front. Another useful waiver-draft pickup was defenseman Al MacNeil, who turned in a steady season on the blue line and helped groom some of the younger defensemen. The waiver draft cost the Rangers forward John Brenneman, who went to Toronto; a bigger loss was caused by the back problems that sidelined center Jean Ratelle for most of the first two months and limited his effectiveness throughout the season. Former college star Red Berenson and rookie Larry Mickey were among those who tried—and failed—to pick up the scoring slack in Ratelle's absence.

Orland Kurtenbach was a key addition in 1966–67.

Ranger Lists

Most Games Played as a Ranger

1,160
Harry Howell
1,065
Rod Gilbert
982
Ron Greschner
945
Walt Tkaczuk
862
Jean Ratelle
838
Vic Hadfield
810
Jim Neilson
719
Andy Bathgate
698
Steve Vickers
671
James Patrick

Madison Square Garden

The current Madison Square Garden owes its name to three predecessors and the start of its hockey history to a team that's long since defunct. When promoter Tex Rickard was making plans for the third Madison Square Garden—the first one not actually built in Madison Square—there were no provisions for ice-making equipment. Rickard, a promoter whose specialty was boxing, had no interest in Canada's national game. Nor did the group of millionaires bankrolling the new building on Eighth Avenue between 49th and 50th Streets much care for the sport.

But with some persuasion from Col. John S. Hammond, a hockey enthusiast who was one of Rickard's favorite partners and confidants, Rickard changed his mind and made provisions to have ice-making equipment put into the Garden, which went up on the site of some old trolley car barns in the astonishingly fast time of 249 days. Howie Morenz, the reigning superstar of his day, came to town with the Montreal Canadiens to play the first hockey game at the Garden on December 15, 1925, beating the New York Americans, owned by "Big Bill" Dwyer, 3-1 before a packed house of more than 17,000.

The Americans continued to draw well—so well that Rickard quickly decided the Garden should own its own team. One year after the Americans' debut, the Rangers skated onto the Garden ice for the first time, beating the Canadiens' intra-city rivals, the Maroons, 1-0.

The Rangers shared the Garden with the Americans until their rivals folded in 1942. The Garden also hosted bicycle races, college and pro basketball, ice shows, rodeos, prize fights—and the circus, which became the bane of Ranger fans. "The Greatest Show On Earth" arrived every spring like clockwork, bumping the Rangers if they were still alive in the playoffs. They won the 1940 Stanley Cup despite playing most of the se-

ries in Toronto, and were forced to play all of the 1950 finals out of town (playing two "home" games in Toronto and the other five contests in Detroit) because Garden management could not bump the circus.

By 1960, the third Garden was 35 years old. On November 3, as the Rangers were losing to Boston, Garden president Irving Mitchell Felt was announcing plans for a fourth Madison Square Garden, a $116 million complex that would be built over Penn Station.

On February 11, 1968, the Rangers said goodbye to their old home by playing to a 3-3 tie with Detroit before a nostalgic sellout crowd. Prior to the game, the greatest collection of hockey talent ever assembled in one place took a last turn around the Garden ice. The 59 immortals included old Ranger heroes like the Cook brothers, Frank Boucher, Ching Johnson, Dave Kerr and Bryan Hextall, plus more recent stars like Andy Bathgate. Jean Ratelle had the honor of scoring the last goal in the old building.

That same night, the fourth Madison Square Garden had its grand opening with a "Salute to the USO," starring Bing Crosby and Bob Hope. The Rangers' Garden IV debut came a week later. Wayne Hicks of the Flyers got the first goal, but the Rangers got the first victory, beating Philadelphia 3-1 before a sellout crowd of 17,250, who reveled in the wider, padded seats and more spacious accommodations offered in the new arena.

Madison Square Garden III.

Madison Square Garden IV.

The Garden finished an extensive renovation in September 1991, a process that saw the arena completely overhauled, including new scoreboards and video boards, improved seating and concessions and luxury suites. Less than three years later, the Garden hosted an event Ranger fans had been waiting a lifetime for—another Stanley Cup triumph, the team's first since 1940 and the first ever won by the Rangers at home.

In all, Madison Square Garden now hosts more than four million people at approximately 400 events each year—including the more than 750,000 fans who turn out to see their favorite hockey team.

—1967 1968—

TIME CAPSULE

- **October 12, 1967:**
  The St. Louis Cardinals beat Boston 7-2 in Game 7 of the World Series, ending the Red Sox's "Impossible Dream" season one victory short of their first championship since 1918.

- **January 23, 1968:**
  North Korea seized the Naval intelligence ship U.S.S. Pueblo off its coast, holding the crew of 83 hostage for 11 months.

- **April 4, 1968:**
  Dr. Martin Luther King Jr. was assassinated in Memphis, Tennessee, setting off a week of rioting around the nation.

1967-1968
FINAL STANDINGS

East Division	W	L	T	PTS	GF	GA
Montreal	42	22	10	94	236	167
RANGERS	39	23	12	90	226	183
Boston	37	27	10	84	259	216
Chicago	32	26	16	80	216	222
Toronto	33	31	10	76	209	176
Detroit	27	35	12	66	245	257

West Division Winner—Philadelphia

PLAYOFF RESULTS
Quarterfinals: Chicago defeated Rangers 4-2
LEADING PLAYOFF SCORER
Rod Gilbert (5-0-5)
STANLEY CUP CHAMPION
Montreal Canadiens

SEASON SNAPSHOT

Most Goals:
Jean Ratelle (32)
Most Assists:
Rod Gilbert (48)
Most Points:
Jean Ratelle (78)
Most Power-Play Goals:
Jean Ratelle (10)
Most Shorthanded Goals:
Reg Fleming (1)
Most Penalty Minutes:
Reg Fleming (132)
Power Play:
46/217, 21.2%, 7 SHGA
Penalty-Killing:
181/223, 81.2%, 1 SHG
Most Wins, Goaltender:
Ed Giacomin (36)
Lowest Goals-Against Average:
Ed Giacomin (2.44)
Most Shutouts:
Ed Giacomin (8)
NHL All-Stars:
Ed Giacomin, G (Second Team);
Jim Neilson, D (Second Team);
Rod Gilbert, RW (Second Team)
Rangers In All-Star Game:
Ed Giacomin, G;
Harry Howell, D;
Don Marshall, LW

The 1967-68 Season in Review

The Rangers bid good-bye to the old Madison Square Garden and said hello to the new one as a team on the rise. They showed their play of the previous season was no fluke by racing off to a 6-1-3 start and playing solid hockey through the rest of the season. Goaltender Ed Giacomin proved that his All-Star form of 1966-67 was no accident, ringing up eight shutouts and posting a 2.44 goals-against average. The offense got a boost from a now-healthy Jean Ratelle. Freed from his back problems, Ratelle blossomed into a star with 32 goals and led the team with 78 points, one more than linemate Rod Gilbert. Ratelle got the last goal in the old Garden, giving the Rangers a 3-3 tie with Detroit on February 11. One week later, the Rangers opened the new Garden with a 3-1 win over Philadelphia,

Jean Ratelle led the Rangers with 32 goals and 78 points. Photo by Ed Sheehan.

and the victories kept coming, as a 12-3-1 finish cemented second place, the Rangers' best showing in a decade. New York won the first two games of its playoff series at home against the Blackhawks, but dropped the next two in Chicago and lost a disheartening 2-1 decision at home in Game 5 when a shot from near center ice by Bobby Schmautz beat Giacomin. The Blackhawks closed out the series at home—but even the loss couldn't diminish the growing feeling that the Rangers were a team headed higher.

MAGIC MOMENT   *February 24, 1968*

Rod Gilbert had the biggest night of his career in his home town.

As a Montreal native, there was no place Rod Gilbert wanted more desperately to play well than at the Forum. On the night of February 24, 1968, Gilbert put on a show that any of the Canadiens' fabled greats would have been proud of. With his hair flying in the breeze, Gilbert ripped four shots past Rogie Vachon as the Rangers routed the Canadiens 6-1, ending Montreal's 20-game unbeaten streak at home. Gilbert pounded a 20-footer past Vachon in the first period, connected twice more in the second and flicked home a loose puck early in the third to join a select group of Rangers ever to score four goals in a road game. He also had an assist for a five-point night while linemate and fellow Montreal-area native Jean Ratelle scored once and set up three of Gilbert's goals. Gilbert finished with 16 shots on goal, an NHL record, and was denied a fifth goal only by the superb work of Vachon. His performance was so brilliant that even the Forum fans, though disappointed with the result, wound up cheering for the local kid who got away.

RANGER LEGEND
Reggie Fleming

Emile Francis got tired of seeing Reggie Fleming belting his players all over the ice—so in January, he sent John McKenzie to the Bruins for the player who, in less than 24 hours prior to the trade, played a key role in Boston's 3-1 win over the Blueshirts at MSG. On January 9, 1966, he was a Ranger. "He's just the type of forward we need," Francis said after the trade. "He's got a lot of brawn and makes good use of it." On a team that historically had been pushed around by bigger, tougher opponents, Fleming's willingness to hit anyone and take on all comers quickly made him a crowd favorite at the Garden. But while Fleming was more than willing to take on any and all challengers, he provided the Rangers

with an enforcer who, as it turned out, could score a bit, too. He had 10 goals in just 35 games after being acquired, then added 15 and 17 goals in his first two full seasons with the Rangers. Not that he forgot the way to the penalty box; Fleming had 122 minutes in penalties in those first 35 games, then added 146, 132 and 138 in the next three seasons. But to Francis, the extra ice his linemates got because Reggie was out there keeping an eye on everyone was at least as important as any puck he ever put into the net. Fleming had been criticized in Chicago, an earlier stop, for taking too many penalties; though he came to New York saying he wanted to prove he was more than just a fighter, Reggie's reputation as a "bad boy" came along with him. Fleming was hit with 540 penalty minutes in only 241 games with the Rangers—a huge total in an era before teams like Boston's "Big Bad Bruins" and Philadelphia's "Broad Street Bullies" began piling up record amounts of penalty time. "I don't look for anybody," he once said of the way he played the game, "but I don't back away from anybody, either."

Reggie Fleming File

- **BORN:**
  April 21, 1936; Montreal, Quebec
- **ACQUIRED:**
  Trade from Boston for John McKenzie, January 10, 1966
- **FIRST SEASON WITH RANGERS:**
  1965-66

- **BEST SEASON WITH RANGERS:**
  1966-67, 61 GP, 15-16-31, 146 PIM
- **TOTALS WITH RANGERS:**
  Regular season: 241 GP, 50-49-99, 540 PIM
  Playoffs: 13 GP, 0-4-4, 22 PIM

CURTAIN CALL
March 3, 1968

Hockey teams don't play doubleheaders. But Garden fans who couldn't get enough of their favorite sport did get a chance to see two NHL games for the price of one on March 3, 1968. With the Philadelphia Flyers homeless because of damage to the Spectrum and a national TV game on tap against Oakland, the contest was moved to the Garden, with fans holding tickets to the Rangers' game that night admitted free (as were Flyer fans with tickets for the game). Amazingly, 12,127 fans showed up on short notice for the 1-1 tie, with most rooting for the underdog Seals. The night game was pretty special, too: Ed Giacomin, facing Chicago for the first time since the Blackhawks blasted him for six goals on November 22, shut out the Hawks 4-0 before a screaming sellout crowd to move into sole possession of second place. The Rangers' checking was so fierce that Giacomin, who had sat while Don Simmons played in the previous four meetings with Chicago, faced only 13 shots as the Rangers won their fifth straight game.

Jean Ratelle and the Rangers beat Chicago in the second game at MSG on March 3, 1968. Photo by T. Makita.

NEW YORK
Ice Exchange

The addition of six new teams saw a number of crowd favorites head out of town. Among the 19 players lost by the Rangers were backup goaltender Cesare Maniago (to Minnesota) and center Earl Ingarfield (to Pittsburgh). Rod Seiling, potentially the most damaging loss, was quickly reacquired by the Rangers in a prearranged trade and finally earned a full-time spot on the blue line. Veteran goaltender Don Simmons joined the Rangers as Ed Giacomin's backup, while former captain and crowd favorite Camille Henry, traded away in 1965, was brought back at midseason. The Rangers got a solid two-way veteran when they landed Ron Stewart, a long-time Maple Leaf, in an early-season deal with St. Louis for Red Berenson, Ron Attwell and Barclay Plager. Stewart helped the Rangers rank among the NHL's best penalty-killing teams over the next few seasons. Garden fans also got a look at the future (and a spelling lesson) when a rugged young center named Walt Tkaczuk played his first two NHL games.

Ron Stewart gave the Rangers a skilled checker and penalty-killer.

—1968  1969—

- **October 10, 1968:**
  The Detroit Tigers rallied from a three-games-to-one deficit to beat the St. Louis Cardinals and win the World Series for the first time since 1945.

- **November 5, 1968:**
  Richard Nixon narrowly defeated Hubert Humphrey to win the presidential election.

- **January 12, 1969:**
  The New York Jets stunned the Baltimore Colts 16-7 in the Super Bowl at Miami's Orange Bowl, giving the AFL its first victory in the title game.

1968-1969
FINAL STANDINGS

East Division	W	L	T	PTS	GF	GA
Montreal	46	19	11	103	271	202
Boston	42	18	16	100	303	221
RANGERS	41	26	9	91	231	196
Toronto	35	26	15	85	234	217
Detroit	33	31	12	78	239	221
Chicago	34	33	9	77	280	246

West Division Winner—St. Louis

PLAYOFF RESULTS
Montreal defeated Rangers 4-0
LEADING PLAYOFF SCORER
Vic Hadfield (2-1-3)
Jim Neilson (0-3-3)
STANLEY CUP CHAMPION
Montreal Canadiens

SEASON SNAPSHOT

Most Goals:
Jean Ratelle (32)
Most Assists:
Rod Gilbert (49)
Most Points:
Jean Ratelle (78)
Most Power-Play Goals:
Bob Nevin (11)
Most Shorthanded Goals:
Ron Stewart (2)
Most Penalty Minutes:
Reg Fleming (138)
Power Play:
56/275, 20.4%, 9 SHGA
Penalty-Killing:
188/223, 84.3%, 4 SHG
Most Wins, Goaltender:
Ed Giacomin (37)
Lowest Goals-Against Average:
Ed Giacomin (2.55)
Most Shutouts:
Ed Giacomin (7)
NHL All-Stars:
Ed Giacomin, G (Second Team)
Rangers In All-Star Game:
Ed Giacomin, G;
Bob Nevin, RW;
Rod Gilbert, RW

The 1968-69 Season in Review

Two years after he talked Bernie Geoffrion back onto the ice as a player, Emile Francis named the Boomer as his successor behind the bench in order to spend more time on his duties as GM. It looked like a perfect marriage for the first eight weeks of the season; the Rangers won 16 of their first 23 games, including a 4-2 victory in Geoffrion's first game as coach in the Montreal Forum on December 4. But then the wheels came off: The Rangers went 0-6-2 in their next eight games and Geoffrion's ulcers began to flare up. He stepped down in mid-January, with Francis returning as coach. The move appeared to revitalize the Rangers, who reeled off a five-game winning streak and wound up a solid third behind Montreal and the surprising Boston Bruins. The pairing of Jean Ratelle and Rod Gilbert again sparked the offense, as the boyhood friends combined for 61 goals and 155 points. There was optimism entering the playoffs against Montreal; in addition to the Rangers' strong finish, they had won the season series from the Canadiens for the first time

Vic Hadfield set new career highs with 26 goals and 66 points. Photo by Ed Sheehan.

since 1947-48. But the defending Stanley Cup champs won the first two games at home and completed the sweep with two wins in the new Madison Square Garden, leaving the Rangers still looking for their first playoff series win since 1950.

MAGIC MOMENT

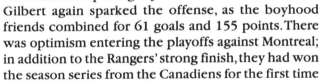
February 23, 1969

Bob Nevin had one of the Rangers' three goals in 38 seconds against Boston. Photo by Barton Silverman.

Just as the Rangers had risen from the rubble of the early '60s to become a contender by decade's end, so had the Boston Bruins—and as the Bruins got better, one of the teams they enjoyed beating was the Rangers. On January 2, 1969, the Bruins practically chased the Rangers out of the Garden, beating them 4-2 and doing their best to physically intimidate the Blueshirts. For the rematch, though, Emile Francis was back at the helm—and it was the Rangers doing the hitting and scoring. Rookies Brad Park and Dennis Hextall notched their first NHL goals, Walt Tkaczuk, Rod Gilbert and Don Marshall each had a pair of goals, and Bob Nevin added one as the Rangers matched the largest shutout victory in their history, 9-0. Nevin, Tkaczuk and Park capped off the celebration by setting a team mark for the fastest three goals, connecting in a 38-second span to seal the rout. Park leaped in the air and landed somewhat ungracefully after finally getting his first goal, then admitted afterward that, "I didn't know what I was doing." The Rangers certainly did.

RANGER LEGEND
Jean Ratelle

The nickname "Gentleman Jean" was a perfect description for Jean Ratelle, the best center in team history between Frank Boucher's retirement to Mark Messier's arrival. Emile Francis, who coached Ratelle in juniors before taking over the Rangers, once said "Ratelle was the closest thing I had ever seen to Jean Beliveau." The analogy was nearly perfect: Both were tall, rangy centers who were good skaters, deft passers, and accurate shooters. Like his boyhood friend and long-time linemate, Rod Gilbert, Ratelle overcame major back surgery to become an NHL star. Ratelle was a 21-goal scorer in 1965-66 on a last-place team, missed nearly half of 1966-67 with back problems, then blossomed into an offensive force, scoring 32 goals in each of three straight seasons. He declined slightly to 26 goals and 72 points in 1970-71, but really broke out in 1971-72, scoring 109 points (still a team record) in only 63 games; a broken ankle suffered when he was hit by Dale Rolfe's slap shot in early March may have cost him the scoring title (he finished third). Many fans also contend it cost the Rangers the Stanley Cup—Ratelle made it back for the finals but was basically ineffective trying to play on one good leg. He never matched his scoring outburst of 1971-72 again, but was still among the NHL's best centers, piling up more than 90 points in two of the next three seasons. Thus, Ranger fans were stunned when Ratelle was sent to Boston in November 1975 in the trade that brought Phil Esposito to the Big Apple; Ratelle went on to play 5 1/2 more seasons in Boston, finishing his 20-year career with an average of nearly a point a game and earning a berth in the Hockey Hall of Fame. Ratelle is still second to Gilbert on the all-time Ranger list for goals (336) and points (817).

Jean Ratelle File

- **BORN:**
  October 3, 1940; Lac St. Jean, Quebec
- **ACQUIRED:**
  Product of Rangers organization
- **FIRST SEASON WITH RANGERS:**
  1960-61
- **BEST SEASON WITH RANGERS:**
  1971-72, 63 GP, 46-63-109, 4 PIM

- **TOTALS WITH RANGERS:**
  Regular season: 862 GP, 336-481-817, 192 PIM
  Playoffs: 65 GP, 9-33-42, 14 PIM
- **HONORS:**
  Masterton Trophy, 1970-71
  Lady Byng Trophy, 1971-72
  Second-team All-Star, 1971-72
  All-Star Game 1969-70, 1970-71, 1971-72, 1972-73
  Players' Player Award, 1967-68, 1968-69, 1969-70, 1970-71, 1974-75
- **NHL MILESTONES:**
  1,281 Games Played; 491 Goals; 776 Assists; 1,267 Points

The Rangers' locker room at the old Madison Square Garden.

Emile Francis was the Rangers' general manager for more than a decade and had three stints as coach.
Photo by Melchior DiGiacamo.

Ed Giacomin became a fan favorite while sparking the revival of the Rangers in the late '60s and early '70s.

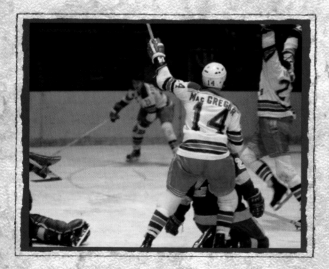

Key acquisitions like Bruce MacGregor (#14) helped the Rangers make the 1972 finals. Photo by Barton Silverman.

Rod Gilbert holds the Rangers' records for goals and points. Photo by George Kalinsky.

Our fans are just as passionate.

Whatever playing field they're on, our lineup of GMC trucks will always inspire spirited applause.
An exciting proposition for up-front fanatics everywhere.

GMC

COMFORTABLY IN COMMAND™

SEE YOUR TRI-STATE
GMC DEALER TODAY

*Chuck Rayner (left) is among more than two dozen
Rangers in the Hockey Hall of Fame.
Photo by George Kalinsky.*

*Three generations of great Rangers goalies (left to right):
Chuck Rayner, Gump Worsley, Gilles Villemure, and Ed Giacomin.*

Phil Esposito was booed
heartily as a Bruin,
but Garden fans grew
to love him. He received
a standing ovation at
his final game.
Photo courtesy of
Jerry Liebman Studio.

Kelly Kisio, a hard-working
two-way center, preceded
Mark Messier as captain.
Photo by Bruce Bennett.

Brian Mullen grew up in New York
and knew the Garden inside and
out before joining the Rangers.
Photo by Bruce Bennett.

McDonald's® salutes the New York Rangers

70 Years on Ice

The McDonald's Owner/Operators of the tri-state area are proud to salute the New York Rangers for 70 years of action and thrills at the Garden. McDonald's appreciates the New York Rangers continued support of the Ronald McDonald House Charities.®

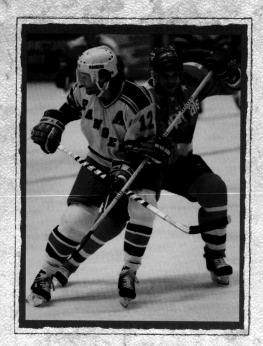

Don Maloney holds the
Rangers' record with nine
game-winning goals in a season.
Photo by Dan Burns.

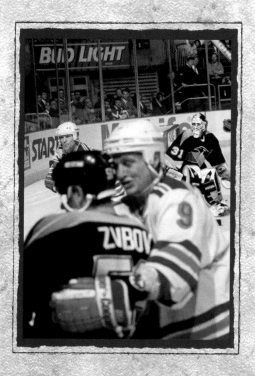

Adam Graves, here battling
ex-Ranger Sergei Zubov, owns
the Rangers' single-season
record with 52 goals.
Photo by Bruce Bennett.

Stephane Matteau's goal beat
the Devils to send the Rangers
to the 1994 finals, triggering a
wild celebration at the Garden.
Photo by Bruce Bennett.

NEW YORK RANGERS

A Proud Tradition

HP congratulates the NY Rangers on a winning tradition.

1994 STANLEY CUP CHAMPIONS

*Craig MacTavish won the final faceoff as
the Rangers ended their Stanley Cup drought.
Photo by Jeffrey Markowitz.*

*Neil Smith's hard work paid off
with a Stanley Cup in 1994.*

The 1994 Stanley Cup Champion New York Rangers.

The Rangers brought the Stanley Cup for a visit to President Clinton.

The Stanley Cup Parade was a day Ranger fans had awaited for more than a half-century. Photo by Jim Leary.

CURTAIN CALL

February 9, 1969

Emile Francis was a goalie during his playing days. But he hadn't played in an NHL game since 1952, when he filled in for the Rangers after Charlie Rayner went down with a knee injury—and hadn't played anywhere since finishing his career in the old Western League in 1960. But when a blizzard struck the New York area Sunday morning, February 9, Francis was ready. With three of his players stranded by the snow and unable to get into Manhattan for that night's game against the Flyers, the 43-year-old Francis made sure he was there early—contract at the ready. With no sign of snowbound starter Ed Giacomin, Francis inked himself to a $1 contract, just in case he might be needed. As it turned out, Francis' role was limited to coaching; backup Don Simmons made his way to the Garden and played as the Rangers rallied for a 3-3 tie in a game that was played in a largely empty Garden. But his preparedness didn't go without notice: "That," wrote columnist Dick Young in the *Daily News*, "explains why Emile Francis IS the manager."

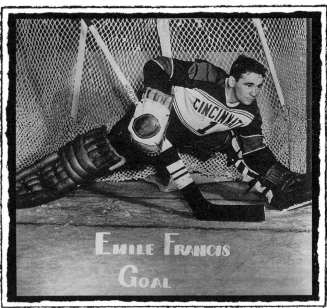

Emile Francis was ready to play if needed when the blizzard hit.

NEW YORK Ice Exchange

Brad Park gave the Rangers an offensive presence on the blue line.

Emile Francis had a lot of the pieces of the puzzle assembled, but one thing he hadn't found was an offensive defenseman— someone who could match the firepower Bobby Orr gave Boston. That all changed when Brad Park, a 21-year-old first-year pro, got the call from Buffalo. Park couldn't match Orr's numbers, but he gave the Rangers a real leader on the back line, a quarterback for the power play and a future star. One of the players who helped Park learn the ropes was veteran Harry Howell, playing his 17th season with the Rangers. But Howell's back was causing him increasing pain; he played only 56 games and was sold to Oakland at the end of the season rather than retire. In what looked like a minor off-season deal, Francis acquired Dave Balon, a former Ranger, from Minnesota. Balon went on to have a pair of 30-goal seasons in New York after being teamed with another new arrival, rookie center Walt Tkaczuk; the third member of the future "Bulldog Line," Bill Fairbairn, had a one-game cup of coffee before sticking for good the next season.

Ranger Lists

Most wins by goaltender, one season

42
Mike Richter, 1993-94
37
Ed Giacomin, 1968-69
36
Ed Giacomin, 1967-68
35
Ed Giacomin, 1969-70
32
Gump Worsley, 1955-56
31
John Vanbiesbrouck, 1985-86
30
Ed Giacomin, 1966-67
30
Ed Giacomin, 1973-74

Ed Giacomin

Ed Giacomin more than paid his dues to get to Broadway. Maybe that's why the Garden faithful related so well to him. After all, how many modern-day Hockey Hall of Famers had their road to immortality make stops in two Eastern League cities and detour for five years in Providence?

It was with the Reds of the AHL that coach Fernie Flaman encouraged Giacomin to work on his stickhandling and puck-handling abilities—traits almost unheard of in a goalie of that era. Still, Giacomin appeared doomed to remaining a minor-league star until Emile Francis stepped in, sending four players to the Reds for the 26-year-old goaltender in the summer of 1965.

There was a starting job to be won, but Giacomin didn't win it immediately. His eagerness to come out of his net and play the puck sometimes got him into trouble while playing behind a last-place team in 1965-66. But a year later, things were different: Giacomin and the Rangers were the toast of the NHL after a hot start put them in first place at Christmas. Both cooled off, but Giacomin still wound up with nine shutouts and a first-team All-Star berth as the Rangers made the playoffs for the first time in five seasons.

Garden fans took to Giacomin. The chants of "Ed-die, Ed-die" echoed through the Garden from the late '60s well into the '70s as Giacomin piled up honors: five straight All-Star berths, six trips to the All-Star Game and the 1971 Vezina Trophy, which he shared with Gilles Villemure.

Giacomin was the last line of

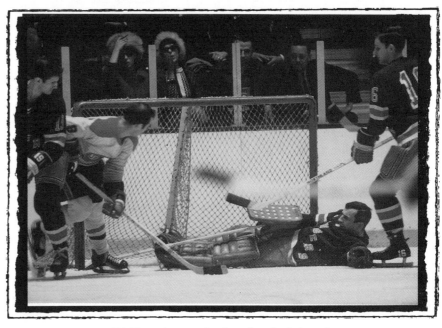

Ed Giacomin stops the Canadiens in their tracks.

defense on some of the best Ranger teams ever—the 1970-71 and 1971-72 squads were among the NHL's elite but could never get past the final hurdle. "Not winning the Stanley Cup is the thing that hurts most," he remembered prior to having his No. 1 retired in 1989, "but I go to outings and stand next to Bill Gadsby, who played 21 seasons and never won a Stanley Cup, and I don't feel so bad."

If there was any doubt about the feelings New York fans had for Giacomin, they were dispelled on the night of November 2, 1975. Two nights earlier, Giacomin had been put on waivers and claimed by Detroit. Now he was back, wearing a Red Wing uniform and facing players who had been his teammates. Giacomin tried hard not to look up at the fans during the National Anthem, perhaps fearing they'd see his tears. When

the puck dropped, much of the crowd rooted for him, not the Rangers. The cheers were for "Eddie, Ed-die," not for the home side. He won the game 6-4—and when Wayne Dillon scored on him, Dillon apologized.

Giacomin finished his career in Detroit in 1978 and was inducted into the Hockey Hall of Fame in 1987. Two years later, Garden fans got one last chance to salute the most popular Ranger goaltender of all time when Giacomin's No. 1 was hoisted to the rafters.

"The warmth I felt from the people that day [of his Garden return] was unbelievable," Giacomin remembered in the *Daily News* a few days before his number was retired. "I said, 'Everybody in this building loves me.'" It has been more than two decades since he left, but that love hasn't disappeared.

—1969 1970—

TIME CAPSULE

- **October 16, 1969:**
  Baseball's loveable losers, the New York Mets, capped one of the most amazing seasons in history by beating the Baltimore Orioles 5-3 to win the World Series in five games.

- **March 18, 1970:**
  The first major postal strike in United States history began.

- **May 8, 1970:**
  The New York Knicks won their first NBA championship, beating Los Angeles 113-99 in Game 7 of the finals at Madison Square Garden. Willis Reed, who missed Game 6 with a leg injury, made a dramatic entrance just prior to the game and inspired the club with a pair of early baskets.

1969-1970
FINAL STANDINGS

East Division	W	L	T	PTS	GF	GA
Chicago	45	22	9	99	250	170
Boston	40	17	19	99	303	221
Detroit	40	21	15	95	246	199
RANGERS	38	22	16	92	246	189
Montreal	38	22	16	92	244	201
Toronto	29	34	13	71	222	242

West Division Winner—St. Louis

PLAYOFF RESULTS

East Semifinals: Boston defeated Rangers 4-2

LEADING PLAYOFF SCORER

Rod Gilbert (4-5-9)

STANLEY CUP CHAMPION

Boston Bruins

SEASON SNAPSHOT

Most Goals:
Dave Balon (33)
Most Assists:
Walt Tkaczuk (50)
Most Points:
Walt Tkaczuk (77)
Most Power-Play Goals:
Jean Ratelle (10)
Most Shorthanded Goals:
Ron Stewart (4)
Most Penalty Minutes:
Dave Balon (100)
Power Play:
52/295, 17.6%, 7 SHGA
Penalty-Killing:
229/269, 85.1%, 7 SHG
Most Wins, Goaltender:
Ed Giacomin (35)
Lowest Goals-Against Average:
Ed Giacomin (2.36)
Most Shutouts:
Ed Giacomin (6)
NHL All-Stars:
Brad Park, D (First Team);
Ed Giacomin, G (Second Team)
Rangers In All-Star Game:
Ed Giacomin, G,
Rod Gilbert, RW

The 1969-70 Season in Review

All of GM/coach Emile Francis' hard work in rebuilding the Rangers finally looked like it would put them over the top in 1969-70. With Ed Giacomin in goal, Brad Park anchoring the defense and three solid lines up front, the Rangers were riding high. They came into Detroit on February 19 in first place at 32-11-11—but left minus Park, who fractured his ankle in the 3-3 tie. Without their defensive leader, the Rangers went into a free fall, going nine games without a win at one point after going the first 60 without losing back-to-back games. The Rangers tumbled out of first place and fell behind Montreal in the race for the last playoff spot in the East. Park returned for the final week of the season, but it looked like that wouldn't be enough when the Blueshirts lost 6-2 at Detroit on the final Saturday of the season. They needed

L. to R. Dave Balon, Walt Tkaczuk and Bill Fairbaim formed the "Bulldog Line".
Photo by Dan Baliotti.

a miracle to get in—and they got one. A 9-5 win over Detroit, combined with Montreal's loss at Chicago, gave the Rangers the last playoff spot on goal differential. But the Rangers appeared drained after their late playoff run: They lost the first two playoff games against Boston, won two emotion-filled games at home, then dropped Games 5 and 6 as the Bruins went on to end their Cup drought—while the Rangers' dry spell reached 30 years.

Magic Moment   April 5, 1970

The Rangers took the ice for the final game of the season knowing they not only had to win to keep their playoff hopes alive, they had to win *big*. Montreal led New York by two points; more importantly, the Canadiens had scored five more goals, meaning that for the Rangers to advance, they had to score early and often. That's just what they did. Rod Gilbert beat Roger Crozier 36 seconds into the game. The Wings tied it at 3:08, but rookie Jack Egers sandwiched two goals around one by Dave Balon to make it 4-1 after one period. Gilbert scored again early in the second period, and now the crowd was euphoric. A pair by Ron Stewart made it 7-3 after two periods; fans began planning to find ways to listen to the Hawks-Canadiens game on radio (one zealot even flew to Chicago for the contest). Balon added two more early in the third for a 9-3 lead, but even that wasn't enough for coach Emile Francis; he pulled Ed Giacomin mid-

Jack Egers had two goals in the Rangers'
miracle comeback.

way through the third period for an extra attacker to try for more. It didn't work; the Red Wings hit the empty net twice. Still, the 9-5 win (behind a team-record 65 shots) put the heat on the Canadiens, who lost 10-2 that night in Chicago, putting the Rangers into the playoffs for the fourth straight year.

As a link between the "Rise of the Rangers" years in the late '60s and the Shero-Patrick-Brooks era of the early 1980s, Walt Tkaczuk holds a unique position in New York hockey lore. It took a while for New York fans to learn how to saw his name: He was TAY-chuk when he came up before the pronunciation was changed to Ka-CHOOK. Either way, he was a major offensive force in his first few seasons, posting 77 and 75 points in his first two full NHL campaigns, leading the club in scoring both times. Though he finished his career with six 20-goal seasons, Tkaczuk never matched his early offensive output again. Instead, he became one of the most valuable two-way centers in the NHL—still capable of contributing offensively, but more intent on preventing the other team's top-scoring center from running wild. The "Bulldog Line," with Bill Fairbairn on the right and Dave Balon (and later Steve Vickers) on the left became a Garden favorite. Tkaczuk was among the hardest players in the NHL to knock off his skates, and his battle with Boston's Phil Esposito in the 1972 finals was a classic, with Tkaczuk helping hold Espo without a goal in the six-game series. Tkaczuk also became one of the NHL's top penalty-killers, teaming with Fairbairn to form one of the league's most effective shorthanded duos for most

Walt Tkaczuk (with Referee Bryan Lewis).

of the 70s. Tkaczuk's offensive numbers declined as his career went on and he was cast in a checking role—ironically, the acquisition of former rival Esposito helped cut into Tkaczuk's offensive production. An eye injury midway through the 1981-82 season forced him to retire, but he's still among the Rangers' all-time leaders in games played (945), goals (227), assists (451) and points (678).

Walt Tkaczuk File

- **BORN:**
  September 29, 1947; Emsdetten, Germany
- **ACQUIRED:**
  Product of Rangers organization
- **FIRST SEASON WITH RANGERS:**
  1967-68
- **BEST SEASON WITH RANGERS:**
  1969-70, 76 GP, 27-50-77, 38 PIM

- **TOTALS WITH RANGERS:**
  Regular Season: 945 GP, 227-451-678, 556 PIM
  Playoffs: 93 GP, 19-32-51, 119 PIM
- **HONORS:**
  All-Star Game, 1969-70
  West Side Assn. Rangers MVP, 1969-70, 1977-78
  Players' Player Award, 1972-73

CURTAIN CALL

Terry Sawchuk

Perhaps the most frustrating part of the early years in Emile Francis' efforts to rebuild the Rangers was the inability to find a goaltender who could give Ed Giacomin a breather—in hopes that Giacomin's play at playoff time would improve. Cesare Maniago, Gilles Villemure and Don Simmons couldn't do the job, so in 1969, Francis turned to goaltending legend Terry Sawchuk, hoping that the NHL's all-time leader in shutouts, could help. But it didn't work out that way, as Giacomin still wound up playing 70 of the 76 games. Sawchuk finished with a 3-1-2 record and a 2.91 goals-against average in just eight regular-season appearances, and lost his only playoff decision. Sawchuk did have one last hurrah: On February 1, he recorded his 103rd and last career shutout as the Rangers blanked Pittsburgh 6-0 at Madison Square Garden. Sawchuk died in an accident during the following off-season and was voted into the Hockey Hall of Fame the following year.

Terry Sawchuk finished his career as a Ranger.

NEW YORK Ice Exchange

Emile Francis knew he had a talented nucleus, especially when defenseman Brad Park showed his rookie season was no fluke. But he kept tinkering, trying to find the rest of the pieces that would add up to a Stanley Cup champion. He added two future Hall of Famers: Terry Sawchuk came from Los Angeles to back up Ed Giacomin in goal and long-time Toronto star Tim Horton added toughness and experience on defense after Park's broken ankle. The Rangers' farm system produced a gem in right wing Bill Fairbairn, a two-way player who scored 22 times and filled out the "Bulldog Line" with Walt Tkaczuk and Dave Balon. Francis also added Ted Irvine, a big, physical winger, from Los Angeles late in the season for youngsters Juha Widing and Real Lemieux. But the addition that excited Rangers fans the most came in the final two weeks, when left wing Jack Egers came up from Omaha. Egers' booming slap shot produced three goals in six games, including two in the season finale, and three more in the playoffs.

Tim Horton added experience on defense.

Ranger Lists

Longest Unbeaten Streaks

19
11/23/39 - 1/13/40

16
2/6/72 - 3/11/72

16
1/7/73 - 2/11/73

14
11/7/69 - 12/10/69

14
10/16/71 - 11/14/71

13
1/3/35 - 2/5/35

11
12/10/31 - 1/5/32

11
2/20/71 - 3/14/71

1970  1971

TIME CAPSULE

- **December 23, 1970:**
  The World Trade Center was topped in New York to become the world's tallest building.

- **January 25, 1971:**
  Charles Manson and three of his followers were convicted of the 1969 murders of actress Sharon Tate and six others.

- **March 11, 1971:**
  Boston's Phil Esposito set the NHL record for goals in a season when he scored his 59th against Los Angeles' Denis DeJordy. Esposito, who became a Ranger in 1975, finished with 76 goals.

1970-1971

FINAL STANDINGS

East Division	W	L	T	PTS	GF	GA
Boston	57	14	7	121	399	207
RANGERS	49	18	11	109	259	177
Montreal	42	23	13	97	291	216
Toronto	37	33	8	82	248	211
Buffalo	24	39	15	63	217	291
Vancouver	24	46	8	56	229	296
Detroit	22	45	11	55	209	308

West Division Winner—Chicago

PLAYOFF RESULTS

Quarterfinals: Rangers defeated Toronto 4-2

Semifinals: Chicago defeated Rangers 4-3

LEADING PLAYOFF SCORER

Vic Hadfield (8-5-13)

STANLEY CUP CHAMPION

Montreal Canadiens

SEASON SNAPSHOT

Most Goals:
Dave Balon (36)

Most Assists:
Walt Tkaczuk (49)

Most Points:
Walt Tkaczuk (75)

Most Power-Play Goals:
Dave Balon (9)

Most Shorthanded Goals:
Ron Stewart (2)

Most Penalty Minutes:
Ted Irvine (137)

Power Play:
60/234, 25.4%, 3 SHGA

Penalty-Killing:
212/253, 83.8%, 5 SHG

Most Wins, Goaltender:
Ed Giacomin (27)

Lowest Goals-Against Average:
Ed Giacomin (2.16)

Most Shutouts:
Ed Giacomin (8)

NHL Award Winners:
Ed Giacomin/Gilles Villemure (Vezina Trophy)
Jean Ratelle (Masterton Trophy)
Bill Jennings (Lester Patrick Trophy)

NHL All-Stars:
Ed Giacomin, G (First Team)
Brad Park, D (Second Team)

Rangers In All-Star Game:
Ed Giacomin, G; Gilles Villemure, G; Brad Park, D;
Jim Neilson, D; Dave Balon, LW; Jean Ratelle, C

The 1970-71 Season in Review

It was a season for the record books. The Rangers set 15 team records and finished with 109 points, still the second-highest total in team history—though still only good enough for second place in the East behind the powerful Boston Bruins. Goalie Ed Giacomin, who had carried the load himself for most of the past four seasons, was aided by the permanent arrival of Gilles Villemure and posted his best season with a 2.16 goals-against average and eight shutouts in just 45 games. Villemure, Giacomin's roommate on the road, added four more shutouts and a 2.30 average. The result was the Rangers' first Vezina Trophy since Dave Kerr won it in 1939-40. The Rangers made Madison Square Garden the most inhospitable place in the NHL for visitors, going 24 games before losing at home and setting a team mark with only two Garden losses. The Rangers downed Toronto in six games in the opening round to win a playoff series for the first time since 1950, taking the clincher on Bob Nevin's overtime goal. Pete Stemkowski was a hero for the Rangers in the semis against Chicago, scoring a pair of overtime goals—including a triple-overtime tally at the Garden that sent the series to a seventh game. But the Rangers couldn't hold a 2-1 lead at Chicago Stadium, and the 4-2 loss provided a too-soon

Dave Balon had a career year with 36 goals in 1970-71.

ending to the best season in team history—while serving notice that they would be a power to be reckoned with next season.

MAGIC MOMENT

April 29, 1971

The Rangers' record-setting season appeared headed for an untimely ending early in Game 6 of the semifinals against Chicago. The Blackhawks, riding the momentum gained from an overtime win in Game 5, jumped out to a 2-0 lead when Dennis Hull connected midway through the first period and Chico Maki beat Ed Giacomin 1:54 into the second. But the Rangers refused to quit. Rod Gilbert's goal with 7:07 gone in the middle period gave them life and Jean Ratelle's tally early in the third period sent the game into overtime. The Blackhawks appeared to have the game won when Bill White's shot off the post came out to a wide-open Stan Mikita—who hit the other post ("I should have just slid it in," Mikita remembers). The Rangers' longest game in 33 years went on into a third overtime before coming to a sud-

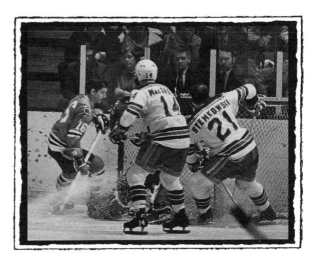

Pete Stemkowski's triple OT goal beats Chicago. Photo by Paul Bereswill.

den conclusion: Ted Irvine raced in and fired Tim Horton's dump-in at Tony Esposito. Espo stopped it, but Pete Stemkowski tucked in the rebound at 1:29 for one of the most famous wins in Rangers history, setting off a wild celebration and sending the series to a seventh game.

RANGER LEGEND
Gilles Villemure

It took Gilles Villemure four tries to stick in New York, but his arrival and the Rangers' emergence into the NHL's elite were no coincidence. Villemure got his first taste of the NHL in 1963-64, when he played five games as a 23-year-old. He also had brief callups in 1967-68 (when he notched his first NHL shutout) and 1968-69, but spent most of his time in the minors before GM Emile Francis, seeking to cut Ed Giacomin's workload after a couple of disappointing playoffs, promoted Villemure, now 30, from Buffalo of the AHL, where he had won two straight MVP awards. The move worked perfectly: Giacomin re-

Photo by Bruce Bennett.

corded his best season with a 2.16 goals-against average and eight shutouts, while Villemure proved to be no night off for opposing shooters, posting a 2.30 goals-against average and four shutouts. The total of 12 shutouts were the most posted by the Rangers since 1928-29, when John Ross Roach had 13 during a much less offensively-minded era. The goaltending tandem produced the Rangers' first Vezina Trophy in 31 years and their first playoff series victory since 1950. One season later, they led the Rangers to the finals in 1971-72. Giacomin and Villemure were such a good team that both were named to play in the 1971 and 1973 All-Star Games, the only times one team has ever placed two goaltenders in the midseason classic. Villemure's stand-up play was a perfect complement to Giacomin's acrobatic style, as the two formed one of the NHL's most effective pairings through the first half of the 1970s. Villemure, whose off-season passion was harness racing, was dealt to Chicago after the 1974-75 season for Doug Jarrett, finishing his Ranger career with a superb 2.62 goals-against average and 13 shutouts.

Gilles Villemure File

- **BORN:**
  May 30, 1940, Trois Rivieres, Quebec
- **ACQUIRED:**
  Product of Rangers organization
- **FIRST SEASON WITH RANGERS:**
  1963-64
- **BEST SEASON WITH RANGERS:**
  1971-72, 24-7-4, 2.09 goals-against average, 3 shutouts

- **TOTALS WITH RANGERS:**
  Regular season: 184 GP, 96-54-21, 2.62 goals-against average, 13 shutouts
  Playoffs: 14 GP, 5-5, 2.93 goals-against average, 0 shutouts
- **HONORS:**
  Vezina Trophy (shared with Ed Giacomin), 1970-71
  All-Star Game, 1970-71, 1972-73, 1973-74

CURTAIN CALL
Frank Paice

The 1970-71 season was Rangers trainer Frank Paice's 25th season in New York, earning the Montreal native an award for "Long And Meritorious Service To New York Hockey" from local hockey writers. Paice actually started his career as a stickboy for visiting teams at the Montreal Forum. Two years later, he became the stickboy for the old Montreal Maroons and remained with the team in various capacities until the club folded in 1938. He served in the Canadian Air Force during World War II, then joined the Eastern League's New York Rovers, a Ranger farm club, as trainer in 1946. Two years later, he was promoted to the Rangers—and remained with the team for 29 years, spanning the eras from the old six-team NHL through expansion and the WHA, and from the old Madison Square Garden to the new before retiring in 1977.

Frank Paice served as the Rangers' trainer for 29 seasons.

NEW YORK
Ice Exchange

With the Rangers' farm system producing a bumper crop of young talent, GM Emile Francis began to use it to fill in some of the holes on the parent club, mostly by dealing with Detroit. Center Pete Stemkowski came from the Wings in October for defenseman Larry Brown—who came back to the Rangers three months later, along with forward Bruce MacGregor, a fine skater and penalty-killer, in a deal that sent popular defenseman Arnie Brown and two youngsters to Detroit. MacGregor and Stemkowski teamed with Ted Irvine to form an excellent third line. Dale Rolfe, a perfect complement for Brad Park on the back line, was lifted from the Wings

Dale Rolfe was one of several players acquired from Detroit in 1970-71.

in March for young forward Jim Krulicki. Francis picked up another usable checker midway through the season when he sent Syl Apps, whose path at center was blocked by the likes of Jean Ratelle and Walt Tkaczuk, to Pittsburgh for pesky winger Glen Sather, who quickly became a fan favorite.

Ranger Lists

Vezina Trophy Winners

Dave Kerr
1939-40

**Ed Giacomin/
Gilles Villemure**
1970-71

John Vanbiesbrouck
1985-86

(Note: Trophy awarded to primary goaltender(s) of team allowing fewest goals through 1980-81; now an award voted by NHL general managers to the league's top goaltender.)

—1971  1972—

TIME CAPSULE

- **September 21, 1971:**
  Baseball's Washington Senators announced that the franchise would move to Arlington, Texas for the 1972 season.

- **February 21, 1972:**
  President Richard Nixon began his historic visit to mainland China.

- **May 26, 1972:**
  Soviet leader Leonid Brezhnev and President Nixon signed a treaty on antiballistic missile systems.

1971-1972
FINAL STANDINGS

East Division	W	L	T	PTS	GF	GA
Boston	54	13	11	119	330	204
RANGERS	48	17	13	109	317	192
Montreal	46	16	16	108	307	205
Toronto	33	31	14	80	209	208
Detroit	33	35	10	76	261	262
Buffalo	16	43	19	51	203	289
Vancouver	20	50	8	48	203	297

West Division Winner—Chicago

PLAYOFF RESULTS
Quarterfinals: Rangers defeated Montreal 4-2

Semifinals: Rangers defeated Chicago 4-0

Finals: Boston defeated Rangers 4-2

LEADING PLAYOFF SCORER
Bobby Rousseau (6-11-17)

STANLEY CUP CHAMPION
Boston Bruins

SEASON SNAPSHOT

Most Goals:
Vic Hadfield (50)
Most Assists:
Jean Ratelle (63)
Most Points:
Jean Ratelle (109)
Most Power-Play Goals:
Vic Hadfield (23)
Most Shorthanded Goals:
Bill Fairbairn (4)
Most Penalty Minutes:
Vic Hadfield (142)
Power Play:
60/257, 23.3%, 10 SHGA
Penalty-Killing:
238/282, 84.4%, 14 SHG
Most Wins, Goaltender:
Ed Giacomin/Gilles Villemure (24)
Lowest Goals-Against Average:
Gilles Villemure (2.09)
Most Shutouts:
Gilles Villemure (3)
Award Winners:
Jean Ratelle (Lady Byng Trophy)
NHL All-Stars:
Rod Gilbert, RW (First Team)
Brad Park, D (First Team)
Jean Ratelle, C (Second Team)
Vic Hadfield, LW (Second Team)
Rangers In All-Star Game:
Gilles Villemure, G; Brad Park, D;
Rod Seiling, D; Jean Ratelle, C;
Vic Hadfield, LW; Rod Gilbert, RW

The 1971-72 Season in Review

Almost from the start, it was obvious that 1971-72 was going to be a special season. An early 11-0-3 roll, highlighted by a record-setting 12-1 crushing of the California Golden Seals, moved the Rangers into first place in the East Division, where they stayed until late January. The trio of Jean Ratelle between Vic Hadfield and Rod Gilbert became the league's most feared line, quickly earning the sobriquet "GAG (Goal-A-Game) Line" and later the "TAG (Two-A-Game) Line." Boston passed them, but the Rangers stayed right on the tail of the front-running Bruins until disaster hit on March 1, when Ratelle's ankle was broken by teammate Dale Rolfe's shot during a routine 4-1 win over the Seals. That ended all hopes of catching Boston, but the Rangers still matched their team-record point total of 109, set the year before. They capped their highest-scoring regular season ever when Hadfield scored his team-record 49th and 50th goals in the season finale against Montreal on national television. The Rangers ousted defending

Jean Ratelle set a team record in 1971-72 with 109 points. Photo by Jerry Liebman.

champion Montreal in six games, then swept the Western Conference champion Blackhawks in four straight to earn their first trip to the finals since 1950. But the injury to Ratelle finally took its toll against Boston, which eliminated the Rangers in six games.

MAGIC MOMENT *April 23, 1972*

The Rangers went through their first 46 seasons without recording a sweep in a best-of-seven series. There was no sign that would change as they entered the semifinals for a return match against Chicago, which had beaten them in seven games a year earlier. But the Rangers, playing without Jean Ratelle and facing the prospect of playing the first two games in Chicago Stadium, reacted like champions. A 3-2 win in the opener and a 5-2 triumph in Game 2 sent the Rangers back home looking for the kill. Dale Rolfe's goal made the difference in a 3-2 victory in Game 3, setting up a Sunday night Rangers fans had been dreaming of for years. Bobby Hull gave the Blackhawks an early lead, but the Rangers scored three times before Pat Stapleton scored to make it a one-goal game again. But Vic Hadfield connected at 16:25 and Gene Carr, mired in a season-long slump, lit up the Garden with a spectacular goal for a 5-2 margin. Bobby Rousseau's third-period goal was icing on the cake as the Rangers completed the first 4-0 sweep in their history and earned a trip to the finals for the first time in 22 years.

Rod Gilbert and Vic Hadfield led the sweep over Chicago. Photo by Barton Silverman.

RANGER LEGEND
Vic Hadfield

No one paid much attention when the Rangers took Vic Hadfield from Chicago in the 1961 waiver draft. The big left wing bounced back and forth between the parent club and the minors until making his mark in 1963-64 by leading the NHL with 151 penalty minutes. Hadfield hadn't shown a whole lot offensively in his early years with the Blueshirts, but armed with a curved stick and a fearsome slap shot, he began making goalies nervous, hitting the 20-goal mark for four straight seasons. Expectations for Hadfield kept growing, and he showed he was ready for the next step in the 1971 playoffs, tying a team record with eight goals, including a hat trick against Toronto, and setting the team points mark with 13. When Bob Nevin was dealt to Minnesota that summer, Hadfield was named captain—and seldom has a player ever responded better to an increase in responsibility. With Jean Ratelle in the middle and Rod Gilbert on his right, Hadfield turned into the Rangers' first 50-goal scorer while forming one-third of the NHL's best line, a unit that amassed a franchise-record 312 points. The last two goals came on the final day

Vic Hadfield was the first Ranger to score 50 goals.

of the season at the Garden in a national TV game against Montreal. With Ratelle and Gilbert setting him up, Hadfield set a team mark that still stands with 23 power-play goals while earning second-team All-Star honors, then excelled again in the postseason as the Rangers made their first trip to the finals in 22 years. Hadfield couldn't keep up that kind of production; he dropped off to 28 and 27 goals in the two following seasons before being dealt to Pittsburgh, but his place in the hearts of Rangers fans remains bright. He wound up with 262 goals and 572 points (as well as 1,036 penalty minutes) to show for his 13 seasons in the Big Apple.

Vic Hadfield File

- **BORN:**
  October 4, 1940; Oakville, Ontario
- **ACQUIRED:**
  Drafted from Chicago, June 1961
- **FIRST SEASON WITH RANGERS:**
  1961-62
- **BEST SEASON WITH RANGERS:**
  1971-72, 78 GP, 50-56-102, 142 PIM

- **TOTALS WITH RANGERS:**
  Regular season: 839 GP, 262-310-572, 1,036 PIM
  Playoffs: 61 GP, 22-19-41, 104 PIM
- **HONORS:**
  Second-team All-Star, 1971-72
  Players' Player Award, 1971-72
- **NHL MILESTONES:**
  1,002 Games Played

CURTAIN CALL
Bill Chadwick

Bill Chadwick was well-known to New York hockey fans before he ever picked up a microphone. Born in the Big Apple, Chadwick went on to a Hall of Fame career as a referee despite losing the sight in one eye in an on-ice accident that ended his dreams of reaching the NHL as a player. Chadwick invented and perfected the hand signals officials use to indicate penalties and was the first American to make it big in the NHL as an official. As the Rangers returned to the spotlight in the late '60s and early '70s, a whole new generation of New York hockey fans came to know Chadwick as a colorful, sometimes caustic, but always lively analyst, first on radio with Marv Albert (who dubbed him "The Big Whistle," a tag that stuck), then on Channel 9 and the MSG Network, where he worked mostly with play-by-play man Jim Gordon into the early 1980s.

Bill Chadwick had a Hall of Fame career as a referee before becoming a broadcaster.

NEW YORK
Ice Exchange

Bobby Rousseau led the Rangers in playoff scoring.

GM Emile Francis knew he had to do some tinkering after 1971's heartbreaking semifinal loss to Chicago. He needed someone from a winning background—and as a veteran of the Montreal Canadiens, Bobby Rousseau knew what it took to win. Montreal had sent Rousseau to Minnesota in 1970, and the Rangers got him a year later for Bob Nevin, whose production had fallen off. Rousseau contributed 21 goals along with superb special-teams play, then led the team in playoff scoring. Francis' other major move didn't turn out as well. Impressed with blond-tressed rookie Gene Carr during an early-season meeting with St. Louis, Francis traded off some of the Rangers' top young talent to get him. Carr had blazing speed, but never found the scoring touch the Rangers had hoped for—his biggest contribution was limiting Montreal speedster Yvan Cournoyer to a pair of goals in the Rangers' first-round playoff win.

Ranger Lists

Most Points, One Season

109
Jean Ratelle, 1971-72
107
Mark Messier, 1991-92
106
Vic Hadfield, 1971-72
103
Mike Rogers, 1981-82
102
Brian Leetch, 1991-92
99
Mark Messier, 1995-96
97
Rod Gilbert, 1971-72
97
Rod Gilbert, 1974-75
94
Jean Ratelle, 1972-73
91
Jean Ratelle, 1974-75
91
Mark Messier, 1992-93

—1972 1973—

TIME CAPSULE

- **October 10, 1973:**
  The New York Mets beat the Cincinnati Reds 7-2 in the fifth and deciding game of the National League playoffs; with an 82-79 record, the Mets became the poorest regular-season finisher to win a pennant in either league.

- **November 7, 1972:**
  The Republican Party enjoyed the biggest landslide in its history as Richard Nixon was reelected president over George McGovern.

- **May 10, 1973:**
  The New York Knicks beat the Los Angeles Lakers 102-93 to win the NBA title in five games, avenging a loss to L.A. the year before.

1972-1973

FINAL STANDINGS

East Division	W	L	T	PTS	GF	GA
Montreal	52	10	16	120	329	184
Boston	51	22	5	107	330	235
RANGERS	47	23	8	102	297	208
Buffalo	37	27	14	88	257	219
Detroit	37	29	12	86	265	243
Toronto	27	41	10	64	247	279
Vancouver	22	47	9	53	233	339
NY Islanders	12	60	6	30	170	347

West Division Winner—Chicago

PLAYOFF RESULTS
Quarterfinals: Rangers defeated Boston 4-2
Semifinals: Chicago defeated Rangers 4-1

LEADING PLAYOFF SCORERS
Walt Tkaczuk (7-2-9) Steve Vickers (5-4-9)
Jean Ratelle (2-7-9) Bill Fairbairn (1-8-9)

STANLEY CUP CHAMPION
Montreal Canadiens

SEASON SNAPSHOT

Most Goals:
Jean Ratelle (41)
Most Assists:
Rod Gilbert (59)
Most Points:
Jean Ratelle (94)
Most Power-Play Goals:
Jean Ratelle (11)
Most Shorthanded Goals:
Bill Fairbairn (2)
Most Penalty Minutes:
Dale Rolfe (74)
Power Play:
54/238, 22.7%, 5 SHGA
Penalty-Killing:
211/250, 84.4%, 5 SHG
Most Wins, Goaltender:
Ed Giacomin (26)
Lowest Goals-Against Average:
Gilles Villemure (2.29)
Most Shutouts:
Ed Giacomin (4)
NHL Award Winners:
Steve Vickers (Calder Trophy)
NHL All-Stars:
Brad Park, D (Second Team)
Rangers In All-Star Game:
Ed Giacomin, G;
Gilles Villemure, G;
Brad Park, D,
Jean Ratelle, C

Coming off a trip to the finals, Rangers fans were expecting big things in 1972-73—especially when GM Emile Francis met the fledgling WHA's challenge head-on by paying to keep his stars while Boston lost goalie Gerry Cheevers and forward Johnny McKenzie to the upstart league. Though the goals didn't come as easily as they had the previous season, the Rangers used an early 12-1-1 streak to get into a three-way race with Montreal and Boston. A 16-game unbeaten streak that included 10 straight wins (including three straight 6-0 shutouts) kept the heat on Montreal for a while, but the Canadiens pulled away, leaving the Rangers to battle Boston for second. The Rangers appeared to have it locked up, only to end with an 0-4-1 slide and see the Bruins, behind the goaltending of Jacques Plante, edge past them, earning home-ice advantage for their return match in the opening round of the playoffs. But the Rangers made short work of the defending champs, winning three times in Boston and routing Plante on the way to a five-game triumph. Hopes were even

Brad Park was an All-Star for the fourth straight year. Photo by Paul Bereswill.

higher when the Rangers opened the semifinals with an easy win in Chicago, but the Hawks got even by winning Game 2, then stunned sellout crowds at the Garden with two more victories before avenging the previous spring's sweep in five games.

MAGIC MOMENT

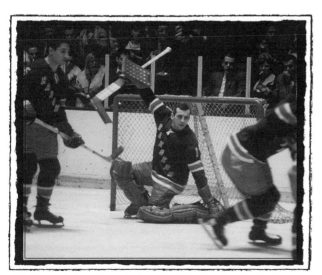

Ed Giacomin had his only playoff shutout vs. Boston.

Ed Giacomin entered the 1973 playoffs with 43 regular-season shutouts, but he had yet to hold an opponent scoreless in his 43 postseason contests. He didn't figure to do so in Game 4 of the quarterfinals, either—not with regulars like Dale Rolfe and Vic Hadfield sidelined with injuries the previous night. But instead of complaining, the Rangers attacked, shutting down Boston and racing to a 2-0 lead on goals by Rod Gilbert and Pete Stemkowski. Bobby Rousseau and Steve Vickers made it 4-0 after two periods. Then it was Giacomin's turn. Fast Eddie kept the Bruins at bay in the third period, even though three penalties gave Boston 4:35 of consecutive power-play time, including a pair of two-man advantages. Not even a whack across the neck from Carol Vadnais could deter Giacomin. A few minutes later, he was accepting the congratulations of his teammates and the plaudits of the crowd. It was the first (and only) playoff shutout of his career—and the first by a Ranger since Chuck Rayner blanked Montreal to close out the semifinals on April 6, 1950.

RANGER LEGEND
Steve Vickers

It's usually pretty hard for a rookie to earn a regular berth on a veteran team that's just been to the Stanley Cup finals, but Steve Vickers made it look easy. Blessed with strength and an excellent scoring touch, "Sarge" needed only one season in the minors before cracking the lineup of a team coming off a trip to the championship round. Vickers earned a spot as the left wing on the "Bulldog Line" and wasted little time showing that he belonged in the NHL; less than two months into his first season, he became the first player in league history ever to record back-to-back hat tricks. Despite missing 15 games with injuries, he finished the season as the first Ranger rookie to score 30 goals in a season. That was enough to earn him the Calder Trophy as the NHL's top rookie, an award no Ranger had won for nearly two decades. Vickers showed his first NHL season was no fluke by getting 34 goals in his second season; playing on the left side with Jean Ratelle and Rod Gilbert in 1974-75, he connected for 41 goals and earned a second-team All-Star berth. Vickers added 30 goals in 1975-76 and set a Ranger record by ringing up seven points (three goals and four assists) in a game against Washington on February 18, 1976. He also set a team record for accuracy when he rebounded from three subpar seasons with a 29-goal campaign in 1979-80—scoring his 29 goals on just 98 shots, a 29.6 shooting percentage that eclipsed the mark set during the previous season by Ulf Nilsson. Vickers excelled in converting rebounds, and Garden fans knew that when Vickers set up in his "office," just outside the crease, good things were likely to happen. Vickers averaged nearly 25 goals per season in his decade with the Rangers and is among the top 10 on the team's all-time list in goals, assists and points.

Steve Vickers File

- **BORN:**
  April 21, 1951; Toronto, Ontario
- **ACQUIRED:**
  Rangers first-round pick in 1971 Entry Draft
- **FIRST SEASON WITH RANGERS:**
  1972-73
- **BEST SEASON WITH RANGERS:**
  1974-75, 80 GP, 41-48-89, 64 PIM

- **TOTALS WITH RANGERS:**
  Regular season: 689 GP, 246-340-586, 330 PIM
  Playoffs: 56 GP, 20-18-38, 44 PIM
- **HONORS:**
  Calder Trophy, 1972-73
  Second-team All-Star, 1974-75
  All-Star Game, 1974-75, 1975-76

CURTAIN CALL
Hockey Expands in New York

For the first time since 1942, there was more than one New York hockey team. Expansion brought the New York Islanders into the NHL. With Long Island always a hotbed of Ranger rooters, there was the promise of an intense rivalry once the newcomers improved; for the first season, though, the Rangers swept all six meetings, ending with a pair of 6-0 shutouts in February. Part of the Islanders' problem was the fact that they had been plundered by the brand-new World Hockey Association. Fans who couldn't get Ranger tickets (as hard then as it is now) could see former Ranger star Camille Henry behind the bench of the New York Raiders, the WHA's entry in the Big Apple. The Raiders started well, but ran out of scoring down the stretch and missed the playoffs. The biggest loser was Henry, who had dreams of coming back to the Rangers as coach and figured the WHA might be a shortcut. It wasn't; the Raiders had to abandon the Garden the next season and wound up in Cherry Hill, N.J. Henry never coached again, unable to understand why the players of a later era didn't love the game the way he did.

The Rangers went 6-0 vs. their new local rivals, the Islanders, in 1972-73.

NEW YORK
Ice Exchange

With Dave Balon now gone from the left side of the "Bulldog Line," Steve Vickers got a chance to play—and made the most of it. The first-year left wing rang up 30 goals on the way to the Calder Trophy as the NHL's top rookie. Aside from Vickers, though, the Rangers generally went with the team that had gone to the finals the year before—at least until injuries started to take their toll, particularly on defense. The Rangers added Ron Harris, a defenseman who could also play up front, for some toughness. They also gave some playing time to promising rookie blueliners like Lawrence Sacharuk and Randy Legge. Young forwards like Mike Murphy, Jerry Butler and Curt Bennett, also made their NHL debuts. In the first transaction between New York's old and new clubs, the Rangers also sold veteran right wing Ron Stewart to the Islanders; the two clubs still have never made a player-for-player deal.

Ron Stewart was the first player to go from the Rangers to the Islanders. Photo by Paul Bereswill.

Rod Gilbert

The sign hanging at Madison Square Garden on March 9, 1977 said it all. "Rod Gilbert: No. 7 on the ice, No. 1 in our hearts."

Few New York athletes in any sport have connected with Big Apple fans the way Gilbert did. From his first big night in the NHL, when he scored two goals in a playoff game against Toronto in 1962, to his present job as the Rangers' director of community relations, Gilbert and New York have been inseparable.

The numbers show that Gilbert is the highest-scoring player in Rangers history: the only one with more than 400 goals and 1,000 points. What they don't show is the bond he enjoyed with those who watched him.

"I love being a hockey player," he remembered a few days before Rod Gilbert Night in March 1977. "I love New York. It's the greatest city in the world. But you have to give love to be loved. It's that way with people. It's that way with New York City."

Gilbert loved New York; he moved into Manhattan in the mid-1960s, when most of the team lived on Long Island. Off the ice, he earned a reputation as one of New York's most eligible bachelors for more than a decade before marrying in the early '70s. But on the ice, he earned a different reputation: as a speedy right wing with a rocket shot who would

Vic Hadfield (11), Jean Ratelle (19) and Rod Gilbert formed the "GAG Line," one of the most potent units in Rangers history. Photo by Barton Silverman.

Rod Gilbert became the Rangers' all-time leading goal scorer when he notched number 273. Photo by Bob Glass.

become a Hall of Famer.

His career nearly derailed in 1965-66, when he underwent a second spinal fusion operation. That cost him half a season, but he rebounded in 1966-67 with 28 goals and had back-to-back 77-point seasons as the Rangers rose toward the top of the NHL.

He finally hit the 30-goal mark in 1970-71, but that was just a warmup for the greatest season any Ranger line ever put together. Gilbert, boyhood friend Jean Ratelle and left wing Vic Hadfield spent 1971-72 filling the net like no line in Ranger history. Ratelle had 109 points despite missing the last month of the season with a broken ankle, Hadfield became a 50-goal scorer and Gilbert erupted for 43 goals and 97 points, setting a team scoring record for right wings and winning the nod as a first-team All-Star.

Cleveland of the fledgling World Hockey Association chased him with a five-year contract worth $300,000 annually, but Rod opted to stay in New York. Hartford came calling in 1975 with another big-bucks offer, but "it was the same story," Gilbert

remembered. "I wanted to stay in New York."

As the Rangers' fortunes waned in the mid-1970s, Gilbert was the last link to the powerhouse teams of earlier in the decade. Unlike the stars he played with—Ratelle, Brad Park, Ed Giacomin and Vic Hadfield—he remained a Ranger to the end.

Rod Gilbert Night on March 9, 1977, was an emotional affair. "My friends, and I think all of you here tonight are my friends, you have given me a home, friendship, respect and love, and that's more important than fame," he told the sellout crowd at the Garden. "For these things, I will always be grateful."

Gilbert then went out and scored a goal to help the Rangers beat Minnesota; he finished the season with 75 points in 77 games. But when he got off to a slow start in 1977-78, GM John Ferguson, an old rival from their playing days, released him, ending his days as a player. Gilbert has worked in a variety of posts for the Rangers since then. He's still the team's highly visible symbol of class and dignity.

—1973 1974—

TIME CAPSULE

- **December 6, 1973:**
  Gerald Ford was sworn in as vice president after Spiro Agnew's resignation on October 10.

- **April 8, 1974:**
  Hank Aaron hit his record-breaking 715th home run, topping Babe Ruth's career mark of 714.

- **August 8, 1974:**
  President Richard M. Nixon announced his resignation in a televised address. Gerald Ford was sworn in the next day.

1973-1974

FINAL STANDINGS

East Division	W	L	T	PTS	GF	GA
Boston	52	17	9	113	349	221
Montreal	45	24	9	99	293	240
RANGERS	40	24	14	94	300	251
Toronto	35	27	16	86	274	230
Buffalo	32	34	12	76	242	250
Detroit	29	39	10	68	255	319
Vancouver	24	43	11	59	224	296
Islanders	19	41	18	56	182	247

West Division Winner—Philadelphia

PLAYOFF RESULTS

Quarterfinals: Rangers defeated Montreal 4-2
Semifinals: Philadelphia defeated Rangers 4-3

LEADING PLAYOFF SCORERS

Pete Stemkowski (6-6-12)
Brad Park (4-8-12)

STANLEY CUP CHAMPION

Philadelphia Flyers

SEASON SNAPSHOT

Most Goals:
Rod Gilbert (36)
Most Assists:
Brad Park (57)
Most Points:
Brad Park (82)
Most Power-Play Goals:
Rod Gilbert (16)
Most Shorthanded Goals:
Walt Tkaczuk/Bill Fairbairn (3)
Most Penalty Minutes:
Brad Park (148)
Power Play:
66/222, 29.7%, 2 SHGA
Penalty Killing:
45/239, 81.2%, 9 SHG
Most Wins, Goaltender:
Ed Giacomin (30)
Lowest Goals-Against Average:
Ed Giacomin (3.07)
Most Shutouts:
Ed Giacomin (5)
NHL All-Stars:
Brad Park, D, (First Team)
Rangers In All-Star Game:
Brad Park, D

The 1973-74 Season Review

After starting out 3-0-1, the Rangers went on a seven-game winless skid (0-6-1). Then, they caught fire, and before it was extinguished, they had lost only three of 22 games (12-3-7). But new head coach Larry Popein found out that even a run like that wasn't enough, because the Rangers lost five of their next eight, and after a 7-2 loss in Buffalo on January 10, he was replaced. So after watching 41 games since giving up the coaching reins, GM Emile Francis put his coaching hat back on. Did it help? Did it help! The Blueshirts lost just twice in 22 games (17-2-3), including winning streaks of five and eight games, before they came back to earth, losing eight of their last 15 before hitting the playoff trail. Two players had career highs in scoring: Brad Park with 25 goals and 82 points (both team records for defensemen), and Pete Stemkowski, with 25 and 70, respectively. Ed Giacomin appeared in 56 games, winning 30 and posting five shutouts. After beating Montreal in

Pete Stemkowski had his best season as a Ranger with 25 goals and 70 points. Photo by Barton Silverman.

six games in the quarterfinals, the Rangers ran into a brick wall known as the Philadelphia Flyers, and lost a seven-game series in which the home team won every game. The seventh game was a heartbreaker; the Rangers led early but the Flyers, sparked by Dave Schultz, the pugilistic leader of the "Broad Street Bullies," wound up with a 4-3 victory that put them into the finals, where they upset the Boston Bruins to win the Stanley Cup.

MAGIC MOMENT — *April 16, 1974*

Just as they had two years earlier, the Rangers and Montreal Canadiens split the first four games of their opening-round playoff series. The fifth game, played at the Montreal Forum, finished up with the type of drama that makes playoff hockey great. The Canadiens took a 1-0 lead when Henri Richard scored 49 seconds into the game. New York's Bruce MacGregor tied the game at 12:43. After a scoreless second period, the Rangers were controlling play in the third when Murray Wilson scored at 5:24 to put the Canadiens ahead 2-1. The game came down to the final minute, and with Ed Giacomin pulled for a sixth attacker, MacGregor got the Rangers even with 16 seconds left in regulation. To cap the comeback, Pete Stemkowski won a draw in the Canadiens' end early in overtime and sent a pass to Ron Harris, a defenseman playing right wing. Harris one-timed a bullet past Montreal

Ron Harris' OT goal helped the Rangers beat Montreal.

goalie Bunny Larocque, and the Rangers took a commanding 3-2 lead in the series, which they wrapped up at home two nights later. It was the second straight playoff series between these two teams that the Blueshirts won, both times ending the Canadiens' reign as Stanley Cup champions.

RANGER LEGEND
Brad Park

Forever inexorably linked to comparisons with Bobby Orr, Brad Park managed to forge his own identity with the Rangers—despite the constant comparisons. While playing defense, Park had a knack for joining the rush at the right time, a skill Orr had popularized. Park could shoot, pass and skate as well as any forward, but could also play solid positional hockey and throw as mean a hip check as any defensive-minded rearguard. Park made his debut as a Ranger during the 1968-69 season after being drafted second overall from Toronto of the OHA in 1966. He scored his first NHL goal on February 23 in a 9-0 romp over the Bruins at home, and wound up his rookie season with three goals and 23 assists in 54 games. Assorted knee and ankle problems only allowed Park to play one complete and injury-free season (1973-74), and that year he led the team in scoring (25-57-82). Park was also brutally honest, as coach/GM Emile Francis found out. Park held out during all of training camp in 1970 and missed the opening game when he felt Francis' contract offer was lower than his worth. Francis gave in, and in the next negotiations, Park's play—plus the emergence of the WHA—earned him a new deal estimated to be about $1 million for five years, the highest contract dollar-wise ever in the league at that time. Park was named captain to start 1974-75, but after a frustrating season that ended with the first-round playoff upset loss to the Islanders, he became expendable. On November 7, 1975, Park was part of what many called the biggest trade in Rangers' history up to that time: He, Jean Ratelle and Joe Zanussi were sent to Boston for Phil Esposito and Carol Vadnais. Park, one of the Boston Garden Gallery Gods' favorite targets as a Ranger, became immensely popular during his eight productive seasons in Boston before finishing his playing career in Detroit. He retired in 1985 and was inducted into the Hockey Hall of Fame in 1988.

Brad Park File:

- **BORN:**
  July 6, 1948; Toronto, Ontario
- **ACQUIRED:**
  Rangers first-round pick in the 1966 Entry Draft.
- **FIRST SEASON WITH RANGERS:**
  1968-69
- **BEST SEASON WITH RANGERS:**
  1973-74, 78 GP, 25-57-82, 148 PIM

- **TOTALS WITH RANGERS:**
  Regular season: 465 GP, 95-283-378, 738 PIM
  Playoffs: 64 GP, 12-32-44, 129 PIM
- **HONORS:**
  First-team All-Star, 1969-70, 1971-72, 1973-74
  Second-team All-Star, 1970-71, 1972-73
  All-Star Game, 1969-70, 1970-71, 1971-72, 1972-73, 1973-74, 1974-75;
- **NHL MILESTONES:**
  1,113 Games Played

CURTAIN CALL
Penalty Shots

Montreal Canadiens forward Yvan Cournoyer finished off an amazing run of penalty shots against the Rangers over a seven-year stretch. Starting with Boston defenseman Dallas Smith on December 21, 1966 and ending with Cournoyer on December 29, 1973, the Rangers faced 12 penalty shots in a row without taking one themselves. Four of the 12 shooters cashed in: Boston's John Bucyk, Oakland's Norm Ferguson, Los Angeles' Butch Goring and Montreal's Jacques Lemaire. Three of the 12 shooters were Pittsburgh Penguins, but neither Charlie Burns, Keith McCreary nor Ron Schock could beat Ed Giacomin. It was not until February 1, 1976 that Greg Polis attempted the first Ranger penalty shot in nearly a decade, ending the streak (he missed). The last previous Ranger penalty shot took place on November 5, 1966 when Bob Nevin beat Toronto's Terry Sawchuk at Maple Leaf Gardens. Ironically, the 12 straight penalty shots against the Blueshirts were sandwiched between a pair of streaks that had the Rangers get six straight penalty-shot calls, both before and after the dirty dozen.

Yvan Cournoyer had the last of 12 straight penalty shots against the Rangers.

NEW YORK
Ice Exchange

Hello, Larry Popein; Goodbye, Larry Popein (almost sounds like a Beatles tune). Popein was in the Rangers' system as a player for more than six seasons, and coached their Providence team to the AHL championship in 1973. He was promoted to the parent club on June 4, 1973 to give Emile Francis a breather from holding both the coaching and general manager's roles. But Francis' choice to replace himself as bench boss didn't quite work out the way "The Cat" wanted it to, so on January 11, it was time to climb out from behind the desk and get back behind the bench. But before Francis made his way back, he made a deal on November 30 to solidify his defense, sending Tom Williams, Mike Murphy and Sheldon Kannegiesser to Los Angeles for hard-hitting rearguard Gilles Marotte and forward Real Lemieux. Built like a fireplug, Marotte spent 2 1/2 seasons with the Rangers. Glen Sather, a checking forward and fan favorite since coming to New York in 1970, was sent to the Blues in late October as Francis reacquired left wing Jack Egers.

Larry Popein's tenure as coach didn't last long.

—1974 NEW YORK RANGERS 1975—

⌛ TIME CAPSULE

- **September 8, 1974:**
  President Ford pardoned former President Richard Nixon for any crimes he may have committed while in office, calling for an end to the Watergate episode.

- **October 30, 1974:**
  Muhammad Ali recaptured the heavyweight title with an eighth-round knockout of George Foreman in Zaire.

- **February 21, 1975:**
  Former White House aides H.R. Haldeman and John Ehrlichman and former Attorney General John Mitchell were sentenced to 30 months in prison each for their roles in the Watergate affair.

1974-1975 FINAL STANDINGS

Patrick Division	W	L	T	PTS	GF	GA
Philadelphia	51	18	11	113	293	181
RANGERS	37	29	14	88	319	276
NY Islanders	33	25	22	88	264	221
Atlanta	34	31	15	83	243	233

Other Division Winners:

Smythe— Vancouver

Norris—Montreal

Adams—Buffalo

PLAYOFF RESULTS
Preliminary Round: Islanders defeated Rangers 2-1
LEADING PLAYOFF SCORERS
Steve Vickers (2-4-6)

Jean Ratelle (1-5-6)
STANLEY CUP CHAMPION
Philadelphia Flyers

SEASON SNAPSHOT

Most Goals:
Steve Vickers (41)
Most Assists:
Rod Gilbert (61)
Most Points:
Rod Gilbert (97)
Most Power-Play Goals:
Jean Ratelle/Steve Vickers (16)
Most Shorthanded Goals:
Fairbairn/Sanderson/Butler (2)
Most Penalty Minutes:
Derek Sanderson (106)
Power Play:
84/296, 28.4%, 7 SHGA
Penalty-Killing:
241/295, 81.7%, 6 SHG
Most Wins, Goaltender:
Gilles Villemure (22)
Lowest Goals-Against Average:
Gilles Villemure (3.16)
Most Shutouts:
Gilles Villemure (2)
NHL All-Stars:
Steve Vickers, LW (Second Team)
Rangers In All-Star Game:
Brad Park, D;
Steve Vickers, LW;
Rod Gilbert, RW

The 1974-75 Season in Review

The nucleus of the team that had made the Rangers into an NHL powerhouse was getting older, so GM Emile Francis began bringing in some new blood. Ron Greschner and Rick Middleton were among the newcomers who helped the Rangers to a second-place finish in the four-team Patrick Division as the league split into four divisions due to the latest round of expansion. The Rangers reached the Christmas holiday just two games over .500 before reeling off eight straight victories to take control of second place in the division and managed to play well enough the rest of the way to hold off the upstart Islanders for the runner-up spot. Under the new playoff format, which called for a best-of-three preliminary round, the first all-New York playoff series since 1938 began at the Garden with a

The Rangers opened their season against Washington in the Caps' NHL debut. Photo by Bruce Bennett.

stunning 3-2 victory by the Islanders. The Rangers retaliated by shellacking the Isles 8-3 in the first playoff game at the Nassau Coliseum, but the Islanders jumped to a quick 3-0 lead in Game 3 against Gilles Villemure. Ed Giacomin's insertion sparked the team and the Rangers dominated the final 20 minutes, scoring three times to send the game into overtime. But the end was as quick as it was stunning. J.P. Parise took a pass from Jude Drouin and directed it past Giacomin just 11 seconds into overtime, sending the Islanders to the quarterfinals and the Rangers home for the summer. As it turned out, it was the real beginning of one of hockey's great rivalries—and the end of an era for the Rangers.

MAGIC MOMENT   *November 17, 1974*

The California Seals proved to be the perfect tonic for a Ranger team that was mired in an early-season slump. With Rick Middleton becoming the first Ranger rookie to get four goals in a game, the Rangers burst out of the Patrick Division cellar with a 10-0 rout of the hapless Seals. Middleton had the game's first goal, scored again in the opening period and added two more tallies in the third period. Three of the four goals came on assists from center Pete Stemkowski, who was more than impressed by the rookie's skills. "He knows what to do around the net," said Stemmer, who had a goal of his own (set up by Middleton). "He has tremendous puck sense for a kid just coming up." While Middleton was enjoying the best night of his young career, veteran Derek Sanderson was enjoying one of the last big nights of his: Sanderson, a long-time Ranger tormentor during his days with the Boston Bruins, set up two goals by Jerry Butler and another by Rod Gilbert as the Rangers posted the biggest shutout victory in their history, sparking a 15-5-4 surge.

Rick Middleton's four goals fueled the biggest shutout win in Ranger history.

211

New York hockey fans literally watched Ron Greschner grow up. He arrived in the Big Apple as a 19-year-old kid from Goodsoil, Saskatchewan, a second-round draft pick joining a veteran team that had come close to winning the Stanley Cup but was ready for some new blood. "Gresch" left 16 years later with virtually all of the Rangers' scoring records for defensemen. Greschner spent just seven games in the minor leagues before being called up by GM Emile Francis to bolster a defense corps that had been depleted by injury and age. His skating and passing skills were obvious; he was an offensive force in his younger years, scoring 20 goals in four different seasons, but gradually grew into an excellent two-way player who saw time at forward as well as on the blue line. But perhaps more amazingly, the kid from the small town in Western Canada grew not only to accept New York, but to enjoy it. "I think anybody who says something negative about New York doesn't deserve to play here," he said late in his career. "It's a fascinating city; there's always something going on." Greschner co-owned restaurants in the Big Apple, ran a hockey school, became involved in charity work and married supermodel Carol Alt, whom he had met in the early 1980s while struggling to overcome the back problems that dogged him for much of his career. His affection for New York was returned—it was a sweet affair for 16 years. Like Harry Howell, and Rod Gilbert the only men to play more seasons with the Rangers, Greschner was never a member of a Stanley Cup champion; due to injuries, he came up 18 games short of reaching the 1,000-game mark for his career. When he was healthy, though, few Ranger backliners were ever better.

Ron Greschner File

BORN:
December 22, 1954; Goodsoil, Saskatchewan

ACQUIRED:
Rangers' second-round pick in 1974 Entry Draft

FIRST SEASON WITH RANGERS:
1974-75

BEST SEASON WITH RANGERS:
1977-78, 78 GP, 24-48-72, 100 PIM

TOTALS WITH RANGERS:
Regular Season: 982 GP, 179-431-610, 1,226 PIM
Playoffs: 84 GP, 17-32-49, 100 PIM

HONORS:
All-Star Game, 1979-80
Players' Player Award, 1977-78

CURTAIN CALL
The Good Guy Award

Ted Irvine won the first "Good Guy" Award.

Any writer who's covered more than one sport can tell you that hockey players are the most enjoyable athletes to deal with among the four major team sports. The Rangers' chapter of the Professional Hockey Writers Association, which dates to the late 1920s, instituted the Good Guy Award in 1974-75 to honor the Ranger it deemed most cooperative with the media. The award can be won only once. Ted Irvine was honored as the first winner, followed by Ron Harris and John Davidson (who's now one of the more famous media members covering the team). Among the award's other winners are a Hall of Famer (Rod Gilbert), a future Hall of Famer (Mark Messier), a brother tandem (Dave Maloney won in 1978-79; two years later, it was Don's turn), and even a non-player—team president and general manager Neil Smith was honored in 1994. The 1996 winner, goaltender Glenn Healy, has his own place in the award's lore: Healy, a former Islander, is the only player ever to win Good Guy Awards as a member of both teams.

NEW YORK
Ice Exchange

With the nucleus of his team getting older, GM Emile Francis knew he had to make changes after the 1974 playoff disappointment. Shockingly enough, the first player to go was captain Vic Hadfield, who went to Pittsburgh for defenseman Nick Beverly. Rookie defenseman Lawrence Sacharuk went to St. Louis for left wing Greg Polis, who scored 26 goals in his first season on Broadway. Two rookies, Ron Greschner and Rick Middleton, made their debuts in what turned out to be long and productive NHL careers, while forward Bert Wilson got his first full chance in the NHL. But one addition had to have Ranger fans shaking their heads. Derek Sanderson was among the most hated of the Bruins when Boston beat the Rangers in the 1970 and 1972 playoffs; two years later, he was a Ranger—and a productive one, too. Sanderson scored 25 goals, added 25 assists and led the team with 106 penalty minutes in his one full season in New York.

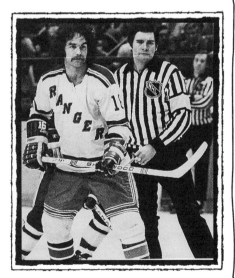

Derek Sanderson (with referee Bruce Hood) had 25 goals in his one season as a Ranger.

Ranger Lists
Most Career Victories by a Goaltender

266
Ed Giacomin

204
Gump Worsley

200
John Vanbiesbrouck

157
Dave Kerr

149
Mike Richter

123
Chuck Rayner

96
Gilles Villemure

90
John Davidson

213

Rangers - Islanders Rivalry

The Rangers had New York all to themselves for 30 years. That all changed in 1972, when the New York Islanders joined the NHL, giving the Blueshirts a local rival for the first time since the Americans went out of business in 1942.

There wasn't much of a rivalry at first. The Islanders set NHL records for futility in their first season and their mountain of defeats included a six-game sweep by the Rangers. The Islanders improved in 1973-74 and tied the Rangers for second place the next season, but a lot of Garden fans still didn't take them seriously.

That all changed on April 11, 1975. The two teams met in the playoffs for the first time, and the Islanders shocked the Garden crowd by winning the opener. The Rangers avoided elimination by breezing to an 8-3 victory at the Nassau Coliseum in Game 2. The Islanders raced to a 3-0 lead in Game 3, but the Rangers stormed back in the third period to send the game into overtime. However, before many of the fans were even seated, the Isles' J.P. Parise silenced the crowd by scoring 11 seconds into the extra period, sending the Rangers home early.

The rivalry was on. It took four years, but the Rangers got revenge,

knocking the Islanders (who had finished with the best record in the NHL) out of the semifinals in 1979. The Islanders beat the Rangers three straight times in the early 1980s on their way to the Stanley Cup before the teams played their best series ever—a best-of-five matchup in the 1984 division semifinals.

The Rangers gained a split at Nassau Coliseum, winning Game 2 on Glen Hanlon's 45-save shutout. They demolished the Islanders 7-2 in Game 3 and were 20 minutes away from winning the series. But their 1-0 third-period lead disappeared as the Islanders scored four goals to even the series and send it to a fifth game at the Coliseum— perhaps the most exciting contest the two teams have ever played.

The Rangers dominated play throughout, but trailed 2-1 until Don Maloney's disputed "stick-above-the-shoulder goal" in the

The Rangers stunned the Islanders in the 1979 semifinals. Photo by Jerry Liebman.

last minute of regulation sent the game into overtime.

The Rangers had three glorious chances to score in the overtime, including one which saw Bob Brooke break in alone on Billy Smith only to be denied. Not long after Brooke was stopped, Ken Morrow's screened shot from the right circle gave the Islanders the win.

The Rangers have won the two postseason meetings since then, including a 4-0 sweep that started the run to the 1994 Stanley Cup. Beating the Islanders to start the trip to the championship made it just a little more special for most Ranger fans. And to this day, the rivalry lives on.

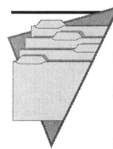

Rangers-Islanders Rivalry File:

RANGERS RECORD: Regular Season: 151 GP, 66-71-14, 535 GF, 545 GA
Playoffs: 39 GP, 19-20-0, 132 GF, 129 GA

SERIES SWEEPS: Regular Season: For - 1 (1972-73, 6-0-0)
Playoffs: For - 1 (1994, 4-0)
Against - 1 (1981, 0-4)

PLAYERS WHO PLAYED FOR BOTH TEAMS:
Bill Berg, Don Blackburn, Paul Boutilier, Arnie Brown, Pat Conacher, Mike Donnelly, Patrick Flatley, Ray Ferraro, Greg Gilbert, Jari Gronstrand, Glenn Healy, Raimo Helminen, Troy Loney, Don Maloney, Bert Marshall, Mike McEwen, Brian Mullen, Pat Price, Ron Stewart, Steve Weeks.

The All-Ranger Team
Second Era (1951-75)

Goaltender
Ed Giacomin (1965-75)

No one was more instrumental in the rise of the Rangers than Giacomin, who Emile Francis referred to as the most important acquisition he ever made. Rescued from Providence of the AHL, Giacomin became one of the most popular Rangers of his era, the team's all-time leader in shutouts and the only Ranger ever to make five straight postseason All-Star teams. The fans' affection for him knew no bounds: The Garden crowd cheered him all night long when he faced the Rangers for the first time after his stunning departure in 1975.

Defense
Harry Howell (1953-69)

It took years for Garden fans to fully appreciate Howell's controlled but effective style on the back line. He wasn't flashy, wasn't a fighter, wasn't a big scorer; he just did the job while breaking in enough defense partners to stock a few franchises. Howell wore No. 3 for 17 seasons and a team-record 1,160 games, and won the Norris Trophy at the age of 34 in 1966-67 thanks to the best offensive season of his career. The only sad note in Howell's Hall of Fame career is that he holds the mark for the most games played without winning a Stanley Cup.

Defense
Brad Park (1968-75)

It was Park's blessing—and his curse—to have been the second-best defenseman in the NHL during his time with the Rangers. Neither he nor his team was able to escape the shadow of Bobby Orr and the Bruins, which tends to make people forget just how good Park was. A terrific puck-carrier with good passing skills and a booming slap shot, yet also capable of clearing the slot in front of his own net, Park was a three-time first-team All-Star and probably the best defenseman never to win the Norris Trophy.

Center
Jean Ratelle (1960-75)

He was a gentleman on and off the ice; but put a hockey stick in his hands and Ratelle was also a slick passer and deadly shooter. He still holds the Rangers record for points in a season with 109, a total that would have been much higher except for the broken ankle that sidelined him for the last month of the 1971-72 season and most of the playoffs. He's still the Rangers' No. 2 all-time scorer with 336 goals and 481 assists for 817 points, trailing only boyhood friend Rod Gilbert.

Jean Ratelle

Wing
Andy Bathgate (1952-64)

The best forward to wear Ranger blue between World War II and the expansion era, Bathgate put up big numbers despite playing without a lot of offensive help for much of his time in the Big Apple. Bathgate led the Rangers in scoring for eight consecutive seasons. His penalty-shot goal in 1962 against Detroit is one of the most famous moments in team history; the trade that sent him to Toronto in 1964 gave him a taste of Stanley Cup champagne while providing the youth that helped the Rangers eventually rebuild.

Wing
Rod Gilbert (1960-78)

The successor to Bathgate as the Rangers' offensive star, Gilbert holds almost all of the team's scoring records despite playing much of his career with a bad back. He was (and still is) beloved by Rangers fans as much for his classy demeanor as for his on-ice accomplishments. He was the first Ranger to make New York City his permanent home and is in his fourth decade with the team, serving as director of community relations and manager of the team's alumni association.

Coach
Emile Francis
(1965-68; 1969-73; 1974-75)

As general manager, Francis rebuilt a team that had been going nowhere for two decades into a powerhouse; as a coach, he piloted the club into the NHL's top ranks. His only failures were an inability to win the Stanley Cup and to find a coach as good as he was, which would have let him fully concentrate on his duties as general manager. "The Cat" holds the team records for games coached (654) and victories (347); if there were a record for time spent promoting hockey, he'd hold that one, too.

Emile Francis

—1975 1976—

IME CAPSULE

- **October 1, 1975:**
  Muhammad Ali retained his heavyweight crown by defeating Joe Frazier in the "Thrilla in Manilla."

- **July 4, 1976:**
  The United States celebrated its bicentennial.

- **July 20, 1976:**
  Viking I landed on Mars, almost a year after its launch.

1975-1976
FINAL STANDINGS

Patrick Division	W	L	T	PTS	GF	GA
Philadelphia	51	13	16	118	348	209
Islanders	42	21	17	101	297	190
Atlanta	35	33	12	82	262	237
RANGERS	29	42	9	67	262	333

Other Division Winners:

Adams–Boston

Norris–Montreal

Smythe–Chicago

PLAYOFF RESULTS

Rangers did not qualify

STANLEY CUP CHAMPION

Montreal Canadiens

SEASON SNAPSHOT

Most Goals:
Rod Gilbert (36)
Most Assists:
Steve Vickers (53)
Most Points:
Rod Gilbert (86)
Most Power-Play Goals:
Phil Esposito (16)
Most Shorthanded Goals:
Phil Esposito/Bill Fairbairn/Bill Collins (1)
Most Penalty Minutes:
Carol Vadnais (104)
Power Play:
67/323, 20.7%, 11 SHGA
Penalty Killing:
68/277, 75.5%, 3 SHG
Most Wins, Goaltender:
John Davidson (22)
Lowest Goals-Against Average:
John Davidson (3.97)
Most Shutouts:
John Davidson (3)
Rangers In All-Star Game:
Steve Vickers, LW;
Carol Vadnais, D

The 1975-76 Season in Review

The Rangers' 50th season in the NHL was one of their most tumultuous. No one knows exactly how much the shock of losing Ed Giacomin, Jean Ratelle and Brad Park had on the club, but the Rangers finished below .500 and missed postseason play for the first time in 10 seasons. In the first half, the Rangers were streaky. They lost 8 of 10 games early, but ran off a seven-game unbeaten streak two weeks later. It was late February when the Blueshirts hit bottom with a 2-11-3 skid. John Davidson, in his first season on Broadway, won 22 games. Davidson, who had come from St. Louis during the summer, got the chance to play after Ed Giacomin was waived on Halloween night after going 0-3-1 in his first four decisions; backups Dunc Wilson (5 wins) and rookie Doug Soetaert (2) helped little. A week after Giacomin was let go,

Phil Esposito was part of the 1975-76 overhaul.

GM Emile Francis, desperate to inject some life into his team, swapped Brad Park and Jean Ratelle to Boston for Phil Esposito and Carol Vadnais—a deal that stunned fans in Boston and the Big Apple alike. Despite losing his long-time linemate and friend, Rod Gilbert stood out again, leading the team offensively with 36 goals and 86 points. Steve Vickers dropped from 41 goals last season to 30 this season, but he raised his assist total from 48 to 53. Vickers also set a team record by picking up seven points (three goals, four assists) in a single game, an 11-4 home win on February 18 against the lowly Capitals. By that time, John Ferguson had replaced both coach Ron Stewart and GM Francis in the third major shakeup of a wild season. The Blueshirts were 15-20-4 when Ferguson took over, but they continued to slide, going 14-22-5 the rest of the way.

MAGIC MOMENT   *November 2, 1975*

Ranger fans are among the most loyal in hockey. But on Sunday, November 2, 1975, the Rangers could have been the Islanders for all the Garden faithful cared—because their favorite player wasn't wearing a Ranger uniform any more. In probably the most unpopular move any Ranger management ever made, Giacomin was waived on Halloween and claimed by the Detroit Red Wings. Unfortunately for the Rangers, their next home game was against those same Red Wings—and who would be starting in goal but Giacomin, though he had to convince GM Alex Delvecchio and coach Doug Barkley to give him the start over Jim Rutherford. The crowd cheered Giacomin from the moment he hit the ice. The noise rendered the National Anthem inaudible as Giacomin fought unsuccessfully to blink back tears during the thunderous ovation. The cheers for Giacomin continued throughout the game, while the Rangers were booed practically every time they touched the puck. Many of the fans turned their back on the Blueshirts in a show of protest over losing Giacomin, and they

Ranger fans cheered Ed Giacomin when he returned to the Garden with the Red Wings. Photo courtesy of Hockey Hall of Fame.

erupted in cheers for every Giacomin save and every Detroit goal. The only thing Giacomin lost was 13 pounds; he kept his dignity and rode the waves of emotion to a 6-4 victory.

RANGER LEGEND
Pete Stemkowski

You could call him "Stemmer." You could even call him "The Polish Prince." With a name and a personality like Pete Stemkowski, there's nowhere to hide—and that's just the way he wanted it. The Winnipeg-born Stemkowski started his career in Toronto, and then was moved to Detroit as part of a deal in which he was a throw-in; the big names in the trade included Frank Mahovlich, Carl Brewer, Norm Ullman and Paul Henderson. Stemmer became a Ranger on Halloween night in 1970, coming from the Red Wings for defenseman Larry Brown. Stemkowski was a perfect fit as a No. 3 center behind Jean Ratelle and Walt Tkaczuk and wound up forming an effective third line with Ted Irvine and fellow ex-Wing Bruce MacGregor. Though Stemmer's best season on Broadway was 1973-74, when he finished with career highs for goals (25) and points (70), most Ranger fans remember him as the goal-scorer in the famous triple-overtime contest against Chicago in Game 6 of the 1971 semifinals. Often forgotten is the fact that he also had the winner in overtime of Game 1 at Chicago Stadium—making him one of only three Rangers, along with Don Raleigh in the 1950 finals against Detroit and Stephane Matteau in the 1994 semis against the Devils, to score twice in overtime in the same series. In addition to his on-ice skills, Stemkowski was regarded as one of the Rangers' (if not the NHL's) top practical jokers. Despite playing mostly on checking units during his time in New York, Stemkowski compiled more than 300 points before being released by GM John Ferguson after the 1976-77 season. He played one year for Los Angeles before retiring to go into broadcasting—first as sports director of WGBB Radio on Long Island, and more recently, as the television color commentator of the San Jose Sharks.

Pete Stemkowski File

- **BORN:**
  August 25, 1943; Winnipeg, Manitoba
- **ACQUIRED:**
  From Detroit for Larry Brown, Oct. 31, 1970.
- **FIRST SEASON WITH RANGERS:**
  1970-71

- **BEST SEASON WITH RANGERS:**
  1973-74, 78 GP, 25-45-70, 74 PIM
- **TOTALS WITH RANGERS:**
  Regular season: 496 GP, 113-204-317, 379 PIM
  Playoffs: 55 GP, 18-18-36, 73 PIM

CURTAIN CALL
John Ferguson

John Ferguson became coach and general manager in 1975-76.

For their first 49 1/2 seasons, the Rangers hired strictly from within. Every coach had been a Ranger player and every general manager had had Ranger ties. John Ferguson had neither when he took over both jobs on January 7, 1976 after coach Ron Stewart and GM Emile Francis were let go. Ironically, Ferguson had turned down the Rangers coaching job the previous summer, saying he did not want to come to New York without long-term security (Francis reportedly had offered him just a one-year contract). Ferguson was Montreal's enforcer in the 1960s and early 1970s, amassing 1,214 penalty minutes in eight seasons—but playing on five Cup-winning teams. He had never been a coach or general manager before coming to the Big Apple, and his success as a player with the Canadiens never translated into championships in New York. The Rangers made the playoffs only once in Ferguson's 2 1/2 seasons as GM, losing in the first round under Jean-Guy Talbot's coaching in 1977-78. That spelled the end for both, as the Rangers returned to the "Family Ties" tradition by hiring Fred Shero as coach and GM.

NEW YORK Ice Exchange

GM Emile Francis knew an overhaul was in order after the stunning loss to the Islanders in April 1975. Little did he know he'd be part of the turnover. Francis handed the coaching reins to Ron Stewart and began the overhaul in June by acquiring young goaltender John Davidson from St. Louis along with Bill Collins for wingers Ted Irvine, Jerry Butler and Bert Wilson. The turnover continued on October 18 when Gilles Villemure was sent to Chicago for defenseman Doug Jarrett. Then came Halloween night, when the entire team was put on waivers, and Detroit's claim of Ed Giacomin was not contested. Seven days later, long-time Rangers and fan favorites Jean Ratelle and Brad Park were sent to rival Boston for long-time nemesis Phil Esposito plus defenseman Carol Vadnais. But Francis wasn't around long enough to see the results of his efforts: On January 6, upper management replaced both "The Cat" and Stewart with former Montreal tough-guy John Ferguson, who had no experience in either job.

Carol Vadnais came to the Rangers in the blockbuster deal with Boston.

Ranger Lists

Most Losses in a Season

44
1984-85

42
1975-76

41
1965-66

39
1992-93

38
1963-64

38
1964-65

38
1985-86

38
1986-87

—1976 1977—

TIME CAPSULE

- **October 14, 1976:**
  Chris Chambliss' dramatic ninth-inning home run gave the New York Yankees a 7-6 victory over Kansas City in Game 5 of the American League playoffs for their first pennant in 12 years.

- **November 2, 1976:**
  Jimmy Carter defeated incumbent Gerald Ford in the presidential election.

- **January 17, 1977:**
  A 10-year halt on capital punishment in the United States ended when Gary Gilmore was executed by a Utah firing squad.

1976-1977
FINAL STANDINGS

Patrick Division	W	L	T	PTS	GF	GA
Philadelphia	48	16	16	112	323	213
NY Islanders	47	21	12	106	288	193
Atlanta	34	34	12	80	264	265
RANGERS	29	37	14	72	272	310

Other Division Winners:

Smythe—St. Louis

Norris— Montreal

Adams—Boston

PLAYOFF RESULTS
Rangers did not qualify

STANLEY CUP CHAMPION
Montreal Canadiens

SEASON SNAPSHOT

Most Goals:
Phil Esposito (34)
Most Assists:
Phil Esposito (46)
Most Points:
Phil Esposito (80)
Most Power-Play Goals:
Phil Esposito (15)
Most Shorthanded Goals:
Ron Greschner (2)
Most Penalty Minutes:
Nick Fotiu (174)
Power Play:
60/290, 20.7%, 16 SHGA
Penalty-Killing:
213/268, 79.5%, 6 SHG
Most Wins, Goaltender:
John Davidson (14)
Lowest Goals-Against Average:
John Davidson (3.54)
Most Shutouts:
John Davidson/Doug Soetaert (1)
Rangers In All-Star Game:
Phil Esposito, C;
Rod Gilbert, RW;
Don Murdoch, RW

The 1976-77 Season in Review

L. to R. Rod Gilbert, John Ferguson, Phil Esposito.

The Rangers were a team in transition in 1976-77. From new players to new uniforms, John Ferguson's first full season in New York was marked by change. The season got off to a promising start: One rookie, Dan Newman, got the game-winner on opening night against the North Stars, while another, Don Murdoch, set a team record with five goals in the return match at Minnesota on October 12. But the Rangers struggled the rest of the way, never winning more than three straight games. The offense wasn't a major problem: Phil Esposito led the team with 34 goals and 80 points, while Murdoch had 32 goals and four other players broke the 20-goal barrier. But the Rangers were bedeviled for much of the season by defensive problems—they allowed 45 more goals than third-place Atlanta and a whopping 117 more than the second-place Islanders. The defense was young and the goaltending inconsistent. Still, the Rangers were at the .500 mark through the first 43 games, but one slump in late January and another that ran from late February through mid-March spelled doom for their playoff hopes. The Rangers got some hope for the future from Murdoch, whose ankle injury limited him to 59 games and probably cost him the Calder Trophy, and other youngsters like defensemen Mike McEwen and Dave Maloney, but the season ended just as the previous one had—too early.

MAGIC MOMENT

The Rangers had high hopes for Don Murdoch, who had been their No. 1 draft pick the previous June. But there's no way they could have expected him to do what he did in Minnesota in the fourth game of his NHL career. Murdoch, who was still 13 days short of his 20th birthday, equaled a league record set by Howie Meeker when he tallied five times in a 10-4 victory over the North Stars. He was the first Ranger ever to get five in one game. "I never had this many in a game in juniors or anywhere," he said of his big night. "But you have to give the team credit, not just me." Amazingly, Murdoch missed out on the Rangers' four-goal first period, but connected three times in the second period against Gary Smith on a rebound, a 25-footer following a breakaway, and during a power play. He added two more late in the third period for the milestone, getting the last with just five seconds left in the game. Murdoch went on to set a team record for goals by a rookie with 32, despite missing more than a quarter of the season with an ankle injury.

Don Murdoch became the first Ranger to get five goals in a game.

RANGER LEGEND
Phil Esposito

It's almost impossible for today's Big Apple fans to comprehend the shock waves generated by the Rangers-Bruins trade that brought Phil Esposito to the Big Apple. Not only were Brad Park and Jean Ratelle regarded as fixtures by the Garden faithful, but Esposito was the Bruin they disliked above all others in a rivalry that was as heated as any in Ranger history. As often happens, though, emotions can change quickly when a player changes jerseys. It didn't take long for "Espo" to become almost as popular in New York as he had been in Boston. Though Esposito didn't score as he once had in Boston, where he set offensive records in the early 1970s, he still knew where the net was. He tallied at least 30 goals in each of his five full seasons in New York, including a high of 42 in 1978-79, when his scoring and leadership were instrumental in leading the Rangers to their first trip to the finals since 1972. By then, Espo was the "old man" on a line that included youngsters Don Murdoch and Don Maloney. That trio put up 52 points in the playoffs, the highest total ever by a three-man unit in team history. In 1979-80, his last full season, Esposito led the team in scoring for the fourth time in as many

Photo by Jack Mecca.

years with 34 goals and 44 assists for 78 points. He recorded his 13th straight 30-goal season and surpassed the 700-goal mark, a level previously exceeded only by Gordie Howe. By the time he retired in 1981, he was the No. 2 scorer in NHL history with 717 goals and 1,590 points (he finished the 1995-96 season still fourth on both lists)—and it was almost impossible to remember that he had once been the opposing player Garden fans had loved to hate. He stayed with the Rangers as a broadcaster, coach and GM well into the '80s.

Phil Esposito File

- **BORN:**
  February 20, 1942; Sault Ste. Marie, Ontario
- **ACQUIRED:**
  Trade from Boston with Carol Vadnais for Jean Ratelle, Brad Park and Joe Zanussi; November 7, 1975
- **FIRST SEASON WITH RANGERS:**
  1975-76
- **BEST SEASON WITH RANGERS:**
  1977-78, 79 GP, 38-43-81, 53 PIM

- **TOTALS WITH RANGERS:**
  Regular season: 422 GP, 184-220-404, 263 PIM
  Playoffs: 30 GP, 11-16-27, 33 PIM
- **HONORS:**
  Lester Patrick Trophy, 1978
  All-Star Game, 1976-77, 1977-78, 1979-80
  West Side Assn. Rangers MVP, 1978-79
  Players' Player Award, 1976-77
- **NHL MILESTONES:**
  1,282 Games Played; 717 Goals; 873 Assists; 1,590 Points

CURTAIN CALL
Rod Gilbert Night

Rod Gilbert loved being a hockey player and loved playing for the Rangers. He appreciated New York fans—and the feeling was mutual. On March 9, 1977, a sellout crowd turned out to honor Gilbert, the highest-scoring and perhaps most popular Ranger forward of all time. Gilbert's former "GAG Line" partners, Vic Hadfield and Jean Ratelle, were there, as was Andy Bathgate, Gilbert's predecessor as the Rangers' top scorer and fan favorite, and Harry Howell, the only other Ranger player who had been honored with a night while active. In his speech, Gilbert sounded as appreciative as the fans had been. "My friends, and I think that all of you here tonight are my friends," he said, "you have given me a home, friendship, respect and love, and that's more important than fame. For these things, I will always be grateful." It was one of the most emotional nights in Ranger history. Gilbert capped his big night by scoring a goal and adding an assist as the Rangers downed the Minnesota North Stars 6-4.

Few Rangers have been as beloved by New York fans as Rod Gilbert.

NEW YORK
Ice Exchange

With the nucleus of the squad that had come close a few times in the early 1970s starting to fade, GM/coach John Ferguson continued the process of renovating the team. Two of the newcomers paid off handsomely: Don Murdoch set a team record for rookies with 32 goals despite playing in only 59 games due to an ankle injury, while defenseman Mike McEwen had 14 goals and 43 points. Another newcomer, goalie Gilles Gratton, made more of a splash with his wild mask and outrageous behavior than he did in the net. While the new players were settling in, 1976-77 was the last hurrah for two popular veterans, Bill Fairbairn and Pete Stemkowski, both of whom played their final seasons in New York. With Esposito now the key to the offense, Ferguson decided to bring in Espo's long-time Boston linemate, Ken Hodge, to help him. The price was Rick Middleton, who had scored 46 goals in his first two NHL seasons. But the deal turned out to be one of the costliest in team history; Hodge never found the magic he enjoyed in Boston, while Middleton went on to score more than 400 goals for the Bruins.

Gilles Gratton made a big splash with his mask, but couldn't solve the Rangers' goaltending problems.

223

—1977 1978—

TIME CAPSULE

- **October 18, 1977:**
  Reggie Jackson tied a World Series record with three home runs as the New York Yankees beat the Los Angeles Dodgers 8-4 to win the World Series in six games for their first championship since 1962.

- **February 8, 1978:**
  Egyptian president Anwar el-Sadat began a six-day visit to the United States, advancing the prospects for a Mideast peace settlement.

- **February 15, 1978:**
  Leon Spinks stunned the boxing world by winning a 15-round decision over Muhammad Ali to capture the heavyweight championship.

1977-1978

FINAL STANDINGS

	W	L	T	PTS	GF	GA
NY Islanders	48	17	15	111	334	210
Philadelphia	45	20	15	105	296	200
Atlanta	34	27	19	87	274	252
RANGERS	30	37	13	73	279	280

Other Division Winners:

Smythe—Chicago

Norris—Montreal

Adams—Boston

PLAYOFF RESULTS
Buffalo defeated Rangers 2-1
LEADING PLAYOFF SCORER
Don Murdoch (1-3-4)
STANLEY CUP CHAMPION
Montreal Canadiens

SEASON SNAPSHOT

Most Goals:
Pat Hickey (40)
Most Assists:
Ron Greschner (48)
Most Points:
Phil Esposito (81)
Most Power-Play Goals:
Phil Esposito (21)
Most Shorthanded Goals:
Greg Polis (4)
Most Penalty Minutes:
Carol Vadnais (115)
Power Play:
78/279, 28.0%, 6 SHGA
Penalty-Killing:
196/244, 80.3%, 10 SHG
Most Wins, Goaltender:
John Davidson (14)
Lowest Goals-Against Average:
John Davidson (3.18)
Most Shutouts:
Wayne Thomas (4)
Rangers In All-Star Game:
Carol Vadnais, D;
Phil Esposito, C

The 1977-78 Season in Review

John Ferguson decided that two jobs were one too many, so he brought old friend Jean-Guy Talbot in to run the bench while he dedicated himself to finding talent. The Rangers made Talbot a winner in his debut with a 6-3 victory over Vancouver at the Garden. But as they had for the previous two seasons, the Rangers struggled, following highs like consecutive shutouts at St. Louis and Minnesota with a seven-game winless streak. The season's most stunning development came in late November, when Rod Gilbert, the Rangers' all-time leading scorer but with only two goals in 19 games, was released by Ferguson. Gilbert weighed the possibility of continuing his playing career with another team, but eventually accepted a front-office job with the Rangers. Through all the struggles, the Rangers' power play was among the league's best, converting 28 percent of its chances and helping the team to its first playoff berth since 1975. Buffalo won the opener 4-1, but Don Murdoch's overtime goal gave the Rangers a 4-3 win in Game 2—their first home playoff win since beating the Flyers in Game 6 of the 1974 semifinals. However, the Sabres won the deciding game 4-1, and that proved to be the last game for both Ferguson and Talbot, both of whom were relieved of their jobs on June 2.

Walt Tkaczuk bounced back with 26 goals in 1977-78.

MAGIC MOMENT

February 25, 1978

John Ferguson told Rangers fans at a party that he had a big surprise for the game the next night at the Montreal Forum. That "surprise" turned out to be the NHL debut of Swedish goaltender Hardy Astrom, who admitted that even he was surprised when he got the call to take on the NHL's most powerful team. Not that he was scared. "It was my first game in the NHL, but I had played big games before with Sweden. I had beaten the Russians in Moscow and the Czechs in Prague. I thought I had a good chance of beating the Canadiens in Montreal" he said. Astrom might have been the only one: The Rangers hadn't won in Montreal for six years and the Canadiens were riding a then-record 28-game unbeaten streak. But amazingly, Astrom was as good as his word: He made 29 saves and the Rangers scored twice in each period on the way to an almost-easy 6-3 victory. Unfortunately for Astrom, that win turned out to be exactly half of his victory total for the Rangers. He split four decisions for New York, went back to Sweden for one season, then played three seasons for Colorado before going home for good.

Hardy Astrom stunned the Canadiens at the Forum in his first NHL game.

RANGER LEGEND
Ron Duguay

With his long hair and infectious smile, Ron Duguay was a hit with Garden fans almost from the moment he first took the ice. As one of two first-round picks by the Rangers in 1977, Duguay quickly showed he could play. With his hair flying in the breeze, Duguay came right out of juniors and rang up 20 goals as a rookie. He bumped that figure up to 27 goals in his second season and 28 in his third, then hit the 40-goal mark in 1981-82, helping the Rangers to their best showing in a decade. His speed and ability to find holes in the defense were ideally suited to coach Herb Brooks' swirling, skate-and-pass style of play. Though he was 6-2 and 210 pounds, Duguay's biggest strength was his skating: he was one of the fastest players ever to put on a Ranger jersey and turned into one of the NHL's busiest breakaway artists. His speed also made him one of the NHL's most dangerous penalty-killers. Duguay's good looks quickly made him a female heartthrob and helped him become a hit off the ice, too: He and Phil Esposito were among the stars of a memorable Sasson jeans commercial in the late 1970s and early 1980s, and he also signed a

modeling contract with a top New York agency. Duguay later co-owned a restaurant on the Upper East Side, and once journeyed to Korea to serve as a judge at the Miss Universe Pageant. A lot of fans were heartbroken when Duguay was dealt to the Detroit Red Wings after slumping to 19 goals in 1982-83. He had his two best offensive seasons for the Red Wings before being sent to Pittsburgh in March 1986 and eventually returning to New York in January 1987. But Duguay never recaptured the scoring touch of his earlier days, tallying just 13 times in 82 games before being traded to Los Angeles in February 1988 and finishing his NHL career on the West Coast.

Ron Duguay File

- **BORN:**
  July 6, 1957; Sudbury, Ontario
- **ACQUIRED:**
  Rangers' first-round pick in 1977 Entry Draft
- **FIRST SEASON WITH RANGERS:**
  1977-78

- **BEST SEASON WITH RANGERS:**
  1981-82, 72 GP, 40-36-76, 82 PIM
- **TOTALS WITH RANGERS:**
  Regular season: 499 GP, 164-176-340, 370 PIM
  Playoffs: 69 GP, 28-19-47, 103 PIM
- **HONORS:**
  All-Star Game, 1981-82

CURTAIN CALL
Uniform Changes

John Ferguson's penchant for change covered more than the players on the roster. In 1976-77 and 1977-78, the Rangers who took the ice looked nothing like the previous teams that called Madison Square Garden home. Instead of the familiar diagonal "RANGERS" on the front of the jersey, their uniforms carried a team crest on the chest, along with a large blue-and-red stripe that went from one sleeve to the other. Ferguson, one of the NHL's toughest players during his career with Montreal, said at the time that he adopted the new uniforms to make his players look bigger. If that didn't work, they could always rely on larger numbers: Phil Esposito, who wore No. 7 in Boston and took No. 12 and then No. 5 after coming to New York (Rod Gilbert already had No. 7), switched to No. 77. His long-time linemate, Ken Hodge, opted

L. to R. Don Murdoch, Walt Tkaczuk, Steve Vickers in the late 70s uniforms. Photo by Jerry Liebman Studio.

for No. 88 when Steve Vickers, who had No. 8, Hodge's number in Boston, declined to make a change. Goalie John Davidson also went for the double-digit approach briefly, becoming the first NHL player to wear 00 on his back before reverting to his previous No. 30.

NEW YORK Ice Exchange

The release of Rod Gilbert in November cut the last major tie with the teams of the early 1970s. Instead, the Rangers gave significant playing time to their two No. 1 draft picks, forwards Lucien DeBlois and Ron Duguay, both of whom hit the 20-goal mark in their first NHL seasons. A lesser-heralded winger, Eddie Johnstone, delighted Garden fans with his drive and hustle and quickly became a crowd favorite while scoring 13 goals despite spending most of his time as a checker. It was fade-out time for a number of veterans; Ken Hodge, Bill Goldsworthy, Don Awrey and Dallas Smith were among those who finished up long careers. GM John Ferguson's best move was perhaps his least-appreciated at the time: He brought in veteran goaltender Wayne Thomas, a former Canadien, on waivers from Toronto; Thomas managed only 12 wins while splitting time with John Davidson, but four of them were shutouts.

Wayne Thomas had four shutouts in his first season as a Ranger. Photo by Jerry Liebman Studio.

—1978 1979—

TIME CAPSULE

- **September 15, 1978:**
  Muhammad Ali became the first three-time heavyweight champion in history, regaining his title by winning a 15-round decision over Leon Spinks in New Orleans.

- **November 18, 1978:**
  More than 900 people, including 211 children, were found dead in Guyana. Jim Jones, leader of a religious sect, led the group in a mass suicide by poison.

- **March 27, 1978:**
  Magic Johnson led Michigan State past Larry Bird and Indiana State in the NCAA title game, foreshadowing their numerous meetings in the pros.

1978-1979

FINAL STANDINGS

Patrick Division	W	L	T	PTS	GF	GA
NY Islanders	51	15	14	116	358	214
Philadelphia	40	25	15	95	281	248
RANGERS	40	29	11	91	316	292
Atlanta	41	31	8	90	327	280

Other Division Winners:

Smythe—Chicago   Norris—Montreal

Adams—Boston

PLAYOFF RESULTS

Preliminary Round: Rangers defeated Los Angeles 2-0

Quarterfinals: Rangers defeated Philadelphia 4-1

Semifinals: Rangers defeated Islanders 4-2

Finals: Montreal defeated Rangers 4-1

LEADING PLAYOFF SCORERS

Phil Esposito (8-12-20)   Don Maloney (7-13-20)

STANLEY CUP CHAMPION

Montreal Canadiens

SEASON SNAPSHOT

Most Goals:
Phil Esposito (42)

Most Assists:
Anders Hedberg (45)

Most Points:
Phil Esposito/Anders Hedberg (78)

Most Power-Play Goals:
Phil Esposito (14)

Most Shorthanded Goals:
Nilsson/Duguay/Talafous/Dave Maloney (2)

Most Penalty Minutes:
Nick Fotiu (190)

Power Play:
75/306, 24.5%, 12 SHGA

Penalty-Killing:
233/311, 74.5%, 9 SHG

Most Wins, Goaltender:
John Davidson (20)

Lowest Goals-Against Average:
John Davidson (3.52)

Most Shutouts:
Wayne Thomas (1)

Rangers In All-Star Game:
Anders Hedberg, RW; Ulf Nilsson, C
(Challenge Cup)

The 1978-79 Season in Review

Everything old was new again in 1978-79. Frustrated by a Stanley Cup drought that was nearing four decades, management lured Fred Shero from Philadelphia, where he had coached the Flyers into one of the most feared—and successful—teams in NHL history. Shero, a former Ranger player and minor-league coach, took over as general manager and coach. The Rangers also went back to the future by returning to their long-time jersey style with "RANGERS" on the front of the home uniforms. Management showed money was no object by shelling out top dollar to land a pair of WHA stars, Anders Hedberg and Ulf Nilsson. Both Swedes quickly dismissed any skeptics with their knowledge, speed and two-way skills. Shero piloted the team to a 40-29-11 record, its best since 1973-74. A late slump, partly fueled by a broken ankle that sidelined Nilsson, left fans wondering if Shero still had his touch, but the doubters disappeared as the Rangers rode the goaltending of John Davidson to beat Los Angeles and oust the Flyers. Davidson then put on one of the great goaltending displays in team history as the Rangers upset the Islanders to make the finals for the first time since 1972. Davidson excelled again as the

John Davidson led the Rangers to the finals. Photo by Ray Amati.

Rangers stunned Montreal in the opener. But the Canadiens regrouped to win Games 2 and 3, then captured Game 4 in overtime at the Garden before wrapping up the series back at the Forum for their fourth straight Cup.

MAGIC MOMENT *May 8, 1979*

John Davidson and the Rangers stunned the Islanders. Photo by Jerry Liebman Studio.

Most experts gave the Rangers little chance of upsetting the powerful Islanders in the 1979 semifinals. Not only had the Isles finished ahead of Montreal in the race for the best regular-season record, but the Rangers were still hampered by the ankle injury that had sidelined center Ulf Nilsson late in the season. But John Davidson, playing the series of his life in goal, enabled the Rangers to survive a pair of overtime defeats and take a 3-2 lead when Anders Hedberg's goal won Game 5. Davidson held the fort in the first period of Game 6, allowing only a goal by Mike Bossy as the Isles dominated. But the Rangers, as they had all series, refused to give up. Don Murdoch tied the game at 5:03 of the middle period and Ron Greschner put them ahead to stay less than four minutes later. The rest of the night belonged to Davidson and the Rangers' defense, who stifled the suburbanites at every turn as the clock slowly ran down. "Those last seconds lasted two hours," said Murdoch. But they finally did run out, triggering a New Year's Eve in May celebration inside and outside the Garden—one that not even a final-round loss to the Canadiens could diminish.

RANGER LEGEND
Anders Hedberg and Ulf Nilsson

They came as a pair, and to Rangers fans, Anders Hedberg and Ulf Nilsson will be forever intertwined as the first Swedes to make a big splash at the Garden. Nilsson, a slick center, and Hedberg, a speedy right wing, terrorized the WHA with Winnipeg while playing with former NHL star Bobby Hull. When their contracts were up after 1977-78, the Rangers spent what was then considered a fortune to bring them both to the Big Apple. Though neither put up WHA-like numbers, both were a big hit with the fans and teammates due to their solid skills, intelligence and personalities. There

Anders Hedberg (L.). Photo by John Tremmel.

are those who think the Rangers might have won the Cup in 1979 had Nilsson's ankle not been broken when he was checked by Denis Potvin late in the season. That was the first of numerous injuries that ultimately forced Nilsson to retire in 1983, having averaged a point a game as a Ranger—but in only 170 contests, leaving Ranger fans to wonder what he could have done if he'd been healthy. Hedberg went on to record four 30-goal seasons and spent seven seasons as one of the most reliable wingers ever to wear a Ranger jersey. His dedication was rewarded with the Masterton Trophy in 1985, his final NHL season, before he stepped into the front office.

Ulf Nilsson

Ulf Nilsson File
- **BORN:**
  May 11, 1950; Nynashahn, Sweden
- **ACQUIRED:**
  Signed as free agent, June 1978
- **FIRST SEASON WITH RANGERS:**
  1978-79
- **BEST SEASON WITH RANGERS:**
  1978-79, 59 GP, 27-39-66, 21 PIM
- **TOTALS WITH RANGERS:**
  Regular season: 170 GP, 57-112-169, 85 PIM
  Playoffs: 25 GP, 11-10-21, 32 PIM
- **HONORS:**
  Players' Player Award, 1978-79

Anders Hedberg File
- **BORN:**
  February 25, 1951; Ornskoldsvik, Sweden
- **ACQUIRED:**
  Signed as free agent, June 1978
- **FIRST SEASON WITH RANGERS:**
  1978-79
- **BEST SEASON WITH RANGERS:**
  1978-79, 80 GP, 33-45-78, 33 PIM
- **TOTALS WITH RANGERS:**
  Regular season: 465 GP, 172-225-397, 144 PIM
  Playoffs: 58 GP, 22-24-46, 31 PIM
- **HONORS:**
  Masterton Trophy, 1984-85
  West Side Assn. Rangers MVP, 1979-80

CURTAIN CALL
Fred Shero

The banner headline in the New York *Daily News* read "A Shero's Welcome." That pretty much summed up the way Ranger fans felt about Fred Shero's return to New York in June 1978. Shero was born and bred a Ranger, playing parts of three seasons with the club in the late 1940s and coaching (successfully) in New York's farm system. He became well-known both for his innovative techniques and his willingness to learn from other systems, including the Soviet model of play. But with Emile Francis as coach/GM, there was nowhere for Shero to go in the Big Apple; instead, he took his talents to Philadelphia, where he turned the Flyers into the Broad Street Bullies, the first expansion team to capture the Stanley Cup. The Rangers gave up a No. 1 pick to bring Shero back home, and were rewarded with a surprising trip to the finals, their first in seven years, following a stunning upset of the Islanders in the semi-finals.

Fred Shero led the Rangers to the finals in 1979.

NEW YORK
Ice Exchange

Don Maloney gave the Rangers an offensive boost. Photo by John Tremmel.

Fred Shero, Anders Hedberg and Ulf Nilsson would have been enough additions for most clubs. But the Rangers also got a big boost from out of nowhere in mid-season when captain Dave Maloney's kid brother, Don, joined the team. The younger Maloney scored on his first NHL shot against Boston on February 14 and wound up with 26 points in 28 games while teaming with Phil Esposito and Don Murdoch. He added 20 points in the playoffs, setting an NHL record for rookies. Another key pickup was Bobby Sheehan, who came off hockey's discard pile and wound up playing 15 playoff games after not getting into a regular-season contest. Sheehan's speed played a big part in the victories over the Flyers and Islanders. Another unheralded pickup, forward Pierre Plante, added solid checking skills that fit in well with Shero's system.

—1979 1980—

TIME CAPSULE

- **November 4, 1979:**
  Iranian revolutionaries seized the U.S. embassy in Teheran, taking some 90 hostages, including 65 Americans.

- **February 22, 1980:**
  The United States hockey team beat the heavily favored Soviet Union 4-3 in the medal round at the Olympics in Lake Placid, N.Y. Two days later, the Americans beat Finland to win the gold medal.

- **May 18, 1980:**
  Mount St. Helens in Washington erupted for the first time since 1857. The volcanic fallout wiped out approximately 120 square miles of forest.

1979-1980

FINAL STANDINGS

Patrick Division	W	L	T	PTS	GF	GA
Philadelphia	48	12	20	116	327	254
Islanders	39	28	13	91	281	247
RANGERS	38	32	10	86	308	284
Atlanta	35	32	13	83	282	269
Washington	27	40	13	67	261	293

Other Division Winners:

Adams—Buffalo

Norris—Montreal

Smythe—Chicago

PLAYOFF RESULTS

Preliminaries: Rangers defeated Atlanta 3-1

Quarterfinals: Philadelphia defeated Rangers 4-1

LEADING PLAYOFF SCORER

Ron Duguay (5-2-7)

STANLEY CUP CHAMPION

New York Islanders

SEASON SNAPSHOT

Most Goals:
Phil Esposito (34)
Most Assists:
Don Maloney (48)
Most Points:
Phil Esposito (78)
Most Power-Play Goals:
Phil Esposito (13)
Most Shorthanded Goals:
Ron Duguay (3)
Most Penalty Minutes:
Dave Maloney (186)
Power Play:
79/304, 26.0%, 7 SHGA
Penalty Killing:
54/303, 82.2%, 8 SHG
Most Wins, Goaltender:
John Davidson (20)
Lowest Goals-Against Average:
John Davidson (3.17)
Most Shutouts:
John Davidson (2)
NHL Award Winners:
Fred Shero (Lester Patrick Award)
Rangers In All-Star Game:
Phil Esposito, C;
Ron Greschner, D

The 1979-80 Season Review

After coming oh-so-close in 1979, there was a lot of pressure on Fred Shero and company to bring home the Stanley Cup. But the season was a roller-coaster, alternating between unbeaten and winless streaks. The high point was winning 10 of 12 games between February 20 and March 16, a stretch that included an eight-game home winning streak. But the team only won three of its last 10 after that run, heading into the playoffs on a down note. Captain Dave Maloney placed himself 11th on the team's single-season penalty minutes list with 186, and Ron Greschner's 21 goals were four behind Brad Park for the most goals by a defenseman in a season. Phil Esposito had a five-game goal scoring streak just prior to their 10-in-12 run, and the team managed to score 10 goals against Edmonton and allow the same amount on Long Island. Espo led the club with 34 goals and 78 points. Ron Duguay went on a tear in the playoffs, and wound up with five goals and two assists in nine games. After dispatching Atlanta in four games in the first round of the playoffs (and simultaneously dispatching the Flames to their new home in Calgary), the Rangers took only one game from the Flyers in the second round, thus ending a season of promise much too soon for their liking.

Ron Duguay had a strong playoff in 1979-80 with five goals. Photo by George Kalinsky.

Magic Moment
January 14, 1980

The Rangers set a team mark for the fastest three goals scored when they hosted Colorado on January 14, 1980, in the first game between the two teams at Madison Square Garden since the 5-for-1 deal that brought Barry Beck to the Big Apple. The Rangers appeared to be in command when Doug Sulliman scored at 7:52 of the first period. Eddie Johnstone connected just five seconds later and Warren Miller scored 23 seconds after that, giving the Rangers three goals in 28 seconds. Unfortunately for the Rangers, they couldn't preserve the lead and the game wound up in a 6-6 tie. The Rangers' mark was eight seconds short of the NHL record set by the Boston Bruins in 1971, when John Bucyk, Ed Westfall, and Ted Green scored in a 20-second span during an 8-3 victory over Vancouver. Three years after setting the team mark, the Rangers would wind up in the record books for the fastest three goals scored by two teams when Mark Pavelich and Ron Greschner scored in a 9-second span against Minnesota and North Stars forward Willi Plett scored six seconds later, all in a 7-5 Ranger loss at Met Center on February 10, 1983.

Ed Johnstone (R) was part of the fastest three goals in Ranger history. Photo by John Tremmel.

CAPTAIN CRUNCH
Barry Beck

Barry Beck was playing in relative obscurity in Denver for the woeful Colorado Rockies, but his size and skills suggested that he wouldn't be there for long. As a rookie, he had 22 goals, 38 assists, and more importantly, 89 penalty minutes. He stood 6-foot-3 and was listed at 215 pounds—but played like he was 6-8 and 250. His offensive skills and size, combined with the Rockies' woes, made him a popular topic of conversation in trade talks. A lot of teams wanted Beck, but on November 2, 1979, the Rangers got him. GM Fred Shero traded away five players to get him—including three who were an integral part of the chemistry that had carried the Rangers to the finals the previous spring. So it was bye-bye Lucien DeBlois, Mike McEwen, Pat Hickey, Bobby Sheehan, and Dean Turner, and hello "Bubba." It wasn't the first time Beck was traded for a quintet of players; It had happened to him in juniors. Beck gained much of his toughness from his growing up in Vancouver as a self-described "ornery young punk." Averaging 111 penalty minutes in his seven seasons in a Rangers uniform, Beck played solidly for New York, but never lived up to his billing as the final piece

Photo by John Tremmel.

to the Stanley Cup puzzle. He sits eighth on the team's all-time penalty minute list, and his 231 minutes in 1980-81 is the fifth-highest single-season penalty minute total in team history. Though he never shot the puck enough for broadcaster Bill Chadwick's liking, Beck did score 66 times, and wound up with an average of 38 points in his seven seasons on Broadway. Those totals might have been higher, but Beck was never the same after suffering a shoulder injury in Game 4 of the first round of the 1984 playoffs against the Islanders when Patrick Flatley drilled him (cleanly) into the boards. Though he tried to play through them, the shoulder problems persisted and worsened, and eventually forced Beck to leave the Rangers to heal. He tried a brief comeback with the Los Angeles Kings after the Rangers traded him for future considerations prior to the 1989-90 season, but after scoring just one goal in 52 games with the Kings. Beck decided after season's end to call it a career.

Barry Beck File

- **BORN:**
  June 3, 1957; Vancouver, British Columbia
- **ACQUIRED:**
  From Colorado for Pat Hickey, Lucien DeBlois, Mike McEwen, Bobby Sheehan, Dean Turner and future considerations (Bobby Crawford), Nov. 2, 1979.
- **FIRST SEASON WITH RANGERS:**
  1979-80

- **BEST SEASON WITH RANGERS:**
  1979-80, 61 GP, 14-45-59, 98 PIM
- **TOTALS WITH RANGERS:**
  Regular season: 415 GP, 66-173-239, 775 PIM
  Playoffs: 51 GP, 10-23-33, 77 PIM
- **HONORS:**
  All-Star Game, 1981-82

CURTAIN CALL

Larry "Ratso" Sloman

For better or worse, the season was chronicled by Larry "Ratso" Sloman in a controversial book published under the title *Thin Ice: A Season in Hell with the New York Rangers.* Hockey's answer to *Ball Four,* Sloman's book depicted the Rangers as a carefree, fun-loving bunch who were as flamboyant off the ice as they were on it. Books written about the Rangers are hard to come by. Aside from Sloman's tell-all, *Daily News* writer Barry Meisel released a book called *Losing The Edge: The Rise and Fall of the Stanley Cup Champion New York Rangers* after the 1994 Cup triumph. But the book focused less on the success of the Rangers and concentrated more on the Neil Smith-Mike Keenan rift. Meisel's colleague, Frank Brown, combined with the publisher of the book you're reading now to chronicle the 1992-93 season, when the Rangers supposedly had a shot to win it all. Instead, Brown wrote a solid book on a season gone wrong entitled *Broadway Blues.* Though Brown missed the boat by one year, the book did have a wry selling point: it retailed, cleverly enough, for $19.40.

Thin Ice detailed a season that didn't end the way Ranger fans had hoped.

NEW YORK Ice Exchange

The landmark deal that brought Barry Beck to Broadway didn't cost the Rangers any of their top guns, but it did deprive them of some of the key players who had contributed to the run to the Stanley Cup finals the previous spring. Pat Hickey, Lucien DeBlois and Mike McEwen had logged a lot of ice time, while Bobby Sheehan had an excellent playoff series after working his way back to the NHL and tough-guy Dean Turner was considered a good prospect. Also, 1979 was the

The Rangers lost Nick Fotiu to Hartford in the expansion draft.. Photo by Stamatia Chalos.

year that the four WHA teams joined the NHL, and as a result, there was an expansion draft. The Rangers lost fan favorite and native son Nick Fotiu to Hartford in that draft, though he returned in January 1981 in a deal for a draft pick. The Rangers also picked up Olympian Dave Silk after the U.S. Olympic team shocked the world by winning a gold medal. Silk skated in two games without scoring a point, but made the team the following season and contributed 14 goals and 26 points.

Ranger Lists
Best Power Play %
Since the 1967
Expansion

1973-74
66 goals
222 attempts
29.7%

1974-75
84 goals
296 attempts
28.4%

1977-78
78 goals
279 attempts
28.0%

1979-80
79 goals
304 attempts
26.0%

1970-71
60 goals
234 attempts
25.6%

1980 — 1981

TIME CAPSULE

- **November 4, 1980:**
  Ronald Reagan was elected the 40th president of the United States, beating incumbent Jimmy Carter.

- **January 20, 1981:**
  American hostages were freed by terrorists who took over the U.S. embassy in Teheran.

- **February 26, 1981:**
  The Boston Bruins and Minnesota North Stars set NHL records for most penalties (84) and most penalty minutes in a game (406).

1980-1981
FINAL STANDINGS

	W	L	T	PTS	GF	GA
NY Islanders	48	18	14	110	355	260
Philadelphia	41	24	15	97	313	249
Calgary	39	27	14	92	329	298
RANGERS	30	36	14	74	312	317
Washington	26	36	18	70	286	317

Other Division Winners:

Adams—Buffalo

Norris—Montreal

Smythe—St. Louis

PLAYOFF RESULTS
Preliminary Round: Rangers defeated Los Angeles 3-1
Quarterfinals: Rangers defeated St. Louis 4-2
Semifinals: Islanders defeated Rangers 4-0
LEADING PLAYOFF SCORER
Ron Duguay (8-9-17)
STANLEY CUP CHAMPION
New York Islanders

SEASON SNAPSHOT

Most Goals:
Anders Hedberg/ Eddie Johnstone (30)
Most Assists:
Ron Greschner (41)
Most Points:
Anders Hedberg (70)
Most Power-Play Goals:
Anders Hedberg (7)
Most Shorthanded Goals:
Don Maloney (5)
Most Penalty Minutes:
Barry Beck (231)
Power Play:
63/351, 17.9%, 12 SHGA
Penalty Killing:
83/392, 78.8%, 14 SHG
Most Wins, Goaltender:
Doug Soetaert (16)
Lowest Goals-Against Average:
Wayne Thomas (3.40)
Most Shutouts:
Steve Baker (2)
Rangers In All-Star Game:
Eddie Johnstone, RW

The 1980-81 Season in Review

Nobody expected the Rangers to get off to a 3-12-3 start, and when they did, management decided that changes had to be made, most notably the coach and GM. Unfortunately for Fred Shero, he wore both hats. On November 19, Shero was ousted from both roles, and two days later, Lester Patrick's grandson Craig assumed both jobs. Patrick made a difference, guiding the team to a playoff spot by going 26-23-11 in his 60-game coaching stint, including a 6-2-2 stretch to end the season. Highlights included Eddie Johnstone's surprising 30-goal output, while Don Maloney hit his eventual career high with 29 tallies. Nick Fotiu rejoined the team after Hartford plucked him in the 1979 draft involving the WHA merger and scored five goals and sat in the sin bin for 91 minutes, while Phil Esposito came to a sudden decision in midseason and opted to retire. John Davidson, hampered by injuries, was just 1-7-1 before having to sit out the rest of the season. The bulk of the work in net went to Doug Soetaert, who wound up at .500 (16-16-7) with a 3.93 goals-against average. Backup Steve Baker had the only two shutouts of the season, and was 10-6-5 with a 3.48 goals-against average After a season in which they finished six

Doug Soetaert led the Rangers with 16 victories in 1980-81.

games under .500, little was expected from the Rangers in the playoffs. Instead, they surprised the Kings in the first round, and then ignored St. Louis' four-game regular-season sweep to shock the Blues in six games to make the semifinals. That's where the fun ended, though—the Islanders swept the Rangers in the semifinals on the way to their second straight Stanley Cup.

MAGIC MOMENT   *April 17, 1981*

Few things are rarer than a penalty-shot goal in a playoff game. There had been only one in NHL history until the Rangers visited St. Louis for Game 2 of the 1981 quarterfinals. With the Rangers already down a game, the Blues jumped out to 2-0 and 3-2 leads before the Rangers took command in the third period. New York evened the score when referee Dave Newell awarded Anders Hedberg a penalty shot after he was tripped by Blues defenseman Jack Brownschidle while on a breakaway at 8:29 of the final period. Hedberg skated deliberately towards goalie Mike Liut, and got within six feet of him before flipping a wrist shot into the left side of the net. The Rangers went on to score three more goals and win the game 6-4, sparking them to a six-game upset of the Blues, who had finished second in the regular-season standings. Prior to Hedberg's goal, the only successful penalty shot in Stanley Cup play was scored by Wayne Connelly of Minnesota on April 9, 1968. He beat Terry Sawchuk of Los Angeles, a game the North Stars won 7-5. Hedberg's postseason penalty shot was only the 10th in NHL history, and one of the eight misses was taken by the Rangers' Alex Shibicky in 1937.

Anders Hedberg's penalty shot goal sparked the Rangers past St. Louis. Photo by John Tremmel.

GRIT TIMES TWO
Eddie Johnstone and Nick Fotiu

Nick Fotiu. Photo by John Tremmel.

They were hardly superstars, but Eddie Johnstone and Nick Fotiu were two of the Rangers' most popular players as the team ventured into a new decade. Johnstone and Fotiu were pure grit, blessed with a lot of heart. 1980-81 was Johnstone's career season, as he scored 30 goals and was the Blueshirts' sole representative at the All-Star game in Los Angeles. Johnstone would also score 30 goals in 1981-82 despite playing in only 68 games. He remained a Ranger until June 13, 1983, when he was dealt along with Ron Duguay and Eddie Mio to Detroit for Willie Huber, Mike Blaisdell and Mark Osborne. He stayed with the Red Wings until his retirement after the 1986-87 season. Fotiu was a story of hometown boy who makes good. Born on Staten Island, Fotiu was a product of the old New Hyde Park Arrows of the Met Junior League. He debuted with the Rangers in time for the 1976-77 season, and tallied four goals and a career season-high 174 penalty minutes. His Rangers total of 970 career penalty minutes put Fotiu fifth on the Rangers' all-time list. GM Fred Shero left him unprotected in the WHA merger draft, and Hartford grabbed him. After 1 1/2 seasons with the Whalers, Fotiu was traded back to Broadway for a fifth-round draft pick. Fotiu did lead the league in one category: tossed pucks. When the team skated in the pre-game warmup, Fotiu would toss some vulcanized rubber into the seats, which delighted and endeared him to the Garden faithful. Fotiu's second tour of duty lasted until the summer of 1985, when he was sent to Calgary. After two seasons with the Flames, he skated for the Flyers and Oilers before calling it quits in 1989. Fotiu has become a successful minor-league coach, and it's not impossible he could reappear in the NHL some day behind the bench.

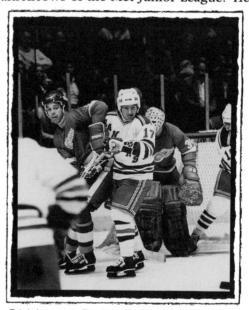

Ed Johnstone. To the left is Detroit Red Wings defenseman Willie Huber, who would soon become a Ranger. Photo by John Tremmel.

Eddie Johnstone File
- **BORN:**
  March 2, 1954; Brandon, Manitoba
- **ACQUIRED:**
  Rangers sixth-round pick in 1974 Entry Draft
- **FIRST SEASON WITH RANGERS:**
  1975-76
- **BEST SEASON WITH RANGERS:**
  1980-81, 80 GP, 30-38-68, 100 PIM
- **TOTALS WITH RANGERS:**
  Regular season: 371 GP, 109-125-234, 319 PIM
  Playoffs: 53 GP, 13-9-22, 83 PIM
- **HONORS:**
  All-Star Game, 1980-81
  West Side Assn. Rangers MVP, 1980-81

Nick Fotiu File
- **BORN:**
  May 25, 1952; Staten Island, N.Y.
- **ACQUIRED:**
  Signed as a free agent, July 23, 1976.
- **FIRST SEASON WITH RANGERS:**
  1976-77
- **BEST SEASON WITH RANGERS:**
  1981-82, 70 GP, 8-10-18, 151 PIM
- **TOTALS WITH RANGERS:**
  Regular season: 455 GP, 41-62-103, 970 PIM
  Playoffs: 24 GP, 0-3-3, 27 PIM

CURTAIN CALL
Crumb Bum Award

Toots Shor, proprietor of one of New York's legendary saloons, with the Rangers' blessing, established a "Crumb Bum" award to be given to the Blueshirt who does a lot to help the children of the city. The first winner of the "Crumb Bum" award was defenseman Ed Hospodar. Subsequent winners include Barry Beck, Nick Fotiu, the Maloney brothers, Ron Greschner, John Vanbiesbrouck, Pierre Larouche, Guy Lafleur, Carey Wilson, Mike Gartner, Kris King, Adam Graves, Brian Leetch, Mark Messier and Jeff Beukeboom. The "Crumb Bum" was one of several awards created to reward their players for their hard work both on and off the ice. Other team-created awards include the Steven McDonald Extra Effort Award, the Fan Club Ceil Seidel Award, and the Lars-Erik Sjoberg Award. To New Yorkers, McDonald's award is self-explanatory, Seidel, who was a long-time member of the Fan Club, was honored after her murder in 1994. The Sjoberg Award is given to the best rookie in the Rangers training camp.

Ed Hospodar won the first "Crumb Bum" award.

NEW YORK
Ice Exchange

The firing of coach/GM Fred Shero and the hiring of Craig Patrick on November 19 caused a change in philosophy as well as personnel. While Shero's last act was to trade defenseman Mario Marois to Vancouver for forward Jere Gillis, Patrick's only trade was the one that brought Nick Fotiu back from Hartford. Patrick chose to stick with the team he was left with, and his confidence paid off as they reached the semifinals. Perhaps more stunning than Shero's firing was Phil Esposito's midseason decision to call it a career. Espo left with career totals of 717 goals and 1,590 points, both second only to Gordie Howe at that time. A total of 30 players played in at least one regular-season game, and the 31st (John Hughes), participated solely in three playoff games. Among them were No. 1 draft pick Doug Sulliman, a rookie with a lot of promise. He lasted two seasons on Broadway before being traded to Hartford along with Chris Kotsopoulous for Mike Rogers just before the 1981-82 season started.

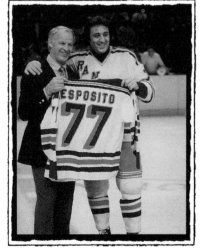

Phil Esposito ended his NHL career in 1980-81. Photo by Jerry Liebman Studio.

Rangers On The Air

What do Monty Hall and Phil Esposito have in common? Well, both have been noted for making lots of deals; both are proud Canadians—and both have served as "voices" of the Rangers. Hall was a between-periods commentator on radio between 1958 and 1960, and Esposito did television commentary from 1981 to 1986.

Through the years, the Rangers have employed some of the most notable names in New York sports broadcasting history. Marty Glickman, Marv Albert, Bob Wolff, Jim Gordon, Win Elliot, Tim Ryan, Bill Mazer and Sal Marchiano are among those who've brought Ranger action to New York fans on radio and television.

Although games were carried sporadically on a Garden-run station, WMSG, during the 1930s, the first regular radio broadcast season of the Rangers was 1939-40, when WHN carried home games with Bert Lee behind the microphone, a position he held until the mid-1950s. The Rangers were part of the first televised hockey game in 1940, and first appeared regularly on television during the 1945-46 season, when WCBW (now WCBS-TV) showed some of their games with Bob Edge doing the play-by-play.

The first Rangers' road game to be broadcast back to New York came on December 15, 1951, when Lee and Ward Wilson journeyed to Toronto to

Marv Albert has done the Rangers on radio for 30 years. His son Ken, now shares the job.

describe the Leafs' 4-1 victory over the Rangers. There was another first in 1958, when WINS did all 70 games. Marv Albert, the man of so many broadcast hats, began calling the Rangers on a regular basis in 1966-67. The current season is his 30th with the team.

In 1969-70, the Rangers began showing home games on the Madison Square Garden Network, which has grown into one of the largest regional cable networks in the United States. WOR (later WWOR) televised road games from 1965 to 1989, when MSG Network began showing all Ranger games, except for those that are nationally televised.

The 1973-74 season marked the debut of two of the most famous Ranger broadcast teams—Albert with Sal (Red Light) Messina on radio and Gordon with Hall of Fame referee Bill (The Big Whistle) Chadwick on television. Chadwick had previously been paired with Albert on radio?

Sam Rosen and John Davidson have spent 10 straight seasons together on television with the Rangers, a tenure highlighted by their call of the run to the 1994 Stanley Cup. Albert's son, Kenny, is now in his second season of radio play-by-play with Messina, having replaced Howie ("Matteau...Matteau...Matteau") Rose, who spent six years behind the microphone.

Win Elliot was a popular Ranger voice on radio and television.

Rangers Radio Outlets

1930s-WMSG
1939-40 to 1947-48-WHN
1948-49 to 1954-55-WMGM
1955-56 to 1959-60-WINS
1961-62-WINS
1962-63 to 1964-65-WCBS
1965-66 to 1969-70-WHN
1970-71 to 1973-74-WNBC
1974-75 to 1983-84-WNEW
1984-85-WPAT/WGBB/WFAS
1985-86 to 1987-88-WNBC
1988-89 to present-WFAN*

Primary station; WMCA, WPAT, WEVD and WXRK have broadcast games when conflicts arose with other events

Rangers TV Outlets

1945-46 to 1946-47-WCBW
1947-48-WCBS
1948-49 to 1957-58-WPIX
1956-57 to 1958-59-CBS
(part of netwrok package)
1962-63 to 1964-65-WPIX
1965-66 to 1987-88-WOR
(later WWOR, road games)
1969-70 to 1987-88-MSG Network
(home games)
1988-89 to present-MSG Network

Primary Ranger Broadcasters

Radio

1939-54-Bert Lee
1944-57-Ward Wilson
1959-63-Jim Gordon
1963-65-Win Elliot
1965-66-Norm Jarry
1966-present-Marv Albert
1969-74 Bill Chadwick
1974-present-Sal Messina
1984-88-Mike Emrick
1989-95-Howie Rose
1995-present-Ken Albert

Television

1945-47-Bob Edge
1948-69-Win Elliot*
1953-59-Bud Palmer
1954-74-Bob Wolff*
1966-84-Jim Gordon*
1973-81-Bill Chadwick
1981-86-Phil Esposito
1984-present-Sam Rosen
1986-present-John Davidson

Did not work all seasons during these years

—1981  1982—

TIME CAPSULE

- **September 21, 1981:**
  Sandra Day O'Connor became the first female member of the United States Supreme Court.

- **March 29, 1982:**
  Michael Jordan and the North Carolina Tar Heels edged Georgetown to win the NCAA basketball title, their first under coach Dean Smith.

- **June 25, 1982:**
  Secretary of State Alexander Haig resigned following disagreements with President Ronald Reagan.

1981-1982

FINAL STANDINGS

Patrick Division	W	L	T	PTS	GF	GA
NY Islanders	54	16	10	118	385	250
RANGERS	39	27	14	92	316	306
Philadelphia	38	31	11	87	325	313
Pittsburgh	31	36	13	75	310	337
Washington	26	41	13	65	319	338

Other Division Winners:

Adams—Montreal

Smythe—Edmonton

Norris—Minnesota

PLAYOFF RESULTS

Patrick Semifinals: Rangers defeated Philadelphia 3-1

Patrick Finals: Islanders defeated Rangers 4-2

LEADING PLAYOFF SCORER

Robbie Ftorek (7-4-11)

STANLEY CUP CHAMPION

New York Islanders

SEASON SNAPSHOT

Most Goals:
Ron Duguay (40)
Most Assists:
Mike Rogers (65)
Most Points:
Mike Rogers (103)
Most Power-Play Goals:
Mark Pavelich (12)
Most Shorthanded Goals:
Mark Pavelich (3)
Most Penalty Minutes:
Ed Hospodar (152)
Power Play:
68/306, 22.2%, 12 SHGA
Penalty-Killing:
244/319, 76.5%, 7 SHG
Most Wins, Goaltender:
Steve Weeks (23)
Lowest Goals-Against Average:
Ed Mio (3.56)
Most Shutouts:
Steve Weeks (1)
Rangers In All-Star Game:
Barry Beck, D;
Ron Duguay, RW

The 1981-82 Season in Review

A reverse pairing of the combination that led the United States to Olympic glory in 1980 turned the Rangers into contenders in 1981-82. General manager Craig Patrick, an assistant coach under Herb Brooks with the gold medal-winning U.S. squad, hired his old boss to relieve him behind the bench, and the results were impressive. Using a more European-flavored, speed-and-passing game, Brooks piloted the Rangers to 92 points and a second-place finish in the Patrick Division. Center Mike Rogers, acquired from Hartford, threatened the team scoring record before finishing with 103 points, while fan favorite Ron Duguay finally lived up to his promise with 40 goals. Two other newcomers, center Mark Pavelich (33 goals, 76 points) and defenseman Reijo Ruotsalainen (18 goals, 56 points), also turned into key producers as the Rangers overcame the loss of two key veterans, goalie John Davidson and right wing Anders Hedberg, both of whom were sidelined by injury (Davidson wound up having to retire). The Rangers ousted third-place Phila-

Ron Duguay's 40 goals helped the Rangers to a second-place finish. Photo by Jerry Liebman Studio.

delphia in the opening round and gave the defending Stanley Cup champion Islanders all they could handle, but wound up losing in six games as their archrivals went on to a third straight title. Still, the improved showing augured well for the future.

MAGIC MOMENT *April 8, 1982*

Mikko Leinonen set a Ranger single-game playoff record with six assists. Photo by George Kalinsky.

Mikko Leinonen was the Rangers' "other" Finnish rookie in 1981-82, the one with at least a passing command of English but without the speed and shot belonging to countryman Reijo Ruotsalainen. He had only 11 goals and 19 assists while playing in 53 of 80 regular-season games. But Game 2 of the Patrick Division semifinals thrust Leinonen into the spotlight—and splattered him across the NHL and Rangers' record books. With his team in trouble after a first-game loss at home to Philadelphia in the best-of-five series, Leinonen revived the Rangers and set a playoff record with six assists as New York routed the Flyers 7-3. "Everything he touched turned to gold," said captain Barry Beck after Leinonen set up the game-tying goal in the first period, added three more assists in the second period and another pair in the third. Leinonen broke the NHL playoff record for assists in a game, tied the league single-game mark for points and set team marks for assists and points in a game. "I didn't know about the records," the quiet Finn said. "When you know where the guys are, it's easy to look for them." The Rangers went on to sweep two games in Philadelphia and eliminate the Flyers for the second of three straight seasons.

MISTER ROGERS
Mike Rogers

Herb Brooks liked players who could skate and shoot. Mike Rogers fit the bill perfectly. At 5-8 and 175 pounds, Rogers wasn't going to out-muscle too many people. But he was fast on his feet and averaged nearly a point a game in five seasons with Edmonton and New England in the World Hockey Association. When the Whalers joined the NHL in 1979, Rogers showed he was good enough to play with the big boys, too. He rang up 44 goals and 105 points in 1979-80, and followed with a 40-goal, 105-point effort in 1980-81. Despite the gaudy offensive numbers, the Whalers weren't always happy with Rogers' defensive play. They made him available and GM Craig Patrick landed the slick center on the eve of the 1981-82 season for defenseman Chris Kotsopoulos and forwards Doug Sulliman (a former No. 1 pick) and Gerry McDonald. Rogers was an immediate hit at the Garden, picking up where he had left off with the Whalers. He started hot and stayed that way, threatening to

rewrite the Rangers' scoring records for most of the season before settling for a 103-point campaign, third-best in team history. He set club records for assists (65) and point-scoring streak (16 games) that lasted until the arrival of Brian Leetch. Though Rogers never put up those kind of numbers again, he also led the team in scoring the next season with 29 goals and 76 points while tying another team mark with five shorthanded goals. His production dropped to 61 and 64 points over the next two seasons, but he was still among the team's most productive forwards. In all, Rogers wound up averaging nearly a point a game during his five seasons in New York, finishing with 117 goals and 308 points in just 316 games.

Mike Rogers File

- **BORN:**
  October 24, 1954; Calgary, Alberta
- **ACQUIRED:**
  Traded by Hartford for Chris Kotsopoulos, Gerry McDonald and Doug Sulliman, October 2, 1981
- **FIRST SEASON WITH RANGERS:**
  1981-82

- **BEST SEASON WITH RANGERS:**
  1981-82, 80 GP, 38-65-103, 43 PIM
- **TOTALS WITH RANGERS:**
  Regular season: 316 GP, 117-191-308, 142 PIM
  Playoffs: 14 GP, 1-10-11, 6 PIM
- **HONORS:**
  West Side Assn. Rangers MVP, 1981-82

CURTAIN CALL

December 5, 1981

The Rangers drafted John Vanbiesbrouck in June 1981 with an eye toward the future. They never dreamed that future would come so soon. But with injuries leaving the Rangers undermanned in goal, they summoned the 18-year-old from Sault Ste. Marie in the Ontario Hockey League for a one-game cameo, a meeting with the Colorado Rockies in Denver on December 5, 1981. The kid from Detroit showed little nervousness as he backstopped the Rangers to a 2-1 victory—a night that he's never forgotten. "One of my memories is how well (Colorado goalie) Glenn Resch played. He was terrific," Vanbiesbrouck remembered years later. "Another is the goal I gave up: It was early in the game. Nick Fotiu was playing left wing at the time and he felt bad because he hadn't made a good play—he came up to me after the game and said 'I'm really sorry' because he thought I would have had a shutout otherwise. I was just thrilled to get the win." It was the first of his 200 victories as a Ranger.

John Vanbiesbrouck won his NHL debut as an 18-year-old. Photo by Bruce Bennett.

NEW YORK Ice Exchange

Despite a surprising trip to the semifinals in 1981, GM Craig Patrick knew he needed more talent—and used all possible avenues to find it. His best move came just days before the season, when he acquired speedy center Mike Rogers from Hartford for Chris Kotsopoulos, Doug Sulliman and Gerry McDonald. Rogers became the Rangers' first 100-point scorer in a decade. Mark Pavelich, a 1980 Olympian ignored by the NHL, signed as a free agent and chipped in with 33 goals and 76 points. Two Finnish rookies, defenseman Reijo Ruotsalainen and center Mikko Leinonen, also became solid contributors. Needing a goalie when injuries forced John Davidson to retire, the Rangers found a productive tandem in holdover Steve Weeks, who won 23 games, and Ed Mio, who went 13-6-3 after being acquired from Edmonton in December.

Reijo Ruotsalainen gave the Rangers an offensive boost.

245

—1982 1983—

- **October 20, 1982:**
  The St. Louis Cardinals won the World Series, beating the Milwaukee Brewers in seven games.

- **December 2, 1982:**
  Barney Clark was the first successful recipient of an artificial heart transplant. He died on March 23, 1983.

- **March 2, 1983:**
  More than 125 million viewers, the largest TV audience ever at the time, tuned in to watch the final episode of M*A*S*H.

1982-1983

FINAL STANDINGS

Patrick Division	W	L	T	PTS	GF	GA
Philadelphia	49	23	8	106	326	240
NY Islanders	42	26	12	96	302	226
Washington	39	25	16	94	306	283
RANGERS	35	35	10	80	306	287
New Jersey	17	49	14	48	230	330
Pittsburgh	18	53	9	45	257	394

Other Division Winners:

Adams—Boston

Smythe—Edmonton

Norris—Chicago

PLAYOFF RESULTS

Patrick Semifinals: Rangers defeated Philadelphia 3-0

Patrick Finals: Islanders defeated Rangers 4-2

LEADING PLAYOFF SCORER

Anders Hedberg (4-8-12)

STANLEY CUP CHAMPION

New York Islanders

SEASON SNAPSHOT

Most Goals:
Mark Pavelich (37)

Most Assists:
Reijo Ruotsalainen (53)

Most Points:
Mike Rogers (76)

Most Power-Play Goals:
Don Maloney (14)

Most Shorthanded Goals:
Mike Rogers (5)

Most Penalty Minutes:
Dave Maloney (132)

Power Play:
71/317, 22.4%, 8 SHGA

Penalty-Killing:
237/312, 76.0%, 12 SHG

Most Wins, Goaltender:
Ed Mio (16)

Lowest Goals-Against Average:
Ed Mio (3.45)

Most Shutouts:
Ed Mio (2)

Rangers In All-Star Game:
Don Maloney, LW

The 1982-83 Season in Review

The Rangers' strong showing against the Islanders the previous spring led to high expectations for 1982-83, and for the first half of the season, the club seemed intent on delivering. A 15-5-2 run from mid-November through early January counteracted a slow start and left Rangers fans anticipating a return matchup with the Islanders—this time with a different outcome. But perhaps bored by the assurance they would make the playoffs (New Jersey and Pittsburgh were out of the race by Christmas), the Rangers were inconsistent the rest of the way, ultimately dropping to .500 for the season with a closing-night loss to Washington. Finishing fourth sent the Rangers against the division-champion Flyers for the fourth time in five years. Flyers coach Bob McCammon had derided some of the Rangers' smallish forwards as "Smurfs" after the tiny blue cartoon characters, but this time, the "Smurfs" had the last laugh, winning the first two games in Philadelphia before embarrassing the Flyers 9-3 to sweep the series. That set up a meeting with the Islanders for the third straight year—but just as they had the year before, the Rangers had to be satisfied with a good effort. The series was tied after the Rangers won Games 3 and 4 at home, but the Isles won Game 5 at the Coliseum before closing out the series with a 5-2 victory at the Garden.

Don Maloney matched his career high with 29 goals in 1982-83. Photo by Ray Amati.

MAGIC MOMENT

April 17, 1983

Beating the Islanders in the playoffs is always special. But the victory over their archrivals in Game 3 of the 1983 Patrick Division finals might have been the wildest game the two have ever played in the postseason. For two periods, the game was a laugher: The Rangers routed their old nemesis, Billy Smith, and took a 7-2 lead into the final 20 minutes. But nothing in a Ranger-Islander game is ever easy, as the Rangers soon learned. Billy Carroll, Mike Bossy and Anders Kallur all scored unassisted goals to make it 7-5, and Denis Potvin's power-play goal with 43 seconds left made it a one-goal game. The Islanders pressed for the equalizer, and looked like they had it when Bossy shoved the puck past Eddie Mio with seven seconds to play. But the gasp of shock quickly turned into cheers when referee Bruce Hood waved off the goal, saying he had blown the whistle before the puck went in. The Rangers ran out the clock and

Mark Pavelich and the Rangers held off Mike Bossy and the Islanders in a furious finish. Photo by John Tremmel.

went home with their first Garden playoff win over the Isles since eliminating them in 1979. "We didn't do it the right way," defenseman Tom Laidlaw said. "But we did it. We won."

RANGER LEGEND
Dave and Don Maloney

Dave Maloney

They played different positions—Dave was a defenseman, Don a left wing—but the Maloney brothers shared one trait: Neither wasted much time earning a regular job with the Rangers. Dave, the Rangers' No. 1 pick in the 1974 draft, was an NHL regular before his 20th birthday after coming to New York to stay late in 1975-76. By October 1978, he was a 22-year-old captain, the youngest in Rangers history, and wound up playing 605 games on the Rangers' backline over a decade. Kid brother Don (two years younger) was the Rangers' top choice in 1978 and spent just half a season in the minors before earning a call-up. He electrified Garden fans by scoring on his first shot in his NHL debut against Boston on February 14, averaged nearly a point a game, and added a rookie playoff-record 20 points to help fuel the Rangers' stunning run to the finals. He followed that with five straight 20-goal seasons, and still holds or shares the team single-season record for game-winning goals (9 in 1980-81) and shorthanded goals (5, also in 1980-81), as well as the team mark for fastest three goals in a game, ringing up a hat trick in just 2:30 against Washington on February 21, 1981. Don, one of the hardest workers ever to wear a Ranger jersey, had a goal in the 1983 All-Star Game at the Nassau Coliseum and followed that by earning the MVP award at the 1984 game at the Meadowlands with a one-goal, three-assist performance. He also scored one of the most memorable goals in team history, swatting a loose puck out of the air and into the net in the final minute of regulation time to send Game 5 of the 1984 opening-round playoff series against the Islanders into overtime, though the Isles eventually won the game, 3-2.

Don Maloney

Dave Maloney File

- **BORN:**
  July 31, 1956, Kitchener, Ontario
- **ACQUIRED:**
  Rangers' first pick in 1974 draft
- **FIRST SEASON WITH RANGERS:**
  1974-75
- **BEST SEASON WITH RANGERS:**
  1982, 78 GP, 8-42-50, 132 PIM
- **TOTALS WITH RANGERS:**
  Regular season: 605 GP, 70-225-295, 1,113 PIM
  Playoffs: 48 GP, 7-17-24, 91 PIM
- **HONORS:**
  West Side Assn. Rangers MVP, 1976-77

Don Maloney File

- **BORN:**
  September 5, 1958, Lindsay, Ontario
- **ACQUIRED:**
  Rangers' first pick (second round) in 1978 draft
- **FIRST SEASON WITH RANGERS:**
  1978-79
- **BEST SEASON WITH RANGERS:**
  1979-80, 79 GP, 25-48-73, 97 PIM
- **TOTALS WITH RANGERS:**
  Regular season: 653 GP, 195-307-502, 739 PIM
  Playoffs: 85 GP, 22-35-57, 91 PIM
- **HONORS:**
  All-Star Game, 1982-83, 1983-84 (MVP)
  Players' Player Award: 1979-80, 1980-81, 1986-87

CURTAIN CALL
Herb Brooks

Herb Brooks had never coached or played in the pros before being named as coach of the Rangers in June 1981. But the lack of experience at the NHL level didn't seem to bother anyone—not after what he had accomplished a year earlier. Brooks earned a place in hockey history by leading the United States to the 1980 Olympic title, upsetting the powerful Soviet Union in the semifinals and rallying to beat Finland to take the gold. There was immediate speculation that Brooks would wind up with the Rangers; instead, he coached for a year in Switzerland before joining his former Olympic assistant, Craig Patrick. Brooks was an immediate hit—the Rangers had a 92-point season in 1981-82 (earning coach of the year honors from *The Sporting News* for Brooks) and bettered that with a 93-point campaign two years later. His teams used the swirling, speed-oriented system he had used with the Olympic team while incorporating the best of North American hockey. He became the fastest Ranger coach to 100 victories when New York beat Detroit on January 16, 1984, and is one of only six New York coaches to reach the 100-victory mark.

Herb Brooks (L.) and Bill Chadwick (R.). Herb Brooks led the Rangers to a pair of 90-point seasons. Photo by Bill Mitchell Photography.

NEW YORK
Ice Exchange

Glen Hanlon beefed up the Rangers' goaltending corps.

After doing some major retooling in 1981-82, GM Craig Patrick was less active in 1982-83. He took a gamble on former Czech and WHA star Vaclav Nedomansky, who had 12 goals in 35 games, and added a solid checker in Kent-Erik Andersson. Chris Kontos, the Rangers' No. 1 pick in the 1982 draft, got significant playing time, as did former U.S. Olympian Rob McClanahan, who had 22 goals in his first full NHL season. Brooks and Patrick added another of their 1980 players, defenseman Bill Baker, as well as Scot Kleinendorst to help take up the slack as injuries limited Ron Greschner to just 10 games. With injuries finally sending goalie John Davidson into retirement, the Rangers beefed up their goaltending corps at midseason by getting Glen Hanlon from St. Louis along with Nedomansky for defenseman Andre Dore. Hanlon got most of his work as Ed Mio's backup, but took over the No. 1 job the next season.

Ranger Lists

Most Playoff Points, Career

Brian Leetch
67 GP, 26 G, 53 A, 79 Pts

Mark Messier
55 GP, 26 G, 42 A, 68 Pts

Rod Gilbert
79 GP, 34 G 33 A, 57 Pts

Don Maloney
85 GP, 22 G, 35 A, 57 Pts

Walt Tkaczuk
93 GP, 19 G, 32 A, 51 Pts

Steve Vickers
68 GP, 24 G, 25 A, 49 Pts

Ron Greschner
84 GP, 17 G, 32 A, 49 Pts

Ron Duguay
69 GP, 28 G, 19 A, 47 Pts

Anders Hedberg
58 GP, 22 G, 24 A, 46 Pts

Brad Park
64 GP, 12 G, 32 A, 44 Pts

New York Rangers– New Jersey Devils Rivalry

When the New Jersey Devils moved from Denver to East Rutherford, N.J., in 1982, they were eager to establish a serious rivalry with the Rangers. It took 12 years to accomplish that feat—just about one year for every mile between the Garden and the Meadowlands.

There were two reasons why the rivalry took so long to build: the established Ranger-Islander feud, and the Devils' own struggles—they didn't even make the playoffs until 1988. Still, nothing establishes a rivalry better than playoff action, and when the two teams finally met in postseason play for the first time in the Patrick Division semifinals of 1992, emotions ran high on both sides before the Rangers emerged victorious in seven games.

Their next playoff get-together was a classic—the 1994 Eastern Conference finals, in which the Rangers again triumphed in seven games. The Devils, who finished second in the overall standings behind the Rangers, looked to be in the driver's seat with a 3-2 lead in games and a 2-0 lead late in the second period of Game 6. But

Mark Messier, who had guaranteed a Ranger victory, delivered on that promise with a hat trick in a 4-2 come-from-behind victory. Game 7 was another classic, with the Devils forcing overtime by scoring in the final seconds of regulation before Stephane Matteau's double-overtime goal sent the Rangers on to the finals.

With the Devils now among the NHL's elite, the trans-Hudson rivalry is among the NHL's fiercest. The Devils are no longer patsies for their big-city rivals, although ironically, the only series sweep by either team came in 1993-94, when the Devils set a team record for points, but earned none against the Rangers. Over the last two seasons, New Jersey is 5-2-2.

Though there's still no team Ranger fans would rather see lose than the Islanders, the Devils are now a solid second in that regard.

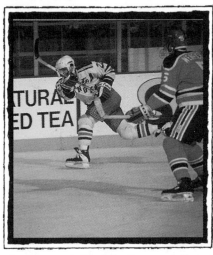

The Rangers, led by Mike Gartner, outlasted the Devils in the first round in 1992. Photo by Bruce Bennett.

Stephane Matteau was the hero of the 1994 Rangers-Devils Series. Photo by Bruce Bennett.

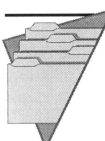

Rangers-Devils Rivalry File:

RANGERS RECORD: Regular Season: 128 GP. 69-45-14, 513 GF, 417 GA
Playoffs: 14 GP, 8-6-0, 46 GF, 41 GA (Rangers won both series 4-3)

SERIES SWEEPS: Regular Season: For - 1 (1993-94, 6-0-0)
Playoffs: None

PLAYERS WHO PLAYED FOR BOTH TEAMS:

Dave Barr, Bob Brooke, Joe Cirella, Pat Conacher, Bruce Driver, Troy Mallette, George McPhee, Corey Millen, Bernie Nicholls, Dave Pichette, Walt Poddubny, Steve Richmond, Rejo Richmond, Doug Sulliman, Peter Sundstrom, Esa Tikkanen, Carol Vadnais, Pat Verbeek.

—1983  1984—

⏳ TIME CAPSULE

- **October 23, 1983:**
  A truck filled with explosives blew up outside the U.S. Marine headquarters in Beirut, Lebanon, killing 241 Marine and Navy personnel.

- **April 23, 1984:**
  Federal researchers announced the identification of a virus thought to cause acquired immunity deficiency syndrome (AIDS).

- **May 8, 1994:**
  The Soviet Olympic committee withdrew from the Summer Olympics, which opened in July in Los Angeles.

1983-1984
FINAL STANDINGS

Patrick Division	W	L	T	PTS	GF	GA
NY Islanders	50	26	4	104	357	269
Washington	48	27	5	101	308	226
Philadelphia	44	26	10	98	350	290
RANGERS	42	29	9	93	314	304
New Jersey	17	56	7	41	231	350
Pittsburgh	16	58	6	38	254	390

Other Division Winners:

Adams—Boston

Norris—Minnesota

Smythe—Edmonton

PLAYOFF RESULTS
Patrick Semifinals: Islanders defeated Rangers 3-2
LEADING PLAYOFF SCORER
Mark Pavelich (2-4-6)
STANLEY CUP CHAMPION
Edmonton Oilers

SEASON SNAPSHOT

Most Goals:
Pierre Larouche (48)
Most Assists:
Mark Pavelich (55)
Most Points:
Mark Pavelich (82)
Most Power-Play Goals:
Pierre Larouche (19)
Most Shorthanded Goals:
Don Maloney/Mike Rogers (3)
Most Penalty Minutes:
Dave Maloney (168)
Power Play:
74/291, 25.1%, 13 SHGA
Penalty-Killing:
271/347, 78.1%, 12 SHG
Most Wins, Goaltender:
Glen Hanlon (28)
Lowest Goals-Against Average:
Glen Hanlon (3.51)
Most Shutouts:
Glen Hanlon (1)
Rangers In All-Star Game:
Pierre Larouche, C;
Don Maloney, LW

The Rangers picked the wrong year to have their best season in a decade. Some excellent shopping by GM Craig Patrick and a superb coaching effort by Herb Brooks highlighted a 93-point season, the Rangers' best since the early 1970s. Pierre Larouche, signed as a free agent, was an instant hit with 48 goals. A couple of ex-Red Wings, Mark Osborne and Willie Huber, plus Swedish rookies Jan Erixon and Peter Sundstrom and post-Olympic additions James Patrick and Bob Brooke all contributed, while Glen Hanlon was solid in goal. The power play was among the NHL's best and the Rangers were especially good when the going got tight, winning 17 of 26 one-goal games. While their 93 points would have won the Norris Division in a breeze, in the powerful Patrick, it was only good for a fourth-place finish and an opening-round rematch with the Islanders. The Rangers had the four-time champs on the ropes, winning 3-0 in Game 2 at the Nassau Coliseum and 7-2 at home in Game 3. They led 1-0 entering the final period of Game 4 before the Islanders rallied to win, then forced

Mark Pavelich led the Rangers with 82 points. Photo by John Tremmel.

overtime in Game 5 when Don Maloney scored in the final minute of regulation. But after Billy Smith stopped Bob Brooke's breakaway in overtime, Ken Morrow's shot from the right circle eluded Hanlon, leaving the Rangers proud of their effort but disappointed with the outcome.

MAGIC MOMENT

April 10, 1984

For three straight seasons, the Rangers' season had ended at the hands of their archrivals from Long Island. Herb Brooks & Co. were determined the streak would not reach four years. They had the Islanders down for the count after winning Game 3 at the Garden, but missed a chance for the kill when the Isles rallied to win Game 4, setting up a showdown game in the best-of-five series. Again, it was the Blueshirts who carried the play and scored first on Ron Greschner's goal at 12:06. Mike Bossy tied the game on a breakaway late in the period, and the Islanders went ahead on Tomas Jonsson's tally midway through the third period. But Don Maloney batted the puck out of the air and past Billy Smith with 39 seconds left in regulation to tie it. (Maloney said years later that his stick was probably over his shoulder, but the goal stood). The Rangers had a chance to win it all when Bob Brooke broke in alone in overtime, but Smith made the save of the series. Ken Morrow then broke the Rangers' hearts when his harmless-looking shot from the right circle beat Glen Hanlon at 8:56. Smith paid Hanlon the ultimate compliment; notorious for skipping the post-series handshakes, Smith sought out his opposite number and congratulated him.

Pierre Larouche faces off against Brent Sutter of the Islanders in the 1984 playoffs.

LUCKY PIERRE
Pierre Larouche

His nickname was "Lucky Pierre," but when it came to putting the puck in the net, Pierre Larouche was a lot more than lucky. Larouche had been a 50-goal scorer with both Pittsburgh (where for a time he roomed with Vic Hadfield, the first Ranger to score 50 times in a season) and Montreal early in his career, but was available for the taking when GM Craig Patrick signed him as a free agent in September 1983 after a disappointing stint with Hartford. For one shining season, Larouche's scoring magic returned; he scored early and often and threatened Hadfield's team scoring mark before finishing with 48 goals—still a Rangers record for a center—and helping the Blueshirts to their best season in a decade. He also had two goals for the victorious Wales Conference team at the All-Star Game, a feat previously accomplished only by Wally Hergesheimer and Andy Bathgate. Larouche also became a fan favorite, and was a popular guest speaker who delighted audiences with his Quebec accent and English malaprops. But Larouche's luck ran out after 1983-84. Injuries dogged him for much of the rest of his time in New York, though he still averaged more than a point a game when he was able to play. He had 20 goals in just 27 games in 1985-86 after being recalled from the minors at mid-season, then added 8 goals and 9 assists in 16 playoff games giving the team an offensive boost that fueled a surprising run to the semifinals. After scoring 28 times in 1986-87, Larouche was off to a good start in 1987-88, with 12 points in 10 games, when a back injury sidelined him for the season and ultimately forced him to retire just five goals short of 400 for his career.

Pierre Larouche File

- **BORN:**
  November 16, 1955; Taschereau, Quebec
- **ACQUIRED:**
  Signed as a free agent, September 1983
- **FIRST SEASON WITH RANGERS:**
  1983-84

- **BEST SEASON WITH RANGERS:**
  1983-84, 77 GP, 48-33-81, 22 PIM
- **TOTALS WITH RANGERS:**
  Regular season: 253 GP, 123-120-243, 59 PIM
  Playoffs: 27 GP, 14-12-26, 8 PIM
- **HONORS:**
  All-Star Game, 1983-84

CURTAIN CALL
Swedes on Broadway

The Rangers were the first NHL team to ice a Swedish-bred player when Ulf Sterner played four games for them in 1965. By the mid-80s, the Rangers were enjoying great success with Swedish talent, thanks largely to the efforts of former WHA star Lars-Erik Sjoberg, whose contacts in his homeland paid off. The Rangers signed two of Sjoberg's former Winnipeg teammates, Anders Hedberg and Ulf Nilsson, in 1978, then began to mine younger talent. Peter Sundstrom and Jan Erixon were picked in 1981 and joined the Rangers two years later, while Tomas Sandstrom was the Rangers' second pick in the 1982 draft and was among the NHL's top rookies in 1984-85. Other Sjoberg successes included defensemen Kjell Samuelsson in 1984 and Ulf Dahlen, the Rangers' top pick in 1985. Sjoberg died in 1987, but his eventual successor, Christer Rockstrom, was instrumental in the Rangers' selection of Mattias Norstrom in the second round in 1992, as well as Niklas Sundstrom, the Rangers' top pick in 1993 and one of the NHL's top rookies in 1995-96.

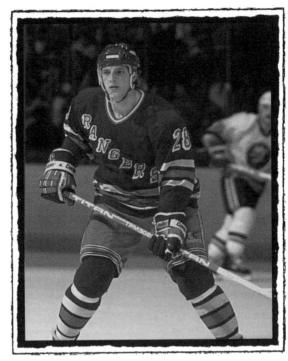

Tomas Sandstrom was one of Lars-Erik Sjoberg's discoveries.

NEW YORK
Ice Exchange

James Patrick joined the Rangers after the Olympics.

Everything GM Craig Patrick touched in 1983-84 seemed to turn out right. He struck gold by signing center Pierre Larouche, who had worn out his welcome in three cities despite a superb scoring touch. Larouche barely missed breaking Vic Hadfield's single-season goal-scoring record, finishing with 48. Patrick won another gamble when he dealt fan favorites Ron Duguay, Ed Mio and Ed Johnstone to Detroit for forwards Mark Osborne and Mike Blaisdell and defenseman Willie Huber; Osborne and Huber became solid contributors. The Rangers' success with Swedish players continued, as rookies Peter Sundstrom and Jan Erixon teamed with Larouche to form the team's most effective line. More reinforcements arrived after the Olympics in the form of defenseman James Patrick and forward Bob Brooke, both of whom became immediate contributors.

Ranger Lists

Most Goals By Position, One Season

Center - 48
Pierre Larouche
1983-84

Left Wing - 52
Adam Graves
1993-94

Right Wing - 49
Mike Gartner
1990-91

Defenseman - 25
Brad Park
1973-74

ME CAPSULE

- **October 7, 1984:**
  The San Diego Padres completed a rally from a two-game deficit to beat the Chicago Cubs, becoming the first team to win a best-of-five series after dropping the first two games.

- **November 6, 1984:**
  President Ronald Reagan was reelected, beating Walter Mondale in the largest Republican landslide ever.

- **March 4, 1985:**
  The Environmental Protection Agency ordered a ban on leaded gasoline.

1984-1985

FINAL STANDINGS

Patrick Division	W	L	T	PTS	GF	GA
Philadelphia	53	20	7	113	348	241
Washington	46	25	9	101	322	240
NY Islanders	40	34	6	86	345	312
RANGERS	26	44	10	62	295	345
New Jersey	22	48	10	54	264	346
Pittsburgh	24	51	5	53	276	385

Other Division Winners:

Adams—Montreal

Norris—St. Louis

Smythe—Edmonton

PLAYOFF RESULTS
Patrick Semifinals: Philadelphia defeated Rangers 3-0
LEADING PLAYOFF SCORERS
Don Maloney (4-0-4)

Mike Rogers (0-4-4)
STANLEY CUP CHAMPION
Edmonton Oilers

SEASON SNAPSHOT

Most Goals:
Tomas Sandstrom (29)
Most Assists:
Reijo Ruotsalainen (45)
Most Points:
Reijo Ruotsalainen (73)
Most Power-Play Goals:
Reijo Ruotsalainen (10)
Most Shorthanded Goals:
Peter Sundstrom/Barry Beck (2)
Most Penalty Minutes:
George McPhee (139)
Power Play:
72/305, 23.6%, 8 SHGA
Penalty-Killing:
269/333, 80.8%, 9 SHG
Most Wins, Goaltender:
Glen Hanlon (14)
Lowest Goals-Against Average:
Glen Hanlon (4.18)
Most Shutouts:
John Vanbiesbrouck (1)
NHL Award Winners:
Anders Hedberg (Masterton Trophy)
Rangers In All-Star Game:
Anders Hedberg, RW

The 1984-85 Season in Review

Far too many of the things that went right in 1983-84 turned sour in 1984-85. The Rangers got off to a good enough start and were 7-4-1 after Reijo Ruotsalainen's overtime goal beat the Islanders 5-4 on November 9. But by then, the injury jinx was in the process of wiping out much of the core of the team. Mark Pavelich broke his ankle in the second game against Minnesota and was gone until after Christmas. Ron Greschner was lost in late October with a shoulder separation that cost him 31 games, while Don Maloney broke his leg in mid-November and missed more than three months, Pierre Larouche's scoring touch fell victim to a variety of ailments that cost him 15 games and hampered him in numerous others, while Anders Hedberg missed 19 games with injuries, then retired to the front office after the season. A 4-15-4 slide helped drop the Rangers into last place before Christmas, and when the club struggled into January, GM Craig Patrick relieved

Anders Hedberg won the Masterton Trophy in 1984-85. Photo by Stamatia Chalos.

coach Herb Brooks, his former boss with the 1980 "Miracle On Ice" team, and went behind the bench himself. The Rangers played in fits and starts under Patrick, but managed to make the playoffs as some of their injured players got well. However, they proved to be no match for the division-champion Flyers in the playoffs, bowing out in three straight after Mark Howe's overtime goal won the series opener.

MAGIC MOMENT
February 15, 1985

Mike Rogers scored twice in the Rangers' record-setting burst.

The Edmonton Oilers came into Madison Square Garden not having lost to the Rangers in almost five years. Nothing that happened in the game's first 15 minutes suggested that this night would be any different. The Oilers, led by Wayne Gretzky's 55th goal, took a quick 3-1 lead, triggering a chorus of boos from the home fans. But the Rangers quickly turned the boos into cheers. Over the next 3 minutes, 22 seconds, New York routed Grant Fuhr while setting a team record for the fastest five goals—breaking the mark of 3:46 set against the Americans on January 13, 1942. The first four goals were scored in a span of 1:38, erasing a team mark that had stood since the Rangers got four in a 2:10 span against Chicago in March 1952. Mike Rogers scored twice in the outburst, while Mark Pavelich, Ron Greschner and rookie Grant Ledyard had the other goals. "They did to us what we usually do to other teams," said Gretzky. The Oilers twice got within one, but third-period tallies by Pierre Larouche and Reijo Ruotsalainen proved to be enough for an 8-7 victory on a night to remember.

REXI
Reijo Ruotsalainen

Probably no Ranger at any position, and certainly no defenseman, has ever had Reijo Ruotsalainen's combination of speed and blazing shot. Ruotsalainen was among the smallest Rangers to play on the blue line, but he made up for his lack of size (5-8 and 170 pounds) with incredible speed and a slap shot that terrified goaltenders (and, until he learned to control it, kept fans behind the end glass alert, too). Teammate Pierre Larouche joked that Ruotsalainen had "the hardest shot I've ever been hit with." But his ability was no joke: Ruotsalainen dazzled everyone with his skating ability and shot from the day he entered the NHL and used those skills to join the play regularly, ranking among the league leaders in scoring among defensemen while flourishing under the coaching of Herb Brooks, who loved small, fast players. Ruotsalainen also had a knack for being on the ice at the right time, too: He was plus-17 or better three times in a four-year stretch from 1982-83 to 1985-86. He never scored less than 16 goals in a season, so the Rangers, seeking to put his offensive skills to greater use, began moving him around. By 1984-85, Ruotsalainen was splitting time between defense and left wing. He responded with his best season, scoring a career-high 28 goals and adding 45 assists for a team-high 73 points—while averaging better than a point a game during his time as a forward and leading the team in six categories. The Finnish native, whose father helped coach Finland's 1984 Olympic team, played only five seasons in New York before being dealt to Edmonton and eventually returning home to play, but few Ranger fans who saw him fly up ice or let go with one of his bullet-like shots will ever forget "Rexi."

Reijo Ruotsalainen File

- **BORN:**
  April 1, 1960; Oulu, Finland
- **ACQUIRED:**
  Rangers' sixth-round pick in 1980 Entry Draft.
- **FIRST SEASON WITH RANGERS:**
  1981-82
- **BEST SEASON WITH RANGERS:**
  1984-85, 80 GP, 28-45-73, 32 PIM

- **TOTALS WITH RANGERS:**
  Regular Season: 389 GP, 99-217-316, 154 PIM
  Playoffs: 43 GP, 11-16-27, 22 PIM
- **HONORS:**
  All-Star Game, 1985-86
  Players' Player Award, 1984-85

CURTAIN CALL
The "Other" Patricks

Stephen Patrick. Photo by Ray Amati.

Neither James nor brother Stephen Patrick are related to the clan that goes back to the Rangers' patriarch, Lester Patrick. But when GM Craig Patrick (Lester's grandson) dealt for Stephen Patrick in mid-December, he set up the 13th brother combination in Rangers' history. Both were first-round picks, with Stephen going to Buffalo in 1980 and James being picked by the Rangers a year later. Among their "Firsts as Rangers:" First time both assisted on the same goal: December 30, 1984 in St. Louis, when they combined to set up Tomas Sandstrom; First Time One Patrick Set Up The Other: February 22, 1985, when James had the only assist on his older brother's goal; First Time Both Got Concurrent Penalties: March 26, at Pittsburgh, when the Winnipeg natives each got two minutes for roughing. Injuries cut Stephen's career short, but his younger brother was a fixture on the Rangers' blue line for a decade.

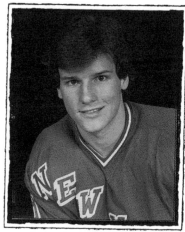

James Patrick.

NEW YORK
Ice Exchange

Former captain Dave Maloney was dealt to Buffalo in 1984-85. Photo courtesy of Jerry Liebman Studio.

Though it didn't always pay off on the scoreboard in 1984-85, the Rangers succeeded in adding more young talent. Two 1984 Olympians, defenseman James Patrick and forward Bob Brooke, showed that their impressive cameos the previous season were not flukes, with Brooke playing everywhere on the ice except goal. Another Olympian, Sweden's Tomas Sandstrom, came out of nowhere to score a team-leading 29 goals and make the NHL's All-Rookie team. Two other youngsters, Dave Gagner and Kelly Miller, also started what proved to be long NHL careers. John Vanbiesbrouck, a star in the Rangers' farm system, showed he could play at the NHL level, performing better than his 12-24-3 record and 4.22 goals-against average would indicate. The Rangers added size up front in December when they traded Dave Maloney, their former captain, to Buffalo for Steve Patrick and Jim Wiemer.

Ranger Lists

Most Decisive Road Wins

11-2
at New Jersey
Oct. 25, 1984
11-3
at Pittsburgh
Nov. 25, 1992
11-4
at Minnesota
Dec. 4, 1976
11-4
at Washington
March 24, 1978
9-2
at Ottawa
Jan. 28, 1933
9-2
at Minnesota
Feb. 15, 1975
8-1
Four times/last at Minnesota,
Dec. 30, 1974
7-0
Four times/last at Toronto,
March 22, 1958

 1985 1986 —

TIME CAPSULE

- **September 11, 1985:**
  Cincinnati's Pete Rose broke Ty Cobb's major-league record for career hits when he stroked No. 4,192, a single in a game against San Diego.

- **January 26, 1986:**
  The Chicago Bears capped one of the most dominant seasons in NFL history by routing the New England Patriots 46-10 to win Super Bowl XX.

- **January 28, 1986:**
  Seven astronauts were killed when the space shuttle Challenger exploded just 74 seconds after lift-off from Cape Canaveral, Florida.

1985-1986

FINAL STANDINGS

Patrick Division	W	L	T	PTS	GF	GA
Philadelphia	53	23	4	110	335	241
Washington	50	23	7	107	315	272
NY Islanders	39	29	12	90	327	284
RANGERS	36	38	6	78	280	276
Pittsburgh	34	38	8	76	313	305
New Jersey	28	49	3	59	300	374

Other Division Winners:

Adams—Quebec

Norris—Chicago

Smythe—Edmonton

PLAYOFF RESULTS

Patrick Semifinals: Rangers defeated Philadelphia 3-2

Patrick Finals: Rangers defeated Washington 4-2

Wales Conference Finals: Montreal defeated Rangers 4-1

LEADING PLAYOFF SCORER

Pierre Larouche (8-9-17)

STANLEY CUP CHAMPION

Montreal Canadiens

SEASON SNAPSHOT

Most Goals:
Tomas Sandstrom (25)
Most Assists:
Mike Ridley (43)
Most Points:
Mike Ridley (65)
Most Power-Play Goals:
Sandstrom/MacLellan/Pavelich (8)
Most Shorthanded Goals:
Tomas Sandstrom/Bob Brooke (2)
Most Penalty Minutes:
Bob Brooke (111)
Power Play:
73/362, 20.2%, 4 SHGA
Penalty-Killing:
284/365, 77.8%, 9 SHG
Most Wins, Goaltender:
John Vanbiesbrouck (31)
Lowest Goals-Against Average:
John Vanbiesbrouck (3.32)
Most Shutouts:
John Vanbiesbrouck (3)
NHL Award Winners:
John Vanbiesbrouck (Vezina Trophy)
NHL All-Stars:
John Vanbiesbrouck, G (First Team)
Rangers In All-Star Game:
Reijo Ruotsalainen, D

The 1985-86 Season in Review

I f ever a regular season was a tuneup for the playoffs, it was 1985-86. Under new coach Ted Sator, an assistant under Mike Keenan at Philadelphia, the Rangers bounced up and down during the regular season, and despite the Vezina Trophy-winning goaltending of John Vanbiesbrouck, they didn't lock up a playoff berth until the final weekend of the season. Finishing fourth earned a return match with the Flyers, who had swept New York the previous spring. This time, though, things were different: Vanbiesbrouck was superb as the Rangers stunned the Flyers, winning the decisive fifth game 5-2 at the Spectrum. Brian MacLellan won the opener of the Patrick Division finals against Washington in overtime and after the Capitals won Games 2 and 3, Bob Brooke capped a Rangers comeback with another overtime goal that tied the series. Vanbiesbrouck did the rest as the Rangers won Game 5 in Washington and closed out the Caps with a 2-1 win at the Garden. Unfortunately, they ran into a goaltender even hotter than Vanbiesbrouck in the semifinals, as Montreal beat the Rangers in five games behind rookie Patrick Roy, who went on to lead the Canadiens to their 23rd Stanley Cup.

John Vanbiesbrouck won the Vezina Trophy in 1985-86. Photo by Bruce Bennett.

MAGIC MOMENT

April 23, 1986

For all intents and purposes, the Rangers' season was ready to end. They trailed 2-1 in games and were down 5-3 to the Washington Capitals 7:45 into the third period of Game 4 after giving up an embarrassing shorthanded goal to Greg Smith on a bad line change. But the Rangers refused to die. Willie Huber atoned for the shorthanded gaffe with a goal on the same power play to make it 5-4. Then Bob Brooke took over. The 1984 U.S. Olympian converted Brian MacLellan's pass with 2:35 left in regulation, sending the Garden into bedlam and the game into overtime. The Rangers missed one chance when Mike Allison's tip hit the post 1:32 into overtime. But Brooke didn't miss at 2:40, when he intercepted Scott Stevens' pass and fired from 30 feet. "I just tossed it at the net," the former Yale star said. "It hit Smith's left skate. When it went in, I felt something special." So did the Rangers, who had gone 0-7-6 in overtime during the regular season but were suddenly alive and even after their second OT victory of the series. Two games later, the Capitals were his-

Bob Brooke's overtime goal sparked the Rangers past Washington. Photo by Bruce Bennett.

tory and the Rangers were headed for the semifinals as Patrick Division champions.

RANGER LEGEND
John Vanbiesbrouck

No one can ever say that John Vanbiesbrouck hasn't earned everything he's gotten in the NHL. He gave Rangers fans a taste of his talent during a one-game callup from juniors in December 1981, beating the Colorado Rockies 2-1 in Denver as an 18-year-old ("Still one of my greatest thrills," he remembered years later). Then it was back to juniors for two more seasons, plus another in the old Central Hockey League, where he led Tulsa to the title, before he got a shot at the big club. His challenging, aggressive style and quickness won him a lot of fans at the Garden, where "Beezer" was an immediate hit. But it wasn't like anyone handed him a job; Vanbiesbrouck had to beat out popular Glen Hanlon. He did so in 1985-86, becoming the first Ranger in 15 years to win the Vezina Trophy as the NHL's top goaltender. His play also keyed the Rangers' surprising playoff run to the semifinals, a feat they hadn't accomplished in five years. Despite that, he kept having to fend off competitors for his job; first Bob Froese in 1986-87, then Mike Richter in 1989-90. He and Richter eventually wound up splitting the job virtually down the middle for four seasons. Expansion ended

that: Faced with being allowed to protect only one goalie, the Rangers dealt Beezer to Vancouver, which lost him to Florida in the expansion draft. Vanbiesbrouck enjoyed a homecoming of sorts at the 1994 All-Star Game, where he and Richter were two of the three goaltenders selected to the Eastern Conference squad. Though he admitted being disappointed at missing the Rangers' run to the 1994 championship, Vanbiesbrouck got a taste of the finals two years later when he backstopped Florida's stunning run to the title round.

John Vanbiesbrouck File

- **BORN:**
  September 4, 1963, Detroit, Michigan
- **ACQUIRED:**
  Rangers fourth-round pick in 1981 Entry Draft
- **FIRST SEASON WITH RANGERS:**
  1981-82
- **BEST SEASON WITH RANGERS:**
  1991-92, 45 GP, 27-13-3, 2.85 goals-against average, 2 shutouts

- **TOTALS WITH RANGERS:**
  Regular season: 449 GP, 200-177-47, 3.45 goals-against average, 16 shutouts
  Playoffs: 38 GP, 13-20, 3.25 goals-against average, 2 shutouts
- **HONORS:**
  Vezina Trophy, 1985-86
  First-team All-Star, 1985-86
  West Side Assn. Rangers MVP, 1985-86
  Players' Player Award, 1985-86
  Steven McDonald Extra Effort Award, 1989-90

CURTAIN CALL

Ted Sator

Ted Sator had been a success everywhere he'd worked, both internationally and in North America, where he spent 1984-85 as an assistant under Mike Keenan as the Flyers went to the Stanley Cup finals. Certainly, no Ranger coach had ever worked harder —or worked his players harder. At a time when offense was king, Sator had his Rangers working overtime at the defensive end, a strategy that paid off when 22-year-old John Vanbiesbrouck turned into a Vezina Trophy winner in goal. Sator was a big believer in nutrition and conditioning (something that was reinforced by working for Keenan after running the NHL's conditioning program), rather than in fiery speeches and emotion. The Rangers struggled through his first season, but caught fire in the playoffs, making the semifinals for the first time since 1981. Unfortunately for Sator, the man who hired him, Craig Patrick, wasn't around by the start of the 1986-87 season, having been succeeded by Phil Esposito—one of hockey's most emotional players. Their approaches didn't coincide, and a 5-10-4 start wound up costing Sator his job.

Ted Sator led the Rangers to the 1986 semifinals.

NEW YORK
Ice Exchange

GM Craig Patrick's young talent kept on coming. Three rookies—Mike Ridley, Kelly Miller and Raimo Helminen—earned roster spots and made immediate impressions. The most unlikely of these was Ridley, who not only became one of the few players ever to jump straight from a Canadian college to the NHL, but went on to lead the team in scoring. He teamed well with Miller, a star at Michigan State. The Rangers picked up some toughness for the stretch run by sending Stephen Patrick to Quebec for Wilf Paiement, who broke a bone in his left foot in his second game as a Ranger, but returned in time to get seven points in eight games down the stretch and added 10 points in 16 playoff games. Defenseman Larry Melnyk, obtained from Edmonton for Mike Rogers, also added muscle.

Mike Ridley led the Rangers in scoring as a rookie.

The Rangers didn't get the regular-season scoring help they had hoped for when they landed Brian MacLellan from Los Angeles for Grant Ledyard and Roland Melanson (obtained earlier the same day from Minnesota) on December 9; however, MacLellan did score the overtime winner in Game 1 of the Patrick Division finals against Washington.

Ranger Lists

Most Assists by a Goaltender

Game

2 - Ed Giacomin
3/19/72 vs. Toronto

2 - John Vanbiesbrouck
1/8/85 at Winnipeg

2 - Mike Richter
2/23/90 at Washington

2 - Mike Richter
10/29/92 vs. Quebec

Season

5 - John Vanbiesbrouck
1984-85

5 - John Vanbiesbrouck
1986-87

5 - Mike Richter
1993-94

Ranger Fans: The World's Best

The love affair between the Rangers and their fans didn't take long to blossom. The combination of their early success, the then-new Madison Square Garden and Lester Patrick's success in teaching the game to the local media and fans quickly made the Garden THE place to be seen. Among the regulars who frequented Rangers games in the team's early years were celebrities like George Raft, Lucille Ball and bandleader Cab Calloway, who used to pop into the Garden to catch a period or two between shows and would introduce players who came into his nightclub.

The Rangers' drawing power far outlasted their on-ice success. Fans still flocked to the Garden even as the team struggled in the 1940s. But the advent of television and the years of losing eventually began taking their toll. To stir up interest, GM Frank Boucher had a letter distributed in the upper reaches of the Garden, inviting recipients to join the new Rangers Fan Club. "We'll be lucky to get

The Steven McDonald Extra Effort Award honors New York City police officer Steven McDonald, who was shot during the line of duty.
Photo by George Kalinsky.

100 people," Boucher said.

He was wrong. About 300 fans— not all from the Garden's upper reaches—showed up at the first meeting on January 15, 1951 to meet with Boucher and the players. Over the years, members have included celebrities like bandleader Skitch Henderson and 'F-Troop' star Larry Storch, as well as thousands of fans who simply wanted to show the world their true (Ranger) colors.

The Fan Club's membership has fluctuated over the years (it's now about 800 and rising), and boasts members throughout the North America and overseas. The club sponsors an annual dinner dance and periodic road trips that give the Rangers support in out-of-town rinks.

Perhaps the most loyal of Fan Club members was Ceil Seidel. Ranger fans and the Fan Club were her family and kept her young.

The lowest point of the Rangers' greatest season, 1993-94, came late in the season when she was murdered in her apartment building as she prepared to leave for a game. The Fan Club instituted the Ceil Seidel Award the following season.

Like Ceil Seidel, Steven McDonald was a lifelong Ranger fan. As a 25-year-old New York City police officer, he was shot in the line of duty and paralyzed. He spent 18 months in the hospital, watching videotapes of each Ranger game, and touched the players who visited him with his courage. The first Steven McDonald Extra Effort Award (voted on by fans) was given in 1987-88, and McDonald is there each spring when the new winner is honored.

They're just a few examples of what everyone connected with the team already knows: There are no other fans like Ranger fans.

Rangers Fan Club logo.

—1986 1987—

- **October 27, 1986:**
  The New York Mets beat the Boston Red Sox 8-5 to win the World Series in seven games for their first championship since 1969.

- **November 22, 1986:**
  Twenty-year-old Brooklyn native Mike Tyson became the youngest heavyweight champion ever when he knocked out Trevor Berbick.

- **January 25, 1987:**
  The New York Giants won their first NFL championship since 1956 by demolishing the Denver Broncos 39-20 in the Super Bowl at Pasadena, California.

1986-1987

FINAL STANDINGS

Patrick Division	W	L	T	PTS	GF	GA
Philadelphia	46	26	8	100	310	245
Washington	38	32	10	86	285	278
NY Islanders	35	33	12	82	279	281
RANGERS	34	38	8	76	307	323
Pittsburgh	30	38	12	72	297	290
New Jersey	29	45	6	64	293	368

Other Division Winners:

Adams—Hartford

Norris—St. Louis

Smythe—Edmonton

PLAYOFF RESULTS
Patrick Semifinals: Phildelphia defeated Rangers 4-2
LEADING PLAYOFF SCORER
Pierre Larouche (3-2-5)
Ron Greschner (0-5-5)
STANLEY CUP CHAMPION
Edmonton Oilers

SEASON SNAPSHOT

Most Goals:
Walt Poddubny/Tomas Sandstrom (40)
Most Assists:
Walt Poddubny (47)
Most Points:
Walt Poddubny (87)
Most Power-Play Goals:
Tomas Sandstrom (13)
Most Shorthanded Goals:
Don Maloney (3)
Most Penalty Minutes:
Larry Melnyk (182)
Power Play:
75/375, 20.0%, 15 SHGA
Penalty-Killing:
308/379, 81.3%, 12 SHG
Most Wins, Goaltender:
John Vanbiesbrouck (18)
Lowest Goals-Against Average:
John Vanbiesbrouck (3.63)
Rangers In All-Star Game:
Tomas Sandstrom, RW
(Rendez-Vous 1987)

The 1986-87 Season in Review

Phil Esposito came aboard as general manager in July 1986 and wasted little time reshaping the Rangers in a series of deals that earned him the nickname "Trader Phil." Espo reeled in Walt Poddubny, a 40-goal scorer, goaltender Bob Froese, superstar forward Marcel Dionne and future captain Kelly Kisio, as well as bringing back fan favorite Ron Duguay. Esposito also changed coaches after a slow start, replacing Ted Sator with Tom Webster. But health problems, including surgery for an inner-ear problem, eventually forced Webster to step down after just 16 games, and Esposito wound up holding two jobs for most of the season. The Rangers responded, going 24-19-0 under their GM/coach to finish fourth. The offense was led by Poddubny and Tomas Sandstrom, who gave the Rangers a pair of 40-goal scorers for the first time since 1971-72; the problems came on defense. Still, the Rangers approached the opening round of the playoffs against the Flyers with confidence—a feeling bolstered by a 3-0 shutout win at the Spectrum in the opener.

John Vanbiesbrouck led the Rangers with 18 wins. Photo by Stamatia Chalos.

The teams split the first four games before Philadelphia took command with a 3-1 victory in Game 5 and closed out the series behind a 5-0 shutout at the Garden by Ron Hextall, who ultimately won the Conn Smythe Trophy as playoff MVP.

MAGIC MOMENT *December 31, 1986*

New Year's Eve is a night to get dressed up ... and who are the Rangers to disagree. Thus, for the last game of 1986, tuxedos were the order of the evening—from coach Phil Esposito on down (even the broadcast team went formal). With the Islanders in town, there was certainly no trouble getting the crowd up, even though both teams had been struggling. The Islanders proved to be troublesome guests, tying the game late in the first period on a goal by Patrick Flatley and twice taking one-goal leads in the second. But Tomas Sandstrom, on the way to his first 40-goal season, wouldn't let the Rangers lose. He scored once in the second period, then tied the game early in the third. Despite outgunning the Isles badly, the Rangers were unable to beat Kelly Hrudey again through regulation time and the first four minutes in overtime. But with 53 seconds left, the Isles' Bryan Trottier was called for slashing. Sandstrom needed only 30 seconds to get the Garden faithful off to an early start on their revelry, beating Hrudey to give the Rangers a 4-3 win. Sandstrom had something to celebrate, too—his first career hat trick.

Tomas Sandstorm beat the Islanders with a New Year's Eve hat trick. Photo by Steve Berman.

SWEDISH SNIPER
Tomas Sandstrom

The Rangers had to wait two years for Tomas Sandstrom to finish his obligations in Sweden (including a stint in carpentry school and a berth on the Swedish bronze-medal team at the 1984 Sarajevo Olympics). But Sandstrom was well worth the wait. The big right wing wasted little time making an impact, scoring his first NHL goal with 1:09 left in his debut with the Rangers to give New York a tie with Hartford on October 11, 1984. Sandstrom went on to score a team-leading 29 goals and earn a berth on the NHL's All-Rookie Team. He led the Rangers in goals again in 1985-86 with 25, then broke out with a 40-goal season in 1986-87 despite breaking his ankle in the first game of Rendez-Vous 1987 and ultimately playing only 64 times in the 80-game season. His 40 goals often came in bunches; Sandstrom set a team record by collecting four hat tricks. He dropped off to 28 goals in 1987-88

Tomas Sandstrom vs. the Detroit Red Wings' Mike O'Connell.

(plus one in the All-Star Game), but bounced back with his best overall season in 1988-89, scoring 32 goals and adding 56 assists for a team-high 88 points (while setting a career high in penalty minutes with 148), then added three more goals and two assists in four playoff games. Sandstrom's feisty style of play won him plenty of fans among the Garden faithful, if not among opposing defensemen and forwards, and he averaged more than 28 goals a season during his 5 1/2 years with the club before going to Los Angeles in the trade that brought Bernie Nicholls to the Rangers during the All-Star break in January 1990. Sandstrom played 4 1/2 seasons in Los Angeles, notching a career high of 45 goals in 1990-91 while skating mostly with Wayne Gretzky, before moving on to Pittsburgh in 1994—making him one of the few players to play on a line with both Gretzky and Mario Lemieux.

Tomas Sandstrom File

- **BORN:**
  September 4, 1964; Jakobstad, Finland
- **ACQUIRED:**
  Rangers second-round pick in 1982 draft
- **FIRST SEASON WITH RANGERS:**
  1984-85
- **BEST SEASON WITH RANGERS:**
  1988-89, 79 GP, 32-56-88, 148 PIM

- **TOTALS WITH RANGERS:**
  Regular season: 407 GP, 173-207-380, 563 PIM
  Playoffs: 29 GP, 8-12-20, 52 PIM
- **HONORS:**
  All-Star Game, 1986-87, 1987-88
  West Side Assn. Rangers MVP, 1984-85

CURTAIN CALL

Coaching Carousel

Tom Webster, a former WHA star, had paid his dues on the way up the coaching ladder, finally earning the chance at an NHL job when Phil Esposito hired him to replace Ted Sator 19 games into the 1986-87 season. Little did Webster know that his stint with the Rangers wasn't going to last long. Webster was still getting to know his players when he came down with an ear infection that prevented him from flying and forced him to have surgery. Esposito, still a rookie as a general manager, eventually wound up behind the bench—and his players responded. They went 8-3 in their first 11 games under Esposito before Webster's return. With Webster still unable to fly due to the ear problems, plans originally called for Esposito to coach when Webster couldn't travel. "Basically, it comes down to this," goalie John Vanbiesbrouck said. "If we win, there will be no trouble. If we lose, there might be." They did lose—and there was trouble. With the team responding better to Esposito, Trader Phil finally decided to become Coach Phil as well, rallying the Rangers into the playoffs. Webster's 16-game stint is the shortest of any full-time coach in team history.

Health problems curtailed Tom Webster's coaching career with the Rangers.

NEW YORK Ice Exchange

From the moment he moved from the broadcast booth to the GM's office, Phil Esposito was determined to overhaul the Rangers. Ted Sator, hired by Espo's predecessor, Craig Patrick, was gone after the Rangers started 5-10-4; his replacement, Tom Webster, lasted only 16 games due to a health condition that made flying an impossibility, and Esposito wound up coaching the second half of the season. Espo's best acquisition was getting center Walt Poddubny from Toronto for Mike Allison; Poddubny turned into a 40-goal scorer. Espo sought a second solid goaltender and got one from the Flyers by dealing defenseman Kjell Samuelsson for Bob Froese.

Seeking more scoring, Esposito dealt Kelly Miller and Mike Ridley for former 50-goal scorer Bobby Carpenter on January 1. But when Carpenter didn't produce as expected, Espo got someone with a proven track record, sending Carpenter and defenseman Tom Laidlaw to the Kings in March for Marcel Dionne, one of the NHL's top offensive players for more than a decade.

Phil Esposito wasted little time revamping the Rangers. Photo by Ray Amati.

Ranger Lists

Most goals, one season

Goals	Season
321	1991-92
319	1974-75
317	1971-72
316	1978-79
316	1981-82
314	1983-84
312	1980-81
310	1988-89
308	1979-80
307	1986-87

—1987 1988—

TIME CAPSULE

- **October 19, 1987:**
  The worst crash in the modern history of the New York Stock Exchange occurred when the Dow Jones Industrial Average dropped 508 points.

- **November 18, 1987:**
  President Reagan was blamed for failing in his constitutional duty by the congressional committee report on the Iran-Contra affair.

- **February 5, 1988:**
  A federal grand jury in Miami indicted Panamanian Gen. Manuel Noriega in connection with illegal drug dealings.

1987-1988
FINAL STANDINGS

Patrick Division	W	L	T	PTS	GF	GA
NY Islanders	39	31	10	88	308	267
Washington	38	33	9	85	281	249
Philadelphia	38	33	9	85	292	292
New Jersey	38	36	6	82	295	296
RANGERS	36	34	10	82	300	283
Pittsburgh	36	35	9	81	319	316

Other Division Winners:

Adams—Montreal

Norris—Detroit

Smythe—Calgary

PLAYOFF RESULTS
Rangers did not qualify

STANLEY CUP CHAMPION
Edmonton Oilers

SEASON SNAPSHOT

Most Goals:
Walt Poddubny (38)

Most Assists:
Kelly Kisio (55)

Most Points:
Walt Poddubny (88)

Most Power-Play Goals:
Marcel Dionne (22)

Most Shorthanded Goals:
Kisio/Cyr/Nemeth/Erixon (1)

Most Penalty Minutes:
Michel Petit (223)

Power Play:
111/491, 22.6%, 11 SHGA

Penalty-Killing:
341/423, 80.6%, 5 SHG

Most Wins, Goaltender:
John Vanbiesbrouck (27)

Lowest Goals-Against Average:
John Vanbiesbrouck (3.38)

Most Shutouts:
John Vanbiesbrouck (2)

Rangers In All-Star Game:
Tomas Sandstrom, RW

The 1987-88 Season in Review

A hot finish couldn't quite make up for a slow start in what turned out to be a season of disappointment for the Rangers. After a 2-0-1 start, the Rangers went 9-19-3 until Christmas as new coach Michel Bergeron struggled to find a successful combination. But things began to click after the holidays, as a 5-0-1 streak got the Rangers back in the playoff hunt in the tightly packed Patrick Division. An 0-6-1 slide slowed things down, but then the Rangers found their form. John Vanbiesbrouck's hot goaltending and a record-setting power play (111 goals) fueled a stretch drive that saw the Rangers go 16-8-3 in their final 27 games. Included in that streak was a 6-1 wipeout of the Stanley Cup champion Edmonton Oilers. The Rangers had no 40-goal scorers, but seven players had at least 23 goals and defenseman James Patrick added 17. The race for the final playoff spot came down to the last night of the season, with the Rangers, Penguins and Devils scrambling for the final berth. Vanbiesbrouck's 3-0 shutout of Quebec eliminated the Penguins and sent the Rangers to the locker room hoping Chicago could help them out. The Blackhawks, playing at home, came close, but John MacLean's overtime goal put the Devils in and the Rangers out—leaving New York with the thin consolation of being one of the few teams to finish over .500 but miss out on postseason play.

Kelly Kisio had his best season with 78 points in 1987-88. Photo by Bruce Bennett.

MAGIC MOMENT October 23, 1987

The Rangers had to wait two years for Ulf Dahlen to arrive. Their No. 1 pick in the 1985 draft was a highly regarded prospect, but had to finish his commitment in Sweden before coming to the NHL, so it was not until the fall of 1987 that Dahlen arrived in New York. He wasn't exactly an immediate sensation; coach Michel Bergeron scratched him in five of the Rangers' first seven games. But with the team struggling, Dahlen got his chance on October 23 at the Garden—and he made the most of it. The rookie right wing lit up the crowd with the Rangers' only hat trick of 1987-88, helping carry the Rangers to a resounding 7-3 victory over the Blackhawks. The hat trick was a sign of more to come: Dahlen delivered 29 goals to finish fourth among all rookies in the NHL and fourth on the Rangers' all-time rookie scoring list. He had 19 of those goals in the second half, helping to fuel the Rangers' stretch run. Dahlen had 2 1/2 productive seasons in New York before being dealt to Minnesota for Mike Gartner in March 1990.

Ulf Dahlen had the Rangers' only hat trick in 1987-88.

A CLASS ACT
Marcel Dionne

For a player who was supposed to be on his last legs, Marcel Dionne showed a lot of life after GM Phil Esposito brought him to New York. Dionne was already one of the NHL's all-time scoring leaders in a career that saw him break the 50-goal mark six times and the 100-point barrier on eight occasions when he arrived in the Big Apple in March 1987—and he wasted little time showing he still had the magic touch. Though seeing limited ice time, Dionne gave the Rangers' offense a major boost in 1987-88 by scoring 31 goals and 65 points in only 67 games; his 22 power-play goals were a key reason why the team set an NHL mark with 111 extra-man tallies. Dionne, the last player to win the Art Ross Trophy as the NHL's top scorer (137 points in 1979-80) before the Gretzky-Lemieux era began, also passed a number of milestones in 1987-88, becoming only the fourth NHL player to hit the 700-goal mark and surpassing 1,000 assists and 1,700 points as well. (Of the four players who have surpassed the 700-goal mark, two—Dionne and Esposito—both reached the milestone with the Rangers. A third, Wayne Gretzky, joined the Rangers for 1996-97). Dionne's presence was a boost off the ice as well—he took rookie Brian Leetch into his home

when the young defenseman joined the team after the 1988 Olympics and helped the former No. 1 pick make the transition to the NHL (something he had done previously for young players while with the Kings). The Rangers knew Dionne was someone special; though he had been with them for less than a season, they honored him with a night on February 29, 1988. Dionne retired after the 1988-89 season with 731 goals, currently third on the all-time list, and 1,771 points; he was elected to the Hall of Fame in 1992.

Marcel Dionne File

- **BORN:**
  August 3, 1951; Drummondville, Quebec
- **ACQUIRED:**
  Traded by Los Angeles with Jeff Crossman for Bobby Carpenter and Tom Laidlaw, March 10, 1987.
- **FIRST SEASON WITH RANGERS:**
  1986-87

- **BEST SEASON WITH RANGERS:**
  1987-88, 67 GP, 31-34-65, 54 PIM
- **TOTALS WITH RANGERS:**
  Regular season: 118 GP, 42-56-98, 80 PIM
  Playoffs: 6 GP, 1-1-2, 2 PIM
- **NHL MILESTONES:**
  731 Goals; 1,040 Assists; 1,771 Points; 1,348 Games Played

CURTAIN CALL

Michel Bergeron

As general manager, Phil Esposito was never reluctant to go after the people he wanted—including coaches. With no desire to remain as both coach and GM after filling both roles for the second half of 1986-87, Espo went out and got the best coach he could find, giving Quebec a No. 1 draft pick for the right to sign Michel Bergeron, who had led the Nordiques to seven straight playoff appearances. The Rangers and Bergeron took some time to get used to each other, but Bergeron's strategy and motivational skills showed down the stretch, when the Rangers were one of the NHL's hottest teams. Despite missing the playoffs on the final night of the season, they finished with their best record since 1983-84, cut their goals-against by 40 and set an NHL record with 111 power-play goals. Bergeron had the Rangers in first place for much of the 1988-89 season, but a late slide cost him his job despite a pair of over-.500 seasons.

The Rangers finished over .500 under Michel Bergeron, but missed the playoffs.

NEW YORK
Ice Exchange

John Ogrodnick gave the offense a boost.

Coach Michel Bergeron wasn't the only new Ranger to come from Quebec. Former 50-goal scorer John Ogrodnick rejoined his old coach and gave the offense a boost with 22 goals. He and local favorite Brian Mullen, a New York City native acquired from Winnipeg during the summer, joined Kelly Kisio as one of the Rangers' most effective lines. They helped pick up the slack caused by a back injury that sidelined Pierre Larouche for all but 10 games and ultimately forced him to retire. New York also got a lift from the arrival of Ulf Dahlen, its No. 1 draft pick in 1985, while rookie defensemen Norm Maciver and Mark Tinordi were helpful additions on the blue line. Seeking more toughness, the Rangers swapped positions in the first round with Montreal at midseason to acquire Chris Nilan, who became a fan favorite the moment he stepped on the ice. The end of the 1988 Olympics brought help in the form of defenseman Brian Leetch, their top pick in 1986. The Rangers liked what they saw, as Leetch chipped in with 14 points in 17 games.

Ranger Lists

Most Power-Play Goals, One Season

111
1987-88

103
1989-90

96
1993-94

91
1990-91

85
1995-96

85
1988-89

84
1974-75

81
1991-92

—1988 1989—

TIME CAPSULE

- **November 8, 1988:**
  Vice President George Bush defeated Massachusetts Gov. Michael Dukakis in the presidential election.

- **January 22, 1989:**
  The San Francisco 49ers defeated the Cincinnati Bengals 20-16 to win the Super Bowl on Joe Montana's last-minute touchdown pass to John Taylor.

- **March 24, 1989:**
  The Exxon Valdez oil tanker struck a reef in Prince William Sound, Alaska, leaking more than one million barrels of crude oil into the water.

1988-1989
FINAL STANDINGS

Patrick Division	W	L	T	PTS	GF	GA
Washington	41	29	10	92	305	259
Pittsburgh	40	33	7	87	347	349
RANGERS	37	35	8	82	310	307
Philadelphia	36	36	8	80	307	285
New Jersey	27	41	12	66	281	325
NY Islanders	28	47	5	61	265	325

Other Division Winners:

Adams—Montreal

Norris—Detroit

Smythe—Calgary

PLAYOFF RESULTS
Patrick Division Semifinals: Pittsburgh defeated Rangers 4-0
LEADING PLAYOFF SCORER
Brian Leetch (3-2-5)
STANLEY CUP CHAMPION
Calgary Flames

SEASON SNAPSHOT

Most Goals:
Tony Granato (36)
Most Assists:
Tomas Sandstrom (56)
Most Points:
Tomas Sandstrom (88)
Most Power-Play Goals:
Tomas Sandstrom (11)
Most Shorthanded Goals:
Tony Granato (4)
Most Penalty Minutes:
Rudy Poeschek (199)
Power Play:
85/457, 18.6%, 17 SHGA
Penalty-Killing:
286/371, 77.1%, 13 SHG
Most Wins, Goaltender:
John Vanbiesbrouck (28)
Lowest Goals-Against Average:
John Vanbiesbrouck (3.69)
Most Shutouts:
Bob Froese (1)
NHL Award Winners:
Brian Leetch (Calder Trophy)
Rangers In All-Star Game:
Brian Mullen, RW

The 1988-89 Season in Review

The 1988-89 season should have been subtitled "New Faces On Broadway." With the memory of the previous spring's disappointment on his mind, GM Phil Esposito infused youth into his roster and came up big when defenseman Brian Leetch won the Calder Trophy as the NHL's top rookie and forward Tony Granato set a team rookie record with 36 goals. The Rangers also got a boost from the comeback of Guy Lafleur, who contributed 18 goals following a 3 1/2-year layoff that was long enough to allow him to qualify for induction to the Hall of Fame before reporting to camp. An early seven-game winning streak moved the Rangers into first place and a 10-1-2 surge in midseason put them back on top at the end of January. One more surge in late February put the Rangers in first place again in early March, but a late slump dropped them back to third entering the final weekend. Esposito then stunned the team and the city by fixing coach Michel Bergeron and going back behind the bench himself. But the move didn't work: The Rangers dropped their last two games and were swept in four straight by Pittsburgh in the opening round of the playoffs. A few weeks later, Esposito was also let go, ending an association with the Rangers that had begun with his arrival in a trade from Boston in 1975.

Tomas Sandstrom led the Rangers with 88 points.

MAGIC MOMENT   *Ed Giacomin Night*

Ed Giacomin's Night was one of the most emotional ever at the Garden.

In the Rangers' first 64 years, there may not have been a more emotional night than March 15, 1989—Ed Giacomin Night. Fourteen years after they let him go on waivers, the Rangers retired Giacomin's No. 1, placing him among only a handful of NHL goaltenders to earn that honor, and raised his sweater to the rafters of the Garden to join long-time teammate Rod Gilbert's No. 7. For one more night, the chant of "Ed-die, Ed-die" echoed through the Garden, just as it had in the late 1960s and early 1970s, when Giacomin's play was a key to the rise of the Rangers. Giacomin, now white-haired but otherwise looking very much like the cat-quick goaltender of a generation earlier, made an emotional speech to thank the fans for their support over the years, then posed with long-time running mate Gilles Villemure, with whom he won the 1970-71 Vezina Trophy, and predecessors Chuck Rayner and Gump Worsley in a meeting of four great Ranger goaltenders and award-winners.

HOME AT LAST
Brian Mullen

No one was better prepared to be a New York Ranger than Brian Mullen. After all, Brian and his brother, Joe, knew Madison Square Garden inside out—their father worked on the maintenance crew at the Garden for decades and Brian was a stickboy for the Rangers from 1977-79, getting a close-up view of the miracle victory over the Islanders and the run to the finals against Montreal. Brian, who grew up within walking distance of the Garden, started out playing roller hockey, then moved to the ice and was a star in the local Metropolitan Junior Hockey Association before being drafted in the seventh round by Winnipeg in 1980. He went to the University of Wisconsin for two years, helping the Badgers win the 1981 NCAA championship, then spent five productive seasons in Winnipeg, averaging just under 25 goals per season with the Jets before coming to the Rangers in the summer of 1987 for a pair of draft choices. He became the second New Yorker (after Nick Fotiu) to make the Rangers—and the first to represent the team in the All-Star Game when, in January 1989, he was picked by Wales Conference

Photo by Bruce Bennett.

coach Terry O'Reilly and lined up opposite older brother Joe, who made the Campbell Conference team while playing with the Calgary Flames. Though he didn't score as much as his big brother, Brian Mullen had 25, 29 and 27 goals in his first three seasons with the Rangers, mostly while playing on a line with Kelly Kisio and John Ogrodnick. Mullen averaged 25 goals and more than 60 points in his four seasons at the Garden before he was lost to San Jose in the expansion draft in 1992. He spent one season with the Sharks and another with the Islanders before his career was cut short by illness.

Brian Mullen File

- **BORN:**
  March 16, 1962; New York City
- **ACQUIRED:**
  Trade by Winnipeg for two draft picks, June 8, 1987
- **FIRST SEASON WITH RANGERS:**
  1987-88

- **BEST SEASON WITH RANGERS:**
  1989-90, 76 GP, 27-41-68, 42 PIM
- **TOTALS WITH RANGERS:**
  Regular season: 307 GP, 100-148-248, 188 PIM
  Playoffs: 19 GP, 2-7-9, 12 PIM
- **HONORS:**
  All-Star Game, 1988-89

CURTAIN CALL

Guy Lafleur

Guy Lafleur had nothing to prove by making a comeback; his career with Montreal had assured him of entrance into the Hockey Hall of Fame as soon as he was eligible. But Lafleur wanted to play again—and Rangers GM Phil Esposito was more than happy to give his old rival the chance. With his helmetless head standing out among younger teammates, Lafleur showed that sitting out for almost four years hadn't robbed him of his skills. "The Flower" wasn't up to the 30-minute-a-game pace of his youth—but he was no slouch, finishing with 18 goals and 45 points despite missing nearly a month with a broken foot. Though he scored in his first game against Montreal in October, no night meant more to Lafleur than February 4, 1989, when he made his return to the Forum. Ovations rocked the building as Lafleur flashed his old magic, scoring twice as the Rangers took an early lead before losing 7-5. The Rangers accommodated Lafleur after the season by sending him to Quebec, where he finished his career. But the vision of Lafleur flashing down right wing in a Rangers uniform, even if only for one season, was not something those who saw it will soon forget.

Guy Lafleur made a successful comeback in 1988-89. Photo by James Bozman.

NEW YORK
Ice Exchange

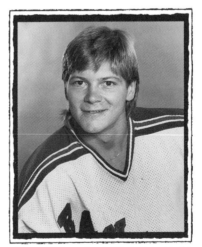

Carey Wilson had 55 points in 41 games.

GM Phil Esposito went after both young and old blood to help get the Rangers back into the playoffs—and was rewarded both ways. The old blood came from Hall of Famer Guy Lafleur, who played well in his return to the NHL after nearly four seasons on the sidelines. The youth infusion came from Brian Leetch and Tony Granato, who gave the Rangers their best rookie twosome in years. Leetch won the Calder Trophy and Granato led the team with 36 goals. Another future star, goaltender Mike Richter, bounced up and down between the parent club and the minors before making his NHL debut in Game 4 of the playoffs against Pittsburgh. Esposito's best trade came the day after Christmas when he dealt former linemate Don Maloney, one of the team's most popular veterans, plus Brian Lawton and Norm Maciver to Hartford for center Carey Wilson, who scored 55 points in only 41 games. The Rangers also landed some much-needed veteran help on defense when they picked up Mark Hardy from Minnesota in early December.

Ranger Lists

Most Goals by Rookie One Season

36
Tony Granato, 1988-89
35
Tony Amonte, 1991-92
33
Mark Pavelich, 1981-82
32
Don Murdoch, 1976-77
32
Darren Turcotte, 1989-90
30
Steve Vickers, 1972-73
29
Tomas Sandstrom, 1984-85
29
Ulf Dahlen, 1987-88
26
Wally Hergesheimer, 1951-52
26
Mike Allison, 1980-81

Neil Smith

It didn't take Neil Smith long to realize he wasn't going to make it big as an NHL player. As an executive, however, he's a Ranger immortal.

Ironically, the Rangers might even owe the Islanders something for Smith. The Isles drafted him in 1974, and after much persistence on Smith's part, eventually hired him as a scout. When assistant GM Jim Devellano went to Detroit as general manager in 1982, Smith went as the head of pro scouting. He eventually became GM of the Wings' top farm team, which won two AHL titles under his aegis.

At age 35, Smith didn't realistically figure to have much of a chance to land the Rangers' GM job after Phil Esposito departed in 1989. But when big names like Scotty Bowman and Herb Brooks dropped out of contention for the job, Smith jumped at his big chance. Ranger fans have been saying "thank you" ever since.

Smith's first task was finding a coach. With a lot of young talent on the way, Smith wanted someone who could serve as a stabilizing influence on a franchise that had been in upheaval, as well as a coach who could work with an emerging group of youngsters. He found the right man in Roger Neilson, whose style belied the fact that he was 20 years older than the man he would be working for.

Smith also overhauled the front office and the scouting staff. As someone who began as a scout, "My philosophy had been to build through the draft. It took me about five minutes to find out that philosophy wouldn't work in New York," he said. "I found out we would have to use the draft to accumulate assets."

Smith's willingness to pull the trigger on big deals brought the Rangers Bernie Nicholls and Mike Gartner—and the team's first division title in 48 years. Ranger fans were delighted with a first-round blitz of the Islanders, but an injury to All-Star defenseman Brian Leetch contributed to a swift ouster by Washington in the second round.

A disappointing finish in 1990-91 and a first-round loss to Washington left Smith vowing to make changes. He kept his word.

Smith signed Adam Graves as a free agent from Edmonton in September, but that was just a warmup for October 4, 1991. Mark Messier wanted more money than the Oilers were willing to pay, and GM Glen Sather was willing to deal. Smith landed one of hockey's greatest leaders for Nicholls and two prospects.

"Messier came and we were totally different," said Smith. That was an understatement: The Rangers set a team record with 50 victories and finished first overall for the first time in 50 years. But with their momentum slowed by a players' strike and Messier battling nagging injuries, the Rangers lost a 2-1 lead in the second round and fell to Pittsburgh in six games.

However, the Rangers' improvement had not been lost on top management. On June 19, he was named president of the team—the first man ever to hold the titles of president and general manager at the same time.

But not much went right in 1992-93, when injuries and a late slump resulted in the Rangers missing the playoffs. Neilson was replaced at midseason, and Smith hired Mike Keenan as coach practically before the Garden ice had melted.

The Keenan-Smith-Messier troika, combined with Smith's willingness to make bold moves when necessary, proved magical. For the second time in three years, the Rangers finished first overall, but this time, there would be no playoff failure. They routed the Islanders and Capitals, rallied to beat New Jersey and held off a determined Vancouver team to win their first Stanley Cup in 54 years.

Neil Smith built the Rangers into a Stanley Cup winner in 1994.
Photo by Bruce Bennett.

Through his first seven seasons in New York, Smith's teams have a 271-200-67 record and have won three division titles, two Presidents' Trophies and the treasured Stanley Cup. He has turned the Rangers into one of the NHL's model organizations on and off the ice—an accomplishment that was rewarded in June 1996 with a new six-year contract that will carry him into the next century as the leader of the Rangers. At the end of that contract, Smith will have been the Rangers' chief executive for 13 years—more than Hall of Famer Emile Francis and longer than anyone except franchise patriarch Lester Patrick, who ran the team for its first 20 seasons.

"My biggest thrill," he said after the new deal was reached, "is to think that somewhere down the road, someone will remember that through his formative years, the man running his favorite club was Neil Smith, just the way I thought of Emile Francis." That's the kind of stability that makes champions.

—1989 — 1990—

TIME CAPSULE

- **October 17, 1989:**
  An earthquake measuring 6.9 on the Richter scale hit the San Francisco Bay Area, killing more than 60 people.

- **February 28, 1990:**
  Black nationalist Nelson Mandela met with President Bush just two weeks after being released following 27 years in a South African prison.

- **May 31, 1990:**
  Russian president Mikhail Gorbachev met with President Bush at a summit in Washington.

1989-1990
FINAL STANDINGS

Patrick Division	W	L	T	PTS	GF	GA
RANGERS	36	31	13	85	279	267
New Jersey	37	34	9	83	295	288
Washington	36	38	6	78	284	275
NY Islanders	31	38	11	73	281	288
Pittsburgh	32	40	8	72	318	359
Philadelphia	30	39	11	71	290	297

Other Division Winners:

Adams—Boston

Norris—Chicago

Smythe—Calgary

PLAYOFF RESULTS
Patrick Semifinals: Rangers defeated Islanders 4-1
Patrick Finals: Washington defeated Rangers 4-1
LEADING PLAYOFF SCORER
Bernie Nicholls (7-5-12)
STANLEY CUP CHAMPION
Edmonton Oilers

SEASON SNAPSHOT

Goals:
John Ogrodnick (43)
Assists:
Brian Leetch (45)
Points:
John Ogrodnick (74)
Power-Play Goals:
John Ogrodnick (19)
Shorthanded Goals:
Brian Mullen (3)
Penalty Minutes:
Troy Mallette (305)
Power Play:
103/442, 23.3%, 8 SHGA
Penalty-Killing:
285/362, 78.7%, 7 SHG
Most Wins, Goaltender:
John Vanbiesbrouck (19)
Lowest Goals-Against Average:
John Vanbiesbrouck (3.38)
Most Shutouts:
John Vanbiesbrouck (1)
Rangers In All-Star Game:
Brian Leetch, D

The 1989-90 Season in Review

T he shocking four-game sweep by Pittsburgh in the spring of 1989 turned the Rangers upside down. Out went Phil Esposito as coach and GM; in came 35-year-old Neil Smith, who had led the Detroit Red Wings' top farm team to two AHL titles. Smith tabbed Roger Neilson, one of the NHL's best teachers, as coach, and the Rangers were off and running, starting 8-1-3. A mid-season slump dropped the Rangers into the division basement, but Neilson kept things together and the team rebounded with a 20-7-5 stretch from mid-January to late March, capped by a 7-4 victory in Quebec on March 27 that gave the Rangers their first division title since 1942. The drive to the top was fueled by key pickups like Bernie Nicholls and Mike Gartner, as well as the goaltending of John Vanbiesbrouck and newcomer Mike Richter and the defensive play of James Patrick and second-year star Brian Leetch. Ironically, though, it was one of the Rangers' best outings—an 8-2 rout of Toronto—that wound up being the most costly game of the season. With the game well in hand, Leetch fell awkwardly in the corner at Maple Leaf Gardens and broke his ankle. The Rangers, even without Leetch, needed only five games to beat the Islanders. But his absence showed severely against Washington, which beat the Rangers in five games.

Mike Richter and John Vanbiesbrouck backstopped the Rangers to the Patrick Division title. Photo by Bruce Bennett.

Magic Moment
April 13, 1990

The New York Islanders spent the early 1980s winning four Stanley Cups and 19 straight playoff series—torturing the Rangers in the process. The Isles beat the Rangers four straight times from 1981-84, so when the teams met in the Patrick Division semifinals in 1990, Ranger fans were looking for revenge—and they got it. The Rangers won 2-1 and 5-2 at the Garden to take a two-game lead, lost Game 3 in double overtime on Long Island, then took command with a 6-1 win at Nassau Coliseum. Game 5 found Ranger fans ready to celebrate, and their heroes were only too glad to oblige. Normand Rochefort's shorthanded goal triggered a three-goal second period for a 5-2 lead that had the Garden rocking. Third-period goals by Jeff Norton and Randy Wood quieted the party briefly, but Mike Gartner's goal at 11:44, just 26 seconds after Wood scored, completed the first playoff hat trick by a Ranger in 10 years and proved to be the margin of victory. The Garden erupted as Mike Richter made a final save to preserve the 6-5 victory that gave the Rangers bragging rights over their local rivals for the first time since 1979—and a trip to the division finals.

The Rangers beat the Islanders in the playoffs for the first time since 1979.

RANGER LEGEND
Brian Leetch

The Rangers had been waiting more than a decade, since the trade of Brad Park in 1975, to find a defenseman with the kind of two-way skills Brian Leetch exhibits on a nightly basis. Leetch was the Rangers' No. 1 pick (ninth overall) in the 1986 draft, but he didn't turn pro until after one year at Boston College and another with the 1988 U.S. Olympic team, for whom he served as captain. Perhaps it was appropriate that Leetch played his first NHL game on February 29—it was obvious right away that he was something special. He was an immediate hit, winning the Calder Trophy as the NHL's top rookie in 1988-89 and leading all first-year players in scoring. Only a broken ankle was able to slow him in 1989-90, when he was a key factor in the Rangers' division title run; he showed there were no ill effects by making the NHL's Second All-Star team in 1990-91, then winning the Norris Trophy as the NHL's top defenseman in 1991-92 while becoming the first Ranger rearguard to break the 100-point mark. After an injury-filled 1992-93 season in which the Rangers missed the playoffs, Leetch changed his style under Mike Keenan, improving his defensive play while doing a better job of picking his spots offensively. He had a solid regular season, then stepped up his game in the playoffs, leading all players in scoring and becoming the first American to win the Conn Smythe Trophy as playoff MVP, helping lead the Rangers' run to the Stanley Cup. Leetch excels at the transition game, turning the puck from defense to offense by breaking up an opponent's attack and setting up teammates for scoring opportunities. He's a superb passer and precise shooter. At the age of 28, Leetch is already the Rangers' all-time playoff scoring leader, has made four postseason All-Star teams, and should be at the top of his game for years to come.

Brian Leetch File

- **BORN:**
  March 3, 1968; Corpus Christi, Texas
- **ACQUIRED:**
  Rangers' first pick in 1986 Entry Draft
- **FIRST SEASON WITH RANGERS:**
  1987-88
- **BEST SEASON WITH RANGERS:**
  1991-92, 80 GP, 22-80-102, 26 PIM
- **TOTALS WITH RANGERS:**
  Regular season: 485 GP, 112-375-487, 255 PIM
  Playoffs: 56 GP, 25-47-72, 20 PIM

- **HONORS:**
  Calder Trophy, 1988-89
  Norris Trophy, 1991-92
  Conn Smythe Trophy, 1994
  First-team All-Star, 1991-92
  Second-team All-Star, 1990-91, 1993-94, 1995-96
  All-Star Game, 1989-90, 1991-92, 1992-93, 1993-94, 1995-96
  West Side Assn. Rangers MVP, 1988-89, 1990-91

CURTAIN CALL
Roger Neilson

Roger Neilson's instructional skills and game preparation were just what Neil Smith was looking for when the Rangers' new GM went shopping for a coach in the summer of 1989. Neilson, long known for his skills as a teacher and his use of videotape for instruction and preparation, proved to be a perfect tonic for a club that had been overhauled. He kept the team from panicking during a mid-season collapse that sent the Rangers to the basement and got maximum production from everyone to lead the Rangers to their first division title in 48 years. A late-season slump cost the Rangers a second straight title in 1990-91, but following the acquisition of Mark Messier in the fall of 1991, Neilson piloted the Rangers to their first 50-win season in 1991-92, winning the President's Trophy in the process. In all, the Rangers won 141 games during Neilson's 3 1/2 seasons behind the bench, putting him fourth on the all-time victory list and helping build the nucleus of the team that was to end New York's Stanley Cup drought.

Roger Neilson coached the Rangers to a division title.

NEW YORK
Ice Exchange

Bernie Nicholls helped the Rangers to their first title since 1942. Photo by George Kalinsky.

Anyone who might have doubted that new GM Neil Smith would be willing to take risks had those doubts dispelled well before the end of his first full season. Smith and coach Roger Neilson gave full-time jobs to rookies like Darren Turcotte, Troy Mallette and Mark Janssens while getting good mileage out of pickups like Kris King. With his team in the hunt for a division title, Smith made a pair of huge deals, picking up high-scoring center Bernie Nicholls from Los Angeles at the All-Star break for Tomas Sandstrom and Tony Granato, then dealing promising winger Ulf Dahlen to Minnesota for Mike Gartner near the trading deadline in March. Nicholls gave the Rangers a threat in the middle, while Gartner proved that he was far from washed up, helping the Rangers to the Patrick Division title by scoring 11 goals in his 12 games with New York before going on to record three straight 40-goal seasons.

Ranger Lists

Most Wins By A Coach

342
Emile Francis
(1965-75)

281
Lester Patrick
(1926-39)

179
Frank Boucher
(1939-48)

141
Roger Neilson
(1989-93)

131
Herb Brooks
(1981-85)

118
Phil Watson
(1955-59)

The Greatest Moments in the Rangers' First 70 Years

June 14, 1994
The Jinx Is Over

One banner said it for everyone who has ever rooted for the Rangers: "Now I Can Die In Peace." Nos. 1a and 1b are Mark Messier's delivering on his promise by scoring a natural hat trick to beat New Jersey in Game 6 of the Eastern Conference final, and Stephane Matteau's double-overtime winner in Game 7 against the Devils.

Ending the 54-year Stanley Cup drought was the thrill of a lifetime for Rangers fans. Photo by Bruce Bennett.

April 7, 1928
Lester Patrick Saves The Day

When goaltender Lorne Chabot was cut in Game 2 of the finals against the Montreal Maroons, the Rangers' coach and general manager put on the pads. Patrick backstopped the Rangers to a 2-1 overtime victory, creating a Ranger legend and sparking the Rangers to their first Stanley Cup—in only their second year of existence.

April 13, 1940
The Rangers Win Their Third Stanley Cup

Lester Patrick had set up the victory party long before Bryan Hextall's overtime winner gave the Rangers Cup No. 3. Little did he know it would be the last celebration of its type for more than a half-century.

April 29, 1971
A Long Night's Victory

Pete Stemkowski's goal 1:29 into the third overtime gave the Rangers a series-evening triumph over Chicago. It's the Rangers' longest game since 1939. No Ranger victory at the Garden ever took longer.

November 2, 1975
Goodbye, Eddie

Ranger fans, the most loyal in hockey, cheered departed hero Ed Giacomin on to victory with Detroit against their own team, just two days after he had been waived by GM Emile Francis.

November 1, 1959
The Debut of the Mask

The face of the NHL literally changed when Montreal goaltender Jacques Plante was cut by Andy Bathgate's shot. Plante returned to the ice wearing a mask and backstopped the Canadiens to victory. He never played another game without one—and by the early 1970s, no one else would, either.

March 14, 1962
Andy Bathgate's Penalty Shot

"The Garden's grimy old steelwork rang with a million-decibel shout of jubilation," was the way *Sports Illustrated* described Bathgate's penalty-shot goal against Detroit's Hank Bassen in a game that keyed the Rangers' playoff drive.

Brian Leetch became the first American to win the Conn Smythe Trophy as playoff MVP.

— 1990 1991 —

IME CAPSULE

- **January 16, 1991**
  American and Allied planes attacked Iraq's communications system and chemical weapons plants. Less than six weeks later, they claimed victory after pushing back the Iraqi army from Kuwait.

- **March 3, 1991**
  Los Angeles policemen stopped and beat African-American motorist Rodney King, an event recorded on videotape by an observer.

- **June 12, 1991**
  Michael Jordan led the Chicago Bulls to their first NBA title, beating the Los Angeles Lakers in five games.

1990-1991
FINAL STANDINGS

Patrick Division	W	L	T	PTS	GF	GA
Pittsburgh	41	33	6	88	342	305
RANGERS	36	31	13	85	297	265
Washington	37	36	7	81	258	258
New Jersey	32	33	15	79	272	264
Philadelphia	33	37	10	76	252	267
NY Islanders	25	45	10	60	223	290

Other Division Winners

Adams—Boston

Norris—Chicago

Smythe—Los Angeles

PLAYOFF RESULTS
Patrick Semifinals: Washington defeated Rangers 4-2
LEADING PLAYOFF SCORER
Bernie Nicholls (4-3-7)
STANLEY CUP CHAMPION
Pittsburgh Penguins

SEASON SNAPSHOT

Most Goals
Mike Gartner (49)
Most Assists
Brian Leetch (72)
Most Points
Brian Leetch (88)
Most Power-Play Goals
Mike Gartner (22)
Most Shorthanded Goals
Jan Erixon (3)
Most Penalty Minutes
Troy Mallette (252)
Power Play
91/389, 23.4%, 10 SHGA
Penalty-Killing
289/362, 79.8%, 9 SHG
Most Wins, Goaltender
Mike Richter (21)
Lowest Goals-Against Average
Mike Richter (3.12)
Most Shutouts
John Vanbiesbrouck (3)
NHL Award Winners
Rod Gilbert (Lester Patrick Trophy)
NHL All-Stars
Brian Leetch, D (Second Team)
Rangers In All-Star Game
Brian Leetch, D;
Darren Turcotte, C

The 1990-91 Season in Review

Year 2 of the Neil Smith/Roger Neilson regime picked up where Year 1 had left off—with the Rangers in first place. The Rangers opened with two road losses, then won 11 of their next 12 games to race into first place in the Patrick Division. Neilson had great success alternating his goaltenders, John Vanbiesbrouck and Mike Richter, while getting superlative play from defenseman Brian Leetch and a balanced attack led by center Bernie Nicholls and right wing Mike Gartner, whose 49 goals left him one short of Vic Hadfield's single-season Rangers record. In all, the Rangers led the division for a team-record 153 days, including 146 in a row. But a slump down the stretch and a surge by Pittsburgh enabled the Penguins to pass the Rangers in the final two weeks of the season. The Rangers started well in the playoffs against Washington, leading 2-1 thanks to Richter's 6-0 shutout in Game 3. But after losing Game 4 in Washington, they were unable to recover from a heartbreaking 5-4 overtime loss in Game 5 at the Garden and saw their season come to a premature end one game later. Still, by finishing second after coming in first in 1989-90, the Rangers had their best back-to-back finishes since ending up first in 1926-27, their inaugural season, and second in 1927-28, when they won their first Stanley Cup.

Mike Gartner had 49 goals in 1990-91, one short of the team record. Photo by Bruce Bennett.

MAGIC MOMENT

October 12, 1990

John Vanbiesbrouck was at his best in shutting out Montreal.

It had been more than 20 years (October 18, 1970) since Ranger fans had seen a regular-season shutout win over the Montreal Canadiens at the Garden. On the second Friday night of the new season, John Vanbiesbrouck gave them a night to remember. Brian Leetch's goal midway through the opening period gave the Rangers the lead —and Vanbiesbrouck took it from there. With the cries of "Bee-zer, Bee-zer" growing louder by the minute, Vanbiesbrouck, one of the few Rangers left from the 1986 semifinal loss to Montreal, played one of the finest games of his career. The Canadiens had numerous scoring chances while outshooting the Rangers 29-17 through two periods, but thanks to Vanbiesbrouck, the Rangers still had that 1-0 lead. Beezer remained brilliant throughout the third period while Mike Gartner added a power-play goal and an empty-netter to seal the 3-0 victory. Vanbiesbrouck, to the acclaim of the Garden faithful, was named the No. 1 star after a 41-save effort that ranks with any in club history.

HUSTLE PAYS OFF
Kelly Kisio

Few Rangers ever played with as much heart—or as much consistency—as Kelly Kisio. His size (5-foot-9 and 183 pounds) probably helped keep him from being drafted despite consecutive 60-goal seasons as a junior. That didn't stop Kisio from pursuing an NHL career: He signed with Detroit as a free agent in 1979 and made it with the Red Wings as a regular four years later after stops in the American Hockey League, International Hockey League, Central Hockey League and a season in Switzerland. The Rangers, needing a solid two-way center, got him from Detroit in the summer of 1986 by dealing away goaltender Glen Hanlon. The trade proved to be as popular as it was successful: Kisio had four straight 20-goal seasons and recorded 110 goals in five campaigns with the Rangers despite seeing only limited power-play time. In all, he recorded seven straight seasons with more than 20 goals and 60 points, including Ranger bests of 26 goals (1988-89) and 78 points (1987-88). His all-out effort and willingness to sacrifice for the team didn't go unnoticed: Kisio was named the Rangers' 21st captain on Christmas Eve in 1987—nine months after he had volunteered to give up his No. 16 to allow future Hall of Famer Marcel Dionne to wear it after

Photo by Bruce Bennett Studios.

Dionne came over from Los Angeles in March 1987. Garden fans and the media knew they were watching someone special who left everything he had on the ice every night: The fans voted him a co-winner of the Steven McDonald Extra Effort award in 1990, while the local hockey writers honored him with their "Good Guy" award the same year.

Kelly Kisio File

- **BORN:**
  September 19, 1959; Peace River, Alberta
- **ACQUIRED:**
  Traded by Detroit with Lane Lambert, Jim Leavins and a draft pick for Glen Hanlon and two draft picks, July 29, 1986
- **FIRST SEASON WITH RANGERS:**
  1986-87

- **BEST SEASON WITH RANGERS:**
  1987-88, 77 GP, 23-55-78, 88 PIM
- **TOTALS WITH RANGERS:**
  Regular season: 336 GP, 110-195-305, 415 PIM
  Playoffs: 18 GP, 2-9-11, 19 PIM
- **HONORS:**
  Players' Player Award, 1989-90
  Steven McDonald Extra Effort Award, 1989-90

CURTAIN CALL

Wayne Cashman

To Garden fans who spent the late 1960s and early 1970s booing him as a member of the "Big Bad Bruins," it must have come as quite a shock to see Wayne Cashman as part of the Rangers' revival. "Cash" spent 16 seasons with the Rangers' New England rivals before retiring in 1983, and was one of the Bruins that Ranger fans despised most. His biggest night against the Rangers was Game 6 of the 1972 finals, when he had two goals as the Bruins won the Stanley Cup at the Garden. But four years after hanging up his skates, Cashman joined the Rangers as a scout for the New England area—an assignment that lasted all of four months, when he was promoted to assistant coach. He even served as head coach on occasion when illness sidelined Tom Webster. His role under Roger Neilson included supervising game preparation and special teams; during his six years with the Rangers, their power play was among the NHL's best, setting a team record with 111 goals in 1987-88 and averaging a conversion rate of better than 20%.

Wayne Cashman has become one of the NHL's most valuable assistants.

NEW YORK Ice Exchange

After the major overhaul of a year earlier, the Rangers made few big moves as they headed into 1990-91. The most important was also the least expensive: for $1, GM Neil Smith landed sharpshooter Ray Sheppard, a Calder Trophy runnerup two seasons earlier in Buffalo who had fallen out of favor with Sabres management. Sheppard chipped in with 24 goals and gave the Rangers a solid No. 2 scorer on right wing behind Mike Gartner. The Rangers also got some help on the blue line by acquiring Joe Cirella on waivers from Quebec. Smith's biggest move came at the trading deadline, when he acquired more toughness by dealing forward Kevin Miller and two minor leaguers to Detroit for enforcer Joe Kocur, but suspensions and an injury limited Kocur to only five games after the trade.

Ray Sheppard got 24 goals for the Rangers, after coming to New York for less than the price of a subway token. Photo by Bruce Bennett.

Ranger Lists

Most Goals, Season

52
Adam Graves, 1991-92
50
Vic Hadfield, 1971-72
49
Mike Gartner, 1990-91
48
Pierre Larouche, 1983-84
47
Mark Messier, 1995-96
46
Jean Ratelle, 1971-72
45
Mike Gartner, 1992-93
43
Rod Gilbert, 1971-72
43
John Ogrodnick, 1989-90
42
Phil Esposito, 1978-79

—1991 1992—

TIME CAPSULE

- **November 7, 1991**
  NBA star Magic Johnson retired after announcing that he had tested positive for HIV.

- **April 1, 1992**
  National Hockey League players went on strike for the first time in league history, shutting down the league for nearly two weeks.

- **May 22, 1992**
  More than 50 million TV viewers tuned in to watch Johnny Carson's final appearance as host of the "Tonight Show."

1991-1992
FINAL STANDINGS

Patrick Division	W	L	T	PTS	GF	GA
RANGERS	50	25	5	105	328	246
Washington	45	27	8	98	330	275
Pittsburgh	39	32	9	87	343	308
New Jersey	38	31	11	87	289	259
NY Islanders	34	35	11	79	291	299
Philadelphia	32	37	11	75	252	273

Other Division Winners:

Adams—Montreal

Norris—Detroit

Smythe—Vancouver

PLAYOFF RESULTS
Patrick Semifinals: Rangers defeated New Jersey 4-3
Patrick Finals: Pittsburgh defeated Rangers 4-2
LEADING PLAYOFF SCORER
Mike Gartner (8-8-16)
STANLEY CUP CHAMPION
Pittsburgh Penguins

SEASON SNAPSHOT

Most Goals:
Mike Gartner (40)
Most Assists:
Brian Leetch (80)
Most Points:
Mark Messier (107)
Most Power-Play Goals:
Mike Gartner (15)
Most Shorthanded Goals:
Mark Messier/Adam Graves (4)
Most Penalty Minutes:
Tie Domi (246)
Power Play:
81/387, 20.9%, 12 SHGA
Penalty-Killing:
335/395, 84.8%, 14 SHG
Most Wins, Goaltender:
John Vanbiesbrouck (27)
Lowest Goals-Against Average:
John Vanbiesbrouck (2.85)
Most Shutouts:
Mike Richter (3)
NHL Award Winners:
Mark Messier (Hart Trophy);
Brian Leetch (Norris Trophy)
NHL All-Stars:
Brian Leetch, D (First Team);
Mark Messier, C (First Team)
Rangers In All-Star Game:
Mike Richter, G;
Brian Leetch, D;
Mark Messier, C

The 1991-92 Season in Review

John Vanbiesbrouck and Mike Richter backstopped the Rangers to their first President's Trophy. Photo by Bruce Bennett.

General Manager Neil Smith knew that changes had to be made after his team's early departure from the playoffs in the spring of 1991. He wanted players who were used to winning, so what better place to shop than Edmonton, where the Oilers still had the nucleus of a dynasty—but not the payroll to keep it. Smith signed Adam Graves as a free agent during the summer, but saved his biggest deal for the first week of the season when he reeled in Mark Messier, perhaps the NHL player most synonymous with winning. Messier debuted on October 5 in Montreal and promptly led the Rangers to a 2-1 overtime win—their first triumph at the Forum in nearly seven years. Messier proved to be everything Smith could have wanted. With Brian Leetch quarterbacking the attack from the blue line, the Rangers rolled to the President's Trophy as the NHL's regular-season champion, the first time they'd finished No. 1 overall in 50 years. The Rangers appeared not to be bothered by any after-effects from the players strike in their two remaining regular-season games, but had to struggle before subduing the stubborn Devils in seven games in the first round. New York jumped to a 2-1 lead against Pittsburgh, but with Messier hampered by a bad back, they lost Game 4 in overtime and dropped the next two games to the revitalized Penguins, who went on to win a Stanley Cup many Rangers fans thought would be theirs.

MAGIC MOMENT October 4-5, 1991

Neil Smith's first two teams had come in first and second, but the Rangers' GM knew that he had to make a major move to get the kind of talent and leadership necessary to win a Stanley Cup. He got the chance in the opening days of the 1991-92 season due to Mark Messier's holdout. The Edmonton captain, a key to the Oilers' five Stanley Cups from 1984-90, wanted a lot more money than the now budget-conscious franchise wanted to pay. Smith seized the opportunity and worked out a deal in which the Rangers sent center Bernie Nicholls and young forwards Steven Rice and Louie DeBrusk to the Oilers for Messier, who wasted no time showing that he was intent on turning the Rangers into winners. With barely enough time to get to know his new teammates, Messier took the ice in Montreal, where the Rangers hadn't won in more than six years, and willed the team to a 2-1 overtime victory, setting up Doug Weight's game-tying goal. The victory was the first step on a path that led the Rangers to a regular-season title in 1991-92 and a Stanley Cup two years later.

Mark Messier led the Rangers to the Stanley Cup three years after coming to New York.

RANGER LEGEND
Mark Messier

If there's one word that describes Mark Messier, it's "winner." That's why GM Neil Smith was more than willing to pay the price to land Messier from the Edmonton Oilers at the start of the 1991-92 season. Messier had inherited the captaincy in Edmonton when Wayne Gretzky was dealt away in 1988; in New York, he didn't have to wait, officially getting the title at the Rangers' home opener, his second game as a Ranger. Messier quickly set about turning his teammates into winners while showing the Garden faithful that his reputation as one of the NHL's most dominant players was well-earned. His 107 points were just two short of the team single-season record, and he became the first Ranger in 33 years to win the Hart Trophy as the league's Most Valuable Player. Between his leadership and his on-ice skills, Messier was the primary factor in the Rangers' No. 1 overall finishes in 1992 and 1994, as well as the 1994 Stanley Cup—in which he appropriately scored the winning goal. He reached a milestone early in the 1995-96 season when he scored his 500th career goal and went on to finish with 47 tallies, losing a chance at

breaking the 50-goal barrier when injuries slowed him in the final weeks of the season. Off the ice, Messier and New York have embraced each other; Messier quickly became one of the most popular athletes in the Big Apple, appearing on television, radio and even getting to throw out the first ball at Yankee Stadium. Mark, in turn, has raised hundreds of thousands of dollars for the his favorite charity, the Tomorrow's Children's Fund, after establishing the Mark Messier Point Club. For 1996-97, he'll be reunited with long-time Edmonton teammate and friend Wayne Gretzky, giving the Rangers a pair of future Hall of Famers in the middle.

Mark Messier File

- **BORN:**
  January 18, 1961; Edmonton, Alberta
- **ACQUIRED:**
  From Edmonton with future considerations for Bernie Nicholls, Steven Rice and Louie DeBrusk, October 4, 1991.
- **FIRST SEASON WITH RANGERS:**
  1991-92
- **BEST SEASON WITH RANGERS:**
  1991-92, 79 GP, 35-72-107, 73 PIM

- **TOTALS WITH RANGERS:**
  Regular season: 350 GP, 147-287-434, 386 PIM
  Playoffs: 55 GP, 26-42-68, 63 PIM
- **HONORS:**
  Hart Trophy, 1991-92
  First-team All-Star, 1991-92
  All-Star Game, 1991-92, 1992-93, 1993-94, 1995-96
  West Side Assn. Rangers MVP, 1994-95, 1995-96
  Steven McDonald Extra Effort Award, 1994-95, 1995-96
- **NHL MILESTONES:**
  1,201 Games Played, 539 Goals; 929 Assists; 1,468 Points

CURTAIN CALL
Larry Pleau

Larry Pleau has helped build up the Rangers farm system.

When Neil Smith took over as general manager in 1989, one of his first priorities was player development. Much of that task fell to Larry Pleau, whose hockey resume included just about every job but driving a Zamboni. Pleau broke into the NHL with Montreal in 1969-70 and spent parts of three seasons with the Canadiens before becoming the first player ever signed by the WHA's New England (now Hartford) Whalers. He had four 25-goal seasons with the Whale before retiring in 1979, then served as assistant coach, head coach and director of player personnel. Pleau then spent 3 1/2 seasons running the Whalers' top farm team at Binghamton before coming back to Hartford in 1987-88 for another stint as coach. Pleau has been with the Rangers for seven seasons, assisting Smith with the development of amateur talent and overseeing the day-to-day operation of the scouting department. Under Pleau's guidance, the Rangers have been able to restock their farm system and use youngsters in key trades while adding players like Alexei Kovalev, Sergei Nemchinov and Niklas Sundstrom to the parent club—with more young talent on the way.

NEW YORK Ice Exchange

Mark Messier might have been Neil Smith's best acquisition ever, but he was far from the only productive one. Smith took advantage of the Oilers' failure to sign talented young forward Adam Graves, inking him to a deal that cost him only Troy Mallette as compensation. Graves proved to be a perfect fit as Messier's left wing, showing a previously undiscovered scoring touch while refusing to allow opponents to take liberties with his linemates or anyone else in a Ranger jersey. The Messier deal cost the Rangers center Bernie Nicholls and prospects Louie DeBrusk and Steven Rice, but as future considerations, the Rangers later got defenseman Jeff Beukeboom from the Oilers for David Shaw. Beukeboom's size and strength made him a perfect fit with Brian Leetch on the Rangers' No. 1 defensive unit. The Rangers lost Kelly Kisio and Brian Mullen to expansion, but got a big boost from forward Tony Amonte, whose 35 goals helped him finish second in the Calder Trophy balloting, and Doug Weight, who showed plenty of promise at center.

Adam Graves blossomed as a scorer after coming to the Rangers. Photo by Bruce Bennett.

Ranger Lists

Hart Trophy Winner (NHL MVP)

Buddy O'Connor
1947-48

Chuck Rayner
1949-50

Andy Bathgate
1958-59

Mark Messier
1991-92

—1992 1993—

- **November 3, 1992:**
  Bill Clinton was elected president, defeating incumbent George Bush and independent challenger Ross Perot.

- **February 26, 1993:**
  New York's World Trade Center was bombed by terrorists.

- **April 19, 1993:**
  Nearly 100 people died in a fire that ended the 51-day standoff between the Branch Davidians and federal agents in Waco, Texas.

1992-1993

FINAL STANDINGS

Patrick Division	W	L	T	PTS	GF	GA
Pittsburgh	56	21	7	119	367	268
Washington	43	34	8	93	325	286
NY Islanders	40	37	7	87	335	297
New Jersey	40	37	7	87	308	299
Philadelphia	36	37	11	83	319	319
RANGERS	34	39	11	79	304	308

Other Division Winners:

Adams—Boston

Norris—Chicago

Smythe—Vancouver

PLAYOFF RESULTS

Rangers did not qualify

STANLEY CUP CHAMPION

Montreal Canadiens

SEASON SNAPSHOT

Most Goals:
Mike Gartner (45)
Most Assists:
Mark Messier (66)
Most Points:
Mark Messier (91)
Most Power-Play Goals:
Mike Gartner/Tony Amonte (13)
Most Shorthanded Goals:
Darren Turcotte (3)
Most Penalty Minutes:
Jeff Beukeboom (153)
Power Play:
77/420, 18.3%, 18 SHGA
Penalty-Killing:
362/446, 81.2%, 12 SHG
Most Wins, Goaltender:
John Vanbiesbrouck (20)
Lowest Goals-Against Average:
John Vanbiesbrouck (3.31)
Most Shutouts:
John Vanbiesbrouck (4)
Rangers In All-Star Game:
Brian Leetch, D;
Kevin Lowe, D;
Mark Messier, C;
Mike Gartner, RW

The 1992-93 Season in Review

Maybe it was the hangover from the disappointing loss to Pittsburgh the previous spring, but whatever the reason, 1992-93 was one of those seasons where almost nothing seemed to go right for the Rangers. It started out OK, with New York going 9-4-1, but inconsistency and injuries began taking their toll. The biggest injury came on Dec. 17, when Brian Leetch missed a check and injured his neck and shoulder during a 4-3 win in St. Louis. Leetch missed 34 games and his absence may have helped cost coach Roger Neilson his job. Neilson, who had led the Rangers to their first President's Trophy the previous season, was replaced by Ron Smith on January 4, but the Rangers continued to struggle until mid-February, when a 7-2-2 run moved New York into a tie for second. But with the Rangers starting to gel, they took two hits from the weather: a blizzard canceled a game in Washington after a stirring victory in Chicago, and Leetch soon went down for a second time, breaking his ankle in a fall on some ice outside his apartment not long after the blizzard. Losing Leetch again appeared to take something out of the Rangers; they dropped 10 of their last 11 and fell out of the playoff race, missing the postseason for the first time since 1988. GM Neil Smith wasted little time hiring Mike Keenan as coach and beginning a shakeup that was to pay the ultimate dividend a year later.

Alexei Kovalev had 20 goals in his first full NHL season. Photo by Bruce Bennett.

MAGIC MOMENT

Mike Gartner's 4 goals earned him All-Star Game MVP honors. Photo by Bruce Bennett.

Mark Messier's sprained wrist turned out to be a bonanza for Mike Gartner. The Rangers' speedy right wing got a chance to play in his sixth All-Star Game when he was named to the Wales Conference team as a replacement for Messier, one of five All-Stars idled by injury or illness. Gartner, who won the fastest skater competition the night before the game at the Montreal Forum, was off to the races early in one of the wildest All-Star contests ever played, scoring twice in the first 3:37 and completing a hat trick at 13:22 as the Wales Conference raced to a 6-0 lead after the opening period. Gartner got his record-tying fourth goal 3:33 into the second period of what turned out to be a 16-6 victory, and though he was unable to get the fifth goal that would have given him an All-Star Game record, he was an easy winner in the MVP balloting. Upon being presented with a new car, he was asked if he owed anything to Messier. Gartner allowed that he'd give the team captain a big handshake—but not the car.

295

RANGER LEGEND
Mike Gartner

When the Rangers got Mike Gartner from Minnesota for Ulf Dahlen at the trading deadline in March 1990, much was made of the fact that GM Neil Smith was giving up a lot of age in his quest for immediate results. Dahlen may have been younger (Gartner was one of the last survivors of the World Hockey Association), but Gartner's legs, shot and drive quickly convinced any doubters that Smith had made the right move. Gartner scored twice in his Ranger debut against Philadelphia and totaled 11 goals in 12 games after coming to New York, helping the Rangers to their first division title in 48 years. He then became the only Ranger ever to record three straight 40-goal seasons—part of his NHL-record 15 straight seasons with 30 or more goals. His 49-goal effort in 1990-91 still stands as a team record for right wings and was just one short of Vic Hadfield's team record; his 45 goals in 1992-93 were fifth on the team list and made him the first Ranger since Wally Hergsheimer in the early 1950s to lead the club in goal-scoring for three straight seasons. The 1991-92 season was a milestone campaign for Gartner; he reached 500 goals, 500 assists, 1,000 points and 1,000

Photo by Bruce Bennett.

games played, the only player ever to reach all four milestones in the same season. Christmas came a day late in 1993; Gartner hit the 600-goal mark on Dec. 26, tallying against the New Jersey Devils during an 8-3 victory at the Garden. To those who doubted that his speed would last, Gartner won the fastest skater title for the second time in his career at the All-Star skills competition in 1993, then set a record while winning the same event three years later in Boston.

Mike Gartner File

- **BORN:**
  October 29, 1959; Ottawa, Ontario
- **ACQUIRED:**
  Traded by Minnesota for Ulf Dahlen, March 6, 1990
- **FIRST SEASON WITH RANGERS:**
  1989-90
- **BEST SEASON WITH RANGERS:**
  1991-92, 76 GP, 40-41-81, 55 PIM

- **TOTALS WITH RANGERS:**
  Regular season: 322 GP, 173-113-286, 231 PIM
  Playoffs: 29 GP, 14-12-26, 16 PIM
- **HONORS:**
  All-Star Game, 1992-93
- **NHL MILESTONES:**
  1,290 Games Played, 664 Goals, 1,245 Points

CURTAIN CALL

Ron Smith

When Roger Neilson was hired as coach of the Rangers in August 1989, one of the first people he brought on board was Ron Smith, his top assistant at previous stops in Toronto, Buffalo and Vancouver. After two seasons in New York, Smith was named coach of the Rangers' top farm team in Binghamton, piloting the AHL team to a first-place finish in 1991-92. Smith had Binghamton on course for the best season in team history when GM Neil Smith promoted him to run the parent club when Neilson was let go on January 4, 1993. The Rangers struggled for a while after the move, but Smith appeared to have everyone moving in the right direction before a broken ankle sidelined All-Star defenseman Brian Leetch for the last 14 games. The resulting late-season fade cost Smith any chance at the coaching job for 1993-94, but the Rangers saw him again the following spring in the Stanley Cup finals as an assistant coach with Vancouver.

Ron Smith coached the Rangers for the second half of the 1992-93 season. Photo courtesy of Bruce Bennett.

NEW YORK
Ice Exchange

GM Neil Smith began the season with most of the 1991-92 team intact, but that didn't last long. Two more former Oilers, Kevin Lowe and Esa Tikkanen, also came to New York. Lowe, one of the NHL's best defensive defensemen, came in a pre-Christmas deal for prospect Roman Oksiuta, while Tikkanen, one of the NHL's top checking forwards and a solid offensive contributor, was acquired at the trading deadline for center Doug Weight. Two Russian rookies, forward Alexei Kovalev and defenseman Sergei Zubov, also made the roster and showed promise. Kovalev notched 20 goals and Zubov stepped in when Brian Leetch was hurt and showed the potential to join the NHL's elite on the blue line. Smith also acquired center Ed Olczyk from Winnipeg for Tie Domi and Kris King and added role players John McIntyre and Mike Hartman.

Kevin Lowe joined former Edmonton teammates such as Mark Messier in New York. Photo by Bruce Bennett.

Ranger Lists

Most Shorthanded Goals, one season

5
Don Maloney
1980-81
5
Mike Rogers
1982-83
4
Ron Stewart
1969-70
4
Bill Fairbairn
1971-72
4
Greg Polis
1977-78
4
Tony Granato
1988-89
4
Mark Messier
1991-92
4
Adam Graves
1991-92

In the great tradition of the Heisman Memorial Trophy Award, THE DOWNTOWN ATHLETIC CLUB, "Home of the Heisman," salutes another great sports tradition—

THE NEW YORK RANGERS
1994 Stanley Cup Champions

The Biggest Deals in the Rangers' First 70 Years

Mark Messier from Edmonton for Bernie Nicholls, Louie DeBrusk, Steven Rice and $1.5 million, plus future considerations (which became Jeff Beukeboom for David Shaw), October 4, 1991. A lot of NHL general managers felt Messier's tank was almost empty after winning five Stanley Cups in Edmonton. Not Neil Smith, who considered the deal a safe gamble. Messier won the Hart Trophy in his first season in New York—and led the Rangers to a Stanley Cup two years later.

Getting Mark Messier was the key to Neil Smith's Stanley Cup strategy.

Signing Wayne Gretzky, July 20, 1996. No, he's not the player he was in the mid-1980s. But he's still Wayne Gretzky, the greatest offensive force hockey has ever seen. Having him in New York, even at a late stage of his career, figures to be a treat for everyone who loves the Rangers.

Phil Esposito and Carol Vadnais from Boston for Jean Ratelle, Brad Park and Joe Zanussi, November 7, 1975. If there were a category for Most Unthinkable Deal, this would be the runaway winner. The Bruins were the Rangers' fiercest rivals, and the trade, which marked the end of the nucleus of the Rangers' powerhouse squads of the early '70s, shocked both fans and players. Espo originally considered not reporting, but grew to love his new organization.

Arnie Brown, Bill Collins, Dick Duff, Bob Nevin and Rod Seiling from Toronto for Andy Bathgate and Don McKenney, February 22, 1964. The biggest Ranger deal ever to that time. Bathgate was by far their best player, but the Rangers weren't winning with him. Seiling, Brown and Nevin became regulars as the rebuilt Rangers returned to prominence in the late '60s.

Ed Giacomin claimed on waivers by Detroit. John Davidson was the Rangers' goalie of the future, so when he couldn't make a trade for Giacomin, GM Emile Francis waived him. He was picked up by Detroit, who happened to be the Rangers' next opponent at the Garden. The fans cheered him on to a 6-4 victory.

Jacques Plante, Phil Goyette and Don Marshall from Montreal for Gump Worsley, Dave Balon, Leon Rochefort and Len Ronson, June 4, 1963. The huge deal marked a swap of unhappy 34-year-old goalies. Plante vowed to make the Rangers a contender, but they didn't even make the playoffs in his two unsuccessful seasons, while Worsley wound up on four Cup winners in Montreal.

Ken Hodge from Boston for Rick Middleton, May 26, 1976. An easy winner as the worst trade in team history. The Rangers traded Middleton's future (more than 400 goals) for Hodge's past. The Esposito-Hodge tandem that flourished in Boston was a bust in New York, with Hodge scoring just 23 times in 96 games and finishing his career in the minors.

Players and fans alike were stunned by the trade that brought Phil Esposito to the Rangers.

—1993 RANGERS 1994—

TIME CAPSULE

- **October 6, 1993:**
  Michael Jordan shocked the sports world by announcing his retirement from the Chicago Bulls, whom he had led to three straight NBA titles.

- **October 23, 1993:**
  Joe Carter's three-run homer in the bottom of the ninth inning gave the Toronto Blue Jays a six-game victory over the Philadelphia Phillies and their second straight World Series title.

- **January 17, 1994:**
  An earthquake in Southern California killed 57 people.

1993-1994

FINAL STANDINGS

Atlantic Division	W	L	T	PTS	GF	GA
RANGERS	52	24	8	112	299	231
New Jersey	47	25	12	106	306	220
Washington	39	35	10	88	277	263
NY Islanders	36	36	12	84	282	264
Florida	33	34	17	83	233	233
Philadelphia	35	39	10	80	294	314
Tampa Bay	30	43	11	71	224	251

Other Division Winners:

Northeast—Pittsburgh

Central—Detroit

Pacific—Calgary

PLAYOFF RESULTS
Eastern Quarterfinals: Rangers defeated Islanders 4-0
Eastern Semifinals: Rangers defeated Washington 4-1
Eastern Finals: Rangers defeated New Jersey 4-3
Stanley Cup Finals: Rangers defeated Vancouver 4-3
LEADING PLAYOFF SCORER
Brian Leetch (11-23-34)
STANLEY CUP CHAMPION
NEW YORK RANGERS

SEASON SNAPSHOT

Most Goals:
Adam Graves (52)
Most Assists:
Sergei Zubov (77)
Most Points:
Sergei Zubov (89)
Most Power-Play Goals:
Adam Graves (20)
Most Shorthanded Goals:
Adam Graves/Steve Larmer (4)
Most Penalty Minutes:
Jeff Beukeboom (170)
Power Play:
96/417, 23.0%, 5 SHGA
Penalty-Killing:
368/435, 84.6%, 20 SHG
Most Wins, Goaltender:
Mike Richter (42)
Lowest Goals-Against Average:
Mike Richter (2.57)
Most Shutouts:
Mike Richter (5)
NHL Award Winners:
Brian Leetch (Conn Smythe Trophy)
NHL All-Stars:
Brian Leetch, D (Second Team);
Adam Graves, LW (Second Team)
Rangers In All-Star Game:
Mike Richter, G; Brian Leetch, D;
Mark Messier, C; Adam Graves, LW

The 1993-94 Season in Review

The Longest Season in Rangers History Ended in Triumph — at Last!

Camp began early because the Rangers opened their exhibition season in London, beating Toronto in a two-game series that earned them their first championship in a season that was full of them. The Rangers stumbled a bit coming out of the gate, going 4-5-0 and dropping back-to-back games to newcomers Anaheim and Tampa Bay. However, the October 22 loss to the Lightning was their last for more than a month. The Rangers went 12-0-2 before a loss on Long Island, then tacked on a 6-0-1 streak to take command of the Atlantic Division race.

Along the way, the Rangers found time to host the All-Star Game. The Rangers' four representatives—Mark Messier, Brian Leetch, Adam Graves and Mike Richter—played key roles as the Eastern Conference outscored the West 9-8. Messier had a goal and two assists, but Richter, who was brilliant in the second period, became the second Ranger in as many years to earn the MVP award.

Fueled by a team-record 52 goals by Adam Graves, the Rangers stayed in front the rest of the way, holding off a challenge from New Jersey by completing a sweep of the Devils with a 4-2 win at the Meadowlands on April 2. They finished with team records for points (112) and wins (52) while winning the President's Trophy, giving them two titles for the season—but not the one Ranger fans were looking for.

The playoffs started with a series for the Madison Square Garden faithful to savor. The Rangers embarrassed their archrivals, the Islanders, in one of the most one-sided sweeps on record. Richter started the series with back-to-back 6-0 shutouts and Messier ended it with a breakaway goal that capped a 5-2 victory at the Nassau Coliseum, where the Rangers had never fared well.

Then it was time to pay back the Washington Capitals, who had ousted the Rangers in 1990 and 1991. Leetch came to the fore, dominating play at both ends of the ice and scoring the series-winning goal with 3:28 remaining in Game 5 to close out the Caps.

New Jersey, which hadn't been able to beat the Rangers during the regular season, found a way to do it in Game 1 of the Eastern Conference finals—tying the game with 43 seconds left in regulation and winning on Stephane Richer's goal at 15:23 of double overtime—the first of three games in the series to go into two overtimes. Messier and Richter helped the Rangers get even with a 4-0 win in Game 2 and Stephane Matteau, one of five players acquired at the trading deadline, scored an unassisted goal 6:13 into the second overtime for a 3-2 win in Game 3. The Devils evened the series with a 3-1 win in Game 4, then played their best game of the series, a 4-1 win that left New York one game from another summer of disappointment.

Mike Richter.

That's when Messier stepped up. He made a Joe Namath-like guarantee of victory, then backed it up with a natural hat trick to rally his team to a 4-2 win at the Meadowlands.

It was hard to believe there could be any more drama left, but there was. Leetch's goal midway through the second period stood up as the lone tally in Game 7—until Valeri Zelepukin spoiled the burgeoning celebration by jabbing the puck past Richter with 7.7 seconds left. Both teams had plenty of chances, but neither could score until Matteau's bad-angled backhander trickled into the net 4:24 into the second overtime, setting off a New Year's Eve-style celebration.

On paper, the Rangers were markedly better than their opponents in the finals. But someone forgot to tell the Vancouver Canucks they were supposed to lose. Kirk McLean's 52-save effort in the opener kept the Canucks in the game until Greg Adams scored at 19:26 of overtime to give the Canucks a 3-2 win. The Rangers won the next three games, including a pair in Vancouver, setting up the night Rangers fans had been dreaming of for more than a half-century.

But again, the Canucks spoiled the party, silencing the Garden by winning 6-3 after blowing a 3-0 lead in the third period. Vancouver then went home and dominated, winning 4-1 and sending everyone back to the Big Apple.

Again, Leetch took command, opening the scoring midway through the first period. Graves' power-play goal less than four minutes later had the Garden rocking, but Trevor Linden quieted the crowd when he scored a shorthanded goal early in the second period. Messier jammed a loose puck past McLean late in the period to restore the two-goal margin, which proved to be just enough when Linden scored again in the third period.

Richter did the rest, stopping the swarming Canucks down the stretch (once with some help from the goal post). As Craig MacTavish, another of GM Neil Smith's late acquisitions, won the final faceoff and the clock ran out, Madison Square Garden erupted as never before. For the first time in 54 years, the Rangers were on top of the NHL. The drought was over!

MAGIC MOMENT *May 25, 1994*

Mark Messier backed up his promise. Photo by Bruce Bennett.

Mark Messier has never been one to go down without a fight. Thus, when the Rangers faced elimination heading into Game 6 of the semifinals, Messier put his neck in the noose, declaring to all who would listen that the Rangers would beat New Jersey at the Meadowlands to force a seventh and deciding game. The guarantee was splattered all over the New York papers—but the Devils weren't impressed. Riding a wave of emotion, New Jersey raced to a 2-0 lead and were prevented from putting the game away only by the brilliance of Mike Richter. That's when Messier began to put his money where his mouth was. He set up Alexei Kovalev for the Rangers' first goal late in the second period, giving his team life. In the third period, Messier was everywhere, scoring the tying goal at 2:48 and putting the Rangers ahead to stay at 12:12. With Glenn Anderson off for slashing and the Devils' net empty, Messier completed a natural hat trick by shooting the puck 160 feet into the vacated cage to cap one of the greatest individual performances in Rangers history—and show that he was a man of his word.

MAGIC MOMENT

The only bad part about the Rangers' miraculous comeback in Game 6 was that it didn't win the semifinal series against New Jersey. Nor were the Devils willing to roll over. With a raucous full house looking on in the latest game ever played at the Garden (at least by the calendar), Mike Richter and the Devils' Martin Brodeur matched save for save until a brilliant individual effort by Brian Leetch opened the scoring midway through the second period. Leetch's goal stood up until the final seconds of regulation time, when the Devils pulled Brodeur for an extra attacker. With the Garden crowd counting down the seconds, the Devils' Valeri Zelepukin shocked everyone by jamming in a rebound with 7.7 seconds left to force the third overtime game of the series. It turned out to be the third double-overtime game of the series when Brodeur and Richter

Stephane Matteau scored to beat New Jersey in the semifinals.

took turns robbing opposing shooters. Then, in a flash, Stephane Matteau, who had the double-overtime winner in Game 4, picked up a dump-in, circled the net, and flicked the puck toward Brodeur—then saw his harmless-looking shot trickle into the net. Matteau was mobbed by his teammates as the Garden erupted in triumph—and relief.

MAGIC MOMENT

There was no wiggle room left. The Rangers had wasted two chances to end their 54-year Stanley Cup drought, losing Game 5 against the Canucks at the Garden and being soundly beaten back in Vancouver. But the home-ice edge, something the Rangers had battled for all season, proved to be just the tonic for dispelling any doubts. The Rangers took the play to the Canucks right away and were rewarded when Brian Leetch converted a sensational pass from Sergei Zubov at 11:02. Adam Graves, bothered by back pain throughout the series, made it 2-0 with a power-play goal at 14:45, and the fans were raising the Garden roof. They put it back on when Trevor Linden scored a shorthanded goal early in the second period, but erupted again when Messier scored on the power play at 13:29 for a 3-1 lead. The Rangers and their fans thought the third period was being played in slow motion—even more so after Linden's power-play goal cut the margin to 3-2. Each second seemed like a minute, each minute like a period ... and each Vancouver shot a potential goal. The Canucks came at the Rangers in waves, but each time, Mike Richter was equal to the challenge. It all came down to one final faceoff with 1.6 seconds left. Craig MacTavish won the draw, put the puck into the corner—and a celebration unlike any New York had ever seen was under way. As Marv Albert, who had broadcast the Rangers for nearly three decades, put it: "The Rangers win the Stanley Cup; words that a lot of people thought they would never hear in their lifetime."

Mark Messier holds the Stanley Cup. Photo courtesy of Bruce Bennett.

303

RANGER LEGEND
Adam Graves

Neil Smith knew he was getting a character player when he signed Adam Graves as an agent in the summer of 1991. Little did he know he'd wind up with a 50-goal scorer, too. Graves had only 16 goals in 139 games before signing with the Rangers after the Edmonton Oilers were unwilling to meet his price, then went without a goal for his first month as a Ranger. But former teammate Mark Messier told anyone who would listen that Graves would become an offensive force—and he was right on the money. After the slow start, Graves

Adam Graves set a team record with 52 goals in 1993-94.

finished his first season in New York with 26 goals, improved to 36 in 1992-93, then hit the jackpot in 1993-94, setting a team record with 52. Appropriately, the record-tying and record-breaking goals both came in Edmonton, with Messier setting up No. 50. "It couldn't have come any other way," Graves said of being set up by Messier, his friend and linemate. "He's been such an influence on my career." Graves added 10 goals in the playoffs, including a power-play goal in Game 7 of the finals that gave the Rangers a 2-0 lead. At least as important is Graves' willingness to stick up for his teammates; he's able to keep opponents from taking liberties without piling up an excessive number of penalty minutes. Off the ice, Graves has given his time and energy to numerous charities. He was the first Ranger to win the King Clancy Trophy for community service and won the *USA Weekend* "Most Caring Athlete" Award in 1994. Graves had back surgery in the fall of 1994 and was at less than full strength when play resumed after the lockout, but still had 17 goals in the regular season and four more in the playoffs, then had 22 in 1995-96 and another seven in the playoffs, where he was a key in the Rangers' comeback against the Canadiens.

Adam Graves File

- **BORN:**
  April 12, 1968, Toronto, Ontario
- **ACQUIRED:**
  Signed as free agent from Edmonton, Sept. 3, 1991
- **FIRST SEASON WITH RANGERS:**
  1991-92
- **BEST SEASON WITH RANGERS:**
  1993-94, 84 GP, 52-27-79, 127 PIM
- **TOTALS WITH RANGERS:**
  Regular season: 377 GP, 153-139-292, 565 PIM
  Playoffs: 53 GP, 26-15-41, 58 PIM

- **HONORS:**
  Second-team All-Star, 1993-94
  King Clancy Trophy (for leadership and community service), 1993-94
  All-Star Game: 1993-94
  West Side Assn. Rangers MVP: 1992-93, 1993-94
  Players' Player Award: 1991-92, 1992-93, 1994-95
  Steven McDonald Extra Effort Award: 1991-92, 1992-93, 1993-94

CURTAIN CALL
Mike Keenan

Photo by Bruce Bennett.

Mike Keenan once told a reporter that "everyone should take a year away from work. You'll look at life a lot differently." But one season away from hockey was too much for Keenan, who was signed by the Rangers before the ice had melted following 1992-93's disappointing fadeout. Keenan led the Blackhawks to the 1992 finals as coach and general manager. He began the next season as GM only, then left the Hawks on Nov. 6, 1992. After just over six months on the sidelines, GM Neil Smith signed him as coach on April 17, 1993.

Keenan was a proven winner—he came to New York with a .590 winning percentage—and made it clear he was aiming for nothing less than a Stanley Cup, the one NHL accomplishment he had yet to achieve. He even showed his players videotapes of ticker-tape parades during the preseason to get them in the right frame of mind. On the ice, he followed his pattern of sticking with one goalie and was rewarded when Mike Richter blossomed into a star. His special teams were brilliant, ranking among the top three on the power play and penalty-killing. When all else failed, he still

had Messier, Leetch, Graves, Richter and the rest of perhaps the most talented cast in Rangers history. The reward came June 14, when Keenan and the Rangers both got the championship they had been waiting for—the Stanley Cup.

The marriage didn't last long; Keenan left for St. Louis less than a month later—after a dispute that had to be mediated by NHL Commissioner Gary Bettman. But he left the Rangers as champions, accomplishing what he had been brought in to do.

NEW YORK Ice Exchange

Glenn Healy gave the Rangers a solid backup in goal. Photo by Bruce Bennett.

GM Neil Smith and Coach Mike Keenan knew they had a good team. That wasn't enough. They wanted a champion—and they were willing to roll the dice to do it.

The John Vanbiesbrouck/Mike Richter goaltending combo was broken up by expansion. Unable to keep both, the Rangers dealt Vanbiesbrouck to Vancouver for defenseman Doug Lidster, who became a valuable fill-in. Smith filled the No. 2 goaltending job by landing the rights to Glenn Healy, who had been let go in the expansion draft after leading the Islanders to the Cup semifinals in 1993, in a deal with Tampa Bay.

But those were just warmups. Keenan wanted Steve Larmer, one of his most reliable players in Chicago; to get him, Nick Kypreos and Barry Richter, the Rangers dealt away popular veterans James Patrick and Darren Turcotte. Larmer fit in perfectly, quietly scoring 21 goals and 60 points while living up to his billing as one of the league's top checkers.

With the Devils threatening as the trading deadline approached, Smith and Keenan went for it all. Five separate deals brought grinders Stephane Matteau and Brian Noonan and former Edmonton Oilers Glenn Anderson and Craig MacTavish to the Rangers, while scorers Tony Amonte and Mike Gartner were among those dealt away. All four newcomers played key roles in the Stanley Cup triumph.

Ranger Lists
Most Wins, One Season

Wins	Season
52	1993-94
50	1991-92
49	1970-71
48	1971-72
47	1972-73
42	1983-84
41	1968-69
40	1973-74
40	1978-79

—1994 1995—

NEW YORK RANGERS

⧖ IME CAPSULE

- **October 1, 1994:**
  The scheduled start of the NHL season was postponed by a lockout after players and owners failed to reach agreement on a new contract. The dispute was not settled until January, with the season ultimately reduced to 48 games.

- **November 5, 1994:**
  Forty-five-year-old George Foreman became the oldest heavyweight champion in history by knocking out Michael Moorer.

- **March 19, 1995:**
  Michael Jordan, who retired to play minor-league baseball, returned to the NBA with the Chicago Bulls.

1994-1995

FINAL STANDINGS

Atlantic Division	W	L	T	PTS	GF	GA
Philadelphia	28	16	4	60	150	132
New Jersey	22	18	8	52	136	121
Washington	22	18	8	52	136	120
RANGERS	22	23	3	47	139	134
Florida	20	22	6	46	115	127
Tampa Bay	17	28	3	37	120	144
NY Islanders	15	28	5	35	126	158

Other Division Winners:

Northeast—Quebec

Pacific—Calgary

Central—Detroit

PLAYOFF RESULTS
Eastern Quarterfinals: Rangers defeated Quebec 4-2
Eastern Semifinals: Philadelphia defeated Rangers 4-0
LEADING PLAYOFF SCORER
Brian Leetch (6-8-14)
STANLEY CUP CHAMPION
New Jersey Devils

SEASON SNAPSHOT

Most Goals:
Adam Graves (17)
Most Assists:
Mark Messier (39)
Most Points:
Mark Messier (53)
Most Power-Play Goals:
Adam Graves (9)
Most Shorthanded Goals:
Mark Messier (3)
Most Penalty Minutes:
Nick Kypreos (93)
Power Play:
40/200, 20.0%, 3 SHGA
Penalty-Killing:
177/211, 83.9%, 5 SHG
Most Wins, Goaltender:
Mike Richter (14)
Lowest Goals-Against Average:
Glenn Healy (2.36)
Most Shutouts:
Mike Richter (2)

The 1994-95 Season in Review

The afterglow of the Stanley Cup triumph was short-lived. First, coach Mike Keenan left for St. Louis after a squabble that eventually had to be decided by NHL Commissioner Gary Bettman; then the lockout that wiped out the first three months of the NHL season delayed their Cup celebration. The night Ranger fans had anticipated all summer, the raising of the championship banner before the home opener, was delayed until January 20, when the shortened 48-game season began. The ceremonies gave Ranger fans enough memories to last a lifetime—but Buffalo spoiled the party with a 2-1 victory. After a slow start, an 11-4-2 stretch put the Rangers among the league leaders, but they were dogged by inconsistency and nagging injuries (especially to Mark Messier) the rest of the way, not clinching a playoff berth until

The Rangers' Cup celebration on opening night didn't last through the season. Photo by Bruce Bennett.

Glenn Healy's 2-0 shutout at Philadelphia in the next-to-last game of the abbreviated 48-game season. The Rangers proved the value of playoff experience by ousting the youthful Quebec Nordiques, the Eastern Conference regular-season champs, in the opening round behind the play of Alexei Kovalev and Sergei Nemchinov. But overtime losses in Games 1 and 2 of the Eastern semifinals at Philadelphia, the second of which came despite a hat trick by Brian Leetch, left the Rangers reeling, and the Flyers applied the knockout punch with two more wins at the Garden.

MAGIC MOMENT January 20, 1995

It was the moment Ranger fans had waited a lifetime for—and not even having it pushed back for more than three months was going to spoil their fun. Due to the lockout, the raising of the Stanley Cup banner and the celebrating that went along with it were pushed back more than three months, from October 3 to January 20. It was well worth the wait. Amid pomp and circumstance befitting a once-in-a-lifetime occasion, the Stanley Cup was lowered from the ceiling to a waiting group of Rangers, who took it for one last turn around the ice. Raising the championship banner to the ceiling brought more noise from a crowd that had come ready to celebrate. Unfortunately for the Rangers, the party had to end: It was time for a new season to begin and the Buffalo Sabres, led by Grant Fuhr's goaltending, put a damper on the evening with a 2-1 victory. But they could never ruin the night—not for Ranger fans who had waited an eternity for Lord Stanley to come calling at the Garden.

The Rangers raised the championship banner at their home opener.

307

RANGER LEGEND
Steve Larmer

If there was ever a player who let his actions on the ice talk for him, it was Steve Larmer. But the play of the skillful right wing spoke volumes. Larmer had been one of the NHL's most consistent right wings for more than a decade when the Rangers acquired him from Chicago in November, 1994 after a contract dispute cost him a chance at the NHL's all-time consecutive games-played record; his mark of 884 in a row is third on the all-time list. Larmer, who was 32, quickly picked up the nickname "Grandpa"—but his consistent two-way play showed he was anything but old as he played a key role in helping the Rangers end their Stanley Cup drought. Larmer had the game-winning goal in his Ranger debut and kept producing; the Rangers were 44-17-7 when he was in the lineup, and he ended the season with 60 points in 68 games, plus 16 more points in the playoffs. Larmer started the 1994-95 season just the way he had ended the previous one—scoring well and checking efficiently, this time on a line with Mark Messier and Adam Graves. He surpassed two milestones late in the season, playing in his 1,000th NHL game on April 20 against Hartford and ringing up his 1,000th point when he set up Brian Noonan's goal on March 8 against

New Jersey. But back trouble began to slow him down, and his offensive production dropped after the arrival of Pat Verbeek from Hartford moved him off Messier's line. Still, he finished with 14 goals in the shortened season and added two more in the playoffs. GM Neil Smith felt Larmer had plenty of hockey left in him, but Larmer disagreed and went quietly off into retirement in Peterborough, Ontario, where he had first played junior hockey 18 years earlier.

Steve Larmer File

- **BORN:**
  June 16, 1961, Peterborough, Ontario
- **ACQUIRED:**
  Acquired in three-way trade from Chicago; Rangers got Larmer, Nick Kypreos and Barry Richter from Hartford for Darren Turcotte and James Patrick, Nov. 2, 1993
- **FIRST SEASON WITH RANGERS:**
  1993-94

- **BEST SEASON WITH RANGERS:**
  1993-94, 68 GP, 21-39-60, 41 PIM
- **TOTALS WITH RANGERS:**
  Regular-season: 115 GP, 35-54-89, 57 PIM
  Playoffs: 33 GP, 11-9-20, 20 PIM
- **NHL MILESTONES:**
  1,006 Games Played; 441 Goals; 1,012 Points

CURTAIN CALL

Colin Campbell

Maybe it was Colin Campbell's destiny to coach the New York Rangers—after all, he started his pro career with the WHA's Vancouver Blazers under the tutelage of Ranger legends Andy Bathgate and Phil Watson. Campbell, a defensive defenseman with plenty of heart, played one season in the WHA and 11 more in the NHL before retiring in 1985 to become an assistant coach with Detroit. After five years with the Wings, he became an assistant under Roger Neilson in 1990, coached the Rangers' top farm team in Binghamton for the second half of 1992-93 and returned to the Rangers as an associate coach under Mike Keenan for the Stanley Cup season of 1993-94. When Keenan left the Rangers in the summer of 1994, GM Neil Smith didn't wait long to anoint Campbell as his replacement. Campbell was hindered by the lockout, but piloted the Rangers into the playoffs and a first-round upset of conference champion Quebec, then led the Rangers to second place in the Atlantic Division and a 96-point finish in his second season.

Colin Campbell had led the Rangers to the second round of the playoffs in both seasons as a coach.

NEW YORK
Ice Exchange

Pat Verbeek added offense after joining the Rangers.

Mike Keenan's departure for St. Louis not only resulted in Colin Campbell stepping up to the head coaching job, it had its effects on the ice, too. As part of the arrangement that allowed Keenan to leave, the Rangers got talented center Petr Nedved from the Blues while Doug Lidster and Esa Tikkanen headed west. Nedved looked superb in the preseason, but was never the same after the players returned following the lockout, winding up with only 11 goals in what turned out to be his only season in New York. With Adam Graves and Steve Larmer hampered by back problems, the Rangers sought scoring help by dealing defensemen Glen Featherstone and Michael Stewart, plus a No. 1 pick, to Hartford for right wing Pat Verbeek, who quickly meshed with Messier to produce 10 goals in 19 games and help the Rangers earn a playoff berth.

Ranger Lists
Playoff Hat Tricks By Rangers

Frank Boucher:
April 9, 1932 at Toronto
Bryan Hextall:
April 3, 1940 vs. Toronto
Pentti Lund:
April 2, 1950 vs. Montreal
Vic Hadfield:
April 21, 1970 vs. Chicago
Steve Vickers:
April 10, 1973 vs. Boston
Ron Duguay:
April 20, 1980 vs. Philadelphia
Mike Gartner:
April 13, 1990 vs. Islanders
Bernie Nicholls:
April 19, 1990 at Washington
Mike Gartner:
April 27, 1992 vs. New Jersey
Mark Messier:
May 27, 1994 at New Jersey
Brian Leetch:
May 22, 1995 at Philadelphia

—1995 1996—

⏳ TIME CAPSULE

- **October 8, 1995:**
  Edgar Martinez's two-run double in the 11th inning gave the Seattle Mariners a 6-5 victory over the New York Yankees in the fifth and deciding game of the AL divisional playoff series, spoiling the Yankees' first postseason appearance since 1981.

- **March 9, 1996:**
  George Burns, a New Yorker who was already a show business veteran when the Rangers were formed in 1926, passed away at the age of 100.

- **June 16, 1996:**
  Michael Jordan capped his basketball comeback by leading the Chicago Bulls to an 87-75 victory over Seattle in Game 6 of the NBA Finals, wrapping up their fourth title in six years.

1995-1996
FINAL STANDINGS

Atlantic Division	W	L	T	PTS	GF	GA
Philadelphia	45	24	13	103	282	208
RANGERS	41	27	14	96	272	237
Florida	41	31	10	92	254	234
Washington	39	32	11	89	234	204
Tampa Bay	38	32	12	88	238	248
New Jersey	37	33	12	86	215	202
NY Islanders	22	50	10	54	229	315

Other Division Winners:

Northeast—Pittsburgh

Central—Detroit

Pacific—Colorado

PLAYOFF RESULTS
Eastern Quarterfinals: Rangers defeated Montreal 4-2
Eastern Semifinals: Pittsburgh defeated Rangers 4-1
LEADING PLAYOFF SCORERS
Mark Messier (4-7-11)
STANLEY CUP CHAMPION
Colorado Avalanche

SEASON SNAPSHOT

Most Goals:
Mark Messier (47)
Most Assists:
Brian Leetch (70)
Most Points:
Mark Messier (99)
Most Power-Play Goals:
Pat Verbeek (17)
Most Shorthanded Goals:
Niklas Sundstrom (2)
Most Penalty Minutes:
Jeff Beukeboom (220)
Power Play:
85/429, 19.8%,, 12 SHGA
Penalty-Killing:
406/495, 82.0%, 6 SHG
Most Wins, Goaltender:
Mike Richter (24)
Lowest Goals-Against Average:
Mike Richter (2.68)
Most Shutouts:
Mike Richter (3)
NHL All-Stars:
Brian Leetch, D (Second Team)
Rangers In All-Star Game:
Brian Leetch, D;
Mark Messier, C;
Pat Verbeek, RW

The 1995-96 Season in Review

In the wake of a disappointing playoff loss to Philadelphia, GM Neil Smith remodeled his roster, seeking more size to combat teams like the Flyers and adding more experience. With Mark Messier scoring goals as he hadn't in more than a decade, the Rangers took off out of the gate, going 11-5-1 over their first 17 games and adding a 7-0-3 streak before Christmas to take first place in the Atlantic Division. A 10-1-5 burst that carried the Rangers through January was fueled by their dominance at home, where they tied a team mark by going unbeaten for 24 games, winning 18 and tying six. The Rangers won a showdown for first place in Florida on February 25, but then hit the skids, and a rib injury to Messier in the final weeks of the season triggered a season-ending five-game losing streak that enabled Philadelphia to climb past them into first place. Things looked bad after Montreal won the first two playoff games, but the Rangers stunned the Canadiens by winning four in a row, including three games in Montreal, where they hadn't won since 1991. That led to a second-round meeting with the Penguins, and the Rangers came back to the Garden for Game 3 in high spirits after splitting the first two games in Pittsburgh. But a fluke goal by Mario Lemieux triggered a 3-2 win for Pittsburgh, and the Penguins rode Lemieux and Jaromir Jagr's scoring to a five-game victory.

Brian Leetch led all NHL defensemen in scoring in 1995-96.
Photo by Bruce Bennett.

MAGIC MOMENT   November 6, 1995

Mark Messier celebrates his 500th NHL goal.

It was somehow appropriate that Mark Messier's 500th career goal came against the Calgary Flames; after all, Messier spent more than a decade as a troop leader with the Edmonton Oilers in the "Battle of Alberta." But Messier reached the milestone in true New York style: He did it with a hat trick, in a comeback victory, with his parents, grandmother, sister and some friends in the stands, and with his former coach, Glen Sather, at the Garden. Messier scored No. 498 in the second period, got No. 499 early in the third, and rocked the Garden when his wrist shot from the right circle eluded Rick Tabaracci at 12:32 of the final period as the Rangers rallied for a 4-2 victory. "I was well aware of No. 500," he said later. "I was well aware that not many people had done it, and that the people who have done it have been great and have had great careers. But I've never really, in my own mind, put a lot of emphasis on goals and assists. I put the emphasis on doing what it takes to win." Rangers fans let him know how they felt with what observers called the longest ovation since the Stanley Cup banner was raised 11 months earlier. Messier went on to a 47-goal season.

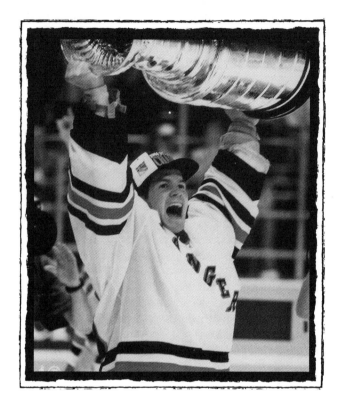

For a while, Mike Richter must have thought his name was "VanRichterBrouck." That's the tag some writers gave to the Rangers' two-headed goalie rotation in the early 1990s, when Richter and John Vanbiesbrouck shared the No. 1 job. It was almost an embarrassment of riches: Both were top-flight goaltenders, and neither was able to bump the other one out of the starting job. In 1990-91, they set an NHL record by alternating starts for 76 straight games before Richter was named the starter for the playoffs; he also was named a finalist for the Vezina Trophy. The two-headed goalie system lasted for two more years, during which Richter made the All-Star Game in 1992 and the Rangers finished first overall for the first time in 50 years, until expansion forced GM Neil Smith to make a choice. "It was the best thing for Mike and for John. They both needed to be No. 1," said former coach Roger Neilson, who initiated the alternating system. Smith's choice was Richter, who responded to the added responsibility of being No. 1 by posting his best season ever, setting a team record with 42 victories, recording a 2.57 goals-against average and a career-best five shutouts. He earned MVP honors in the All-Star Game at the Garden, backstopped the Rangers to their best finish ever, then played every game in the playoffs and matched NHL records with 16 victories and four shutouts as the Rangers ended their Stanley Cup drought. Richter appeared to be on the way to another banner season in 1995-96, but injured his groin less than two minutes from the end of his fifth consecutive victory, an 8-3 triumph in Edmonton on December 30, and wasn't able to play regularly again until mid-March, though he still finished with 24 wins. Off the ice, Richter has been honored for his considerable charitable work with the Thurman Munson Award and the Sloan-Kettering Award Of Courage. Having just turned 30, and coming off an MVP effort in the World Cup, Richter's skills should keep the Rangers' goaltending solid into the next millennium.

Mike Richter File

- **BORN:**
  September 22, 1966, Abington, Pennsylvania
- **ACQUIRED:**
  Second-round pick in 1985 Entry Draft
- **FIRST SEASON WITH RANGERS:**
  1988-89
- **BEST SEASON WITH RANGERS:**
  1993-94, 68 GP, 42-12-6, 2.57 goals-against average, 5 shutouts

- **TOTALS WITH RANGERS:**
  Regular season: 291 GP, 149-91-28, 2.99 goals-against average, 14 shutouts
  Playoffs: 61 GP, 32-27, 2.83 goals-against average, 6 shutouts
- **HONORS:**
  All-Star Game, 1992-93, 1993-94
  Players' Player Award, 1990-91

CURTAIN CALL
The Comeback

Montreal may be a nice place to live, but the Rangers have never particularly enjoyed visiting there. They were 55-183-35 at the Forum, their worst record at any visiting building, and were beaten 4-2 by the Canadiens in the opener at the new Molson Centre on March 17. Thus, Ranger fans were more than a little bit nervous when Montreal won the first two games of their opening-round playoff series at the Garden. The Rangers had never rebounded from an 0-2 deficit, but proving there's a first time for everything, they evened the series with 2-1 and 4-3 victories in Montreal, where they hadn't won since Mark Messier's debut on October 5, 1991 and were 1-20-3 since 1983. A 3-2 win back at the Garden put the Rangers ahead for the first time in the series, and they put the Canadiens away on April 28 with perhaps the best spurt any Ranger team has ever had in Montreal—a four-goal outburst in the first period that drained the life out of the Canadiens and their fans, leading to a 5-3 victory that capped the finest comeback in the Rangers' first 70 years.

Mark Messier led the comeback against Montreal.
Photo by Bruce Bennett.

NEW YORK
Ice Exchange

Standing pat is not a Neil Smith trademark. The Rangers' GM reacted to a sweep by Philadelphia with a flurry of moves designed to make his team bigger and faster. He raided his local rivals for two veterans, center Ray Ferraro (Islanders) and

Jari Kurri came to the Rangers in a late-season deal.

defenseman Bruce Driver (Devils), and made a major deal with Pittsburgh, bringing in left wing Luc Robitaille and defenseman Ulf Samuelsson for defenseman Sergei Zubov and forward Petr Nedved, who had failed to blossom in the Big Apple. Stephane Matteau, a playoff hero 18 months earlier, was sent to St. Louis in December for center Ian Laperriere; Laperriere and Ferraro, along with young defenseman Mattias Norstrom were dealt to Los Angeles at the trading deadline for three veterans: forwards Jari Kurri and Shane Churla and defenseman Marty McSorley. The Rangers' most effective rookie was center Niklas Sundstrom, their top pick in 1993, who checked efficiently all season long and showed promise as a scorer in the playoffs.

Ranger Lists

Longest home unbeaten streaks

24
10/24/95 - 2/15/96

24
10/14/70 - 1/31/71

18
11/28/39 - 2/25/40

18
1/5/69 - 3/30/69

18
10/17/71 - 12/29/71

16
10/24/93 - 1/5/94

13
11/25/41 - 2/5/42

12
12/28/69 - 2/25/70

The Great One Arrives...

New York's sporting history has been graced by most of the great ones—Babe Ruth, Lou Gehrig, Willie Mays, Lawrence Taylor, Willis Reed and a host of Ranger stars among them. But not until now has the Big Apple been blessed with The Great One.

Wayne Gretzky is one of those athletes who transcend their sport. He owns virtually every NHL offensive record and was part of a dynasty that produced four Stanley Cups in five years for the Edmonton Oilers in the mid-1980s. On July 20, 1996, he brought his quest for a fifth Cup to New York, signing a two-year deal that reunited him with long-time friend and teammate Mark Messier.

"I always thought that if you had an opportunity to bring Babe Ruth to New York, you ought to do it," Madison Square Garden president Dave Checketts said of his and Rangers president Neil

Smith's reasons for bringing No. 99 to New York. "Now we're bringing Wayne Gretzky to New York so that he and Mark Messier together can finish what have been astounding careers. We want another Stanley Cup here at the Garden. Our chances have been greatly enhanced."

Gretzky cited the presence of Messier as a deciding factor in coming to New York. "What tipped the scales was the chance to play with Mark and with a team centered on winning a championship," he said. "I wanted to come here and I'm thrilled that they wanted me."

At 35, Gretzky is not the offensive force he was in the 1980s with

Wayne Gretzky and Mark Messier will try to lead the Rangers to the same kind of success they had in Edmonton in the 1980s. Photo by Bruce Bennett.

the Oilers. But even a "bad" year from Gretzky usually means more than 100 points, and he's intent on showing he's got something left to show his new home fans.

"I think people in New York will be surprised to see how much I've got left," he said. Garden fans can hardly wait to see if he's right.

The Future

Ranger fans should have a lot to look forward to over the next few years.

With Mark Messier and Wayne Gretzky in the middle, the Rangers will have a future Hall of Famer at the center for almost of every game during the next couple of seasons. They'll take the pressure off players like Niklas Sundstrom, the 21-year-old Swede who was one of the Rangers top checkers and showed some scoring skills in the playoffs.

Three other key members of the team, Brian Leetch (28), Adam Graves (28) and Mike Richter (30) are in their prime and should have several more top-flight seasons left.

For the long-term future, there are youngsters like Christian Dube, the Rangers' first pick in the 1995 entry draft and one of the top scorers in Canadian junior hockey, as well as the Ferraro twins, Peter and Chris. Both Long Island natives were 100-point scorers in the minors in 1995-96 and played well in brief callups to the big club. They have the potential to be solid NHL players for a number of years.

On defense, the Rangers have high hopes for their latest No. 1 draft pick, Jeff Brown, as well as promising youngsters such as Eric Cairns, winner of the Lars-Erik Sjoberg Trophy as the top rookie in training camp prior to the

Peter Ferraro has been impressive in brief appearances with the Rangers. Photo by Bruce Bennett.

1996-97 season. In goal, there's 1994's No. 1 pick, Dan Cloutier, who excelled in juniors and may be pushing Richter for playing time before too long.

The All-Ranger Team
Third Era (1976-present)

Goaltender
Mike Richter
(1989-present)

Richter will go down in history as the goaltender who ended the Rangers' Stanley Cup drought in 1994. But there's a lot more: He's been an All-Star Game MVP, stopped a penalty shot in the Stanley Cup finals, posted a team-record 42-win season and a 20-game unbeaten streak, as well as leading the United States to the World Cup title. An intensely dedicated athlete, Richter should be at the top of his game for several years to come.

Mike Richter

Defense
Brian Leetch
(1988-present)

Leetch broke a Rangers drought of more than two decades when he won the Calder Trophy in 1988-89 and he's been picking up honors ever since—the one he undoubtedly enjoys most is the Conn Smythe Trophy as MVP of the Rangers' run to the Cup in 1994. No Ranger rearguard has ever been quicker in making the transition from defense to offense; few have run the power play as well or possessed his passing skills and on-ice vision.

Defense
Ron Greschner
(1974-90)

Had injuries, mostly to his back, not hampered him for much of his career, Greschner would have been the second Ranger to reach the 1,000-game mark. Greschner's offensive skills were what got him to the NHL at age 19; he developed into an excellent two-way player who remained productive right up until his retirement, setting franchise offensive records for defensemen along the way.

Center
Mark Messier
(1991-present)

The Rangers knew how to skate, pass and score; Messier taught them how to win. GM Neil Smith brought him in specifically to end the Rangers' half-century Cup drought, and end it he did, scoring the Cup-winning goal in Game 7 of the 1994 finals. Messier took to New York as if he were born to the task of leading the Rangers to the promised land, providing leadership skills that were perhaps even more important than his immense on-ice skills.

Mark Messier

Wing
Adam Graves
(1991-present)

He plays like Messier's younger brother—not as fast or skilled, perhaps, but every bit as relentless and team-oriented. Graves blossomed into a scorer after arriving in New York, setting the franchise record of 52 goals in 1993-94 while riding shotgun for Messier on left wing. He thrives in the most punishing places on the ice, and woe to an opponent who tries to take liberties with a teammate when Graves is on the ice.

Wing
Mike Gartner (1989-94)

In 1989, Gartner was regarded by many as a short-term player whose best years were behind him. Nothing could have been more wrong. Gartner scored at least 40 goals in each of his three full seasons with the Rangers, while serving as a role model with his work ethic, intelligence and class. One of the few sad notes of the 1994 championship season was that Gartner, who was dealt to Toronto at the trading deadline, wasn't around for the big moment.

Coach
Mike Keenan
(1993-94)

Neil Smith knew what he was getting when he hired Mike Keenan after the 1992-93 season—a controversial coach who invariably wore out his welcome despite his teams' success. Keenan's style angered many, but he did what none of the 24 men who had preceded him were able to do: coach the Rangers to a Stanley Cup. Even the storm clouds that surrounded his departure a month after the victory can never alter that.

SOURCES

Boucher, Frank & Frayne, Trent. (1973). *When the Rangers Were Young.* New York: The Cornwall Press Inc.

Diamond, Dan. (1991). *The Official National Hockey League 75th Anniversary Commemorative Book.* Toronto, Canada: McClelland & Stewart Inc.

Diamond, Dan, Ed. (1994). *The National Hockey League's Official Book of the Six-Team Era.* Toronto, Canada: McClelland & Stewart Inc.

Fischler, Stan. (1995). *Coaches: The Best NHL Coaching Legends from Lester Patrick to Pat Burns.* New York: Warwick Publishing Inc.

Fischler, Stan. (1978). *Kings of the Rink.* New York: Dodd, Mead.

Hollander, Zander, Ed. (1994). *The Complete Encyclopedia of Hockey, Fourth Edition.* New York: Visible Ink (a division of Gale Research).

Isaacs, Neil, D. (1977). *Checking Back.* New York: W.W. Norton & Company Inc.

Irvin, Dick. (1995). *In the Crease.* Toronto, Canada: McClelland & Stewart Inc.

MacFarlane, Brian. (1989). *One Hundred Years of Hockey.* Toronto, Canada: Deneau Publishers.

National Hockey League & Diamond, Dan. (1990). *Hockey: The Official Book of the Game.* New York: BDD Promotional Book Company, Inc.

Pearson, Mike. (1995). *Illini: Legend, Lists & Lore: 100 Years of Big Ten Heritage.* Champaign, Il: Sagamore Publishing.

Professional Sports Team Histories: Hockey, Volume 4. (1994). New York: Gale Research Inc.

Romain, Joseph, & Diamond, Dan. (1987). *The Pictorial History of Hockey.* New York: W.H. Smith Publishers Inc. (Gallery Books).

Whitehead, Eric. (1980). *The Patricks: Hockey's Royal Family.* Garden City, New York: Doubleday Press.

Worsely, Lorne & Moriarity, Tim. (1975). *They Call Me Gump.* New York: Associated Press Inc.

TEAM AND LEAGUE BOOKS

National Hockey League. (1980-96). *The National Hockey League Official Guide & Record Book.* New York: National Hockey League.

New York Rangers. (1966-96). *New York Rangers Media Guides.* New York: New York Rangers.

NEWSPAPERS:
The New York Times
The New York Daily News
The New York Post
The New York Journal-American
Newsday
The Toronto Star
The Toronto Sun
The Montreal Gazette

PERIODICALS:
The Hockey News, 1947-96
Sports Illustrated, 1962
Hockey Pictorial
New York Rangers Game Programs (1942-present)

(A complete listing of all the New York Ranger players from 1926-27 through 1995-96.)

#	Name & Position	Yrs. Played	REGULAR SEASON					PLAYOFFS				
			GP	G	A	PTS	PIM	GP	G	A	PTS	PIM
A												
4	Taffy Abel (D)	1926-27 - 1928-29	110	10	6	16	147	16	1	1	2	30
19	Doug Adam (LW)	1949-50	4	0	1	1	0	-	-	-	-	-
17	Lloyd Ailsby (D)	1951-52	3	0	0	0	2	-	-	-	-	-
15	Clint Albright (C)	1948-49	59	14	5	19	19	-	-	-	-	-
17	George Allen (D)	1938-39	19	6	6	12	10	7	0	0	0	4
14	Mike Allison (C)	1980-81-1985-86	266	63	102	165	297	32	4	9	13	48
18	Bill Allum (D)	1940-41	1	0	1	1	0	-	-	-	-	-
33, 31	Tony Amonte (RW)	1991-92-1993-94	234	84	99	183	135	15	3	8	11	4
36	Glenn Anderson (RW)	1993-94	12	4	2	6	12	23	3	3	6	42
24	Kent-Erik Andersson (RW)	1982-83-1983-84	134	13	35	48	22	9	0	0	0	0
5	Peter Andersson (D)	1992-93-1993-94	39	5	12	17	20	-	-	-	-	-
25	Steve Andrascik (RW)	1971-72	-	-	-	-	-	1	0	0	0	0
18	Paul Andrea (RW)	1965-66	4	1	1	2	0	-	-	-	-	-
17	Lou Angotti (C)	1964-65-1965-66	91	11	10	21	22	-	-	-	-	-
20	Hub Anslow (LW)	1947-48	2	0	0	0	0		-	-	-	-
6	Syl Apps (C)	1970-71	31	1	2	3	11	-	-	-	-	-
10	Dave Archibald (C)	1989-90	19	2	3	5	6	-	-	-	-	-
16	Oscar Asmundson (C)	1932-33-1933-34	94	7	16	23	28	9	0	2	2	4
9	Walt Atanas (RW)	1944-45	49	13	8	21	40	-	-	-	-	-
24	Ron Attwell (C)	1967-68	4	0	0	0	2	-	-	-	-	-
10	Oscar Aubuchon (LW)	1943-44	38	16	12	28	4	-	-	-	-	-
6	Don Awrey (D)	1977-78	78	2	8	10	38	3	0	0	0	6
2	Thomas Ayres (D)	1935-36	28	0	4	4	38	-	-	-	-	-
B												
15	Pete Babando (LW)	1952-53	29	4	4	8	4	-	-	-	-	-
21	Mike Backman (RW)	1981-82-1983-84	18	1	6	7	18	10	2	2	4	2
6	Bill Baker (D)	1982-83	70	4	14	18	64	2	9	9	9	0
11, 22, 8, 17	Dave Balon (LW)	1959-60-1962-63; 1968-69-1971-72	361	99	113	212	284	29	5	6	11	38
25	Jeff Bandura (D)	1980-81	2	0	1	1	0	-	-	-	-	-
11	Dave Barr (C)	1983-84	6	0	0	0	2	-	-	-	-	-
22, 14, 17	Jimmy Bartlett (LW)	1955-56; 1958-59-1959-60	126	19	14	33	174	-	-	-	-	-
	Cliff Barton (RW)	1939-40	3	0	0	0	0	-	-	-	-	-
12, 10, 9, 16	Andy Bathgate (RW)	1952-53-1963-64	719	272	457	729	444	22	9	7	16	19
16	Frank Bathgate (C)	1952-53	2	0	0	0	2	-	-	-	-	-
21	Frank Beaton (LW)	1978-79-1979-80	25	1	1	2	43	-	-	-	-	-
5, 3	Barry Beck (D)	1979-80-1985-86	415	66	173	239	775	49	10	22	32	77
23	John Bednarski (D)	1974-75-1976-77	99	2	18	20	114	1	0	0	0	17
19	Danny Belisle (RW)	1960-61	4	2	0	2	0	-	-	-	-	-
29	Bruce Bell (D)	1987-88	13	1	2	3	8	-	-	-	-	-
2	Harry Bell (D)	1946-47	1	0	1	1	0	-	-	-	-	-
20, 5	Joe Bell (LW)	1942-43; 1946-47	62	8	9	17	18	-	-	-	-	-
15	Lin Bend (C)	1942-43	8	3	1	4	2	-	-	-	-	-
20	Curt Bennett (C)	1972-73	16	0	1	1	11	-	-	-	-	-
17, 27	Ric Bennett (LW)	1989-90-1991-92	15	1	1	2	13	-	-	-	-	-
14	Doug Bentley (LW)	1953-54	20	2	10	12	2	-	-	-	-	-

#	Name & Position	Yrs. Played	REGULAR SEASON					PLAYOFFS				
			GP	G	A	PTS	PIM	GP	G	A	PTS	PIM
22, 10	Max Bentley (C)	1953-54	57	14	18	32	15	-	-	-	-	-
24	Red Berenson (C)	1966-67-1967-68	49	2	6	8	4	4	0	1	1	2
18	Bill Berg (LW)	1995-96	18	2	1	3	27	10	1	0	1	0
23	Jeff Beukeboom (D)	1991-92-1995-96	332	15	49	64	735	55	2	12	14	113
25	Nick Beverley (D)	1974-75-1976-77	126	4	23	27	67	-	-	-	-	-
6	Bob Blackburn (D)	1968-69	11	0	0	0	0	-	-	-	-	-
23	Don Blackburn (LW)	1969-70-1970-71	4	0	0	0	0	1	0	0	0	0
18	Mike Blaisdell (RW)	1983-84-1984-85	48	6	6	12	42	-	-	-	-	-
38	Jeff Bloemberg (D)	1988-89-1991-92	43	3	6	9	25	7	0	3	3	5
6, 3	Tim Bothwell (D)	1978-79-1981-82	62	4	10	14	32	9	0	0	0	8
21	Dick Bouchard (RW)	1954-55	1	0	0	0	0	-	-	-	-	-
17, 7	Frank Boucher (C)	1926-27-1937-38; 1943-44	533	152	261	413	114	52	16	18	34	12
2, 12	Leo Bourgault (D)	1926-27-1930-31	155	17	11	28	219	20	1	1	2	18
29	Phil Bourque (LW)	1992-93-1993-94	71	6	15	21	47	-	-	-	-	-
27	Paul Boutilier (D)	1987-88	4	0	1	1	6	-	-	-	-	-
15, 2	Jack Bownass (D)	1958-59-1959-60; 1961-62	76	3	7	10	58	-	-	-	-	-
8	William Boyd (RW)	1926-27-1928-29	95	8	1	9	56	9	0	0	0	2
15	Doug Brennan (D)	1931-32-1933-34	123	9	7	16	152	16	1	0	1	21
18	John Brenneman (LW)	1964-65-1965-66	33	3	3	6	20	-	-	-	-	-
32	Stephane Brochu (D)	1988-89	1	0	0	0	0	-	-	-	-	-
13	Bob Brooke (C)	1983-84-1986-87	175	35	36	71	214	24	6	9	15	43
37	Paul Broten (RW)	1989-90-1992-93	194	27	33	60	194	24	2	3	5	14
4	Arnie Brown (D)	1964-65-1970-71	460	33	98	131	545	29	0	7	7	23
16	Harold Brown (RW)	1945-46	13	2	1	3	2	-	-	-	-	-
4, 21	Larry Brown (D)	1969-70-1970-71	46	1	4	5	18	11	0	1	1	0
14	Stanley Brown (LW)	1926-27	24	6	2	8	14	2	0	0	0	0
17, 24	Jeff Brubaker (LW)	1987-88	31	2	0	2	78	-	-	-	-	-
12	Glenn Brydson (RW)	1935-36	30	4	12	16	9	-	-	-	-	-
19	Bucky Buchanan (C)	1948-49	2	0	0	0	0	-	-	-	-	-
4	Hy Buller (D)	1951-52-1953-54	179	22	55	77	209	-	-	-	-	-
14	Kelly Burnett (C)	1952-53	3	1	0	1	0	-	-	-	-	-
24, 27	Gary Burns (LW)	1980-81-1981-82	11	2	2	4	18	5	0	0	0	6
15	Norman Burns (C)	1941-42	11	0	4	4	2	-	-	-	-	-
17, 20	Jerry Butler (RW)	1972-73-1974-75	112	24	26	50	130	15	1	2	3	41
15	Jerry Byers (LW)	1977-78	7	2	1	3	0	-	-	-	-	-

C

#	Name & Position	Yrs. Played	GP	G	A	PTS	PIM	GP	G	A	PTS	PIM
5, 2	Larry Cahan (D)	1956-57-1958-59; 1961-62-1964-65	303	19	39	58	337	14	0	0	0	16
14	Patsy Callighen (D)	1927-28	36	0	0	0	32	9	0	0	0	0
14	Angus Cameron (C)	1942-43	35	8	11	19	0	-	-	-	-	-
38	Terry Carkner (D)	1986-87	52	2	13	15	120	1	0	0	0	0
11	Bob Carpenter (C)	1986-87	28	2	8	10	20	-	-	-	-	-
9, 20	Gene Carr (C)	1971-72-1973-74	138	18	23	41	90	17	1	4	5	21
11	Lorne Carr (RW)	1933-34	14	0	0	0	0	-	-	-	-	-
14	Gene Carrigan (C)	1930-31	33	2	0	2	13	-	-	-	-	-
18	Bill Carse (C)	1938-39	1	0	1	1	0	6	1	1	2	0
	Gerald Carson (C)	1928-29	14	0	0	0	5	5	0	0	0	0
26	Jay Caufield (RW)	1986-87	13	2	1	3	45	3	0	0	0	12
	Bill Chalmers (C)	1953-54	1	0	0	0	0	-	-	-	-	-
36	Todd Charlesworth (D)	1989-90	7	0	0	0	6	-	-	-	-	-
11	Rick Chartraw (D)	1982-83-1983-84	30	2	2	4	41	9	0	2	2	6
6	Bob Chrystal (D)	1953-54-1954-55	132	11	14	25	112	-	-	-	-	-
22	Shane Churla (LW)	1995-96	10	0	0	0	26	11	2	2	4	14
15	Hank Ciesla (C)	1957-58-1958-59	129	8	20	28	37	6	0	2	2	0
18, 6	Joe Cirella (D)	1990-91-1992-93	141	7	18	25	258	19	0	6	6	49
32	Dan Clark (D)	1978-79	4	0	1	1	6	-	-	-	-	-
6	Bruce Cline (RW)	1956-57	30	2	3	5	10	-	-	-	-	-
15	Bill Collins (RW)	1975-76	50	4	4	8	38	-	-	-	-	-
5, 16	Mac Colville (RW)	1935-36-1941-42; 1945-46-1946-47	353	71	104	175	132	40	9	10	19	14

#	Name & Position	Yrs. Played	REGULAR SEASON					PLAYOFFS				
			GP	G	A	PTS	PIM	GP	G	A	PTS	PIM
6	Neil Colville (C)	1935-36-1941-42;										
		1944-45-1948-49	464	99	166	265	213	46	7	19	26	33
6	Les Colwill (RW)	1958-59	69	7	6	13	16	-	-	-	-	-
6, 16	Charles Conacher, Jr. (LW)	1954-55-1955-56	93	21	18	39	22	-	-	-	-	-
15, 5	Jim Conacher (C)	1951-52-1952-53	33	2	5	7	4	16	1	1	2	2
28	Pat Conacher (C)	1979-80; 1982-83	22	0	6	6	8	3	0	1	1	2
15	Bert Connolly (LW)	1934-35-1935-36	72	12	13	25	33	4	1	0	1	0
20	Cam Connor (RW)	1979-80-1982-83	28	1	6	7	81	10	4	0	4	16
5	Bill Cook (RW)	1926-27-1936-37	475	228	138	366	386	46	13	12	25	66
6	Fred "Bun" Cook (LW)	1926-27-1935-36	433	154	139	293	436	46	15	3	18	57
10	Hal Cooper (RW)	1944-45	8	0	0	0	2	-	-	-	-	-
11, 12	Joe Cooper (D)	1935-36-1937-38;										
		1946-47	154	5	13	18	136	-	-	-	-	-
2, 17	Art Coulter (D)	1935-36-1941-42	287	18	67	85	332	37	2	5	7	46
18	Danny Cox (LW)	1933-34	15	5	0	5	2	2	0	0	0	0
32	Bob Crawford (RW)	1985-86-1986-87	14	1	2	3	12	7	0	1	1	8
16	Dave Creighton (C)	1955-56-1957-58	210	55	87	142	125	16	5	5	10	4
14	Brian Cullen (C)	1959-60-1960-61	106	19	40	59	12	-	-	-	-	-
17	Ray Cullen (C)	1965-66	8	1	3	4	0	-	-	-	-	-
19	Bob Cunningham (C)	1960-61-1961-62	4	0	1	1	0	4	0	1	1	0
2	Ian Cushenan (D)	1959-60	17	0	1	1	12	-	-	-	-	-
22	Paul Cyr (LW)	1987-88-1988-89	41	4	13	17	43	-	-	-	-	-
D												
16, 9	Ulf Dahlen (LW)	1987-88-1989-90	189	71	60	131	106	4	0	0	0	0
5	Hank Damore (C)	1943-44	4	1	0	1	2	-	-	-	-	-
4	Gordon Davidson (D)	1942-43-1943-44	51	3	6	9	8	-	-	-	-	-
8	Ken Davies (C)	1947-48	-	-	-	-	-	1	0	0	0	0
16	Billy Dea (LW)	1953-54	14	1	1	2	2	-	-	-	-	-
35, 23,	Lucien DeBlois (RW)	1977-78-1979-80;										
32		1986-87-1988-89	326	57	79	136	297	18	2	0	2	12
16	Val Delory (LW)	1948-49	1	0	0	0	0	-	-	-	-	-
24	Ab DeMarco (D)	1969-70-1972-73	104	8	21	29	19	-	-	-	-	-
15	Ab DeMarco (C)	1943-44-1946-47	182	67	86	153	36	9	0	1	1	2
5	Tony Demers (RW)	1943-44	1	0	0	0	0	-	-	-	-	-
14	Jean Paul Denis (RW)	1946-47; 1949-50	10	0	2	2	2	-	-	-	-	-
11	Victor Desjardins (C)	1931-32	48	3	3	6	16	7	0	0	0	0
2	Tommy Dewar (D)	1943-44	9	0	2	2	4	-	-	-	-	-
14	Herb Dickenson (LW)	1951-52-1952-53	48	18	17	35	10	-	-	-	-	-
4	Bob Dill (D)	1943-44-1944-45	76	15	15	30	135	-	-	-	-	-
8, 15	Cecil Dillon (RW)	1930-31-1938-39	409	160	121	281	93	38	13	9	22	15
9, 11	Wayne Dillon (C)	1975-76-1977-78	216	43	66	109	58	3	0	1	1	0
16	Marcel Dionne (C)	1986-87-1988-89	118	42	56	98	80	6	1	1	2	2
44	Per Djoos (D)	1991-92-1992-93	56	2	19	21	42	-	-	-	-	-
3	Gary Doak (D)	1971-72	49	1	10	11	2	-	-	-	-	-
28	Tie Domi (RW)	1990-91-1992-93	82	5	4	9	526	6	1	1	2	32
22	Mike Donnelly (LW)	1986-87-1987-88	22	3	3	6	8	-	-	-	-	-
27, 2	Andre Dore (D)	1978-79-1982-83;										
33		1984-85	139	8	38	46	153	10	1	1	2	16
8	Jim Dorey (D)	1971-72	1	0	0	0	0	6	0	1	1	19
33	Bruce Driver (D)	1995-96	66	3	34	37	42	11	0	7	7	4
16	Jim Drummond (D)	1944-45	2	0	0	0	0	-	-	-	-	-
9	Dick Duff (LW)	1963-64-1964-65	43	7	13	20	22	-	-	-	-	-
6	Marc Dufour (RW)	1963-64-1964-65	12	1	0	1	2	-	-	-	-	-
44, 10	Ron Duguay (C)	1977-78-1982-83;										
		1986-87-1987-88	499	164	176	340	370	69	28	19	47	103
19	Craig Duncanson (RW)	1992-93	3	0	1	1	0	-	-	-	-	-
25	Andre Dupont (D)	1970-71	7	1	2	3	21	-	-	-	-	-
18	Duke Dutkowski (D)	1933-34	29	0	3	3	16	2	0	0	0	0
	Henry Dyck (LW)	1943-44	1	0	0	0	0	-	-	-	-	-
E												
2	Frank Eddolls (D)	1947-48-1951-52	260	18	34	52	88	13	0	1	1	4
6	Pat Egan (D)	1949-50-1950-51	140	10	21	31	120	12	3	1	4	6

#	Name & Position	Yrs. Played	GP	G	A	PTS	PIM	GP	G	A	PTS	PIM
			REGULAR SEASON					PLAYOFFS				
20	Jack Egers (RW)	1969-70-1971-72;										
		1973-74	111	13	14	27	72	16	4	1	5	16
20	Jan Erixon (LW)	1983-84-1992-93	556	57	159	216	167	58	7	7	14	16
77, 12, 5	Phil Esposito (C)	1975-76-1980-81	422	184	220	404	263	30	11	15	26	33
5, 30	Jack Evans (D)	1948-49-1951-52;										
3		1943-54-1957-58	407	15	38	53	670	16	1	1	2	22
5	Bill Ezinicki (RW)	1954-55	16	2	2	4	22	-	-	-	-	-
F												
24	Trevor Fahey (LW)	1964-65	1	0	0	0	0	-	-	-	-	-
10, 14	Bill Fairbairn (RW)	1968-69-1976-77	536	138	224	362	161	52	13	21	34	29
3	Dave Farrish (D)	1976-77-1978-79	217	6	41	47	225	10	0	2	2	14
6	Glen Featherstone (D)	1994-95	6	1	0	1	18	-	-	-	-	-
32	Tony Feltrin (D)	1985-86	10	0	0	0	21	-	-	-	-	-
42, 25	Paul Fenton (LW)	1986-87	8	0	0	0	2	-	-	-	-	-
14	Chris Ferraro (RW)	1995-96	2	1	0	1	0	-	-	-	-	-
21, 17	Peter Ferraro (C)	1995-96	5	0	1	1	0	-	-	-	-	-
21	Ray Ferraro (C)	1995-96	65	25	29	54	82	-	-	-	-	-
41	Peter Fiorentino (D)	1991-92	1	0	0	0	0	-	-	-	-	-
12	Dunc Fisher (RW)	1947-48-1950-51	142	21	37	58	82	13	3	4	7	14
6	Sandy Fitzpatrick (C)	1964-65	4	0	0	0	2	-	-	-	-	-
9	Reg Fleming (LW)	1965-66-1968-69	241	50	49	99	540	13	0	4	4	22
18	Gerry Foley (RW)	1956-57-1957-58	137	9	14	23	91	9	0	1	1	2
14	Val Fonteyne (LW)	1963-64-1964-65	96	7	19	26	6	-	-	-	-	-
8	Lou Fontinato (D)	1954-55-1960-61	418	22	57	79	939	15	0	1	1	19
4	Harry "Yip" Foster (D)	1929-30	31	0	0	0	10	-	-	-	-	-
18	Herb Foster (LW)	1940-41; 1947-48	5	1	0	1	5	-	-	-	-	-
22	Nick Fotiu (LW)	1976-77-1978-79;										
		1980-81-1984-85	455	41	62	103	970	24	0	3	3	27
6	Archie Fraser (C)	1943-44	3	0	1	1	0	-	-	-	-	-
8, 38	Robbie Ftorek (C)	1981-82-1984-85	170	32	55	87	112	14	8	4	12	11
G												
4	Bill Gadsby (D)	1954-55-1960-61	457	58	212	270	411	16	2	5	7	10
9	Dave Gagner (C)	1984-85-1986-87	80	11	16	27	47	-	-	-	-	-
8	Dutch Gainor (C)	1931-32	46	3	9	12	9	7	0	0	0	2
17, 12	Cal Gardner (C)	1945-46-1947-48	126	28	36	64	103	-	-	-	-	-
15	Dudley Garrett (D)	1942-43	23	1	1	2	18	-	-	-	-	-
22	Mike Gartner (RW)	1989-90-1993-94	322	173	113	286	231	29	14	12	26	16
9	Fern Gauthier (RW)	1943-44	33	14	10	24	0	-	-	-	-	-
7, 10	Guy Gendron (LW)	1955-56-1957-58;										
		1961-62	272	38	41	79	217	22	6	3	9	21
5	Bernie Geoffrion (RW)	1966-67-1967-68	117	22	41	63	53	5	2	1	3	0
12	Ken Gernander (C)	1995-96	10	2	3	5	4	6	0	0	0	0
17	Greg Gilbert (LW)	1993-94	76	4	11	15	29	23	1	3	4	8
7, 16	Rod Gilbert (RW)	1960-61-1977-78	1065	406	615	1021	508	79	34	33	67	43
6	Curt Giles (D)	1986-87-1987-88	74	2	17	19	60	5	0	0	0	6
16	Randy Gilhen (C)	1991-92-1992-93	73	10	9	19	22	13	1	2	3	2
6	Jere Gillis (LW)	1980-81-1981-82	61	13	19	32	20	14	2	5	7	9
8	Howie Glover (RW)	1963-64	25	1	0	1	9	-	-	-	-	-
19	Pete Goegan (D)	1961-62	7	0	2	2	6	-	-	-	-	-
12	Bill Goldsworthy (RW)	1976-77-1977-78	68	10	13	23	55	-	-	-	-	-
14	Leroy Goldsworthy (D)	1929-30	44	4	1	5	16	4	0	0	0	2
11	Hank Goldup (LW)	1942-43-1945-46	103	34	46	80	69	-	-	-	-	-
16	Billy Gooden (LW)	1942-43-1943-44	53	9	11	20	15	-	-	-	-	-
19, 16	Jack Gordon (C)	1948-49-1950-51	36	3	10	13	0	9	1	1	2	7
11	Benoit Gosselin (LW)	1977-78	7	0	0	0	33	-	-	-	-	-
9, 20	Phil Goyette (C)	1963-64-1968-69;										
		1971-72	397	98	231	329	51	26	2	4	6	6
18, 39	Tony Granato (RW)	1988-89-1989-90	115	43	45	88	217	4	1	1	2	21
23	Norm Gratton (LW)	1971-72	3	0	1	1	0	-	-	-	-	-
9, 11	Adam Graves (LW)	1991-92-1995-96	377	153	139	292	565	53	26	15	41	58
2	Alex Gray (RW)	1927-28	43	7	0	7	28	9	1	0	1	0
4	Ron Greschner (D)	1974-75-1989-90	982	179	431	610	1226	84	17	32	49	106

#	Name & Position	Yrs. Played	GP	G	A	PTS	PIM	GP	G	A	PTS	PIM
			REGULAR SEASON					**PLAYOFFS**				
5	Jari Gronstrand (D)	1987-88	62	3	11	14	63	-	-	-	-	-
2	Jocelyn Guevremont (D)	1979-80	20	2	5	7	6	-	-	-	-	-
20, 12	Aldo Guidolin (D)	1952-53-1955-56	182	9	15	24	117	-	-	-	-	-
H												
11	Vic Hadfield (LW)	1961-62-1973-74	839	262	310	572	1036	62	22	19	41	106
19	Wayne Hall (LW)	1960-61	4	0	0	0	0	-	-	-	-	-
6, 25	Allan Hamilton (D)	1965-66; 1967-68-1969-70	81	0	5	5	54	6	0	0	0	0
6	Ken Hammond (D)	1988-89	3	0	0	0	0	-	-	-	-	-
22	Ted Hampson (C)	1960-61-1962-63	183	14	40	54	16	6	0	1	1	0
2, 6	John Hanna (D)	1958-59-1960-61	177	6	26	32	204	-	-	-	-	-
6	Pat Hannigan (RW)	1960-61-1961-62	109	19	23	42	58	4	0	0	0	2
14	Mark Hardy (D)	1987-88-1992-93	284	7	52	59	409	52	4	14	18	128
3	Ron Harris (D)	1972-73-1975-76	146	6	30	36	64	24	4	3	7	25
17	Ed Harrison (LW)	1950-51	4	1	0	1	2	-	-	-	-	-
18	Mike Hartman (RW)	1992-93-1994-95	39	1	1	2	80	-	-	-	-	-
2	Doug Harvey (D)	1961-62-1963-64	151	10	61	71	144	-	-	-	-	-
12	Gordie Haworth (C)	1952-53	2	0	1	1	0	-	-	-	-	-
19	Mark Heaslip (RW)	1976-77-1977-78	48	6	10	16	65	3	0	0	0	0
26, 40	Randy Heath (LW)	1984-85-1985-86	13	2	4	6	15	-	-	-	-	-
12	Andy Hebenton (RW)	1955-56-1962-63	560	177	191	368	75	22	6	5	11	8
15	Anders Hedberg (RW)	1978-79-1984-85	465	172	225	397	144	58	22	24	46	31
23	Bill Heindl (LW)	1972-73	4	1	0	1	0	-	-	-	-	-
3, 14	Ott Heller (D)	1931-32-1945-46	647	55	176	231	465	61	6	8	14	61
23	Raimo Helminen (C)	1985-86-1986-87	87	12	34	46	12	-	-	-	-	-
21	Camille Henry (LW)	1953-54-1954-55; 1956-57-1964-65 1967-68	637	256	222	478	78	22	3	7	10	5
18	Wally Hergesheimer (RW)	1951-52-1955-56; 1958-59	310	112	77	189	94	5	1	0	1	0
15	Orville Heximer (LW)	1929-30	19	1	0	1	4	-	-	-	-	-
6	Bryan Hextall (C)	1962-63	21	0	2	2	10	-	-	-	-	-
12, 19	Bryan Hextall (RW)	1936-37-1943-44; 1945-46-1947-48	449	187	175	362	227	37	8	9	17	19
21	Dennis Hextall (C)	1967-68-1968-69	13	1	4	5	25	2	0	0	0	0
17, 12	Bill Hicke (RW)	1964-65-1966-67	137	18	33	51	58	-	-	-	-	-
28	Greg Hickey (LW)	1977-78	1	0	0	0	0	-	-	-	-	-
16, 14 24	Pat Hickey (LW)	1975-76-1979-80; 1981-82	370	128	129	257	216	21	3	7	10	6
14	Ike Hildebrand (RW)	1953-54	31	6	7	13	12	-	-	-	-	-
8, 18	Dutch Hiller (LW)	1937-38-1940-41; 1943-44	200	49	70	119	116	23	3	4	7	11
16	Jim Hiller (RW)	1993-94		2	0	0	0	7	-	-	-	-
2	Wayne Hillman (D)	1964-65-1967-68	219	6	42	48	185	6	0	0	0	2
88	Ken Hodge (RW)	1976-77-1977-78	96	23	45	68	51	-	-	-	-	-
22	Jerry Holland (LW)	1974-75-1975-76	37	8	4	12	6	-	-	-	-	-
17	Greg Holst (C)	1975-76-1977-78	11	0	0	0	0	-	-	-	-	-
6	Miloslav Horava (D)	1988-89-1990-91	79	5	17	22	38	2	0	1	1	0
3	Tim Horton (D)	1969-70-1970-71	93	3	23	26	73	19	2	5	7	32
6, 11	Bronco Horvath (C)	1955-56-1956-57; 1962-63	114	20	34	54	78	5	1	2	3	34
23	Ed Hospodar (D)	1979-80-1980-81	122	8	23	31	442	19	3	0	3	135
16, 11	Vic Howe (RW)	1950-51; 1953-54-1954-55	33	3	4	7	10	-	-	-	-	-
3	Harry Howell (D)	1952-53-1968-69	1160	82	263	345	1147	34	3	2	5	30
21, 5	Ron Howell (D)	1954-55-1955-56	4	0	0	0	4	-	-	-	-	-
27	Willie Huber (D)	1983-84-1987-88	238	28	58	86	284	28	5	5	10	33
15	Mike Hudson (C)	1993-94	48	4	7	11	47	-	-	-	-	-
28	John Hughes (D)	1980-81	-	-	-	-	-	3	0	1	1	6
21	Jody Hull (RW)	1990-91-1991-92	50	5	8	13	12	-	-	-	-	-
5	Fred Hunt (RW)	1944-45	44	13	9	22	6	-	-	-	-	-

321

#	Name & Position	Yrs. Played	REGULAR SEASON					PLAYOFFS				
			GP	G	A	PTS	PIM	GP	G	A	PTS	PIM
25	Larry Huras (D)	1976-77	1	0	0	0	0	-	-	-	-	-
32	Mike Hurlbut (D)	1992-93	23	1	8	9	16	-	-	-	-	-
11	Ron Hutchinson (C)	1960-61	9	0	0	0	0	-	-	-	-	-

I

#	Name & Position	Yrs. Played	GP	G	A	PTS	PIM	GP	G	A	PTS	PIM
10	Earl Ingarfield (C)	1958-59-1966-67	527	122	142	264	201	10	3	2	5	2
4	Ron Ingram (D)	1963-64-1964-65	19	1	3	4	10	-	-	-	-	-
27	Ted Irvine (LW)	1969-70-1974-75	378	86	91	177	438	60	10	18	28	102
2	Ivan Irwin (D)	1953-54-1955-56; 1957-58	151	2	26	28	214	5	0	0	0	8

J

#	Name & Position	Yrs. Played	GP	G	A	PTS	PIM	GP	G	A	PTS	PIM
29	Don Jackson (D)	1986-87	22	1	0	1	91	-	-	-	-	-
14	Jeff Jackson (LW)	1986-87	9	5	1	6	15	6	1	1	2	16
14	Jimmy Jamieson (D)	1943-44	1	0	1	1	0	-	-	-	-	-
15, 47, 27	Mark Janssens (C)	1987-88-1991-92	157	14	15	29	338	15	5	1	6	16
28	Doug Jarrett (D)	1975-76-1976-77	54	0	4	4	23	-	-	-	-	-
8	Pierre Jarry (LW)	1971-72	34	3	3	6	20	-	-	-	-	-
10, 17	Larry Jeffrey (LW)	1967-68-1968-69	122	3	10	13	27	7	0	0	0	2
15, 39	Chris Jensen (RW)	1985-86-1987-88	53	7	11	18	23	-	-	-	-	-
2	Joe Jerwa (D)	1930-31	33	4	7	11	72	4	0	0	0	4
6, 5	Don Johns (D)	1960-61; 1962-63-1964-65	148	2	21	23	70	-	-	-	-	-
3	Ching Johnson (D)	1926-27-1936-37	403	38	48	86	798	54	2	7	9	159
24	Jim Johnson (C)	1964-65-1966-67	8	1	0	1	0	-	-	-	-	-
17, 14	Ed Johnstone (RW)	1975-76; 1977-78-1982-83	371	109	125	234	319	53	13	10	23	83
6	Bob Jones (LW)	1968-69	2	0	0	0	0	-	-	-	-	-
16	Bing Juckes (LW)	1947-48; 1949-50	16	2	1	3	6	-	-	-	-	-
19	Bill Juzda (D)	1940-41-1941-42; 1945-46-1947-48	187	11	25	36	178	12	0	1	1	13

K

#	Name & Position	Yrs. Played	GP	G	A	PTS	PIM	GP	G	A	PTS	PIM
11, 15	Bob Kabel (C)	1959-60-1960-61	48	5	13	18	34	-	-	-	-	-
17	Alex Kaleta (LW)	1948-49-1950-51	181	32	37	69	84	10	0	3	3	0
26	Sheldon Kannegiesser (D)	1972-73-1973-74	12	1	3	4	6	1	0	0	0	2
25	Alexander Karpovtsev (D)	1993-94-1995-96	154	9	39	48	114	31	1	5	6	16
21	Mike Keating (LW)	1977-78	1	0	0	0	0	-	-	-	-	-
10, 11	Butch Keeling (LW)	1928-29-1937-38	455	136	55	191	250	47	11	11	22	32
6	Ralph Keller (D)	1962-63	3	1	0	1	6	-	-	-	-	-
6	Dean Kennedy (D)	1988-89	16	0	1	1	40	-	-	-	-	-
16	Bill Kenny (D)	1930-31	6	0	0	0	0	-	-	-	-	-
12	Tim Kerr (RW)	1991-92	32	7	11	18	12	8	1	0	1	0
19, 12	Kris King (LW)	1989-90-1992-93	249	27	33	60	733	29	6	2	8	88
25	Steven King (RW)	1992-93	24	7	5	12	16	-	-	-	-	-
16	Bobby Kirk (RW)	1937-38	39	4	8	12	14	-	-	-	-	-
6	Bob Kirkpatrick (C)	1942-43	49	12	12	24	6	-	-	-	-	-
11, 16	Kelly Kisio (C)	1986-87-1990-91	336	110	195	305	415	18	2	9	11	19
3	Scot Kleinendorst (D)	1982-83-1983-84	53	2	11	13	43	6	0	2	2	2
26	Joe Kocur (RW)	1990-91-1995-96	278	14	15	29	537	48	2	4	6	84
23	Chris Kontos (C)	1982-83-1984-85	78	12	16	28	65	-	-	-	-	-
6	Mike Korney (RW)	1978-79	18	0	1	1	18	-	-	-	-	-
16	Dick Kotanen (D)	1948-49; 1950-51	2	0	0	0	0	-	-	-	-	-
24	Chris Kotsopoulos (D)	1980-81	54	4	12	16	153	-	-	-	-	-
27	Alexei Kovalev (RW)	1992-93-1995-96	270	80	100	180	361	44	16	23	39	42
6	Steve Kraftcheck (D)	1951-52-1952-53	127	10	18	28	75	-	-	-	-	-
12	Joe Krol (LW)	1936-37; 1938-39	2	1	1	2	0	-	-	-	-	-
22	Jim Krulicki (LW)	1970-71	27	0	2	2	6	-	-	-	-	-
15	Dolph Kukulowicz (C)	1952-53-1953-54	4	1	0	1	0	-	-	-	-	-
18	Stu Kulak (RW)	1986-87	3	0	0	0	0	-	-	-	-	-
19, 14	Eddie Kullman (RW)	1947-48-1948-49; 1950-51-1953-54	343	56	70	126	298	6	1	0	1	2
17	Alan Kuntz (LW)	1941-42; 1945-46	45	10	12	22	12	6	1	0	1	2
17	Jarri Kurri (RW)	1995-96	14	1	4	5	2	11	3	5	8	2

#	Name & Position	Yrs. Played	REGULAR SEASON					PLAYOFFS				
			GP	G	A	PTS	PIM	GP	G	A	PTS	PIM
25	Orland Kurtenbach (C)	1960-61; 1966-67-1969-70	198	30	61	91	191	15	2	4	6	50
	Larry Kwong (RW)	1947-48	1	0	0	0	0	-	-	-	-	-
19	Bill Kyle (C)	1949-50-1950-51	3	0	3	3	0	-	-	-	-	-
15, 6	Gus Kyle (D)	1949-50-1950-51	134	5	8	13	235	12	1	2	3	30
19	Nick Kypreos (LW)	1993-94-1995-96	128	7	12	19	272	13	0	2	2	8

L

#	Name & Position	Yrs. Played	GP	G	A	PTS	PIM	GP	G	A	PTS	PIM
15	Michel Labadie (RW)	1952-53	3	0	0	0	0	-	-	-	-	-
18, 19	Gordon Labossiere (C)	1963-64-1964-65	16	0	0	0	12	-	-	-	-	-
17	Max Labovitch (RW)	1943-44	5	0	0	0	4	-	-	-	-	-
20	Guy Labrie (D)	1944-45	27	2	2	4	14	-	-	-	-	-
32, 37	Daniel Lacroix (C)	1993-94-1995-96	30	2	2	4	30	-	-	-	-	-
22	Nathan LaFayette (C)	1994-95-1995-96	17	0	0	0	0	8	0	0	0	2
10	Guy Lafleur (RW)	1988-89	67	18	27	45	12	4	1	0	1	0
15	Jason Lafreneiere (C)	1988-89	38	8	16	24	6	3	0	0	0	17
2	Tom Laidlaw (D)	1980-81-1986-87	510	20	99	119	561	38	2	9	11	52
14	Lane Lambert (RW)	1986-87	18	2	2	4	33	-	-	-	-	-
21, 16 22	Jean Paul Lamirande (D)	1946-47-1947-48; 1949-50	48	5	5	10	26	8	0	0	0	4
16	Jack Lancien (D)	1946-47-1947-48; 1949-50-1950-51	63	1	5	6	35	6	0	1	1	2
12	Myles Lane (D)	1928-29	24	2	0	2	24	-	-	-	-	-
15	Darren Langdon (LW)	1994-95-1995-96	82	8	5	13	237	2	0	0	0	0
4	Al Langlois (D)	1961-62-1963-64	173	13	34	47	184	6	0	1	1	2
22	Ian Laperriere (C)	1995-96	28	1	2	3	53	-	-	-	-	-
10	Edgar Laprade (C)	1945-46-1954-55	500	108	172	280	42	18	4	9	13	4
28	Steve Larmer (RW)	1993-94-1994-95	115	35	54	89	57	23	9	7	16	14
20	Claude Larose (LW)	1979-80-1981-82	25	4	7	11	2	2	0	0	0	0
10,24	Pierre Larouche (C)	1983-84-1987-88	253	123	120	243	59	26	14	12	26	8
39	Steve Larouche (LW)	1995-96	1	0	0	0	0	-	-	-	-	-
19	Norm Larson (RW)	1946-47	1	0	0	0	0	-	-	-	-	-
44	Jim Latos (RW)	1988-89	1	0	0	0	0	-	-	-	-	-
18	Phil Latreille (RW)	1960-61	4	0	0	0	2	-	-	-	-	-
39	Peter Laviolette (D)	1988-89	12	0	0	0	6	-	-	-	-	-
17	Brian Lawton (C)	1988-89	30	7	10	17	39	-	-	-	-	-
2	Hal Laycoe (D)	1945-46-1946-47	75	1	14	15	31	-	-	-	-	-
24	Jim Leavins (D)	1986-87	4	0	1	1	4	-	-	-	-	-
18	Al Lebrun (D)	1960-61; 1965-66	6	0	2	2	4	-	-	-	-	-
18	Albert Leduc (D)	1933-34	10	0	0	0	6	2	0	0	0	0
30	Grant Ledyard (D)	1984-85-1985-86	69	10	21	31	73	3	0	2	2	4
2	Brian Leetch (D)	1987-88-1995-96	567	127	445	572	285	67	26	53	79	24
5	Roger Leger (D)	1943-44	7	1	2	3	2	-	-	-	-	-
4	Randy Legge (D)	1972-73	12	0	2	2	2	-	-	-	-	-
28	Mikko Leinonen (C)	1981-82-1983-84	159	31	77	108	69	19	2	11	13	28
14, 9	Real Lemieux (LW)	1969-70; 1973-74	62	4	6	10	51	-	-	-	-	-
18	Tony Leswick (LW)	1945-46-1950-51	368	113	89	202	420	18	5	6	11	20
14	Joe Levandoski (RW)	1946-47	8	1	1	2	0	-	-	-	-	-
11	Alex Levinsky (D)	1934-35	21	0	4	4	6	-	-	-	-	-
22	Danny Lewicki (LW)	1954-55-1957-58	280	76	90	166	107	16	0	4	4	8
27	Dale Lewis (LW)	1975-76	8	0	0	0	0	-	-	-	-	-
26	Igor Liba (LW)	1988-89		10	2	5	7	15	-	-	-	-
6	Doug Lidster (D)	1993-94; 1995-96	93	5	11	16	83	16	3	0	3	16
28	Bill Lochead (LW)	1979-80	7	0	0	0	4	-	-	-	-	-
14	Troy Loney (LW)	1994-95	4	0	0	0	0	1	0	0	0	0
25	Jim Lorentz (C)	1971-72	5	0	0	0	0	-	-	-	-	-
4	Kevin Lowe (D)	1992-93-1995-96	217	10	38	48	262	42	1	5	6	36
19	Odie Lowe (C)	1948-49-1949-50	4	1	1	2	0	-	-	-	-	-
14	Don Luce (C)	1969-70-1970-71	21	1	3	4	8	5	0	1	1	4
9	Pentti Lund (RW)	1948-49-1950-51	182	36	41	77	38	12	6	5	11	0

M

#	Name & Position	Yrs. Played	GP	G	A	PTS	PIM	GP	G	A	PTS	PIM
2, 8, 14	Kilby MacDonald (LW)	1939-40-1940-41; 1943-44-1944-45	151	36	34	70	47	15	1	2	3	4

#	Name & Position	Yrs. Played	REGULAR SEASON					PLAYOFFS				
			GP	G	A	PTS	PIM	GP	G	A	PTS	PIM
14	Parker MacDonald (LW)	1956-57-1957-58; 1959-60	119	15	18	33	54	7	2	3	5	2
19, 17	Hub Macey (LW)	1941-42-1942-43	18	6	8	14	0	1	0	0	0	0
12, 14	Bruce MacGregor (RW)	1970-71-1973-74	220	62	73	135	44	52	10	14	24	14
37	Norm Maciver (D)	1986-87-1988-89	66	9	26	35	28	-	-	-	-	-
11	Bill MacKenzie (D)	1934-35	20	1	0	1	10	3	0	0	0	0
2	Reg Mackey (D)	1926-27	34	0	0	0	16	1	0	0	0	0
14	Mickey MacIntosh (F)	1952-53	4	0	0	0	4	-	-	-	-	-
26	Brian MacLellan (LW)	1985-86	51	11	21	43	47	16	2	4	6	15
12	Bob MacMillan (RW)	1974-75	22	1	2	3	4	-	-	-	-	-
6	Al MacNeil (D)	1966-67	58	0	4	4	44	4	0	0	0	2
14	Craig MacTavish (C)	1993-94	12	4	2	6	11	23	1	4	5	22
2	John Mahaffy (C)	1943-44	28	9	20	29	0	-	-	-	-	-
16, 26	Troy Mallette (LW)	1989-90-1990-91	150	25	26	51	557	15	2	2	4	99
26	Dave Maloney (D)	1974-75-1984-85	605	70	225	295	1113	48	7	17	24	91
12	Don Maloney (LW)	1978-79-1988-89	653	195	307	502	739	85	22	35	57	99
5	Felix Mancuso (RW)	1942-43	21	6	8	14	13	-	-	-	-	-
16	Jack Mann (C)	1943-44-1944-45	9	3	4	7	0	-	-	-	-	-
19	Ray Manson (LW)	1948-49	1	0	1	1	0	-	-	-	-	-
14	Henry Maracle (F)	1930-31	11	1	3	4	4	4	0	0	0	0
39	Todd Marchant (C)	1993-94	1	0	0	0	0	-	-	-	-	-
42	Dave Marcinyshyn (D)	1992-93	2	0	0	0	2	-	-	-	-	-
29	Ray Markham (C)	1979-80	14	1	1	2	21	7	1	0	1	24
25	Mario Marois (D)	1977-78-1980-81	166	15	52	67	356	28	0	6	6	34
6	Gilles Marotte (D)	1973-74-1975-76	180	10	66	76	131	15	0	2	2	10
4	Bert Marshall (D)	1972-73	8	0	0	0	14	6	0	1	1	8
22	Don Marshall (LW)	1963-64-1969-70	479	129	141	270	40	15	3	2	5	2
17	Clare Martin (D)	1951-52	15	0	1	1	8	-	-	-	-	-
16	Charles Mason (RW)	1934-35-1935-36	74	6	14	20	44	4	0	1	1	0
32	Stephane Matteau (LW)	1993-94-1995-96	85	11	10	21	49	32	6	4	10	30
26	Brad Maxwell (D)	1986-87	9	0	4	4	6	-	-	-	-	-
34	Jim Mayer (RW)	1979-80	4	0	0	0	0	-	-	-	-	-
12	Sam McAdam (LW)	1930-31	4	0	0	0	0	-	-	-	-	-
20	Dunc McCallum (D)	1965-66	2	0	0	0	2	-	-	-	-	-
28	Dan McCarthy (C)	1980-81	5	4	0	4	4	-	-	-	-	-
9, 39	Rob McClanahan (LW)	1981-82-1983-84	141	33	43	76	77	19	4	10	14	14
39	Shawn McCosh (C)	1994-95	5	1	0	1	2	-	-	-	-	-
21	Bill McCreary (LW)	1953-54-1954-55	10	0	2	2	2	-	-	-	-	-
19	Bill McDonagh (LW)	1949-50	4	0	0	0	2	-	-	-	-	-
14	Bob McDonald (RW)	1943-44	1	0	0	0	0	-	-	-	-	-
6	Bucko McDonald (D)	1943-44-1944-45	81	7	15	22	14	-	-	-	-	-
11	John McDonald (RW)	1943-44	43	10	9	19	6	-	-	-	-	-
22, 28	Mike McDougal (RW)	1978-79; 1980-81	3	0	0	0	0	-	-	-	-	-
6, 27	Mike McEwen (D)	1976-77-1979-80; 1985-86	242	42	92	134	141	18	2	11	13	8
18	Sandy McGregor (RW)	1963-64	2	0	0	0	2	-	-	-	-	-
14	John McIntyre (C)	1992-93	11	1	0	1	4	-	-	-	-	-
25	Tony McKegney (RW)	1986-87	64	29	17	46	56	6	0	0	0	12
17	Don McKenney (C)	1962-63-1963-64	76	17	33	50	10	-	-	-	-	-
14	John McKenzie (RW)	1965-66	35	6	5	11	36	-	-	-	-	-
14, 19 18, 12	Jack McLeod (RW)	1949-50-1952-53; 1954-55	106	14	23	37	12	7	0	0	0	0
4, 6	Mike McMahon (D)	1963-64-1965-66; 1971-72	61	0	13	13	50	-	-	-	-	-
21, 37	George McPhee (LW)	1982-83-1986-87	109	21	24	45	247	29	5	3	8	69
16	Brian McReynolds (C)	1990-91	1	0	0	0	0	-	-	-	-	-
55, 36	Marty McSorley (D)	1995-96	9	0	2	2	21	4	0	0	0	0
12	Dick Meissner (RW)	1963-64-1964-65	36	3	5	8	0	-	-	-	-	-
30	Larry Melnyk (D)	1985-86-1987-88	133	4	21	25	281	22	1	2	3	50
28, 29	Joby Messier (D)	1992-93-1994-95	25	0	4	4	24	-	-	-	-	-
11	Mark Messier (C)	1991-92-1995-96	350	147	287	434	386	55	26	42	68	63
18, 12, 9	Larry Mickey (RW)	1965-66-1967-68	19	0	2	2	2	-	-	-	-	-

#	Name & Position	Yrs. Played	GP	G	A	PTS	PIM	GP	G	A	PTS	PIM
			REGULAR SEASON					**PLAYOFFS**				
11	Nick Mickoski (LW)	1947-48-1954-55	362	88	93	181	129	14	1	6	7	2
9	Rick Middleton (RW)	1974-75-1975-76	124	46	44	90	33	3	0	0	0	2
12	Jim Mikol (D)	1964-65	30	1	3	4	6	-	-	-	-	-
4	Hib Milks (LW)	1931-32	45	0	4	4	12	7	0	0	0	0
32, 23	Corey Millen (C)	1989-90-1991-92	19	4	5	9	12	6	1	2	3	0
40, 10	Kelly Miller (RW)	1984-85-1986-87	117	19	36	55	76	19	3	4	7	6
32, 26	Kevin Miller (RW)	1988-89-1990-91	103	20	37	57	67	1	0	0	0	0
24	Warren Miller (RW)	1979-80	55	7	6	13	17	6	1	0	1	0
21	Bill Moe (D)	1944-45-1948-49	261	11	42	53	163	1	0	0	0	0
5	Lloyd Mohns (D)	1943-44	1	0	0	0	0	-	-	-	-	-
24	Randy Moller (D)	1989-90-1991-92	164	7	38	49	378	16	1	8	9	43
16	Larry Molyneaux (D)	1937-38-1938-39	45	0	1	1	20	3	0	0	0	8
32	Sergio Momesso (LW)	1995-96	19	4	4	8	30	11	3	1	4	14
15	Hartland Monahan (RW)	1974-75	6	0	1	1	4	-	-	-	-	-
40	Jayson More (D)	1988-89	1	0	0	0	0	-	-	-	-	-
11	Howie Morenz (C)	1935-36	19	2	5	7	6	-	-	-	-	-
8	Elwin Morris (D)	1948-49	18	8	1	1	8	-	-	-	-	-
2	Jim Morrison (D)	1960-61	19	1	6	7	6	-	-	-	-	-
21	Mark Morrison (C)	1981-82; 1983-84	10	1	1	2	0	-	-	-	-	-
19	Brian Mullen (RW)	1987-88-1990-91	307	100	148	248	188	18	2	5	7	12
14	Don Murdoch (RW)	1976-77-1979-80	221	97	93	190	110	21	8	8	16	16
9	Murray Murdoch (LW)	1926-27-1936-37	508	84	108	192	197	66	10	15	25	30
14	Mike Murphy (RW)	1972-73-1973-74	31	6	5	11	5	10	0	0	0	0
15, 10	Ron Murphy (LW)	1952-53-1956-57	207	41	60	101	141	10	0	1	1	2
18	Vic Myles (D)	1942-43	45	6	9	15	57	-	-	-	-	-
N												
34	Vaclav Nedomansky (RW)	1982-83	35	12	8	20	0	-	-	-	-	-
10	Petr Nedved (C)	1994-95	46	11	12	23	26	10	3	2	5	6
15	Jim Neilson (D)	1962-63-1973-74	810	60	238	298	766	65	2	16	18	61
13	Sergei Nemchinov (C)	1991-92-1995-96	355	99	107	206	139	52	7	15	22	20
47	Steve Nemeth (C)	1987-88	12	2	0	2	2	-	-	-	-	-
21	Lance Nethery (C)	1980-81-1981-82	38	11	12	23	12	14	5	3	8	9
8	Bob Nevin (RW)	1963-64-1970-71	505	168	174	342	105	33	6	12	18	8
24	Dan Newman (LW)	1976-77-1977-78	100	14	21	35	59	3	0	0	0	4
9	Bernie Nicholls (C)	1989-90-1991-92	104	37	73	110	116	15	11	8	19	24
25	Graeme Nicolson (D)	1982-83	10	0	0	0	9	-	-	-	-	-
-30	Chris Nilan (RW)	1987-88-1989-90	85	11	14	25	332	8	0	2	2	57
19, 11	Ulf Nilsson (C)	1978-79-1982-83	170	57	112	169	85	25	8	14	22	27
16	Brian Noonan (RW)	1993-94-1994-95	57	18	15	33	38	27	4	7	11	25
14, 5	Mattias Norstrom (D)	1993-94-1995-96	43	2	6	8	13	3	0	0	0	0
O												
14	Warren Oatman (LW)	1928-29	27	1	1	2	10	6	0	0	0	0
5	Buddy O'Connor (C)	1947-48	238	62	102	164	12	18	5	6	11	4
25	John Ogrodnick (LW)	1987-88-1991-92	338	126	128	254	106	20	8	3	11	0
12	Eddie Olczyk (LW)	1992-93-1994-95	103	18	22	40	58	1	0	0	0	0
19, 20	Mark Osborne (LW)	1983-84-1986-87 1994-95	253	61	74	135	32	7	1	0	1	2
P												
11	Wilf Paiement (RW)	1985-86	8	1	6	7	13	16	5	5	10	45
14	Aldo Palazzari (RW)	1943-44	12	2	0	2	0	-	-	-	-	-
2	Brad Park (D)	1968-69-1975-76	465	95	283	378	738	64	12	40	52	121
27	Joe Paterson (LW)	1987-88-1988-89	41	1	4	5	149	-	-	-	-	-
6	Larry Patey (C)	1983-84-1984-85	16	1	3	4	16	5	0	1	1	6
3	James Patrick (D)	1983-84-1993-94	671	104	363	467	541	63	5	26	31	62
9, 18	Lynn Patrick (LW)	1934-35-1942-43; 1945-46	455	145	190	335	270	44	10	6	16	22
2, 15	Muzz Patrick (D)	1937-38-1940-41; 1945-46	166	5	26	31	133	25	4	0	4	34
11	Stephen Patrick (RW)	1984-85-1985-86	71	15	21	36	100	1	0	0	0	0
16, 40	Mark Pavelich (C)	1981-82-1985-86	341	133	185	318	326	23	7	17	24	14
18	Jim Pavese (D)	1987-88	14	0	1	1	48	-	-	-	-	-
12, 16	Mel Pearson (LW)	1959-60; 1961-62 1962-63-1964-65	36	2	5	7	25	-	-	-	-	-

#	Name & Position	Yrs. Played	REGULAR SEASON					PLAYOFFS				
			GP	G	A	PTS	PIM	GP	G	A	PTS	PIM
3	Fern Perreault (LW)	1947-48; 1949-50	3	0	0	0	0	-	-	-	-	-
4	Frank Peters (D)	1930-31	44	0	0	0	59	4	0	0	0	2
21	Garry Peters (C)	1965-66	63	7	3	10	42	-	-	-	-	-
24, 17	Michel Petit (D)	1987-88-1988-89	133	17	49	66	377	4	0	2	2	27
11	Gordon Pettinger (C)	1932-33	35	1	2	3	18	8	0	0	0	0
32	Dave Pichette (D)	1987-88	6	1	3	4	4	-	-	-	-	-
2, 16	Alf Pike (C)	1939-40-1942-43; 1945-46-1946-47	234	42	77	119	145	21	4	2	6	12
2, 25	Bob Plager (D)	1964-65-1966-67	29	0	5	5	40	-	-	-	-	-
24	Pierre Plante (RW)	1978-79	70	6	25	31	37	18	0	6	6	20
8	Walt Poddubny (C)	1986-87-1987-88	152	78	97	175	125	6	0	0	0	8
29, 41	Rudy Poeschek (RW)	1987-88-1989-90	68	0	2	2	256	-	-	-	-	-
14	Bud Poile (RW)	1949-50	28	3	6	9	8	-	-	-	-	-
19	Johnny Polich (RW)	1939-40-1940-41	3	0	1	1	0	-	-	-	-	-
20	Greg Polis (LW)	1974-75-1978-79	275	65	76	141	196	3	0	0	0	6
19	Larry Popein (C)	1954-55-1960-61	402	75	127	202	150	16	1	4	5	6
11, 2	Babe Pratt (D)	1935-36-1942-43	307	27	97	124	299	39	9	8	17	70
17	Dean Prentice (LW)	1952-53-1962-63	666	186	236	422	263	19	2	7	9	20
18	Wayne Presley (RW)	1995-96	61	4	6	10	71	-	-	-	-	-
15	Noel Price (D)	1959-60-1960-61	7	0	0	0	4	-	-	-	-	-
47	Pat Price (D)	1986-87	13	0	2	2	49	6	0	1	1	27
17	Jean Pusie (D)	1933-34	19	0	2	2	17	-	-	-	-	-
Q												
12	Leo Quenneville (F)	1929-30	25	0	3	3	10	3	0	0	0	0
R												
7, 9	Don Raleigh (C)	1943-44; 1947-48-1955-56	535	101	219	320	96	18	6	5	11	6
19, 14	Jean Ratelle (C)	1960-61-1975-76	862	336	481	817	192	65	9	33	42	14
5	Mel Read (C)	1946-47	6	0	0	0	8	-	-	-	-	-
11	William Regan (D)	1929-30-1930-31	52	2	1	3	53	8	0	0	0	2
11	Oliver Reinikka (F)	1926-27	16	0	0	0	0	-	-	-	-	-
5	Leo Reise, Jr. (D)	1952-53-1953-54	131	7	20	27	124	-	-	-	-	-
2	Leo Reise, Sr. (D)	1929-30	12	0	1	1	8	-	-	-	-	-
10	Steven Rice (RW)	1990-91	11	1	1	2	4	2	2	1	3	6
18	Dave Richardson (LW)	1963-64-1964-65	41	3	2	5	25	-	-	-	-	-
29	Barry Richter (D)	1995-96	4	0	1	1	0	-	-	-	-	-
41	Steve Richmond (D)	1983-84-1985-86	77	2	12	14	263	4	0	0	0	12
18	Mike Ridley (C)	1985-86-1986-87	118	38	63	101	89	16	6	8	14	26
4	Vic Ripley (LW)	1933-34-1934-35	39	5	14	19	12	2	1	0	1	4
19	Alex Ritson (LW)	1944-45	1	0	0	0	0	-	-	-	-	-
21	Wayne Rivers (RW)	1968-69	4	0	0	0	0	-	-	-	-	-
5	Doug Robinson (LW)	1964-65-1966-67	73	16	26	42	10	-	-	-	-	-
20	Luc Robitaille (LW)	1995-96	77	23	46	69	80	11	1	5	6	8
25, 24	Mike Robitaille (D)	1969-70-1970-71	15	1	1	2	15	-	-	-	-	-
16	Leon Rochefort (RW)	1960-61; 1962-63	24	5	4	9	6	-	-	-	-	-
5	Normand Rochefort (D)	1988-89-1991-92	112	7	15	22	108	-	-	-	-	-
12	Edmond Rodden (F)	1930-31	24	0	3	3	8	-	-	-	-	-
17, 27	Mike Rogers (C)	1981-82-1985-86	316	117	191	308	142	14	1	10	11	6
5	Dale Rolfe (D)	1970-71-1974-75	244	13	66	79	190	50	5	17	22	59
19	Len Ronson (LW)	1960-61	13	2	1	3	10	-	-	-	-	-
9	Paul Ronty (C)	1951-52-1954-55	260	45	114	159	62	-	-	-	-	-
2, 15	Jim Ross (D)	1951-52-1952-53	62	2	11	13	29	-	-	-	-	-
22	Bobby Rousseau (RW)	1971-72-1974-75	236	41	116	157	30	38	9	22	31	15
15	Ronnie Rowe (LW)	1947-48	5	1	0	1	0	-	-	-	-	-
8	Jean-Yves Roy (RW)	1994-95	3	1	0	1	2	-	-	-	-	-
44	Lindy Ruff (D)	1988-89-1990-91	83	3	12	15	135	10	0	3	3	29
29	Reijo Ruotsalainen (D)	1981-82-1985-86	389	99	217	316	154	43	11	16	27	22
19	Duane Rupp (D)	1962-63	2	0	0	0	0	-	-	-	-	-
16	Church Russell (LW)	1945-46-1947-48	90	20	16	36	12	-	-	-	-	-
S												
21	Simo Saarinen (D)	1984-85	8	0	0	0	8	-	-	-	-	-
4, 3 2, 5	Larry Sacharuk (D)	1972-73-1973-74;- 1975-76-1976-77	75	9	11	20	18	-	-	-	-	-

#	Name & Position	Yrs. Played	REGULAR SEASON					PLAYOFFS				
			GP	G	A	PTS	PIM	GP	G	A	PTS	PIM
26, 8	Kjell Samuelsson (D)	1985-86-1986-87	39	2	6	8	60	9	0	1	1	8
5	Ulf Samuelsson (D)	1995-96	74	1	18	19	122	11	1	5	6	16
16, 4	Derek Sanderson (C)	1974-75-1975-76	83	25	25	50	110	3	0	0	0	0
5	Chuck Sands (C)	1943-44	9	0	2	2	0	-	-	-	-	-
28	Tomas Sandstrom (RW)	1984-85-1989-90	407	173	207	380	563	29	8	12	20	52
6	Glen Sather (LW)	1970-71-1973-74	188	18	24	42	193	38	0	2	2	47
17	Chuck Scherza (C)	1943-44-1944-45	27	5	5	10	29	3	0	1	1	6
18	Ken Schinkel (RW)	1959-60-1963-64; 1966-67	265	34	55	89	77	6	0	1	1	0
11	Lawrence Scott (F)	1927-28	23	0	1	1	6	-	-	-	-	-
21, 2	Earl Seibert (D)	1931-32-1935-36	202	27	41	68	338	-	-	-	-	-
16	Rod Seiling (D)	1963-64-1974-75	644	50	198	248	425	54	3	6	9	47
16	George Senick (LW)	1952-53	13	2	3	5	8	-	-	-	-	-
6, 5	Eddie Shack (RW)	1958-59-1960-61	141	16	26	42	236	-	-	-	-	-
18	Joe Shack (LW)	1942-43; 1944-45	70	9	27	36	20	-	-	-	-	-
27, 21	David Shaw (D)	1987-88-1991-92	240	17	57	74	314	10	0	2	2	41
6	Bobby Sheehan (C)	1978-79	-	-	-	-	-	15	4	3	7	8
23	Ray Sheppard (RW)	1990-91	59	24	23	47	21	-	-	-	-	-
	Johnny Sherf (LW)	1937-38	-	-	-	-	-	1	0	0	0	0
3	Fred Shero (D)	1947-48-1949-50	145	6	14	20	137	13	0	2	2	8
4	Alex Shibicky (LW)	1935-36-1941-42; 1945-46	322	110	91	201	161	40	12	12	24	12
4	Alex "Babe" Siebert (LW)	1932-33-1933-34	55	9	11	20	56	8	1	0	1	12
16	Dave Silk (RW)	1979-80-1982-83	141	30	33	63	112	9	2	4	6	4
41	Mike Siltala (RW)	1986-87-1987-88	4	0	0	0	0	-	-	-	-	-
21	Reg Sinclair (RW)	1950-51-1951-52	139	38	31	69	103	-	-	-	-	-
20, 11	Ed Slowinski (RW)	1947-48-1952-53	291	58	74	132	63	16	2	6	8	6
14, 20, 10	Clint Smith (C)	1936-37-1942-43	281	80	115	195	12	31	4	5	9	2
15	Dallas Smith (D)	1977-78	29	1	4	5	23	1	0	1	1	0
21	Don Smith (RW)	1949-50	10	1	1	2	0	1	0	0	0	0
19	Floyd Smith (RW)	1960-61	29	5	9	14	0	-	-	-	-	-
17	Stan Smith (C)	1939-40-1940-41	9	2	1	3	0	-	-	-	-	-
12	Art Somers (LW)	1931-32-1934-35	145	19	37	56	82	19	1	5	6	18
16	Glen Sonmor (LW)	1953-54-1954-55	28	2	0	2	21	-	-	-	-	-
15, 16, 21	Irv Spencer (D)	1959-60-1961-62	131	4	20	24	81	1	0	0	0	2
19	Red Staley (C)	1948-49	1	0	1	1	0	0	-	-	-	-
8	Allan Stanley (D)	1948-49-1954-55	307	23	56	79	272	12	2	5	7	10
4	Wally Stanowski (D)	1948-49-1950-51	146	3	14	17	54	-	-	-	-	-
4	Harold Starr (D)	1934-35-1935-36	45	0	0	0	38	4	0	0	0	2
21	Bud Stefanski (C)	1977-78	1	0	0	0	0	-	-	-	-	-
21	Pete Stemkowski (C)	1970-71-1976-77	496	113	204	317	379	55	16	18	24	75
5	Ulf Sterner (LW)	1964-65	4	0	0	0	0	-	-	-	-	-
16	Gaye Stewart (LW)	1951-52-1952-53	87	16	27	43	30	-	-	-	-	-
12	Ron Stewart (RW)	1967-68-1972-73	306	44	37	81	74	37	4	3	7	4
13	Jack Stoddard (RW)	1951-52-1952-53	80	16	15	31	31	-	-	-	-	-
21	Blaine Stoughton (RW)	1983-84	14	5	2	7	4	-	-	-	-	-
21	Neil Strain (LW)	1952-53	52	11	13	24	12	-	-	-	-	-
15, 10	Art Stratton (C)	1959-60	18	2	5	7	2	-	-	-	-	-
10	Art Strobel (LW)	1943-44	7	0	0	0	0	-	-	-	-	-
9	Doug Sulliman (RW)	1979-80-1980-81	63	8	8	16	34	3	1	0	1	0
7	Red Sullivan (C)	1956-57-1960-61	322	59	150	209	300	6	1	2	3	4
24	Niklas Sundstrom (C)	1995-96	82	9	12	21	14	11	4	3	7	4
25	Peter Sundstrom (RW)	1983-84-1985-86	206	48	62	110	70	9	1	3	4	2
5	Bill Sweeney (C)	1959-60	4	1	0	1	0	-	-	-	-	-

T

#	Name & Position	Yrs. Played	GP	G	A	PTS	PIM	GP	G	A	PTS	PIM
19	Dean Talafous (RW)	1978-79-1981-82	202	42	60	102	91	19	4	7	11	11
26, 35	Ron Talakoski (RW)	1986-87-1987-88	9	0	1	1	33	-	-	-	-	-
15	Bill Taylor (C)	1947-48	2	0	0	0	0	-	-	-	-	-
19	G. Bill Taylor (C)	1964-65	2	0	0	0	0	-	-	-	-	-
12	Ralph Taylor (D)	1929-30	24	2	0	2	28	4	0	0	0	10
18, 5	Ted Taylor (LW)	1964-65-1965-66	8	0	1	1	6	-	-	-	-	-
17	Spence Thatchell (D)	1942-43	1	0	0	0	0	-	-	-	-	-
8, 10	Paul Thompson (LW)	1926-27-1930-31	216	35	33	68	144	24	3	2	5	40

#	Name & Position	Yrs. Played	GP	G	A	PTS	PIM	GP	G	A	PTS	PIM
			REGULAR SEASON					**PLAYOFFS**				
14	Fred Thurier (C)	1944-45	50	16	19	35	14	-	-	-	-	-
10	Esa Tikkanen (LW)	1992-93-1993-94	98	24	37	61	132	23	4	4	8	34
6	Mark Tinordi (D)	1987-88	24	1	2	3	50	-	-	-	-	-
18, 17	Walt Tkaczuk (C)	1967-68-1980-81	945	227	451	678	556	93	19	32	51	119
12	Zellio Toppazzini (RW)	1950-51-1951-52	71	15	14	29	31	-	-	-	-	-
14	Wes Trainor (RW)	1948-49	17	1	2	3	6	-	-	-	-	-
14	Guy Trottier (RW)	1968-69	2	0	0	0	0	-	-	-	-	-
4	Rene Trudell (RW)	1945-46-1947-48	129	24	28	52	72	5	0	0	0	2
8	Darren Turcotte (C)	1988-89-1993-94	325	122	133	255	183	25	6	8	14	10
6	Dean Turner (D)	1978-79	1	0	0	0	0	-	-	-	-	-
17	Norm Tustin (LW)	1941-42	18	2	4	6	0	-	-	-	-	-
V												
5, 2	Carol Vadnais (D)	1975-76-1981-82	485	56	190	246	690	54	5	16	21	65
11	Sparky Vail (D)	1928-29-1929-30	50	4	1	5	18	10	0	0	0	2
16,17	Pat Verbeek (RW)	1995-96	88	51	46	97	147	21	7	12	19	32
40	Dennis Vial (D)	1990-91	21	0	0	0	61	-	-	-	-	-
8	Steve Vickers (LW)	1972-73-1981-82	698	246	340	586	330	68	24	25	49	58
11	Carl Voss (C)	1932-33	10	2	1	3	4	-	-	-	-	-
W												
15	Frank Waite (F)	1930-31	17	1	3	4	4	-	-	-	-	-
14, 36	Gord Walker (LW)	1986-87-1987-88	19	2	4	6	19	-	-	-	-	-
25	Peter Wallin (RW)	1980-81-1981-82	52	3	14	17	14	14	2	6	8	6
	Eddie Wares (RW)	1936-37	2	2	0	2	0	-	-	-	-	-
14	Billy Warwick (LW)	1942-43-1943-44	14	3	3	6	16	-	-	-	-	-
8	Grant Warwick (RW)	1941-42-1947-48	293	117	116	233	179	6	0	1	1	2
7, 15	Phil Watson (RW)	1935-36-1942-43; 1944-45-1947-48	546	127	233	360	471	36	7	20	29	51
21	John Webster (LW)	1949-50	14	14	0	0	4	-	-	-	-	-
39	Doug Weight (C)	1991-92-1992-93	118	23	47	70	78	4	3	2	4	0
24	Jay Wells (D)	1991-92-1994-95	186	5	23	28	277	43	0	2	2	38
12	Len Wharton (D)	1944-45	1	0	0	0	0	-	-	-	-	-
41	Simon Wheeldon (C)	1987-88-1988-89	11	0	2	2	6	-	-	-	-	-
17, 39	Rob Whistle (D)	1985-86	32	4	2	6	10	3	0	0	0	2
19	Sherman White (C)	1946-47; 1949-50	4	0	2	2	0	-	-	-	-	-
14	Doug Wickenheiser (C)	1988-89	1	1	0	1	0	-	-	-	-	-
20	Juha Widing (C)	1969-70	44	7	7	14	10	-	-	-	-	-
6, 24	Jim Wiemer (D)	1984-85-1985-86	29	7	3	10	32	9	1	0	1	6
17	Tom Williams (LW)	1971-72-1973-74	25	1	3	4	6	-	-	-	-	-
14	Bert WIlson (LW)	1973-74-1974-75	66	6	2	8	68	-	-	-	-	-
17	Carey Wilson (C)	1988-89-1989-90	82	30	51	81	102	14	3	3	6	2
16	Johnny Wilson (LW)	1960-61-1961-62	96	25	15	40	38	6	2	2	4	4
4	Bob Wood (D)	1950-51	1	0	0	0	0	-	-	-	-	-
14	Bill Wylie (C)	1950-51	1	0	0	0	0	-	-	-	-	-
Y												
19, 39	Tom Younghans (RW)	1981-82	47	3	5	8	17	2	0	0	0	0
Z												
31	Rob Zamuner (C)	1991-92	9	1	2	3	2	-	-	-	-	-
24	Joe Zanussi (D)	1974-75	8	0	2	2	4	-	-	-	-	-
21	Sergei Zubov (D)	1992-93-1994-95	165	30	126	156	51	32	8	22	30	2

GOALTENDERS

#	Name	Years Played	REGULAR SEASON						PLAYOFFS					
			W-L-T	GP	Min	GA	AVG	SO	W-L-T	GP	MINS	GA	AVG	SO
A														
1	Andy Aitkenhead	1932-33 - 1934-35	47-43-16	106	6570	257	2.42	11	6-3-1	10	608	15	1.48	3
1	Lorne Anderson	1951-52	1-2-0	3	180	18	6.00	0	-	-	-	-	-	-
31	Hardy Astrom	1977-78	2-2-0	4	240	14	3.50	0	-	-	-	-	-	-
B														
35	Steve Baker	1979-80 - 1982-83	20-20-11	57	3081	190	3.70	3	7-7	14	826	55	4.00	0
1	Gordie Bell	1955-56	-	-	-	-	-	-	1-1	2	120	9	4.50	0
1	Bill Beveridge	1942-43	4-10-3	17	1020	89	5.24	1	-	-	-	-	-	-
1	Lionel Bouvrette	1942-43	0-1-0	1	60	6	6.00	0	-	-	-	-	-	-
1	Johnny Bower	1953-54 - 1954-55; 1956-57	31-35-11	77	4620	202	2.62	5	-	-	-	-	-	-
1	Steve Buzinski	1942-43	2-6-1	9	560	55	5.89	0	-	-	-	-	-	-
C														
1	Lorne Chabot	1926-27 - 1927-28	41-25-14	80	5037	135	1.61	21	2-3-2	8	441	11	1.50	1
D														
30, 00 35	John Davidson	1975-76 - 1982-83	93-90-25	222	12,449	742	3.58	7	16-13	30	1802	73	2.43	1
1	Bob DeCourcy	1947-48	0-0-0	1	29	6	12.41	0	-	-	-	-	-	-
1	Dave Dryden	1961-62	0-1-0	1	40	3	4.50	0	-	-	-	-	-	-
F														
1, 16	Emile Francis	1948-49 - 1951-52	7-9-5	22	1280	68	3.19	0	-	-	-	-	-	-
1	Jimmy Franks	1942-43	5-14-4	23	1380	103	4.48	0	-	-	-	-	-	-
33	Bob Froese	1986-87 - 1989-90	36-43-8	98	5350	324	3.63	1	1-3	6	237	18	4.56	0
G														
1	Bruce Gamble	1958-59	0-2-0	2	120	6	3.00	0	-	-	-	-	-	-
1	Bert Gardiner	1935-36; 1938-39	1-0-0	1	60	1	1.00	0	3-3	6	433	12	2.00	0
1, 30	Ed Giacomin	1965-66 - 1975-76	266-169-90	539	31,646	1441	2.73	49	29-35	65	3834	180	2.82	5
33	Gilles Gratton	1976-77	11-18-7	41	2034	143	4.22	0	-	-	-	-	-	-
H														
1	Glen Hanlon	1982-83 - 1985-86	56-56-13	138	7690	473	3.69	0	-	-	-	-	-	-
30	Glenn Healy	1993-94 - 1995-96	35-32-14	90	4820	228	2.84	5	2-1	7	298	14	2.82	0
1,20	Jim Henry	1941-42; 1945-46 - 1947-48	47-44-17	109	6583	346	3.15	4	2-4	6	360	13	2.17	1
31	Corey Hirsch	1992-93	1-2-1	4	224	14	3.75	0	-	-	-	-	-	-
J														
1	Percy Jackson	1934-35	0-1-0	1	60	8	8.00	0	-	-	-	-	-	-
K														
1	Dave Kerr	1934-35 - 1940-41	157-110-57	324	20,230	698	2.07	40	17-13-3	32	2376	56	1.41	7
44	Terry Kleisinger	1985-86	0-2-0	4	191	14	4.40	0	-	-	-	-	-	-
1	Julian Klymkiew	1958-59	0-0-0	1	19	2	6.32	0	-	-	-	-	-	-
L														
1	Harry Lumley	1943-44	0-0-0	1	20	0	0.00	0	-	-	-	-	-	-
M														
30	Cesare Maniago	1965-66 - 1966-67	9-19-4	34	1832	108	3.54	2						

			REGULAR SEASON						PLAYOFFS					
#	Name	Years Played	W-L-T	GP	Min	GA	AVG	SO	W-L-T	GP	MINS	GA	AVG	SO
1	Ken McAuley	1943-44 - 1944-45	17-64-15	96	5740	537	5.61	1	-	-	-	-	-	-
1	Jack McCartan	1959-60 - 1960-61	3-7-2	12	680	43	3.79	1	-	-	-	-	-	-
31	Peter McDuffe	1972-73 - 1973-74	4-2-1	7	400	19	2.85	0	-	-	-	-	-	-
1	Joe Miller	1927-28	-	-	-	-	-	-	2-1	3	180	3	1.00	1
41	Ed Mio	1981-82 - 1982-83	29-24-11	66	3865	225	3.49	2	9-6	16	923	60	3.90	0

O

#	Name	Years Played	W-L-T	GP	Min	GA	AVG	SO	W-L-T	GP	MINS	GA	AVG	SO
1	Dan Olesevich	1961-62	0-0-1	1	40	2	3.00	0	-	-	-	-	-	-

O

#	Name	Years Played	W-L-T	GP	Min	GA	AVG	SO	W-L-T	GP	MINS	GA	AVG	SO
23,1	Marcel Paille	1957-58 - 1962-63 1964-65	33-52-21	107	6342	362	3.42	2	-	-	-	-	-	-
16	Lester Patrick	1927-28	1-0-0	1	46	1	1.30	0	1-0	1	46	1	1.30	0
	Marcel Pelletier	1962-63	0-1-1	2	40	4	6.00	0	-	-	-	-	-	-
1	Jacques Plante	1963-64 - 1964-65	32-52-13	98	5838	329	3.38	5	-	-	-	-	-	-

R

#	Name	Years Played	W-L-T	GP	Min	GA	AVG	SO	W-L-T	GP	MINS	GA	AVG	SO
34	Jamie Ram	1995-96	0-0-0	1	27	0	0.00	0	-	-	-	-	-	-
1	Chuck Rayner	1945-46 - 1952-53	123-181-73	377	22,488	1122	2.99	24	9-9	18	1135	46	2.43	1
35	Mike Richter	1989-90 - 1995-96	149-91-28	291	16,418	817	2.99	14	32-27	61	3575	169	2.84	6
35	Curt Ridley	1974-75	1-1-0	2	81	7	5.19	0	-	-	-	-	-	-
1	John Ross Roach	1928-29 - 1931-32	80-63-37	180	11,310	407	2.16	30	9-10	21	1421	48	2.03	6
1	Al Rollins	1959-60	1-3-4	8	480	31	3.88	0	-	-	-	-	-	-

S

#	Name	Years Played	W-L-T	GP	Min	GA	AVG	SO	W-L-T	GP	MINS	GA	AVG	SO
30	Terry Sawchuk	1969-70	3-1-2	8	412	20	2.91	1	0-1	3	80	6	4.50	0
1	Joe Schaefer	1959-60 - 1960-61	0-1-0	2	86	8	5.58	0	-	-	-	-	-	-
31, 35	Ron Scott	1983-84 - 1987-88	3-7-4	16	796	51	3.84	0	-	-	-	-	-	-
30	Don Simmons	1965-66; 1968-68 - 1968-69	7-9-4	21	997	58	3.49	0	-	-	-	-	-	-
1, 31 / 1, 33	Doug Soetaert	1975-76 - 1980-81 1986-87	35-40-15	103	5226	372	4.27	1	-	-	-	-	-	-
1	Doug Stevenson	1944-45	0-4-0	4	240	20	5.00	0	-	-	-	-	-	-

T

#	Name	Years Played	W-L-T	GP	Min	GA	AVG	SO	W-L-T	GP	MINS	GA	AVG	SO
25	Dave Tataryn	1976-77	1-1-0	2	80	10	7.50	0	-	-	-	-	-	-
1	Wayne Thomas	1977-78 - 1980-81	34-43-11	94	5288	320	3.63	5	0-1	1	60	4	4.00	0

V

#	Name	Years Played	W-L-T	GP	Min	GA	AVG	SO	W-L-T	GP	MINS	GA	AVG	SO
34	John Vanbiesbrouck	1981-82; 1983-84 - 1992-93	200-177-47	449	25,380	1458	3.45	16	13-20	38	1939	105	3.25	2
30, 1	Gilles Villemure	1963-64 - 1967-68 1970-71 - 1975-76	96-54-21	184	10,472	457	2.62	13	5-5	14	656	32	2.93	0

W

#	Name	Years Played	W-L-T	GP	Min	GA	AVG	SO	W-L-T	GP	MINS	GA	AVG	SO
31	Steve Weeks	1980-81 - 1983-84	42-33-14	94	5313	339	3.83	1	1-2	5	141	10	4.26	0
1, 31	Dunc Wilson	1974-75 - 1975-76	6-11-3	23	1260	89	4.24	0	-	-	-	-	-	-
1	Hal Winkler	1926-27	3-4-1	8	514	16	1.87	2	-	-	-	-	-	-
1	Lorne Worsley	1952-53 - 1962-63	204-271-101	583	34,675	1789	3.10	24	5-15	20	1245	87	4.19	0

**Denotes Playoff Statistics

Rangers Career Leaders

GOALS		WINS		PENALTY MINUTES	
Rod Gilbert	406	Ed Giacomin	266	Ron Greschner	1226
Jean Ratelle	336	Lorne Worsley	204	Harry Howell	1147
Andy Bathgate	272	John Vanbiesbrouck	200	Dave Maloney	1113
Vic Hadfield	262	Dave Kerr	157	Vic Hadfield	1036
Camille Henry	256	*Mike Richter	125	Nick Fotiu	970
Steve Vickers	246	Chuck Rayner	123	Lou Fontinato	939
Bill Cook	228	Gilles Villemure	96	Ching Johnson	798
Walt Tkaczuk	227	John Davidson	93	Barry Beck	775
Don Maloney	195	John Ross Roach	80	Jim Neilson	766
Bryan Hextall	187	Glen Hanlon	56	Don Maloney	739
Dean Prentice	186	*Active Rangers		Brad Park	738
Phil Esposito	184			Kris King	733
Ron Greschner	179	**ASSISTS**		Carol Vadnais	690
Andy Hebenton	177	Rod Gilbert	615	Jack Evans	670
Mike Gartner	173	Jean Ratelle	481	Tomas Sandstrom	563
Tomas Sandstrom	173	Andy Bathgate	457	Tom Laidlaw	561
Anders Hedberg	172	Walt Tkaczuk	451	Troy Mallette	557
Bob Nevin	168	Ron Greschner	431	Walt Tkaczuk	556
Ron Duguay	164	*Brian Leetch	375	Arnie Brown	545
Cecil Dillon	160	James Patrick	363	James Patrick	541
Bun Cook	154	Steve Vickers	340	Reg Fleming	540
Frank Boucher	152	Vic Hadfield	310	Tie Domi	526
		Don Maloney	307	*Jeff Beukeboom	515
GAMES		Brad Park	283	Rod Gilbert	508
Harry Howell	1160	Harry Howell	263		
Rod Gilbert	1065	Frank Boucher	261	**SHUTOUTS**	
Rod Greschner	982	Jim Neilson	238	Ed Giacomin	49
Walt Tkaczuk	945	Dean Prentice	236	Dave Kerr	40
Jean Ratelle	862	*Mark Messier	235	John Ross Roach	30
Vic Hadfield	838	Phil Watson	233	Chuck Rayner	24
Jim Neilson	810	Phil Goyette	231	Lorne Worsley	24
Andy Bathgate	719	Anders Hedberg	225	Lorne Chabot	21
Steve Vickers	698	Dave Maloney	225	John Vanbiesbrouck	16
James Patrick	671	Bill Fairbairn	224	Gilles Villemure	13
Dean Prentice	666	Camille Henry	222	Andy Aitkenhead	11
Don Maloney	653	Phil Esposito	220	*Mike Richter	11
Ott Heller	647	Don Raleigh	219		
Rod Seiling	644	Reijo Ruotsalainen	217		
Camille Henry	637	Bill Gadsby	212		
Dave Maloney	605	Tomas Sandstrom	207		
		Pete Stemkowski	204		

Rangers Year-By-Year Scoring Leaders

Year	Goals		Assists		Points	
1926-27	33	Bill Cook	15	Boucher	37	Bill Cook
1927-28	23	Boucher	14	Bun Cook	35	Boucher
1928-29	15	Bill Cook	16	Boucher	26	Boucher
1929-30	29	Bill Cook	36	Boucher	62	Boucher
1930-31	30	Bill Cook	27	Boucher	42	Bill Cook
1931-32	33	Bill Cook	23	Boucher	47	Bill Cook
1932-33	28	Bill Cook	28	Boucher	50	Bill Cook
1933-34	18	Bun Cook	30	Boucher	44	Boucher
1934-35	25	Dillon	32	Boucher	45	Boucher
1935-36	18	Dillon	18	Boucher	32	Dillon
1936-37	22	Keeling	18	N. Colville	31	Dillon
1937-38	21	Dillon	25	Watson	39	Dillon
1938-39	24	Shibicky	23	Heller	41	C. Smith
1939-40	24	Hextall	28	Watson	39	Hextall
1940-41	26	Hextall	28	N. Colville	44	Hextall
					44	Lynn Patrick
1941-42	32	Lynn Patrick	37	Watson	56	Hextall
1942-43	27	Hextall	39	Lynn Patrick	61	Lynn Patrick
1943-44	21	Hextall	33	Hextall	54	Hextall
1944-45	24	DeMarco	30	DeMarco	54	DeMarco
1945-46	20	DeMarco	27	DeMarco	47	DeMarco
1946-47	27	Leswick	25	Laprade	41	Leswick
1947-48	24	O'Connor	36	O'Connor	60	O'Connor
	24	Leswick				
1948-49	18	Laprade	24	O'Connor	35	O'Connor
1949-50	22	Laprade	25	Leswick	44	Laprade
	25	Raleigh	44	Leswick		
1950-51	20	Mickoski	24	Raleigh	39	Raleigh
					39	Sinclair
1951-52	26	Hergesheimer	42	Raleigh	61	Raleigh
1952-53	30	Hergesheimer	38	Ronty	59	Hergesheimer
1953-54	27	Hergesheimer	33	Ronty	46	Ronty
1954-55	29	Lewicki	32	Raleigh	53	Lewicki
1955-56	24	Prentice	47	Bathgate	66	Bathgate
	24	Hebenton				
1956-57	27	Bathgate	50	Bathgate	77	Bathgate
1957-58	32	Henry	48	Bathgate	78	Bathgate

1958-59	40	Bathgate	48	Bathgate	88	Bathgate
1959-60	32	Prentice	48	Bathgate	74	Bathgate
1960-61	29	Bathgate	48	Bathgate	77	Bathgate
1961-62	28	Bathgate	56	Bathgate	84	Bathgate
1962-63	37	Henry	46	Bathgate	81	Bathgate
1963-64	29	Henry	43	Bathgate	65	Goyette
1964-65	25	Gilbert	36	Gilbert	61	Gilbert
1965-66	29	Nevin	33	Nevin	62	Nevin
1966-67	28	Gilbert	49	Goyette	61	Goyette
1967-68	32	Ratelle	48	Gilbert	78	Ratelle
1968-69	32	Ratelle	49	Gilbert	78	Ratelle
1969-70	33	Balon	50	Tkaczuk	77	Tkaczuk
1970-71	36	Balon	49	Tkaczuk	75	Tkaczuk
1971-72	50	Hadfield	63	Ratelle	109	Ratelle
1972-73	41	Ratelle	59	Gilbert	94	Ratelle
1973-74	36	Gilbert	57	Park	82	Park
1974-75	41	Vickers	61	Gilbert	97	Gilbert
1975-76	36	Gilbert	53	Vickers	86	Gilbert
1976-77	34	Esposito	48	Gilbert	80	Esposito
1977-78	40	Hickey	48	Greschner	81	Esposito
1978-79	42	Esposito	45	Hedberg	78	Esposito
					78	Hedberg
1979-80	34	Esposito	50	Beck	78	Esposito
1980-81	30	Hedberg	41	Greschner	70	Hedberg
	30	Johnstone				
1981-82	40	Duguay	65	Rogers	103	Rogers
1982-83	37	Pavelich	53	Ruotsalainen	76	Rogers
1983-84	48	Larouche	53	Pavelich	82	Pavelich
1984-85	29	Sandstrom	45	Ruotsalainen	73	Ruotsalainen
1985-86	25	Sandstrom	43	Ridley	65	Ridley
1986-87	40	Poddubny	47	Poddubny	87	Poddubny
	40	Sandstrom				
1987-88	38	Poddubny	55	Kisio	88	Poddubny
1988-89	36	Granato	56	Sandstrom	88	Sandstrom
1989-90	43	Ogrodnick	45	Leetch	74	Ogrodnick
1990-91	49	Gartner	72	Leetch	88	Leetch
1991-92	40	Gartner	80	Leetch	107	Messier
1992-93	45	Gartner	66	Messier	91	Messier
1993-94	52	Graves	77	Zubov	89	Zubov
1994-95	17	Graves	39	Messier	53	Messier
	17	Verbeek				
1995-96	47	Messier	70	Leetch	99	Messier

Rangers Single-Season Leaders

GOALS

*Adam Graves	1993-94	52
Vic Hadfield	1971-72	50
Mike Gartner	1990-91	49
Pierre Larouche	1983-84	48
*Mark Messier	1995-96	47
Jean Ratelle	1971-72	46
Mike Gartner	1992-93	45
Rod Gilbert	1971-72	43
John Ogrodnick	1989-90	43
Phil Esposito	1978-79	42
Jean Ratelle	1972-73	41
Steve Vickers	1974-75	41
Pat Verbeek	1995-96	41
Andy Bathgate	1958-59	40
Pat Hickey	1977-78	40
Ron Duguay	1981-82	40
Walt Poddubny	1986-87	40
Tomas Sandstrom	1986-87	40
Mike Gartner	1991-92	40

POINTS

Jean Ratelle	1971-72	109
*Mark Messier	1991-92	107
Vic Hadfield	1971-72	106
Mike Rogers	1981-82	103
*Brian Leetch	1991-92	102
*Mark Messier	1995-96	99
Rod Gilbert	1971-72	97
Rod Gilbert	1974-75	97
Jean Ratelle	1972-73	94
Jean Ratelle	1974-75	91
*Mark Messier	1992-93	91
Steve Vickers	1974-75	89
Sergei Zubov	1993-94	89
Andy Bathgate	1958-59	88
Walt Poddubny	1987-88	88
Tomas Sandstrom	1988-89	88
*Brian Leetch	1990-91	88
Walt Poddubny	1986-87	87
Rod Gilbert	1975-76	86

ASSISTS

*Brian Leetch	1991-92	80
Sergei Zubov	1993-94	77
*Brian Leetch	1990-91	72
*Mark Messier	1991-92	72
*Brian Leetch	1995-96	70
*Mark Messier	1992-93	66
Mike Rogers	1981-82	65
Jean Ratelle	1971-72	63
Rod Gilbert	1974-75	61
Rod Gilbert	1972-73	59
*Mark Messier	1993-94	58
Brad Park	1973-74	57
James Patrick	1991-92	57
Andy Bathgate	1961-62	56
Vic Hadfield	1971-72	56
Tomas Sandstrom	1988-89	56
*Brian Leetch	1993-94	56
Jean Ratelle	1974-75	55
Kelly Kisio	1987-88	55
Rod Gilbert	1971-72	54
Jean Ratelle	1972-73	53
Steve Vickers	1975-76	53
Reijo Ruotsalainen	1982-83	53
Mark Pavelich	1983-84	53
*Mark Messier	1995-96	52
Andy Bathgate	1956-57	50
Walt Tkaczuk	1969-70	50
Rod Gilbert	1975-76	50
Walt Poddubny	1987-88	50

GOALS BY A ROOKIE

Tony Granato	1988-89	36
Tony Amonte	1991-92	35
Mark Pavelich	1981-82	33
Don Murdoch	1976-77	32
Darren Turcotte	1989-90	32
Steve Vickers	1972-73	30
Tomas Sandstrom	1984-85	29
Ulf Dahlen	1987-88	29
Wally Hergesheimer	1951-52	26
Mike Allison	1980-81	26

*Active Rangers

WINS

*Mike Richter	1993-94	42
Ed Giacomin	1968-69	37
Ed Giacomin	1967-68	36
Ed Giacomin	1969-70	35
Lorne Worsley	1955-56	32
John Vanbiesbrouck	1985-86	31
Ed Giacomin	1966-67	30
Ed Giacomin	1973-74	30
Jim Henry	1941-42	29
John Bower	1953-54	29
Chuck Rayner	1949-50	28
Glen Hanlon	1983-84	28
John Vanbiesbrouck	1988-89	28

PIM

Troy Mallette	1989-90	305
Kris King	1989-90	286
Troy Mallette	1990-91	252
Tie Domi	1991-92	246
Barry Beck	1980-81	231
*Shane Churla	1995-96	231
Michel Petit	1987-88	223
*Jeff Beukeboom	1995-96	220
Ed Hospodar	1980-81	214
Lou Fontinato	1955-56	202
Rudy Poeschek	1988-89	199
Nick Fotiu	1978-79	190
Dave Maloney	1979-80	186
Tie Domi	1990-91	185
Larry Melynk	1986-87	182
Chris Nilan	1988-89	177
*Darren Langdon	1995-96	175
Nick Fotiu	1976-77	174

GOALS BY A DEFENSEMAN

Brad Park	1973-74	25
Brad Park	1971-72	24
*Brian Leetch	1988-89	23
*Brian Leetch	1993-94	23
*Brian Leetch	1991-92	22
Ron Greschner	1977-78	21
Ron Greschner	1979-80	21
Ron Greschner	1980-81	20
Carol Vadnais	1975-76	20
Mike McEwen	1978-79	20
Reijo Ruotsalainen	1983-84	20

SHUTOUTS

John Ross Roach	1928-29	13
Lorne Chabot	1927-28	11
Lorne Chabot	1926-27	10
John Ross Roach	1931-32	9
Ed Giacomin	1966-67	9
Dave Kerr	1935-36	8
Dave Kerr	1937-38	8
Dave Kerr	1939-40	8
Ed Giacomin	1967-68	8
Ed Giacomin	1970-71	8

POWER-PLAY GOALS

Vic Hadfield	1971-72	23
Marcel Dionne	1987-88	22
Mike Gartner	1990-91	22
Phil Esposito	1977-78	21
*Adam Graves	1993-94	20
Pierre Larouche	1983-84	19
John Ogrodnick	1989-90	19
*Brian Leetch	1993-94	17
Pat Verbeek	1995-96	17
Rod Gilbert	1973-74	16
Jean Ratelle	1974-75	16
Steve Vickers	1974-75	16
Phil Esposito	1975-76	16
Phil Esposito	1976-77	15
Darren Turcotte	1990-91	15
Mike Gartner	1991-92	15

SHORTHANDED GOALS

Don Maloney	1980-81	5
Mike Rogers	1982-83	5
Mike Gartner	1993-94	5
Ron Stewart	1969-70	4
Bill Fairbairn	1971-72	4
Greg Polis	1977-78	4
Tony Granato	1988-89	4
*Adam Graves	1991-92	4
*Mark Messier	1991-92	4
*Adam Graves	1993-94	4
Steve Larmer	1993-94	4

Rangers In Hockey Hall of Fame

Builders

Gen. John Reed Kilpatrick (1960)
Thomas Lockhart (1965)
William Jennings (1975)
Emile Francis (1982)

Players (33)

Howie Morenz (April 1945)
Lester Patrick (April 1945)
Bill Cook (August 1952)
Frank Boucher (April 1958)
Ching Johnson (April 1958)
Babe Siebert (June 1961)
Earl Seibert (June 1963)
Doug Bentley (June 1964)
Max Bentley (August 1966)
Babe Pratt (August 1966)
Neil Colville (September 1967)
Bryan Hextall (June 1969)
Bill Gadsby (June 1970)
Terry Sawchuk (August 1971)
Bernie Geoffrion (August 1972)
Doug Harvey (August 1973)
Chuck Rayner (August 1973)

Art Coulter (August 1974)
Andy Bathgate (September 1978)
Jacques Plante (September 1978)
Harry Howell (September 1979)
Lynn Patrick (September 1980)
Gump Worsley (September 1980)
Rod Gilbert (September 1982)
Phil Esposito (September 1984)
Jean Ratelle (September 1985)
Ed Giacomin (June 1987)
Guy Lafleur (September 1988)
Buddy O'Connor (September 1988)
Brad Park (September 1988)
Clint Smith (September 1991)
Marcel Dionne (September 1992)
Edgar Laprade (September 1993)
Fred "Bun" Cook (September 1995)

Rangers Management

Rangers Presidents

John S. Hammond	(1926 thru 1931-32)
William F. Carey	(1932-33)
John Reed Kilpatrick	(1933-34)
John S. Hammond	(1934-35)
John Reed Kilpatrick	(1935-36 thru 1959-60)
John J. Bergen	(1960-61 thru 1961-62)
William M. Jennings	(1962-63 thru 1980-81)
John H. Krumpe	(1981-82 thru Dec. 31, 1986)
Richard H. Evans	(Jan. 1, 1987 to June 28, 1990)
John C. Diller	(June 29, 1990 to April 22, 1991)
Neil Smith	(June 19, 1992 to present)

Rangers General Managers

Lester Patrick	(1926-27 thru 1945-46)
Frank Boucher	(1946-47 thru 1954-55)
Muzz Patrick	(1955-56 thru 1963-64)
Emile Francis	(1964-65 to Jan. 6, 1976)
John Ferguson	(Jan. 7, 1976 to June 2, 1978)
Fred Shero	(June 2, 1978 to Nov. 21, 1980)
Craig Patrick	(Nov. 21, 1980 to July 14, 1986)
Phil Esposito	(July 14, 1986 to May 24, 1989)
Neil Smith	(July 17, 1989 to present)

Rangers Coaches & Records

		GC	W	L	T	PCT.
Lester Patrick	(1926-27 thru 1938-39)	604	281	216	107	.554
Frank Boucher	(1939-40 - 12/21/48)	486	166	243	77	.412
Lynn Patrick	(12/21/48 thru 1949-50)	107	40	51	16	.449
Neil Colville	(1950-51 - 12/6/51)	93	26	41	26	.419
Bill Cook	(12/6/51 thru 1952-53)	117	34	59	24	.393
Frank Boucher	(1953-54 - 1/6/54)	39	13	20	6	.410
Muzz Patrick	(1/6/54 thru 1954-55)	105	35	47	23	.443
Phil Watson	(1955-56 - 11/12/59)	294	118	124	52	.490
Alf Pike	(11/18/59 thru 1960-61)	123	36	66	21	.378
Doug Harvey	(5/30/61 thru 1961-62)	70	26	32	12	.457
Muzz Patrick	(9/7/62 - 12/28/62)	34	11	19	4	.382
Red Sullivan	(12/28/62 - 12/5/65)	196	58	103	35	.385
Emile Francis	(12/5/65 - 6/4/68)	193	81	82	30	.497
Bernie Geoffrion	(6/4/68 - 1/17/69)	43	22	18	3	.547
Emile Francis	(1/17/69 - 6/4/73)	344	202	88	54	.666
Larry Popein	(6/4/73 - 1/11/74)	41	18	14	9	.549
Emile Francis	(1/11/74 - 5/19/75)	117	59	39	19	.585
Ron Stewart	(5/19/75 - 1/7/76)	39	15	20	4	.436
John Ferguson	(1/7/76 - 8/22/77)	121	43	59	19	.434
Jean-Guy Talbot	(8/22/77 - 6/2/78)	80	30	37	13	.456
Fred Shero	(6/2/78 - 11/22/80)	180	82	74	24	.522
Craig Patrick	(11/22/80 - 6/4/81)	60	26	23	11	.525
Herb Brooks	(6/4/81 - 1/21/85)	285	131	113	41	.532
Craig Patrick	(1/21/85 - 6/19/85)	35	11	22	2	.343
Ted Sator	(6/19/85 - 11/21/86)	99	41	48	10	.465
*Phil Esposito	(1986-87)	43	24	19	0	.558
*Tom Webster	(1986-87)	16	5	7	4	.474
*Wayne Cashman/Ed Giacomin	(1986-87)	2	0	2	0	.000
Michel Bergeron	(6/18/87 - 4/1/89)	158	73	67	18	.518
Phil Esposito	(4/1/89 - 5/24/89)	2	0	2	0	.000
Roger Neilson	(8/15/89 - 1/4/93)	280	141	104	35	.566
Ron Smith	(1/4/93 - 4/16/93)	44	15	22	7	.421
Mike Keenan	(4/17/93 - 7/24/94)	84	52	24	8	.667
Colin Campbell	(8/10/94 - present)	130	63	50	17	.550

*(Due to illness to Tom Webster, head coaching situation changed several times during season.)

Rangers' All-Time Draft

Round/Overall	Name	Position	Team/League
1963			
1/4	Al Osborne	RW	Weston, Jr. B
2/10	Terry Jones	C	Weston, Midg.
3/15	Mike Cummings	LW	Georgetown, OHL Midget
4/20	Campbell Alleson	D	Portage La Praire, Jr. B
1964			
1/3	Robert Graham	D	Toronto, Midget
2/9	Tim Ecclestone	C	Etobicoke, Jr. B
3/15	Gordon Lowe	D	Toronto, Midget
4/21	Syl. Apps	C	Kingston, Midget
1965			
1/1	Andre Veilleux	RW	Montreal, Jr. B
2/6	George Surmay	G	Winnipeg, MJHL
3/10	Michel Parizeau	LW	Montreal, Jr. B
1966			
1/2	Brad Park	D	Toronto, OHA
2/8	Joey Johnston	C	Peterborough, OHA
3/14	Don Luce	C	Kitchener, OHA
4/20	Jack Egers	LW	Kitchener, Jr. B
1967			
1/6	Robert Dickson	LW	Chatham, OHL
2/15	Brian Tosh	D	Smith Falls, Jr. A
1968			
3/19	Bruce Buchanan	D	Weyburn, WHL
1969			
1/8	Andre Dupont	D	Montreal, OHA
2/12	Pierre Jarry	C	Ottawa, OHA
3/23	Bert Wilson	LW	London, OHA
4/35	Kevin Morrison	RW	St. Jerome, QMJHL
5/47	Bruce Hellemond	D	Moose Jaw, WHL
6/59	Gordon Smith	D	Cornwall, QMJHL
1970			
1/11	Normand Gratton	RW	Montreal, OHA
2/25	Mike Murphy	RW	Toronto, OHA
3/39	Wendell Bennett	RW	Weyburn, SJHL
4/53	Andre St. Pierre	D	Drummondville, QMJHL
5/67	Gary Coalter	RW	Hamilton, OHA
6/81	Duane Wylie	C	St. Catharines, OHA
7/94	Wayne Bell	G	Estevan, WHL
8/106	Pierre Brind'Amour	LW	Montreal, OHA

Round/Overall	Name	Position	Team/League
1971			
1/10	Steve Vickers	LW	Toronto, OHA
1/13	Steve Durbano	D	Toronto, OHA
2/27	Tom Williams	LW	Hamilton, OHA
3/41	Terry West	C	London, OHA
4/55	Jerry Butler	RW	Hamilton, OHA
5/69	Fraser Robertson	D	Lethbridge, AJHL
6/83	Wayne Wood	G	Montreal, OHA
7/96	Doug Keeler	C	Ottawa, OHA
7/97	Jean-Denis Royal	D	St. Jerome, QMJHL
9/109	Eugene Sobchuk	C	Regina, WHL
10/110	Jim Ivison	D	Brandon, WHL
11/111	Andre Peloffy	C	Rosemount, QMJHL
12/112	Elston Evoy	C	Sault Ste. Marie, OHA
13/114	Gerald Lacompte	D	Sherbrooke, QMJHL
14/115	Wayne Forsey	LW	Swift Current, WHL
15/116	Bill Forrest	D	Hamilton, OHA
1972			
1/10	Al Blanchard	RW	Kitchener, OHA
1/15	Bob MacMillan	C	St. Catharines, OHA
2/21	Larry Sacharuk	D	Saskatoon, WHL
2/31	Rene Villemure	LW	Shawinigan, QMJHL
3/48	Gerry Teeple	C	Cornwall , QMJHL
4/63	Doug Horbul	LW	Calgary, WHL
5/78	Marty Gateman	D	Hamilton, OHA
6/95	Ken Ireland	C	New Westminster, WHL
7/111	Jeff Hunt	RW	Winnipeg, WHL
8/127	Yvon Blais	LW	Cornwall, QMJHL
9/137	Pierre Archambault	D	St. Jerome, QMJHL
1973			
1/14	Rick Middleton	RW	Oshawa, OHA
2/30	Pat Hickey	LW	Hamilton, OHA
3/46	John Campbell	LW	Sault Ste. Marie, OHA
4/62	Brian Movik	D	Calgary, WHL
5/78	Pierre Laganiere	RW	Sherbrooke, QMJHL
6/94	Dwayne Pentland	D	Brandon, WHL
1974			
1/14	Dave Maloney	D	Kitchener, OHA
2/32	Ron Greschner	D	New Westminster, WHL
3/50	Jerry Holland	LW	Calgary, WHL
4/68	Boyd Anderson	LW	Medicine Hat, WHL
5/86	Dennis Olmstead	C	Univ. of Wisc., WCHA
6/104	Eddie Johnstone	RW	Medicine Hat, WHL
7/122	John Memryk	G	Winnipeg, WHL
8/139	Greg Holst	C	Kingston, OHA

Round/Overall	Name	Position	Team/League
9/156	Claude Arvisais	C	Shawinigan, QMJHL
10/171	Ken Dodd	LW	New Westminster, WHL
11/186	Ralph Krentz	LW	Brandon, WHL
12/198	Larry Jacques	RW	Ottawa, OHA
13/208	Tom Gastle	LW	Peterborough, OHA
14/218	Eric Brubacher	C	Kingston, OHA
15/224	Russell Hall	RW	Winnipeg, WHL
16/227	Bill Kriski	G	Winnipeg, WHL
17/230	Kevin Treacy	RW	Cornwall, QMJHL
18/233	Ken Gassoff	C	Medicine Hat, WHL
19/236	Clifford Bast	D	Medicine Hat, WHL
20/239	Jim Mayer	RW	Mich. Tech, WCHA
21/241	Warren Miller	RW	Univ. of Minn., WCHA
22/243	Kevin Walker	D	Cornell University, ECAC
23/245	Jim Warner	RW	Minnesota, Midwest Jr.

1975

Round/Overall	Name	Position	Team/League
1/12	Wayne Dillon	C	Toronto, WHA
2/30	Doug Soetaert	G	Edmonton, WHL
3/48	Greg Hickey	LW	Hamilton, OHA
4/66	Bill Cheropita	G	St. Catharines, OHA
5/84	Larry Huras	D	Kitchener, OHA
6/102	Randy Koch	LW	Univ. of Vermont, ECAC
7/120	Claude Larose	LW	Sherbrooke, QMJHL
8/138	Bill Hamilton	RW	St. Catharine's, OHA
9/154	Bud Stefanski	C	Oshawa, OHA
10/169	Dan Beaulieu	LW	Quebec, QMJHL
11/184	John McMorrow	C	Providence Coll., ECAC
12/195	Tom McNamara	G	Univ. of Vermont, ECAC
13/200	Steve Roberts	D	Providence Coll., ECAC
13/201	Paul Dionne	D	Princeton Univ., ECAC
14/205	Cecil Luckern	RW	U. of New Hamp., ECAC
15/209	John Corriveau	RW	U. of New Hamp., ECAC
16/212	Tom Funke	LW	Fargo, Midwest Jr.

1976

Round/Overall	Name	Position	Team/League
1/6	Don Murdoch	RW	Medicine Hat, WHL
2/24	Dave Farrish	D	Sudbury, OHA
3/42	Mike McEwen	D	Toronto, OHA
4/60	Claude Periard	LW	Trois Rivieres , QMJHL
5/78	Doug Gaines	C	St. Catharines, OHA
6/96	Barry Scully	RW	Kingston, OHA
7/112	Remi Levesque	LW	Quebec, QMJHL

1977

Round/Overall	Name	Position	Team/League
1/8	Lucien DeBlois	RW	Sorel, QMJHL
1/13	Ron Duguay	C	Sudbury, OHA
2/26	Mike Keating	LW	St. Catharines, OHA
3/44	Steve Baker	G	Union College, Ind.
4/62	Mario Marois	D	Quebec, QMJHL
5/80	Benoit Gosselin	LW	Trois Rivieres, QMJHL
6/98	John Bethel	LW	Boston University, ECAC
7/116	Robert Sullivan	C	Chicoutimi, QMJHL
8/131	Lance Nethery	LW	Cornell University, ECAC
9/146	Alex Jeans	RW/C	Univ. of Toronto, OUAA
10/157	Peter Raps	LW	West. Mich. Univ., CCHA
11/164	Mike Brown	RW	West. Mich. Univ., CCHA

Round/Overall	Name	Position	Team/League
12/171	Mark Miler	LW	Univ. of Michigan, WCHA

1978

Round/Overall	Name	Position	Team/League
2/26	Don Maloney	LW	Kitchener, OHA
3/43	Ray Markham	C	Flin Flon, WHL
3/44	Dean Turner	D	Univ. of Michigan, WCHA
4/59	Dave Silk	RW	Boston University, ECAC
4/60	Andre Dore	D	Quebec, OHL
5/76	Mike McDougal	RW	Port Huron, IHL
6/93	Tom Laidlaw	D	North. Mich Univ., CCHA
7/110	Dan Clark	D	Milwaukee, IHL
8/127	Greg Kostenko	D	Ohio State Univ., CCHA
8/144	Brian McDavid	D	Sudbury, OHA
9/161	Mark Rodrigues	G	Yale University, ECAC
10/176	Steve Weeks	G	North. Mich. Univ., CCHA
11/192	Pierre Daigneault	LW	St. Laurent Coll., QUAA
12/206	Chris McLaughlin	D	Dartmouth Coll. , ECAC
13/217	Todd Johnson	C	Boston University, ECAC
13/223	Dan McCarthy	C	Sudbury, OHA

1979

Round/Overall	Name	Position	Team/League
1/13	Doug Sulliman	LW	Kitchener, OHA
2/34	Ed Hospodar	D	Ottawa, OHA
4/76	Pat Conacher	C	Saskatoon, WHL
5/97	Dan Makuch	RW	Clarkson College, ECAC
6/118	Stan Adams	C	Niagara Falls, OHA

1980

Round/Overall	Name	Position	Team/League
1/14	Jim Malone	C	Toronto, OHA
2/35	Mike Allison	C	Sudbury, OHA
4/77	Kurt Kleinendorst	C	Providence Coll., ECAC
5/98	Scot Kleinendorst	D	Providence Coll., ECAC
6/119	Reijo Ruotsalainen	D	Karpat, Finnish
7/140	Bob Scurfield	C	West. Mich. Univ., CCHA
8/161	Bart Wilson	D	Toronto, OHA
9/182	Chris Wray	RW	Boston College, ECAC
10/203	Anders Backstrom	D	Brynas, Swedish

1981

Round/Overall	Name	Position	Team/League
1/9	James Patrick	D	Prince Albert, SJHL
2/30	Jan Erixon	RW	Skelleftea, Swedish
3/50	Peter Sundstrom	LW	Bjorkloven, Swedish
3/51	Mark Morrison	C	Victoria, WHL
4/72	John Vanbiesbrouck	G	Sault Ste. Marie, OHA
6/114	Eric Magnuson	C	RPI, ECAC
7/135	Mike Guentzel	D	Coleraine H.S., (MN)
8/156	Ari Lahtenmaki	RW	IFK Helsinki, Finnish
9/177	Paul Reifenberger	RW/C	Anoka H.S., (MN),
10/198	Mario Proulx	G	Providence Coll., ECAC

1982

Round/Overall	Name	Position	Team/League
1/15	Chris Kontos	C	Toronto , OHL
2/36	Tomas Sandstrom	RW	Farjestads, Swedish
3/57	Corey Millen	C	Cloquet H.S., (MN)
4/78	Chris Jensen	C	Kelowna, BCJHL
6/120	Tony Granato	C	Northwood Prep (NY)
7/141	Sergei Kapustin	LW	Central Red Army, USSR
8/160	Brian Glynn	C	Buffalo, NAJHL

Round/Overall	Name	Position	Team/League
8/162	Jan Karlsson	D	Kiruna, Swedish
9/183	Kelly Miller	C	Mich. St. Univ., CCHA
10/193	Simo Saarinen	D	IFK Helsinki, Finnish
10/204	Bob Lowes	C	Prince Albert, SJHL
11/225	Andy Otto	D	Northwood Prep, (NY)
12/246	Dwayne Robinson	D	U. of N. Hamp., Hockey E.

1983

Round/Overall	Name	Position	Team/League
1/12	Dave Gagner	C	Brantford, OHL
2/33	Randy Heath	LW	Portland, WHL
3/49	Vesa Salo	D	Lukko, Finnish
3/53	Gordon Walker	LW	Portland, WHL
4/73	Peter Andersson	D	Orebo IK, Swedish
5/93	Jim Andonoff	RW	Belleville, OHL
6/113	Bob Alexander	D	Rosemount H.S., (MN)
7/133	Steve Orth	C	St. Cloud Tech H.S., (MN)
8/153	Peter Marcov	LW	Welland, Ont. Jr. B
9/173	Paul Jerrard	D/RW	Notre Dame H.S., (Sask.)
11/213	Bryan Walker	D	Portland, WHL
12/233	Ulf Nilsson	G	Skelleftea, Sweden

1984

Round/Overall	Name	Position	Team/League
1/14	Terry Carkner	D	Peterborough, OHL
2/35	Raimo Helminen	C	Ilves, Finnish
4/77	Paul Broten	C	Roseau H.S., (MN)
5/98	Clark Donatelli	LW	Stratford, Ont. Jr. B
6/119	Kjell Samuelsson	D	Leksand, Swedish
7/140	Tom Hussey	LW	St. Andrew's H.S., (Ont.)
8/161	Brian Nelson	C	Wilmar H.S., (MN)
9/182	Ville Kentala	LW	IFK Helsinki, Finnish
9/188	Heinz Ehlers	C	Leksand, Swedish
10/202	Kevin Miller	C	Redford, NAJHL
11/223	Tom Lorentz	C	Brady H.S. (MN)
12/243	Scott Brower	G	Lloydminster, SJHL

1985

Round/Overall	Name	Position	Team/League
1/7	Ulf Dahlen	C	Ostersund, Swedish
2/28	Mike Richter	G	Northwood Prep (NY)
3/49	San Lindstahl	G	Sodertalje, Swedish
4/70	Pat Janostin	D	Notre Dame H.S., (Sask.)
5/91	Brad Stepan	LW	Hastings H.S., (MN)
6/112	Brian McReynolds	C	Orillia, OHL
7/133	Neil Pilon	D	Kamloops, WHL
8/154	Larry Bernard	LW	Seattle, WHL
9/175	Stephane Brochu	D	Quebec, QMJHL
10/196	Steve Nemeth	C	Lethbridge, WHL
11/217	Robert Burakovski	LW	Leksand, Swedish
12/238	Rudy Poeschek	D	Kamloops, WHL

1986

Round/Overall	Name	Position	Team/League
1/9	Brian Leetch	D	Avon Old Farms HS, (CT)
3/51	Bret Walter	C	Univ. of Alberta, CWUAA
3/53	Shaun Clouston	RW	Univ. of Alberta, CWUAA
4/72	Mark Janssens	C	Regina, WHL
5/93	Jeff Bloemberg	D	North Bay, OHL
6/114	Darren Turcotte	C	North Bay, OHL
7/135	Robb Graham	RW	Guelph, OHL

Round/Overall	Name	Position	Team/League
8/156	Barry Chyzowski	C	St. Albert, AJHL
9/177	Pat Scanlon	LW/C	Cretin H.S., (MN)
10/198	Joe Ranger	D	London, OHL
11/219	Russell Parent	D	S. Winnipeg, MJHL
12/240	Soren True	LW	Skobakken, Denmark

1987

Round/Overall	Name	Position	Team/League
1/10	Jayson More	D	New Westminster, WHL
2/31	Daniel Lacroix	LW	Granby, QMJHL
3/46	Simon Gagne	RW	Laval, QMJHL
4/69	Michael Sullivan	C	Boston U., Hockey East
5/94	Erik O'Borsky	C	Yale University, ECAC
6/115	Ludek Cajka	D	Dukla Jihlava, Czech.
7/136	Clint Thomas	D	RPI, ECAC
8/157	Chuck Wiegand	C	Essex Junction HS, (VT)
9/178	Eric Burrill	RW	Tartan H.S., (MN)
10/199	David Porter	LW	North. Mich. U., WCHA
10/205	Bret Barnett	RW	Wexford, Ont. Jr. B
11/220	Lance Marciano	D	Choate H.S., (CT)

1988

Round/Overall	Name	Position	Team/League
2/22	Troy Mallette	C	Sault Ste. Marie, OHL
2/26	Murray Duval	D	Spokane, WHL
4/68	Tony Amonte	RW	Thayer Academy, (MA)
5/99	Martin Bergeron	C	Drummondville, QMJHL
6/110	Dennis Vial	D	Hamilton, OHL
7/131	Mike Rosati	G	Hamilton, OHL
8/152	Eric Couvrette	LW	St. Jean, QMJHL
9/173	Patrick Forrest	D	St. Cloud State
10/194	Paul Cain	C	Cornwall, OHL
10/202	Eric Fenton	C	N. Yarmouth Prep, (MA).
11/215	Peter Fiorentino	D	Sault Ste. Marie, OHL
12/236	Keith Slifstein	RW	Choate H.S., (CT)

1989

Round/Overall	Name	Position	Team/League
1/20	Steven Rice	RW	Kitchener, OHL
2/40	Jason Prosofsky	RW	Medicine Hat, WHL
3/45	Rob Zamuner	C	Guelph, OHL
3/49	Louie DeBrusk	LW	London, OHL
4/67	Jim Cummins	RW	Michigan State, CCHA
5/88	Aaron Miller	D	Niagara Scenics, NAHL
6/118	Joby Messier	D	Michigan State, CCHA
7/139	Greg Leahy	C	Portland, WHL
8/160	Greg Spenrath	LW	Tri-City, WHL
9/181	Mark Bavis	C	Cushing Academy, USS
10/202	Roman Oksiuta	RW	Khimik Voskresensk, Rus.
11/223	Steve Locke	LW	Niagara Falls, OHL
12/244	Ken MacDermid	LW	Hull, QMJHL

1990

Round/Overall	Name	Position	Team/League
1/13	Michael Stewart	D	Michigan State, CCHA
2/34	Doug Weight	C	Lake Superior St., CCHA
3/55	John Vary	D	North Bay, OHL
4/69	Jeff Nielsen	RW	Grand Rapids H.S., (MN)
4/76	Rick Willis	LW	Pingree Prep, (MA)
5/85	Sergei Zubov	D	CSKA, Sov. Elite
5/99	Lubos Rob	C	Budejovice, Czech.

Round/Overall	Name	Position	Team/League
6/118	Jason Weinrich	D	Springfield H.S., (MA)
7/139	Bryan Lonsinger	D	Choate H.S., (CT)
8/160	Todd Hedlund	RW	Roseau H.S., (MN)
9/181	Andrew Silverman	D	Beverly H.S., (MA)
10/202	Jon Hillebrandt	G	Monona Grove H.S., (WI)
11/223	Brett Lievers	C	Wayzata H.S., (MN)
12/244	Sergei Nemchinov	C	Soviet Wings, Sov. Elite

1991

Round/Overall	Name	Position	Team/League
1/15	Alexei Kovalev	LW	Dynamo Moscow, USSR
2/37	Darcy Werenka	D	Lethbridge, WHL
5/96	Corey Machanic	D	U. of Vermont, USC
6/125	Fredrik Jax	RW	Leksand, Swedish
6/128	Barry Young	D	Sudbury, OHL
7/147	John Rushin	C	Kennedy, USS
8/169	Corey Hirsch	G	Kamloops, WHL
9/191	Vjateslav Uvaev	D	Spartak Moscow, USSR
10/213	Jamie Ram	G	Michigan Tech, CCHA
11/235	Vitali Chinakov	C	Torpedo Jaroslav, USSR
12/257	Brian Wiseman	C	Univ. of Michigan, CCHA

1992

Round/Overall	Name	Position	Team/League
1/24	Peter Ferraro	C	Waterloo, USJHL
2/48	Mattias Norstrom	D	AIK, Swedish
3/72	Eric Cairns	D	Detroit, OHL
4/85	Chris Ferraro	RW	Waterloo, USJHL
5/120	Dimitri Starostenko	RW	CSKA Moscow, CIS
6/144	Davide Dal Grande	D	Ottawa, Tier 2,
7/168	Matt Oates	LW	Miami, Ohio, CCHA
8/192	Mickey Elick	D	Univ. of Wisc., WCHA
9/216	Dan Brierley	D	Choate H.S., (CT)
10/240	Vladimir Vorobiev	RW	Met. Cherepovets, CIS

1993

Round/Overall	Name	Position	Team/League
1/8	Niklas Sundstrom	C	MoDo, Swedish
2/34	Lee Sorochan	D	Lethbridge, WHL
3/61	Maxim Galanov	D	Lada Togilatti, CIS
4/86	Sergei Olympijev	C	Dynamo Minsk, CIS
5/112	Gary Roach	D	Sault Ste. Marie, OHL
6/138	Dave Trofimenkoff	G	Lethbridge, WHL
7/162	Serei Kondrashkin	RW	Cheropovets, CIS
7/164	Todd Marchant	C	Clarkson Univ., ECAC
8/190	Eddy Campbell	D	Omaha Jr. A, Tier 2

Round/Overall	Name	Position	Team/League
9/216	Ken Shepard	G	Oshawa, OHL
10/242	Andrei Kudinov	C	Chelyabinsk, CIS
11/261	Pavel Komarov	D	Nizhni Novgorod, CIS
11/268	Maxim Smelnitski	C	Chelyabinsk, CIS

1994

Round/Overall	Name	Position	Team/League
1/26	Dan Cloutier	G	Sault Ste. Marie, OHL
2/52	Rudolf Vercik	LW	Slovan Bratislava, Slovakia
3/78	Adam Smith	D	Tacoma, WHL
4/100	Alexander Korobolin	D	Chelyabinsk, Russian Elite
4/104	Sylvain Blouin	D	Laval, QMJHL
5/130	Martin Ethier	D	Beauport, QMJHL
6/135	Yuri Litvinov	C	Kryjla Sovetov, Russian Elite
6/156	David Brosseau	C	Shawinigan, QMJHL
7/182	Alexei Lazarenko	W	CSKA, Russian Elite
8/208	Craig Anderson	D	Park Center H.S., MN
9/209	Vitali Yeremeyev	G	Ust-Kamenogorsk, Rus.
9/234	Eric Boulton	LW	Oshawa, OHL
10/260	Radoslav Kropac	RW	Slovan Bratislava, Slovakia
11/267	Jamie Butt	LW	Tacoma, WHL
11/286	Kim Johnsson	D	Malmo, Swedish

1995

Round/Overall	Name	Position	Team/League
2/39	Christian Dube	C	Sherbrooke, QMJHL
3/65	Mike Martin	D	Windsor, OHL
4/91	Marc Savard	C	Oshawa, OHL
5/110	Alexei Vasiljev	D	Yaroslavl, CIS
5/117	Dale Purinton	D	Tacoma, WHL
6/143	Peter Slamiar	RW	Zvolen, Jr., Slovakia
7/169 NCHA	Jeff Heil	G	U. Wisconsin-River Falls
8/195	Ilja Gorohov	D	Yaroslavl, CIS
9/221	Bob Maudie	C	Kamloops, WHL

1996

Round/Overall	Name	Position	Team/League
1/22	Jeff Brown	D	Sarnia, OHL
2/48	Daniel Goneau	LW	Granby, QMJL
3/76	Dmitri Subbotin	LW	CSKA Moscow
5/131	Colin Pepperall	LW	Niagara Falls, CHL
6/158	Ola Sandberg	D	Djurgarden, Swedish
7/185	Jeff Dessner	D	Taft, USHS
8/211	Ryan McKie	D	London, OHL
9/237	Ronnie Sundin	D	Vastra F. Goteborg, EUR

Rangers Record Against All National Hockey League Teams Since 1926

New York Rangers vs.	GP	W	L	T	GF	GA	PTS
Chicago Blackhawks	559	228	234	97	1610	1646	553
Boston Bruins	568	215	259	94	1659	1825	524
Detroit Red Wings(a)	556	207	246	103	1543	1691	517
Toronto Maple Leafs	537	191	252	94	1518	1707	476
Montreal Canadiens	548	166	294	88	1428	1879	420
Philadelphia Flyers	177	73	70	34	554	558	180
Pittsburgh Penguins	158	79	65	18	637	583	176
New Jersey Devils (K.C./Colorado)	128	69	45	14	513	417	152
St. Louis Blues	108	68	27	15	415	287	151
New York Islanders	151	66	71	14	535	545	146
Dallas Stars (Minnesota)	109	63	27	19	403	313	145
Vancouver Canucks	94	68	18	8	410	265	144
Washington Capitals	131	58	58	15	488	487	131
Los Angeles Kings	105	55	36	14	400	330	124
Buffalo Sabres	102	38	46	18	349	370	94
Calgary Flames (Atlanta)	89	30	45	14	295	361	74
Ottawa Senators (b)	46	30	7	9	150	92	69
Colorado Avalanche (Quebec)	54	27	21	6	220	195	60
Hartford Whalers	55	26	23	6	216	184	58
Phoenix Coyotes (Winnipeg)	47	25	18	4	200	183	54
Edmonton Oilers	46	18	23	5	173	183	41
Tampa Bay Lightning	17	10	5	2	65	61	22
San Jose Sharks	9	8	0	1	49	23	17
Florida Panthers	14	7	5	2	40	31	16
Anaheim Mighty Ducks	4	1	3	0	13	15	2
Defunct Teams (c)	246	152	58	36	811	521	340
Totals	**4664**	**1978**	**1955**	**731**	**14694**	**14752**	**4687**
Home							
Detroit Red Wings (a)	277	132	87	58	854	711	322
Boston Bruins	286	124	108	54	868	802	302
Chcago Blackhawks	280	117	108	55	832	795	289
Toronto Maple Leafs	269	112	101	56	824	787	280
Montreal Canadiens	274	111	109	54	798	799	276
Philadelphia Flyers	89	41	27	21	300	258	103
New York Islanders	75	45	22	8	299	227	98
Pittsburgh Penguins	81	42	32	7	333	288	91
St. Louis Blues	54	42	6	6	231	123	90
New Jersey Devils (K.C./Colorado)	64	38	16	10	277	198	86
Dallas Stars (Minn.)	55	34	11	10	197	150	78

Vancouver Canucks	48	36	7	5	220	119	77
Washington Capitals	65	33	26	6	263	234	72
Los Angeles Kings	52	32	15	5	210	151	69
Buffalo Sabres	50	23	15	12	176	138	58
Calgary Flames (Atlanta)	45	20	20	5	160	162	45
Colorado Avalanche (Quebec)	26	17	6	3	112	74	37
Hartford Whalers	28	16	9	3	121	85	35
Ottawa Senators (b)	23	13	5	5	68	50	31
Phoenix Coyotes (Winnipeg)	23	13	8	2	110	93	28
Edmonton Oilers	23	6	13	4	88	94	16
Tampa Bay Lightning	9	5	3	1	36	36	11
Florida Panthers	7	3	2	2	18	16	8
San Jose Sharks	4	3	0	1	22	11	7
Anaheim Mighty Ducks	2	1	1	0	7	5	2
Defunct Teams (c)	123	80	26	17	425	258	177
Totals	**2332**	**1139**	**783**	**410**	**7849**	**6664**	**2688**

Road

Chicago Blackhawks	279	111	126	42	778	851	264
Boston Bruins	282	91	151	40	791	1023	222
Toronto Maple Leafs	268	79	151	38	694	920	196
Detroit Red Wings (a)	279	75	159	45	689	980	195
Montreal Canadiens	274	55	185	34	630	1080	144
Pittsburgh Penguins	81	37	33	11	304	295	85
Philadelphia Flyers	88	32	43	13	254	300	77
Dallas Stars (Minn.)	54	29	16	9	206	163	67
Vancouver Canucks	46	32	11	3	190	146	67
New Jersey Devils (K.C./Colorado)	64	31	29	4	237	219	66
St. Louis Blues	56	26	21	9	184	164	61
Washington Capitals	66	25	32	9	225	253	59
Los Angeles Kings	53	23	21	9	190	179	55
New York Islanders	76	21	49	6	236	318	48
Ottawa Senators (b)	23	17	2	4	82	42	38
Buffalo Sabres	52	15	31	6	173	232	36
Calgary Flames (Atlanta)	44	10	25	9	135	199	29
Phoenix Coyotes (Winnipeg)	24	12	10	2	90	90	26
Edmonton Oilers	23	12	10	1	85	89	25
Colorado Avalanche (Quebec)	28	10	15	3	108	121	23
Hartford Whalers	27	10	14	3	95	99	23
San Jose Sharks	8	5	2	1	28	25	11
Tampa Bay Lightning	5	5	0	0	27	12	10
Florida Panthers	7	4	3	0	22	15	8
Anaheim Mighty Ducks	2	0	2	0	6	10	0
Defunct Teams (c)	123	72	32	19	386	263	163
Totals	**2332**	**839**	**1172**	**321**	**6845**	**8088**	**1999**

(a) includes records of Detroit Cougars and Detroit Falcons

(b) includes records of Ottawa Senators

(c) Teams are: Brooklyn and New York Americans, Cleveland Barons (Calif.), Montreal Maroons, Philadelphia Quakers, Pittsburgh Pirates, and St. Louis Eagles

Rangers Year-By-Year Scoring Statistics

1926-27	GP	A	A	PTS	PIM
Bill Cook	44	33	4	37	58
Frank Boucher	44	13	15	28	17
Bun Cook	44	14	9	23	42
Taffy Abel	44	8	4	12	78
Paul Thompson	43	7	3	10	12
Murray Murdoch	44	6	4	10	12
Stan Brown	24	6	2	8	14
Billy Boyd	41	4	1	5	40
Ching Johnson	27	3	2	5	66
Leo Bourgault	20	1	1	2	28
Lester Patrick	1	0	0	0	2
Ollie Reinikka	16	0	0	0	0
Reg Mackey	34	0	0	0	16

1927-28	GP	G	A	PTS	PIM
Frank Boucher	44	23	12	35	14
Bun Cook	44	14	14	28	45
Bill Cook	43	18	6	24	42
Ching Johnson	43	10	6	16	146
Murray Murdoch	44	7	3	10	14
Paul Thompson	41	4	4	8	22
Leo Bourgault	37	7	0	7	72
Alex Gray	43	7	0	7	30
Billy Boyd	43	4	0	4	11
Taffy Abel	22	0	1	1	28
Laurie Scott	23	0	1	1	6
Patsy Callighen	36	0	0	0	32

1928-29	GP	G	A	PTS	PIM
Frank Boucher	44	10	16	26	8
Bill Cook	43	15	8	23	41
Bun Cook	43	13	5	18	70
Paul Thompson	44	10	7	17	38
Murray Murdoch	44	8	6	14	18
Butch Keeling	43	6	3	9	35
Leo Bourgault	44	2	3	5	59
Sparky Vail	18	3	0	3	16
Taffy Abel	44	2	1	3	41
Myles Lane	24	2	0	2	24
Russ Oatman	27	1	1	2	10
Ching Johnson	9	0	0	0	14
Jerry Carson	10	0	0	0	5
Billy Boyd	11	0	0	0	5

1929-30	GP	G	A	PTS	PIM
Frank Boucher	42	26	36	62	16
Bill Cook	44	29	30	59	56
Bun Cook	43	24	18	42	55
Butch Keeling	44	19	7	26	34
Murray Murdoch	44	13	13	26	22
Paul Thompson	44	7	12	19	36
Leo Bourgault	44	7	6	13	54
Ching Johnson	30	3	3	6	82
Leroy Goldsworthy	44	4	1	5	16
Leo Quenneville	25	0	3	3	10
Ralph Taylor	24	2	0	2	28
Sparky Vail	32	1	1	2	2
Orville Heximer	19	1	0	1	4
Leo Reise	14	0	1	1	8

Bill Regan	10	0	0	0	4
Harry Foster	31	0	0	0	10

1930-31	GP	G	A	PTS	PIM
Bill Cook	44	30	12	42	39
Frank Boucher	44	12	27	39	20
Bun Cook	44	18	17	35	72
Butch Keeling	44	13	9	22	35
Murray Murdoch	44	7	7	14	8
Paul Thompson	44	7	7	14	36
Joe Jerwa	33	4	7	11	72
Cecil Dillon	25	7	3	10	8
Ching Johnson	44	2	6	8	77
Henry Maracle	11	1	3	4	2
Frank Waite	17	1	3	4	4
Bill Regan	42	2	1	3	49
Eddie Rodden	24	0	3	3	8
Gene Carrigan	33	2	0	2	13
Leo Bourgault	10	0	1	1	6
Sam McAdam	4	0	0	0	0
Ernie Kenny	6	0	0	0	0
Frank Peters	44	0	0	0	59

1931-32	GP	G	A	PTS	PIM
Bill Cook	48	33	14	47	33
Cecil Dillon	48	23	15	38	22
Frank Boucher	48	12	23	35	18
Bun Cook	45	14	20	34	43
Art Somers	48	11	15	26	45
Murray Murdoch	48	5	16	21	32
Butch Keeling	48	17	3	20	38
Ching Johnson	47	3	10	13	106
Norman Gainor	46	3	9	12	9
Earl Seibert	44	4	6	10	88
Doug Brennan	38	4	3	7	40
Vic Desjardins	48	3	3	6	16
Ott Heller	21	2	2	4	9
Hib Milks	45	0	4	4	12

1932-33	GP	G	A	PTS	PIM
Bill Cook	48	28	22	50	51
Bun Cook	48	22	15	37	35
Frank Boucher	46	7	28	35	4
Cecil Dillon	48	21	10	31	12
Art Somers	48	7	15	22	28
Babe Siebert	42	9	10	19	38
Ching Johnson	48	8	9	17	127
Murray Murdoch	48	5	11	16	23
Ozzie Asmundson	48	5	10	15	20
Butch Keeling	47	8	6	14	22
Ott Heller	40	5	7	12	31
Doug Brennan	48	5	4	9	94
Earl Seibert	45	2	3	5	92
Carl Voss	10	2	1	3	4
Gordon Pettinger	35	1	2	3	18

1933-34	GP	G	A	PTS	PIM
Frank Boucher	48	14	30	44	4
Cecil Dillon	48	13	26	39	10
Bun Cook	48	18	15	33	36
Murray Murdoch	48	17	10	27	29

	GP	G	A	PTS	PIM
Bill Cook	48	13	13	26	21
Earl Seibert	48	13	10	23	66
Butch Keeling	48	15	5	20	20
Vic Ripley	35	5	12	17	10
Ozzie Asmundson	46	2	6	8	8
Ching Johnson	48	2	6	8	86
Ott Heller	48	2	5	7	29
Dan Cox	15	5	0	5	2
Art Somers	8	1	2	3	5
Duke Dutkowski	29	0	3	3	16
Jean Pusie	19	0	2	2	17
Babe Siebert	13	0	1	1	18
Albert Leduc	7	0	0	0	6
Lorne Carr	14	0	0	0	0
Doug Brennan	37	0	0	0	18

1934-35	GP	G	A	PTS	PIM
Frank Boucher	48	13	32	45	2
Bill Cook	48	21	15	36	23
Cecil Dillon	48	25	9	34	4
Bun Cook	48	13	21	34	26
Murray Murdoch	48	14	15	29	14
Earl Seibert	48	6	19	25	86
Lynn Patrick	48	9	13	22	17
Bert Connolly	47	10	11	21	23
Butch Keeling	47	15	4	19	14
Charlie Mason	46	5	9	14	14
Ott Heller	47	3	11	14	31
Ching Johnson	26	2	3	5	34
Art Somers	41	0	5	5	4
Alex Levinsky	21	0	4	4	6
Vic Ripley	4	0	2	2	2
Bill MacKenzie	20	1	0	1	10
Harold Starr	30	0	0	0	26

1935-36	GP	G	A	PTS	PIM
Cecil Dillon	48	18	14	32	12
Frank Boucher	48	11	18	29	2
Lynn Patrick	48	11	14	25	29
Butch Keeling	47	13	5	18	22
Bill Cook	44	7	10	17	16
Glenn Brydson	30	4	12	16	7
Ott Heller	43	2	11	13	40
Murray Murdoch	48	2	9	11	9
Bun Cook	26	4	5	9	12
Ching Johnson	47	5	3	8	58
Howie Morenz	19	2	5	7	6
Alex Shibicky	18	4	2	6	6
Art Coulter	23	1	5	6	26
Charlie Mason	28	1	5	6	30
Earl Seibert	17	2	3	5	6
Mac Colville	18	1	4	5	6
Bert Connolly	25	2	2	4	10
Thomas Ayres	28	0	4	4	38
Babe Pratt	17	1	1	2	16
Phil Watson	24	0	2	2	24
Neil Colville	1	0	0	0	0
Joe Cooper	1	0	0	0	0
Harold Starr	15	0	0	0	12

*Did not qualify for playoffs

1936-37	GP	G	A	PTS	PIM
Cecil Dillon	48	20	11	31	13
Phil Watson	48	11	17	28	22
Neil Colville	45	10	18	28	33
Butch Keeling	48	22	4	26	18
Lynn Patrick	45	8	16	24	23
Alex Shibicky	47	14	8	22	30
Frank Boucher	44	7	13	20	5
Mac Colville	46	7	12	19	10
Ott Heller	48	5	12	17	42
Babe Pratt	47	8	7	15	23
Murray Murdoch	48	0	14	14	16
Art Coulter	47	1	5	6	27
Bill Cook	21	1	4	5	6

	GP	G	A	PTS	PIM
Joe Cooper	48	0	3	3	42
Eddie Wares	2	2	0	2	0
Clint Smith	2	1	0	1	0
Bryan Hextall	3	0	1	1	0
Joe Krol	1	0	0	0	0
Ching Johnson	34	0	0	0	2

1937-38	GP	G	A	PTS	PIM
Cecil Dillon	48	21	18	39	6
Clint Smith	48	14	23	37	0
Neil Colville	45	17	19	36	11
Alex Shibicky	48	17	18	35	26
Lynn Patrick	48	15	19	34	24
Phil Watson	48	7	25	32	52
Mac Colville	48	14	14	28	18
Bryan Hextall	48	17	4	21	6
Babe Pratt	47	5	14	19	56
Butch Keeling	39	8	9	17	12
Ott Heller	48	2	14	16	68
Art Coulter	43	5	10	15	80
Bobby Kirk	39	4	8	12	14
Joe Cooper	46	3	2	5	56
Muzz Patrick	1	0	2	2	0
Dutch Hiller	9	0	1	1	2
Frank Boucher	18	0	1	1	2
Larry Molyneaux	2	0	0	0	2
Johnny Sherf	1	0	0	0	0

1938-39	GP	G	A	PTS	PIM
Clint Smith	48	21	20	41	2
Neil Colville	47	18	19	37	12
Phil Watson	48	15	22	37	42
Bryan Hextall	48	20	15	35	18
Alex Shibicky	48	24	9	33	24
Dutch Hiller	48	10	19	29	2
Lynn Patrick	35	8	21	29	25
Mac Colville	48	7	21	28	26
Cecil Dillon	48	12	15	27	6
Ott Heller	48	0	23	23	42
Babe Pratt	48	2	19	21	20
George Allen	19	6	6	12	10
Art Coulter	4	4	8	12	58
Muzz Patrick	48	1	10	11	64
Joe Krol	1	1	1	2	0
Bill Carse	1	0	1	1	0
Larry Molyneaux	43	0	1	1	18

1939-40	GP	G	A	PTS	PIM
Bryan Hextall	48	24	15	39	52
Neil Colville	48	19	19	38	22
Phil Watson	48	7	28	35	42
Alex Shibicky	43	11	21	32	33
Dutch Hiller	48	13	18	31	57
Kilby MacDonald	44	15	13	28	19
Lynn Patrick	48	12	16	28	34
Clint Smith	41	8	16	24	2
Mac Colville	47	7	14	21	12
Ott Heller	47	5	14	19	26
Alf Pike	47	8	9	17	38
Babe Pratt	48	4	13	17	61
Art Coulter	48	1	9	10	68
Muzz Patrick	46	2	4	6	44
Johnny Polich	1	0	0	0	0
Stan Smith	1	0	0	0	0
Cliff Barton	3	0	0	0	0

1940-41	GP	G	A	PTS	PIM
Bryan Hextall	48	26	18	44	16
Lynn Patrick	48	20	24	44	12
Neil Colville	48	14	28	42	28
Phil Watson	40	11	25	36	49
Mac Colville	47	14	17	31	18
Clint Smith	48	14	11	25	0
Alex Shibicky	40	10	14	24	14
Babe Pratt	47	3	17	20	52
Alf Pike	48	6	13	19	23

	GP	G	A	PTS	PIM
Art Coulter	35	5	14	19	42
Dutch Hiller	45	8	10	18	20
Ott Heller	48	2	16	18	42
Kilby MacDonald	47	5	6	11	12
Muzz Patrick	47	2	8	10	21
Stan Smith	8	2	1	3	0
Herb Foster	4	1	0	1	5-
Bill Allum	1	0	1	1	0
Johnny Polich	2	0	1	1	0
Bill Juzda	5	0	0	0	2

1941-42	GP	G	A	PTS	PIM
Bryan Hextall	48	24	32	56	30
Lynn Patrick	47	32	22	54	18
Phil Watson	48	15	37	52	58
Alex Shibicky	45	20	14	34	16
Clint Smith	47	10	24	34	4
Grant Warwick	44	16	17	33	36
Neil Colville	48	8	25	33	37
Mac Colville	46	14	16	30	26
Babe Pratt	47	4	24	28	65
Alf Pike	34	8	19	27	16
Alan Kuntz	31	10	11	21	10
Art Coulter	47	1	16	17	31
Bill Juzda	45	4	8	12	29
Ott Heller	35	6	5	11	22
Hub Macey	9	3	5	8	0
Norman Tustin	18	2	4	6	0
Norman Burns	11	0	4	4	2

1942-43	GP	G	A	PTS	PIM
Lynn Patrick	50	22	39	61	28
Bryan Hextall	50	27	32	59	28
Phil Watson	46	14	28	42	44
Grant Warwick	50	17	18	35	31
Clint Smith	47	12	21	33	4
Bob Kirkpatrick	49	12	12	24	6
Hank Goldup	36	11	20	21	33
Alf Pike	41	6	16	22	48
Angus Cameron	35	8	11	19	0
Ott Heller	45	4	14	18	14
Vic Myles	45	6	9	15	57
Felix Mancuso	21	6	8	14	13
Joe Shack	20	5	9	14	6
Joe Bell	15	2	5	7	6
Hub Macey	9	3	3	6	0
Gordon Davidson	35	2	3	5	4
Lin Bend	8	3	1	4	2
Billy Gooden	12	0	3	3	0
Dudley Garrett	23	1	1	2	18
Babe Pratt	4	0	2	2	6
Billy Warwick	1	0	1	1	4
Spence Thatchell	1	0	0	0	0
*Did not qualify for playoffs

1943-44	GP	G	A	PTS	PIM
Bryan Hextall	50	21	33	54	41
Dutch Hiller	50	18	22	40	15
Ott Heller	50	8	27	35	29
Ab DeMarco	36	14	19	33	2
John Mahaffy	28	9	20	29	0
Oscar Aubuchon	38	15	12	27	4
Fern Gauthier	33	14	10	24	0
John McDonald	43	10	9	19	6
Billy Gooden	41	9	8	17	15
Grant Warwick	18	8	9	17	14
Kilby MacDonald	24	7	9	16	4
Bob Dill	28	6	10	16	66
Frank Boucher	15	4	10	14	2
Bob McDonald	39	5	6	11	14
Billy Warwick	13	3	2	5	12
Chuck Scherza	24	3	2	5	13
Don Raleigh	15	2	2	4	2
Gordon Davidson	16	1	3	4	4
Roger Leger	7	1	2	3	2
Aldo Palazzari	12	2	0	2	0

	GP	G	A	PTS	PIM
Tommy Dewar	9	0	2	2	4
Chuck Sands	9	0	2	2	0
Hank D'Amore	4	1	0	1	2
Jimmy Jamieson	1	0	1	1	0
Archie Fraser	3	0	1	1	0
Tony Demers	1	0	0	0	0
Hank Dyck	1	0	0	0	0
Bob McDonald	1	0	0	0	0
Lloyd Mohns	1	0	0	0	0
Jack Mann	3	0	0	0	0
Max Labovitch	5	0	0	0	0
Art Strobel	7	0	0	0	0
*Did not qualify for playoffs

1944-45	GP	G	A	PTS	PIM
Ab DeMarco	50	24	30	54	10
Grant Warwick	52	20	22	42	25
Hank Goldup	48	17	25	42	25
Fred Thurier	50	16	19	35	14
Fred Hunt	44	13	9	22	6
Joe Shack	50	4	18	22	14
Walt Atanas	49	13	8	21	40
Phil Watson	45	11	8	19	24
Ott Heller	45	7	12	19	26
Kilby MacDonald	36	9	6	15	12
Bob Dill	48	9	5	14	69
Bucko McDonald	40	2	9	11	0
Jack Mann	6	3	4	7	0
Bill Moe	35	2	4	6	14
Chuck Scherza	22	2	3	5	18
Guy Labrie	27	2	2	4	14
Neil Colville	4	0	1	1	2
Alex Ritson	1	0	0	0	0
Len Wharton	1	0	0	0	0
Jim Drummond	2	0	0	0	0
Hal Cooper	8	0	0	0	2
*Did not qualify for playoffs

1945-46	GP	G	A	PTS	PIM
Ab DeMarco	50	20	27	47	20
Grant Warwick	45	19	18	37	19
Edgar Laprade	49	15	19	34	0
Phil Watson	49	12	14	26	43
Tony Leswick	50	15	9	24	26
Alf Pike	33	7	9	16	18
Alex Shibicky	33	10	5	15	12
Lynn Patrick	38	8	6	14	30
Mac Colville	39	7	6	13	8
Cal Gardner	16	8	2	10	2
Neil Colville	49	5	4	9	25
Bill Moe	48	4	4	8	14
Rene Trudell	16	3	5	8	4
Hank Goldup	19	6	1	7	11
Ott Heller	34	2	3	5	14
Bill Juzda	32	1	3	4	17
Church Russell	17	0	5	5	2
Hal Brown	13	2	1	3	2
Muzz Patrick	24	0	2	2	4
Hal Laycoe	17	0	2	2	6
Bryan Hextall	3	0	1	1	0
Alan Kuntz	14	0	1	1	2
Chuck Rayner	40	0	0	0	6
*Did not qualify for playoffs

1946-47	GP	G	A	PTS	PIM
Tony Leswick	59	27	14	41	51
Grant Warwick	54	20	20	40	24
Edgar Laprade	58	15	25	40	9
Bryan Hextall	60	20	10	30	18
Carl Gardner	52	13	16	29	30
Church Russell	54	20	8	28	8
Rene Trudell	59	8	16	24	38
Neil Colville	60	4	16	20	16
Ab DeMarco	44	9	10	19	4
Alf Pike	31	7	11	18	2
Phil Watson	48	6	12	18	17

Name	GP	G	A	PTS	PIM
Bill Moe	59	4	10	14	44
Hal Laycoe	58	1	12	13	25
Joe Bell	47	6	4	10	12
Joe Cooper	59	2	8	10	38
Bill Juzda	45	3	5	8	60
Joe Levandoski	8	1	1	2	0
Jean Paul Lamirande	14	1	1	2	14
Harry Bell	1	0	1	1	0
Jean Paul Denis	6	0	1	1	0
Jack Lancien	1	0	0	0	0
Norm Larson	1	0	0	0	0
Sherman White	1	0	0	0	0
Mel Read	6	0	0	0	8
Mac Colville	14	0	0	0	8

*Did not qualify for playoffs

1947-48	GP	G	A	PTS	PIM
Buddy O'Connor	60	24	36	60	8
Edgar Laprade	59	13	34	47	7
Tony Leswick	60	24	16	40	76
Phil Watson	54	18	15	33	54
Don Raleigh	52	15	18	33	2
Eddie Kullman	51	15	17	32	32
Grant Warwick	40	17	12	29	30
Cal Gardner	58	7	18	25	71
Bryan Hextall	43	8	14	22	18
Rene Trudell	54	13	7	20	30
Frank Eddolls	58	6	13	19	16
Neil Colville	55	4	12	16	25
Bill Moe	59	1	15	16	31
Bill Juzda	60	3	9	12	70
Ed Slowinski	38	6	5	11	2
Church Russell	19	0	3	3	2
Ronnie Rowe	5	1	0	1	0
Fred Shero	19	1	0	1	2
Jean Lamirande	18	0	1	1	6
Herb Foster	1	0	0	0	0
Larry Kwong	1	0	0	0	0
Hub Anslow	2	0	0	0	0
Bing Juckes	2	0	0	0	0
Fern Perrault	2	0	0	0	0
Billy Taylor	2	0	0	0	0

1948-49	GP	G	A	PTS	PIM
Buddy O'Connor	46	11	24	35	0
Alex Kaleta	56	12	19	31	18
Edgar Laprade	56	18	12	30	12
Pentti Lund	59	14	16	30	16
Tony Leswick	60	13	14	27	70
Don Raleigh	41	10	16	26	8
Dunc Fisher	60	9	16	25	40
Nick Mickoski	54	13	9	22	20
Clint Albright	59	14	5	19	19
Jack Gordon	31	3	9	12	0
Allan Stanley	40	2	8	10	22
Ed Kullman	18	4	5	9	14
Fred Shero	59	3	6	9	64
Wally Stanowski	60	1	8	9	16
Bill Moe	60	0	9	9	60
Frank Eddolls	34	4	2	6	10
Neil Colville	14	0	5	5	2
Wes Trainor	17	1	2	3	6
Ed Slowinski	20	1	1	2	2
Ray Manson	1	0	1	1	0
Red Staley	1	0	1	1	0
Elwin Morris	18	0	1	1	8
Dick Kotanen	1	0	0	0	0
Bucky Buchanan	2	0	0	0	0
Val DeLory	1	0	0	0	0
Odie Lowe	1	0	0	0	0
Jack Evans	3	0	0	0	4
Chuck Rayner	58	0	0	0	2

*Did not qualify for playoffs

1949-50	GP	G	A	PTS	PIM
Edgar Laprade	60	22	22	44	2
Tony Lewsick	69	19	25	44	85
Ed Slowinski	63	14	23	37	12
Don Raleigh	70	12	25	37	11
Dunc Fisher	70	12	21	33	42
Buddy O'Connor	66	11	22	33	4
Alex Kaleta	67	17	14	31	40
Pentti Lund	64	18	9	27	16
Nick Mickoski	47	10	10	20	10
Pat Egan	70	5	11	16	50
Jack McLeod	38	6	9	15	2
Fred Shero	67	2	8	10	71
Bud Poile	28	3	6	9	8
Allan Stanley	55	4	4	8	58
Gus Kyle	70	3	5	8	143
Frank Eddolls	58	2	6	8	20
Jean Lamirande	16	4	3	7	6
Jack Lancien	43	1	4	5	27
Bing Juckes	14	2	1	3	6
Odie Lowe	3	1	1	2	0
Don Smith	10	1	1	2	0
Wally Stanowski	37	1	1	2	10
Sherman White	3	0	2	2	0
Doug Adam	4	0	1	1	0
Jean Paul Denis	4	0	1	1	2
Jack Gordon	1	0	0	0	0
Fern Perrault	1	0	0	0	0
Bill Kyle	2	0	0	0	0
Jack Evans	3	0	0	0	2
Bill McDonagh	4	0	0	0	2
Chick Webster	14	0	0	0	4
Chuck Rayner	69	0	0	0	6

1950-51	GP	G	A	PTS	PIM
Reg Sinclair	70	18	21	39	70
Don Raleigh	64	15	24	39	18
Buddy O'Connor	66	16	20	36	0
Nick Mickoski	64	20	15	35	12
Ed Slowinski	69	14	18	32	15
Ed Kullman	70	14	18	32	88
Zellio Toppazzini	55	14	13	27	27
Tony Leswick	70	15	11	26	112
Edgar Laprade	42	10	13	23	0
Allan Stanley	70	7	14	21	75
Pentti Lund	59	4	16	20	6
Jack McLeod	41	5	10	15	2
Pat Egan	70	5	10	15	70
Frank Eddolls	68	3	8	11	24
Alex Kaleta	58	3	4	7	26
Wally Stanowski	49	1	5	6	28
Gus Kyle	64	2	3	5	92
Bill Kyle	1	0	3	3	0
Vic Howe	3	1	0	1	0
Ed Harrison	4	1	0	1	2
Jack Evans	49	1	0	1	95
Jack Gordon	4	0	1	1	0
Jack Lancien	19	0	1	1	8
Dick Kotanen	1	0	0	0	0
Bob Wood	1	0	0	0	0
Bill Wylie	1	0	0	0	0
Dunc Fisher	12	0	0	0	0
Chuck Rayner	66	0	0	0	6

*Did not qualify for playoffs

1951-52	GP	G	A	PTS	PIM
Don Raleigh	70	19	42	61	14
Ed Slowinski	64	21	22	43	18
Paul Ronty	65	12	31	43	16
Gaye Stewart	69	15	25	40	22
Wally Hergesheimer	68	26	12	38	6
Edgar Laprade	70	9	29	38	8
Hy Buller	68	12	23	35	96
Reg Sinclair	69	20	10	30	33
Herb Dickenson	37	14	13	27	8
Eddie Kullman	64	11	10	21	59

Nick Mickoski	43	7	13	20	20
Allan Stanley	50	5	14	19	52
Steve Kraftcheck	58	8	9	17	30
Jim Ross	51	2	9	11	25
Frank Eddolls	42	3	5	8	18
Jack Evans	52	1	6	7	83
Jack Stoddard	20	4	2	6	2
Jack McLeod	13	2	3	5	2
Zellio Toppazzini	16	1	1	2	4
Clare Martin	15	0	1	1	8
Jim Conacher	16	0	1	1	2
Lloyd Ailsby	3	0	0	0	2
Chuck Rayner	53	0	0	0	4

*Did not qualify for playoffs

1952-53	GP	G	A	PTS	PIM
Wally Hergesheimer	70	30	29	59	10
Paul Ronty	70	16	38	54	20
Nick Mickoski	70	19	16	35	39
Jack Stoddard	60	12	13	25	29
Hy Buller	70	7	18	25	73
Neil Strain	52	11	13	24	12
Don Raleigh	55	4	18	22	2
Leo Reise	61	4	15	19	53
Ed Kullman	70	8	10	18	61
Allan Stanley	70	5	12	17	52
Harry Howell	67	3	8	11	46
Steve Kraftcheck	69	2	9	11	45
Dean Prentice	55	6	3	9	20
Pete Babando	30	4	5	9	8
Herb Dickenson	11	4	4	8	2
Aldo Guidolin	30	4	4	8	24
Ed Slowinski	37	2	5	7	14
George Senick	13	2	3	5	8
Jim Conacher	17	1	4	5	2
Ron Murphy	15	3	1	4	0
Edgar Laprade	11	2	1	3	2
Gaye Stewart	18	1	2	3	8
Jim Ross	11	0	2	2	4
Kelly Burnett	3	1	0	1	0
Dolph Kukulowicz	3	1	0	1	0
Gordie Haworth	2	0	1	1	0
Frank Bathgate	2	0	0	0	2
Michel Labadie	3	0	0	0	0
Jack McLeod	3	0	0	0	2
Ian Mackintosh	4	0	0	0	4
Chuck Rayner	20	0	0	0	2
Lorne Worsley	50	0	0	0	2

*Did not qualify for playoffs

1953-54	GP	G	A	PTS	PIM
Paul Ronty	70	13	33	46	18
Don Raleigh	70	15	30	45	16
Wally Hergesheimer	66	27	16	43	42
Camille Henry	66	24	15	39	10
Nick Micoski	68	19	16	35	22
Max Bentley	57	14	18	32	15
Dean Prentice	52	4	13	17	18
Hy Buller	41	3	14	17	40
Harry Howell	67	7	9	16	58
Ed Kullman	70	4	10	14	44
Ivan Irwin	56	2	12	14	109
Ike Hildebrand	31	6	7	13	12
Doug Bentley	20	2	10	12	2
Bob Chrystal	64	5	5	10	44
Jack Evans	44	4	4	8	73
Leo Reise	70	3	5	8	71
Aldo Guidolin	68	2	6	8	51
Edgar Laprade	35	1	6	7	2
Andy Bathgate	20	2	2	4	18
Ron Murphy	27	1	3	4	20
Glen Sonmor	15	2	0	2	17
Billy Dea	14	1	1	2	2
Allan Stanley	10	0	2	2	11
Bill Chalmers	1	0	0	0	0
Vic Howe	1	0	0	0	0

Dolph Kukulowicz	1	0	0	0	0
Bill McCreary	1	0	0	0	0

*Did not qualify for playoffs

1954-55	GP	G	A	PTS	PIM
Danny Lewicki	70	29	24	53	8
Andy Bathgate	70	20	20	40	37
Don Raleigh	69	8	32	40	19
Dean Prentice	70	16	15	31	20
Ron Murphy	66	14	16	30	36
Larry Popein	70	11	17	28	27
Nick Mickoski	18	0	19	19	6
Pete Conacher	52	10	7	17	10
Bill Gadsby	52	8	8	16	42
Harry Howell	70	2	14	16	87
Bob Chrystal	68	6	9	15	68
Paul Ronty	54	4	11	15	10
Edgar Laprade	60	3	11	14	0
Ivan Irwin	60	0	13	12	85
Camille Henry	21	5	2	7	4
Aldo Guidolin	70	2	5	7	34
Wally Hergesheimer	14	4	2	6	4
Vic Howe	29	2	4	6	10
Jack Evans	47	0	5	5	91
Bill Ezinicki	16	2	2	4	22
Lou Fontinato	28	2	2	4	60
Jackie McLeod	11	1	1	2	2
Bill McCreary	8	0	2	2	0
Allan Stanley	12	0	1	1	2
Dick Bouchard	1	0	0	0	0
Ron Howell	3	0	0	0	0
Glen Sonmor	13	0	0	0	4
Lorne Worsley	65	0	0	0	2

*Did not qualify for playoffs

1955-56	GP	G	A	PTS	PIM
Andy Bathgate	70	19	47	66	59
Dave Creighton	70	20	31	51	43
Bill Gadsby	70	9	42	51	84
Danny Lewicki	70	18	27	45	26
Ron Murphy	66	16	28	44	71
Dean Prentice	70	24	18	42	44
Wally Hergesheimer	70	22	18	40	26
Larry Popein	64	14	25	39	37
Andy Hebenton	70	24	14	38	8
Bronco Horvath	66	12	17	29	40
Pete Conacher	41	11	11	22	10
Lou Fontinato	70	3	15	18	202
Harry Howell	70	3	15	18	77
Don Raleigh	29	2	12	13	4
Guy Gendron	63	5	7	12	38
Jack Evans	70	2	9	11	104

1956-57	GP	G	A	PTS	PIM
Andy Bathgate	70	27	50	77	60
Andy Hebenton	70	21	23	44	10
Dean Prentice	68	19	23	42	38
Bill Gadsby	70	4	37	41	72
Dave Creighton	70	18	21	39	42
Danny Lewicki	70	18	20	38	47
Larry Popein	67	11	19	30	20
Camille Henry	36	14	15	29	2
Red Sullivan	42	6	17	23	36
Ron Murphy	33	7	12	19	14
Gerry Foley	69	7	9	16	48
Guy Gendron	70	9	6	15	40
Parker MacDonald	45	7	8	15	24
Lou Fontinato	70	3	12	15	139
Harry Howell	65	2	10	12	70
Larry Cahan	61	5	4	9	65
Jack Evans	70	3	6	9	110
Bruce Cline	30	2	3	5	10
Bronco Horvath	7	1	2	3	4

1957-58

1957-58	GP	G	A	PTS	PIM
Andy Bathgate	65	30	48	78	42
Camille Henry	70	32	24	56	2
Dave Creighton	70	17	35	52	40
Bill Gadsby	65	14	32	46	48
Red Sullivan	70	11	35	46	61
Andy Hebenton	70	21	24	45	17
Larry Popein	70	12	22	34	22
Danny Lewicki	70	11	19	30	26
Guy Gendron	70	10	17	27	68
Dean Prentice	38	13	9	22	14
Parker MacDonald	70	8	10	18	30
Jack Evans	70	4	8	12	108
Harry Howell	70	4	7	11	62
Lou Fontinato	70	3	8	11	152
Hank Ciesla	60	2	6	8	16
Gerry Foley	68	2	5	7	43
Larry Cahan	34	1	1	2	20

1958-59	GP	G	A	PTS	PIM
Andy Bathgate	70	40	48	88	48
Red Sullivan	70	21	42	63	56
Andy Hebenton	70	33	29	62	8
Camille Henry	70	23	35	58	2
Bill Gadsby	70	5	46	51	56
Dean Prentice	70	17	33	50	11
Larry Popein	61	13	21	34	28
Eddie Shack	67	7	14	21	109
Jim Bartlett	70	11	9	20	118
Hank Diesla	69	6	14	20	21
Harry Howell	70	4	10	14	101
Lou Fontinato	64	7	6	13	149
Les Colwill	69	7	6	13	16
John Hanna	70	1	10	11	83
Wally Hergesheimer	22	3	0	3	6
Jack Bownass	35	1	2	3	20
Earl Ingarfield	35	1	2	3	10
Larry Cahan	16	1	0	1	8

*Did not qualify for playoffs

1959-60	GP	G	A	PTS	PIM
Andy Bathgate	70	26	48	74	28
Dean Prentice	70	32	34	66	43
Andy Hebenton	70	19	27	46	4
Red Sullivan	70	12	25	37	81
Larry Popein	66	14	22	36	16
Bill Gadsby	65	9	22	31	60
Ken Schinkel	69	13	16	29	27
Brian Cullen	64	8	21	29	6
Camille Henry	49	12	15	27	6
Eddie Shack	62	8	10	18	110
Bob Kabel	44	5	11	16	32
Harry Howell	67	7	6	13	58
Lou Fontinato	64	2	11	13	137
Jim Bartlett	44	8	4	12	48
John Hanna	61	4	8	12	87
Art Stratton	18	2	5	7	2
Jack Bownass	37	2	5	7	34
Mel Pearson	23	1	5	6	13
Earl Ingarfield	20	1	2	3	2
Irv Spencer	32	1	2	3	20
Bill Sweeney	4	1	0	1	0
Ian Cushenan	17	0	1	1	22
Dave Balon	3	0	0	0	0
Parker MacDonald	4	0	0	0	0
Noel Price	6	0	0	0	0

*Did not qualify for playoffs

1960-61	GP	G	A	PTS	PIM
Andy Bathgate	70	29	48	77	22
Andy Hebenton	70	26	28	54	10
Camille Henry	53	28	25	53	8
Dean Prentice	56	20	25	45	17
George Sullivan	70	9	31	40	66
Bill Gadsby	65	9	26	35	49
Earl Ingarfield	66	13	21	34	18
Brian Cullen	42	11	19	30	6
Johnny Wilson	56	14	12	26	24
Pat Hannigan	53	11	9	20	24
Ted Hampson	69	6	14	20	4
Harry Howell	70	7	10	17	62
Floyd Smith	29	5	9	14	0
John Hanna	46	1	8	9	34
Irv Spencer	56	1	8	9	30
Ken Schinkel	38	2	6	8	18
Don Johns	63	1	7	8	34
Jim Morrison	19	1	6	7	6
Lou Fontinato	53	2	3	5	100
Jean Ratelle	3	2	1	3	0
Len Ronson	13	2	1	3	10
Eddie Shack	12	1	2	3	17
Dave Balon	13	1	2	3	8
Danny Belisle	4	2	0	2	0
Bob Kabel	4	0	2	2	2
Al Lebrun	4	0	2	2	4
Rod Gilbert	1	0	1	1	2
Bob Cunningham	3	0	1	1	0
Larry Popein	4	0	1	1	0
Noel Price	1	0	0	0	2
Wayne Hall	4	0	0	0	0
Phil Latreille	4	0	0	0	2
Ron Hutchinson	9	0	0	0	0

*Did not qualify for playoffs

1961-62	GP	G	A	PTS	PIM
Andy Bathgate	70	28	56	84	44
Dean Prentice	68	22	38	60	20
Earl Ingarfield	70	26	31	57	18
Andy Hebenton	70	18	24	42	10
Camille Henry	60	23	15	38	8
Doug Harvey	69	6	24	30	42
Ken Schinkel	65	7	21	28	17
Ted Hampson	68	4	24	28	10
Guy Gendron	69	14	11	25	71
Al Langlois	69	7	18	25	90
Pat Hannigan	56	8	14	22	34
Harry Howell	66	6	15	21	89
Dave Balon	30	4	11	15	11
John Wilson	40	11	3	14	14
Jean Ratelle	31	4	8	12	4
Irv Spencer	43	2	10	12	31
Larry Cahan	57	2	7	9	85
Vic Hadfield	44	3	1	4	22
Pete Goegan	7	0	2	2	6
Bob Cunningham	1	0	0	0	0
Rod Gilbert	1	0	0	0	0
Mel Pearson	3	0	0	0	2
Jack Bownass	4	0	0	0	4

1962-63	GP	G	A	PTS	PIM
Andy Bathgate	70	35	46	81	54
Camille Henry	60	37	23	60	8
Dean Prentice	68	19	34	53	22
Earl Ingarfield	69	19	24	43	40
Doug Harvey	68	4	35	39	92
Andy Hebenton	70	15	22	37	8
Rod Gilbert	70	11	20	31	20
Harry Howell	70	5	20	25	55
Dave Balon	70	11	13	24	72
Don McKenney	21	8	16	24	4
Bronco Horvath	41	7	15	22	34
Jean Ratelle	48	11	9	20	8
Larry Cahan	56	6	14	20	47
Jim Neilson	69	5	11	16	38
Al Langlois	60	2	14	16	62
Ken Schinkel	69	6	9	15	15
Vic Hadfield	36	5	6	11	32
Leon Rochefort	23	5	4	9	6
Ted Hampson	46	4	2	6	2
Don Johns	6	0	4	4	6
Bryan Hextall	21	0	2	2	10
Mel Pearson	5	1	0	1	6
Duane Rupp	2	0	0	0	0

*Did not qualify for playoffs

1963-64	GP	G	A	PTS	PIM
Phil Goyette	67	24	41	65	15
Rod Gilbert	70	24	40	64	62
Andy Bathgate	56	16	43	59	26
Camille Henry	68	29	26	55	8
Harry Howell	70	5	31	36	75
Jim Neilson	69	5	24	29	93
Earl Ingarfield	63	16	11	26	26
Don McKenney	55	9	17	26	6
Vic Hadfield	68	14	11	25	151
Val Fonteyne	69	7	18	25	4
Don Marshall	70	11	12	23	8
Al Langlois	61	5	8	13	45
Larry Cahan	53	4	8	12	80
Don Johns	57	1	9	10	20
Bob Nevin	14	5	4	9	9
Dick Duff	14	4	4	8	2
Dick Meissner	35	3	5	8	0
Jean Ratelle	15	0	7	7	6
Dave Richardson	34	3	1	4	21
Ron Ingram	16	1	3	4	8
Doug Harvey	14	0	2	2	10
Marc Dufour	10	1	0	1	2
Howie Glover	25	1	0	1	9
Rod Seiling	2	0	1	1	0
Mike McMahon	18	0	1	1	16
Sandy McGregor	2	0	0	0	2
Ken Schinkel	4	0	0	0	0
Gordon Labossiere	15	0	0	0	12

*Did not qualify for playoffs

1964-65	GP	G	A	PTS	PIM
Rod Gilbert	70	25	36	61	52
Phil Goyette	52	12	34	46	6
Vic Hadfield	70	18	20	38	102
Camille Henry	48	21	15	36	20
Don Marshall	69	20	15	35	2
Jean Ratelle	54	14	21	35	14
Bob Nevin	64	16	14	30	28
Earl Ingarfield	69	15	13	28	40
Rod Seiling	68	4	22	26	44
Doug Robinson	21	8	14	22	2
Harry Howell	68	2	20	22	63
Lou Angotti	70	9	8	17	20
Bill Hicke	40	6	11	17	26
Jim Neilson	62	0	13	13	58
Dick Duff	29	3	9	12	20
Arnie Brown	58	1	11	12	145
Wayne Hillman	22	1	8	9	26
John Brenneman	22	3	3	6	6
Larry Cahan	26	0	5	5	32
Jim Mikol	30	1	3	4	6
Dave Richardson	7	0	1	1	4
Don Johns	22	0	1	1	4
Val Fonteyne	27	0	1	1	2
Trevor Fahey	1	0	0	0	0
Jim Johnson	1	0	0	0	0
Gordon Labossiere	1	0	0	0	0
Mike McMahon	1	0	0	0	0
Dick Meissner	1	0	0	0	0
Marc Dufour	2	0	0	0	0
Billy Taylor	2	0	0	0	0
Ron Ingram	3	0	0	0	2
Sandy Fitzpatrick	4	0	0	0	2
Ulf Sterner	4	0	0	0	0
Ted Taylor	4	0	0	0	4
Mel Pearson	5	0	0	0	4
Bob Plager	10	0	0	0	18

*Did not qualify for playoffs

1965-66	GP	G	A	PTS	PIM
Bob Nevin	69	29	33	62	10
Don Marshall	69	26	28	54	6
Jean Ratelle	67	21	30	51	10
Phil Goyette	60	11	31	42	6

	GP	G	A	PTS	PIM
Earl Ingarfield	68	20	16	36	35
Vic Hadfield	67	16	19	35	112
Harry Howell	70	4	29	33	92
Bill Hicke	49	9	18	27	21
Rod Gilbert	34	10	15	25	20
Reggie Fleming	35	10	14	24	122
Jim Neilson	65	4	19	23	84
Doug Robinson	51	8	12	20	8
Wayne Hillman	68	3	17	20	70
Lou Angotti	51	6	12	18	14
Rod Seiling	52	5	10	15	24
Mike McMahon	41	0	12	12	34
John McKenzie	35	6	5	11	36
Garry Peters	63	7	3	10	42
Arnie Brown	64	1	7	8	106
Bob Plager	18	0	5	5	22
Ray Cullen	8	1	3	4	0
Paul Andrea	4	1	1	2	0
Jim Johnson	5	1	0	1	0
Ted Taylor	4	0	1	1	2
Al Lebrun	2	0	0	0	0
Dunc McCallum	2	0	0	0	2
Allan Hamilton	4	0	0	0	0
Larry Mickey	7	0	0	0	2
John Brenneman	11	0	0	0	14

*Did not qualify for playoffs

1966-67	GP	G	A	PTS	PIM
Phil Goyette	70	12	49	61	6
Rod Gilbert	64	28	18	46	12
Don Marshall	70	24	22	46	4
Bob Nevin	67	20	24	44	6
Bernie Geoffrion	58	17	25	42	42
Harry Howell	70	12	28	40	54
Orland Kurtenbach	60	11	25	36	58
Earl Ingarfield	67	12	22	34	12
Vic Hadfield	69	13	20	33	80
Reg Fleming	61	15	16	31	146
Jim Neilson	61	4	11	15	65
Wayne Hillman	67	2	12	14	43
Arnie Brown	69	2	10	12	61
Jean Ratelle	41	6	5	11	4
Bill Hicke	48	3	4	7	11
Red Berenson	30	0	5	5	2
Al MacNeil	58	0	4	4	44
Rod Seiling	12	1	1	2	6
Larry Mickey	4	0	2	2	0

1967-68	GP	G	A	PTS	PIM
Jean Ratelle	74	32	46	78	18
Rod Gilbert	73	29	48	77	12
Phil Goyette	73	25	40	65	10
Bob Nevin	74	28	30	58	20
Don Marshall	70	19	30	49	2
Vic Hadfield	59	20	19	39	45
Orland Kurtenbach	73	15	20	35	82
Jim Neilson	67	6	29	35	60
Harry Howell	74	5	24	29	62
Arnie Brown	74	1	25	26	83
Reg Fleming	73	17	7	24	132
Bernie Geoffrion	59	5	16	21	11
Camille Henry	36	8	12	20	0
Rod Seiling	71	5	11	16	44
Ron Stewart	55	7	7	14	19
Larry Jeffrey	47	2	4	6	15
Wayne Hillman	62	0	5	5	46
Red Berenson	19	2	1	3	2
Larry Mickey	4	0	2	2	0
Allan Hamilton	2	0	0	0	0
Walt Tkaczuk	2	0	0	0	0

1968-69	GP	G	A	PTS	PIM
Jean Ratelle	75	32	46	78	26
Rod Gilbert	66	28	49	77	22
Vic Hadfield	73	26	40	66	108
Bob Nevin	71	31	25	56	14

	GP	G	A	PTS	PIM
Phil Goyette	67	13	32	45	8
Jim Neilson	76	10	34	44	95
Don Marshall	74	20	19	39	12
Walt Tkaczuk	71	12	24	36	28
Dave Balon	75	10	21	31	57
Ron Stewart	75	18	11	29	20
Brad Park	54	3	23	26	70
Arnie Brown	74	10	12	22	48
Rod Seiling	73	4	17	21	73
Reg Fleming	72	8	12	20	138
Harry Howell	56	4	7	11	36
Larry Jeffrey	75	1	6	7	12
Dennis Hextall	13	1	4	5	25
Bill Fairbairn	1	0	0	0	0
Bob Jones	2	0	0	0	0
Orland Kurtenbach	2	0	0	0	2
Guy Trottier	2	0	0	0	0
Wayne Rivers	4	0	0	0	0
Bob Blackburn	11	0	0	0	0
Allan Hamilton	16	0	0	0	8

1969-70	GP	G	A	PTS	PIM
Walt Tkaczuk	76	27	50	77	38
Jean Ratelle	75	32	42	74	28
Dave Balon	76	33	37	70	100
Bill Fairbairn	76	23	33	56	23
Vic Hadfield	71	20	34	54	69
Rod Gilbert	72	16	37	53	22
Bob Nevin	68	18	19	37	8
Brad Park	60	11	26	37	98
Arnie Brown	73	15	21	36	78
Rod Seiling	76	5	21	26	68
Ron Stewart	76	14	10	24	14
Don Marshall	57	9	15	24	6
Jim Neilson	62	3	20	23	75
Orland Kurtenbach	53	4	10	14	47
Tim Horton	15	1	5	6	16
Allan Hamilton	59	0	5	5	54
Jack Egers	6	3	0	3	2
Don Luce	12	1	2	3	8
Larry Brown	15	0	3	3	8
Ted Irvine	17	0	3	3	10
Don Blackburn	3	0	0	0	0
Ab DeMarco	3	0	0	0	0
Mike Robitaille	4	0	0	0	8

1970-71	GP	G	A	PTS	PIM
Walt Tkaczuk	77	26	49	75	48
Jean Ratelle	78	26	46	72	14
Rod Gilbert	78	30	31	61	65
Dave Balon	78	36	24	60	32
Bob Nevin	78	21	25	46	10
Pete Stemkowski	68	16	29	45	61
Vic Hadfield	63	22	22	44	38
Brad Park	68	7	37	44	114
Ted Irvine	76	20	18	38	137
Jim Neilson	77	8	24	32	69
Bill Fairbairn	56	7	23	30	32
Rod Seiling	68	5	22	27	34
Bruce MacGregor	27	12	13	25	4
Tim Horton	78	2	18	20	57
Jack Egers	60	7	10	17	50
Arnie Brown	48	3	12	15	24
Ron Stewart	76	5	6	11	19
Dale Rolfe	14	0	7	7	23
Andre Dupont	7	1	2	3	21
Syl Apps	31	1	2	3	11
Glen Sather	31	2	0	2	52
Mike Robitaille	11	1	1	2	7
Larry Brown	31	1	1	2	16
Jim Krulicki	27	0	2	2	6
Ab DeMarco	2	0	1	1	0
Don Luce	9	0	1	1	0
Don Blackburn	1	0	0	0	0

1971-72	GP	G	A	PTS	PIM
Jean Ratelle	63	46	63	109	4
Vic Hadfield	78	50	56	106	142
Rod Gilbert	73	43	54	97	64
Brad Park	75	24	49	73	130
Walt Tkaczuk	76	24	42	66	65
Bill Fairbairn	78	22	37	59	53
Bobby Rousseau	78	21	36	57	12
Rod Seiling	78	5	36	41	62
Bruce MacGregor	75	19	21	40	22
Jim Neilson	78	7	30	37	56
Ted Irvine	78	15	21	36	66
Pete Stemkowski	59	11	17	28	53
Gene Carr	59	8	8	16	25
Dale Rolfe	68	2	14	16	67
Glen Sather	75	5	9	14	77
Ab DeMarco	48	4	7	11	4
Gary Doak	49	1	11	12	23
Dave Balon	16	4	5	9	2
Pierre Jarry	34	3	3	6	20
Phil Goyette	8	1	4	5	0
Jack Egers	17	2	1	3	14
Ron Stewart	13	0	2	2	2
Norm Gratton	3	0	1	1	0
Jim Dorey	1	0	0	0	0
Mike McMahon	1	0	0	0	0
Tom Williams	3	0	0	0	2
Jim Lorentz	7	0	0	0	0
Steve Andrascik	1	0	0	0	2

1972-73	GP	G	A	PTS	PIM
Jean Ratelle	78	41	53	94	12
Rod Gilbert	76	25	59	84	25
Walt Tkaczuk	76	27	39	66	59
Bill Fairbairn	78	30	33	63	23
Vic Hadfield	63	28	34	62	60
Pete Stemkowski	78	22	37	59	71
Steve Vickers	61	30	23	53	37
Brad Park	52	10	43	53	51
Bobby Rousseau	78	8	37	45	14
Rod Seiling	72	9	33	42	36
Dale Rolfe	72	7	25	32	74
Bruce MacGregor	52	14	12	26	12
Glen Sather	77	11	15	26	64
Ted Irvine	53	8	12	20	54
Jim Neilson	52	4	16	20	35
Gene Carr	50	9	10	19	50
Ab DeMarco	51	3	13	16	15
Ron Harris	45	3	10	13	17
Mike Murphy	15	4	4	8	5
Randy Legge	12	0	2	2	2
Bill Heindl	4	1	0	1	0
Jerry Butler	8	1	0	1	4
Larry Sacharuk	8	1	0	1	0
Sheldon Kannegiesser	3	0	1	1	0
Tom Williams	8	0	1	1	0
Ron Stewart	11	0	1	1	0
Curt Bennett	16	0	1	1	11
Bert Marshall	8	0	0	0	14

1973-74	GP	G	A	PTS	PIM
Brad Park	78	25	57	82	148
Rod Gilbert	75	36	41	77	20
Pete Stemkowski	78	25	45	70	74
Jean Ratelle	68	28	39	67	16
Walt Tkaczuk	71	21	42	63	58
Bill Fairbairn	78	18	44	62	12
Steve Vickers	75	34	24	58	18
Vic Hadfield	77	27	28	55	75
Bobby Rousseau	72	10	41	51	4
Ted Irvine	75	26	20	46	105
Bruce MacGregor	66	17	27	44	6
Rod Seiling	68	7	23	30	32
Gilles Marotte	46	2	17	19	28
Jerry Butler	26	6	10	16	24
Dale Rolfe	48	3	12	15	56

	GP	G	A	PTS	PIM
Ron Harris	63	2	12	14	25
Jim Neilson	72	4	7	11	38
Larry Sacharuk	23	2	4	6	4
Gene Carr	29	1	5	6	15
Sheldon Kannegiesser	12	1	3	4	6
Jack Egers	28	1	3	4	6
Mike Murphy	16	2	1	3	0
Tom Williams	14	1	2	3	4
Bert Wilson	5	1	1	2	2
Glen Sather	2	0	0	0	2
Real Lemieux	7	0	0	0	0

1974-75	GP	G	A	PTS	PIM
Rod Gilbert	76	36	61	97	22
Jean Ratelle	79	36	55	91	26
Steve Vickers	80	41	48	89	64
Bill Fairbairn	80	24	37	61	10
Pete Stemkowski	77	24	35	59	63
Brad Park	65	13	44	57	104
Derek Sanderson	75	25	25	50	106
Ron Greschner	70	8	37	45	93
Greg Polis	76	26	15	41	55
Rick Middleton	47	22	18	40	19
Walt Tkaczuk	62	11	25	36	34
Gilles Marotte	77	4	32	36	69
Ted Irvine	79	17	17	34	66
Jerry Butler	78	17	16	33	102
Nick Beverley	54	3	15	18	19
John Bednarski	35	1	10	11	37
Dale Rolfe	42	1	8	9	30
Ron Harris	34	1	7	8	22
Bert Wilson	61	5	1	6	66
Bobby Rousseau	8	2	2	4	0
Bob MacMillan	22	1	2	3	4
Dave Maloney	4	0	2	2	0
Joe Zanussi	8	0	2	2	4
Jerry Holland	1	1	0	1	0
Rod Seiling	4	0	1	1	0
Hartland Monahan	6	0	1	1	4

1975-76	GP	G	A	PTS	PIM
Rod Gilbert	70	36	50	86	32
Steve Vickers	80	30	53	83	40
Phil Esposito	62	29	38	67	28
Rick Middleton	77	24	26	50	14
Carol Vadnais	64	20	30	50	104
Wayne Dillon	79	21	24	45	10
Pete Stemkowski	75	13	28	41	49
Gerg Polis	79	15	21	36	77
Pat Hickey	70	14	22	36	36
Walt Tkaczuk	78	8	28	36	56
Bill Fairbairn	80	13	15	28	8
Ron Greschner	77	6	21	27	93
Giles Marotte	57	4	17	21	34
Jean Ratelle	13	5	10	15	2
Larry Sacharuk	42	6	7	13	14
Jerry Holland	36	7	4	11	6
John Bednarski	59	1	8	9	77
Nick Beverley	63	1	8	9	46
Bill Collins	50	4	4	8	38
Brad Park	6	2	4	6	23
Dave Maloney	21	1	3	4	66
Doug Jarrett	45	0	4	4	19
Eddie Johnstone	10	2	1	3	4
Ron Harris	3	0	1	1	0
Greg Holst	2	0	0	0	0
Dale Lewis	8	0	0	0	0
Derek Sanderson	8	0	0	0	4

*Did not qualify for playoffs

1976-77	GP	G	A	PTS	PIM
Phil Esposito	80	34	46	80	52
Rod Gilbert	77	27	48	75	50
Ken Hodge	78	21	41	62	43
Don Murdoch	59	32	24	56	47
Steve Vickers	75	22	31	53	26
Walt Tkaczuk	80	12	38	50	38
Carol Vadnais	74	11	37	48	131
Ron Greschner	80	11	36	47	89
Wayne Dillon	78	17	29	46	33
Mike McEwen	80	14	29	43	38
Pat Hickey	80	23	17	40	35
Greg Polis	77	16	23	39	44
Bill Goldsworthy	61	10	12	22	43
Dave Maloney	66	3	18	21	100
Dave Farrish	80	2	17	19	102
Dan Newman	41	9	8	17	37
Pete Stemkowski	61	2	13	15	8
Nick Fotiu	70	4	8	12	174
Bill Fairbairn	9	1	2	3	0
Mark Heaslip	19	1	0	1	31
Larry Huras	1	0	0	0	0
Larry Sacharuk	2	0	0	0	0
John Bednarski	5	0	0	0	0
Greg Holst	5	0	0	0	0
Nick Beverley	9	0	0	0	2
Doug Jarrett	9	0	0	0	4

*Did not qualify for playoffs

1977-78	GP	G	A	PTS	PIM
Phil Esposito	79	38	43	81	53
Pat Hickey	80	40	33	73	47
Ron Greschner	78	24	48	72	100
Walt Tkaczuk	80	26	40	66	30
Steve Vickers	79	19	44	63	30
Don Murdoch	66	27	28	55	41
Carol Vadnais	80	6	40	46	115
Ron Duguay	71	20	20	40	43
Lucien DeBlois	71	22	8	30	27
Ed Johnstone	53	13	13	26	44
Greg Polis	37	7	16	23	12
Dave Maloney	56	2	19	21	63
Dave Farrish	80	2	17	19	102
Mike McEwen	57	5	13	18	52
Wayne Dillon	59	5	13	18	52
Dan Newman	59	5	13	18	22
Mark Heaslip	29	5	10	15	31
Rod Gilbert	19	2	7	9	6
Nick Fotiu	59	2	7	9	105
Don Awrey	78	2	6	8	38
Ken Hodge	18	2	4	6	8
Dallas Smith	29	1	4	5	23
Jerry Byers	7	2	1	3	0
Mario Marois	8	1	1	2	15
Bill Goldsworthy	7	0	1	1	12
Greg Hickey	1	0	0	0	0
Mike Keating	1	0	0	0	0
Bud Stefanski	1	0	0	0	0
Greg Holst	4	0	0	0	0
Benoit Gosselin	7	0	0	0	33

1978-79	GP	G	A	PTS	PIM
Phil Esposito	80	42	36	78	37
Anders Hedberg	80	33	45	78	33
Pat Hickey	80	34	41	75	56
Ulf Nilsson	59	27	39	66	21
Ron Duguay	79	27	36	63	35
Mike McEwen	80	20	38	58	35
Ron Greschner	60	17	36	53	6
Steve Vickers	66	13	34	47	24
Carol Vadnais	77	8	37	45	86
Walt Tkaczuk	77	15	27	42	38
Don Murdoch	40	15	22	37	6
Pierre Plante	70	6	25	31	37
Mario Marois	71	5	26	31	153
Dean Talafous	68	13	16	29	29
Lucien DeBlois	62	11	17	28	26
Dave Maloney	76	11	17	28	151
Don Maloney	28	9	17	26	39
DaveFarrish	71	1	19	20	61
Ed Johnstone	30	5	3	8	27
Nick Fotiu	71	3	5	8	190

	GP	G	A	PTS	PIM
Dan Clark	4	0	1	1	6
Mike Korney	18	0	1	1	18
Tim Bothwell	1	0	0	0	2
Mike McDougal	1	0	0	0	0
Dean Turner	1	0	0	0	0
Frank Beaton	2	0	0	0	0
Andre Dore	2	0	0	0	0

1979-80	GP	G	A	PTS	PIM
Phil Esposito	80	34	44	78	73
Don Maloney	79	25	48	73	97
Anders Hedberg	80	32	39	71	21
Steve Vickers	75	29	33	62	38
Barry Beck	61	14	45	59	98
Ron Greschner	76	21	37	58	103
Ulf Nilsson	50	14	44	58	20
Ron Duguay	73	28	22	50	37
Walt Tkaczuk	76	12	25	37	36
Dave Maloney	77	12	25	37	186
Eddie Johnstone	78	14	21	35	60
Mario Marois	79	8	23	31	142
Dean Talafous	55	10	20	30	26
Carol Vadnais	66	3	20	23	118
Warren Miller	55	7	6	13	17
Claude Larose	25	4	7	11	2
Doug Sulliman	31	4	7	11	2
Tim Bothwell	45	4	6	10	20
Jocelyn Guevremont	20	2	5	7	6
Pat Conacher	17	0	5	5	4
Cam Connor	12	0	3	3	37
Ray Markham	14	1	1	2	21
Frank Beaton	23	1	1	2	43
Ed Hospodar	20	0	1	1	76
Andre Dore	2	0	0	0	0
Dave Silk	2	0	0	0	0
Jim Mayer	4	0	0	0	0
Bill Lochead	7	0	0	0	4

1980-81	GP	G	A	PTS	PIM
Anders Hedberg	80	30	40	70	52
Ed Johnstone	80	30	38	68	100
Ron Greschner	74	27	41	68	112
Mike Allison	75	26	38	64	83
Steve Vickers	73	19	39	58	40
Don Maloney	61	29	23	52	99
Dave Maloney	79	11	36	47	132
Ulf Nilsson	51	14	25	39	42
Ron Duguay	50	17	21	38	83
Barry Beck	75	11	23	34	231
Dean Talafous	50	13	17	30	28
Tom Laidlaw	80	6	23	29	100
Walt Tkaczuk	43	6	22	28	28
Dave Silk	59	14	12	26	58
Lance Nethery	33	11	12	23	12
Carol Vadnais	74	3	20	23	91
Jere Gillis	35	10	10	20	4
Ed Hospodar	61	5	14	19	214
Chris Kotsopoulos	54	4	12	16	153
Nick Fotiu	27	5	6	11	91
Peter Wallin	12	1	5	6	2
Doug Sulliman	32	4	1	5	32
Dan McCarthy	5	4	0	4	4
Gary Burns	11	2	2	4	18
Cam Connor	15	1	3	4	44
Andre Dore	15	1	3	4	15
Mario Marois	8	1	2	3	46
Jeff Bandura	2	0	1	1	0
Tim Bothwell	3	0	1	1	0
Mike McDougal	2	0	0	0	0
John Hughes	3	0	1	1	6

1981-82	GP	G	A	PTS	PIM
Mike Rogers	80	38	65	103	43
Ron Duguay	72	40	36	76	82
Mark Pavelich	79	33	43	76	67
Ed Johnstone	68	30	28	58	57
Don Maloney	54	22	36	58	73
Reijo Ruotsalainen	78	18	38	56	27
Dave Maloney	64	13	36	49	105
Barry Beck	60	9	29	38	108
Dave Silk	64	15	20	35	39
Robbie Ftorek	30	8	25	33	24
Mikko Leinonen	53	11	19	30	18
Pat Hickey	53	15	14	29	32
Mike Allison	48	7	15	22	74
Tom Laidlaw	79	3	18	21	104
Andre Dore	56	4	16	20	64
Nick Fotiu	70	8	10	18	151
Ron Greschner	29	5	11	16	16
Rob McClanahan	22	5	9	14	10
Dean Talafous	29	6	7	13	8
Jere Gillis	26	3	9	12	16
Ed Hospodar	41	3	8	11	152
Peter Wallin	40	2	9	11	12
Tom Younghans	47	3	5	8	17
Tim Bothwell	13	0	3	3	10
Mark Morrison	9	1	1	2	0
Mike Backman	3	0	2	2	4
Anders Hedberg	4	0	1	1	0
Lance Nethery	5	0	0	0	0

1982-83	GP	G	A	PTS	PIM
Mike Rogers	71	29	47	76	28
Mark Pavelich	78	37	38	75	52
Don Maloney	78	29	40	69	88
Reijo Ruotsalainen	77	16	53	69	22
Anders Hedberg	78	25	34	59	12
Mikko Leinonen	78	17	34	51	23
Dave Maloney	78	8	42	50	132
Rob McClanahan	78	22	26	48	46
Ron Duguay	72	19	25	44	58
Ed Johnstone	52	15	21	36	27
Barry Beck	66	12	22	34	112
Robbie Ftorek	61	12	19	31	41
Kent-Erik Andersson	71	8	20	28	14
Nick Fotiu	72	8	13	21	90
Vaclav Nedomansky	35	12	8	20	0
Mike Allison	39	11	9	20	37
Bill Baker	70	4	14	18	64
Chris Kontos	44	8	7	15	33
Scot Kleinendorst	30	2	9	11	8
Tom Laidlaw	80	0	10	10	75
Ron Greschner	10	3	5	8	0
Ulf Nilsson	10	2	4	6	2
Rick Chartraw	26	2	2	4	37
Mike Backman	7	1	3	4	6
Dave Silk	16	1	1	2	15
Pat Conacher	5	0	1	1	4
Cam Connor	1	0	0	0	0
Graeme Nicolson	10	0	0	0	9

1983-84	GP	G	A	PTS	PIM
Mark Pavelich	77	29	53	82	96
Pierre Larouche	77	48	33	81	22
Anders Hedberg	79	32	35	67	16
Don Maloney	79	24	42	66	62
Mike Rogers	78	23	38	61	45
Reijo Ruotsalainen	74	20	39	59	26
Ron Greschner	77	12	44	56	117
Mark Osborne	73	23	28	51	88
Peter Sundstrom	77	22	22	44	24
Barry Beck	72	9	27	36	134
Dave Maloney	68	7	26	33	168
Jan Erixon	75	5	25	30	16
Mikko Leinonen	28	3	23	26	28
Willie Huber	42	9	14	23	60
Mike Allison	45	8	12	20	64
Kent-Erik Andersson	63	5	15	20	8
Tom Laidlaw	79	3	15	18	62
Rob McClanahan	41	6	8	14	21
Nick Fotiu	40	7	6	13	115
Mike Blaisdell	36	5	6	11	31
James Patrick	12	1	7	8	2
Blaine Stoughton	14	5	2	7	4

	GP	G	A	PTS	PIM
Steve Richmond	26	2	5	7	110
Robbie Ftorek	31	3	2	5	22
Bob Brooke	9	1	2	3	4
Larry Patey	9	1	2	3	4
George McPhee	9	1	1	2	11
Scot Kleinendorst	23	0	2	2	35
Mike Backman	8	0	1	1	8
Chris Kontos	46	0	1	1	38
Mark Morrison	1	0	0	0	0
Rick Chartraw	4	0	0	0	4
Dave Barr	6	0	0	0	2

1984-85	GP	G	A	PTS	PIM
Reijo Ruotsalainen	80	28	45	73	32
Mike Rogers	78	26	38	64	24
Pierre Larouche	65	24	36	60	8
Tomas Sandstrom	74	29	29	58	51
Anders Hedberg	64	20	31	51	10
Ron Greschner	48	16	29	45	42
Mark Pavelich	48	14	31	45	29
Peter Sundstrom	76	18	25	43	34
James Patrick	75	8	28	36	71
Stephen Patrick	43	11	18	29	63
Jan Erixon	66	7	22	29	33
George McPhee	49	12	15	27	139
Don Maloney	37	11	16	27	32
Barry Beck	56	7	19	26	75
Mike Allison	31	9	15	24	17
Grant Ledyard	42	8	12	20	53
Robbie Ftorek	48	9	10	19	35
Bob Brooke	72	7	9	16	79
Willie Huber	49	3	11	14	55
Dave Gagner	38	6	6	12	16
Chris Kontos	28	4	8	12	24
Tom Laidlaw	61	1	11	12	52
Nick Fotiu	46	4	7	11	54
Mark Osborne	23	4	4	8	33
Jim Wiemer	22	4	3	7	30
Andre Dore	25	0	7	7	35
Randy Heath	12	2	3	5	15
Steve Richmond	34	0	5	5	90
Dave Maloney	16	2	1	3	10
Kelly Miller	5	0	2	2	2
Mike Blaisdell	12	1	0	1	11
Larry Patey	7	0	1	1	12
Simo Saarinen	8	0	0	0	8

1985-86	GP	G	A	PTS	PIM
Mike Ridley	80	22	43	65	69
Reijo Ruotsalainen	80	17	42	59	47
Tomas Sandstrom	73	25	29	54	109
Ron Greschner	78	20	28	48	104
Bob Brooke	79	24	20	44	111
James Patrick	75	14	29	43	88
Mark Pavelich	59	20	20	40	82
Mark Osborne	62	16	24	40	80
Raimo Helminen	66	10	30	40	10
Kelly Miller	74	13	20	33	52
Brian MacLellan	51	11	21	32	47
Don Maloney	68	11	17	28	56
Pierre Larouche	28	20	7	27	4
Peter Sundstrom	53	8	15	23	12
Jan Erixon	31	2	17	19	4
Tom Laidlaw	68	6	12	18	103
Willie Huber	70	7	8	15	85
Mike Allison	28	2	13	15	22
Barry Beck	25	4	8	12	7
Dave Gagner	32	4	6	10	19
Larry Melnyk	46	1	8	9	65
George McPhee	30	4	4	8	63
Wilf Paiement	8	1	6	7	13
Rob Whistle	32	4	2	6	10
Chris Jensen	9	1	3	4	0
Jim Wiemer	7	3	0	3	2
Bob Crawford	11	1	2	3	10
Randy Heath	1	0	1	1	0

	GP	G	A	PTS	PIM
Kjell Samuelsson	9	0	0	0	10
Tony Feltrin	10	0	0	0	21

1986-87	GP	G	A	PTS	PIM
Walt Poddubny	75	40	47	87	49
Tomas Sandstrom	64	40	34	74	60
Kelly Kisio	70	24	40	64	73
Pierre Larouche	73	28	35	63	12
Don Maloney	72	19	38	57	117
James Patrick	78	10	45	55	62
Tony McKegney	64	29	17	46	56
Ron Greschner	61	6	34	40	62
Willie Huber	66	8	22	30	70
Jan Erixon	68	8	18	26	24
Ron Duguay	34	9	12	21	9
Curt Giles	61	2	17	19	50
Larry Melnyk	73	3	12	15	182
Terry Carkner	52	2	13	15	120
Chris Jensen	37	6	7	13	21
Lucien DeBlois	40	3	8	11	27
Marcel Dionne	14	4	6	10	6
George McPhee	21	4	4	8	34
Jeff Jackson	9	5	1	6	15
Dave Gagner	10	1	4	5	12
Jay Caufield	13	2	1	3	45
Mike Donnelly	5	1	1	2	0
Pat Price	13	0	2	2	37
Gord Walker	1	1	0	1	2
Don Jackson	22	1	0	1	91
Norm Maciver	3	0	1	1	0
Jim Leavins	4	0	1	1	4
Mike Siltala	1	0	0	0	0
Stu Kulak	3	0	0	0	0
Ron Talakoski	3	0	0	0	24
Paul Fenton	8	0	0	0	2

1987-88	GP	G	A	PTS	PIM
Walt Poddubny	77	38	50	88	76
Kelly Kisio	77	23	55	78	88
Tomas Sandstrom	69	28	40	68	95
Marcel Dionne	67	31	34	65	54
James Patrick	70	17	45	62	52
Brian Mullen	74	25	29	54	42
John Ogrodnick	64	22	32	54	16
Ulf Dahlen	70	29	23	52	26
Don Maloney	66	12	21	33	60
Michel Petit	64	9	24	33	223
David Shaw	68	7	25	32	100
Lucien DeBlois	74	9	21	30	103
Jan Erixon	70	7	19	26	33
Norm Maciver	37	9	15	24	14
Paul Cyr	40	4	13	17	41
Jari Gronstrand	62	3	11	14	63
Brian Leetch	17	2	12	14	0
Pierre Larouche	10	3	9	12	13
Ron Duguay	48	4	4	8	23
Chris Nilan	22	3	5	8	96
Ron Greschner	51	1	5	6	82
Gord Walker	18	1	4	5	17
Mike Donnelly	17	2	2	4	8
Mark Hardy	19	2	2	4	31
Dave Pichette	6	1	3	4	4
Joe Paterson	21		3	4	65
Bruce Bell	13	1	2	3	8
Mark Tinordi	24	1	2	3	50
Steve Nemeth	12	2	0	2	2
Jeff Brubaker	31	2	0	2	78
Simon Wheeldon	5	0	1	1	4
Ron Talakoski	6	0	1	1	12
Chris Jensen	7	0	1	1	2
Mark Janssens	1	0	0	0	0
Rudy Poeschek	1	0	0	0	2
Curt Giles	13	0	0	0	10

*Did not qualify for playoffs

1988-89	GP	G	A	PTS	PIM
Tomas Sandstrom	79	32	56	88	148
Brian Leetch	68	23	48	71	50
Brian Mullen	78	29	35	64	60
Tony Granato	78	36	27	63	140
Kelly Kisio	70	26	36	62	91
Carey Wilson	41	21	34	55	45
James Patrick	68	11	36	47	41
Guy Lafleur	67	18	27	45	12
Ulf Dahlen	56	24	19	43	50
John Ogrodnick	60	13	29	42	14
Lucien DeBlois	73	9	24	33	107
Michel Petit	69	8	25	33	154
Jason Lafreniere	38	8	16	24	6
Marcel Dionne	37	7	16	23	20
Brian Lawton	30	7	10	17	39
David Shaw	63	6	11	17	88
Jan Erixon	44	4	11	15	27
Chris Nilan	38	7	7	14	177
Mark Hardy	45	2	12	14	45
Don Maloney	31	4	9	13	16
Ron Greschner	58	1	10	11	94
Darren Turcotte	20	7	3	10	4
Norm Maciver	26	0	10	10	14
Kevin Miller	24	3	5	8	2
Normand Rochefort	11	1	5	6	18
Lindy Ruff	13	0	5	5	31
Rudy Poeschek	52	0	2	2	199
Miloslav Horava	6	0	1	1	0
Simon Wheeldon	6	0	1	1	2
Joe Paterson	20	0	1	1	84
Stephane Brochu	1	0	0	0	0
Paul Cyr	1	0	0	0	2
Jim Latos	1	0	0	0	0
Jayson More	1	0	0	0	0
Mark Janssens	5	0	0	0	0
Jeff Bloemberg	9	0	0	0	0
Peter Laviolette	12	0	0	0	6

1989-90	GP	G	A	PTS	PIM
John Ogrodnick	80	43	31	74	44
Brian Mullen	76	27	41	68	42
Darren Turcotte	76	32	34	66	32
Kelly Kisio	68	22	44	66	105
James Patrick	73	14	43	57	50
Brian Leetch	72	11	45	56	26
Bernie Nicholls	32	12	25	37	20
Troy Mallette	79	13	16	29	305
Carey Wilson	41	9	17	26	57
Mike Gartner	12	11	5	16	6
Mark Hardy	54	0	15	15	94
Miloslav Horava	45	4	10	14	26
Kris King	68	6	7	13	286
Mark Janssens	80	5	8	13	161
Jan Erixon	58	4	9	13	8
Randy Moller	60	1	12	13	139
David Shaw	22	2	10	12	22
Ron Greschner	55	1	9	10	53
Lindy Ruff	56	3	6	9	77
Paul Broten	32	3	5	8	26
Jeff Bloemberg	28	3	3	6	25
Dave Archibald	19	2	3	5	6
Kevin Miller	16	0	5	5	2
Normand Rochefort	31	3	1	4	24
Chris Nilan	25	1	2	3	59
Ric Bennett	6	1	0	1	5
Corey Millen	4	0	0	0	2
Todd Charlesworth	7	0	0	0	6
Rudy Poeschek	15	0	0	0	55

1990-91	GP	G	A	PTS	PIM
Brian Leetch	80	16	72	88	42
Bernie Nicholls	71	25	48	73	96
Mike Gartner	79	49	20	69	53
Darren Turcotte	74	26	41	67	37
Brian Mullen	79	19	43	62	43

	74	10	49	59	58
James Patrick	74	10	49	59	58
John Ogrodnck	79	31	23	54	10
Ray Sheppard	59	24	23	47	21
Kevin Miller	63	17	27·	44	63
Kelly Kisio	51	15	20	35	58
Kris King	72	11	14	25	156
Jan Erixon	53	7	18	25	8
Randy Moller	61	4	19	23	161
Troy Mallette	71	12	10	22	252
Mark Janssens	69	9	7	16	172
Jody Hull	47	5	8	13	10
David Shaw	77	2	10	12	89
Paul Broten	28	4	6	10	10
Normand Rochefort	44	3	7	10	35
Miloslav Horava	29	1	6	7	12
Mark Hardy	70	1	5	6	89
Corey Millen	4	3	1	4	0
Steven Rice	11	1	1	2	4
Jeff Bloemberg	3	0	2	2	0
Joe Cirella	19	1	0	1	52
Tie Domi	28	1	0	1	185
Lindy Ruff	14	0	1	1	27
Brian McReynolds	1	0	0	0	0
Joey Kocur	5	0	0	0	36
Ric Bennett	6	0	0	0	6
Dennis Vial	21	0	0	0	61
Tony Amonte	2	0	2	2	2
Doug Weight	1	0	0	0	0

1991-92	GP	G	A	PTS	PIM
Mark Messier	79	35	72	107	76
Brian Leetch	80	22	80	102	26
Mike Gartner	76	40	41	81	55
James Patrick	80	14	57	71	54
Tony Amonte	79	35	34	69	55
Adam Graves	80	26	33	59	139
Sergei Nemchinov	73	30	28	58	15
Darren Turcotte	71	30	23	53	57
John Ogrodnick	55	17	13	30	22
Doug Weight	53	8	22	30	23
Kris King	79	10	9	19	224
Per Djoos	50	1	18	19	40
Tim Kerr	32	7	11	18	12
Jan Erixon	46	8	9	17	4
Joe Cirella	67	3	12	15	121
Randy Gilhen	40	7	7	14	14
Joey Kocur	51	7	4	11	121
Jeff Beukeboom	56	1	10	11	122
Paul Broten	28	4	6	10	18
Randy Moller	32	2	7	9	78
Mark Hardy	52	1	8	9	65
Tie Domi	42	2	4	6	246
Corey Millen	11	1	4	5	44
Rob Zamuner	9	1	2	3	2
Normand Rochefort	26	0	2	2	31
Eric Bennett	3	0	1	1	2
Jeff Bloemberg	3	0	1	1	0
David Shaw	10	0	1	1	15
Peter Fiorentino	1	0	0	0	0
Bernie Nichols	1	0	0	0	0
Jody Hull	3	0	0	0	2
Mark Janssens	4	0	0	0	5
Jay Wells	11	0	0	0	24

1992-93	GP	G	A	PTS	PIM
Mark Messier	75	25	66	91	72
Tony Amonte	83	33	43	76	49
Mike Gartner	84	45	23	68	59
Adam Graves	84	36	29	65	148
Sergei Nemchinov	81	23	31	54	34
Darren Turcotte	71	25	28	53	40
Alexei Kovalev	65	20	18	38	79
Brain Leetch	36	6	30	36	26
Sergei Zubov	49	8	23	31	4
Eddie Olczyk	46	13	16	29	26
James Patrick	60	5	21	26	61

	GP	G	A	PTS	PIM
Phil Bourque	55	6	14	20	39
Jeff Beukeboom	82	2	17	19	153
Jan Erixon	45	5	11	16	10
Peter Andersson	31	4	11	15	18
Kevin Lowe	49	3	12	15	58
Paul Broten	60	5	9	14	48
Steven King	24	7	5	12	16
Jay Wells	53	1	9	10	107
Joe Cirella	55	3	6	9	85
Joe Kocur	65	3	6	9	131
Mike Hurlbut	23	1	8	9	16
Esa Tikkanen	15	2	5	7	18
Mike Richter	38	0	5	5	2
Per Djoos	6	1	1	2	2
John McIntyre	11	1	0	1	4
Craig Duncanson	3	0	1	1	0
John Vanbiesbrouck	48	0	1	1	18
Dave Marcinyshyn	2	0	0	0	2
Mike Hartman	3	0	0	0	6
Corey Hirsch	4	0	0	0	0
Joby Messier	11	0	0	0	6

1993-94	GP	G	A	PTS	PIM
Sergei Zubov	78	12	77	89	39
Mark Messier	76	26	58	84	76
Adam Graves	84	52	27	79	127
Brian Leetch	84	23	56	79	67
Steve Larmer	68	21	39	60	41
Alexei Kovalev	76	23	33	56	154
Esa Tikkanen	83	22	32	54	114
Sergei Nemchinov	76	22	27	49	36
Kevin Lowe	71	5	14	19	70
Alexander Karpovtsev	67	3	15	18	58
Jeff Beukeboom	68	8	8	16	170
Greg Gilbert	76	4	11	15	29
Mike Hudson	48	4	7	11	47
Jay Wells	79	2	7	9	110
Eddie Olczyk	37	3	5	8	28
Nick Kypreos	46	3	5	8	102
Stephane Matteau	12	4	3	7	2
Glenn Anderson	12	4	2	6	12
Craig MacTavish	12	4	2	6	11
Brian Noonan	12	4	2	6	12
Joe Kocur	71	2	1	3	129
Mike Hartman	35	1	1	2	70
Joby Messier	4	0	2	2	0
Mattias Norstrom	9	0	2	2	6
Glenn Healy	29	0	2	2	2
Doug Lidster	34	0	2	2	33
Jim Hiller	2	0	0	0	7
Daniel Lacroix	4	0	0	0	0
Mike Richter	68	0	0	0	2

1994-95	GP	G	A	PTS	PIM
Mark Messier	46	14	39	53	40
Brian Leetch	48	9	32	41	18
Sergei Zubov	38	10	26	36	18
Adam Graves	47	17	14	31	51
Steve Larmer	47	14	15	29	16
Alexei Kovalev	48	13	15	28	30
Brian Noonan	45	14	13	27	26
Petr Nedved	46	11	12	23	26
Pat Verbeek	19	10	5	15	18
Sergei Nemchinov	47	7	6	13	16
Alexander Karpovtsev	47	4	8	12	30
Jay Wells	43	2	7	9	36
Stephane Matteau	41	3	5	8	25
Kevin Lowe	44	1	7	8	58
Mark Osborne	37	1	3	4	19
Nick Kypreos	40	1	3	4	93
Jeff Beukeboom	44	1	3	4	70
Joey Kocur	48	1	2	3	71
Mattias Norstrom	9	0	3	3	2
Darren Langdon	18	1	1	2	62
Joby Messier	10	0	2	2	18
Glenn Healy	17	0	2	2	2
Jean-Yves Roy	3	1	0	1	2
Shawn McCosh	5	1	0	1	2
Mike Hartman	1	0	0	0	4
Dan Lacroix	1	0	0	0	0
Troy Loney	4	0	0	0	0
Nathan LaFayette	12	0	0	0	0
Dan Lacroix	1	0	0	0	0
Troy Loney	4	0	0	0	0
Mike Richter	35	0	0	0	2

1995-96	GP	G	A	PTS	PIM
Mark Messier	74	47	52	99	122
Brian Leetch	82	15	70	85	30
Pat Verbeek	69	41	41	82	129
Luc Robitaille	77	23	46	69	80
Alexei Kovalev	81	24	34	58	98
Adam Graves	82	22	36	58	100
Ray Ferraro	65	25	29	54	82
Bruce Driver	66	3	34	37	42
Sergei Nemchinov	78	17	15	32	38
Niklas Sundstrom	82	9	12	21	14
Ulf Samuelsson	74	1	18	19	122
Alexander Karpovtsev	40	2	16	18	26
Doug Lidster	59	5	9	14	50
Jeff Beukeboom	82	3	11	14	220
Darren Langdon	64	7	4	11	175
Wayne Presley	61	4	6	10	71
Sergio Momesso	19	4	4	8	30
Nick Kypreos	42	3	4	7	77
Stephane Matteau	32	4	2	6	66
Kevin Lowe	53	1	5	6	76
Ken Gernander	10	2	3	5	4
Jari Kurri	14	1	4	5	2
Daniel Lacroix	25	2	2	4	30
Bill Berg	18	2	1	3	8
Mattias Nordstrom	25	2	1	3	22
Ian Laperriere	28	1	2	3	53
Joe Kocur	38	1	2	3	49
Chris Ferraro	2	1	0	1	0
Marty McSorley	9	0	2	2	21
Barry Richter	4	0	1	1	0
Peter Ferraro	5	0	1	1	0
Mike Richter	41	0	1	1	4
Glenn Healy	44	0	1	1	8
Steve Larouche	1	0	0	0	0
Jamie Ram	1	0	0	0	0
Nathan LaFayette	5	0	0	0	2
Shane Churla	10	0	0	0	26

Year-By-Year
Goaltending Statistics

Season	Goaltender	GP	W	L	T	GA	GAPG	SHO
1926-27	Hal Winkler	8	3	4	1	16	2.00	1
	Lorne Chabot	36	22	9	5	56	1.56	10
1927-28	Lorne Chabot	44	19	16	9	79	1.80	11
1928-29	John Ross Roach	44	21	13	10	65	1.48	13
1929-30	John Ross Roach	44	17	17	10	143	3.25	1
1930-31	John Ross Roach	44	19	16	9	89	1.98	7
1931-32	John Ross Roach	48	23	17	8	112	2.33	9
1932-33	Andy Aitkenhead	48	23	17	8	107	2.23	3
1933-34	Andy Aitkenhead	48	21	19	8	113	2.35	7
1934-35	Andy Aitkenhead	10	3	7	0	37	3.70	1
	Percy Jackson	1	0	1	0	8	8.00	0
	Dave Kerr	37	19	12	6	94	2.54	4
1935-36	Dave Kerr	47	18	17	12	95	2.02	8
	Bert Gardiner	1	1	0	0	1	1.00	0
1936-37	Dave Kerr	48	19	29	9	106	2.21	4
1937-38	Dave Kerr	48	27	15	6	96	2.00	8
1938-39	Dave Kerr	48	26	16	6	105	2.19	6
1939-40	Dave Kerr	48	27	11	10	77	1.60	8
1940-41	Dave Kerr	48	21	19	8	125	2.60	2
1941-42	Jim Henry	48	29	17	2	143	2.98	1
1942-43	Jimmy Franks	23	5	14	4	103	4.48	0
	Bill Beveridge	17	4	10	3	89	5.24	1
	Steve Buzinski	9	2	6	1	55	6.11	0
	Lionel Bouvrette	1	0	1	0	6	6.00	0
1943-44	Ken McAuley	50	6	39	5	310	6.20	0
	Harry Lumley	1	0	0	0	0	0.00	0
1944-45	Ken McAuley	46	11	25	10	227	4.94	1
	Doug Stevenson	4	0	4	0	20	5.00	0
1945-46	Chuck Rayner	41	12	21	7	150	3.75	1
	Jim Henry	11	1	7	2	41	4.10	1
1946-47	Chuck Rayner	58	22	30	6	177	3.05	5
	Jim Henry	2	0	2	0	9	4.50	0
1947-48	Jim Henry	48	17	18	3	153	3.19	2
	Chuck Rayner	12	4	8	0	42	3.65	0
	Bob DeCourcy	1	0	0	0	6	12.41	0
1948-49	Chuck Rayner	58	16	31	11	168	2.90	7
	Emile Francis	2	2	0	0	4	2.00	0
1949-50	Chuck Rayner	69	28	30	11	181	2.62	6
	Emile Francis	1	0	1	0	8	8.00	0
1950-51	Chuck Rayner	66	19	27	20	187	2.83	2
	Emile Francis	5	1	2	1	14	2.80	0
1951-52	Chuck Rayner	53	18	25	10	159	3.00	2
	Emile Francis	14	4	7	3	42	3.00	0
	Lorne Anderson	3	1	2	0	18	6.00	0
1952-53	Chuck Rayner	20	4	9	7	58	2.90	1
	Gump Worsley	50	13	28	9	153	3.06	2
1953-54	Johnny Bower	70	29	31	10	182	2.60	5
1954-55	Gump Worsley	65	15	33	17	197	3.03	4
	Johnny Bower	5	2	2	1	13	2.60	0
1955-56	Gump Worsley	70	32	28	10	203	2.90	4
1956-57	Gump Worsley	68	26	28	14	220	3.24	3
	Johnny Bower	2	0	2	0	7	3.50	0

Season	Goaltender	GP	W	L	T	GA	GAPG	SHO
1957-58	Gump Worsley	37	21	10	14	86	2.32	4
	Marcel Paille	33	11	15	7	102	3.09	0
1958-59	Gump Worsley	67	26	29	12	205	3.07	2
	Marcel Paille	1	0	0	1	4	4.00	0
	Bruce Gamble	2	0	2	0	6	3.00	0
	Julian Klymkiw	1	0	0	0	2	6.32	0
1959-60	Gump Worsley	41	8	25	8	137	3.57	0
	Marcel Paille	17	6	9	2	67	3.94	1
	Al Rollins	8	1	3	4	31	3.88	0
	Jack McCartan	4	2	1	1	7	1.75	0
	Joe Schaefer	1	0	0	0	5	7.69	0
1960-61	Gump Worsley	59	20	29	8	193	3.29	1
	Marcel Paille	4	1	2	1	16	4.00	0
	Jack McCartan	8	1	6	1	36	4.91	1
	Joe Schaefer	1	0	1	0	3	3.83	0
1961-62	Gump Worsley	60	22	27	9	174	2.97	2
	Marcel Paille	10	4	4	2	28	2.80	0
	Dan Olesevich	1	0	0	1	2	3.00	0
	Dave Dryden	1	0	1	0	3	4.50	0
1962-63	Gump Worsley	67	22	34	9	219	3.30	2
	Marcel Paille	3	0	1	2	10	3.33	0
	Marcel Pelletier	2	0	1	1	4	6.00	0
1963-64	Jacques Plante	65	22	35	8	220	3.38	3
	Gilles Villemure	5	0	3	2	18	3.60	0
1964-65	Jacques Plante	33	10	17	5	109	3.37	2
	Marcel Paille	39	10	21	7	135	3.58	0
1965-66	Ed Giacomin	36	8	19	7	128	3.66	0
	Cesare Maniago	28	9	16	3	94	3.50	2
	Don Simmons	11	3	6	3	37	4.52	0
1966-67	Ed Giacomin	68	30	25	11	173	2.61	9
	Cesare Maniago	6	0	3	1	14	3.84	0
1967-68	Ed Giacomin	66	36	20	140	160	2.44	8
	Gilles Villemure	4	1	2	0	8	2.40	1
	Don Simmons	5	2	2	1	8	2.33	0
1968-69	Ed Giacomin	70	37	23	7	175	2.55	7
	Gilles Villemure	4	2	1	1	9	2.25	0
	Don Simmons	5	2	2	1	8	2.33	0
1969-70	Ed Giacomin	70	35	21	14	163	2.36	6
	Terry Sawchuk	8	3	1	2	20	2.91	1
1970-71	Ed Giacomin	45	27	10	7	95	2.16	8
	Gilles Villemure	34	22	8	4	78	2.30	4
1971-72	Ed Giacomin	44	24	10	9	115	2.70	1
	Gilles Villemure	37	24	7	4	74	2.09	3
1972-73	Ed Giacomin	43	26	11	6	125	2.91	4
	Gilles Villemure	34	20	12	2	78	2.29	3
	Peter McDuffe	1	1	0	0	1	1.00	0
1973-74	Ed Giacomin	56	30	15	10	168	3.07	5
	Gilles Villemure	21	7	7	3	62	3.53	0
	Peter McDuffe	6	3	2	1	18	3.18	0
1974-75	Ed Giacomin	37	13	12	8	120	3.48	1
	Gilles Villemure	45	22	14	6	130	3.16	2
	Dunc Wilson	3	1	2	0	13	4.33	0
	Curt Ridley	2	1	1	0	7	5.19	0
1975-76	Ed Giacomin	4	0	3	1	19	4.75	0
	John Davidson	56	22	28	5	212	3.97	3
	Dunc Wilson	20	5	9	3	76	4.22	0
	Doug Soetaert	8	2	2	0	24	5.27	0
1976-77	John Davidson	39	14	14	6	125	3.54	1
	Doug Soetaert	12	3	4	1	58	2.95	1
	Gilles Gratton	41	11	18	7	143	4.22	0
	Dave Tataryn	2	1	1	0	10	7.50	0

Season	Goaltender	GP	W	L	T	GA	GAPG	SHO
1977-78	John Davidson	34	14	13	4	98	3.18	1
	Doug Soetaert	6	2	2	2	20	3.33	0
	Hardy Astrom	4	2	2	0	14	3.50	0
	Wayne Thomas	42	12	20	7	141	3.60	4
1978-79	John Davidson	39	20	12	5	131	3.52	0
	Wayne Thomas	31	15	10	3	101	3.63	1
	Doug Soetaert	17	5	7	3	57	3.80	0
1979-80	John Davidson	41	20	15	4	122	3.17	2
	Steve Baker	27	9	8	6	79	3.41	1
	Wayne Thomas	12	4	7	0	44	3.95	0
	Doug Soetaert	8	5	2	0	33	4.55	0
1980-81	Steve Weeks	1	0	1	0	2	2.00	0
	Wayne Thomas	10	3	6	1	34	3.40	0
	Steve Baker	21	10	6	5	73	3.48	2
	Doug Soetaert	39	16	16	7	152	3.93	0
	John Davidson	10	1	7	1	48	5.14	0
1981-82	John Davidson	1	1	0	0	1	1.00	0
	John Vanbiesbrouck	1	1	0	0	1	1.00	0
	Ed Mio	25	13	6	5	89	3.56	0
	Steve Weeks	49	23	16	9	179	3.77	1
	Steve Baker	6	1	5	0	33	6.03	0
1982-83	John Davidson	2	1	1	0	5	2.50	0
	Steve Baker	3	0	1	0	5	2.94	0
	Glen Hanlon	21	9	10	1	67	3.43	0
	Ed Mio	41	16	18	6	136	3.45	2
	Steve Weeks	18	9	5	3	68	3.92	0
1983-84	John Vanbiesbrouck	3	2	1	0	10	3.33	0
	Glen Hanlon	50	28	14	4	166	3.51	1
	Steve Weeks	26	10	11	2	90	3.97	0
	Ron Scott	9	2	3	3	29	3.59	0
1984-85	Glen Hanlon	44	14	20	7	175	4.18	0
	John Vanbiesbrouck	42	12	24	3	166	4.22	1
1985-86	John Vanbiesbrouck	61	31	21	5	184	3.32	3
	Glen Hanlon	23	5	12	1	65	3.33	0
	Ron Scott	4	0	3	0	11	4.23	0
	Terry Kleisinger	4	0	2	0	14	4.40	0
1986-87	John Vanbiesbrouck	50	18	20	5	161	3.63	0
	Bob Froese	28	14	11	0	92	3.74	0
	Doug Soetaert	13	2	7	2	58	3.99	0
	Ron Scott	1	0	0	1	5	5.00	0
1987-88	John Vanbiesbrouck	56	27	22	7	187	3.38	2
	Bob Froese	25	8	11	3	85	3.53	0
	Ron Scott	2	1	1	0	6	4.00	0
1988-89	John Vanbiesbrouck	56	28	21	4	197	3.69	0
	Bob Froese	30	9	14	4	102	3.78	1
1989-90	Mike Richter	23	12	5	5	66	3.00	0
	Bob Froese	15	5	7	1	45	3.33	0
	John Vanbiesbrouck	47	19	19	7	154	3.38	1
1990-91	Mike Richter	45	21	13	7	135	3.12	0
	John Vanbiesbrouck	40	15	18	6	126	3.35	3
1991-92	John Vanbiesbrouck	45	27	13	3	120	2.85	2
	Mike Richter	41	23	12	2	119	3.11	3
1992-93	John Vanbiesbrouck	40	20	18	7	152	3.31	4
	Corey Hirsch	4	1	2	1	14	3.75	0
	Mike Richter	38	13	19	3	134	3.82	1
1993-94	Mike Richter	68	42	12	6	159	2.57	5
	Glenn Healy	29	10	12	2	69	3.03	2
1994-95	Glenn Healy	17	8	6	1	35	2.36	1
	Mike Richter	35	14	17	2	97	2.92	2
1995-96	Jamie Ram	1	0	0	0	0	0.00	0
	Mike Richter	41	24	13	3	107	2.68	3
	Glenn Healy	44	17	14	11	124	2.90	2

Year-By-Year Playoff Goaltending Statistics

Season	Goaltender	GP	W	L	T	GA	AVG	SHO
1926-27	Lorne Chabot	2	0	1	1	3	1.50	1
1927-28	Lester Patrick	1	1	0	0	1	1.00	0
	Joe Miller	3	2	1	0	3	1.00	1
	Lorne Chabot	6	2	2	1	8	1.33	1
1928-29	John Ross Roach	6	3	2	1	5	0.83	3
1929-30	John Ross Roach	4	1	2	1	7	1.75	0
1930-31	John Ross Roach	4	2	2	0	4	1.00	1
1931-32	John Ross Roach	7	3	4	0	27	3.86	1
1932-33	Andy Aitkenhead	8	6	1	1	13	1.60	2
1933-34	Andy Aitkenhead	2	0	1	1	2	1.00	1
1934-35	Dave Kerr	4	1	1	2	10	2.50	0
1936-37	Dave Kerr	9	6	3	0	10	1.11	4
1937-38	Dave Kerr	3	1	2	0	8	2.67	0
1938-39	Dave Kerr	1	0	1	0	2	2.00	0
	Bert Gardiner	6	3	3	0	12	2.00	0
1939-40	Dave Kerr	12	8	4	0	20	1.67	3
1940-41	Dave Kerr	3	1	2	0	6	2.00	0
1941-42	Jim Henry	6	2	4	0	13	2.17	1
1947-48	Chuck Rayner	6	2	4	0	17	2.83	0
1949-50	Chuck Rayner	12	7	5	0	29	2.42	1
1955-56	Lorne Worsley	3	0	3	-	15	5.00	0
	Gordie Bell	2	1	1	-	9	4.50	0
1956-57	Lorne Worsley	5	1	4	-	22	4.18	0
1957-58	Lorne Worsley	6	2	4	-	28	4.60	0
1961-62	Lorne Worsley	6	2	4	-	22	3.44	0
1966-67	Ed Giacomin	4	0	4	-	14	3.41	0
1967-68	Ed Giacomin	6	2	4	-	18	3.00	0
1968-69	Ed Giacomin	3	0	3	-	10	3.33	0
	Gilles Villemure	1	0	1	-	4	4.00	0
1969-70	Ed Giacomin	5	2	3	-	19	4.13	0
	Terry Sawchuk	3	0	1	-	6	4.50	0
1970-71	Ed Giacomin	12	7	5	-	28	2.21	0
	Gilles Villemure	2	0	1	-	6	4.50	0
1971-72	Ed Giacomin	10	6	4	-	27	2.70	0
	Gilles Villemure	6	4	2	-	14	2.33	0
1972-73	Ed Giacomin	10	5	4	-	23	2.56	1
	Gilles Villemure	2	0	1	-	2	1.97	0
1973-74	Ed Giacomin	13	7	6	-	37	2.82	0
	Gilles Villemure	1	0	0	-	0	0.00	0
1974-75	Ed Giacomin	2	0	2	-	6	2.79	0
	Gilles Villemure	2	1	0	-	6	2.93	0
1977-78	John Davidson	2	1	1	-	7	3.44	0
	Wayne Thomas	1	0	1	-	4	4.00	0
1978-79	John Davidson	18	11	7	-	42	2.28	1
1979-80	John Davidson	9	4	5	-	21	2.33	0
1980-81	Steve Baker	14	7	7	-	55	4.00	0
	Steve Weeks	1	0	0	-	1	4.29	0
1981-82	John Davidson	1	0	0	-	3	5.45	0
	Ed Mio	8	4	3	-	28	3.79	0
	Steve Weeks	4	1	2	-	9	4.25	0
1982-83	Glen Hanlon	1	0	1	-	5	5.00	0
	Ed Mio	8	5	3	-	32	4.00	0
1983-84	Glen Hanlon	5	2	3	-	13	2.53	1
	John Vanbiesbrouck	1	0	0	-	0	0.00	0
1984-85	Glen Hanlon	3	0	3	-	14	5.00	0
	John Vanbiesbrouck	1	0	0	-	0	0.00	0
1985-86	John Vanbiesbrouck	16	8	8	-	49	3.27	1
	Glen Hanlon	3	0	0	-	6	4.80	0
1986-87	Bob Froese	4	1	1	-	10	3.64	0
	John Vanbiesbrouck	4	1	3	-	11	3.38	1
1988-89	Bob Froese	2	0	2	-	8	6.67	0
	Mike Richter	1	0	1	-	4	4.14	0
	John Vanbiesbrouck	2	0	1	-	6	3.36	0
1989-90	Mike Richter	6	3	2	-	19	3.45	0
	John Vanbiesbrouck	6	2	3	-	15	3.02	0
1990-91	Mike Richter	6	2	4	-	14	2.68	1
	John Vanbiesbrouck	1	0	0	-	1	1.15	0
1991-92	John Vanbiesbrouck	7	2	5	-	23	3.75	0
	Mike Richter	7	4	2	-	24	3.50	1
1993-94	Mike Richter	23	16	7	-	49	2.07	4
	Glenn Healy	2	0	0	-	1	0.88	0
1994-95	Mike Richter	7	2	5	-	23	3.59	0
	Glenn Healy	5	2	1	-	13	3.39	0
1995-96	Mike Richter	11	5	6	-	36	3.27	0